L.A.A. de Verteuil

Trinidad

Its geography, natural resources, administration, present condition, and prospects.

Second Edition

L.A.A. de Verteuil

Trinidad

Its geography, natural resources, administration, present condition, and prospects. Second Edition

ISBN/EAN: 9783337424343

Printed in Europe, USA, Canada, Australia, Japan

Cover: Foto ©Suzi / pixelio.de

More available books at **www.hansebooks.com**

TRINIDAD:

Its Geography, Natural Resources, Administration, Present Condition, and Prospects.

BY

L. A. A. DE VERTEUIL, M.D.P.,

CORRESPONDING MEMBER OF THE CENTRAL SOCIETY OF AGRICULTURE OF FRANCE
(MEMBRE CORRESPONDANT DE LA SOCIÉTÉ CENTRALE D'AGRICULTURE).

"The softness and purity of the climate, and the verdure, freshness, and sweetness of the country, appeared to Columbus to equal the delights of early spring in the beautiful province of Valencia, in Spain."—*Washington Irving*, book x., ch. 2.

SECOND EDITION.

CASSELL & COMPANY, Limited:
LONDON, PARIS & NEW YORK.
1884.

CONTENTS.

	PAGE
DEDICATION	v
PREFACE	vii
INTRODUCTION	1

CHAPTER I.—Geographical Description—Position and Area . . 36

CHAPTER II.—Geological View—Mineral Springs, Pitch Deposits—Soil and Vegetation 54

CHAPTER III.—Natural History—Vegetable Kingdom: Timber Woods, Useful and Poisonous Plants—Animal Kingdom: Mammifers, Birds, Reptiles, Fish and Insects, viz., those which merit attention from their utility as food, their singular habits, or noxious and destructive propensities 70

CHAPTER IV.—Climate—Temperature—Rains—Diseases . . 117

CHAPTER V.—Population—Ethnography—Religion—Education—Crime . 153

CHAPTER VI.—General Administration—Government—Civil, Judiciary, Ecclesiastical, and Financial Departments—Means of Communication 188

CHAPTER VII.—Productive Industry—Agriculture—Exportable Articles: Sugar, Cacao, Coffee, &c.—Alimentary Articles: Live Stock, Vegetables, Plantain, Maize, Rice, Manioc, Yams, &c.—Fruits—Commerce 220

CHAPTER VIII.—Topography—Northern Division: Counties of St. George, St. David, St. Andrew, and Caroni 269

CHAPTER IX.—Topography—Southern Division: Counties of Victoria, St. Patrick, Mayaro, and Nariva 301

CHAPTER X.—Prospects of Trinidad—Suggestions . . 334

	PAGE
CHAPTER XI.—Natural History of Trinidad—Zoology—Botany	358
Mammalia	358
Birds.—An Essay on the Ornithology of Trinidad. By Antoine Leotaud, M.D.P.	365
Reptiles	381
Fishes	388
Botany.—Outline of the Flora of Trinidad. By Herman Crüger	395
CHAPTER XII.—Historical Outline	421

APPENDIX.

SUGGESTIONS FOR ORGANIZING A CENTRAL AGRICULTURAL COMMITTEE, AND ESTABLISHING MODEL FARMS IN THE ISLAND OF TRINIDAD	470
MINERAL COALS	481

DEDICATION.

TO THE NATIVES OF TRINIDAD.

IN dedicating this production to you, my countrymen, I can truly say with Montaigne—" C'est icy un livre de bonne foy, lecteur." I am, therefore, anxious that you should find it truthful, if not as interesting or valuable as it might, under other auspices, have been. And yet, it cannot be reasonably expected that, in treating so many and such various subjects, no errors should have crept in; this much, however, I can say—they are not wilful errors.

With all the drawbacks, however—for which I crave your indulgence—I am confident you will find in the work itself material evidences of the great importance of Trinidad in an agricultural as well as a commercial point of view. Numberless, varied, and more than competent are its resources, but they remain undeveloped still; and it assuredly, in a great measure, depends on *you* to render them available, by cheerfully and unhesitatingly throwing off the lethargy of inaction, by resolutely girding yourselves for the arduous enterprise, and by putting forth, in unity of faith and purpose, the collected might, the energy, the perseverance, of a people resolved to yield to no obstacles, and to halt at no issue short of complete and triumphant success.

That many obstacles naturally exist, that not a few have been cast in the way, I have admitted and shown; I have also endeavoured to point out such as can be traced to the influence of former social institutions. Nevertheless, on a careful review of our present social condition, you have no cause for despondency; but let my earnest advice prevail with you to sever all connection with the past by a steady advance in moral and industrial improvement; or if the events of the past cannot but be reverted to, if its trials and struggles, its sufferings and humiliations will, of necessity, intrude—let them rather serve as beacons by which to avoid the shoals, and to steer onward in the current of the future, than as provocations to disunion, or precedents for error.

In conclusion, my opinion on many topics I give up to discussion, but I ask and expect a fair and impartial discussion.

Your friend and devoted servant,
L. A. A. DE VERTEUIL.

PORT-OF-SPAIN, *May*, 1856.

PREFACE.

It is to me somewhat surprising that geographical works, in general, should contain so many and such glaring errors, even respecting countries which certainly ought to be better known. Not to deviate from the subject in hand, and selecting Trinidad as a case in point, I may remark that such errors are of frequent occurrence in some of the best works that have made mention of the island, and also in books of very recent publication.

Adrien Balbi, speaking of Trinidad, has only these few words:—"*Spanish Town* (jadis Puerto España), ville *fortifiée* et commerçante, avec un port et peut-être 10,000 habitants; Saint-Joseph d'Oruña, autrefois capitale : *Charagaramus*, importante par son beau port, et *les chantiers que les Anglais y ont établis*."

Thus Balbi alters the name of the modern capital from *Port-of-Spain* to *Spanish Town;* he terms it *fortified*, whilst it is an open, unprotected town; also, instead of *Chaguaramas*, he writes *Charagaramus*—a misnomer, adopted by all the French geographers—making it, besides, an important place "*on account of the docks therein established by the English.*"

In Mr. Montgomery Martin's book, "The British Colonies," and the volume on the West Indies, published as late as 1854, I find the following erroneous statements :—" The chief ports resorted to, on the Trinidad side (of the Gulf of Paria), are : Chaguaramas Bay, where the extremity of the north-western peninsula, Gaspar Grande, and other islets, form an immense natural dock, sheltered from all weathers and all winds, and

Port-of-Spain, on whose shores stands the capital of the island." Mr. Martin, therefore, classes as one of the chief ports *resorted to*, in the Gulf of Paria, Chaguaramas Bay, whereas vessels never resort thither, except at intervals, to take in ballast. Let me remark here again that Port-of-Spain is the name of the *town*, and not of a *port*. Mr. Martin is likewise committing a glaring error when he says that from Mount Tamana "the lovely and fertile valleys of Maraccas and Las Cuevas extend themselves before the eye," for this good reason, that, between Tamana and those valleys, the northern range rises nearly 1,400 feet above the former. Again, never was *Rio Grande* a *good roadstead*—the only safe harbours, on the whole northern coast, being Las Cuevas and Maraccas Bay, which are not even mentioned in Mr. Martin's work.

In preparing the following pages, my anxious desire has mainly been to make Trinidad better known to the British public in general, and to its own inhabitants in particular. It is really surprising how uninformed even Trinidadians are regarding their own country. Our best schoolboys are able to give the names of the chief rivers, and the position of the principal towns in Great Britain, France, and even in Russia and China; but they are ignorant, perhaps, of the names of the Guataro and Oropuche, or through what county the Caroni has its course. They know that San Fernando exists, but may not be able to say whether it is on the eastern or the western side of the island; they can give the principal boundaries and dimensions of Europe, and its larger kingdoms, but are ignorant of those of their own island-home; they can enumerate the chief productions of England and France, but they do not know what are the agricultural products of their own country.

Not only is such ignorance discreditable, but its effects cannot but be prejudicial to the best interests, and consequently to the advancement, of the colony.

With this view of being serviceable, particularly to my own countrymen, I have entered into details which might otherwise have been overlooked. Being also under the conviction that statistical facts and comparisons make a deeper and more lasting impression on the mind than mere statements, I have taken great pains in preparing a few tables which, I hope, will prove useful in drawing and fixing the attention of those who can judge for themselves, and in circulating correct notions regarding the commercial and agricultural capabilities of Trinidad. I hope that those among us who have fallen from comparative affluence into poverty, will find in this sketch sufficient reasons to encourage them to exertion.

It now remains for me to give a few explanations, and to accomplish a pleasant duty, in tendering my acknowledgments to those who have supplied me with materials for, or have otherwise aided me in, the completion of this work.

During the eight years Lord Harris governed Trinidad, his Lordship invariably manifested the liveliest interest in the welfare of the island, not only as to the development of its natural resources, but also in regard to the intellectual and moral improvement of its inhabitants; and that interest he evinced in various ways, but particularly by directly encouraging useful information, and the diffusion of knowledge among all classes.

After awarding a very liberal prize to the best Essay on the Cultivation of the Sugar-cane and the Manufacture of Sugar, his Lordship proposed for public competition another Essay on the Vegetable and Mineral Resources of Trinidad. Various reasons then prevented me from writing on the subject; the proposals, however, aroused in my mind a strong desire to bring under public notice the natural resources of this important, but comparatively unknown and much neglected, colony; and to that circumstance may be traced the origin of the present work.

My personal knowledge of the topography of the island being somewhat limited, I have availed myself of information drawn from publications on the subject, and especially from the valuable survey made by Captain Columbine of the northern and southern coasts of the island; from the Geological Survey of Messrs.

Wall and Sawkins I have also obtained the elevation of our mountains and a few remarkable spots; from many kind friends I have received most useful and interesting contributions, and, from some, material aid. To these gentlemen, too numerous to be individually mentioned, I offer my most grateful acknowledgments; they are, however, especially due to Mr. John Thatcher. I also acknowledge with pleasure that the Report of MM. Wall and Sawkins on the Geology of Trinidad has greatly assisted me in improving this second edition, by affording most valuable information on the economic geology of the island.

The zoological part of this work is very incomplete; but not only did I not possess the necessary facilities for writing very comprehensively on the subject, but my intention has merely been to give some short descriptive details of those animals which do not exist in the other Antilles, or which deserve peculiar notice (as I have elsewhere stated) either on account of their prominent utility in the way of food, &c., their singular habits, or their noxious qualities and destructive propensities. I hope, therefore, the reader will make allowance for the little information afforded under this head. The botanical part will be found much more complete.

My friend, Dr. Leotaud, has contributed a very interesting memoir on the ornithology of the island. To him also I am indebted for the catalogue of our fishes. The assistance of my friend, Dr. Court, has enabled me to give a pretty complete account of our most remarkable reptiles; and another friend, Mr. Herman Crüger, has kindly furnished a very talented and valuable sketch of the flora of Trinidad.

In the application of names, I have adopted those which I consider as sanctioned by the common consent and usage of the inhabitants, or which were originally given to certain localities. Captain Columbine, in his report, had mistaken a few names: for instance, he writes *Les Couvas* and *Patura* instead of *Las Cuevas* * and *Matura*. I would have given preference to *Guataro*

---

* *Las Cuevas*, a Spanish name signifying *The Caves*.

instead of *Ortoire*, the former being more in unison with the names of the other rivers of the island, which are in general of Indian derivation; but Ortoire is more familiar. The northern point of the north-west peninsula of Trinidad had, apparently, no known designation; I suggested for its distinction that of *Point Mono*, from its proximity to the islet of the same name.

As to the introduction, it contains my personal views and opinions on the future prospects of the Columbian archipelago, and the line of policy which might be adopted for effecting an amelioration in the condition, and a security to the welfare, of its numerous islands. I anticipate that both those views and opinions will meet with opposition; but provided they are not regarded as prejudiced or unreasonable, I shall feel satisfied, at least, in not having been misunderstood; for my utmost endeavours throughout have aimed at being strictly impartial as well as practical.

In the collection and arrangement of the materials of this work, I have encountered more difficulties, labour, and anxiety than I had anticipated. My resources were confined within the narrow limits of local information, and I had, in addition, to contend with an imperfect knowledge of the tongue in which I ventured to write.

Again, being unknown, I have thought it necessary to seek for my opinions the support of those who, from their social position or special knowledge, may be regarded as authorities; hence the cause that so many extracts will be found transcribed in these pages.

TRINIDAD.

INTRODUCTION.

OF the numerous groups of islands which stud the surface of the deep, none is of more intrinsic importance than the Western or Caribbean Archipelago; and it may be questioned whether even the Eastern or Indian Archipelago, which alone can stand in comparison, really does equal it in the totality of its local and relative advantages.

In point of fertility of soil, agricultural productions, similarity of climate, and geographical position, they bear a great resemblance to each other, though they are, of course, not without their individual peculiarities. As a consequence, they may be said to have been always antagonistic in interest, and to have progressed in as constant an opposition.

At one period, the Western Archipelago seemed to have gained the ascendancy; but that ascendancy has been gradually transferred to the East, in proportion as European interest, power, and patronage have been extending in that quarter, and, more particularly, since the abolition of slavery in the West Indies.

The isles of the East certainly do possess many advantages over those of the West; they have greater agricultural and mineral wealth. Gold is found in almost every part, but particularly in Borneo and Sumatra, and no country produces better tin than Banca. Copper and iron are not uncommon, sulphur exists pretty generally, and diamonds are found in Borneo. Copper, only, it seems, is abundant in the Western Archipelago, though traces of gold have been found in Cuba and Hayti; sulphur however, is not scarce, and salt is plentiful and of excellent quality.

Sugar, coffee, cotton, indigo, and tobacco are products of both archipelagos; cotton and indigo of the Eastern particularly; tobacco of the Western. Cinnamon, cloves, nutmegs, and black pepper are indigenous to the East; vanilla, cacao, cochineal, and pimento to the West. Rice forms the basis of the agricultural economy of the Eastern, Indian corn of the Western, Archipelago.

The isles of the East do not import food, but manufactured goods only; Java even exports rice. The isles of the West, on the contrary, import an immense quantity of alimentary articles. This is, again, an advantage the former enjoy over the latter. The evils arising from such an anomalous position will not be felt so long as the population remains scant or limited, and high money-wages are afforded; but should it become more dense, and the same plan be persisted in, the most distressing results may be predicted—amongst others, starvation and its concomitant miseries will be the consequence, unless the cultivation of the "ground-provisions" be pursued on a sufficiently extensive scale.

The Eastern Archipelago lies within the tropics, between $19°$ N. and $11°$ S. latitude, and between $95°$ and $135°$ E. longitude. Its area may be estimated at about 392,000 square miles; that of the Western at about 105,000. The islands of the East, such as Borneo, Java, Sumatra, Celebes, Luzon, are generally of larger dimensions than those of the West.

The total population of the Eastern Archipelago may be computed at 23,000,000 inhabitants, or at the rate of 58·67 to the square mile; that of the Western, at about 3,113,000, or 31·13 to the square mile. Several races inhabit the Eastern Archipelago, viz., the Javano-Malayan and the Hindoo, both of which are again subdivided into many tribes; the Chinese, and also a few Arabians. The prevailing religion is Mahommedan; large numbers of Christians, however, are found in the Spanish, Portuguese, Dutch, and, latterly, the British colonies. The Chinese and Hindoos still adhere to Buddhism and Brahminism. Not exactly slavery, but serfdom exists everywhere, the seigneurial rights of all territory being vested in the sovereigns or hereditary chiefs, and despotism is the only prevailing form of government.

The Western Archipelago is, at present, inhabited by two races, the aborigines or Indian stock being almost entirely extinct. Those two races are the European and the African; widely different in origin, external appearance, and also in habits and prejudices. The representatives of the former are immigrants from Europe; the latter, imported labourers from Africa. The Africans, whilst Europeans continued to be slaveholders, were, for a long time, degraded under the worst form of slavery; but, at the present period, unconditional freedom, and such as was never known to exist in any Asiatic kingdom, practically exists in nearly all the Western isles, and Christianity may be said to form the sole prevailing religion.

In proportion as the natural resources of the Eastern islands become more accessible, a vast aggregate of industrious immigrants are within hail, and at their beck—nay, at their very doors —ready to avail themselves of any inducement afforded. China is the grand source from which population will flow into Luzon, Borneo, Celebes, Java, and Sumatra. The Hindoo race will, in preference, seek a home in Ceylon and the peninsula beyond the Ganges.

From what quarter will emigration issue to stock the Caribbean Archipelago? The United States are, probably, the source from which the African race will, by degrees, drain off into the Western isles, there to form free communities under the joint protection of Europe and America, or to become naturalised subjects of the various governments to which those possessions at present respectively belong. But this is a question which requires mature consideration, and which I shall afterwards more fully examine.

The present condition of the Eastern Archipelago is cheering and highly encouraging; its prospects are those of prosperity and peaceful progress. The present condition of the Western Archipelago is one of hard struggle, and discouraging in the extreme, whilst its prospects are still veiled in obscurity.

The Indian Archipelago is on the highway from Europe to China and Japan, by the Cape of Good Hope and the Suez Canal, and lies between the southern kingdoms of Asia and Australia. Those kingdoms produce similar articles of food and commerce, viz., rice, sugar, cotton, and indigo; Australia, wheat, wool, and gold. But the latter is also capable of producing cotton, indigo, and sugar. However, New Zealand, Van Diemen's Land, and the southern colonies of New Holland, may be regarded as growing and highly promising markets for the Eastern isles.

The Western Archipelago is on the track from Europe, through Central America, to Japan, China, Australasia, and the western coast of America; stretching between the southern States of the great American Republic and the northern shores of South America; and lying opposite the rich countries of Mexico, Guatimala, Nicaragua, &c. The different regions which are in the vicinity of the Western Archipelago produce, or are capable of producing, the same staples which form the basis of its exports; and, most unfortunately, negro slavery is still in those regions the agent of that production. But, as a compensation for all these disadvantages, there is the geographical position of the Archipelago, its proximity to Europe and the rising countries of North America; also, the greater fertility of its islands, whether arising from the composition of the soil, or from the greatest part of their surface being still covered with virgin forests.

The Caribbean isles are in general fertile, some of them remarkably so, and they can be made to yield all intertropical productions, such as sugar, coffee, cotton, indigo, cacao, spices, rice, and the best tobacco in the world. They can also produce, for the support of their own population, an abundance of alimentary substances, particularly plantains, corn, rice, cassada, and other farinaceous roots, with all sorts of vegetables and fruits; also poultry, hogs, and oxen. Some of them abound in beautiful cabinet-woods, and the most durable timber. Their numerous harbours and ports are capable of accommodating vast fleets of merchantmen, and of affording anchorage to the united navies of the entire world. Cuba, alone, possesses, besides many bays and havens, at least a dozen first-class seaports; and the Gulf of Paria, between Trinidad and the province of Cumana, in Venezuela, may be regarded as a truly magnificent harbour, closely and securely sheltered from all winds and weathers. In no part of the world is navigation more easy and safe than in the Caribbean Sea: it is, however, visited, at intervals, by hurricanes, which spread ruin and devastation wherever they are felt. The Antilles are also subject to earthquakes, of which sad records are written in the annals of some of the islands. The climate is generally unhealthy on the seaboard, remittent and intermittent fevers being prevalent; dysentery and yellow fever may also be said to be endemic.

The proximity of the Western isles to Europe, the great capabilities of their soil for producing the tropical staples and other articles of commerce, formerly rendered them of great importance; and, for many years, their possession was warmly disputed by the European powers. For a long period they enjoyed the privilege of supplying Europe with colonial products, and the French colony of St. Domingo then ranked as a queen amongst her sister isles: but after passing through alternations of prosperity and depression, these islands have at length approached a most eventful crisis, and those amongst them that still retain something of their pristine eminence—it grieves me to say—are those which have not abjured the wholesale abominations of slavery. The time, however, has arrived when they, too, must yield and submit to the *fiat* of public opinion.

These islands were, therefore, at a bygone epoch, rich and flourishing; but they were then cursed with the loathsome *lepra* of slavery; nearly all are now free, but many of them fast verging on ruin. By contrasting their present with their former social condition, the philanthropist has reason to rejoice; but, on the other hand, the comparison of their actual state of industrial depression with their past prosperity, cannot but be a subject of anxious reflection to the statesman and philosopher. It behoves these parties, therefore—whether as leaders in the senate, or as deep searchers into the nature of things—to consider it both a profitable and incumbent duty to institute a diligent and persevering inquiry into the various causes which have induced such results, and into the best means for remedying the same, and improving the condition of the emancipated colonies. For these colonies are, by the progression of modern navigation, brought nearer to Europe than they ever were, whilst contiguous to them new markets are rising, viz., the United States, Canada, Nova Scotia, and New Brunswick; they still possess their fertile soils, and their productive capabilities are unimpaired. When the great Columbus sailed from Palos in search of the golden regions of *India* and *Cathay*, he met them on his way; and surely their geographical position has not changed in our days. Ere many years have elapsed, the land section of the great commercial highway to Japan, China, and Australasia; to Oregon, California, and the western shores of Mexico and Central America; to Ecuador, Peru, and Chili, will have been completed—thus establishing a communication between the Pacific and that great Mediterranean Sea of the New World which lies almost within the lap of the Antilles.

The numerous islands which form the Western Archipelago, classed as the Great and Lesser Antilles, are scattered in the form of a horse-shoe, along an arched line running eastward and E.S.E., from the entrance of the Gulf of Mexico, and then curving southward to the mouth of the Orinoco, whence they stretch westward along the northern coast of Venezuela, to the eastern extremity of the Gulf of Maracaibo; they lie between 10° and 27° N. latitude, and 60° and 85° W. longitude—the greatest distance between any adjacent two of them being about 100 miles.

By drawing a line from the Bay of Apalache, through Florida, to Point Galera in Trinidad, and another from Tampico in the Gulf of Mexico, through Yucatan and the Mosquito country, to the mouth of the Atrato, it is found that these two lines run very nearly parallel, and that together with the southern coast of the United States and the northern coast of South America—which also end in a nearly parallel direction, they form an oblong, which comprises within its limits the great Mediterranean Sea of the West. This sea is completely land-locked on the N.W. and S., whilst being bounded on the E. by the chain of the Antilles; a great many outlets are left between these islands, extending as they do over a space of 17° of latitude, or 1,200 miles.

This vast inlet of the Atlantic consists of two distinct basins, viz., the Gulf of Mexico and the Caribbean Sea. The former is nearly of a circular form, being shaped on the N.E. by the western coast of Florida; on the N. by the coasts of Alabama, Mississippi, Louisiana, and Texas, in the United States; on the W.

by those of Mexico, from the mouth of the Rio Grande to Vera-Cruz, whence it is rounded on the S. and S.E. to Cape Catoche in Yucatan, which stretches northwards towards Cape Sable in the extreme S. of Florida. Into the entrance thus narrowed by the approach of these points, Cuba advances so as to hold the key of that most important basin—the Gulf of Mexico, important as being the outlet of the great valley of the West, and of the commercial road from the Pacific through the Isthmus of Tehuantepec.

The Caribbean Sea is more irregular in its formation, and is bounded on the W. by Central America and the Isthmus of Panama; on the S. by New Granada and Venezuela; on the N. by Cuba, Hayti, and Porto Rico; on the E. by the Lesser Antilles, from the Virgin Islands down to Trinidad, which holds the key of the rich and extensive basin of the Orinoco, as does Cuba that of the Gulf of Mexico. This basin is the outlet of the following important rivers:—the San Juan, the Atrato, the Magdalena, and the Orinoco; likewise of the commercial roads from the Pacific through the territory of Nicaragua and the Isthmus of Panama. Lake Maracaibo is also an inlet of its waters.

Lieutenant Maury, speaking of the Gulf of Mexico and the Caribbean Sea, says in rather enthusiastic language, but which is well adapted to my object:—" Nature has scooped out the land in Central America, and cut the Continent nearly in two there, that she might plant between the mouth of the 'King of Rivers' and the 'Father of Waters' an arm of the sea, capable of receiving the surplus produce which the two grandest river-basins on the face of the earth are, some day, to pour out into the *Gulf of Mexico* and the *Caribbean Sea*. These two sheets of water form the great commercial lap of the south. This sea and gulf receive the drainage of all the rivers of note in both Continents, except La Plata on the south, and Columbia on the west; the St. Lawrence, and those of the Atlantic seaboard on the east.

"The Caribbean Sea and the Gulf of Mexico are twin basins. They are seas Mesopotamian, and wholly American. The great equatorial current having its *genesis* in the Indian Ocean, and doubling the Cape of Good Hope, sweeps by the mouth of the Amazon: and, after traversing both the Caribbean Sea and the Gulf of Mexico, meets with the gulf-stream and places the commercial outlet of that river almost as much in the Florida Pass as in the mouth of the Mississippi itself.

"These twin basins are destined by nature to be the greatest commercial receptacles in the world. No age, clime, nor quarter of the globe affords any parallel, or any conditions of the least resemblance, to those which we find in this sea or gulf.

"What other arm of the ocean is between two Continents with opposite seasons? Where is there another gulf-stream, uniting the waters of an Amazon with the waters of a Mississippi, an extra-tropical with an inter-tropical river? Where, in the wide ocean, or the wider world, is there another Mesopotamian sea, that is the natural outlet for a system of river-basins draining an extent of arable and fertile lands greater than the Continent of Europe can contain, that yield all the productions of the torrid and the temperate zones?

"From the Gulf of Mexico, all the great commercial markets of the world are down hill. A vessel bound from the gulf to Europe, places herself in the current of the great stream, and drifts along with it at the rate, for part of the way, of 80 or 100 miles a day.

"And when there shall be established a commercial thoroughfare across the isthmus, the trade-winds of the Pacific will place China, India, New Holland, and all the islands of that ocean down hill also, from this sea of ours. In that case, all Europe must pass by at our very doors on the great highway to the markets both of the East and West Indies.

"This beautiful Mesopotamian sea is in a position to occupy the summit level of navigation, and to become the great commercial receptacle of the world. Our rivers run into it, and float down with their currents the surplus articles of merchandise that are produced upon their banks. Arrived with them upon the bosom of this grand marine basin, there are the currents of the sea and the winds of heaven so arranged by nature, that they drift it and waft it down hill, and down stream, to the great market-places of the world."

This is a spirited, and, to the reflective statesman, a true picture of this Mesopotamian sea, as the talented writer calls it. But the Antilles form its Eastern limits, and, therefore, must evidently participate in its importance.

How is it that these islands, once so eagerly coveted, are, in our days, virtually neglected and disregarded? The present state of depression of the emancipated colonies is evidently the main cause of their being neglected. Capital does not venture where there is little profit to expect, and only precarious security.

The abolition of slavery was one of the most extraordinary social changes recorded in the history of the human race. It will be conceded that the natural and immediate results must have been a greater or less revolution in the relations of the different classes which then constituted colonial society: and I take it for granted that such disorganisation must have influenced temporarily, at least, the welfare of the community.

The revolution produced was instantly felt in the labour

market, the available amount being either directed into new
channels, rendered unsteady, or permanently reduced. The
amount of labour diverted into new channels was not exactly
lost, but was, in many cases, such an exchange as tended to the
detriment of all classes, as shown by the disproportionate number
of carpenters, masons, and other tradesmen, tailors, petty shopkeepers, as compared with the tillers of the soil, etc. The
permanent reduction for agricultural purposes was, on the
contrary, a real loss to the colonies, since the cultivation of
staples is the only foundation of their commerce and of their
prosperity.

One of the greatest difficulties with which the colonists had
to contend was the unsettled state of the labour market. For
whenever, as in the case of cane cultivation, continuous labour is
required and cannot be obtained, the whole system of agricultural
economy suffers thereby; in fact, when the available labour is
not proportionate to the demand, agricultural interests are
imperilled; and such was the position of nearly all the emancipated colonies, whether Danish, French, or British, excepting
Barbadoes and Antigua, where nearly the whole of the land was
under cultivation. Demerara and Trinidad, however, might be
pointed out as exceptions, since their exports have been steadily
increasing for the last fifteen or twenty years; and yet their
example is highly confirmatory of what I have alleged. The
introduction of Asiatics and other labourers has alone prevented
a proportionate decrease or total abandonment of sugar manufacture in those two colonies; and that, so far only as those
labourers were placed under indenture, and their labour thus
rendered regularly available.

It is admitted, as an axiom, that free is cheaper than slave
labour, because, it is said, the freeman finds, in a strong desire
to improve his condition, a stimulus to exertion, which the slave
has not. As a general principle, the admission is correct; but
this, as all other rules, has its exceptions. Undoubtedly, the
freeman ought to be more active and more industrious than the
slave. But indolence and prejudice may prove the deadliest
paralysers of energy in improving any one's condition. To
assert that hired is cheaper than slave labour becomes a paradox,
if taken in an absolute sense; and the best proof of this is the
extension of agriculture in Cuba and Brazil, as compared with
the similar interest in the emancipated colonies. Wherever free
labour is abundant, it is cheaper, as in Hindostan; but wherever
population is scanty and labour not easily procurable, slave
labour then becomes decidedly the cheapest and more gainful,
for this simple reason—it can be concentrated within given
limits and arbitrarily directed, in all cases of emergency and at

the most suitable juncture, to the production of the contemplated results.

I only contend that, as certain effects flow from certain causes, so certain results ought naturally to have succeeded the abolition of slavery; and that these results had necessarily a great influence on the conditions under which the social economy of the West Indies was constituted. In my opinion, measures might have been adopted to counteract some of those results, and to render the Act of Emancipation a boon to the slave-holder as well as to the slave himself.

It was eight years only after the abolition of slavery that the Equalisation Act of 1846 was passed; so that only eight years had been allowed, both to the planters and the emancipated class, for recovering from the shock of a great social revolution, and for settling down from the violent oscillation which had been imparted to the entire social body in the colonies. These eight years, besides, had been a period of unceasing contention and of growing bewilderment.

The planter had to be taught by experience, and by experience only, a totally new system of property management; the emancipated had to be taught that freedom imposed on them new duties and new obligations; that it behove them to become industrious, to obey the laws and submit to prescriptions of which, as slaves, they had no idea. And whatever may have been said to the contrary, both planters and emancipated did prove themselves equal to all reasonable expectations. For who, with the slightest knowledge of human nature, could possibly have expected that the one party would never commit disorders in practice, nor the other be guilty of errors in judgment.

During the time of slavery, free labour, when procurable, was paid at a very high rate; immediately after emancipation, the labouring population considered themselves as entitled to, and actually received, the same high wages; and through fear that the labourers would altogether retire from the cane field, the planter readily paid the amount demanded, in order to keep his property under cultivation, till better days should come. The scarcity of labour in the colonies, and the high price of sugar in the home market, seemed to concur in justifying both the unreasonable demands of the labourers and the imprudent offers of the planters. Things were carried a stage further: the planter, instead of showing himself provident and calculating, began to create a competition in the labour market, by offering enhanced wages to the labourer. Led on by reckless improvidence, and deceived by fallacious appearances, he at once sought to extend his cultures at a moment when the labour market was under a severe strain, and offered the most exorbitant wages for daily task-work. The labourer, seeing his employer yielding at discretion, wantonly indulged in idleness and revelry, or squandered his time in wandering over the country, from place to place, being always certain of procuring shelter and work whereever he preferred remaining, even for a few days.

I have already proved that slave countries can produce sugar and other articles at a cheaper rate than could be effected in the emancipated colonies. As a consequence of the Equalisation Act of 1846 Cuba, Porto-Rico, Brazil, the United States, Mauritius, and the East Indies enormously increased their production; whilst that of the emancipated colonies was retrograding, with the exception of Mauritius, which had been allowed to import labour from India.

Emancipation was not only a political, it was, above all, a philanthropical act; an act of reparation, intended as the means of the regeneration of the oppressed race. As such it ought to have had its consequences; and one of these results surely was to extend its benefits, as far as possible, to the whole African race, by discouraging negro slavery in all countries where it actually existed. The reverse, however, may be said to have at first practically ensued; for, at the very time in which the British money was employed in checking the slave trade on the coasts of Africa, the British Parliament was passing measures which, indirectly but most effectively, favoured that trade, by tendering a premium to slave produce. Certainly it is difficult to say what would have occurred had the British market been closed against slave-growing sugar, or a differential duty been established; but I am justified in concluding, from what has taken place, that such a measure would have been the death-blow of the slave trade, both in Cuba and Brazil.

It has been stated that the "*ci-devant* slave proprietors were, in most instances, impoverished, in many ruined." With regard to Trinidad, the fact was this: by far the greatest part of the compensation grant (£1,390,000) had been applied in liquidating the mortgage and other debts of the planters, so that the majority of them began the new era free from liabilities, many with reserve funds. However, they were soon afterwards involved in fresh difficulties, owing to the exorbitant wages they were compelled to pay, in order to obtain a mere *modicum* of labour, and to the usurious rates of interest paid on capital advanced by merchants and others residing in Great Britain. " I could quote to your lordship," wrote Lord Harris to Earl Grey, in April, 1848, " I could quote estates, so far as their soil is concerned, of great value, and giving previously to emancipation a large income, on which the whole of the redemption money was expended in improvements; which were entirely free from debt at the time, and which are now mortgaged to their full value; and their proprietors, resident creoles too, from being in good circumstances, reduced to the last extremities. In those cases, the want of labour at a fair rate has been the chief cause of their embarrassments; they surely have some claims for assistance from the mother country."

Every one plainly foresaw that the immediate result of emancipation would be a complete disturbance of the labour market, and consequently a paralysis—at least momentary—of the productive powers of these islands. That a fair remuneration would operate as an inducement to exertion was true, but superficial was the mind that would have trusted to that agency alone to continue the active industry of the emancipated. The much misunderstood, because distrusted, planter, coveted not— thought not of the renewal of any law unjust or unfair to the labourer; he called for the interposition of legislative authority to complete the work of emancipation, to exercise a parental interest in the welfare of those who had been snatched from the fetters of slavery to be delivered to the grievous thraldom of their own ignorant and improvident habits. Certainly the planters contemplated a benefit to themselves. And what was that benefit? That the emancipated should continue to labour according to God's divine commands; to labour for their own advantage, by maintaining the agricultural prosperity of the country of which they were resident inhabitants; to labour consequently for the general prosperity of the country with whose progress or decline their own well-being or misery was inseparably interwoven.

There is no doubt that had cane cultivation been discontinued in the West Indies, they would have suffered still more; for, as judiciously observed by the Governor of Jamaica, "the progress and prospects of civilisation in these islands are closely interwoven with the continuation of a branch of industry to which European capital and skill have, from the earliest period of its history, been mainly devoted, and because it seems clear that the same economical conditions required to restore a fair ratio of profit to sugar-planting would be necessary to render any other species of cultivation whatever remunerative." And I will add, because cane cultivation is, from its very nature, better calculated than any other agricultural pursuit in this climate to induce industry and create habits of steadiness, as well as to keep up regular and profitable commercial intercourse with those countries, the influence of which all sensible men must concede is, and will for a long period be, necessary to the development of civilisation in these islands.

After what I have said of the dispositions of the emancipated slaves, it remains for me to add a few remarks on the character of the African race as exhibited in these islands.

Be it the result of slavery or of natural disposition, or of both, the African does not seem to understand the motives and the object of legislation. He would not decide a case on principle, but on circumstantial considerations. Whenever he is wronged, he finds that the law is not severe enough; but, as the offending party, he is amazed at its severity. In his own favour he wishes it to exert a spirit of revenge, and does not seem fully to understand that, in its application, it must be impartial and governed by fixed principles. Should justice be done him, he is unsatisfied and unconvinced, because that justice was not awarded according to his own views; to realise his ideas, the law must avenge him to the utmost extent and independently of all extenuation. So predominant is this peculiar disposition of the African character, that nearly all the heinous crimes he commits have no other cause or source than his misconception of justice. An African labourer who may have received an offensive epithet from his employer, or some other trifling injury, will satiate his revengeful passion by firing a megass or curing-house, or perhaps the dwelling of the offender. It would be unjust to pretend that this is a distinctive characteristic of the African, for it is still more strongly delineated in the Javanese race, and the more civilised inhabitants of Corsica and Italy generally; with this difference, however, that the African aims more at the property, the others mainly at the person. Arson is in the hands of the negro a weapon as redoubtable as it is treacherous.

He seems to nourish a great dread of the watchful eye of a protecting law, and, as a consequence, has the greatest reluctance to aid in the discovery of crime, unless he has very strong personal motives for so doing; it does not concern him. He has besides a sort of supernatural fear of a daring criminal, and the more dangerous to society, the more certain is the culprit of escaping detection and punishment. The fact is this: the African is wanting in moral courage; and he willingly submits to the chance of being deprived of the blessings of civilisation provided he be not required to fulfil the obligations it imposes.

Considered in domestic life he has many defects, and not a few capital faults. Since emancipation, marriages are much more frequent among all classes than they were during the period of slavery; an increased desire exists of engaging in its bonds, for marriage is regarded as a claim to respectability. The respect manifested towards this rite is, so far, a good symptom; but let it be added that in no part of the world perhaps are the obligations of marriage less binding, since a husband and wife very commonly, and too often, by tacit consent, live unblushingly in adulterous intercourse. I need not point out the pernicious consequences which such want of principles must necessarily involve. Whenever domestic associations are not framed on a Christian basis, society is sapped to its very foundations; strife and hatred ensue, children are disowned and abandoned, industry and economy are out of the question, whilst ignorance, vice, and poverty are the inevitable results.

The African is exceedingly—indeed blindly—attached to his offspring; and yet he cannot be said to be a good parent, inasmuch as he is governed by mere caprice—at times indulging and spoiling his child beyond all measure, or, in rage approaching madness, punishing him with the most savage brutality. Should any interference take place, he objects that his child is his own, and he can do with him as he pleases. He is withal exceedingly jealous of his paternal authority, and, of course, feels highly offended should his child be chastised, or even reprimanded, by those who have the authority to do so. Negro children are, as a consequence, self-willed, impudent, and most disobedient. As soon as a youth of this class is able to provide for his own wants, he generally abandons the paternal home, considering himself free from all filial obligations. I must acknowledge, however, that there is of late years a marked improvement in these respects, the relations of children and parents being more cordial. The latter are evidently more anxious about the education of their children, and more cautious in their treatment of them; the former, on the other hand, are more ready to please and assist their parents. This is mostly apparent in the families of small cottagers who attend to their religious duties.

There is another salient defect in the emancipated class, and which became particularly manifest during the prevalence of cholera. Though very punctilious on the score of respectability, the negro is nevertheless exceedingly indolent, and the moment he can rely on the aid of others, will not even endeavour to exert himself. This is to a certain extent common to all creoles. A strong inclination also exists on the part of the negro to consider all acts of benevolence exercised towards him as his due, and not in the light of a favour. I have known individuals of this class who, during the cholera epidemic of 1852, with their small apartments prettily furnished, or receiving abundant aid from their employers, would yet regularly apply for their meals at the charitable soup kitchens established for the relief of the destitute; not that they really required them, but only because they "would have their share." Nor did persons of the same class blush to say, "Since one must die a day, he better die now, as there is no payment asked for either medical attendance, medicines, coffin, grave, or funeral."

Slavery, with its degrading influence, I readily concede, must have contributed largely to the implanting of the above-mentioned defects in the negro character. During slavery marriage was not exactly discouraged; but, as it was generally allowed only between individuals belonging to the same estate, the consequence was that marriages were the rare exceptions and concubinage the general rule. In addition to that, the slave possessing no civil right had no interest, as he had no benefit, in any civil contract; and it is well known that habits contracted during ages cannot be uprooted in a few years. Again, the slave had very little authority over his children, the care of them being left to him only in their infant state; these children, on the other hand, being bound to obey and serve the master, were actually led to cast aside the respect and attention due to the parents. Slavery had, in this as in other cases, a fatal tendency to relax the natural as well as the civil ties, and it is not surprising that its effects are still felt even after forty years of freedom.

I think it therefore due to the negro to say that those vicious features of his character which I have portrayed are more the offspring of ignorance and the consequence of a protracted state of debasing bondage than the effects of a wicked and perverse nature; for, however prominent their faults and, at times, heinous their offences, it is notorious that they do not approach to that degree of moral turpitude which characterises those of the same class in Europe. The crimes committed by the negroes generally spring from sudden impulse and ungovernable passions, and are not the result of base and selfish calculations. Seldom have we heard of life violated for the acquisition of money in Trinidad. They are, besides, charitably disposed, and ever ready to assist the destitute. But if their vices do not assume as dark a shade of moral perversity as those of some Europeans, doubtless their qualities, in regard to all the degrees of social obligations, are far inferior to theirs. Such is my conscientious appreciation of the merits and demerits of the negroes as they are exhibited in these islands. He is and must be responsible to a great extent for his faults, but more responsible still should be those institutions which necessarily tend to debase the human mind. A healthy and highly encouraging change has already taken place since he has been admitted to the enjoyment of those rights which for so many years were the exclusive advantage of a few.

In 1858, when I first published this book, I could say indeed that the West Indian planters had been in general most unmercifully treated, and without regard to the peculiarities of their position by those who had written or spoken on the subject. They were then so recently slave-holders, and must bear the consequences of an unenviable position indeed, and endure the odium attached to the institution. I am ready to recognise that the situation is now different, and that public opinion has undergone a change; yet I believe that the time has not come yet when we should consider as buried in oblivion the many accusations which were heaped on us, especially as there still exists a tendency occasionally to revive them in one shape or the other. I trust, therefore, that I will be excused for insisting in this new edition on what took place as a consequence of the abolition of slavery, and the causes that brought on the ruin of so many families. We are but too easily inclined to judge of the present by what we actually see, without reference to the past, or without taking into account grave difficulties which may no more exist, but which, whilst prevailing, had their effects.

When the West Indians were judged as agriculturists, for instance, neither the climate nor the conditions of inter-tropical agriculture were ever taken into consideration. Their system was weighed according to the rules which were found most applicable to European tillage; and yet the climate and the very nature of inter-tropical cultivation have a very great influence on the most superior methods of conducting agricultural operations.

The almost uncontrollable luxuriance of vegetation within the torrid zone renders it necessary to have labourers constantly engaged in field-work, whilst under temperate zones vegetation is dormant for four or five months in the year, during which recess the labourer may be employed under shelter, and in various occupations. Moreover, under our zone heavy rains or extreme droughts act as an obstacle to certain agricultural operations. Again, nearly all our crops require weedings, an operation which is but seldom performed in Europe, for the cereals, which form the basis of European agriculture, once sown are allowed to grow and arrive at maturity undisturbed; so that the same extent of land requires in these colonies more constant care and attention than, for instance, in England or France. Nearly all our cultivated plants are perennial, which makes it very difficult—if not impossible—to establish a system of rotation of crops, as where annuals are raised. Some of our plants even, such as the cacao and coffee, do not begin to yield a regular crop except after a term of five or eight years' growth; so that, even should an agricultural article become almost valueless in the market, the planter is still under the obligation of continuing its cultivation. And with regard to a sugar estate, its management resembles more that of a manufactory than of a farm, and field operations are suspended more or less for four or five months, in order to manufacture the juice of the cane into sugar. Thus the sugar-planter is subject, at the same time, to all the casualties attendant on the pursuits, both of the manufacturer and the agriculturist. These may be said to be natural conditions which cannot be changed; but there were others of an artificial kind against which the planter had incessantly to struggle.

Under the system of slavery man was regarded and employed as a mere mechanical agent; and the planter who, immediately after emancipation, required skill in the tillage of the soil, and intelligent labourers who could understand and profitably adopt improved and efficient methods, was compelled to rest satisfied with the mechanical aid of the very class he had kept in a state of ignorance and serfdom; and where initiated, active, and willing agents were necessary, he found obtuse, indolent, and, above all, capricious instruments. Of course, this was perhaps the greatest difficulty with which the West Indian planter had to contend, the undesirable bequest of slavery.

Again, on what terms were proprietors compelled to employ those agents? It may be said that during the existence of slavery there were but two distinct classes in the colonies, the slaveholders and the slaves; for many who were not owners of land were nevertheless owners of slaves. Many of the labourers, soon after obtaining their liberty, left their masters' property and began to erect small cottages on unoccupied lands or on small lots purchased by themselves; the majority, however, continued to live on the estates, actually occupying houses and lands free from all rent, and yet exacting from their masters whatever wages they thought proper, the greatest number of them receiving from forty to fifty cents (1s. 8d. to 2s. 1d.) per measured task of field-work.

The task system which had been adopted in Trinidad on nearly all cacao, and on several sugar plantations, during the period of slavery, was almost immediately afterwards enforced on all other estates; and in few cases only did an able labourer take more than four hours to perform the allotment, some of them perfecting two to two tasks and a half per day. In nearly all the colonies, the planters were necessitated to submit to the terms of the labourers. The consequence was that the greater number of planters who had been extricated from their liabilities by the compensation grant became soon involved to very large amounts, especially those who had attempted the introduction of improvements. On several estates the labourers lost their wages, their employers having been utterly ruined; and let me record it here, under those trying circumstances the labouring class, generally, behaved very generously, many of them continuing to work for several months without exacting wages. Lest they should soon be placed in the same position, the other employers, compelled by necessity, began to give less wages and to exact more work; the labourers became dissatisfied, and the emancipated population began gradually to retire from estate field-work. It was about this period, and consequent on this movement, that they were ejected from the houses and land they occupied on estates, and their provision grounds destroyed.

"During the last two years," said Lord Harris, "great exertions have been used by sugar-growers here to lower the cost of production through a diminished rate of wages, and by getting more work performed; this has caused dissatisfaction among the labourers, and increased their migratory and idle inclinations, which has resulted in visible inattention to their provision grounds—an evil of serious import, operating unfavourably against reduced cost of production by rendering the labourer totally dependent upon high money wages to pay for imported articles of consumption; an alarming position to be in, with the prospect of curtailed employment, through sugar cultivation being diminished.

"The general excuse offered by the labourers for their inattention to raising provisions, is that they are liable to be robbed, and turned off estates. True, this is the case; but the latter is invariably caused by their own fickleness and pervert acts." (Lord Harris to Earl Grey, April, 1846.)

Could the planters exercise any control over such circumstances? They did struggle to the utmost of their power, and, as a class, they are more worthy of praise than of blame.

Increased labour is required in the West Indies, whatever may be said to the contrary, and their deficiency in this respect is certainly the greatest obstacle to their progress. Listen to the words of the Governor of Jamaica: "Let us remove all obstacles to their recruiting the ranks of their labourers from other countries; let us go further indeed, and take active steps to set on an immigration of the negro population of the United States at the public expense."

I will quote Governor Barkly once more, for all he says concerning Jamaica is applicable to the other islands :—" Far from deserving the imputation of supineness, and ignorance of their business, which it has been too much the fashion to lavish upon them, I found the planters of Jamaica as eager to introduce new machinery and to adopt new processes of manufacture as any of their competitors, British or foreign, and I have had more opportunities than most persons of observing both; and

c

this, at least, I can safely undertake to assert, that if they fail, it will not, in the majority of instances, be for want of exertions on their part. .... I derive no small hope for the future from the spirit of enterprise and intelligence in which the sugar plantations that remain are carried on."

This assertion of one who has had, as he says, "more opportunities than most persons" of observing the earnestness of the colonists to introduce new machinery and to improve manufacture, must have, in the eyes of impartial judges, more weight than the allegations of those who prefer to echo the accusation brought against us, of "wanting the spirit of progress and improvement," instead of examining into the merits of the case.

Undoubtedly "skill and capital are needed to render the West Indies a remunerative field of production." Skill, I dare say, we will always be able to procure; but how can we expect to allure capital to these islands when our staple produce has become a drug in the market? when we are compelled to compete with countries which actually do grant protection to their own article, and are admitted into the British market on terms of equality with us? when these islands are pointed out as precarious and worthless fields? Let those who take an interest in these colonies and their inhabitants listen to the disinterested appeal of the noble Governor of Jamaica:—"Be it their task to encourage our efforts by every means legislation can present, and to smoothe, as far as lies in their power, the inevitable difficulties of a competition which, aggravated as it unfortunately is at the moment by extraneous circumstances, threatens to prove more formidable than could have been previously anticipated."

The present difficulties, created by unfair European competition, are greater, and our position more precarious, than they were forty years ago, unless the British Government consent to interfere; and the only interference we solicit is this:—That foreign sugar be not admitted to compete with our own produce on terms which are not equal, on account of the protection which it receives in the shape of bounties or drawbacks on exportation. The effect of such protection—but too real, though indirect—is to depress the value of colonial sugar to an unremunerative level, that, as we believe, would not exist under the conditions of fair international free trade. Bounties are granted in France, Belgium, Prussia, Austria, Hungary, Russia, and Holland. These drawbacks are supposed to represent the rates levied on the beetroots or the juice; but as the quantity of sugar extracted from the roots is actually larger than the quantity assessed, any surplus thus obtained is a clear profit to the exporters.

All persons interested in the production and the commerce of cane-sugar have energetically remonstrated against this bounty system; a remedy has become urgent, for, under such conditions, we must succumb in the unequal struggle, and leave an undisputed field to the beet growers. If it be intended to give us any relief, let it be afforded immediately, or it may come too late. Let us all join in the prayer of the West India Committee, and demand that the British West India colonies may not look in vain for redress to Her Majesty's Government. These colonies, in their painful efforts to restore themselves by means of free labour, and their long-continued struggle to hold their own against the slave system of Cuba and Brazil, possess, we conceive, a strong claim for consideration. This is not asking for protection for ourselves, but simply objecting to protection being allowed to our antagonists.

I cannot say what may be the position of the sugar-planters in the other colonies; but I can affirm, as regards Trinidad, that the following estimates are correct:—The expenses for carrying on a sugar estate making 500 hogsheads, or 900,000 lbs. net, of muscovado sugar, may be calculated at £5,500 sterling; value of the estate, £12,000 sterling; at 18s. the hundredweight—the actual price of the article in the home market—£7,231 the 500 hogsheads. I do not reckon molasses, which generally go to pay interests, land-taxes, &c. Deduct £5,500 from these £7,231 sterling, there remains a sum of £1,731; interest on the value of the property, £1,000; amount available for contingencies, improvements, &c., £731.

Now, as a sugar-planter cannot turn his estate into a cacao or other plantation without great loss, he must struggle on, hoping even against hope, till ruin overwhelms him; the estate is then in an abandoned state. This process, which has been going on in Jamaica, Dominica, &c., and which has rendered these colonies nearly worthless, must, I fear, commence in Trinidad and Demerara, for sugar selling at 2 dollars 50 cents the cwt., here, as elsewhere, the result must be the same. Let me, therefore, state, in the words of the *Economist*, that " it is clearly not the interest, even of the consumer, that prices should be lower than the fair relation of supply and demand justifies, inasmuch as such a state of the market would discourage those necessary supplies which may be hereafter required."

The condition of the sugar-market in the United Kingdom is far from encouraging; we cannot go on long producing sugar at the actual low price. The danger is different from what it was thirty years ago, but it is as great. Now, should our ruin be achieved, will not the consumer be exposed to deception, and suffer in turn?

Can we expect that Parliament will ever agree to imposing a counteracting duty on sugars imported into the United Kingdom and which enjoy artificial advantages in the shape of bounty? And yet this would be the most effectual, perhaps the sole, remedy. Of course, whilst crying for help, we should put our shoulders to the wheel; and we are ready to do so.

Various plans may be devised for the encouragement of agriculture. As a general rule, let all financial enactments, be they in the shape of direct or indirect taxation, bear as lightly as possible on land owners; let agricultural implements of every description be admitted duty free, as also draught animals or those of burden; afford effective protection to the growth of staple and other marketable produce, by strictly enforcing the law with respect to the stealing and destruction of agricultural products and cultivated plants; and assist in the diffusion of agricultural knowledge, by establishing experimental farms. In Germany and in France, *Agronomic stations* have largely contributed to the improvement of agriculture, and the cultivation of the beetroot plant particularly. Let us not forget that though our population is purely agricultural, yet the labouring classes, in their ignorance, are prejudiced against field occupations; that, with the exception of a minority of the planters, no others possess even the most elementary notions of agricultural economy. No capital, in my opinion, could be better invested than in the formation and the maintenance of one or two such experimental farms. In the management of these farms, not only should improved methods of cultivation be adopted and chemical researches instituted, but new cultures might also be experimented; for no one will dare to pretend that everything concerning cultural development is known in these islands. Not only the production of arrowroot, tuluman, starch, tobacco, and rice might be encouraged, but the cultivation of vanilla, an indigenous plant, of spices and exportable fruits, might be tried on a large scale. Success at the experimental farm would, no doubt, act as an encouragement to others to embark in the same pursuits.

Besides these measures for the direct encouragement of agriculture, others might be introduced which would exert an indirect influence on the agricultural interests and the general prosperity of the island.

From causes already stated, the emancipated classes felt a strong inclination to retire from field labour and to congregate in towns and villages, where they engaged in petty trade or adopted some handicraft. The number of shopkeepers, tailors, carpenters, etc., became, consequently, out of proportion, compared with the requirements of the country, and almost every small tenement in towns and villages was occupied by some retailer of fruits, charcoal, etc. The stock in trade (?), displayed in trays before their doors, or on stands as apologies for counters, was really ridiculous; and I have no doubt that, had an inventory of articles been taken, in nine cases out of ten, the value of property thus exhibited could not have amounted to ten shillings. Some fruits, a few pounds of charcoal, peas, and plantains, constituted generally the whole stock, and in a large majority of cases the vendor barely managed to eke out a most precarious livelihood: but he was no more a labourer; he was a shopkeeper.

Every individual, I contend, ought to pay for the protection afforded by civil institutions. All pay indirect taxes, thus contributing to uphold the protection afforded to the person of the subject. Those who are owners of property are generally made to pay direct taxes for the security extended to property, or for any other advantages they may derive from the public institutions of the country. Why not make traders pay a small direct tax for the protection extended to their property? A licence I regard as just, and the principle here advocated is partially carried into effect by the licensing of hucksters, carters, boatmen, etc. Such a tax, moreover, would be most opportune in the colonies, since it would have for effect to diminish that enormous number of would-be shopkeepers and irregular dealers of all kinds and grades, who frequently *wind up* after a few months, by being indebted to the merchants who have supplied them, or to the poor cultivator whom they have gulled. The public, evidently, would not suffer from the adoption of such a measure. The competition now existing must be a ruinous one to the *bona fide* grocer, who otherwise might be better stocked, and could more extensively and cheaply meet the demands of customers, were he protected against the idle and dishonest swarm which generally form the bulk of under-sellers in the country districts.

I must acknowledge, however, that in this, as in some other important respects, a change has lately taken place, and the disproportion which so largely existed has a tendency to become more normal. It seems that not a few have been taught by observation and experience that there are more guarantees of success in agricultural than in any other pursuits; and greater security to a steady and industrious family.

I have now come to a most important, to a vital, question— that of immigration. Every facility should be afforded for the acquisition of agricultural labour, by removing all difficulties in the way of immigration from the East; in fact, by opening up every channel through which population may flow, in a continuous stream, into these islands. Excepting two or three which have a comparatively large population, and may therefore rely upon a steady supply of labour, the outcry for an increase of hands has been loud and general from the emancipated colonies; and the only ones that have not succumbed are those which have been able, in some measure, to provide for immigration—viz., Mauritius, British Guiana, and Trinidad.

A comparison of the imports and exports of these three colonies with those of Jamaica, St. Christopher, and Grenada may prove interesting:—

MAURITIUS: POPULATION IN 1881, 360,847.

	IMPORTS.	EXPORTS.
1871	£1,807,000	£3,053,050
1880	2,169,673	3,634,787

BRITISH GUIANA: POPULATION, 252,186.

	IMPORTS.	EXPORTS.
1871	1,898,124	2,748,770
1880	2,008,694	2,617,624

TRINIDAD: POPULATION, 153,128.

	IMPORTS.	EXPORTS.
1871	1,218,024	1,492,811
1880	2,382,268	2,186,512

JAMAICA: POPULATION, 580,853.

	IMPORTS.	EXPORTS.
1871	1,331,185	1,196,531
1880	1,475,197	1,512,978

ST. CHRISTOPHER: POPULATION, 29,169.

	IMPORTS.	EXPORTS.
1871	211,370	283,285
1880	177,245	176,224

GRENADA: POPULATION, 42,403.

	IMPORTS.	EXPORTS.
1871	132,466	153,920
1880	138,619	171,727

These figures may be made to show, for each of the above-named colonies, the proportion per individual of imports and exports:—

	IMPORTS.	EXPORTS.
MAURITIUS	£5·01	£8·47
BRITISH GUIANA	7·52	10·89
TRINIDAD	15·55	14·28
JAMAICA	2·98	2·91
ST. CHRISTOPHER	6·04	6 05
GRENADA	4·05	3·26

They are also, if I am not mistaken, a practical evidence in favour of immigration, and an answer to those who attempt an argument to the contrary; indeed, it would be a work of supererogation to insist upon the necessity of immigration to these colonies.

The class of people we mainly require are agricultural

labourers; skilful mechanics we shall always be able to procure whenever we stand in need of their service. European labourers might find employment in the curing-house or on cacao plantations in healthy localities, in the care of stock or the cultivation of vegetables; but they will never be able to undergo any *hard or exposed work*, more especially field work, in our climate. The only class of labourers that will ever suit our requirements are Africans and Asiatics. I must declare here once and for ever, that I am decidedly opposed to the importation of Africans direct from Africa—at least, in any numbers—because the natives of that continent, ranking no higher than semi-barbarians, require a great deal of care and attention to effect their civilisation, particularly as, from past circumstances, they have every reason to distrust the *Buckras*, or white people. They are besides inclined to retain and propagate their superstitious devices and heathenish practices.

The fate of the White and the Black man is intimately connected, and in these islands, where slavery no more exists, they must rise or fall together. Highly mistaken are those who think that the emancipated Africans are able to carve out their onward destinies by their own unaided efforts, and that the presence of the White man on the same spot with them is an obstacle to their advancement.

The vast and overcrowded peninsula of India teems with an intellectual, mild, and industrious population; but that population is crushed under the tyranny of castes, and is in its native condition most miserable, and no better in a moral point of view, as exhibited in the picture which Sir Emerson Tennent draws of the Tamils of Ceylon: "Their households exhibit none of the endearments and comforts which constitute the charms and attractions of a home. Sensuality and gain are the two passions of their existence, and in the pursuit of them they exhibit a licentiousness so shocking, and practices so inconceivably vile, as would scarcely obtain credence from those who are familiar with the aspects and usages of civilised life even in its lowest and least attractive forms." He is deceitful, and always prepared to take advantage of the unaware.

The Hindoo race is a branch of the great Aryan stock; and the Coolies who have been brought to Mauritius, British Guiana, and Trinidad have been instrumental in saving these valuable possessions from ruin. They have their faults undoubtedly, and are especially confirmed liars. The new comers, who belong to the lowest castes, are filthy in their habits, lazy, and addicted to pilfering. As a class, however, they have proved obedient subalterns, industrious, and steady; and, so far as my personal opinion is concerned, I would say that, though they are not so robust as the negroes, they nevertheless are preferable to all other immigrants, as they have little to learn and nothing to forget or to forgive. It is much to be regretted that one of the conditions imposed on us is to send back the immigrant to his country after he has completed his industrial residence in the colony; that is to say, after he has become acclimatised and has just begun to become imbued with notions of a civilised life. Is the Coolie better off in his own country? No; reliable reports speak to the contrary; and are there not millions of people in India who are kept under such servile and galling degradation, through the prejudices of *caste*, as absolutely to constitute them the most miserable race of beings under the sun? Encourage by all means the emigration of these poor creatures to a land of freedom and Christianity, where their social and moral condition becomes vastly improved. The British Government cannot reasonably demur to the immigration of these people; for, allowing that 2,000,000 should leave India for our shores, can it be said that the country would suffer thereby? Certainly not. And, on the other hand, hundreds of thousands who periodically perish through the joint agencies of famine and hardships would thus be saved.

Several schemes in succession have been adopted and Ordinances passed for the promotion of paid immigration. Our Ordinance on the subject is comprehensive enough, and fully protects the rights of the immigrants. The expenses of their recruiting in India and their passage to Trinidad are defrayed from a common fund. To that fund the Government contributes three-tenths and the planters seven-tenths, by paying indenture fees and an export duty on sugar, molasses, rum, cacao, and coffee. The indenture fees are paid by those who engage the immigrants. This I consider a fair arrangement. However, the question arises whether the Government ought not to pay for the fixed establishment, which costs the sum of £3,612, or the sum of £8,412, including the salaries of the district medical officers, amounting to the sum of £4,800. They are not appointed exclusively to attend the immigrants on estates, as they act as visitors of the poor and paupers, of the police, and in other capacities; in fact, in the interest of the public generally.

A liberal system of public instruction based on sound principles is, I believe, the most powerful instrument for good which any Government can use. Primary instruction should be offered to all. I have heard many persons object to this plan, on the ground that instruction tends to create, in the lower classes, a desire to retire from menial and prædial occupations, and an aspiration to pursuits above their condition. This objection, I confess, is plausible enough, but it will retain its plausibility so long only as the larger mass of the people remain in their present state of ignorance. The knowledge of reading, writing, and arithmetic confers a privilege only in those countries where there exists an unqualified mental darkness. On the other hand, it cannot be denied that the lowest primary instruction is the first step to religious and industrial teaching; that this instruction is the more essential in those countries where it is absolutely necessary to impart to the people both religious and social ideas and habits. But I, at the same time, contend that man has, besides the brain in his head, a heart in his breast; besides an intellect to develop, morals to improve. To this end education must be religious as well as secular; and the state, to be impartial, must leave the former entirely to the clergy, though not without aiding, whenever practicable, in the combination of both. Whatever scheme is adopted, I have come to the conclusion—not without experience founded on diligent observation—that a purely secular education must necessarily conduce to complete indifference in matters of religion, and subsequently to infidelity.

The system of primary schools established by Lord Harris was exclusively secular; ministers of religion were even forbidden the entrance of the schoolroom to impart religious instruction. Such a system could bring forth only poisonous fruits.

In the year 1838 Governor Keate, the successor of Lord Harris, succeeded, against the strong opposition of the Catholic community, in establishing, on the same principle, the Queen's Collegiate School.

In the year 1870 Sir Arthur Gordon made material changes in the scheme of Lord Harris and the arrangements of Governor Keate. Those changes were borrowed from the Irish National System. Government aid was granted, and two classes of schools were formed: (1) Those under the exclusive control of, and entirely supported by, the Government; (2) those assisted by the Government, but under the control of local managers. Religious instruction became permissive in the school premises at certain fixed hours.

Denominational schools of secondary instruction were invited to become affiliated, under certain conditions, to the Queen's Collegiate School, the name of which was changed to that of the Royal College, which, however, remained a purely secular institution with only day pupils. The Catholic school then existing became affiliated, the principal receiving £500, and £500 more being set aside to pay results' fees at the end of each year.

In the year 1875 Sir Henry Irving made further changes, and schools of primary instruction became entitled to the advantages which Sir Arthur Gordon had granted to secondary schools. Private individuals may, if they choose, establish schools of primary instruction, provided these schools are placed under the control of local managers, are open at all times to inspection by officers appointed by Government, and the average daily attendance during the scholastic year is not less than twenty-five. The aid to which they become entitled consists of a capitation grant, (a) for every scholar present on the day of examination who is above the age of five years and under the age of seven years, who has made no less than 200 attendances at the school in the course of the school year, the sum of ten shillings; or, if taught as a *separate department*, the sum of fifteen shillings; (b) for every scholar above the age of seven years, present on the day of examination, who has made no less than 200 attendances at the school in the course of the school year, and who passes the inspector's examination satisfactorily, the sum of twenty-five shillings; (c) and in addition, where plain needlework is regularly taught to the girls in a satisfactory manner, for every girl above the age of five years, who has made 200 attendances, the sum of two shillings.

This system, though taxing to the utmost private resources, has nevertheless been received with approbation, as the most impartial that could be devised. Wards or Government schools are continued wherever they have not been superseded by voluntary or free schools.

It may be truly said that wherever Christianity has obtained an ascendancy, there civilisation has penetrated together with all its blessings; for it seems that Christianity alone holds the secret of man's destinies; and it is remarkable that the civilising influence of religious institutions is in proportion to their accordance with the Christian doctrine. It is the privilege of Christianity to educe civilisation from any material: it is the grand and tried agent which can, with certainty, be brought into operation in all cases and under any form of government.

It may be well for those who have imbibed the truths of the Gospel, who bask in the sunshine of Christian civilisation, and who relish the savoury fruits of the tree planted by their forefathers, to pretend or assume that Christianity has done its work, and must now give precedence to other systems or institutions resulting from, and better adapted to, the progress of ages; but those who pause to consider the progress of humanity in general under the reign of Paganism and Idolatry, or even of Islamism, who witness the supernatural results of Christianity, particularly in its taming and civilising influence on the wildest and most ignorant tribes, are induced to regard it as the chief, because the most powerful and the surest, agent in procuring tranquillity for nations, and rendering them prosperous and happy. I am bound to say that all the agencies which impart life and grandeur to the social agglomerations of modern times, natural justice, mutual assistance, equality in the advantages and burdens of civil society, individual freedom, the steady progress of man, &c.—all are the fruits of Christianity. For it cannot be denied that Christianity has snatched the world from under the baneful yoke of paganism wherever its action has not been forcibly checked; and that the worship of one Holy God, Creator, Saviour, and Sanctifier, with all its rational consequences, all its beneficial emanations, all its social applications, has become, through the teaching of the Gospel, a practical science for all indistinctively, the Vulgate of all nations. It is also certain that wherever Christianity has not yet penetrated, the same frightful superstition and gross idolatry, which in former ages overspread the entire world, are still prevailing; that countries once enlightened by the Christian doctrine, and which, under its influence, shone with all the brightness of intellectual greatness and practical virtues, have since, by repudiating its dictates, sunk into the abjection of degeneracy, and have remained in the darkness which ensued on their extinction of the lamp of Christianity. Asia and Africa will supply many examples of this.

During the period of slavery no sort of religious instruction was afforded to the slaves; and the little they ever learned of Christianity was derived from the prayers taught them by their masters, or the sermons—few and far between—addressed to them on occasional Sundays by the ministers of religion; but even those small crumbs fallen from the table of Christianity have nourished and improved the minds of the wild Africans to the extent we see. And let me remark that those who have received more direct and constant lessons have shown themselves by no means unworthy of their high and holy privileges; whilst, on the contrary, those who have been deprived of these means of instruction have evidently been declining in the scale of morality, civilisation, and comfort. Such being the case, ought not the local authorities and home government aid those who have the peculiar charge of preaching evangelic morality and Scripture truths? Not only will they thus indirectly lead the people to be peaceable, but they will also, by teaching them their duties, contribute to form, of not inapt materials, useful members of society, faithful subjects of the crown, industrious and thrifty communities. Now the question is, how can the Government co-operate in the diffusion of Christianity and aid its ministers?

Simply by being impartial, and by "rendering to Cæsar the things which are Cæsar's, and unto God the things that are God's;" that is to say, by granting full liberty to the ministers of religion in everything pertaining to religion, and by placing at the disposal of the tax-payers, for ecclesiastical purposes, their full share of the funds they may contribute to the general revenue of the country.

I do not wish to enter into an examination of the merits and demerits of Church establishments, but I dare conscientiously affirm that in comparatively newly-settled countries, and particularly in small communities like ours—impoverished as they are, and struggling for their very existence—State Churches are an invidious and impolitic institution. If tax-payers are entitled to a share of the funds contributed by them, it is to such portion as is applicable to the provision of such wants which are most essential, and to the furtherance of those interests which are dearest to human nature.

I am aware that some would prefer the system of voluntary contribution, and do away with all aid from the State. But not only are we not ripe for the voluntary system, but the inhabitants of these dependencies are in too precarious a position to be able to maintain, unaided, a respectable and efficient clergy. The voluntary system has also, in my opinion, the very great inconvenience of placing the minister of religion at the mercy of his flock, and rendering him, to a certain extent, subject to, and dependent on, their pleasure, even in things pertaining to religion.

At the capitulation of the island, the Catholic Church was the only establishment recognised and supported by the State; the Governor had the title and exercised the prerogatives of patron. Sir Ralph Woodford, among others, not only readily accepted the title, but actually performed the obligations of the office. At a later period the Church of England became the State Church, and as such secured all the advantages derivable from the circumstance; it appropriated the largest share of the Ecclesiastical Fund, though the Catholics formed the great majority of the people. They had always protested against this partial arrangement. They naturally enough gave their full support to the measures proposed by Sir Arthur Gordon, with the object of securing equality for all denominations. State aid was proffered to all indistinctively, but was accepted only by the Wesleyan body; and the Ecclesiastical Fund is at present distributed among the Church of England, the Roman Catholic Church, and the Wesleyan body, according to the number of their adherents, as manifested by the census of 1861.

Just at the time emancipation was proclaimed in the British

West Indies a new commercial policy was inaugurated—highly favourable, I consider, to the British consumers, but no less antagonistic to the agricultural interests of these dependencies.

On the other hand, the changes effected in the social condition of these islands required corresponding changes in their general constitution, so as to bring them more closely under the control of the mother country.

As matters now stand, the British West India Islands form six distinct governments, viz., the Bahamas; Jamaica; the Leeward Islands, comprising Antigua, the Virgin Islands, Saint Christopher, Nevis, Montserrat, and Dominica, as a federation; the Windward Islands, viz., Barbadoes, Saint Lucia, Saint Vincent, Grenada, and Tobago; the Island of Trinidad; and the colony of British Guiana. All these colonies are independent one of the other, and have their respective constitutions, varying in each; and not only does each colony differ in method of government, laws, &c., but each has its Governor, or Lieutenant-Governor, and a wholesale staff of public officers. The public establishments of some of these colonies are evidently disproportionate to their resources; and it is morally impossible, besides, that, from their scanty population, men can be selected really capable of framing salutary laws, or acting in other respects as legislators. And so limited are their resources that they cannot expect to command the services of competent persons.

So foreign and remote are the relations existing between the different colonies that the inhabitants of Trinidad are better acquainted with events in Europe, and even in China, than those in Jamaica and the Bahamas. Again, so diversified and dissimilar are their laws in general, and the regulations of their courts of justice in particular, that a barrister of good repute in Trinidad would be obliged to undergo a fresh training before practising in the neighbouring colony of Grenada. And yet the interests of these different islands are nearly identical. They must rise or fall together. It is, therefore, highly essential that these different dependencies should be homogenised, as far as possible—that they should be brought into mutual relations and contact, so that the least advanced may profit by the experience of those that are more precocious—that their natural resources should become known, and their individual wrongs be felt and acknowledged as the wrongs of all: thus, and thus only, will they be able to afford each other aid and support in difficulties and distress. This, however, can be done only by forming a political union of the scattered colonies, with a Federal Colonial Assembly.

I have come to this conclusion after mature reflection, and I am fully convinced that the proposed change would be for the benefit of the colonies, both in a financial and administrative point of view. The general Assembly or Parliament should consist of representatives from all the different islands. These deputies might be elected either by the local legislatures, or by a board of electors holding high elective qualifications. The members of the Federal Assembly would be entitled to a daily allowance, to be contributed by each colony respectively during the whole period of the session; each session to be limited to a certain duration. These sessions should be held on the most central or the most important island, and the deputies should deliberate and decide only on general matters, each colony preserving complete freedom and full right to decide on all local or municipal matters. One of the first acts of the Federal Assembly should be the appointment of commissioners to revise the laws of all the colonies, and to condense them into a general code for the government of the confederacy—each colony, however, retaining full power and authority for local administration, particularly as regards finance and taxation, police regulations, &c. This confederation would absolutely require the appointment of a Governor-General, with a responsible Council. There should be instituted a High Court of Justice, which would constitute a Court of Appeal from the different tribunals, this Court to be supported from a common fund, to be furnished by the colonies jointly, according to their respective population. Lastly, a central lunatic asylum would be established, also a penitentiary for juvenile offenders.

These are my views on the constitutional changes which might be made in these islands; and I am convinced that, by the adoption of some such plan, not only would a regeneration be effected in the general system of government, but an improvement also in their local administration. The most essential laws being framed by an assembly composed of members chosen from among the ablest men in each colony would undoubtedly be better and more closely adapted to the circumstances of all; nor, as at present, would legislation be hurried through, and a fresh Ordinance required for each contingency. The office and duties of the local legislators being circumscribed within narrower and more practical limits, they would devote more attention to the internal administration of each colony, and but little ground would be left vacant for party discussions. A more extended field being also open to men of talent, they would the more likely aspire to becoming members of the Federal Assembly; and complaints which, preferred by the inhabitants of Tobago, Trinidad, Nevis, &c., at present are disregarded, would likely receive some share of attention when urged by a Colonial Parliament.

This suggestion, made in 1858, was partially carried into effect in 1871. By an Act passed in August of that year, the Leeward Islands were united under one Government with a "General Legislative Council," composed of ten elective and ten non-elective members. Curious enough, this Act actually revived the old constitution of the Leeward Islands.

The Governor may, with the consent of the Council, make laws for the dependencies comprising the federation: he may, in like manner, make, with the consent of the Legislative body of any island, laws for the peace, order, and good government thereof.

I must say, however, that, from one reason or the other, this arrangement has not worked so satisfactorily as was anticipated.

In the year 1876 an attempt was made to form a second confederation of the Windward Islands, comprising Barbados, St. Lucia, St. Vincent, Grenada, and Tobago. Barbados, however, manifested such a determined opposition that the Government was obliged to desist.

The prospects of any country depend mainly on its internal resources, its geographical position, and means of communication; finally, upon the dispositions of its inhabitants. The West India islands being small in size, inland communication is neither distant nor on an extensive scale; but, as they are generally rugged, and occasionally mountainous, travelling and cartage are often difficult. I have already mentioned their capabilities as agricultural countries, and given a sufficient estimate of the character of their inhabitants. I shall only add that, by the natural agency of social intercourse and commercial communications, the character of the population would rapidly improve, and a spirit of industry be created; I even consider this result as the necessary consequence of the onward march of events.

Several of the West India islands may be regarded, both from their size and configuration, as unimportant; such, for instance, are all the islands of the Bahama and Virgin groups, Montserrat, Nevis, Tobago, etc.; others, on the contrary, are, either from their size, position, and fertility, of an importance which cannot be underrated; and a few of them, though at present more or less disregarded, must, by force of circumstances, and in the mere progress of time, rise from their present depressed condition to comparative prosperity and wealth. This may be easily predicted of Cuba, Porto Rico, Jamaica, Hayti, and Trinidad.

Cuba never will, never can, become Africanized, as the Americans would say, whether it continues a dependency of the crown of Spain, or be annexed to the States.

Less important than Cuba, Porto Rico is safe enough, since the slave population and the African race do not form the majority of its inhabitants, nor even of the labouring class, more than two-thirds of the field-labourers being freemen.

The condition of Jamaica, though still rather precarious, has nevertheless improved of late years. It is on the route from the United States and Europe to the Pacific; to Japan, China, and the isles of the East, through Central America by the Isthmus of Panama, the Lake of Nicaragua, or even the Isthmus of Tehuantapec.

Trinidad is second, in positional importance, to Cuba alone. From its situation, it commands the country drained by the Orinoco and its affluents, of which immense and teeming basin the Gulf of Paria is the natural outlet. Irrespective of this, its own soil is richly fertile; and by far the largest extent of the island is still covered with virgin forests.

Hayti is divided into two independent states—the negro republic of Hayti to the West, and the mixed republic of Santo Domingo to the East. This island is scarcely second to Cuba in size and fertility, and must, sooner or later, attract European commerce and enterprise.

Of the smaller islands I say nothing, because, though each has its own *status*, and may exercise a certain limited share of influence, they must all follow the general fate of the larger.

Ere the lapse of ten years, the great commercial thoroughfare from Europe and the shores of the Atlantic to the regions bathed by the Pacific, from Chili to the Strait of Behring, and from New Zealand to Japan, an immense extent of rich and populous countries, will be through Central America. The Western Archipelago has been placed by nature on this international highway. These islands must, of necessity, become more and more civilised, either from the direct or indirect intervention of the great commercial nations of the world: the great obstacle of slavery has been removed at last; the foundation has been laid; it now remains to raise the superstructure.

From the preceding postulates it does not appear unreasonable to expect that, in a given time, the Western Archipelago will recover the high position which it once occupied, and which, by nature, it must eventually reoccupy. If, as we may reasonably foresee, the now insignificant West India islands become well settled, they will supply the manufactures of colder climates with raw materials and tropical products, receiving from them, in return, their supply of manufactured goods. "We advise the inhabitants of Cuba," says Ramon de la Sagra, "to increase, by all possible means, the industrious white population; for such may be, some day to come, the commercial and political preponderance of the most important of the Antilles—lying at the entrance of the Gulf of Mexico—that it will change the future destinies of the other islands, by exercising over all a favourable reaction by the combined influence of a well cultivated soil, and the superiority of intelligence of its population of European origin." Such is the encouragement held out to the Cubans by a man of some reputation, and who had spent twelve years of his laborious life in their island.

The change which Ramon de la Sagra expected could have been worked by the Cubans, and the influence of a well cultivated soil, has been partially anticipated in the French colonies of Martinique and Guadeloupe by improved manufacture and the establishment of central usines; and I am glad to say that the example set forth has not been altogether forsaken by Demerara and Trinidad. And it is to be hoped that, ere many years have elapsed, improved manufacture on private estates and central factories, combined with *intensive* and rational culture, will have changed the destinies of the West India Islands.

The establishment of central factories will encourage the formation of a middle-class, by affording to small proprietors the means of manufacturing into sugar whatever quantity of canes they may plant. I have always been convinced that the existence of such a body is a necessary element in the welfare of all communities, but particularly of those which are chiefly or solely addicted to agricultural pursuits. Wherever such a class does not exist there is an immense gap left open, which the lower classes will invariably attempt to fill up, either by forcing themselves through or dragging the higher classes into the same, thus creating permanent danger to the social institutions. This danger is greatly mitigated, if not entirely obviated, when there is a gradation established from the lowest up to the highest. Those who start from below and above to meet midway must interchange ideas in their progress upwards and downwards, and form as an intermediate link between the two extremities of the social scale. The formation of a class of industrious small proprietors was therefore desirable, and ought to have been encouraged, not by granting privileges, as I have heard it contended, but by removing, instead of throwing, obstacles in the way. Such a policy I regard as particularly opportune in countries where, and at a period when, by the progress of events, many families have sunk from comparative affluence into the lowest state of misery. At the time emancipation was proclaimed, it was thought prudent not to open the public lands for competition. The adoption of such a plan was not perhaps unreasonable or impolitic, since it had for its object the protection of cane and other staple cultivation. I would not like to affirm that it succeeded, though it was effective in checking the increase of small proprietors. The crown lands of the colony are now offered for sale under certain restrictions. To the foresight of Sir Arthur Gordon—to his judicious arrangements—we owe the change.

Societies, in their normal evolutions, must pass through certain stages or phases, and wisdom consists not in opposing those natural changes, but in checking and preventing deflections, and in restraining them within certain limits.

One of the phases of this evolution in the West Indian freed communities was evidently the formation of a class of small proprietors, or the aggregation of a certain number of families to that class where it already existed. The inclination to become freeholders must have been particularly strong in the emancipated labourers, both on account of their long dependence and the influence of climate. The desire to become cotters has been well manifested in the great number of *squatters* formerly occupying crown land, and who, since the Government has taken cognisance of their occupancy, have, by the payment of a certain amount, become entitled to and actual owners of the lands which their industry had brought under cultivation. As agriculturists, however, the emancipated slaves may be said to exhibit a partiality for the culture of certain plants—viz., of such which do not require much exertion or unremitting attention; of such as arrive most rapidly to maturity; or of those the product of which does not demand much preparation to render them merchantable, nor the same amount of care in their cultivation, as our more delicate vegetables, for instance. As to those plants which require a large and constant amount of labour to render them exportable, they will cultivate such only when directly compelled by legal enactments, or indirectly by circumstances. This is proved, I believe, not only by the history of the West Indies since emancipation, but also by that of all other inter-tropical countries. And this is, perhaps, the main point from which cane cultivation has received such a check in the emancipated colonies; for it has been kept up or increased only where circumstances compelled the people to work for a livelihood, or where indenture bound them to the sugar estates.

There is no inducement, at present, to increase the production of sugar. If, however, an increased demand should call for increased production, industrious cotters will probably be the principal agents of that production, by adopting the division of labour system, and by the establishment of central factories. The system of central factories I consider as the most rational and also the most beneficial to all parties; and yet I apprehend that its advantages are not fully appreciated, perhaps because it necessitates from the planter immediate sacrifices which he feels disinclined to make, though they must be followed by subsequent advantages.

Here let me conclude this rather lengthy introduction to a mere sketch of the Island of Trinidad. But the fate of my native land being more or less intimately connected with that of the other Antilles, I thought it necessary to offer a few remarks on the natural resources, present condition, and general importance of the isles of which it forms a not inconsiderable unit.

CHAPTER I.

GEOGRAPHICAL DESCRIPTION—POSITION AND AREA.

THE Island of Trinidad is situated between 10° 3' and 10° 50' latitude N., and between 60° 54' and 61° 56' longitude W. of Greenwich; it is separated from the province of Cumana, in the republic of Venezuela, by the Gulf of Paria, together with the Dragon's and Serpent's Mouths. In figure it is an oblong, or of a rectangular shape, with promontories at its four angles—viz., Galera and Galeota to the eastward, and Mono and Icacos to the westward; these two latter stretching for several miles towards the opposite shores of Venezuela, and thus contributing to the formation of the northern and southern boundaries of the Gulf of Paria.

According to Captain Columbine, its principal dimensions are as follows:—

The north side, from Point Galera to Point Mono, 53½ miles.

The eastern side, from Point Galera to Point Galeota, 48¼ miles.

The south side, from Point Galeota to Point Icacos, 65 miles.

The western side from Point Icacos to Point Mono, 49½ miles.

The greatest length of the island, from N. to S., is, from Grand Matelot to Casa Cruz, 50 miles; average length, 48 miles. Greatest breadth, from Galeota to Icacos, 65 miles; average breadth, 35 miles only. The superficial extent or area, according to MM. Wall and Sawkins, is not more than 1,754½ square miles, or 1,122,880 acres.

Trinidad is bounded on the N. by the Caribbean Sea, on the S. by the channel which separates it from the Delta and Caños of the Orinoco, on the E. by the Atlantic Ocean, and on the W. by the Gulf of Paria.

Physical Aspect.—The general aspect of Trinidad is that of

a level country, bearing no resemblance to the other Antilles. Its mountains have not the towering majesty which distinguishes those of St. Vincent, Dominica, Cuba, &c.; they do not present separate summits, cone-shaped, steep, and rugged, but form three ranges running in a parallel line from E. to W., separated by two large valleys or river-basins, and being clothed from their base to their utmost summits with stately forests. The central and southern ranges are accessible on all sides; the northern range, which is abrupt on the sea side, slopes gradually towards the intervening valley; it may be ascended, however, along the ridges or crests which separate the water-courses.

The mountains trending along the whole northern border of the island are in a style of eminent grandeur, stretching southward to the plain, and, in many places, along the gulf, down to the sea; whilst the forms of the hills are strikingly varied by the intersections of the valleys and gullies in opposite directions. The valleys in this range are few, open generally to the south, and transversal. These valleys also present a great uniformity in their general configuration, being contracted in the middle by the convergence of the ridges, and expanding at each extremity. They are level, branching off into smaller vales, and each watered by a stream, from which it commonly takes its name. Such are the valleys of Cuesa or Carenage, Diego-Martin, and Maraval, westward of Port of Spain; the beautiful and rich valley of Santa Cruz to the eastward, as also those of Maraccas and Caura. These latter are shut in, as it were, by the rise of the land at their entrance. This is still more strongly exhibited at the Valley of Arouca, which is blocked up for several miles by high hills, the river flowing between precipitous slopes. Beyond Arouca the valleys are contracted to a very small span—in fact, to mere gorges. There are also, on the north coast, three or four glens, viz.:—Maraccas, Las Cuevas, Chupara, and Rio Grande. The Maraccas Bay Valley, as it is called, to distinguish it from the Valley of Maraccas, is a small semi-circular plain, bounded on almost every side by steep hills, with a stream of fine water; the valley of Las Cuevas is extensive, with a copious stream of water running through it, but completely barred up at its mouth; it is the Quebrada-de-Hierro, or the Iron Ravine, of the old Spanish settlers. Chupara is contracted to a mere gorge by the surrounding mountains; whilst at Rio Grande the land is undulating, and a considerable part of it flat. It does not appear that any other valleys than the above-mentioned are known, except the Valley of Labranche and that of Guaracara, in the central range.

Trinidad, being a comparatively newly-settled island, presents in many parts the appearance of a wild unreclaimed country. It is covered with dense and lofty forests, the heavy appearance of an endless woodland being only broken here and there by vast savannahs, or by the efforts of agricultural industry,—except, perhaps, at the Naparimas, where an extensive district is under uninterrupted cultivation. Even where cacao and coffee are cultivated, the country still preserves the appearance of forest-land, since those plants are protected by the shade of the "Bois Immortel," a tree which attains a considerable size.

A cacao plantation forms of itself a most charming prospect. The trees are planted at twelve or fifteen feet apart, and range from about twenty-five to thirty-five feet in height. The leaves are large and, when young, of a violet-red hue; whilst from the larger branches and the stem hang red, yellow, green, or dark crimson pods,—the "Immortel" itself forming a striking feature in the scenery. In January and February the latter exchanges its leaves for a thick covering of bright red blossoms, the ground underneath being literally carpeted with flowers, whilst birds of various species, and of the most brilliant plumage, join in gay concert above. Several other trees become, at certain periods, like the "Immortel," a regular mass of flowers. Those of the Poui are of a brilliant yellow; of the Roble, an orange colour, and with the fragrancy of the wall-flower; others, again, are white, pink, or violaceous.

The bamboo grows in clusters of hollow jointed reeds, and forms, as it were, an immense sheaf, about fifty feet high, from six to ten feet in diameter, and containing above one hundred stems, surmounted by a foliage resembling an assemblage of waving plumes. Sometimes they grow on each side of a river for several miles, their feathery summits uniting overhead at intervals, in immense arches.

From some of the hills the view is often most beautiful. At the foot of the hill extensive cane-fields; a little further, that red tract marks out a cacao plantation, beyond which is the Caroni savannah; and further yet, the expanse of the placid gulf, with the merchantmen lying at anchor in the roadstead, or beating up for the port.

A person visiting the island would meet with but very few neat, or even comfortable, residences in the country districts, the dwellings of the planters looking rather primitive, whilst the labourers' cottages, or rather cabins, and other estate-buildings, do not contribute to make the aspect of a plantation a very pleasing one. Although nature has liberally supplied a very fine growth of fruit trees, yet the island cannot boast of even a resemblance to an orchard, except at Dr. de. Boissière's residence, Maraval, and at the Government Gardens, to the northward of the town. Several country residences can bear comparison with English and French villas—viz., that of the late Mr. Burnley, Tacarigua; of Mr. L. Agostini, Saint Ann; Zurcher, Dr. de Boissière, and Cipriani, in the neighbourhood of Port of Spain; and several others in the country.

Coasts.—The coasts of Trinidad are bold on the N., bluff on the S., and generally low and flat on the E. and W., where the water also is very shallow.

The north coast is rock-bound, with serried mountains thickly wooded from their summits to the very verge of the sea, which breaks in a heavy surf along the whole extent, and renders landing impossible, except at a few shelving spots; its bearing is W. by S. Passing from E. to W., we may notice the following points or promontories:—Arecife or Reef's Point, Toco, Sanssouci, Rio Grande, Petit and Grand Matelot, Chupara, Pointe-à-Vache, Saut-d'-Eau, and Maqueripe.

The south coast extends from Point Galeota on the E. to Point Icacos on the W. From Galeota to Casa Cruz—a distance of twelve miles and a half—it takes a south-western direction, and then runs due W. Between Points Galeota and Casa Cruz are Grand Cayo and Tablas; and westward of Casa Cruz are the following promontories:—Canary, Pelican, Moruga, La Ceyba, Curao, Negra, Siparia, Roja, Chagonaray, Taparo, Erin, Islote, Galfat, and Quemada.

The eastern coast stretches from Point Galera on the N. to Point Galeota on the S., and appears by nature to be divided into four sections, which respectively bear the names of Cumana, Matura, Cocal, and Mayaro. The first section extends from Galera to Point Salibea—a distance of thirteen miles; it has a south-western direction, and terminates the northern range on the E. Point Galera is low and rocky, with a constant heavy surf breaking on it; from Galera to Cumana the coast is very rocky and wild, with only one landing-place—within Forest Point. Along the Cumana section are the following promontories :—Forest, Cumana, Balandra, Salibea, Paloma, Pointe Noire, and Matura. Ten miles southward of Cumana Point is Point Manzanilla, presenting high cliffs towards the sea, and trending suddenly westward by S. for about two miles. The line of coast from Cumana to Manzanilla is a sandy beach, running S. by E. From Manzanilla to Point Mayaro—a distance of twelve miles—the whole extent consists of a low sandy beach, running S. by E. This section is separated from Mayaro by a lofty promontory, or small peninsula, called Point Radix. It is about two miles in extent, hilly, presenting everywhere to the seaboard high perpendicular cliffs, terminating in two lesser points, viz.: Point Guataro on the N., and Point Mayaro on the S. From Mayaro to Galeota the distance is fourteen miles. Here again the coast is a sandy beach, rising gradually towards Galeota; at a short distance from the sea the ground rises into sloping hillocks. Cape Galeota is a high, rocky promontory, running S.E., and then trending N. by W., so as to form a small peninsula, sloping towards the northern or land side. It is connected with the mainland by a neck of only one mile in breadth, partly covered with mangroves.

The western coast forms a nearly semi-circular curve. The north-western angle of Trinidad, it would seem, has no name: as a suggestion, it may be called Point Mono. It rises in a lofty promontory, about two miles and a half in breadth, with two points encircling a small cove; the northernmost might bear the name of Mono, the southern retaining that of Current Point. From the latter to the town of Port-of-Spain the coast runs E. by S. for about twelve miles, and terminates the western extremity of the northern range. From Port-of-Spain to the mouth of the Guaracara—a stretch of twenty-five miles—it takes a southerly direction, the ground being low, and in many places swampy, and covered with mangroves. From the mouth of the Guaracara to the lagoon of Oropuche—a distance of nearly nine miles—its bearing is S. by W., and from Oropuche to Cape La Brea—a further distance of five miles—it stretches nearly due

W.; from Point La Brea to Point Icacos it runs W. ¼ S. for nearly twenty-four miles. Besides Point Mono and Current Point already mentioned, we meet, westward of Port of Spain, with Punta Gorda, or Big Point, formed of compact limestone, and which divides the port of Chaguaramas from that of Carenage. Southward of Port-of-Spain are the following points or landmarks :—Large Point, Chaguanas, Cascajal, Cangrejos, and Savanetta—all very flat and muddy; Lisas and Pointe-à-Pierres, or Stony Point; south of San Fernando, Sandy Point, very low; Cape La Brea, which succeeds, is formed of hardened pitch, or bitumen. Between La Brea and Icacos we meet with the following points:—Guapo or Fortin, Ligoure, Pointe Noire or Grandeville, Pointe Rouge, Cedros, and Los Gallos, or The Cocks. Icacos, the south-western angle of Trinidad, is a low, sandy peninsula, intersected by several lagoons.

The northern, southern, and eastern coasts are nearly destitute of harbours. "Between the Bocas and Chupara," says Captain Columbine, "there are some large bays, but so much swell sets into them, and the wind is so uncertain and light, close in shore, that it is dangerous to anchor a ship in them, except in those of Maraccas and Las Cuevas.

"Maqueripe is a cove at the northern extremity of the valley of Cuesa; Saut-d'-Eau is a very small sandy cove; Las Cuevas is a sandy bay; the sandy shore on the eastern side of it is richly wooded, almost close to the sea, interrupted by several breaks of the woods filled by long winding slips of sand, and varied by high rocks and smaller rivulets mingling fancifully amongst them. A mile to leeward of Las Cuevas is the deep bay of Maraccas, open to the north, but affording more shelter than any other on this part of the coast. From Las Cuevas to Toco the coast is chiefly rocky and high, with a few sandy bays which generally contain a small river; but the surf is so heavy that these bays are scarcely more accessible than the rocks; the only places which we could find were at Rio Grande, Petit Matelot, Trou Bouilli, and Paria Bay. There is also a very small circular cove about half a mile to the N.E. of Madamas, where a drogher might lie in smooth water with the greatest security, being within the breakers. It is closed round with steep rocky cliffs, and did not appear to have any communication with the surrounding country. It is very difficult to land at Rio Grande

Bay; the early part of the morning is the best time, before the sea-breeze sets in. A heavy sea breaks all along the shore, from Rio Grande to Toco, the few landing places being only small openings amongst the breakers; and even these are not practicable at all times. The Bay of Toco is safe, with good landing."

During the prevalence of the northerly winds, from November to May, a heavy surf breaks constantly along this coast, and it becomes difficult, and even dangerous, to attempt landing, except at Maraccas Bay, and then only in canoes; vessels also that anchor in the bay will often find it a hazardous task to leave their anchorage, the wind being right ahead and the entrance narrow. The depth of water along the northern coast varies from three to twenty-five fathoms, with a good bottom.

The eastern coast is very shallow, with a heavy surf throughout, but particularly at Matura and the Cocal, the depth of water varying from three to ten fathoms. The only anchorages and landing-places are at Forest Point, Cumana, three miles and a half from Point Galera, and in Balandra and Salibea Bays. The former of these two bays is small but safe, and the water bold enough to receive trading schooners and droghers; the latter hardly merits the term of bay, but a vessel might find tolerable shelter within it under cover of a small rocky island. To the S. of Point Manzanilla is a small harbour, completely rock-bound, with a good landing at the mouth of the Lebranche river. This harbour, formed by rocky islets, is of sufficient depth for any vessel not drawing more than nine feet of water; and, although very small, it is the best on the east coast, and, with some little improvement, would afford an available anchorage to droghers. Off Point Manzanilla is a sunken rock called the Carpenter, upon which a slaver struck and was wrecked in the year 1802. Some years ago a sunken rock was discovered by the French steamer "Darien," coming from Cayenne. It is about twenty-three miles off the coast of Matura, due E. of Pointe Noire. There is also a pretty good landing-place to the N. of Point Radix, at the mouth of the river Guataro, called la Chaussée, a well-known place for turtle. The surf, although still very heavy along the sea-board of Mayaro, does not impede the landing on part of the coast—especially under the lee-side of Point Mayaro

—when proper precautions are taken, and strong boats used for the purpose.

The southern coast is generally bluff, and the sea shallow throughout the channel, the depth of water varying from three to twenty-seven fathoms, with excellent bottom. From April to October—during the overflow of the mighty river Orinoco, which discharges part of its waters into the channel—strong currents prevail, bearing westward. Besides the following landing-places, viz.: Moruga, Erin, and Quemada—there is on this coast the small port of Guayaguayare, at the S.E. extremity of the southern coast, between Galeota and Grand Cayo or Pointe Taillée. This latter is a high bluff promontory, forming the western limit of the bay or port of Guayaguayare, whilst Point Galeota forms its eastern boundary. It has a pebbly bar across its entrance, extending from Grand Cayo to Galeota, and is open to the S.S.E. It may, however, be considered a safe harbour, though it cannot admit vessels of above fifty tons, the depth of water being from two to four and a half fathoms only.

The soundings along the western coast are generally very shallow, with exceptions, however, of considerable depth, in a few places, particularly at Chaguaramas, Carenage, and opposite the village of Cocorite, to the westward of Port-of-Spain; also at Pointe-à-Pierres and La Brea. Chaguaramas is a land-locked harbour at the N.W. extremity of the island, extending between Current Point and Punta Gorda. The islet of Gasparil, which stretches nearly from Punta Gorda beyond Current Point, contributes to its formation and protection on the S. There are two entrances to the Bay of Chaguaramas; the north-eastern is sheltered by a small islet called Diego Island; the western entrance is likewise protected by a rock called Little Gasparil, which divides the same into two channels, the one between Little Gasparil and Gasparil Grande affording a passage for large vessels, and the other for smaller craft only. The port of Chaguaramas is perfectly safe at all times, and the water bold. Separated from Chaguaramas by the small rocky peninsula of Punta Gorda is the port of Carenage, well inclosed and as safe as the former. Captain Columbine has the following remarks on Carenage and Chaguaramas:—

"The want of a sufficient depth of water in the Carenage renders it useless for men-of-war.

"The harbour of Chaguaramas is very spacious; but, in case the enemy should have such temporary superiority by sea as to enable him to attack this island, our ships could not be protected here, as the mountainous nature of the country could afford him many points from whence he might easily destroy them.

"The situation which presents itself as the most proper to place naval magazines, with the probability of their being effectually defended, without any extensive works, is the island of Gasparil Grande. It has two principal hills, one to the east end, the other near the middle, affording powerful means of defence. On the south side there is a cove large enough for the purpose of repairing and heaving down a ship of the line, where store-houses to any extent might be erected, covered from the view, though not from the shells, of a besieging enemy. With respect to the security of our fleet, the only place, in my opinion, capable of affording it, is the south side of this island. Westward from the above cove the shore is quite bold, and it should be proper to anchor close to it, in order to cover the ships from hot shots, which the enemy might throw from the outer point of Diego's Isle, a spot which he would occupy with that intent, unless we had works on Chaguaramas heights."

In addition to these two lesser ports, the Gulf of Paria forms one extensive harbour, in which vessels may anchor, from three to twenty fathoms, on a bottom of gravel and mud; in fact, vessels coming to Port-of-Spain very often run into the soft mud, in order to gain a nearer approach to the wharves. Captain Columbine again remarks regarding Port-of-Spain :—" The water in the road of Port-of-Spain is very shallow; a mile and a half off there are only three fathoms; it is extremely foul and muddy there, and near the shore it is proportionally more filthy. The course of the tides, both ebb and flood, being checked by an opposite shore, in the corner where the town stands, they naturally must deposit there much of the mud which they carry along with them : the obvious result is that, in process of time, Port-of-Spain will be an inland town. This operation of nature appears to be going on fast, and to be without remedy."

The Gulf of Paria may be considered as a sort of salt lake, being shut in on the eastward by the island of Trinidad, which thereby breaks the roll of the Atlantic; on the westward by the adjoining part of the province of Cumana; on the northward by the Peninsula of Paria, the north-western angle of Trinidad, and a few intervening islets; on the southward by the corresponding portion of the Delta of the Orinoco, the south-western angle of Trinidad, and some interposed rocks. Passages are formed on the N. and S. between the islets; also between the latter and Trinidad at one extremity, and Venezuela at the other. The northern passages are known as the *Bocas del Dragon*, or the Dragon's Mouths; the southern as the *Bocas de la Sierpe*, or the Serpent's Mouths.

The islet nearest to Trinidad, in the formation of the Dragon's Mouths, is Monos, or Apes' Islet; the next Huevos, or Eggs'; and lastly, Chacachacarreo. These islets present precipitous cliffs to the N., and can be approached only on the gulf side. The different passages or channels known as the Dragon's Mouths bear the respective names of Monos, between the mainland and Monos; Huevos, between Monos and Huevos; Navios, or Ships' Passage, between Huevos and Chacachacarreo; and the Boca Grande, or Grand Mouth or Passage, between Chacachacarreo and Cape Peña, which is the easternmost extremity of the Peninsula of Paria. The Monos Channel gives admittance only to sloops and schooners, or steamers; the depth of water is from ten to twenty fathoms, but the channel is very narrow. Huevos Passage allows entrance to vessels bound inward; the water is very deep and bold—from ten to forty fathoms. The islet of Monos, being very elevated (1,000 feet), shelters the passage from the easterly winds, so that vessels entering run the risk of being becalmed if much in shore of the islet. Boca de Navios, or Ships' Mouth, between Huevos and Chacachacarreo, has a north-western direction, and is the outward-bound passage. The Grande Boca is about twelve miles in breadth; it is the safest passage for vessels bound both inward and outward, and is that which, although more to the leeward of Port of Spain, is chosen by men-of-war and the larger class of merchantmen.

The ebb or flow of the tide determines the direction inward or outward of strong currents in the Dragon's Mouths, and vessels becalmed in the Huevos and Navios passages may be drifted on the rocky sides of either island and wrecked. The southern entrance of the Gulf of Paria is divided into several passages by rocks; those nearest to Point Icacos are known as Los Lobos, or the Wolves; and about the middle of the strait is El Soldado, or the Soldier Rock; the four channels formed by them and the mainland are called the Serpent's Mouths. The former is between Point Icacos and the Wolves; the second between the Wolves and a three-fathoms bank; the third, or middle channel, between the latter and the Soldier; the fourth between the Soldier and the mainland. The main depth in the two first channels is about five fathoms, six in the middle channel, and fifteen in the fourth. Strong currents prevail in the southern as well as in the northern passages.

Mountains.—The island of Trinidad is divided in an E. and W. direction into two basins or drainage-valleys, by three ranges of mountains or high hills, varying from 600 to 3,100 feet above the level of the sea. The northern range is the most elevated, and stretches along the northern shore from Point Galera to Point Mono. This range possesses a breadth of nearly seven miles, occupying an area of 358 square miles. It is divided into two ridges, the subordinate one rising immediately from the sea, and attaining an average elevation of 800 feet; and the main ridge, which varies from 1,600 to 2,000 feet. Several high peaks arise from this ridge—the Tucuche (3,012 feet) in the western section, and the *Cerro de Aripo* (2,740 feet) in the eastern. "The purity of the air," say Messrs. Wall and Sawkins, "the coolness of the nights, and the beauty of the scenery, combine to make this the most agreeable portion of the island. The elevation at which the temperate climate commences under the same parallel on the adjacent continent is stated by Codazzi at 1,925 feet." A temperate climate, therefore, we may enjoy in the northern mountains. There, and especially between the two ridges, where the ground is not so abrupt and rugged, it would be possible to cultivate the more delicate vegetables of Europe; and I have no doubt that habitation in those mountains would prove perfectly healthy.

The southern range seems to be less elevated than the other two, particularly to the westward, where it gradually declines, and terminates in the low sandy point of Icacos. This range does not form a continuous system, but may be considered as commencing at Point Gran Cayo, extending to Canary, from whence its elevation goes on decreasing to the depressions formed by the river Moruga. It rises again after that river, lowering afterwards to the gently undulating land of Siparia. The maximum elevation appears to be at the back of Punta Tablas, where are to be found the Three Sisters—those very mountains which were seen from Columbus's vessel on the 31st July, 1498, as united into one. The appearance struck the great navigator as a singular coincidence, and he gave to the island the name it bears. The highest peak was measured, and ascertained to be 718 feet. The hilly surface may be calculated at 555 square miles. The northern and southern ranges are parallel.

The middle or central range runs W.S.W. from Point Manzanilla to Pointe-à-Pierres. This range measures about thirty-five miles from E. to W., on an average breadth of three and a half miles, its area being represented by 122 square miles. The highest peaks are Tamana, nearly in the centre of the island (1,025 feet); Maharabe, to the westward (952 feet); Mount Harris (903 feet); Lebranche, to the eastward (718 feet); and Carata (532 feet). "The view from Tamana," say Messrs. Wall and Sawkins, "possesses a peculiar charm; it is by far the most comprehensive in the island. The eye luxuriates in every shade of the richest greens. A vast extent of woodlands, from eastern to western sea, from northern to southern hills, without the slightest perceptible trace of cultivation, save where the scarlet flowers of the 'Madre del Cacao' mark the winding course of the Caroni, testifies the supremacy of nature. Scenery more sublime may be readily obtainable; but for loveliness of hues, for exuberance of vegetation, this is a prospect which can scarcely be surpassed."

The distance which separates the northern from the central range is about twelve miles. That tract is flat and rather low to the W.; to the E. it is undulating. From the central to the southern range the distance is eighteen miles, and the intervening country may be described as highly undulating, sometimes cut by precipitous ravines.

Between these three ranges are comprised two basins or drained tracts, extending from E. to W., and which may be denominated the northern and southern basins; the former is generally more level than the latter. Each of these superior basins is by nature subdivided into two secondary basins or plains by a plateau or table-land. The two subdivisions of the northern plain may be called the Oropuche Basin on the E., and the Caroni on the W.: the two sections of the southern plain may likewise be termed the Guataro basin on the E., and the Great Lagoon on the W. To these four basins may be added the following: the Lebranche at the eastern, and the Guaracara basin at the western extremity of the central range. These are two valleys formed by a bifurcation of that range.

Rivers.—These plains are watered and drained by a number of rivers and rivulets, and the flanks of the mountains deeply rent and furrowed by innumerable ravines. Proceeding eastward from Port-of-Spain, we meet in the northern division with the following perennial water-courses: the Aricagua, or San Juan's; the St. Joseph's, the Tacarigua, Arauca, Oropuna, Mujico, Arima, Maturita, Guanape, Mamo, Aripo, and Valencia. All these streams have their sources in the northern range. After receiving the Valencia on the left and the Mamo on the right, as also the Cumuto, from the Tamana ridge, the Aripo river unites with the Guanape, to form the Caroni, of which the Aripo may be regarded as the true origin. The Maturita and Arima are affluents of the Guanape; the other named rivers discharge their waters into the Caroni. The Aripo takes a southerly direction, with a bend to the W.; the course of the Caroni is very nearly due W., and it has its embouchure in the gulf about two miles S. of Port-of-Spain. Besides the above tributaries, the Caroni receives the Tumpuna and Arena from Tamana. It flows through a low and partly swampy district, and has a very winding course. Its banks are high and steep in the former part of its course, and the water shallow. Approaching the swamps the banks are on a level with the adjoining lands; its bed deepens to several feet, and it may be ascended for several miles by the flats of vessels loading or discharging in the harbour.

Proceeding eastward, we meet with the following streams:— The Cuare, with the Turure and La Ceyba, its tributaries; the Oropuche, which receives the Cuare on the right, and the Rio Grande on the left side. They all rise in the northern range, and run in a southerly direction, curving to the E. The Oropuche receives from the central range the Cunapo and its affluent the Guayco; also the Sangre Grande and Sangre Chiquito, which are themselves formed by the aggregation of a number of small ravines. The Oropuche has its outlet nearly in the centre of the Matura coast.

It becomes evident from this description that the dividing table-land lies between Valencia and Cuare, and extends southward to the central range, dividing the waters of the Cumuto from those of the Guayco and Cunapo. It is 219 feet above the level of the sea, and distant thirteen miles from the eastern, and twenty-one miles from the western coast. The greatest elevation of this water-shed, between the affluents of the Ortoire and the Great Lagoon of Oropuche, should be sought at Savannah Grande; it is 230 feet. The distance to the eastern coast is twenty-six miles, and only seven miles to the western. Besides the Oropuche and its affluents, we meet farther eastward with the Matura, Salibea, and Tumpire, which have their mouths in Matura, Salibea, and Cumana bays respectively. The Matura is the largest of these currents, the other two being mere mountain streams.

In addition to the Caroni and its affluents, there are in the Caroni basin several other water-courses worth mentioning, some of them being natural canals or outlets for the waters of the extensive swamp, which forms, as it were, a Delta to the Caroni; such are Blue River and Chaguanas, or Madame Espagnole. The Capparo River, which seems to rise in that part of the central range connecting Tamana and Montserrat, has first a north-westerly course, and discharges its waters into the gulf. Next come the Arena and Couva, both having their sources in the central range, and their outlet in the gulf.

The southern plain is watered by a number of small streams, and a principal river called the Guataro. In the Lagoon basin the following water-courses are worth noticing:—The Cipero, southward of the town of San Fernando, flows from the district of Savannah Grande, and drains part of that of Naparima; about one mile and a half from its mouth is a shipping place, whither flats are sent to take off produce. Eastward of La Brea are the Aripero, the Silver-stream, and the Roussillac; southward, the Bravo or Vossini River, the Guapo, and Capdeville, with a number of smaller ravines. All these water-courses spring from the high land of the interior, and form separate streams which flow into the gulf. Between the Cipero and Aripero, however, lies the Oropuche or Grand Lagoon, which may be considered as the

E

great drain of the lagoon basin. It is an extensive swamp, studded with mounds of a black soil, clothed with rank vegetation, and intersected by channels, expanding at intervals into ponds, covered with reeds, rushes, and other aquatic plants or trees. A great number of streams, flowing from the surrounding undulating districts, supply it with much more water than might be at first imagined. The Lagoon discharges its waters into the gulf by two principal outlets—Mosquito Creek or Blazini's River, and Godineau's River.

The eastern division of the southern plain is drained by the largest river in the colony—the Guataro or Ortoire. Its course is imperfectly known; it may, however, be traced from the Montserrat heights, running southward, then eastward, and its mouth opens on the eastern coast, immediately northward of Point Guataro. Its tributaries are partly from the central range, the principal being the Pure, Bell's Creek, Guanapure, Laranache, Anapa, Guarapiche, and a number of small ravines, and partly from the high lands to the south. The river Guataro is made on Mallett's map to communicate with the Nariva by means of navigable canals, but no such communication exists.

The Lebranche valley is watered by the Lebranche and a few ravines; the Lebranche itself has its source in the group of the same name, and its mouth to the southward of Manzanilla Point. The Guaracara valley is watered by the Guaracara, which descends from the Montserrat Range, and discharges itself into the gulf southward of Point-à-Pierre.

Between Manzanilla and Mayaro, at the basis of the Lebranche group, and parallel with the Cocal, is an extensive swampy tract, cut up by several canals, which concur in the formation of the Nariva. This river, or rather natural canal, runs northward, and nearly parallel with the shore, till it meets with the high land of Morne Calabash, when it curves in an opposite direction southward, to discharge itself nearly in the centre of the Cocal; hence its name of Mitan, or Middle River. The Nariva cannot be said to have any current, since the flow is upwards at high tide, and downwards at low tide only. It is very deep and wide near its mouth, and receives all its waters from the central range.

The rivers on the N. and S. coasts may be regarded in general as unimportant. They are, on the N., Rio Grande, Tiburon, Madamas, Paria, Macapou, Chupara, Las Cuevas, and Maraccas;

on the S. the Lizards and Pilot rivers discharge their waters into the Bay of Guayaguayare; they are both tidal streams. Between Points Canary and Pelican are three small rivers; then comes the Moruga, westward of Point Moruga—a tidal stream also, and the largest of all; and, in succession, La Ceyba, Curao, Siparia, and Erin, to the leeward of the corresponding promontories.

The different water-courses above mentioned present a few general characteristics which require notice. Those that take their rise in the northern range have clear and limpid waters, running over pebbly beds; those from the central range flow between steep banks and over muddy bottoms, their waters being turbid and yellow—as, for instance, the Cumuto and Tumpuno, the Cunapo, Sangre-Chiquito, &c. Several of these streams, but especially those which take their rise in, or only flow through, swampy districts, have dark-coloured waters; such as the Nariva, Mosquito Creek, the Godineau, &c. The water, however, though dark, is perfectly clear, the discoloration arising from the long maceration of leaves, bark, and other vegetable *débris* in water almost stagnant.

Rivers falling into the gulf, particularly the Caroni and Couva, are obstructed at their mouth by *basses* or shallows. The shallow at the entrance of the Caroni extends upwards of a mile into the gulf, and presents somewhat of an impediment to the coastwise navigation. More than once vessels beating up for Port-of-Spain have run aground on its mud-bank. These shallows are formed by the gradual accumulation of stumps, branches, and even entire trees, carried down the stream during the rainy season, and which, sticking in the soft ground, remain to form an embankment with the alluvial deposits; such accumulation and deposits are greatly aided by the nearly constant direction of the prevailing winds, there being no surf at all along the western coast to disturb the formation of such deposits. On the other hand, to the eastward, where a heavy surf incessantly rolls over the beach, also to the northward and southward, where the coast is generally bluff and the shores steep, all the rivers, with the exception of the Lebranche, which empties itself under the cover of a rocky hill, have across their mouths bars of sand, resulting from the antagonism of the waves and the currents of the streams. The consequence is that such of our rivers as are of a depth sufficient to admit small craft can be entered only at high tide, when there is a sufficiency of water on the bars and shallows to allow of their being crossed. During the dry season some of the rivers thus obstructed by bars become lost in the sandy beach, and may be said to *ooze* into the sea. Of this the Oropuche is an instance. The shallow at the mouth of the Caroni sometimes forms a species of dyke from one to two feet high. The beds of many of these rivers are so much beneath the level of the sea through the greater part of their courses that in the dry months they are quite salt; in the wet season, however, the torrents of rain pouring into them force out the salt water, and they become perfectly fresh. The Guataro is said to be salt during the dry season for eighteen miles upwards.

The above brief and general view of the geography of Trinidad shows that the island is of a nearly rectangular form, and that it is divided by nature into two great valleys running east and west, and of almost the same form and extent. As a result of the direction of the middle range, the northern valley is more contracted at its eastern, and the southern at its western, extremity. Each of these two valleys is subdivided into two secondary basins of unequal areas, the Caroni basin being more extensive than that of Oropuche, and the Guataro basin than that of the Great Lagoon.

Well marked is the contrast between these two portions of Trinidad. The northern division is more mountainous, the range in that direction attaining an elevation of two and three thousand feet. The ground rises gradually from each extremity towards the centre, and from the depth of the valley on each side towards the ridges. The southern portion is less mountainous, the middle and southern ranges reaching the height of about 700 feet, whilst intermediately the country exhibits more or less of gradation, a uniformly undulating surface being succeeded on the N. and S.E. by a hilly and, in some parts, a broken region.

In the northern section the rivers are, generally speaking, larger—such as the Matura and Oropuche, to the eastward; the Caroni, Chaguanas, and Couva, to the westward; the only large river in the southern section is the Guataro. Nevertheless, the rivers, which from the southern range flow in a southerly direction, are larger and more numerous than those which from the northern range have a northerly course. The Caroni swamp, in the northern, is corresponded to by the Nariva Lagoon in the southern section; but the Oropuche or Grand Lagoon has not its counterpart in the northern section, unless Oropuche be taken as such.

There are no ports on the eastern coast; but, as a compensation, easy communication may be established with the gulf by means of wheel or even tram-roads; so that the produce from eastern and intervening districts may be easily brought to the shores of the gulf. It was once in project to connect the Oropuche with the Caroni by means of a canal. I fear, however, that canal communications will not answer in a country like ours, where there exist no considerable water-courses, and where the rains are so heavy at one season as to cause partial inundations, and the drought so protracted at another as to dry up the ravines and even portions of the larger streams for several weeks at a time. Under such circumstances, tram-roads deserve a decided preference.

None of the other islands, I believe, offer such advantages as Trinidad in an agricultural point of view. Even its highest summits are not inaccessible to beasts of burden, and there the soil is commonly of excellent quality. The area of the island is about 1,755 square miles, or 1,020,000 acres. Of this quantity not more than 326,597 are appropriated, of which about 100,000 acres only are under cultivation, the rest still belonging to the Crown.

Monotony may be said to be the characteristic feature of the country; and this tameness of scenery arises not so much from a general evenness of surface as from the vast and almost unbroken series of virgin forests which still cover nearly the whole of its extent; and thus this beautiful and fertile colony, capable of supporting, according to a most moderate calculation, 1,000,000 inhabitants, at present maintains the unimportant aggregate of 153,118 individuals.

CHAPTER II.

GEOLOGICAL VIEW—MINERAL SPRINGS, PITCH DEPOSITS—SOIL AND VEGETATION.

The island of Trinidad has evidently been detached from the adjacent peninsula of Paria. Of this we find numerous proofs in the animal and vegetable kingdoms, as also in the geological structure of the island; and this must be evident even to the least initiated.

In the animal kingdom we find the following objects for comparison :—The Howling Monkey and Weeping Ape, among quadrumana; the Tiger-cat, or Ocelot, the Gato-melao, or Taïra, and the Otter, amongst carnivora; the Lapa among rodentia; the Tatou, or Cachicame, with the great and small Sloths, among edentata; the Guazoupita amongst ruminantia; and the Pecari among pachydermata. In the feather tribe, I may mention, among numerous species, the vultures Papa and Urubu; the Crested Gavilan (*Spizaetus ornatus*), the Campanero, and the Yacou, with several pigeons; the Macaw, the Guacharo, the Kamichi, and Red Ibis; also several ducks, &c. The tribe of reptiles supplies the following identical species :—The Morocoy, or land Tortoise, the Galapa, or river Tortoise, among chelonians; the Mapipire and Coral Snakes, the Macaouel and Huillia (boas), among ophidians; the Pipa and Paradoxal frogs amongst batrachians; the Mato (*Salvator Merianæ*), and a few others. We have also several fresh-water fish, which are found on the neighbouring main, viz. : the Cascaradura and Guabine; as also some kinds of insects which are not inhabitants of the other Antilles—among them the Lanthorn and the Parasol-ants.

The analogy between our Flora and that of the peninsula of Paria is also well defined. The stately Moriche Palm, the useful Timite and Carata, adorn the savannahs and woodlands alike of Trinidad and of Venezuela; the Mora Tree forms here, as it does there, immense forests; the Poui, the Cyp, Roble, and

Copaiba may be reckoned among our timber; among our lianes, the Bauhinia and Bambusa (Chusquea), with many Orchids.

The resemblance between the island and the continent, however, becomes more striking still, when we come to consider the geological structure, and consequent surface disposition of the country. We can follow the direction of the mountains of Paria to Cape Galera, through the Dragon's Mouths: the islets which contribute to the formation of the passages representing so many peaks which, having resisted the convulsions of nature, and remained above the waters when the lower parts were submerged, are to us as so many witnesses of a past cataclysm: just as the highest summits between Diego-Martin and Cuesa, and those to the westward of the latter, might probably become if the valley they form were sunk and invaded by the sea. All our valleys are transversal to the northern ridge and directed southward—only a few insignificant glens opening to the north, exactly as in the peninsula of Paria.

"The chain of calcareous mountains of the Brigantine and Cocollar," says Baron von Humboldt, " sends off a considerable branch to the north, which joins the primitive mountains of the coast. This branch bears the name of Sierra de Meapire.

" When standing on the summit of the Cerro de Meapire, we see the mountain currents flow on one side to the Gulf of Paria, and on the other to the Gulf of Carriaco; east and west of the ridge there are low marshy grounds, spreading out without interruption; and if it be admitted that both gulfs owe their origin to the sinking of the earth, and to rents caused by earthquakes, we must suppose that the Cerro de Meapire has resisted the convulsive movements of the globe, and hindered the waters of the Gulf of Paria from uniting with those of the Gulf of Carriaco. But for this rocky dyke, the isthmus itself, in all probability, would have had no existence; and from the Castle of Araya, as far as the Cape of Paria, the whole mass of the mountains of the coast would have formed a narrow island parallel to the island of Margarita."

No such dyke existing where the mountains were rent in formation of the *Bocas*, Trinidad was thus and then severed from the continent; and even at the epoch of its discovery by Columbus, the Indians entertained the opinion that the catastrophe had taken place at a not very remote period. Previous to that event, the Gulf of Paria was, in all probability, a lagoon, or lake, formed in the delta of the Orinoco.

At present, and by the gradual accumulation of deposits from the low plains of the Tigre and the vicinity, the waters of the gulf are receding; "and," according to Baron von Humboldt, "if the level of the soil seems to indicate that the two gulfs of Carriaco and Paria formerly occupied a much more considerable space, we cannot doubt that, at present, the land is progressively extending."

The presence of bitumen on the mainland, in the Gulf of Carriaco, and at El Buen Pastor, near the *Rio Areo*, as also its existence in the Gulf of Paria, and throughout the southern division of the island, is another proof of the geological connection existing between the two countries; and that connection may be traced across the gulf, by drawing a line from La Brea to El Buen Pastor—a distance of 105 miles.

At Manzanilla, between the Point and Oropuche, muriatiferous clay is met with; it is of a smoke-gray colour, like that of Araya, and apparently lies on sandstone. Not only was Captain Columbine deceived during his survey of the eastern coast, but several others have been bitterly disappointed at finding salt rills where they expected fresh water to quench their thirst. "On our first attempt," says Captain Columbine, "to reach the Oropuche, we perceived a few small drains of water on the sides of earthy cliffs along the shore, perfectly salt, although far within the range of the sea, and at least twenty and thirty feet above high-water mark; but three or four days afterwards, rain having fallen, they were found to be fresh."

Baron von Humboldt considers the Brigantine and Cocollar as being of Alpine formation. He says: "Three great parallel chains extend from east to west; the two most northerly chains are primitive, and contain the mica-slate of Mucanao and the San Juan valley, of Maniquarez and of Chaparipari. These we shall distinguish by the names of cordillera of the island of Margarita, and cordillera of Araya. The third chain, the most southerly of the whole, the cordillera of the Brigantine and of the Cocollar, contains rocks only of secondary formation; and what is remarkable enough, though analogous to the geological constitution of the Alps westward of St. Gothard, the primitive chain is much less elevated than that which was composed of secondary rocks." It is evident that our mountains also belong to the same formation.

Excepting Mr. C. Deville, who made but a short stay in Trinidad, no professional geologist has ever visited this island; but that gentleman's work on the Antilles is still in print, and part of it only has yet been published, so that it is rather difficult for me to give any account or comprehensive view of the geology of Trinidad.

Since writing this in 1857, two competent explorers—Mr. Wall, from the Government School of Mines, and Mr. Sawkins, geologist—were appointed to undertake a general survey of the economic geology of Trinidad, an undertaking which they executed with credit to themselves and to the satisfaction, I believe, of the governments which employed them. I am therefore in a position to make this new edition of my book more comprehensive and interesting.

When Messrs. Wall and Sawkins began their survey, not even one-fourth of the island had been recovered from its virgin state, and the uncontrolled luxuriance of the forest vegetation presented an almost impenetrable barrier to their exploration. Many and various were the difficulties they had to contend with. The allowance of £1 a day to cover personal and travelling expenses was barely sufficient for the purpose. They had been at work for two years, and yet they required twelve months more to perfect their work; they were particularly anxious to explore more minutely the coal formation of the island, and to follow up the seams at different places in the coal district. To do this, they required men, not only to carry personal luggage and provisions, but also tools, through the entangled forest; men to build their huts and assist in digging where required. This being hard and unpleasant work, the men asked for high pay, and, upon calculation, Messrs. Wall and Sawkins found that they could not carry on the survey without further assistance; and that assistance was refused, so that the work was not brought to the perfection these gentlemen had contemplated.

In accordance with the principle generally accepted, of naming geological formations which are examined or described for the first time, after the localities where they occur, Messrs. Wall and Sawkins propose to name *Caribbean group* that series of micaceous slates, sandstones, limestones, and slates, which are the constituent strata of the northern littoral range.

They propose to describe as *Older Parian* an indurated formation of lower cretaceous age, occurring in the central range.

They designate as *Newer Parian* that series of tertiary strata which comprises the whole of the southern division of the island.

The most prevalent beds of the Caribbean group consist of mica slates with layers of quartzose matter, at Saint Ann, for instance. There is a considerable variety of sandstones. Calcareous rocks are represented by two varieties in this group, viz.: crystalline limestones, contained in the slates, and alternating with same, as at Monos, for instance; and compact limestones, either completely unconnected with the schistose group, or only associated with its upper strata. The former sometimes occur in massive beds, varying from white to blue in colour. The compact limestones form a portion of the Laventille hills and several of the islands in the gulf. Point Gourde is entirely formed of that variety. It occurs again at Oropuche, at an elevation of 2,000 feet.

The *Older Parian* group consists mainly of a great variety of sandstones; of strata composed of an argillaceous base with equivalents of free silica. When combined with a given proportion of silica, it represents a certain degree of hardness, and forms a species of clay rock, which may be termed Argiline. This substance is extensively quarried at the Naparima hill, and is used, under the name of gravel, to make up the roads in Naparima and some neighbouring districts.

The *Newer Parian* group may be said to reach, northward, the rivers Caroni and Oropuche; it occupies the whole of the southern division of the island—more than two-thirds of its entire surface. It comprises a succession of clays, shales, loose sand, limestones, calcareous sandstones, and marls.

For facility of study, this group has been divided by Messrs. Wall and Sawkins into five series, viz.: (1), the *Caroni*, or *Carbonaceous series*, which extends from Pointe Noire, on the eastern coast, to the gulf. The tract it represents is but slightly elevated above the sea near the gulf.

2nd. The *Naparima Marl*. This series is formed of strata composed of clay, marls, and calcareous sands. A considerable and the best portion of the cultivated district of Naparima belongs to this formation; it also contributes to form the best soil of Oropuche. The series extends from west to east very nearly to the Ortoire, on a breadth of from two to four miles.

3rd. *Tamana* or *Calcareous Series*. The limestones of this series—viz., of Montserrat, Tamana, and Lebranche—vary from granular to crystalline in texture, and form, with sandstone, calcareous sandstones pretty common. The stratum can be traced from Cedar Hill Estate, Savanetta, to Manzanilla, eastern shore. Messrs. Wall and Sawkins are of opinion that the thickness of these strata cannot be less than several hundred feet.

4th. The *Nariva Series* consists of ferruginous clays, forming the substratum of the well-known *red soil*, stiff and retentive, and particularly observable in the county of Victoria.

5th. The *Moruga* or *Arenaceous Series* may be followed up from the southern coast to the Ortoire and the Oropuche lagoon, and from Mayaro, eastern coast, to Guapo and Cedros, western coast. The strata in this series are more or less of light sand; calcareous sandstones, however, are not deficient. This admixture of the calcareous element accounts for the quality of the soil where it exists in certain proportion, as at Guayaguayare, Moruga, Erin, and Cedros, where cacao and the sugar-cane are cultivated to advantage. Asphaltum is extensively disseminated in this series; lignite is found on the southern coast. We should also look for mud volcanoes or salses in this series.

I may be permitted to add a few particulars. Transition limestone prevails not only at La Ventille and the islets in the gulf, but is also met with in the mountains which border our valleys, between Diego-Martin and Cuesa; in the valley of Maraval, particularly on the Moka Estate; between Santa Cruz and Maracas Valley; between the sources of Arima and Oropuche, and more eastward still. At the head of the rivers Aripo and Oropuche there are some caves beautifully ornamented with stalactites and stalagmites; they are haunted by Guacharos, which breed therein. Our limestone is, in general, compact, of a bluish-gray colour, destitute of organic remains, and traversed by veins of calcareous spar. Small crevices occur in the calcareous rocks, lined with a beautiful crystallisation of carbonate of lime of a topaz colour.

Gypsum is not uncommon, and there is a quarry of it near

the town of Saint Joseph, at the foot of the mountain, and adjoining the royal road; this gypsum is very white, containing native sulphur, and perfectly resembling that of Guiria, on the opposite coast of the gulf. There exists another deposit at La Ventille, at a short distance from the town. Lamellar gypsum is found in many places in the southern division, as also granular, and a bank of grayish earthy sulphate of lime is known on the Brechin Castle Estate, ward of Savanetta, within a short distance of Cangrejos Bay.

Sandstone is also abundant, and is exhibited in the limestone formation, as, for instance, near Port-of-Spain, at Maraval, Pointe-à-Pierres, Manzanilla, Quemada, &c. Between Guanape and Aripo, at the foot of the mountains, the soil is composed altogether of silicious pebbles, imbedded in a coarse reddish clay. Blocks of milky quartz, and crystals of hyaline quartz, are found in many parts of the mountainous region, and at the bases of the mountains. "However extraordinary this mixture of sandstone and compact limestone may appear," says Baron von Humboldt, "we cannot doubt that these strata belong to one and the same formation."

The slate, or schistose formation, is also very apparent in the hills forming the valleys of St. Ann and Maraval. Mica slate, talcky and mica schists, are particularly common; the latter sometimes contains garnets, generally of a small size. The admixture of sandstone, schistose and limestone rocks, is well marked at Monos; some of the projections are formed of limestone, others of large slabs of schistose rocks; and mica schists are observed in many localities, as also quartz rocks. In our valleys and the beds of rivers rounded pebbles of quartz-stone, some very large, are found, together with a small flat stone of a bluish soft talc; this is particularly apparent after some of those mountain torrents, swollen by heavy rains, have furrowed the neighbouring ridges. The softer rocks, however, soon disintegrate, and the silicious pebbles alone resist the action of atmospheric agents, and thus predominate in the valleys and beds of rivers.

Lignite has been found to the westward of the river Moruga, near Erin, and apparently occurs in seams, not only in that locality, but in several places also throughout the southern division. A substance nearly allied to lignite has also been found at Savanetta; it is compact, and of a dead, dark fracture; it burns with difficulty, and could not be used as fuel, unless mixed with some other substance.

Bitumen, or fossil pitch, another member of the carboniferous system, exists in inexhaustible abundance throughout the whole extent of the southern division. Point la Brea, in the county of St. Patrick, is formed altogether of hardened pitch, which extends into the gulf. The Pitch Lake, near the village of La Brea, in the same locality, is the great natural curiosity of Trinidad, and is really worth visiting. Soft bitumen also exists within the site of the town of San Fernando, and between Moruga and Guayaguayare; the latter is known by the appellation of "Lagon Bouf," from the peculiar noise produced by the bubbling of the soft bitumen. At Oropuche, Guapo, and Quemada, are likewise small craters of the same substance. About two miles from the Yaro, in the spring of the year, a periodical but brief submarine eruption occurs, throwing up quantities of pitch, with which the beach is afterwards strewn. Many of these bitumen craters exist at the bottom of the gulf, along the line of coast from San Fernando to Irois; their eruptions occasionally agitate the waves, and eject considerable quantities of petroleum. The pitch cast up on the beach is generally in the form of lumps or cakes.

It is to me evident that our pitch deposits must have a submarine communication with those of El Buen Pastor, in the canton of Maturin. "These springs," says Baron von Humboldt, "proceed, probably, from the beds of limestone which form the Brigantine and Cocollar."

There exist, in different parts of the island, what we term *natural* savannas, to distinguish them from *artificial* savannas, or pasture grounds laid out for stock. They exhibit a peculiar vegetation, characterised by a growth of coarse graminaceæ, cyperoids and other plants, studded with stunted dwarf trees, mainly the Chapara (*Curatella*) and Bois-sang (*Vismia*). The surface of these savannas is usually sandy and very poor. Some of them are situated on the flanks and even summits of the mountains; others on low, flat lands. The former may be observed in the northern range, from St. Joseph to Arima; the soil is formed of coarse quartzose gravel and very poor. They are dotted over with blocks of milky quartz, which from a distance appear as so many white sheep or cattle grazing in the pasture.

The soil of the savannas O'Mara and Piarquito, in the ward of Arima, of Arouca and Piarco, in the ward of Arouca, is a coarse, unproductive clay, with a layer of white sand; that of Aripo, Couva, and Savanetta light and poor—that of Aripo, however, rather swampy; the savannas of Erin and Icacos are sandy, but not altogether deficient in organic matter; they produce an abundance of Guinea Grass and another panicum called Caricio. The Caroni savanna, and that at the back of the Cocal, Nariva, differ from those already mentioned, not only because they are partly under water during the wet season, but because their soil being formed, to a great extent, of sedimentary matter, supports a more varied and richer vegetation. These savannas being rather level are very subject to become miry and swampy under the prevalence of the periodical rains, whilst during the dry months of the year they become indurated and everywhere rent into ruts or chasms several feet in depth. It is customary to fire these miniature prairies during the dry season, in order to destroy the rank vegetation which had sprung up during the rains, and thereby induce a fresh and tender growth for the benefit of the stock which is sent to graze therein.

The Caroni and Cocal savannas may be ranged among those swamps which occupy more than one-seventeenth of the area of the island. They are tracts of perfectly plane ground bordering the sea, and extending more or less towards the interior. The section adjacent to the shore is usually flooded by the tide, and thickly overgrown by mangroves; the portion towards the interior is covered with a thick vegetation of graminaceæ, cyperaceæ, and vines. The soil may be considered as made up of vegetable *débris in situ* and sedimentary matter washed down by heavy rains and periodical floods.

SOIL AND VEGETATION.—In its geological formation Trinidad displays much variety. Volcanic rocks, however, are entirely wanting. The soils of the island are generally in accordance with the strata on which they rest, and are formed by the disintegration of those strata. Changes occur in the qualities of our soils to such an extent as to have attracted the attention of the least observant. The character of these soils being very similar over one and the same formation will allow their classification according to their productive capabilities. I should remark here that, notwithstanding the rich vegetation generally prevailing, and the excess of forests, none of the soils really abound in vegetable matter. On the whole, however, they may be rated as of average fertility, and several districts might sustain comparison with the best soils of Cuba and Hayti, whilst a few tracts bear the characteristics of irretrievable barrenness.

There is a great variety of soils in the Caribbean group, but the quality cannot be described as generally good. These soils consist of a variable mixture of clay and sand, or gravel: they are of a better quality when mixed with calcareous matter; the *cerros* of Aripo and Oropuche are illustrations of this fact, as also the *vegas* of Oropuche, Tompuna, Coumuto, and Cunapo. Where sand prevails, the land is very poor. The soil may be said to be of average quality in the counties of St. George and Caroni, and in part of those of St. David and St. Andrew. From Arouca to Guanape it becomes unproductive, being a cold, reddish clay, or poor silicious land, whilst from Guanape to La Ceyba it is a retentive, whitish clay, or a poor sand, supporting a languishing vegetation of ferns, sclerias, cocorits, and bromelias. The whole of this tract may be considered as the worst land in the colony, and not worth the labour of cultivation. On the banks of the Oropuche and Matura the land is excellent; a tract between Oropuche and Manzanilla, known as the Caratal, is equal to any in the colony. Chaguanas, Carapichaima, and Couva, under intelligent tillage, can give remunerative crops of sugar. The total extent represented by these soils is $342\frac{1}{2}$ miles.

In the *Older Parian*, soil generally poor; absence of calcareous matter. Mount Harris and Mount Carata in this group are formed of hard sandstone, and the surrounding tracts are sterile. Area 97 square miles.

In the *Newer Parian* group the Nariva series is composed of stiff ferruginous clay (red soil), not very fertile. In Naparima it is associated with the marl formation, presenting frequent alternations with the same; it is under cane cultivation, less on account of its agricultural capabilities than its close proximity to the black soil.

The Naparima marl series affords soils of excellent quality, friable, and usually black, or of chocolate colour—the *tierra mulata* of Cuba. The great fertility of these soils is undoubtedly attributable to the presence of a large proportion of carbonate of lime with an admixture of carbonate of magnesia. I have not the slightest doubt that the addition, especially of the white marl, to the red soil would materially improve its properties; and since on many estates it is within proximity, it would not cost much to try some essays, especially as there cannot be any apprehension of a bad result. The area occupied by the marl series may be calculated at 75 square miles.

Not inferior to the marl series is the calcareous or Tamana series. This region is imperfectly known, being cultivated only on a small scale, viz., at Manzanilla on the eastward, and at Montserrat on the west. The soil is of excellent quality, of a brownish colour, and friable. All sorts of provisions, particularly roots, grow to perfection; cacao culture is extending in the Montserrat district, and the plant is highly prolific and the produce of as good a quality as anywhere else in the colony. Where not too hilly, as between Montserrat and Tamana, the soil would be well adapted to the cultivation of the sugar-cane. The area may be taken at 86 square miles.

The Caroni series occupies a large surface from east to west, and displays a variety of soils: good, adjacent to the Tamana series; sandy as we approach the Caroni and Oropuche; argillaceous when we approach nearer; then the *vegas*, formed of sedimentary matter. On the eastern coast, and near the Oropuche, we meet better soil, owing to a fair admixture of calcareous drift from the Lebranche and Oropuche elevations. The extent of this series may be calculated at 318 square miles.

In the Moruga, or arenaceous series, the soil may be said to be sandy and yet not unproductive, especially where it is modified by the occurrence of interstratified shales, as at Moruga, Guayaguayare, Erin; or of calcareous sandstone, as at Quemada and part of Cedros. This section occupies more than one fourth of the total area of the island—492 square miles. Cacao and the sugar-cane have been cultivated with some success at Mayaro, Moruga, and Cedros; provisions thrive at Guayaguayare as well as anywhere else in the colony; but this section seems to be well adapted to the culture of cotton and tobacco; also to that of coffee.

The soils of our swamps may be ranged as sedimentary

alluvials with a large admixture of vegetable *débris*. To become tillable, they should be empoldered and drained; this has already been attempted with some success, and I have no doubt that a good portion of them may be recovered for agriculture. They would then become adaptable to the cultivation of the sugarcane, but especially to the production of rice. The Caroni and Nariva swamps might be turned into pasturage. The area of the principal swamp tracts may be estimated as follows: Nariva, 34,560 acres; Caroni, 20,480 acres; Oropuche (west coast), 8,960 acres.

The beaches of Mayaro, Nariva, and Icacos are lined with tracts of blown sand, in which the coco-nut palm thrives admirably.

"The great diversity of soil," observe Messrs. Wall and Sawkins, "from the heaviest (red soil of Naparima) to the lightest (siparia, Erin); from the richest (Naparima marl, Tamana), to the most unpromising (Valencia, Turure), seems to indicate that the country, limited in extent as it may be, is calculated to become the home of a highly varied agriculture. However strong the temptation may be to spread the sugar cultivation into every corner of the island, it should be remembered that a country which is dependent on several staples is infinitely more secure than another which relies on one only." This is a sensible remark, and I shall add that, though in the estimation of certain people it may be a matter of regret that there do exist in the colony such extensive tracts of barren land, I nevertheless consider this, to a certain extent, as a relative advantage, since the chances are that these tracts will never be brought under cultivation; and we shall have thus in store fuel, and even timber, for building purposes; a good area besides remaining covered with forest, we shall not be exposed to suffer from drought, as is the case in some of the older islands.

MINERAL SPRINGS.—Two mineral springs only have been hitherto discovered in the island; one of these is in the valley of Maraccas, at the foot of a high hill, and nearly in the bed of the St. Joseph or Maraccas river; it is a cold spring. According to Dr. T. Davy, "it has a strong smell of sulphuretted hydrogen, and there is a disengagement of gas in bubbles at its surface." From an examination of a portion which he took with him, he found it to contain the following ingredients, viz., "carbonate and sulphate of lime, carbonate of potash, common salt, and traces of silica, and to be impregnated with sulphuretted hydrogen, and that pretty strongly, and with carbonic acid gas: its specific gravity is 1·0016."

The Maraccas spring may be considered as having a rather powerful action on the human frame, since a febrile condition has been invariably produced after a few days' bathing in its waters; such baths, however, have proved very advantageous in several instances, and this spring might be resorted to in many cases of chronic disease.

The other mineral spring is also cold; it has not been analysed by the learned doctor, but Messrs. Crüger and Léotaud, who examined it, found therein the following ingredients to sixteen ounces:—

	Grs.
Muriate of soda	2·349
Sulphate of soda	3·471
Sulphate of lime	6·776
Sulphate of magnesia	6·417
Oxide of iron	6·231

The metallic taste is so strong that it is almost impossible to swallow any quantity of the water: this spring is in the ward of Pointe-à-Pierres, on a small property belonging to M. Desanclos. In the same locality, on the Plaisance Estate, are three springs, one nearly cold, another warm, which is used for bathing, and a third unbearably hot. Dr. Davy found that the hot springs were "slightly impregnated with sulphuretted hydrogen and carbonic acid gas, and contained minute quantities of carbonate of potash, lime, and magnesia, and of silica, with a trace of phosphate of lime; so dilute are they, that their specific gravity does not exceed 1·0003." And yet their medicinal virtues, particularly in cases of rheumatism and nervous debility, have been strikingly displayed in more than one case.

Dr. Davy remarks, besides, that the mud volcanoes may be considered as mineral springs:—"The water, muddy as it is, in its ordinary state, from clay suspended in it, when filtered becomes perfectly clear and transparent. A portion so treated, procured from Cedros, was of specific gravity 1·0147, had a faint bituminous smell, and slight pure saline taste. Its chief ingredient was common salt; it contained, besides, a notable proportion of iodine, probably in the form of hydriodate of soda and carbonate of lime. A specimen of muddy water from the mud volcano in Savanna Grande afforded, on examination, results very similar to the preceding, seeming to indicate a common source and origin. What is worthy of note in the waters of the mud eruptions," adds the Doctor, " is the presence of iodine, a substance of high medicinal powers. Containing it, they may be deserving of trial, and may prove efficacious in all those ailments in the treatment of which iodine has been found to be beneficial."

The vegetation of wild plants furnishes a good criterion whereby to judge of the various degrees of fertility or barrenness of soils. The single family of palms affords sufficient accurate indications of the quality of the land and of its adaptability, or otherwise, to the growth of our various staples : as instances—the Carat is indicative of the best soil, and of its suitableness for the production of sugar; the Mountain-cabbage is a sure characteristic of good land, adapted to the cultivation of cacao and coffee; the *Attalea speciosa*, of a light rich loam, particularly well suited to the production of "ground-provisions;" the Groo-groo, on the other hand, grows in dry silicious lands; the Timite generally in low sandy tracts ; the Cocorite and Palma Real in the worst soils. Any land producing the Carat (*Copernicia*) and Mountain-cabbage (*Oreodoxa*) Palms, the Wild Fig-tree (*Ficus*), Wild Plum-tree (*Spondias*), the Cedar (*Cedrela*), Balizier (*Heliconia*), Sand-box tree (*Hura*), &c., may be pronounced good. Wherever these plants grow in abundance, the soil is very fertile ; the Carat, wild Fig-tree, and Cedar, however, are particularly characteristic of superior lands. The soil is of excellent quality where the Fig-tree, Mountain-cabbage, Plum-tree, Cedar, and Baliziers are plentiful; it may also be considered good whenever any one of the above species is not wanting. On the contrary, wherever the Cocorite, Manaco, Timite, and Groo-groo (Palms), the Mulatto-tree (Cassia), Bois-sang (*Vismia*), the Fox-tail grass, Cortaderas (*Scleria*), Caratas, Pine-apple, and Melastomaceous plants grow in abundance, the soil may be pronounced poor and unproductive. The Poui (*Tecoma*) Balata (*Achras*), Carapa, or *Crapaud* (*Carapa*), and Guatecaro (*Lecythis*) thrive both in good and bad lands; the two former, however, arrive at superior growth in poor sandy soils, the two latter in damp clay-lands.

The vegetation of Trinidad, like that of all inter-tropical

climates, is dense and luxuriant. Some trees attain the loftiest heights, and display the most majestic forms. In the palm family, the Moriche (*Mauritia*) and Mountain-cabbage (*Oreodoxa*) grow perfectly straight like columns, supporting a tuft of fan-like and pinnated leaves: over its humble associates towers the giant Cedar, whilst the noble Balata rears its magnificent trunk, expanding above in vigorous branches clothed with a dark green foliage. The Poui and Bois Immortel periodically change their verdant foliage—the former for a thick covering of pure yellow, the latter of brilliant crimson blossoms; and, in like manner also, the flowering Roble assumes its orange-coloured garment, and spreads far around a delicious perfume. The Ceyba, the Sand-box, and Wild Plum-trees display, on their branches and along their trunks, a thick vegetation of Epidendra and Tillandsias. The underbrush, in some parts, is so thick that a passage must be effected with the cutlass. Bauhinias, Bignonias, and other lianes, are everywhere seen climbing up the trunks of the loftiest trees, whilst from the branches of others depend the twining roots of the Mamure (*Carludovicia*) and the Seguine (*Philodendrum*). The vigorous Matapalo (*Elusia*), accidentally implanted on some tree, sends down into the soil its cable-like root, meanwhile encircling its supporter with an inextricable network of pliant root-stems, which, by a gradual yet rapid growth, eventually stifle and destroy the most luxuriant tree. In copses are met the more humble individuals of the vegetable kingdom—the beautiful Passiflora, the delicate Convolvulus, the more robust Bignonia, and the useful Guaco and Pareira Brava. Poisonous as well as wholesome medicinal plants grow everywhere; and from our forests we may draw an almost inexhaustible supply of valuable timber, as well as cabinet and other woods, applicable to all descriptions of useful purposes.

The culture of only a few of our indigenous vegetables has, as yet, been attempted, though many more might perhaps be cultivated to advantage. Those, however, which—whether indigenous or exotic—form the basis of our agriculture, exhibit the same luxuriance of growth as the spontaneous vegetation.

The sugar-cane, when cultivated in virgin and congenial soils, displays a vigour such as to call forth the admiration even of the casual observer, and how much more to elate the rational hopes of the interested planter. The cacao-tree reaches, in our *vegas*, the height of thirty feet, and yields a successive produce throughout the year; the coffee, as well as the cotton and castor-oil plants, attains the proportion of copse-wood; rice grows to the height of six and seven, maize to that of eighteen, and even twenty, feet; the farinaceous roots of the Manioc, and the tubercles of the Yam mature, in proper localities, to enormous sizes; Plantains furnish, with but little trouble, an abundance of alimentary provision, whilst in rich sandy loams, Pumpkins and Water-melons are reproduced on the same spot for years, without the slightest care. Fruit-trees, when planted, are usually left to their own untended growth and development, unaided even by the pruning-knife; but they fail not, in due season, to pour forth the exuberance of their luscious treasures; the Nutmeg and Cinnamon trees also grow to the fullest perfection. Yet man—neglectful man—satisfied with Nature's proceedings, attempts but feebly to turn to advantage the gratuities of a bountiful Providence.

EARTHQUAKES.—Although there exists no authentic record of Trinidad having ever suffered, to any great extent, from earthquakes, yet the island is not unfrequently visited by those subterranean convulsions; and a year seldom passes away without the recurrence of one or more of such visitations. They were rather numerous during the prevalence of the long and severe drought of the year 1846, when as many as seven shocks were felt in the month of September alone. In October, 1761, the island suffered from a rather severe earthquake, and the mountain to the N.E. of St. Joseph, known by the name of "Cerro de Don Pedro Indio," was rent to a large extent, the fissure or chasm remaining open for a long period. For many years, and until lately, a mass in honour of "Nuestra Señora de la Guadalupe" was celebrated in St. Joseph on the date, and in commemoration, of that event. In September, 1825, the steeple of Trinity Church was thrown down, and the walls of several houses in Port of Spain were dangerously cracked during one of the severest shocks within the memory of the inhabitants.

It has been remarked that earthquakes are more prevalent during the hottest months, namely, in August, September, and October. Their movement is either from S.S.W. to N.N.E., or from E. to W., that is to say, in the direction of the Antillan range, or the Grand Cordillera of Venezuela.

CHAPTER III.

NATURAL HISTORY—VEGETABLE KINGDOM, TIMBER WOODS, USEFUL AND POISONOUS PLANTS—ANIMAL KINGDOM, MAMMIFERS, BIRDS, REPTILES, FISH, AND INSECTS, VIZ., THOSE WHICH MERIT ATTENTION FROM THEIR UTILITY AS FOOD, THEIR SINGULAR HABITS, OR NOXIOUS AND DESTRUCTIVE PROPENSITIES.

THE all-bountiful Creator has everywhere made an abundant provision for the wants of His creatures; and whithersoever man directs his steps in search of a home, he is certain to find food for his sustenance, materials for his clothing and lodging, as also products naturally suited, or artificially adaptable, to commercial purposes. Yet, wherever civilised man migrates and settles, he carries with him, as a matter of necessity, not only those implements and conveniences which an advanced state of civilisation has invented, but likewise those animals he has domesticated, those plants or seeds he has reclaimed from nature, and which he knows will be useful in contributing either to his support or comfort. Thus, the ox, the horse, the sheep, swine, and poultry, were introduced and naturalised in the West Indies; and the sugar-cane, coffee, rice, and other growths, imported and propagated into staples. But in these islands were also found building materials, as well as articles of food and commerce. I have, in the preceding chapter, mentioned the mineral productions which may be, or are already, turned to useful purposes; I shall hereafter fully notice those which the vegetable kingdom supplies for trade and general aliment; but at present I only wish to point out those indigenous plants and animals which have been rendered subservient to our wants, together with those of the former which deserve peculiar mention on account of their noxious or curative properties; and those of the latter which merit attention, either from their singular habits, or destructive propensities and venomous attributes.

VEGETABLE KINGDOM.—Under this division, such plants only will form the objects of notice as serve for building purposes, cabinet-work, &c.; for medicinal purposes, or such as are to be avoided on account of their deleterious properties.

Balata (*Mimusops globosa*, Goertner).—The Balata, or Bullet-wood, is one of our best and most useful timbers. Though a hard wood, Balata is not, however, iron-hard, as are the Poui and a few others: owing to its regularity of grain and freedom from knots, it is easily sawn, and still more so split; and workmen, in general, prefer working it to many others of even less solidity. It is excellent in many respects, but mainly as house-posts and plates, joists or floor-beams and runners, as also for fence-posts, spokes, and even shingles—the latter remarkably durable. The Balata grows to very large sizes, some measuring five and six feet in diameter, whilst the unbranched shaft often rises from fifty to sixty feet.

Poui (*Tecoma serratifolia*, Donal.).—There are three varieties of the Poui, characterised by the colour chiefly, viz., the white, the green, and the black Poui; of these the green is accounted the superior quality. Poui is, unquestionably, our hardest timber, and the Swedish axe alone is fully equal to the task of felling it; it also contains a sort of gummo-resinous substance which, particularly in the black kind, impedes the free action of the saw. The usages to which Poui is applicable are not so numerous as those of Balata; it is mainly employed for ground-posts and other beams in heavy buildings, and is, for such purposes, considered by many as superior to the former: though growing to large sizes, it never attains the proportions of the Balata.

Acoma, or Mastic (*Sideroxylon mastichodendron*, Jacquin).—Between this wood and the Balata there exists the greatest analogy, with the exception of colour—the former being of a light straw, whilst the latter is of a dark red tinge: it possesses a very fine and close, but also a very hard, grain, and may be said to combine the qualities of the two foregoing timbers. It is adapted to almost all purposes, even to the handling and boxing of carpenters' tools, and is, in these respects, perhaps our most available timber. It thrives, generally, in mountainous districts, and attains large dimensions.

Yoke (*Piptademia peregrina*, Bentham).—Very common, and an excellent wood—not so hard and heavy as the preceding ones, but equally durable. It is applicable to all building purposes, and can also be wrought into handsome furniture; its colour is not so dark as that of the mahogany, but is, perhaps, more beautifully variegated. Yoke may be said to be imperishable in the ground: it grows to a large size.

Bois-lézard, Bois-fidèle, or, by corruption, Fiddle-wood (*Vilez divaricata*, Swartz).—This again is an excellent wood, neither too heavy nor too hard, and is employed only for building purposes, as ground and house-posts, plates, joists, rafters, &c. It grows ordinarily to about twelve or eighteen inches, but often much more in diameter; when large, however, it is commonly found to be hollow within.

Epineux Jaune—Yellow Sanders (*Xanthoxyloz clava Herculis*)—which ought not to be confounded with Epineux Blanc, bears a very close resemblance to the Acoma, and is available for the same purposes: it is also valuable to the wheelwright. It is the Satin-wood of the West Indies. Diameter, from twenty-four to thirty inches.

Guatequen, Guatacare (*Lecythis idatimon*).—Very common in damp clay lands, is of intricate grain, very tough, and is available for house-posts, joists, rafters, and even ground-posts, though in the latter it is apt to rot at the surface-line of the earth, especially in damp soils. It is, however, particularly in use for cart-shafts, and generally wherever the quality of toughness is required. Diameter, from two to three feet.

Savonette Jaune (*Sapindus saponaria*).—Though not used as extensively perhaps as it ought to be, the Savonette Jaune is undoubtedly one of our best woods: it is tough, grows to pretty good sizes, and might be employed in all house constructions, as posts, beams, rafters, &c. Its qualities also fit it for felloes and mill-frames. It is very common.

Red Mangrove (*Rhizophora mangle*).—This wood, though not equal to any of the former, is nevertheless used for building purposes, and chiefly for beams and joists: it entered into the construction of many houses in Port of Spain. The same remark is applicable to the Bois-rouge and Contre-vent: the latter may be said to be peculiar to the northern mountains, and is of large size; the two former belong to salt swamps and low lands. They are generally warped in growth.

Fustic, or Bois d'Orange (*Macleira xantoxytlon*), is well known as a dye-wood, and is besides an excellent timber. It lasts a very long time in the ground, but unfortunately does not grow to any very large size, which is an obstacle to its being in more extensive demand : it is, however, invaluable to the wheelwright for naves and felloes, and I have no doubt fine furniture might also be wrought from it. Though in some parts rare, it would appear to be in great abundance all along the southern coast, and in the interior of some of the south-eastern districts.

Angelim (*Andira inermis*).—There exist here at least two different species of Angelim, growing almost everywhere, and of which one is less in bulk than the other : the former furnishes very superior cart-naves ; and the larger species, when sawn into boards and planks, makes excellent flooring : it is also valuable for mill-frames.

Tapana (*Richeria grandis*) grows to a very large size, and is well suited to all building purposes : it is a strong tough wood, and may be sawn into boards for flooring and boat-building; it is, however, chiefly used by wheelwrights for felloes.

Roble (*Platymiscium platystachium*, Bent.).—The Roble grows in great abundance in some parts of the country, and commonly in good soils, where it attains large dimensions. Though not in very extensive use, it is yet an excellent timber—of a dark orange colour, not over hard, and easily sawn into boards and scantling; it can be employed in almost any erection, and furnishes remarkably good and lasting ground-posts. It possesses, when newly wrought, a very agreeable odour, which it preserves indefinitely, and is of sufficiently fine grain and polish to serve for furniture ; in fact, where Locust is scarce, the Roble is used as a very efficient substitute.

Carapa, or, by corruption, Crapaud (*Carapa guianensis*).— Besides the oil which is extracted from the seeds of the Carapa, the tree itself supplies excellent timber. There are two distinct varieties ; both may be sawn into scantling, boards, and planks; they are also split into shingles and staves. The Carapa is very extensively used as beams and rafters, and the lighter coloured species, when well polished, makes fine furniture. Diameter, from two to three feet.

Copaiba (*Copaifera officinalis*) very much resembles the European walnut, and may be applied to the same uses, but is not, perhaps, as much employed as it ought to be. It is an excellent timber, of very large size, and may serve the purposes of the builder, wheelwright, turner, and cabinet-maker.

Locust, or Courbaril (*Hymenæa courbaril*).—This is one of our most valuable woods, and might be used for all building purposes, but mainly in ornamental work; it is, however, almost exclusively used for furniture—such as presses, bedsteads, sideboards, tables, &c., and by wheelwrights for carriage naves. Diameter, five to six feet, and very lofty.

Purple-heart, or Sapatero (*Copaifera pubiflora*).—The Purple-heart is an excellent timber, and may serve in building as beams and rafters; but, from its rich dark colour, it is especially used by cabinet-makers for facing and other ornamentation in the choicer kinds of furniture. The heart-wood is as hard as the Poui itself, whilst the sap, or outer wood, is of a light colour, rather soft, and not durable.

Mora (*Mora excelsa*).—The Mora and Mangrove may be said to be our only *social* trees, and the former is, perhaps, the most abundant of all our timber woods. It is one of the loftiest and largest inhabitants of our forests, but when of any large proportions, is in general hollow, or, at least unsound, in the centre. The Mora has never been much employed, and is not, therefore, in great demand. It is objected that it does not last in the ground beyond three or four years, and on that account has not hitherto been ranked among the valuable timbers. If not recommendable, however, for ground-posts, it is certainly available in some other respects. I have no doubt that it would answer well for the flooring of stables, and in the construction of bridges. One of our Mora forests has been felled (by order of his Excellency the Governor), and the timber brought into notice. I must say that it has not answered expectations, and is now completely neglected. The Mora is not a hard wood, but very much resembles the Angelim both in colour and grain.

Cedar, or Acajou (*Cedrela odorata*).—For all building purposes, except ground-posts, Cedar is, unquestionably, our most valuable wood. It is light, easily wrought, and yet very lasting; also, from its pungent odour and acrid taste, it is generally exempt from the attacks of insects. Cedar is commonly sawn into boards and scantlings, and used for plates and rafters, flooring and wainscoting, inside fittings and outside boarding; for panel-doors and windows, mouldings, and most of the ornamental parts of buildings; it is also split into light, but durable shingles, and wrought up into ordinary furniture. The side-roots or spurs, springing from the trunk, are finely grained, and sometimes richly knotted and variegated—so much so, in fact, as to furnish beautiful slabs, hardly inferior in appearance to mahogany, and which are wrought into the most elegant furniture. It is particularly durable in water, and may be used in boat-building; handsome and valuable canoes are also hollowed from the largest specimens. Cedar thrives in the best soils, and is pretty abundant throughout the island. Diameter, five to ten feet, and in height perhaps the loftiest of our trees.

Black and White Cyp (*Cordia Gerascanthus*, Jacq.), (*Cordia sulcata*, De C.).—The Cyp is not so light as the Cedar, nor is it so variously employed; it, is, however, extensively used for rafters and flooring-boards, and is, with reason, regarded as one of our best woods; it generally grows in the mountainous districts, and does not attain very large proportions.

Laurier, or Laurel-Cyp (*Oreodaphne strumosa*, Griesb.).— The Laurier-Cyp grows only in the mountain districts; it does not last in the ground, but may be sawn into boards and scantlings: it is light and very durable—in fact, quite equal to the Cyp itself. Diameter, from two to three feet, lofty, and as straight as a palm tree.

Olivier (*Chuncoa obovata*) generally thrives in poor land, and is plentiful between Arauca and Aripo, as also at Guapo and Irois: it is not so valuable as the Laurier-Cyp, but can be used for the same purposes—though rather heavy, and with a great tendency to rive. The Olivier grows to a large size, but is then invariably hollow: it is most available when of only twenty-four to thirty-six inches in diameter.

Couroucay or Incense-tree (*Icica Heptaphylla*, Aublet).— Scarce, but valuable for building purposes, besides the gum or gum-resin it contains in great abundance; so are also the Boistan or Surette (*Byrsonima spicata*, Rich.), and the Bois-sang or Blood-wood (*Vismia*); they never attain a very large size, but may be used for rafters.

Aguatapana (*Rhopala montana*).—An excellent timber, growing in the mountains, but never reaching a large bulk: it resembles rose-wood, and might be turned to useful purposes by the cabinet-maker. It is called Beef-wood, on account of its resemblance to a piece of salt beef.

Gasparil (*Esenbeckia*).—Very tough and lasting, and bearing the closest resemblance to box-wood, but, like it, unfortunately of small size; when large enough, it is used for posts in house-building.

Yoke-savanne (*Mimosa*).—Very valuable to the wheelwright.

Calabash (*Crescentia Cujete*).—Light and very tough; excellent in boat-building—particularly as ribs—and in the framework of agricultural implements; useful also to coachmakers.

Tendre Acajou (*Mimosa arborea*).—A soft and yet very durable wood, adapted to all building purposes.

Moussara, or Bread-nut (*Artocarpus incisa*, var. *Mucifera*).— Its seeds are eatable, much resembling the chestnut, when roasted; the wood is scarcely fit for furniture and building: it attains large dimensions, and is pretty abundant.

Galba (*Calophyllum galaba*, Jacq.) is one of our finest forest trees, and when of large size is principally used for the fabric of canoes; though it may also be sawn into scantling, boards, and planks, and is then applicable to all sorts of constructions. It, however, contains a sort of gum-resin, which materially impedes the free action of the saw. When set in rows, the Galba grows thick, and forms excellent hedge fences, which are easily kept down by periodical prunings.

Sand-box Tree (*Hura crepitans*).—The Sand-box tree matures to proportions equal to those of the Ceyba and Cedar: it thrives in the best soils, and near the sea-shore. This wood is only used, as far as I am aware, for canoe-hulls, which are hollowed out according to the dimensions of the trunk or block; but, as it is light and durable, it might also be rendered serviceable in other respects. The Mora, Cedar, Galba, and Sand-box are possessed, in all probability, of the qualities required in ship-building, and, on this account alone, may be reckoned as very valuable.

Manchoneel (*Hippomane mancinilla*).—It is well known that the Manchoneel-tree is a deadly poison: it would also appear to preserve its poisonous qualities for an indefinite period. I know of an instance in which a planter having found, lying on the beach, a Manchoneel tree which, from all appearances, had been there for years, thought he should be able to make it of service in some way or other; but he was soon obliged to desist. The Manchoneel wood is, otherwise, a valuable timber, and might be used in building and ornamental works.

Beside the hitherto enumerated forest trees, there are others which are, or might be, turned to advantage. From the Moricyp, Genipa, Moripa, Caracoli, and Pois-doux (*Inga fæculifera*), also from the Land-grape, Carapa, and even Cedar, are prepared excellent staves; the latter, however, ought to be discarded in this respect on account of its bitter taste and discolouring properties. The Mirobolant (*Hernandia*), Chestnut-tree (*Carolinea*), Mombin, or Wild Plum (*Spondias*), and other soft woods, supply good, cheap, and easily procured headings for hogsheads.

Many other plants are similarly brought into practical and every-day utility, and among them several palms. When arrived at full maturity, the Carat (*Copernicia*) makes very good ground-posts: its leaves, as also those of the Timite (*Manicaria saccifera*) and Cocorite (*Maximiliana Caribea, Attalea regia*), supply a cheap and durable thatch—the two former especially—and are extensively used whenever procurable. It is observable, however, that they are rarely found together in the same parts; and according to their respective prevalence is the distinctive covering of the cottage roofs to be known. The Mountain-cabbage, the Manaco, Groo-groo, Palma Real, and Cocorite, are split into rounded boards, which are employed by the poor for the outer boarding and even flooring of their cottages, and may also be used for inclosing poultry houses and yards, sheep-folds, stable-boarding, &c.: they are cheaper and more durable than White Pine boards. *Cortaderas*, or Sword Grass, Cane-tops, and Fox-tail Grass (*Pennisetum setosum*, Rich.) are also used in thatching.

The black and white Roseau (*Bactris* and *Gynerium*) are made use of as laths for the laying on for thatch; the former also in wattling or forming the framework of *tapia*—a species of very coarse stucco made of grass and clay—whilst the leafy top of the latter, though not so generally employed as it might be, supplies a most excellent thatch-covering, being thick and very durable. The Bamboo (*Nastus Borbonicus*) is extensively used as fuel in lieu of megass in those districts where it is plentiful; for that purpose, it is cut about four feet long, and then split or bruised, to allow a free escape of the air contained in the internodes, lest its expansion should occasion explosions, and thereby damage the furnaces and flues. The Bamboo is also employed as plantings for quickset hedges, and as rods for temporary fences; in the latter by being attached to the posts with some pliant lianes or withes: baskets and fish-nets are commonly made from the stem of this plant, in which branch of industry the Chinese immigrants excel. Its foliage supplies a rich fodder. A vine-like palm (*Desmoncus*) is employed for securing the rods in field-fencing, and might also serve in the manufacture of baskets: the Carib basket—water-tight when well woven—is made of a species of Calathea-Ahoman or Aruma. The fact is, it is a sort of double basket, the leaves of the Cachibou (*Calathea*) being inserted between two coatings of wicker-work. With the twiny roots of the Seguine (*Philodendrum*) are made neat hand-baskets; and the Mamure, split into small strips, serves the purpose of binding the leaves of the Carat and Timite-thatch to the Roseau laths.

From the two plants of the genera *Bauhinia* and *Brownea*, viz., *Pata de Vaca* (*Bauhinia megalandra*, Griesb.) and *Palo-Rosa*, superior hoops have been obtained; and I have no doubt some of our Bignonias, and the indigenous or prickly Bamboo (*Bambusa*) might answer a similar purpose.

The Bois Immortel (*Erythrina*) is invaluable as affording shade and protection to the Cacao, on which account it has been called by the Spaniards "Madre del Cacao," "Mother of the Cacao." There are two species of the *Erythrina*, the *coccinea*, or *Anauco*; and the *umbrosa*, or *Bucare*. The former is a very soft, light wood, rather brittle, and perfectly useless as timber or fuel; the latter is not exactly so soft or brittle: they are propagated by slips or cuttings or from seedlings.

The family of Graminaceæ furnishes excellent fodder, and various species from the genera *Paspalum* (Herbe-lancette), so called from the form of its leaves, which resemble the blade of a lancet. *Panicum* (Herbe-fine), *Andropogon* (Couch-grass), *Cynodon* (Bahama-grass), *Oplismenus*, *Pennisetum*, &c., form, in a great measure, the basis of our pasture-grounds. The Guinea-grass, Bamboo, and Guinea-corn, are excellent fodder for all sorts of cattle; cows thrive well on the Cow-grass (*Alternanthera*), and the Liane-douce (*Convolvulus*)—the latter eagerly sought by swine; to which may be added the Herbe-grasse (*Commelyna vulgaris*), and several plants of the Amarantaceæ family.

From the fibres of the Mahoe (*Sterculia*), Carata (*Bromelia carata*), and Agave are made excellent ropes ; and I have no doubt very useful textile fibres would be procured from various Apocynaceæ and Asclepiadaceæ, among others, from the *Asclepias Curassavica*, and also from the Balais, or Broom-plant (*Sida*), and the Mallow (*Malachra*) ; they should be thickly sown in a good soil, so as to prevent their growth into branches.

Many of our plants are of a poisonous nature, whilst others furnish useful medicinal matters : of those belonging to these two latter classes I have but a limited knowledge.

Poisonous Plants.—The Brinvilliers, or Pink-root (*Spigelia anthelmia*), is a small plant, very common, and generally growing in newly-cleared lands : it is fatal to animals as well as man ; and yet it is a powerful vermifuge, when administered with caution : the *Yongue*, or Stramony, and several other *Daturas*, are strong narcotics. The seeds of several *Euphorbiaceæ*, viz., of the Croton, Sand-box tree, and the Medicinier or Physic-nut (*Iatropha Curcas*) are violent emeto-cathartics : the fruit of the Manchoneel and the roots of the Manioc (*Iatropha Manihot*) are acrid and stupefactive poisons. A species of Seguine (*Caladium Seguinum*, vulg., the *Devil seguine*, which grows in damp places, is strongly caustic, and, wherever applied, causes a violent inflammation, and even ulcers difficult of cure. Several *Apocyna*, *Asclepias*, and *Bryonies* are poisonous emeto-cathartics ; the *Hamelia*, as well as the bulbs of a few Amaryllides, are also poisons.

The catalogue of useful medicinal plants is, nevertheless, much larger than the above. Among emollients may be numbered the following : Herbe-grasse, Prickly-pear (*Tuna*), and the mucilaginous part of the common Aloe ; the buds, flowers, and young fruits of the Ochro (*Hibiscus esculentus*), the leaves of the Gigiree (*Sesamum Orientale*), the *liber*, or inner bark of the Bois d'Orme (*Guazuma ulmifolia*), the Balais-doux (*Scoparia dulcis*), the flowers and roots of our Mallow, the young pods of the Cacao : as external applications, the Aloe, Prickly-pear, and Ochro, the young leaves of the Medicinier, Coco-nut oil, and Cacao-fat, Manioc, Corn-meal, and Rice, in the preparation of emollient poultices.

Lime and sour Orange juices, as also the fruits and young leaves of the Tamarind, serve to prepare very agreeable lemonades; the liquor of the Coco-nut is likewise a pleasant and refreshing drink.

The Canne-de-rivière, or River-cane (*Costus*), Herbe-couresse, or wild Cress (*Peperomia*), Couch-grass, and the flowers and roots of a few amarantaceous herbs are excellent diuretics.

The Lemon-grass (*Andropogon Schænanthus*), Guérit-tout (*Pluchea*), Chardon-bénit (*Eryngium fœtidum*), Cariaquite (*Lantana*) and warm lemonade, may be regarded as excellent diaphoretics.

The Herbe-à-charpentiers, or Carpenter's Grass (*Justicia pectoralis*), several species of ferns, known here by the name of Capillaire (*Adiantum*), and Hart's Tongue (*Scolopendrium*), the Dorstenia, Ceriman (*Monstera*), the bud of the Trumpet-tree (*Cecropia peltata*), and Macornette (*Borreria-suaveolens*), the flowers of the Pigeon-pea and Pumpkin, as also a syrup prepared from the Calabash and the pod of a species of Cassia, are used as pectorals.

The following are regarded as excellent astringents, viz., the inner bark of the Wild Plum, Cashew, Cachiman (*Anona reticulata*), and Mangrove, the green fruit of the Guava (*Psidium*), the buds and leaves of the Guava, Trumpet-wood, Pigeon-pea, and the flowers of the Palo-rosa, the sap of the Blood-wood (*Croton gossypifolium*) and the Liane-tasajo (*Bauhinia*). The Belle-de-nuit (*Mirabilis Jalapa*) applied in a bruised state, in cases of sprains, has a powerful healing action. To the above may be added, as excellent vulneraries, the Herbe-à-charpentiers, the Aloe, Herbe-à-pino (*Eupatorium*), *Hebeclinium macrophyllum*, and a Jussieua, which grows in great abundance in all damp localities. These are also used, together with the pulp of the Tamarind and sour Orange, the Agave, the Pied-poule (*Eleusine Indica*), and even the leaves of the Sand-box tree, as effective detergents.

The following are good hydragogues, viz.: the juice of the Banana tree and the decoction made of its bulbs, the bark of the Petit Branda (*Chioccoca racemosa*), also a bryony, which is rather irritating, and the coffee prepared with the parched seeds of the Stinking-weed (*Cassia Occidentalis*).

The leaves of the Sour-sop (*Anona muricata*) and other Anonæ, I regard as valuable anti-spasmodics, and far superior to the lime flowers. As emmenagogues, the syrup made from the Carata and green Pine-apples, the roots of several Aristolochiaceæ, and of the stinking-weed, are accounted excellent : the Pop-bark, or Poque (*Physalis*), I consider as highly recommendable in the cure of Leucorrhœa.

In dysentery the following are extensively used as astringents: The *liber* of the Cashew, wild Plum, and Mangrove; green Guavas and Liane Tasajo; as sedatives and emollients, Lemonade, the Cashew-apple and Mango, the Prickly-pear, Aloe, Balais-doux, Bois d'Orme, and, almost as a specific, the Toco (*Cratæva Tapia*) ; from the berries of the Hamelia also is prepared a syrup of excellent effect.

The Bitter-ash (*Quassia amara*), Herbe-éguilles (*Rolandra argentea*), Herbe-à-pique (*Calea-lobata*), Grand Trèfle (*Aristolochia*), Fruta de burro (*Uvaria*), Quinquina-pays (*Portlandia hexandra*) are good febrifuges. To these may be added, as excellent stomachics, and very valuable in cases of indigestion, the Secua or Nhandiroba (*Feuillea scandens*), and the Guaco (*Mikania Guaco*) ; as also the leaves of the Aguacate, or Avocado, and Aya-pana, and the seeds of the Guatamare (*Myrospermum*).

The Brinvilliers, and the inner bark of the Angelim (*Andira inermis*), are powerful but rather dangerous anthelmintics, as they have a strong stupefactive action on the brain. The Worm-bush (*Chenopodium ambrosioides*) and the Liane-à-l'ail (*Bignonia alliacea*) are excellent and safe vermifuges. Some persons are prejudiced against the administering of the Cowhage (*Mucuna*) as an anthelmintic : I have, however, prescribed it on several occasions, not only without the slightest ill effect or inconvenience, but with remarkable success. I even urge it as the best remedy against Lumbrics. It ought to be given either in thick syrup, in honey, or well enveloped in some soft substance.

The action and uses of Balsam Capivi are too well known to require any comment : the Liane-paques (*Securidaca*), Lignum-vitæ, and the roots of the Agave, are administered as anti-venereals; and I have invariably found the root of the Pareira-brava (*Cissampelos*) valuable in chronic inflammation of the urinary organs.

Some of the above plants, viz., the Guaco, Secua, Grand-tréfle, as also the musk Ochro (*Hibiscus Abelmoschus*), and the roots of the Manaco, are regarded as excellent antidotes to the bite of serpents and venomous insects, such as scorpions, spiders, and centipedes. They are generally given in some spirit; but, under pressure of necessity, they may be bruised, and the simple juice taken—as in the case of the Guaco and Manaco—the residuum being applied to the wound; or the seeds can be masticated and swallowed, as is practised with the Musk-ochro and Secua. There are, in addition to those already mentioned, many other plants successfully employed in like circumstances; even Lime-juice, both internally and externally, is highly beneficial.

The juice of the root of Yuquilla is an excellent remedy for the cure of chronic ophthalmia; but when used in the acute stage, increases the inflammation: it is the *Bignonia ophthalmica* of Dr. Chisholm. Carapa-oil used in friction is an infallible cure for ticks.

The indigenous trees and plants hitherto enumerated, and of which I now close the catalogue, are those which are ordinarily used in building, in mill, wheel, and cabinet works, as also for medicinal and other purposes. Some of them are met with almost everywhere, and in great abundance; others, as I have already stated, are scarce, and thrive only in certain localities. The Mora and Mangrove, as also the Timite, Carat, and Swordgrass are perhaps the only indigenous plants which grow gregariously: the Cedar thrives in the best lands, whether level or mountainous; the Guatacare and Carapa in damp clay soils; the Cyp and Laurier-cyp in the mountain districts.

Durability is the main characteristic of nearly all our timberwoods: a few only are light and soft, the generality solid and heavy; the hardest of all is the Poui, as also the heaviest. These qualities of extreme solidity and weight are, to a certain extent, a defect; because they exact a larger amount of labour to render the timbers marketable, or even render them unfit for indiscriminate use in ordinary buildings, and for certain purposes in many constructions, such as the lighter roof-work.

Generally speaking, popular opinion and practice do not distinguish or prescribe any fitness or unfitness of seasons for the felling of timber-trees: this I pronounce to be a very serious error. In Europe and other temperate climates, trees are felled in autumn, when the sap is deficient or dormant. It cannot be said that such a season really prevails in tropical regions: there is, however, a period during which vegetative life in general may be said to be at a minimum, particularly in certain trees: the cedar, for instance, remains for several months completely denuded, and the poui and roble lose their foliage immediately before flowering. After the dry season has set in the vegetation becomes everywhere more or less languid for the space of two months, or two months and a half, thus showing a deficiency of sap in vegetable organs : this period commonly embraces a part of February, the months of March and April, with part of May, but is more or less extended, according as the dry season itself is more or less protracted. This is the proper time, in fact the only season, in which trees can advantageously be felled for industrial purposes. Any wood thrown down during the rainy season, but especially during June, July, and August, when there is a renewed vigour in the vegetation, becomes liable to rot, or to the ravages of insects, viz., the termite or white ant, and the beetle.

There exists a popular opinion that the phases of the moon exercise a marked influence on the durability, if not of the harder timber, at least of the softer wood and thatch covering. According to that opinion, wood cut during the *crescent* of the moon does not last so long, and becomes liable to the attacks of insects and the dry rot. Whenever, on the contrary, it is felled during the wane, and especially from the last quarter to two or three days before the new moon, it preserves all its best qualities in durable perfection.

This opinion respecting the influence of the moon at stated periods on the quality of felled timbers has already been the subject of much and varied discussion, but cannot hitherto be considered as fully determined, particularly as regards our climate, where so few, or no scientific experiments have yet been made. It may, however, be mentioned, that this view of the question of lunar control over vegetation is, in a great measure, supported by the celebrated French astronomer Arago; and I must candidly acknowledge that I feel inclined to lean towards the popular opinion, and to admit the reality of that influence within certain limits. Where hard wood is concerned, it is only by many years of observation, and renewed comparative experiments, that it would be possible to arrive at any safe conclusions on the subject; but in the case of soft woods, as the bamboo, for instance, or the timite and carat, that influence becomes perceptible. Bamboo, cut in proper season, and under favourable lunar conditions, lasts for several months, and is scarcely touched by insects; but whenever cut during the crescent of the moon it soon crumbles into dust under their attacks: the same remark is applicable to the timite and carat.

The following considerations may supply, at least, a plausible explanation of the above-mentioned phenomena. When a tree is felled during the active circulation of the sap, it becomes more liable to rot: this is a general and unexceptionable fact, being founded on actual experience. Now, the question is this: Is not the quantity of the sap greater during the increase of the moon, and particularly at the full, when the quantity of light is greater throughout the twenty-four hours, than at any other period? This could be ascertained by experiments. And should the supposition prove correct, the influence of the lunar phases would no longer meet with opposition or ridicule from the incredulous, and the fact once ascertained would be the means of establishing some beneficial principles and rules of guidance in the felling of trees, and concerning other agricultural operations. I may conclude this subject by remarking that, whatever may be the diversity of opinions or of doubts among the scientific and the educated classes generally, this idea of lunar influence, not only on woods, but on the process of planting, weeding, pruning, reaping, &c., is held as an undoubted article of credence by the small proprietors and cottagers; and, what is more to the point, this belief is successfully carried out in the management of their cultivations.

The inexcusable waste of our best timber-woods is really something much to be regretted. Whenever a clearance is made for the purpose of cultivation the under-brush is cut first, and then the larger trees; after a few weeks, the whole mass of vegetation is destroyed by fire, the most valuable timber often becoming the prey of that wholesale destruction. I wish, therefore, to repeat what I have already advised in my essay on the cultivation of the sugar-cane, viz., that proper precautions should be taken for the preservation of the best forest-woods, either by allowing them to stand over, or by felling them after the clearance has been made by fire, the timber being afterwards removed to some safe place for use or sale, as opportunity may offer, or occasion demand.

ANIMAL KINGDOM.—It is not my intention to give here a

detailed account of the various species which the animal kingdom of Trinidad embraces, but only to notice such as deserve attention for their utility, their peculiar habits, or destructive propensities.

Mammals—Quadrumana.—Two species: the red or howling Monkey (*Mycetes barbatus*), and the Sapajou (*Cebus*). The former is a large species, and very common, but extremely shy and untameable. Even when taken young they refuse food, and continue moaning day and night till they die of inanition. The red monkey has a sort of deep resounding yell (hence the term howling), which it emits particularly previous to and during rain and thunderstorms; it is eaten in default of better game, and is even relished by the mixed-breed Indian and Spanish hunters, and the *conuqueros,* who often smoke-dry the flesh entire, as is their custom with other game.

The Sapajou is a small whitish ape, very common in the eastern and southern districts. It is very inquisitive, and not only does not flee at the approach of man, but will remain and examine him with apparent curiosity; its cries, however, prove that it is really alarmed at his presence. Like all other sapajous it has a soft plaintive tone, which has gained for it the name of the *weeping monkey;* contrary to the howling species, it can be rendered remarkably tame, and becomes domesticated in a few days.

Cheiroptera.—Bats may be said literally to swarm in Trinidad, both in town and country; sometimes an immense number of them take their lodgings in the hollow of some large tree, from which they are seen issuing by hundreds to venture on depredatory excursions. Many live on fruits, and some others by sucking the blood, not only of animals, but of man; they are so numerous in some parts, that instances of persons having been bitten several times in the same night are not rare. Although they cut out a portion of the skin in their bite, no pain is occasioned; the only protection against their attacks is light. The loss of blood from numerous or repeated bitings is, at times, so great, that large animals, such as oxen, become immediately enfeebled, and may die within two or three weeks; this, however, happens only at intervals of several years, when great loss in live-stock is occasioned to proprietors of estates. They attack also swine, and even fowls. These vampires are from three genera: *Molossi, Noctilion,* and *Phyllostoma.*

Carnivora—Digitigrada.—Tiger-cat or Ocelot (*Felis Pardalis*).—This is one of the most beautiful of the feline tribe; when full-grown, it is nearly four times as large as the domestic cat. One was killed in the ward of Guanape weighing thirty-three pounds. The ocelot preys upon all sorts of small animals, is particularly fond of poultry, and, in one night, may destroy a dozen or more. It climbs the highest trees, but, when hunted down, or hard pressed by dogs, it backs against the trunk of some tree, and keeps its enemies at bay with its powerful paws.

Gato-Melao, or Wood-dog—Caïra (*Mustela barbara*).—This animal is not common, and its habits are imperfectly known. Like the ocelot, it can ascend the loftiest trees, invariably descending head downwards: it lives upon honey, birds' eggs, &c., and makes terrible havoc amongst fowls; when attacked by dogs, it defends itself fiercely.

Marsupialia. — Opossum, or Manicou (*Didelphis*). — The Opossum is very common here, and feeds upon fruits, birds, and carcases; it is also a great destroyer of poultry, creeps into the roosts at night, and ventures even into towns on its depredations. The Manicou is generally very fat, and its flesh tender, but is not prized as food, except by the lower classes, by whom it is considered rather a delicacy.

Rodentia.—Squirrel (*Sciurus*) very common, and a great enemy to corn, and particularly to the cacao, of which it is very fond: it devours the bean of the latter, which it abstracts after having gnawed a hole in the pod.

Rats (*Mus*).—Multitudes of both rats and mice are met with in all parts of the island. The former, however, are not, as in the older colonies, a pest to the cane-fields; but a peculiar species of a dark colour is a great destroyer of cacao, and also of root-provisions, such as sweet potatoes and yams.

Agouti (*Chloromys acuti*).—Very common, well known, and easily domesticated. The Agouti feeds principally upon seeds and roots, and is partial to corn, the manioc or bitter cassada, and yam. This animal does not of itself burrow, but lives in the hollows of fallen timber, or in the holes at the root of standing trees, particularly the Balata; in dispositions and habits, as well as in the quality of its flesh, it resembles the rabbit; as food, however, it is not much esteemed, being dry and always requiring much seasoning to render it savoury. An exception, notwithstanding, may be made in favour of the Agoutis of our northern valleys.

Lapa, or Lape (*Cavia Paca*).—The Lape is not so common as the Agouti, and seems to prefer the high woods in the vicinity of plantations. It lives upon seeds and fruits, is particularly fond of corn, and, in order to get to the ear, brings down the stalk by gnawing it near the roots. Besides its burrow, which it prepares amongst the roots of some large tree or in hollows under ground, the Lape may be said to have also a place of refuge on the margin of a neighbouring ravine or river; this shelter is, commonly, under the roots of trees forming a sort of vault. When pressed by the dogs the Lape resorts to this stronghold, and, in extremity, to the water itself, from either of which retreats it is sometimes difficult to dislodge it. It has been said that the Lape is amphibious: this is not the case; for, when apparently under water, though the body is completely hidden, the snout is held above the surface for the purpose of breathing. Though capable of being domesticated, the Lape nevertheless seems always to preserve a strong predilection for the haunts and freedom of the wild forest, to which it soon returns if left at liberty. It may be regarded as one of the richest and most delicate dishes in the shape of game, its flesh partaking of the qualities of veal and pork.

Edentata.—Cachicame, Armadillo, or Tatou (*Dasypus*).—The Tatou haunts the high woods, and subsists partly on vegetables, partly on insects; it burrows, closes the entrance of its burrow with leaves, and ventures out at night. Though not very fleet, the Cachicame is not easily caught by dogs on account of its hard shell. When tastily prepared, it forms a very delicate dish.

Great Ant-eater, or Mataperro (*Myrmecophaga tridactyla*).—It lives in the high woods, sleeping the day out in the hollows of fallen or in the foliage of green trees, and crawls about at night in search of food, in obtaining which it insinuates its long filiform tongue into the nests of ants; the insects becoming entangled in the viscid saliva which covers the tongue are then swallowed in a mass; they also lay their tongue on the track of the Parasol-ants, and devour immense numbers of them. The great Ant-eater moves very slowly, and whenever aware of any danger, quickly throws itself on its back, and, in that posture, awaits the attack of its assailant, which it seizes with its powerful arms and fearful claws : these it plunges into the body of its enemy, gradually thrusting more and more deeply until death ensues. Its hold is so tenacious that dogs cannot disengage themselves from the murderous embrace, and must perish unless promptly relieved; hence its Spanish name of *Mataperro,* or the "Dog-killer;" it is also called the "Sloth," or, again, the "Poor-me-one," from its mournful night-cry, which the fancy of the peasant has assimilated to the sound of those syllables. In connection with this animal, the following anecdote was related to me :—An African labourer meeting with a Mataperro in the act of crossing the high road, and mistaking it for an opossum, eagerly seized it by the tail and swung it over his shoulder, congratulating himself on his good fortune; but he had "reckoned without his host," and was compelled to call for immediate assistance, being almost deprived of breath from the embrace of his pseudo-captive.

Pachydermata.—Wild Hog, Cuenco, or Pecari (*Dycotiles*).— There are, it appears, two distinct species of Cuencos : one rather larger than the other. They range in small bands of five or eight, or in larger, of fifty and above; they haunt the high woods, and the smaller species is particularly common towards the eastern coast. When started by the dogs the Pecari takes to flight, but is soon brought to bay against a tree, or in some hollow, or other shelter, where it makes a formidable and often a successful defence with its tusks—frequently wounding, maiming, or killing such as venture within its reach. When in force, and very numerous, they even give chase to the dogs, and the hunters themselves may be compelled to seek refuge in the branches of some tree. This animal, notwithstanding, is easily domesticated, and becomes much attached to its master. When young, and in good season and condition, the Cuenco is most delicate eating.

Ruminantia.—Deer (*Cervus simplicicornis*).—The Deer is very common in all parts of the island, but particularly in the neighbourhood of plantations, where it browses on pease, young maize, the stems and leaves of the manioc, sweet potato, and yam, as also of young cacao plants. The Deer bears in appearance, size, and habits, the greatest resemblance to the roebuck. When captured young it is easily domesticated, and may be seen tamely following those persons who have the care of it. The flesh of this animal very much resembles that of the European deer. It is either shot from an ambuscade, or hunted down by hounds.

Lamantin, or Manati (*Trichecus Manatus*), is scarce, and found only in the rivers of the east and south coasts; it grows to a very large size, and may be regarded as excellent eating.

Cetacea.—Whale or Rorqual (*Balænoptera Boops*).—The Razor-back is not scarce in the gulf from February to May, and is eagerly pursued for the sake of its blubber.

Birds.—The feathered tribes are very numerous in Trinidad, and many birds of different sizes and varied plumage, from the minute crested Humming-bird to the Kamichi and the King of the Vultures, inhabit the forests and swamps of the island; a few only will be mentioned.

Rapaces.—Vultures (*Vultur*).—The King of the Corbeaux (*Vultur Papa*) is a noble and most beautiful specimen; it is met with in the high woods, and does not approach towns or villages.

The Turkey Buzzard (*Cathartes aura*), called by the natives the "Governor" of the corbeaux, is black, with a red head and a strong beak. It inhabits the high woods, and is particularly fond of snakes; it may be said to be always on the wing, though seldom flying very high, but rather skimming along with a gliding movement over the tops of the forest trees.

Carrion-crow, or Corbeau (*Cathartes fœtens*).—Colour and head black, bill less strong than that of the former; gregarious, and very common, but principally in the neighbourhood of towns and plantations, where they congregate in large numbers to feed on the carcases of unburied animals, the offal from slaughter-houses, and other putrid matters. They have been found so useful in cleansing the towns from filth and putridity as to be considered in the light of gratuitous scavengers, and hence are tacitly exempted from being killed; in fact, under the government of Sir Thomas Picton and Sir Ralph Woodford, such an act was punishable by fine. They, however, sometimes prove a great nuisance from the offensive smell which exhales from the localities in which they have established their abodes. They dispose of a dead rat, fowl, or other small animal, in the space of a few minutes; of a dog or cat in a few hours, and, in the country, where animals dying on estates are left exposed, they will consume the carcase of an ox or a horse in less than a week. It is really wonderful how these birds become aware of the presence of carrion. It may be that not one single vulture has been seen for weeks in a locality, but no sooner is an animal dead, even a cat or rat, than some corbeau is seen wheeling in the air above; all on a sudden it sweeps down with a peculiar hissing sound, and, after describing a rapid circle, promptly alights on its prey; others follow, and in a few hours a host of them are collected on the spot. Sometimes the corbeaux, as by some common accord, start in a body to parade (to use the local expression), when numbers of them are seen rising in the air and describing spirals, till they become nearly imperceptible; then one takes the lead, and the others follow in a line, until they arrive at some place of rest or of prey. The Carrion-crow is so familiar that it mixes in the market-places of Port of Spain with the vendors, and sometimes carries away from an incautious seller a piece of fish or flesh.

The Papa, Aura, and Fœtens Vultures, build their nests on the ground, generally near or between the roots of some tree; at each incubation they produce but a pair, which, in their unfledged state, are covered with a purely white down.

Falcons (*Falco*).—There are several species of the Falcon family in Trinidad; they are called here *Gavilans*. The Crested Gavilan (*Spizactus ornatus*) is a large bird, grey in colour, with a large head and an occipital tuft; the tarsi are strong and feathered throughout. This bird is most ferocious, and will pick up a fowl in the poultry-yard and carry it off, even within sight and cry of persons in the neighbourhood. The White Gavilan is somewhat smaller than the crested; it is a great destroyer of chickens, as is also the speckled species, which is still smaller. This latter is very fond of snakes; it always seizes them by the head with the bill, and by the body with the claws, so as neither to be bitten nor infolded; the snake, however, sometimes succeeds in enveloping its enemy within its coils, and thus vanquishes it: this may happen even in the air, as I have myself witnessed. The Black Gavilan lives principally on fish. The Fork-tailed Kite, or Ciseaux (*Falco furcatus*), may be said to be gregarious, as from five to twelve and fifteen are commonly seen together; they are also migratory, being never seen except during a short interval in the rainy season.

Passeres.—The number of passerinæ is very great in Trinidad, but I shall notice a few only. The Tyrants are remarkable for their indomitable courage, and even the Gavilans and Corbeaux yield to their repeated attacks; also, minute and apparently frail as it is, the Humming-bird attacks all other birds, and ultimately succeeds in driving them away from the tree whereon it has built its nest. Our Tanagers are not only conspicuous for their gorgeous plumage, but several of them are excellent warblers; a wren (*Troglodytes eudon*) is known here as the Rossignol, or Nightingale, on account of its note; it is very familiar, and frequently builds under the eaves of houses. The Averano, or Campanero (*Cotinga variegata*), has a very remarkable cry, as being of a purely metallic sound; hence its Spanish appellation of *Campanero*, or Bell-ringer, and its equally common name, among the peasantry, of the *Blacksmith*. The French call it *Capucin*, from a number of dark capillary appendages which hang from the throat of the male, and bear some resemblance to a beard. One of our Cassiques has gained the name of the Mocking-bird, which it really deserves, as it imitates the songs of many of the feathered tribes, and even the sounds made by other animals. Several species are gregarious, and one (*Cassicus cristatus*) particularly so, numbers of the latter constructing their nests close together; these are in the form of long cylindrical bags, made of thready fibres, which the birds generally procure from the balisier. The upper extremity of the nest is formed first, the threads being, meanwhile, allowed to remain pendent; the architect, from within, then draws them up and interweaves them, so as to form a very close and strong shelter, the lower extremity being hemispherical, and thicker than the other parts. It is a curious sight to observe some forty or fifty of these aerial constructions hanging at the extremity of the branches of a large tree, and swinging to and fro with each undulation of the breeze.

Several of our Creepers, or Grimpereaux, are remarkable for their brilliant colours, and out of nineteen species of Humming-birds, not a few exhibit the most dazzling plumage. They extract the nectar from the flowers of the highest trees—the *Erythrina*, the *Inga*, and others—or are seen culling their honeyed food from the *Curassavica*, or the blossoms of our garden-plants; but the habits and beauty of the Humming-birds are too well known to require any further illustration. Amongst several species of Picucules (*Dendrocolaptes*), one is known by the name of Cacao-eater. With its long and strong bill, it pierces a hole in the ripe pod, apparently to suck the sweet mucilage that covers the beans within; and each pod thus attacked, together with its contents, rots on the tree, so that these not uncommonly wholesale depredations often occasion great loss to the cacao planter. The Merle Cavalier, or Black Corn-bird (*Cassicus Ater*), sometimes makes great havoc in the corn-fields, by removing with its bill the husk of the ear; and although it eats but a few grains, the mutilated ear invariably rots from being exposed to the rain or heavy dews.

Very few individuals of the Passerine order are useful as articles of food; though in this respect they are chiefly neglected on account of their small size. The following are occasionally served on our tables, viz.: Longue-queue (*Tyrannus Savanna*), the Campanero, several Tanagers and Thrushes; also a Goat-sucker (*Caprimulgus Caripensis*)—Guacharo or Diablotin. Of the latter, the young only are acceptable, and they are caught in the nest during February and March: the fledged bird is not eatable. Nevertheless all the Passeres have their utility, in destroying an immense number of insects, which otherwise would become an intolerable pest; even the Merle Cavalier and the Merle Corbeau (*Crotophaga ani*) are of notable assistance in clearing the blood-thirsty tick from the hides of oxen, horses, and mules, in the Estates'-pastures.

Syndactyles.—To this order belong the *Voutou* or Mot-mot (*Prionites Brasiliensis*), the Jacamar (*Galbula Paradisea*)—of a beautiful metallic colour—the Ani and Toucan (*Ramphastos*); the latter is very common in the high woods; the Voutou and Toucan serve as food. Trinidad harbours several varieties of Parrots, and among them two Aras or Macaws; they are met with only in the high woods, where they generally perch on the highest trees. There are also two kinds of Parrots proper (*Psittacus*) in the island; they are gregarious, and prefer unfrequented places, though sometimes met with in cacao plantations, whither they resort to eat the green fruit of the *Erythrina coccinea*. Generally speaking, they fly about during the day in search of food, and return in the evening to some favourite spot to sleep; in this they show a preference for the mangroves, and when assembled in some such locality, their loud chattering is absolutely deafening. The Paroquets (*Psittacula*) are mostly found in inhabited localities, and live chiefly on the fruits of the

Ingas. Although gregarious, they are much attached individually, and when one of a pair has been killed, the other will, for several days, haunt the neighbourhood—perching on the summit of some tree—and almost incessantly call for its departed mate. Another kind, known as the seven-coloured Paroquet (*Psittacula Batavica*), is met with everywhere in the island: it lives upon insects and the fruits of the *Clusia*, generally builds in the nests of the Termites, and lays from six to ten eggs. This beautiful bird has never been tamed so as to live in a cage; when taken it refuses food, and consequently dies in a few days. The Ara, though tough, and therefore discarded from the table, is prized as a domestic favourite for its gorgeous plumage; but the Parrot and Paroquet, when young, are much esteemed for the delicacy of their flesh.

Gallinaceæ.—This order is remarkable for furnishing man, here as in other countries, with an abundance of excellent game. At their head is to be placed the Pauji or Yacou (*Penelope*), as the largest gallinacean to be found in Trinidad; it is of the size of a large domestic fowl, and is very choice fare. It lives generally upon berries, and is very stupid; so much so that, if several are met with together, they can be shot in succession, as they do not fly, even after their companions have been killed. They are easily tamed.

Next to the Yacou come the Speckled Ramier (*Columba speciosa*), and the Mangrove Ramier (*Columba rufina*), both of the size of a pigeon. The latter generally seeks its food in the fruits of shrubs, and often on the ground; the other on larger trees, and seldom alights lower. Next to these may be mentioned eight kinds of doves, of which four only are known here as such, whilst the others are designated by the names of partridge and ortolans: the former are chiefly distinguished from the latter by their superior size. In general they prefer cool localities, such as the banks of rivers, particularly as they are fond of bathing, and of drinking pure limpid water. The ortolans are smaller, and their habits somewhat different. The Blue Ortolan (*Peristera cinerea*) is a beautiful bird, of an ashy blue colour, spotted with black: it is not so common as the other, and prefers the high woods. The Red Ortolan, or Ground Dove (*Chamæpelia rufipennis*), is of a reddish-brown colour, barred with black; another species is the smallest, and is found only, it appears, at the Bocas' Islets and at Cedros—it is of a lighter colour. The partridge is, in size, intermediate between the dove and the ortolan. The habits of the blue ortolan are but imperfectly known, from its being so excessively shy; the red ortolan, on the contrary, is familiar and gregarious, and troops of forty and sixty alight at times in the rice-fields, or among the maize-stubble; the smallest species are always seen in pairs, the male and female seeking their food side by side. These doves, particularly the red ortolan, are easily tamed.

A species of Tinamoo (*Tinamus sovi*) is also very common here. It is about the size of a partridge, and is met with almost everywhere in the colony; it seems to prefer copses or underbrush, on the borders of the high woods. The Tinamoo is known here by the appellation of caille, or quail. It is a very difficult shot, unless seen feeding on the ground, as it starts up in flight quite suddenly, and alights at a very short distance; it also runs very rapidly through the underwood. The Tinamoo lays two eggs, of a most beautiful violet colour, and sits with such fondness on them as, in that state, to be easily caught with the hand. This bird has a peculiar tremulous and prolonged whistle, the note of the male being different from that of the female; they are heard early in the morning, at sunset, and also at mid-day, and midnight; and so regularly are their notes timed in general, that they serve as the peasant's chronometer. As I have already stated, all the above gallinaceans are delicate and excellent game; and the ramiers and doves are at times offered for sale in our markets.

Grallatoriæ.—Many species of the Grallatoriæ order are either permanent inhabitants of the island, or visit it at regular intervals. The former consist of herons, known here by the name of Crabiers, or Crab-eaters, and Egrets; several of them are regarded as very good eating, particularly the mountain crab-eater (*Ardea liniata*). The egrets assemble in large flocks in the marshes of the island, and, at certain periods of the year, numbers of them can be seen on the *basses*, or mud-banks of the Caroni and Couva rivers. The mountain crab-eater and the soldado (*Tantalus loculator*) are scarce. The golden (*Charadrius Wilsonii*) and ring plovers (*Charadrius Virginiacus*) visit the island during September, together with hosts of chevaliers, sandpipers, curlews, and even snipes (*Scolopax Gallinago*), as also the surgeon (*Jacana*). The Flamingo, or red Ibis (*Ibis rubra*), and Spoon-bill (*Platalea Aiaia*) are habitual residents, or occasional visitors. They are all of excellent flavour, but some of them, particularly the chevaliers and sandpipers, are little sought after, on account of their diminutive size. Though very common, particularly the wood-hen (*Rallus longirostris*), our Rails are seldom served on table; the same remark is applicable to our water-hens (*Gallinula chloropus* and *Porphirio Tavoua*).

Palmipedes.—Ten different species of ducks are met with in the island, all of them deserving the reputation of being delicate eating: the largest of all is the common duck of the country, or the Musk Duck (*Anas moschata*), commonly, but improperly called the Muscovy Duck: it is a native of Trinidad, as are also the Vingeon (*Anas Dominica*), Ouikiki (*Anas autumnalis, A. viduata*), and the Teal (*Anas discors*); in November and December, other species make their appearance—viz., the Poachard, the Shoveler (*Anas clypeata*); and the Jensen (*Anas Americana*).

Shooting, in our climate, is an occupation less exciting and much more fatiguing than in Europe, though, however, marsh-fowling bears some resemblance in both latitudes. Here is, certainly, no extensive field or meadow through which one can stroll quietly, in company of an intelligent pointer, which has also its share in the sport; no clear wood which one can thread at ease; no park intersected with alleys, in which one can ride or drive. Forests intricated with lianes, "crocs-chien," "devil's guts," or "sword-grass;" marshes and lagoons, overgrown with mangroves, reeds, or rushes, and teeming with mosquitos; mud-banks, deep ponds, and malaria. Such are the attendant difficulties which the sportsman has to encounter and overcome; in addition to which, he must himself go in search of his game, and collect it when killed. Ramier-shooting, however, may be said to be free from all these drawbacks; the sportsman generally awaits them under some tree—the Gommier, or the Surette, for instance—whither they flock to feed, in the afternoon or early in the morning; there he stands in keen look-out, for this sport requires a keen eye and a steady aim. The birds alight, shots are poured in, and after each, the frightened Ramiers take to flight, but soon to return, again and again, as long as they have not satisfied their craving appetite. They are also looked for, during the heat of the day, *in the shade*, that is to say, in some thick part of the forest, near a rivulet, whither they resort, apparently to enjoy the cool, and it would almost appear, to take their *siesta*. Being now *full*, from their morning's feed, after each discharge they flutter to some near tree, where they are easily discovered and followed. The doves are generally killed when feeding on the ground, or on call, in such spots as they frequent for water; the ortolans in rice-fields, or in some copse-wood wherein they assemble. Parrots and paroquets are watched at some tree on which they alight to feed—the former, however, especially in their sleeping-places—where a good number may be shot in a short time.

Marsh-fowling is, on the other hand, irksome and harassing. The crabiers and egrets choosing, generally, some mud-bank, and the fastness of some mangrove swamp, as their habitual haunt, cannot be approached with facility, both because they can discover the enemy at a distance, and take to flight in time to escape, and because it is always difficult, if not impossible, to wade through the mud to get a nearer approach. The red ibis and spoon-bill are sought after in the midst of damp natural savannahs, or in lagoons, where they keep along the border of ponds and rivers, always on the look-out, and ready to take wing; but as they are very heavy in their flight, they are easily shot, whenever within range. Of all our birds, however, the ducks are the most difficult shot, for they are very cunning and extremely fleet, the teal especially. They commonly alight in troops in some secluded pond, in the midst of damp localities or lagoons; and to approach them it is necessary to walk knee-deep in the mud and waist-deep in the water, or, again, to paddle with the greatest precaution in some light canoe. If fortunate enough to come within range, the sportsman has the chance of firing on them while still floating on the water, and again on their starting, so that, as many as from ten to twenty may be brought down at this double shot. Plovers, sandpipers, and other smaller species, are generally killed on the wing; the plovers, seeking damp pasture-grounds and ploughed lands, are easily approached.

At the conquest of the island—a period when the population was scanty, and all sorts of game in great abundance—several *émigrés* from the French colonies, whom I could name, drew a subsistence from the return of their chase, some from the sale of ramiers, others of ducks. Every day they would send to market a few dozen ramiers or ouikikis, which fetched at the rate of sixty cents, or 2s. 6d. per pair. The number of those birds has decreased to such an extent since, that any one now choosing such a orecarious occupation as the chase for a maintenance would inevitably starve.

Reptiles.—Numerous as reptiles are in Trinidad, a few only will be mentioned as deserving notice, either on account of their utility, or of their venomous characteristics. Besides the turtle, both the land and fresh-water tortoises are eaten, and when in good season and condition are not to be despised; the liver of the morocoy (*Testudo tabulata*) is as delicate, or even much richer and choicer than the *foie gras*; it requires the condiments of lime-juice, salt, and pepper, and must be dressed in the frying-pan. Morocoys are sometimes kept in pens, and fattened upon ripe plantains, guavas, &c., for the table. By far the greater number of sea and land tortoises exposed for sale in our markets come from the Main.

The common Iguana (*Iguana tuberculata*), but particularly the Mato (*Salvator Merianæ*), are not to be rejected from the table; the flesh of the latter, both in appearance and taste, very much resembles that of a tender fowl. Some persons are also very fond of iguana eggs: they are nearly cylindrical, with rounded extremities.

The supply of food derived from the great class of reptiles is much greater than is, perhaps, at first thought. From the Spanish Main alone, the town of Port of Spain receives, on an average, 4,000 pounds of turtle per annum, to which we may safely add 4,000 pounds more, as representing the quantity supplied to all other parts, including, however, a quota from the island itself; thus the whole quantity of turtle consumed in the island would amount to 8,000 pounds; if to this we add 1,000 pounds more for morocoys, lizards, matos, we shall then have a grand total of from 9,000 to 10,000 pounds of flesh supplied from the grand class of reptiles.

Although venomous serpents are numerous and common in Trinidad, accidents arising from their bite are of rare occurrence, either because the Mapepire and Cascabel (*Crotalus mutus*, and *Trigonocephalus jararaca*), being very sluggish, are easily avoided, or even do not attack or inflict wounds, except on their being disturbed in the enjoyment of repose; or again, because those

H

who are more exposed to their encounter, such as sportsmen, are in the possession of good antidotes. The guaco, however, and the roots of the manaco palm—both rather common plants—are the favourite remedy for the bite of serpents. Dogs, in the woods, as also horses and mules, in the underbrush, are common victims of the Cascabel and Mapepire. Casualties from the bite of the Coral snake (*Elaps corallinus*) must be very rare, since many persons even regard it as perfectly innocuous: this opinion I myself entertained for a long time, and until I had too convincing a proof of the contrary in the death, within a few hours, of two robust African labourers, under the following circumstances. These two men were at work in a cane-field, on "La Marguerite" Estate, in the ward of St. Joseph; having discovered a coral snake, they laid hold of it by way of amusement. Of the warning given by their fellow-labourers they took no notice, but, on the contrary, continued to tease the reptile, and even put its head into their mouths. They were both bitten, one on the lip, and the other on the tongue; this happened about 1 P.M. The one who had apparently most irritated the snake, soon began to reel about like a drunken man, and was next taken with convulsions; he died about eight o'clock, and the other about nine, the same day. This coral has been preserved by Dr. Court, and measures four feet and a half.

The Clibo or Cribo (*Coluber variabilis*) haunts inhabited places, and is occasionally seen in houses, where, however, it ought to be welcome as a destroyer of rats. It is asserted that this Cribo is the enemy of the poisonous serpents, which it would fight successfully. Some years ago, Mr. Robert Mitchell, now Protector of Immigrants in Demerara, but then Sub-Intendant of Crown Lands, on his way to Blanchisseuse, through the high woods, met with a black Cribo, called by the peones, "Vidua," and was preparing to dispatch it, when he was entreated by a peon who accompanied him not to kill the innocuous beast, as it was a deadly enemy of the venomous snakes, which it would fight and kill. Mr. Mitchell desisted, though not quite satisfied with the assertion of his companion. A short time after, hir view was arrested by the curious appearance of two snakes entwined in a fierce struggle. On a nearer approach, he found that one of the snakes had taken hold of the other by the head, and was in the act of swallowing its antagonist. The peon pointed out that it was a "Vidua" swallowing a Cascabel (*Trigonocephalus jararaca*). Mr. Mitchell would not lose such an occasion, and killed the adder, which had already swallowed up nearly twelve inches of its enemy. He passed a rope round to keep them together, and brought them to town, where I saw them thus tied. As far as I know, they were sent to the British Museum, where, of course, they must have attracted attention. This coluber is very determined, particularly the black kind, and it has been known to give battle, and even chase, to man. When a child, I was once pursued by a clibo, and I also distinctly remember having witnessed one in combat with a gentleman, on which occasion it would stand erect on its tail, and bite at the garments, meanwhile hissing and inflating its neck: the clibo, like the mapepire, also produces a rattling noise by the rapid motion of its tail. The Macajuel (*Boa constrictor*), whenever irritated, inflates its body, and then loudly emits a fetid and sickening breath, which causes a sort of fainting sensation.

Those who have had an opportunity of observing snakes cannot but admit what has been said of their power of fascination. Do they exercise that power under all circumstances? This I do not believe. Can this power be considered as a sort of magnetic emanation from the serpent, which subdues the victim, and as distinct from the indescribable terror with which it inspires the smaller animals? This again I very much doubt. Be it what it may, that power of fascination is exercised both by venomous and non-venomous serpents, and apparently through the instrumentality of the eye: for during the whole time that the victim remains under the influence of the charm, the serpent's eyes are intently fixed on the helpless creature, following all and each of its movements. In relation to this subject I may, perhaps, mention the following cases which were reported to me by trustworthy witnesses. Being struck by the distressing cries proceeding from a bird on a tree, Mr.——, on examination, perceived the poor little creature, leaping from branch to branch, in a state of apparent agony, and uttering incessant plaints; not far from it was a clibo, following all the agitations of the victim by a slow motion of the head, and with fixed and glistening eyes; the bird was so much fascinated, that from leap to leap, it came within reach of the clibo, nearly into its jaw, and was swallowed; on another similar occasion, the charm was broken by striking the clibo, and the bird escaped. The next case is that of a Mapepire and Squirrel. A troop of squirrels was met with in a copse, one of them manifesting all the symptoms of anxious distress, as if actually riveted to the branch to which it clung—there screaming, trembling, and stretching in agony, as if apparently trying to get a firmer hold of the branch, but all to no purpose, for it soon dropped, and on the party approaching, a mapepire was discovered beneath, with the squirrel in its maw.

Ameivas are useful in gardens, when they destroy numbers of mole-crickets. During the whole rainy season, and also after heavy showers, toads of all kinds and sizes unite their varied croakings in discordant concerts—from the most acute falsetto to the gravest bass, occasionally drowned by the accompaniment of a chorus from our larger species; they are generally assisted, in the minor notes, by frogs. Hearken! the loud croak from this cluster of bamboos by the bank of the river, and in the still of the night, is the harsh and solemn "FROG—FROG—FROG" of one of our hylas; another species is often met with in some obscure corner of a house, where its croaking is a sure announcement of coming rain. If placed in a bottle with water, it generally keeps motionless at the bottom during dry weather, but rises to the surface and commences its croak on the slightest indication of a shower.

Fishes.—Out of about fifteen different species of fresh-water fish, only a few are eaten, the others being neglected, from their small size. The largest of those eaten is the guabine (*Erythrinus*), which is regarded by some as a great treat; but, in reality, it is neither a savoury nor a delicate fish, as it never loses a certain taste of mud, and is besides difficult to eat, owing to its flesh being crowded with small bones exactly resembling the letter *y*. The yarrao, which resembles the guabine very much in form, is smaller in size, but has not the same quantity of bones, and on the whole may be said to be delicate eating. Next come a fine little pike (*Gerres*) and barbel (*Mysus*), also the Anne-Marie (*Hypostomus*). Our fresh-water sardines (*Hydrocyon*) are neglected on account of their small size, but, when properly dressed, would bear comparison with the gudgeon. None, however, is so much prized as the cascaradura (*Callicthys*), and it really is delicate eating. Cascaraduras are offered for sale in country and town during the dry season, at which time an enormous quantity is procured from the ponds in the Grand Savannah. The following saying may be noted as expressive of the high opinion the natives entertain of this fish : " He who has eaten cascaraduras must die in the country." It ought not to be confounded with the chat or cat-fish (*Callicthys*), which is not commonly eaten.

Of our salt-water fish, the following are the most common :— The carangue, the Spanish mackerel or carite, the king-fish or tassard, the gar-fish or orphie, and a smaller species called the Balaou (*Hemiramphus*), the barracuta; of these, the king-fish and "*carangue grasse*" are the best. Under the general denomination of *red fish* are sold several species of snappers, red-mouths, and sardes, all very good and delicate. To the above may be added the gruper (*Mesoprion* and *Clinus*), the lebranche and mullets (*Mugil*), the dories or lunes (*Vomer* and *Zeus*), the crapaud, rays, and the conger-eel; a species of caranx, of the size of a sardine, and called here the anchovy; of the last, an immense quantity is taken in the Gulf during July; they are migratory, and disappear in two or three weeks. The zapatero, salmon (*Otolythus*), and cod-fish (*Elacates*), are sold occasionally in our markets, as they keep but for a short time. The dog-headed eel (*Synbranchus*), though, in my opinion, delicate eating, is rejected from the table on account of its resemblance to a snake. I confess, however, that the French proverb, " *La sauce fait manger le poisson*," is applicable to a number of our fresh and salt-water fishes; Madeira or Bordeaux wine, for instance, is the best sauce for crapaud and gruper; king-fish and snappers are served either boiled or stewed; the dories fried mainly, as also the mullet; the lebranche roasted, with the addition of lime-juice and Cayenne pepper.

The variety of our fishes is very great, and yet fish of good quality is rather scarce ; the principal reason is, the impossibility of keeping it fresh for more than a few hours; in fact, the change produced in the quality of the fish is something remarkable, and can be appreciated only by those who have had an opportunity of procuring it just after its capture. The salmon and mullets particularly do not keep long; those which stand better are the king-fish, Spanish mackerel, sardes, snappers, and gruper, also the carangues.

Crustacea.—Crabs, cray-fish, shrimps, and lobsters are common. Besides the sea-crabs, there are in the island two land or fresh-water species—one about the size of a dollar, and of a red colour; it is to be met with only at the beginning of the wet season, at which time it comes forth to breed; it is not eaten, and the Negroes are under an impression that any one eating it will certainly " turn crazy." The other land species is as large as the common crab, and of a dark brown colour; it is called the " mountain crab," from being found on the hills, also along the banks, and even in the beds of rivers and brooks; it is by some much esteemed as an article of food. Among the sea-crabs two kinds are eaten—the blue, which burrows in low lands along the sea-board, and the brown, which lives amidst the rocks. The blue crabs are in such prodigious numbers in some places that the soil is literally furrowed by them; in September they leave their recesses, and betake themselves to the sea, there to deposit their spawn.

The island lobsters, cray-fishes, and shrimps, are much like those of Europe; excellent and very beautiful cray-fish are taken in the Caroni and other rivers, in nets. Both the sea and land crabs are occasionally hurtful, probably from feeding on poisonous substances, more especially the fruits of the Manchoneel tree.

Arachnida.—Spiders are numerous, and some of them of very large size; several kinds frequent the dwellings in towns and villages, spreading their webs almost everywhere in houses, where they are useful in destroying cockroaches and other vermin. Two species are venomous, and one particularly so, viz., the crab-spider (*Aranea avicularia*); it bites most severely—swelling of the part and fever for about twenty-four hours being the result.

There are two species or varieties of scorpions, known as the *grey* and the *black*; they are both venomous, yet very seldom does death follow their sting. A few cases, however, have been known of infants having died from exhaustion occasioned by the violent retching produced by the sting of scorpions; and even adults have been severely affected and weakened. The accidents arising from the bite or sting of scorpions depend evidently upon various causes, and particularly, it would seem, upon the part into which the virus has been instilled, and its more or less complete absorption; it may also vary in effect according to the age, the sex, or other circumstances connected with the animal itself.

Myriapoda.—The mainland, and particularly the islets at the Bocas, have gained a notoriety for the immense size of their centipedes, some of them being more than twelve inches long; the centipedes bite severely, and are venomous, but never to the extent of the scorpions, though the pain is locally more acute. The congori (*Iulus*) is perfectly innocuous to man, but injures fruits and flowers. Ammonia, lime-juice, and the musk-ochro, are excellent remedies for accidents arising from the virus of the above insects, but the guaco is by far the best: the part must be well rubbed with the extract or tincture, and some taken internally. When the plant itself is within reach, let it be pounded or bruised previous to its application to the part affected, the juice being also taken internally at the same time.

Insecta.—The *bête-rouge* is very troublesome from the itching it causes; thousands of them sometimes collect on the heads of horses and other animals.

Ticks (*Ricinus*).—These are very troublesome insects: there are two distinct species—the *tick* and the *garrapato*. The tick is larger, of the size, colour, and appearance of the castor-oil seed; whence its zoological name *Ricinus*. It adheres to the hide of animals, particularly to the inside of the ears, and other denuded parts. The garrapato is smaller, flat, and of a brown colour; it is particularly common in underbrush and the high woods. It sticks to animals exactly like the tick, but its hold is firmer, and when efforts are made to tear it away, it breaks, and its sucker, remaining fixed in the skin, causes an intolerable itching for weeks and months. Ticks and garrapatos sometimes collect by hundreds on the animals allowed to pasture in the natural savannahs; they particularly follow horned cattle, horses, mules, and dogs. Some of these animals may be said to contract at times a tick-disease, hundreds of them being found sticking to the hide a few days after as many had been removed. The best remedy against these insect-pests is the carapa-oil: they die within one or two days after its having been applied.

Chigoes (*Pulex penetrans*) are very common; however, they prefer dry, dusty localities, and multiply particularly where animals herd together for rest: the numbers bred in such spots at certain seasons are sometimes enormous. The chigo is not only troublesome on account of the itching and pain it occasions, but may become, from neglect and uncleanly habits, the cause of dangerous sores, particularly on the toes and soles of the feet.

Of the coleoptera a few only will be mentioned, viz., the cabbage-palm (*Curculio*), called here the *Groo-groo Worm*, of which the larvæ are much esteemed by our *gourmets;* and a longicorn, that lays on young cacao-trees its larvæ, which, by devouring its inner bark, cause the plant to die. Some insects of the weevil genus also occasion great damage in the corn, rice, and even in the corn-meal and flour of provision-stores: another species of the same genus attacks books and papers, and renders it an arduous task to keep them in proper order. The bamboo, which is much used for fences and other purposes, is liable to the ravages of coleoptera, and crumbles to dust in a short time under their attacks. The fig-tree, which otherwise grows and thrives well in the colony, is also attacked by another coleopterous insect, the larva of which is about one inch long, and very much like a caterpillar: it perforates the wood, and takes its lodging in the pith; if not assiduously watched, the tree soon becomes enfeebled, and yields but scanty and insipid fruit. Other insects deposit their larvæ in many of our fruits, such as the guava, the lemon-apple, the sapodilla, the star-apple, soursop, sugar-apple, &c.; but they show a decided preference for the guava, so much so, that seldom is a ripe guava without worms. Some of our vegetables, and particularly the cajan, or pigeon-pea, are also attacked by an insect, the larvæ of which eat into the pod and destroy the bean. I should not pass unnoticed the *Cane Borers*. Insects belonging to various genera go by that name of cane borer, which should be taken as a generic designation for such larvæ as actually pierce or bore the canes. Among *Coleoptera* I may mention a Calandra (*Calandra sacchari*) and a chrysomelida. I have had the opportunity of particularly observing two borers: one, evidently a Hymenoptera, which is, I believe, the most common, but not the most destructive. It commonly bores a small hole near a node in the lower portion of a cane, and deepens a furrow which may extend through several internodes. The plant thus bored does not suffer to any great extent: and yet when many canes are thus perforated in a field, the damage done becomes perceptible. The other borer which I have observed is a Lepidoptera, probably a *Cossus*, perhaps a Pyrale (*Diatræa sacchari ?*). It attacks the young and soft plants, and apparently lays its eggs at the basis of the tender leaves: the caterpillar, which is of good size, eats up the substance of the young sprout, which withers and dies. I have seen whole fields of young canes destroyed by this vermin: it is by far the most destructive of all cane-borers.

Without dwelling on the many kinds of cockroaches, blattæ, or butterflies, which are all numerous and common, it may be stated here that the *Fulgora laternaria* has been found in the island. There are also two kinds of grasshopper or cicada: one smaller, with a gay, thrilling chirp; the other larger, with a tremulous, graduated, and prolonged whistle: the former gaily celebrates the arrival of the dry season, the other is the as melancholy foreteller of heat and rain. Locusts visit the shores at long intervals, and make ravages similar to those of other countries; caterpillars also swarm over some parts of the island at periodical intervals of eight or nine years, laying waste portions of pastures and corn-fields. With regard to these visitations, it has been remarked that both locusts and caterpillars make their appearance after long periods of drought. In the year 1846, caterpillars visited Mayaro and Couva; and in the year 1855 they were depredating Couva and Savanetta. However, the cane-fields thus traversed by these insects have not apparently suffered from such molestations. Butterflies are numerous, and amongst them a few beautiful kinds. It may as well be mentioned here, that there exist in the island two species of caterpillars, the larvæ probably of moths, which, whenever placed in contact with the skin, instantly raise a blister, causing a horrible burning sensation, like that of a hot iron: they are one inch long, and covered with long hairs of a fawn colour.

Mosquitoes (*Culex*) and sand-flies abound in the low marshy parts of the country, particularly near the sea. In some parts of the interior, at Arouca, Arima, and Guanape, they are only seen occasionally, and mosquito nettings to the beds may be dispensed with. There are two distinct species of sand-flies; one very small, of a grey colour; the other nearly double in size, and entirely black: the former is an inhabitant of the sea-shore particularly, the other of the interior. The black sand-fly becomes common at certain periods only: it generally attacks the legs, seldom the face or hands, and its bite occasions an itching sensation, but no bulla, the place being marked by a very small black spot, formed by coagulated blood. The grey sand-fly is by far the most troublesome of all insects : when in swarms they attack men or animals, and, small as they are, cause extreme irritation, whilst the spot bitten swells immediately into a bulla resembling nettle-rash; they creep into the sleeves, penetrate even into the ears and nostrils, animals becoming sometimes unmanageable under their attacks.

Three kinds of breezes, or gad-flies, are found in the islands, and commonly known as horse-flies. One is somewhat smaller than the common fly, and of a grey colour; it bites severely, and is exceedingly numerous during the summer months; it is met with everywhere, especially in towns, and on estates. The second species is of the size of a bee, and of greenish-yellow colour; it is found in the country and on the skirts of the high woods, and comes out generally between four o'clock and sunset; its bite is severe, and sometimes blood trickles in drops from the wound. The third species is larger, of a light brown colour, with large green eyes; its habits are very much like those of the green breeze, or gad-fly.

It will, however, suffice to mention only two kinds of flies which appear to be of the same genus, and even of the same species, as those of Europe, viz., the blue flesh-fly (*Musca vomitoria*) and the viviparous grey fly (*Musca carnaria*). The blue fly, it seems, more especially haunts inhabited places. The grey fly is met with in the high forest, and they must, indeed, be numerous there, for let any putrid substance be exposed, and it is immediately covered with swarms of those flies. These insects are a source of loss to the planters, and an incessant cause of annoyance even to individuals; for the moment an animal presents a raw surface on its hide, however small it may be, they are sure to deposit their larvæ on the spot; they act similarly on the wounds or sores of incautious persons. I remember the case of a man who had some sore in one of his nostrils, and lived near a slaughter-house; being a confirmed drunkard, he one day fell asleep in the open air in front of his dwelling; a few days after he was taken with intense headache, and soon after with hemorrhage from the nose. On examination, it was found that the evil was caused by two or three dozen worms, arising from the above-mentioned fly. They are also invariably deposited on the navel, and not unfrequently on the very lips and gums, of newly-dropped calves, so that the most watchful attendance is required for several days after birth.

Several applications are used in the extirpation of these troublesome insects, such as tobacco, the grated rind of the green bitter orange, and sabadilla; but this latter is by far the surest and best remedy. After the worms have been killed, the part must be protected by turpentine or carapa oil, which is applied once or twice a day till the wound or sore is perfectly healed.

Another injurious insect is the oestrus; it deposits its larvæ in the bodies of animals, and even of human beings. It is known here by the name of *Ver-maringouin*, or *Mosquito-worm*—the people being under the impression that the larva is that of a large mosquito; but the fact is, that no one here has ever seen the mother-insect. The larva of the oestrus has its head at a small aperture immediately under the skin, probably for the purpose of breathing, as it dies within an hour or less if the access of air be efficiently checked. This is done by covering the part with a piece of sticking-plaster.

Of bees, or honey-flies, there are four species: three black, of which one is smaller than the common fly, another larger than the common bee, and the third of an intermediate size. The smaller species build generally in walls, and the other in the hollows of trees. Their honey is very good, and the wax soft and black. The fourth kind, of a light brown colour, and the size of the European bee, has the habits of the two larger black species; none of them sting.

Six or seven species of wasps exist in the island, some of them building very ingenious nests, and several stinging very severely, viz., the common brown wasp, locally called "Jack Spaniard," which builds in houses, and the species called here the Tatou wasp (*Polistes*), from the resemblance of its nest to the barred shell of the armadillo. Of this wasp there are two species; they build their nests against the trunk or the larger branches of trees, with an entrance-hole at the lower extremity. The smaller species of the tatou wasp is more than half an inch long; the larger above one inch. They are of a bluish colour, and fever is generally brought on by their sting.

Termites, or wood-lice (*Termes devastans*).—The wood-lice, or termites, are too well known to require any extended notice; I will only remark that the nymphs, not the grown insect, are destructive. The nymph is of a whitish colour, and without wings. The males and females are provided with very long wings, of a dark-blue colour, and the insects themselves are of a light brown hue, with a brownish dark head; the wings are very readily detached, which operation the animal itself performs with its legs. During, or after, heavy rains, they issue, as it were, from every corner, literally clouding the air, where they become the prey of swallows and other birds. This remark does not apply to the termites only, for cockroaches, ants, and other insects are observed to rush out of retreats, or to abandon their nests in heavy rains, some in a state of visible anxiety, as the cockroaches, for instance, which are seen running or flying in all directions. How to account for this influence of rain? Really, I cannot discover any satisfactory explanation: they are not forced out by inundations, since many live in houses; they do not come forth in search of food, not even, I think, with a view to breeding. The wood-lice are certainly very destructive, but their ravages here are not, by any means, to be compared with those of the white ant in Africa, and southern Asia, particularly. They build their nests in trees, or in houses on the beams and rafters, with covered galleries for communication from one point to another; but they more commonly take their lodging within the wood itself, which they gradually destroy, and that in a very short time, by forming longitudinal excavations throughout the interior. Scantling, boards, &c., thus eaten away, become a mere shell, and break down, though to all external appearance entire and sound. They attack, in preference, the softer woods, and are very partial to white pine, and other foreign timber: but they rarely invade the country growths, and especially our hard woods; hence the inappreciable advantage of the latter for building purposes. I am not aware that the termites of the island ever raise such pyramidal earth-structures as the white ants of Africa and Asia do.

Ants.—Few countries can be said to harbour so many species of ants, and in such numbers, as Trinidad. Although it is not pretended that a description of all can be given, above twenty distinct species are, however, well known. Of these, several tribes inhabit the high woods, and are never seen in towns or dwelling-houses; while others seem to prefer the haunts of man, where they find an abundance of food. They vary in length from

one-twelfth to about three-quarters of an inch; some bite, others
sting; several have a very strong and unpleasant odour; some
raise their hillocks from under ground, others build in decayed,
a few in the hollows of living trees, as, for instance, in the
interior of the soft trumpet-tree, which they pierce in order to
effect a lodging in its internodes; others build a regular kind of
mortared nest against the trunk or larger branches of trees, in
a manner similar to the wasps or termites. Several of the kinds
inhabiting houses deserve a few words of notice. Of these, the
stinging black ants are met with almost everywhere; they form
their nests underground, or at the roots of plants, particularly of
those upon which the "pucerons" feed; they carry numbers of
the latter to the plant, and build along the stems and twigs
covered galleries, besides which they devour the bark of the
roots or stem, so that the plant, both from the attacks of the
"pucerons" and their own devastation, soon perishes. The black
ants sting very severely, and, when disturbed, they rush out in
numbers, and most fiercely. There are two species of the red
stinging ant, one of which, called the sugar-ant, seems to be the
smallest of all the kinds here; they both sting, particularly the
smaller one, and the burning and itching sensation they cause
lasts more than half an hour. They are very fond of sweets and
olive oil, so that it is always necessary to place those articles out
of their reach. The black and red ants move slowly. The
"crazy ant" is black, and is about one-eighth of an inch in
length; it always seems to be in a hurry, moving very rapidly
backwards, forwards, and sideways, as if it were mad; hence its
sobriquet. These ants are particularly fond of syrup and sugar;
they are also carnivorous, and nothing is more amusing than to
observe thousands of them carrying along large cockroaches,
worms, or other dead insects. If they encounter a crawling
worm, immediate notice is circulated among the tribe, and, in a
short time, hundreds of them march to the attack; their huge
adversary rolls and contracts in self-defence, but, although tossed
about, the ants hold fast, fresh recruits come to the rescue, and,
after a struggle of more than half an hour, the giant is subdued,
and carried to the nest, part of the host pulling forwards, and
part raising up, so as to lighten the draft. Once arrived at the
entrance to the nest, which is generally small, and cannot admit
the booty, the ants cut their prey into small pieces, which they

carry down; one only, or a dozen or more, taking charge of each piece, according to the size. The crazy ants neither bite nor sting.

The hunter and parasol ants deserve peculiar notice. The former, or visiting ant, called also *Fourmi chasseuse*, is not, I conceive, the *Atta cephalotes* of Fabricius, because the head is not comparatively large; it is of a brown colour, but the abdomen of a lighter hue than the thorax and head; when full grown it is about one-third of an inch long. This ant is very active and quick in its movements, stings most severely, and may be said to be excessively fierce in its attack. It is exclusively carnivorous, and, after killing its prey, divides it into portions, each ant carrying its share of the spoil. The hunter ants do not build nests, but choose recesses in some decayed tree, or among dry leaves, forming a sort of mass, sometimes two feet in diameter, where they congregate during the dry months; in fact, they are nomadic, being always engaged in some predatory excursions, and preferring the wet to the dry seasons for their expeditions; they carry with them their larvæ close to the body. The army, or tribe, on starting, marches on a frontage of from about five to six feet, by ten feet deep; then follow three or four columns, which afterwards are formed into two, and sometimes only a single section, this rearguard being sometimes half a mile from the expeditionary corps actually engaged in spoliation. The latter beats up the ground, climbing the smaller trees, groping into every hole, under every leaf, and leaving nothing unvisited. Not only insects and the smaller animals fly in every direction, but even the larger species are compelled to give way; for the hunter ants kill every living thing in the way of their march, young birds in their nests, animals too young or too weak to escape, cockroaches, scorpions, crickets, &c., and carry away the larvæ of insects and their nymphs; they dare not penetrate, however, into the nests of the parasol ants, which defend their townships bravely. The hunters are generally accompanied by anis, thrushes, and other birds which feed on insects; and during the bustle of their ravages, there is a sort of crackling, occasioned not only by the movements of the ants themselves, but also by the frightened insects that flee in all directions. The hunter ants sometimes visit houses, where they destroy an immense quantity of vermin; rats, mice, cockroaches, centipedes, scorpions, become their prey, or are obliged to abandon the house. It is well, then, to protect oneself and the young of the domestic animals from their attacks; in fact, the inhabitants sometimes find it the wisest plan to surrender at discretion, evacuate the premises, and leave them to the salutary plundering of these marauders, who, after making a thorough clearance of all vermin, beat an orderly retreat; after this, the inmates may safely re-enter, and for some time will be freed from their former insect annoyances. When the hunter ants meet with a hollow, or a rillet of water, which affords the primary element of a bridge in a blade of grass, or any other slip, they immediately contrive a construction to cross the same in the following manner :—A few of them take a strong hold on the bank; others come forward, and are firmly held by the former by the hind legs; fresh volunteers are attached in like manner by the latter, until a sufficient number has formed a kind of chain or suspension bridge, so as to reach the opposite bank. As, however, this living bridge may have swerved from its direct course, or be slack, those which have reached the other side give a tight strain, so as to restore the original line, and render it a level floor; the bridge is also rendered stronger by fresh ants forming, as it were, two or three floorings, one over the other. It would seem that they manage, by regular reinforcements, to relieve those that have been primarily engaged in forming the bridge, without interfering with its solidity. When the whole tribe has crossed over, the bridge is broken up by a process the reverse to that which had prevailed in its formation.

The parasol ants are very common in the island, and in such numbers in some districts as to discourage cultivators. Is the parasol ant the *Atta cephalotes* of Fabricius? I am inclined to admit this; however, it does not sting, but has strong serrated mandibles. There are three distinct species, one very small, which deserves no peculiar notice, and two others, which may be called the *dark* and the *red;* and not only do they differ in colour, but in size, their habits also being somewhat different. The dark parasol-ant is smaller, particularly the female; it prefers inhabited places, and builds its nest in walls, under the roots of trees, and among rubbish; these nests are never very large. They do not venture out, generally, during the day, but after sunset. With great apparent cunning, when aware of any danger, they remain quite still, and sometimes drop down motionless; they seem also to be more delicate as regards the choice of their food. The red parasol ants are larger in size; they never build in walls, but in the high forest, and particularly in the neighbourhood of plantations: their nests look like so many mounds, some being from two to three feet high, and from twenty to thirty feet in diameter. When they have once settled in a locality they never remove, unless compelled: the nest or township is gradually increased from two or three feet, on the first settlement, to thirty feet in diameter. The parasol ant shows a great deal of discrimination in the selection of a spot wherein to build its nest; generally, it is on a gentle slope, or near the bank of some brook. The nest is composed, according to the extent of the township, of a greater or lesser number of spherical excavations, each of them being, in general, traversed or crossed by a tree-rootlet: they are separated from each other by a rather thick wall, and communication is effected between the different excavations or chambers by passages cut through the walls; these have access also to a larger public passage, which opens out at the lower part of the nest on the declivity. The earth dug from the excavations is accumulated on the nest, so as to give it the mound-like form already mentioned. In each of the chambers are deposited the larvæ and nymphs, in a soft, light substance of a whitish colour; this sort of bed is moulded on the excavation, and is generally laid around the root, which was probably preserved for the purpose. The female ants are also lodged in the same substance, and fresh leaves are therein deposited, undoubtedly for food for the larvæ and nymphs, and also for the females. I suppose they suck the juice of the leaves, the parenchymatous part being left to be prepared into the white substance above mentioned. Several highways diverge from the nest, branching off afterwards in the various directions which lead to the trees or localities whence they procure their food. Their dwellings are kept perfectly clean, all rubbish and dry leaves being carried away, every day, to a place of deposit, through the common passage already noticed, which may be considered as the main sewer of the township; it is about one inch high by three or four inches wide. Not far from the place of deposit is what may be termed the cemetery, to which all dead and enfeebled ants are carried and there deposited.

From these details, which are too incomplete, perhaps, but which are strictly true, it is easily seen that the nests of the parasol-ants are constructed on a well-devised plan. Not only is the spherical form adopted in their underground architecture the best adapted to resist pressure, but thick walls are left between the chambers; a communication, as has been observed, is also established between them, with a common passage or outlet, which serves mainly for the discharge of all impurities, and so constructed as not to interfere with the regular operations of the township, or be a nuisance to the population; in case of inundation, likewise, the water is drained off through the same sewer. So much for the ingenuity and industry of the parasol-ants.

The females are nearly three-quarters of an inch long in the larger species; the labourers vary in size, from one-eighth to two-thirds of an inch. The larger ants seldom go out to forage, and in all such cases never carry their share of the provender, but they seem to act as inspectors to enforce order and rebuke laziness: their principal office, however, seems to be the protection of the township; for the moment any stranger disturbs the fortification, these garrison soldiers come out in large numbers, with their mandibles open, and ready for action.

The parasol-ants do not sting, but bite; their mandibles are like two small saws ending in a sharp point, and which serve to cut or carve out small portions of the leaves which constitute their food; in the same manner they incise the skin, so as to draw blood. These ants venture out after sunset, generally, although during rainy days they come out earlier, and in the morning also, keeping in their nest during the heat of the day. The roads which lead from the nest to the plants they attack are from four to six inches wide; all grasses are cut close to the ground, and every particle of vegetation, as also small gravel, is removed, so that the road remains clear, and perfectly free from all obstacles. Myriads of the parasol-ants traverse these roads at night in search of food; two or more trees may be attacked at the same time, and a branch-road leads to each. The parasol-ants feed in preference on certain particular plants—as the range-tree, the manioc, the yam, the young cacao—and generally are found to select the most delicate herbage: they feed nevertheless on almost any others, whenever those they prefer are not within reach—excepting, however, strongly aromatic plants,

I

such as the pimento, the cinnamon, &c. ; they also select soft rather than coriaceous leaves, and climb to the top of high trees to get at the young and tender leaflets. When arrived at an eligible spot for foraging, they set to work immediately, each ant selecting the margin of a leaf wherefrom to cut a portion; this it does with its mandibles, by the movement of the head, the body being motionless, so that the cut is circular. When the portion is nearly separated, it is grasped by the two first legs, and once cut out, the insect elevates it between the mandibles by one extremity, so that the whole weight of the severed leaf bears backwards, and thus proceeds with its burden homewards. Some of these cuttings are sometimes half an inch in diameter, and when, as is generally the case, in large bands, they present a most singular appearance, each insect seeming gravely to march under shelter of a parasol; hence their name of parasol-ants. A great many of the youngest ants accompany the labourers, and as many as seven I have seen clinging to the cutting of a leaf, in which manner they are carried home by their elders. In severing the leaves, many pieces are dropped from the tree, and taken up by those that are at the foot. After they have stripped a tree or plant bare, they proceed to another; but as soon as the plant first attacked begins to send forth new shoots they return to it, so that after it has been thus deprived of its foliage two or three times, it withers away, or becomes so much enfeebled as to be altogether unproductive. In one single night the parasol-ants will bare a tree of its foliage; and the damage they occasion is such, in some localities, as greatly to discourage the culture of yams, manioc, and other of their favourite plants. The town of Port of Spain may be said to be infested with the *dark parasol-ants*, and it is only by constant watchfulness and unceasing exertions that roses, vines, &c., can be preserved from their attacks; it is sometimes even difficult to reach them so as to insure their destruction, for they often nest in walls, and the very walls of the houses.

Various methods have been tried for destroying these enemies: poisons, fumigations, and lastly water, by way of submerging their abodes, and drowning them. Arsenic, corrosive sublimate mixed up with cassada-meal, orange-rind, &c., have been used as agents in their eradication: for one or two days they readily carry the poisonous substance to the nest, and from the effects of which many die; but they soon detect the mistake, and never touch it again. Fumigations with sulphur, or with sulphur and nitre, are perhaps the simplest means of destroying the parasol-ants. For this purpose, a sort of small furnace is prepared—an old iron kettle being the best: a hole is made at the bottom, and the kettle turned upside down on one of the passages or openings of the township. Sulphur alone, or sulphur mixed with nitre, is placed in it with coals below, and a pair of bellows adapted for keeping up combustion: every aperture or fissure through which the smoke may escape is cemented with clay, and the fumigation then commences: it must continue at intervals for two or three days before there can be an assurance of success. The most certain means perhaps is to dig up the nest to the foundation, and, by pouring on water, to form with the clay a batter of mortar, in which the ants are stifled and buried; but, in this case, the first requisite is a good supply of water; and to dig up a large ants' nest is not a trifle, particularly as the ants become wild when disturbed, and bite unmercifully.

Annelida.—A species of leech has been found here in ponds and brooks: it is of a dark colour, and bears a very great resemblance to the horse-leech.

Testaceæ.—It will only be necessary to mention those which are used as food, and a few terrestrial or fluviatile conchiferæ. Of the former class are oysters, mussels, and two small bivalves called here *Palourdes,* or cockles, and *Chip-chips.* Oysters are generally met with in abundance, adhering to the roots of the mangrove trees, either in small bays, or at the outlets of rivers and creeks: those taken in Scotland Bay, in the first Boca, and at the Rivers Moruga and Guataro, are much esteemed, some of them being very large; but they become sweetish during the rainy season, at which time a large proportion of fresh water is mixed with the salt. Mussels are very large, and are dug from the sand or mud along the sea-shore, as also the Palourdes or cockles, and the chip-chips—the latter a roseate triangular bivalve.

Amongst our terrestrial gasteropoda is a very large helix, about the size of a goose's egg: there are also several fluviatile univalve conchiferæ.

It may perhaps happen that the above details on the animals of Trinidad will be deemed by some tedious and of no practical use, while others will undoubtedly consider them as insignificant, and of no scientific value. To the former I answer, that such details must tend to rouse curiosity in the minds of those who may read this sketch. The latter I refer to the Appendix, where they will find a more extended notice of the grand class of Vertebrata.

CHAPTER IV.

CLIMATE—TEMPERATURE—RAINS—DISEASES.

FOR a long period Trinidad has been, and is still, regarded as very unhealthy; but it is really less so than many other countries similarly situated. For instance, the rate of mortality in this island is one per thirty inhabitants, being less than that of several large towns in Europe, viz., Madrid, Palermo, Naples, Rome, and Vienna. But the rate of mortality is not perhaps a correct criterion of the salubrity of a country; and the greater or less prevalence of ordinary maladies, together with the proportion of the diseased to the total population, ought also to be taken into account. Now, if the salubrity of Trinidad is to be determined by this test, it must be confessed that the island stands lower than several places in which the rate of mortality is actually greater.

The climate of Trinidad is almost identical with that of the other Antilles. It is an inter-tropical, and, at the same time, an insular climate; that is to say, it is cooler than a continental country under the same latitude and of the same altitude, and its temperature more equal. It, however, presents the following peculiarities, when compared with the sister islands: a total exemption from hurricanes, a greater regularity in the periodical returns of seasons, and its being but little subject to the inconveniences arising from droughts and blighting winds; the contrast between the temperature of the day and night is also, perhaps, greater—the latter being deliciously cool from December to April.

In Trinidad, as in other tropical climates, there are only two seasons—the dry, and the wet or rainy. The dry season may be said to commence with January and end with May—five months; while the rainy season sets in with June, and lasts to the middle of December. February, March, and April are the driest months of the year. The heat of the sun is then scorching. The grass becomes parched, the leaves of plants wither, and the smaller streams are dried up; but after the first showers at the end of May or the beginning of June, the face of the country is completely altered in an incredibly short time, and the vegetation looks everywhere green and luxuriant. There is seldom a sudden alteration from dry to wet, or from wet to dry. The change from the dry to the rainy season is generally characterised by a calm and close atmosphere, with occasional showers, from the middle of May to the 10th of June, at which time dark clouds begin to stretch along the horizon, accompanied by remote thunder, and soon followed by heavy rains. In July and August the rain falls in torrents; and the soil being soon saturated to the utmost, the rivers are everywhere overflowed, ravines rush foaming down the hills, the roads are in many localities almost impassable, and even plantations are frequently damaged by its violence. The rain often continues to pour for hours, whilst the crash of electricity is incessant, and almost deafening. Showers are still frequent in September, but not heavy; and from the end of that month to the 20th of October, there are generally very fine days—that short period of dry weather being called the fall, or Michaelmas summer. At the end of October showers become more frequent, and, although not of daily occurrence, are very heavy in November. The northerly wind, which commences ordinarily in October, becomes steadier in December, veering to the east-north-east, with occasional squalls during the day, and the skies clearing almost immediately after. This change marks the transition from the wet to the dry season.

The prevailing winds, from January to June, are from east, veering to north-north-east, after sunset; and to east-south-east quarter south after nine o'clock P.M. From June to October, the winds are variable, blowing, however, from south-south-west and west-north-west. Southerly winds are always accompanied by heavy rain. In October, the wind shows a tendency to change to east and north-east, to settle at the north-north-east in November and December, and then to veer round to east-south-east.

By climate, I do not mean any astronomically defined zone or region, but the combined action of all the changes which may take place in the atmosphere and at the surface of the soil, and which actually produce, or are capable of producing, in our organs certain permanent or only transient modifications : such as light, the amount of electric tension and barometrical pressure, the temperature resulting from the geographical position, as also humidity, and those emanations or exhalations which are designated by the names of *effluvia, miasma,* or *malaria.*

Of light, I will say nothing, except that it has a powerful influence on the healthy development of vegetable and animal life, on the greater or less amount of colouring matter in the leaves of plants, and in the complexion of man.

The appreciation of the influence of electric tension on the human body is a matter of greater difficulty; but its indirect action must be powerful, since it is evidently connected with all atmospherical phenomena.

The variations of the barometrical pressure being indicative of the density of the air, and, consequently, of the mass of respirable principle therein contained, are an important element in the appreciation of climatic influence. On this point, I may remark that, between the tropics, the horary oscillations of the barometer are very regular, and present two *maxima*—at 9 or $9\frac{1}{2}$ A.M., and at $10\frac{1}{2}$ or $10\frac{3}{4}$ P.M.; and two *minima*—at 4 and $4\frac{1}{2}$ P.M., and 4 A.M. "Their regularity is so great," says Baron von Humboldt, "that in the day-time especially the hour may be ascertained from the height of the mercurial column, without an error, on the average, of more than fifteen or seventeen minutes. I have found the regularity of the ebb and flow of the aerial ocean undisturbed by storms, hurricanes, rain, and earthquakes."

Amongst the various and numerous causes which modify the mean annual temperature of the island, and all tending to its depression, the following may be taken into consideration: its insular position, its peculiar disposition into two grand sectional valleys, running east and west, between three almost parallel ridges; and the extensive woods, which covering nearly the whole of its surface, influence the temperature by acting as a shield against the direct bearing of the sun's rays by radiation, and even by augmenting the atmospherical humidity.

Three series of thermometrical observations, made at different periods and localities, give $80.73°$ as the mean temperature of Trinidad. Two of those series comprise a period of five years each; the third period, extending from 1870 to 1880, comprises ten years. In Captain Tulloch's "Statistical Reports," &c., I have found the first series of observations; they were probably taken at St. James's Barracks. The others were taken at the Royal Gaol, Port-of-Spain, and the Botanic Gardens, St. Ann.

AVERAGE OF FIVE YEARS. Capt. Tulloch.				AVERAGE OF FIVE YEARS. Royal Gaol.		
Months.	Max.	Med.	Min.	Max.	Med.	Min.
January	85·50	78·50	71	86	81·80	74·40
February	86	79	71	86·60	82·40	73
March	87	79	70	89	83	77·60
April	88	80	71·50	91	84·40	79·60
May	87·50	80	73	93·20	85·60	79·20
June	87	81	75	90	84·60	79
July	84	79	74·50	89·60	84·60	80
August	84·50	79·50	74	91·60	84·60	80
September	85	79·50	73	92	85	80·40
October	84·50	79	73	90·60	85	79·60
November	84	78·50	72·50	89·40	84	79
December	82	77	72·50	87·80	83	76·40

Botanic Gardens, Saint Ann. Ten years (1870–1880).			
Months.	Maximum.	Mean.	Minimum.
January	80·73	79·24	64·7
February	87·4	79·8	63·8
March	87·9	80·5	65·1
April	89·1	82·0	66·1
May	89·9	82·7	67·8
June	87·9	81·0	68·8
July	88·3	81·0	69·2
August	88·4	81·0	69·3
September	88·4	81·6	69·2
October	89·5	81·8	68·8
November	88·3	81·1	68·3
December	86·5	80·0	66·6

The mean yearly temperature, according to the first series, is 79°; and 84° according to the second; third series, 80·97°. The second series of observations was made in town, at the Royal Gaol, and may be said to give the temperature of Port-of-Spain, not of the country generally. The maxima are

88°, 93°, and 95·5°; and the minima, 70°, 73°, and 60·1°, for the three periods respectively. The greatest daily variations were 17°, 14°, and 30·9°, corresponding to the months of March, May, and April. The highest temperature was 95·5° in April, 1878; lowest, 60·1° in January, 1878. The mean annual temperature of the neighbouring region of Venezuela varies, according to Codazzi, from 70·90° to 81·14°.

In the first period, the hottest months are June, May, and April; in the second, May, September, and October; in the third, March, April, and May. The months which exhibit a *maximum* of temperature are April, May, and March; those showing a *minimum* are January, February, and December. The coldest months are, in the first period, December, November, and January; in the second, January, February, March, and December; in the third, January, December, and February. The temperature of June and July is more uniform; and that greater uniformity is a consequence of the heavy rains which fall during those months and produce a refreshing action on the atmosphere, whilst the bright sun and parching breezes of March, April, and even May, have for result an increase of temperature during the day.

There is also a *maximum* and *minimum* of daily temperature; and the following table shows their daily variations, at the Royal Gaol, for a term of two years.

Months.	Hours.				
	6 a.m.	9 a.m.	12 a.m.	3 p.m.	6 p.m.
January . . .	78·40	82	84	82	80
February . . .	78	84	85	85	80·60
March	79	83	85	85·50	81
April	81	84	87	87·70	82
May	82	86	88	87·50	82·40
June	79	86	87	87	82
July . . .	82	82·60	86	87	82·30
August . . .	82	85	86	86·60	82·20
September . .	82	85	87·50	88	82·75
October . . .	81	85·50	87	87	82
November . .	81	85	86	84	82
December . .	80	84	85	85	81
Average . . .	80·45	84·32	86·12	86·00	81·69

By comparing the figures of this table, it will be found that the hour which exhibits the *minimum* temperature is 6 A.M., and that which presents the *maximum* is 3 P.M. Now, although the temperature is two degrees lower at 9 A.M. than at noon and 3 P.M., it may yet be affirmed that the heat is excessive from that hour to 4 P.M. The above table shows also that the increase is more gradual than the decrease of temperature—the former being 5·67°, within six hours, viz., from 6 in the morning to 12 noon; and the latter 4·31° within three hours, viz., from 3 to 6 P.M. The mean temperature, in the sun, may be estimated at 124° Farenheit.

The thermometer gives neither a fair indication of the sensation felt by, nor of the impression made upon, the human frame by a high temperature. They both depend greatly on the rarefaction of the air and the hygrometric state of the atmosphere; so that the sensation of oppression, and the general prostration caused by a high temperature, are increased by sultry weather, and rendered more painful than when the air is comparatively dry, pure, and agitated. The influence of winds in connection with the temperature is very remarkable. The northerly wind, even when light, being comparatively cold, produces an unpleasant feeling of chill, whereas the easterly breeze, however strong, never produces that sensation; on the contrary, it is agreeable, cool, and refreshing, and may be said to be bracing.

The southerly wind has a depressing effect; still more so the westerly.

Humidity.—The influence of atmospheric moisture on vegetable life is too well known to require any comment. Its influence on our own organs is, perhaps, as powerful, though less apparent. Temperature, atmospheric pressure, the prevailing winds, and the condition of a country, whether as cultivated or still covered with forests — all these greatly influence the actual quantity of moisture contained in the atmosphere.

I am not in possession of such hygrometric observations as would enable me to give any definite information on the subject; but the quantity of rain which falls throughout the year may serve as a test for appreciating the humidity of our climate. It will be seen, from the following returns, that such quantity may be estimated at 66 inches 28 hundredths *per annum*.

Petit Morne Estate (Naparima),	3 years (71—73)	...	...	71·73
Corynth Estate ,,	5 years (68—72)	...	...	68·75
Williamsville Estate ,,	,, ,,	...	...	67·09
Taruba Estate ,,	,, ,,	...	...	65·19
Les Efforts Estate ,,	,, ,,	...	...	63·36
Union Hall Estate ,,	,, ,,	...	...	67·70
El Socorro Estate (Cimaronero)	,, ,,	...	...	57·69
Endeavour Estate (Chaguanas),	11 years (68—79)	...	...	69·74
Botanic Gardens (Saint Ann),	15 years (62—76)	...	...	65·25
	General Average	...	...	66·28

In the first edition of this book, I had given such quantity as 70·30 inches. It was compiled from observations published by Captain Tulloch in his "Statistical Report" for the years 1825, 1826, 1827; from those of Dr. J. Davy, in his work on the West Indies, from the years 1847 to 1852 inclusive, and taken at the St. James's Barracks; also from observations made at the Royal Gaol, from 1850 to 1854 inclusive.

The months which exhibit a *minimum* of rain are April, March, and February; and those wherein the *maximum* quantity falls are August, July, and September. It would appear, from six years' observation by Ramon de la Sagra, that the mean annual quantity of rain which falls at Havanna is 109 inches; it is 72 inches on the north coast of Venezuela (Codazzi); from 118 to 128 in Hindustan, near the coast (Humboldt); 90·75 inches in Ceylon (western coast). In Paris it was found by Arago to be 20 inches; in London, by Howard, 25 inches; in Geneva, 30·50 inches (Humboldt).

By taking separately the first five months of the year allotted to the dry season, and the seven last months which comprise the wet, we have the following results: 1·98 inch per month for the first five months; 7·78 inches during the last seven months. We may, therefore, conclude that June, July, August, September, October, November, and December are very humid, and the climate generally damp. The greatest quantity of rain which fell during any month, pending the period of fifteen years, was 15·18 inches, viz., in August, 1876; in the same month of 1851, the quantity reached 16·81 inches. No rain, by the rain-gauge, in January, 1862, and May, 1873; only 4 hundredths in April, 1864; and 7 hundredths in February, 1872.

Average quantity of rainfall in Demerara (5 years), 75·62 ; Berbice, 70·53 ; St. Vincent (8 years), 99·36 ; St. Christopher (13 years), 52·23 ; Barbadoes (26 years), 57·74.

I have already stated that the aforesaid physical agencies—but particularly light, heat, and humidity—exercised the greatest influence on animal as well as vegetable life ; I will now briefly examine their influences on our own organs.

Heat.—Besides its well-known debilitating effect on the human body, a high temperature seems to have a powerful action in modifying certain functions. Under such temperature, the cerebral activity is diminished, as well as the muscular power, and the digestive organs are greatly enfeebled. Cutaneous exhalation is much increased, and becomes apparent under the form of perspiration ; in fact, it is brought to its *summum* in a warm and damp atmosphere. Perspiration has, for effect, a diminution of the quantity of heat produced in the human body by natural processes—nor does it act as a debilitating cause, to the extent that is generally supposed ; for prostration of strength is relieved by an abundant natural perspiration, and its increase, when the air is not too damp, results in a counteraction of the effects of a high temperature. I may adduce, as a proof of what I advance, that individuals in robust health are generally those who perspire the most. It is a principle in physiology, that the greater the activity of an organ the more liable it becomes to disease ; and, as a consequence, cutaneous affections must be more frequent and serious in a warm than in a temperate climate.

Humidity.—Warm air contains, even when comparatively dry, a larger contingent of water than cold damp air. This aqueous admixture increases the volume of air, and diminishes its specific gravity ; as an inference, warm damp air contains less of the respirable element than any other. The warmer the atmosphere the larger the quantity of water which it can hold in suspension. A damp atmosphere—the temperature being equal, or even greater—produces a peculiar feeling of chill, widely differing from the bracing effect caused by a cold, dry air. The sensation produced by the former is keener, and seems to penetrate the whole system, thereby producing chilliness and involuntary shivering from within, with a bluish paleness externally ; in fact, a damp atmosphere acts by diminishing the power of producing heat, and the symptoms evinced very much resemble those of an incipient attack of intermittent fever.

The influence of a damp, warm atmosphere on the various functions is still more distinctly observable than that of a dry, warm air. The proportion of the colouring matter decreases in the blood, thereby showing that hematosis is modified by humidity. As a result of these modifications of the blood, the different organs are variously affected, and, among others, the stomach: its digestive power is weakened, and, generally, a lesser proportion of food is required to satisfy the appetite—gentle stimulants and tonics then become necessary.

The hepatic secretion is much diminished, and the quantity of bile secreted may not only become insufficient for the process of healthy digestion, but even its very quality may become so much altered as to constitute a pathological state. As a consequence of the alterations caused in hematosis, and the digestive functions, nutrition becomes impaired.

The glandular system is, also, particularly modified; its activity is much increased, and individuals, having lived for a certain period in a damp locality, may be said to be placed under the same conditions as those who are of a lymphatic temperament. If, together with these natural coincidents, are combined those of insufficient non-animal diet, bad lodgings, and the appurtenances of filth, the consequences speedily become apparent: inflammation of the lymphatic glands and vessels, ulcers, chronic eczema, and even leprosy, according to individual constitution, must be the deplorable results.

Light.—It is not very easy to obtain practical information as to the influence on man of this physical agent, when considered separately from air and heat; but we are warranted in concluding, analogically, from its effects on the healthy growth of plants, and the metamorphoses of batracians, that it must materially influence certain functions. I do not, therefore, hesitate to affirm, that the evil effects of confinement in dark rooms or dwellings must be partly attributed to the absence or want of light; whilst to the presence of that agent may be partly traced the beneficial results of exercise in the open air, particularly in the case of those who have the misfortune of being born with a lymphatic temperament.

Besides the general influence exercised on the human frame

by a high temperature combined with humidity, there may exist in the air certain substances which, in the form of miasmatic emanations, become a most material element in the development of maladies, and the sanitary condition of a country.

A warm, damp atmosphere is the condition naturally most favourable to the decomposition of organic substances, either animal or vegetable; and as the gaseous exhalations evolved from such decompositions are more readily held in suspension in such an atmosphere, it may be considered, where suitable affinities exist, as highly predisposing to very serious diseases, and especially to the almost innumerable series of periodical affections.

Emanations arising from the decomposition of vegetable matters are particularly noxious; and yet, when they are allowed to decay in a dry air, they do not disengage any deleterious principles. In order to generate those principles, they must undergo the process of decay in stagnant water, thus forming swamps. Swamp-water is, generally, fetid; but fetidity is no positive mark of the deleterious qualities of a swamp.

Swamps or marshes are created by collections of standing water, either fresh or salt; it may be said, however, that purely salt-water marshes do not exist, since they are almost invariably formed by an admixture of fresh with salt-water. The latter are much more dangerous than merely fresh or salt-water swamps, whereas this admixture has for result to aid in the decomposition of the organic matter contained in both.

The following are the conditions necessary for the formation of swamp effluvia: a damp, warm air, the ground neither too dry nor too deeply covered with water. Hence the atmosphere of these watery tracts always contains more or less of moisture, but more during the night than the day; it also holds in suspension during the former period certain substances which do not seem to exist therein during the latter, so that the disengagement, or at least the condensation, of marsh emanations is less during the day, and greater at night, but particularly at sunset and sunrise. Their chemical nature has not yet been ascertained by analysis; however, they have been found to contain ammoniacal components, and, therefore, must be of an organic or vegeto-animal nature. No doubt their mode of operating is complex ; but in order to account for the identical effects produced by the atmosphere of swampy places, and from the consideration of the processes of vegeto-animal decay which are uninterruptedly going on in such localities, we are led to admit that they give rise to certain noxious principles, which we call *effluvia, miasma,* and *malaria*. Now, are these substances the elements of the noxious influence of swamps? This would appear to be highly probable.

The specific gravity of effluvia seems to be greater than that of pure air, for they do not spread beyond a certain height. It would seem, also, that they are soluble in the globular moisture, actually saturating the air, so that they become condensated by the coolness of the night, and fall with the dew—the popular dread of dew-damps being proved thereby to be well founded.

Local circumstances may greatly influence the condensation of effluvia; for instance, whenever a swamp exists in a deep valley, abuts on a hill or mountain, or is skirted by forests, the miasmas evolving therefrom are likely to accumulate in the locality. The direction of variable or prevailing winds, also, aids materially in the spreading of malaria, and may thus modify the salubrity of a whole district.

Hills, mountains, and forests may therefore act as a protection against, or, on the contrary, as an aggravation of the noxious influence of a swamp, according as it is situated to the leeward or windward of the tract. In fact, it often happens that the miasmatic influence is almost *null* in the locality of the swamp itself, whilst it becomes very noxious at a certain distance, particularly whenever any barrier obtrudes, in the shape of hills and mountains to the leeward. Localities to the windward are comparatively exempt and safe.

The formation of effluvia is more abundant when a larger section of a marsh remains uncovered, or exposed to the direct action of the solar rays; so that, in our island, the deleterious influence of most of our swamps is materially tempered during the rainy season, when their ground surface is overflowed by pluvial waters.

We are naturally induced to admit the existence of *telluric* effluvia, as manifested by the prevalence of remittent and intermittent fever, when forest and brush lands are brought under tillage, and deeply furrowed by the plough.

Nearly the whole surface of Trinidad may be said to be covered with virgin forests; many swamps, formed by an admixture of fresh with salt water, exist all along the island shores, particularly on the western coast. The average quantity of rain which falls throughout the year may be estimated at 70 inches; the mean annual temperature 81°. The climate may thus be classed as at the same time humid and warm, and, consequently, highly debilitating; certain precautions, therefore, become necessary to counteract the effects of such a temperature on the general constitution.

Persons coming to Trinidad may avoid, to a certain extent, the diseases resulting from the climate, and become acclimatised or *seasoned*, as it is said, by submitting to a few rules deducible from the foregoing considerations. The climate being both warm and humid, such rules must be a combination of those which are respectively applicable to a warm, and to a humid climate.

Diet.—It is, in my opinion, of great importance that no preconceived system with respect to diet should be assumed or enforced; and I regard as a great mistake the adoption of, and submission to, certain theoretical dietetic prescriptions, without due preparation or gradual transition. The best plan is, as far as practicable, to follow one's previous regimen, if found to have agreed with the constitution, and, by degrees, to substitute those changes or modifications which observation may suggest, or experience sanction.

The almost exclusive use of vegetable food is, by some hygienists, strongly recommended to persons inhabiting a warm climate. Such a diet may suit an *exclusively warm* climate, and be acceptable to those individuals who spend their time in the *dolce far niente*, and enjoy a long *siesta* during the mid-day heat; but individuals living in damp localities, and leading an active life, would soon become enfeebled and invalided by indulging in a purely vegetable diet. In such a climate, and with such habits, I consider the use of animal food, and particularly of fresh meat, as even amounting to a necessity. This observation is also applicable to the inconsiderate use of fruits, encouraged by the same parties. Not that I consider fruits, in their own nature, unwholesome; for the poorest classes here, at certain seasons of the year, live almost exclusively on mangoes, avocado pears, oranges, and cashews; and that, at least, without apparent ill effects. I am, on the contrary, therefore, inclined to encourage the moderate use of the cooling produce of the orchard, when maturely ripened. But the indiscriminate and immoderate use of fruits would soon produce its debilitating effects on the digestive organs. Neither should the use of spices be indulged in habitually, except, perhaps, that of black pepper in swampy localities.

Whenever wholesome spring water can be got, it is by far the best drink; but this, as also rain water, ought always to be filtered, and the latter rendered more digestible by the addition of a little wine or spirit. Generally speaking, water only, or wine and water, ought to form the basis of common drink; pure wine or spirit is to be allowed only in exceptional cases, and when the body has been chilled by exposure to wet or cold damps. Beer and porter, however, form a wholesome beverage, particularly in swampy places. As a general rule, no fermented liquors should be taken in the intervals of meals; and the custom of passing wine after dinner ought to be discountenanced by all persons having pretensions to sobriety. I may boldly decry this as a faulty habit, inasmuch as it tends to accustom individuals to the immoderate use of fermented liquors. By the abuse or even the incautious use of such, the digestive organs, and the stomach especially, soon become deranged; a craving for drink, and repugnance to food, are the first symptoms; disturbed sleep and retching in the morning soon follow, as also general dyspepsia. Meanwhile, the liver becomes affected, together with the nervous system—a step further, *delirium tremens* supervenes as a complication, and, as a sequel, intellectual prostration and moral degradation; finally, a miserable death closes the scene.

Violent exercise immediately before meals is injurious; muscular action causing a diversion of the blood and nervous energy to the limbs and the surface generally. If any quantity of food be received ere equilibrium be restored, the stomach is then taken at a disadvantage; as a rule, therefore, at least half an hour's rest should be allowed before partaking of food. Again, immediately after meals, the digestive functions are in the highest degree of activity; all perturbing causes should then be carefully avoided, and only gentle exercise indulged in.

J

Fatigue of whatever kind, and especially from 10 A.M. to 3 P.M., is injurious, and may bring on fever, which generally takes the adynamic form; but regular exercise is absolutely necessary. Persons who lead a life of general physical inaction soon find that their appetite decreases, whilst their sensibility increases to a morbid extent; they become debilitated, and subject to nervous affections, and, if otherwise of a nervous temperament, highly excitable, and even hypochondriacal. When these individuals come to the determination of regularly taking foot or horse exercise, they gain by degrees a better and more regular appetite; the nervous symptoms subside, ultimately to disappear.

Moderation in eating, drinking (as also in the use of stimulants), and exercise, form the great secret for preserving health in Trinidad. Two meals per diem are sufficient; something, however, must be taken early in the morning, such as chocolate, tea, or coffee, particularly in marshy localities; neither would I object to chocolate or tea at night after an early dinner. Regularity in the hours of meals is also of paramount importance.

Attention ought likewise to be paid to clothing, in the materials of which thick cotton should be preferred to linen; it answers admirably as an under-shirt. Cotton is no good conductor of caloric, and is particularly useful in retaining perspiration within proper limits; it is also preferable to flannel, which is heavy, and irritates the skin. In our climate, indeed, cotton is fully as good a protective as woollens, since in the system is required not so much the preservation of warmth as the prevention of cold; for it is most essential that perspiration should not be checked.

The cold bath has for effect to diminish the temperature of the body by a merely physical action; but it is also one of the best cooling agents, as it, at the same time, diminishes the power productive of heat. Cold bathing, therefore, must be highly beneficial; but it ought to be of short duration—a few minutes only; and persons who are in a position to do so should bathe every day, since experience has proved that such practice is an almost sure guarantee of sound good health.

During sleep perspiration is augmented, though, at the same time, the power of producing heat is diminished; as a consequence, there is less reaction against physical agents, and greater risk of being assailed by disease. It is, therefore, very imprudent to sleep with open windows, or, at least, with such as admit a current of air to pass over the sleeping body. And yet this is a practice generally followed, with a view to enjoying the cool of the night. Sleeping in the open air has not the same ill effects.

Besides these general rules, there are others which are specially applicable to persons living within the limits of marshy places. The effluvia arising from such localities exercise their influence on the natives as well as strangers; and the suggestions I am about to offer are intended for both classes of persons.

Any individual dwelling near a marsh ought to make use of animal food, drink beer and porter, or spirits and water in the proportion of one pint of the former and thirty of the latter: the water should be filtered through charcoal. If engaged in rural avocations, before going out in the morning he should take some strong coffee, chocolate, or tea, with a little bread; in fact, he ought never to commence his labours with an empty stomach. Again, he should not venture out at an early hour when the dew is still abundant on the field, or during rain, unless dressed in coarse woollen garments—say serge trousers and a flannel jacket: both should be made large. He should not follow the practice of wearing socks, and, on coming home—even for a short time—he should change his wet for dry shoes. If possible, he should avoid exposure to the action of effluvia either at sunrise or sunset, as they condense at night and seem to evolve or disperse with renewed energy in the morning; and, as the human frame is more liable to be acted upon during slumber, all outer entrances to dwellings ought to be closed before sunset, and re-opened some time after sunrise—particularly those of the sleeping-room; screens made of canvas, or metallic sheets, should be also placed at the draughts of doors and windows, as a protection against the introduction of miasma.

Individuals should be very careful in protecting themselves against humidity, for I have come to the conclusion that this is one of the most active causes of disease. It is humidity, and not heat, which may be said to be productive of fever. Yellow fever may arise during the rainy season, as also dysentery. Many localities, under the same latitude, which enjoy the privilege of a dry atmosphere, are salubrious. Such are, for instance, Cumana and the Island of Margarita, both of which enjoy a very dry though warm climate; such are, also, the islets in the Gulf of Paria. The Portuguese, and other white immigrants, have no objection to field-work during the heat of the day; but they have much dread of rain, and of humidity generally. They all agree in saying, "that the sun will not cause fever, whilst rain invariably does so."

In order, therefore, to allow of a free and speedy drainage, houses should be built on a gentle elevation; whilst carefully-made and well-paved gutters should carry off the surplus water. Dwelling-houses should be raised on brick or stone pillars, to give free access to a current of air beneath the flooring, and means of ventilation provided by a sufficient number of windows and of ventilators in the upper part of the apartments. The sleeping-rooms should be as large as possible; and, finally, it is very important that houses should be protected on the marsh side by a plantation of trees, always, however, at a certain distance from the dwellings: bamboos would answer admirably.

As may have been anticipated from the above remarks, Trinidad is mainly subject to those diseases which belong to a warm damp climate, viz., to fevers and dysenteries. These are, in fact, the most prevalent maladies; and the observation made by Annesley, that two-thirds of the deaths in tropical regions are caused by the effects of marsh effluvia, is fully borne out in Trinidad.

Remittent and intermittent fevers attack all classes; the female sex and the aged, however, are less subject to them. They are particularly prevalent amongst children—convulsions being one of the most common symptoms in severe cases.

Europeans and unacclimatised persons, as well as children, are commonly attacked with the remittent, and native adults with the intermittent type. Congestions of the different organs, but mainly abdominal plethora, accompany remittent fevers. These may under unfavourable conditions terminate in black vomit; thus showing the great analogy, almost the identity of nature, in the remittent and yellow fevers. And though Trinidad is, perhaps, more subject to remittent fever than the Great Antilles, Vera Cruz, and New Orleans, yet yellow fever—that plague of the west, which may be said to be endemic in some of the above-mentioned places—visits our shores only at long intervals, and with little effect. The mortality from that cause has been particularly insignificant among seamen. The most frequent types of the remittent fevers are the *bilious, double quotidian*, and *double tertian*, which latter often terminates in the intermittent.

The most common types of intermittent fevers are the *quotidian, double tertian*, and *tertian;* the *quartan* is of very rare occurrence, but the *octan* and the *quinquedecimal* forms are rather frequent. The return of the latter types coinciding generally with certain changes of the moon, many have been induced to ascribe an influence to that planet as connected with the return of this fever.

Periodical fevers, either remittent or intermittent, are in certain places endemic throughout the whole year; regular epidemical *recrudescences*, however, occur at certain periods—generally at a change of season. The localities most liable to fever are those skirting the sea, or lying to the leeward of swamps; the interior districts may be said to enjoy comparative immunity from periodical fevers, and the occasional cases which there occur may, in general, be traced to some direct cause. Though the harbour of Port-of-Spain is to the leeward of the great Caroni swamp, the shipping, nevertheless, is almost exempt from fever. This is attributable to the fact, that no barrier exists to leeward in the shape of land, either level or elevated; and the effluvia are thus carried away several miles westward before any such obstruction intervenes.

Individuals inhabiting a salubrious locality are almost certainly attacked with remittent fever by resorting, even for a short period, to a swampy spot; should they stay there a few days only, fever will often declare itself even after a return to their former place of residence. It then, generally, terminates in the octan or quinquedecimal form, and may last for months. A change of air and sea-bathing are, sometimes, the only remedies.

Persons living in marshy districts are very liable to an attack of remittent fever by removal to a healthier locality. Intermittent, but remittent fevers particularly, when not attended to in time, or not properly treated, may end in malignant fever, generally in the apoplectic or algid form; this commonly happens from the third to the fifth day. It sometimes, however, exhibits the malignant character at the very first onset. Intermittent fever is often *masked*—the neuralgic form being the most frequent. The appearance of pain—sometimes very severe—in a limb, or any other part of the body, preceded or accompanied by cold hands and feet, or even by regular ague, and followed by either a gentle or profuse perspiration—after three, six, twelve, or more hours' duration—and a complete remission of the predominant symptoms, are sure indications of the nature of the complaint. Quinine is the surest, if not the sole remedy. It has been said of verminous affections, that they are Proteus-like; but remittent and intermittent fevers are the real Protean malady.

Dysentery.—Next to fever, dysentery is the most prevalent disease in Trinidad; it is even endemic in a few localities which are otherwise regarded as healthy. Every ten or twelve years, however, there are returns of epidemic dysentery. The disease commonly begins at the commencement of the wet season, viz., in July and August, and lasts for several months; so that atmospheric moisture seems to have an undeniable influence on the production of dysentery.

It has also been remarked that, in those localities wherein dysentery is endemic, there is always a coincidence between the breaking out of the distemper and the overflow of rivers after the first heavy showers. This is mainly apparent in our valleys and such other districts as are covered with high woods.

Dysentery may appear under four different forms, constituting, as it were, four distinct species, and having different seats:—The *mucous* or *gastric*, in which the stomach, and the *bilious* or *hepatic*, in which the liver, evidently participates; the *inflammatory*, which seems to attack the whole of the intestinal tube; and the *putrid*, or *adynamic*, known here by the name of *Bicho*, which has its seat in the *rectum* and *descending colon*. Each variety of this malady requires a different treatment. Chronic dysentery also is not unfrequent.

Dysentery attacks all classes and ages; the Europeans and the foreign whites are, however, far less subject to it than the natives and the coloured class. This may be attributed to the different mode of living of the two classes. Europeans and other whites generally enjoy more comforts, are better lodged and fed, and more cleanly in their habits; besides which, they are not so much exposed as the coloured people.

Eruptive fevers.—Measles, small-pox, and scarlatina reign epidemically every ten or twelve years; scarlatina less frequently than small-pox, and small-pox less again than measles. Measles and scarlatina are not so dangerous as in Europe, the convalescence particularly requiring less attention and caution. Small-pox has proved very fatal on various occasions. Vaccination may not infallibly act as a preservative, but it invariably modifies the characteristics of the eruption to such an extent as to render it comparatively harmless. Lately vaccination has been made compulsory, and vaccinators appointed to the different districts of the colony; re-vaccination is also encouraged.

Hooping-cough is of frequent occurrence, but not dangerous, except when altogether neglected, or accompanied with *bronchitis*. The latter affection, but particularly *tracheitis* and *laryngitis*, become very common during the season in which the chill northerly winds prevail. *Croup*, or *angina membranacea*, is of very rare occurrence, for what is termed here croup is either *angina stridulosa* or *angina ædematosa*, both of which simulate croup. *Angina ædematosa* almost invariably commences under the form of an inflammation of the *pharynx*, which afterwards extends to the *glottis*.

Sore-throat is one of the most frequent, and may be also reckoned one of the most serious, diseases which prevail in Trinidad. The *ædematous* variety is rather common, and by the extension of the ædema to the *glottis* may prove fatal in a few hours.

Diphtheria, almost unknown in the island for a long period, has for the last ten years prevailed epidemically on several occasions, and with disastrous results. There exists also a peculiar form of sore-throat, or *pharyngitis*, which may be termed remittent *pharyngitis*. The sufferer feels comparatively easy during the day, but an exacerbation invariably takes place in the evening, most distressing at about ten or eleven o'clock. If overlooked, or not properly treated, it may terminate fatally, especially in young children. Quinine is the remedy, and to it the disease yields very readily.

Pneumonia and *pleuritis* are of comparatively rare occurrence, and exposure to a draught of air, or cold bathing, the body being warm, will rather cause an attack of bilious remittent fever than an inflammation of either the lungs or pleura. Consumption is no uncommon malady; it comes to a fatal termination with great rapidity.

Ophthalmia, and the inflammation of the *cornea* especially, is rather frequent; its apparent cause is cold, as it generally occurs during the dry season, and consequent on exposure to chill and damp of night.

Hepatitis, and other complaints of the liver, are rather prevailing, and abscesses of that organ are often the consequence. Dr. Clark, an army surgeon, and a resident for many years in the different West India Islands, told me that he found inflammation of the liver more prevalent in Trinidad than in any other of the islands. A sort of atrophy of that organ is also a common disease; the result is a diminution in the quantity, with an alteration of the quality, of the bile, and a consequent diarrhœa, which may be said to be incurable. Chronic ulcerative *enteritis* is not unfrequent, and generally proves very dangerous.

Of all inflammations, however, the most common is that of the *lymphatic* glands and vessels; it often terminates in suppuration or in *elephantiasis*.

Ulcers, particularly of the legs and feet, are a disgustingly common sight. They attack almost exclusively those who travel or labour, as many of the poorer classes do, with bare feet or legs; but they may also generally and justly be considered as the consequence of neglect and filthiness. They are also frequently caused by certain insects, viz., *chigoes* and *bêtes-rouges*. The latter, almost invisibly small, attack the legs, producing much itching and cutaneous irritation; the former penetrate into the toes, heels, and soles of the feet, causing also an itching sensation, and, if not extracted in time, produce first a very small ulcer, which soon increases by its own extension, or the formation of fresh ones, so as almost to honeycomb the edges and surface of the soles. By constant irritation and exposure they assume an unhealthy appearance, the bones by degrees become diseased, whilst the inflammation sometimes extends to the whole foot; at this stage amputation is found to be the only remedy. Newly arrived Africans and Coolies, and even native labourers, are particularly liable to these ulcers.

Leprosy is, unfortunately, very prevalent, and of late years appears to be on the increase. There are two forms of that cruel and loathsome malady—the anæsthetic, or dry form, and the tubercular.

The primary apparent symptom of *anæsthetic* leprosy is a weakness of the extensor muscles of both the upper and lower extremities; as a consequence, a feebleness in walking is ordinarily experienced in one foot; sometimes in both. The fingers gradually curve in the palms of the hands. Any individual exhibiting these symptoms may be said to be *doomed*.

The first symptom of the tubercular form is a discoloration of the skin, together with the appearance on the loins and posterior part of the thighs of blotches; these are soon followed by the swelling of the fingers and the development of tubercles on the face and other parts.

Both forms of leprosy are, in my opinion, but a peculiar modality of *scrofulose*. Not only is leprosy hereditary, but, like consumption, it may be said to be incurable. The remark has also been made that seldom are there not instances of consumption in those families in which cases of leprosy have occurred. It is a popular opinion that venereal affections may have an influence in developing leprosy; and let me say that such opinion is rational, since those affections are well known to have a marked action on the glandular, osseous, and cutaneous systems.

It is much to be apprehended that the malady will continue to spread, and thereby entail an increasing amount of misery. Parents should, therefore, be awakened to the necessity of checking all predispositions to the lymphatic temperament by strict attention to food, habitation, cleanliness, and exercise in the open air.

An asylum was established under the government of Sir Henry McLeod, and is still maintained at the public expense, for the reception of lepers who are not in a position to support themselves. But as it is left to their option to enter the asylum or not, those only who make application are admitted, and of course lepers who prefer a mendicant life are seen going their rounds and begging, not only on the highways, but in the very streets of Port-of-Spain. Surely this ought not to be tolerated.

I say that lepers should not be allowed to be at large, at least such as are not in a position to maintain themselves.

The contagiousness of leprosy is at this present moment warmly discussed, and though generally decided in the negative, is nevertheless one of those points which should not be regarded as settled. *Adhuc sub judice lis est.* There are facts, few in number it may be, but there are facts which militate in favour of contagion; also parallel facts which seem to prove that segregation is a sure barrier against the propagation of the disease. But the important point is not whether leprosy is *contagious,* but under what condition it is *propagated.* There is no doubt that its *propagation* may be traced to the following causes or circumstances: 1st, Intermarriages of or with leprous persons; 2nd, Hereditary transmission; and 3rd, Co-habitation.

We find in the report of Dr. Tilbury Fox and T. Farquhar the following statements: "We have no doubt," they say, "that in Syria the leprosy is mainly propagated by the intermarriage of the leprous or those hereditarily tainted. Of 623 cases to which reference is made in the leprosy report of the College of Physicians, 287 were known to be hereditary; and it is no doubt probable that this is not a correct proportion, since leprous taints in families are as much as possible concealed." Dr. Davidson, speaking of leprosy in Madagascar, remarks, "It certainly deserves notice that, while the laws of Madagascar excluded leprous persons from society, the disease was kept within bounds, but after this law was permitted to fall into disuse, it has spread to an almost incredible degree. This is, no doubt, due in part to lepers being allowed to marry without hindrance; but the natives are also strongly impressed with the conviction that the disease is inoculable." But the series of facts reported by Dr. Hillebrand is more striking still. Leprosy was thought to be unknown in the Sandwich Islands till 1859, and cannot be traced back further than the year 1852, or at the earliest 1848. Dr. Hillebrand has been at Honolulu since 1851. As it appears, the disease was imported by the Chinese; in 1848 and in 1853 there existed only one single leper in Honolulu; in 1864 the number had increased to 250; within a period of ten years 1,570 lepers had been admitted into the asylum. In the year 1873 the total number amounted to 1,750. Dr. Hillebrand observes that "the natives are of a very social disposition, much given to visiting each other, and that hospitality is considered as a sacred duty by them. . . About one-fourth avow contact with other lepers as a cause." The reporters remark on this subject: "The disease arises in a clean nation, is unnoticed at first, and spreads slowly. . . It so happens that the hygienic state of the natives and the colony has improved, and not deteriorated. Animal food is within the reach of all; labour is in great demand and well paid for. The natives are clad now like Europeans; formerly scantily, if at all. The climate is, perhaps, the finest in the world; taxation is light. Yet, notwithstanding, leprosy spreads, and has spread, from and around known lepers as from centres of contagion." They wind up with the following remark: "It appears, then, that in searching for the cause of leprosy, we must make allowance for a large amount of *propagated* disease through intermarriage, hereditary transmission, and contact with the affected—for, in fact, disease propagated from individual to indiviual." Nothing, as it appears, has been attempted to check the spreading of the disease, and it has spread fearfully.

Let us [now turn to some other places where measures more or less stringent have been enforced, and let us compare the result. In New Brunswick the disease made its first appearance about the year 1815; in 1844 twenty-two persons afflicted with leprosy were found out, and most stringent measures immediately adopted. "Within the last ten or twelve years," says Dr. Gordon, "the disease has decreased, owing to the greater care and attention taken in separating the lepers. In 1863 the total number was twenty-two, and now cannot be more than forty."

In Curacao most stringent measures have been enforced for the last forty years, and the number of lepers in that island has for the last twenty years varied between ten and thirteen.

In another Dutch colony, Surinam, the adoption of similar measures had the same beneficial results, and the number of lepers is smaller there than it is in French or British Guiana.

Lepers, from the very nature of their malady, are shunned by those amongst whom they live, and cannot find employment; except such as have personal resources, they must become mendicants. There is no doubt that a country where leprosy prevails to any extent is more or less dreaded as a resorting place. I have, therefore, come to the conclusion that lepers should be sequestered and admitted into proper asylums, where they would be well housed, properly fed, and kindly nursed.

I will conclude with another quotation from Drs. Fox and Farquhar's report: "The presence of the disease (in Europe) was clearly in greatest part, if not entirely, to be accounted for by its introduction through the Crusaders from the East, and its propagation by intercommunication of the leprous with the healthy. The extinction of leprosy was effected, we believe, in all probability by the enforced segregation of lepers so sedulously ensured by the Church and State."

Yaws, Pians, Frambœsia.—This is another skin disease to which I am anxious to call the earnest attention of the Government.

Yaws is a disease *sui generis*, which is propagated by contagion, and has a tendency to spread among the people of the same locality, and may easily extend to remote districts by intercommunication. It is peculiar to the African race, and may be said to be an importation from Africa, where it widely prevails. The duration of the disease generally extends over several years, and I even doubt very much whether its cure is ever spontaneous. When properly treated it lasts from two to four months. People suffering from yaws do not exactly become disabled, but the disease tells sorely on their constitution, and they become enfeebled and apathetic; intercourse with them is carefully avoided by prudent persons. I am, therefore, led to advocate, with regard to yaws, the adoption of the same stringent measures which I have suggested with regard to leprosy. People suffering from yaws should be forcibly sent to hospitals or asylums, there to be treated. Except in a few exceptional cases, this measure should not be extended to persons in good circumstances, as they are anxious to be cured. As a rule, confinement could not be protracted beyond two or four months, after which time the patients would be restored to their families and occupations; and the far greater number of yaws patients being under the age of fifteen, sequestration could not be regarded by them as a very great hardship, especially in view of the great benefit conferred and the advantages resulting to the whole community.

Lunacy prevails to a very great extent. There were on the 31st December, 1878, in the Lunatic Asylum 182 unfortunate subjects, 94 males, 88 females; under care during the same year, 266; in 1880, 229.

For many years we had no asylum for the reception of lunatics, and those considered as dangerous were confined in a separate ward in the Royal Gaol. A colonial asylum, however, was established in 1858, and the lunatics removed thereto. In the year 1876 a comprehensive ordinance was passed, and provisions were made for the care and custody of all classes of lunatics.

I will conclude this notice of the principal diseases of the island by the following remark. Nearly all the diseases in Trinidad—no matter what may be the nature of the complaint—have a tendency to assume the remittent or intermittent form, as a complication.

Intermittent sore-throat and dysentery are very common, and remittent pneumonia is not rare. An individual accidentally confined to the sick room—for instance, from a broken leg or any other cause—is almost certain to get an attack of intermittent fever after having been laid up for two or three weeks. Quinine, combined with some other co-efficient medicines, is a certain cure.

I may say, in addition, that *sporadic* cases of disease are the exception, whilst the *epidemic* form the rule. It is evident that the latter type is determined by the existence of certain conditions which we cannot always discover or fully appreciate; but which, nevertheless, become apparent in the uniformity of their pathological effects. These conditions may subsist for a shorter or longer period; but, during the whole time of their persistence, prevalent diseases undergo some uniform modification, and also exhibit a few characteristic and identical symptoms which cause them to bear a sort of resemblance to each other, and for the cure of which the same treatment is generally successful, although otherwise the diseases may be of a different nature. And not only do these conditions vary at long intervals, but sometimes more than once in the same year; so that the treatment which has been most successful against fever in the commencement of the year, will not be so effectual at a later period.

The pathological phenomena exhibited in Trinidad are highly illustrative of the doctrine of *medical constitutions*, so admirably advocated by Hippocrates among the ancients, and by Sydenham, as well as others, among the moderns.

Immediately after, and on several occasions since emancipation, attempts were made for securing medical aid to the class of artisans in towns, of labourers located on estates, and of small settlers generally, on their contributing the small sum of ten cents per week for each working person—children and old people being attended gratuitously; incredible, however, as it may appear, these attempts have invariably failed. After a few weeks, or two or three months at the utmost, such of the subscribers who had not been subject to any attack during that period withdrew their subscription, on the pretext that it was not fair they should pay for the doctor while they enjoyed good health. But these very people, when ailing, are unwilling, and in most cases unable, to pay the fee; and they then throw themselves into the hands of male and female quacks, or *obeah* practisers, who bleed, cup, prescribe *nostrums,* and give their own personal attendance, exacting more or less from their dupes, according to their own *status* or reputation in quackery or obeahism. They are punctually paid—chiefly from a superstitious dread infused into the minds of their patients—but always retire in time from any unprofitable field. How many accidents occur, how many lives are lost, in consequence of this perverse neglect! As regards midwives, matters are still worse; for not only do they indulge in the most silly and disgusting manœuvres in ordinary instances, but they have recourse to most abominable practices—(such as flogging, suspension, &c.), in protracted cases of accouchement, the child or mother, or both, being but too often the untimely victims of these self-confident *commères*. Their directions regarding the management of infants, are barbarous in the extreme.

There is a provision in the Medical Ordinance, that no one shall practise as a midwife in Port-of-Spain without a license granted by the Medical Board; and, in the rural districts, without a certificate signed by the medical practitioner of the locality; but as the enforcement of the law is left to the midwives already licensed, and to the members of the profession, with the view only of affording them an opportunity of protecting their own interest, that wise proviso remains unexecuted. Surely the Government ought to interfere, if merely for the sake of the public welfare.

A ward of six beds for accouchement might be set aside at the Colonial Hospital; all women or young girls desirous of practising as midwives could be admitted as pupils and act as assistants. Lectures would be delivered to them, on regular days, and after a certain time they would be admitted to examination, and, if found qualified, would receive their license to practise in the colony. I once made the suggestion; it was received with approbation, but nothing has been done yet.

There are now in the island two hospitals, one in Port-of-Spain, equal, I believe, to any in the West Indies, and the other in San Fernando. They were built for the accommodation of 250 patients; it is seldom, however, when that number is not exceeded. There were in the Colonial Hospital, 31st December, 1877, 276 patients, and 105 in the San Fernando Hospital. Daily average in 1880, 433; San Fernando, 130. The Colonial Hospital staff consists of a resident surgeon, with two assistants, two dispensers, a consulting physician, and a consulting surgeon. At San Fernando, there are a resident surgeon, an assistant, and a dispenser.

No patients are admitted into the hospitals unless some party be responsible for the sum of one shilling a day, which is charged for every poor patient; two shillings are exacted for sailors, who are not considered as poor persons.

It was once proposed that each ward should have its own hospital; and this is still considered as feasible. Such proposition must have emanated from, and it can only be entertained by, persons who never reflected on the necessary expenses consequent on the establishment of a hospital, on however limited a scale. Besides bedsteads, bedding, cloth, and other requisites, a large annual sum is required for defraying the salaries of the medical attendant, superintendent, and dispensers; also the hire of a cook, washerwoman, and at least one nurse. Neither should it be overlooked that the smaller the establishment the larger the proportionate expenses. One hospital for each county is just the utmost required and possible. Numerous facts and extensive observations having proved the great influence that extraneous causes may exercise on the salubrity of towns and country districts generally, the importance of sanitary measures was at once rendered palpable; and, in our days, it is regarded as almost a necessity that a Board of Health consisting of special men should be established in all well-organised communities, for the purpose of watching over the public health. The general Board of Health of the island consists of eleven members, with the Governor as president. There are two sanitary inspectors appointed for the boroughs of Port-of-Spain and San Fernando: wardens are sanitary inspectors in their respective wards.

144 TRINIDAD.

RAINFALL.
Annual Rainfall, 1862-1876.—St. Ann's Observatory, County of St. George.

Year.	January. Inches	January. 100ths	February. Inches	February. 100ths	March. Inches	March. 100ths	April. Inches	April. 100ths	May. Inches	May. 100ths	June. Inches	June. 100ths	July. Inches	July. 100ths	August. Inches	August. 100ths	September. Inches	September. 100ths	October. Inches	October. 100ths	November. Inches	November. 100ths	December. Inches	December. 100ths	Total Rainfall in each year in inches.
1862	...	...	...	66	...	77	...	25	1	41	8	47	10	36	9	57	11	97	6	60	10	06	3	08	63·23
1863	1	54	2	71	1	45	...	85	1	26	9	12	10	12	10	53	12	11	6	24	4	30	6	57	66·83
1864	2	51	...	53	...	36	...	04	8	15	4	96	7	17	12	06	8	04	6	53	5	94	6	61	62·90
1865	2	62	3	20	1	07	7	98	3	22	5	64	10	35	14	83	7	32	14	62	4	81	9	62	85·29
1866	2	24	3	91	1	44	1	09	1	45	6	59	7	83	12	34	5	87	10	11	8	17	6	82	67·86
1867	1	31	3	36	...	83	...	32	2	33	5	30	12	20	15	21	10	45	7	87	...	67	2	71	66·56
1868	2	06	6	82	3	20	...	64	4	17	7	78	11	35	6	73	5	46	4	66	8	31	1	03	56·21
1869	...	08	...	93	...	74	...	41	...	69	5	62	10	17	8	74	8	86	5	15	6	30	5	87	53·46
1870	2	61	...	56	1	46	1	51	4	65	8	81	11	91	9	00	10	63	3	98	5	94	8	29	69·35
1871	6	62	...	40	2	89	...	92	3	97	8	84	11	73	12	97	10	87	4	37	10	73	3	27	74·09
1872	1	45	...	07	...	74	...	39	3	14	7	09	5	45	10	82	3	07	4	80	9	89	3	04	49·95
1873	1	78	1	08	1	98	5	53	...	...	4	31	5	04	8	37	5	80	10	34	3	48	1	31	44·02
1874	3	47	1	96	3	67	...	16	2	61	12	28	12	28	11	20	9	38	6	42	3	66	4	29	76·20
1875	3	39	...	91	...	56	...	42	2	61	4	15	12	62	7	22	11	95	10	85	3	74	2	48	60·90
1876	3	26	1	03	1	78	1	67	6	65	11	17	12	23	15	18	12	03	7	04	5	95	3	96	81·95
Aver. Monthly Rainfall to '73	2	25	1	85	1	41	1	32	2	87	6	87	9	47	10	93	8	12	7	10	6	55	4	85	978·89
Do. to '76	2	33	1	74	1	52	1	54	3	08	7	33	10	06	10	98	8	72	7	30	6	13	4	59	65·25

Hy. PRESTOE, Government Botanist.   Average Annual Rainfall for 15 years—1862-76

RAINFALL.

TABLE OF ELEVEN YEARS' OBSERVATION WITH THE RAIN-GAUGE AT THE ST. JAMES'S BARRACKS AND THE ROYAL GAOL.

MONTHS.	St. James's Barracks.										Royal Gaol.					General Average
	1825.	1826.	1827.	1847.	1848.	1849.	1850.	1851.	1852.	Average.	1850.	1851.	1852.	1853.	1854.	Average	
January .	"	2·42	2·42	5·54	3·69	1·95	2·97	1·14	4·77	3·21	3·72	2·99	2·95	0·52	0·83	2·20	2·70
February .	"	0·95	0·95	0·56	2·69	0·70	0·90	1·70	2·25	1·39	1·21	0·76	3·05	4·30	2·51	2·37	1·88
March . .	2·17	0·45	0·45	1·54	0·37	2·20	0·82	0·67	2·34	1·32	1·27	0·79	1·88	2·18	0·83	1·39	1·35
April . .	5·91	Monthly fall not specified.	0·25	1·82	2·22	2·90	3·97	0·07	2·00	2·39	6·78	1·79	2·25	1·36	0·00	2·44	2·41
May . . .	6·93		6·50	1·97	8·16	9·00	6·35	5·23	4·97	6·14	5·48	5·33	4·06	3·30	3·80	4·39	5·26
June . . .	7·20		8·86	3·91	6·53	13·67	8·89	11·36	6·28	8·83	6·18	12·35	5·03	6·20	4·90	6·93	7·63
July . . .	8·37		7·86	10·34	14·38	7·30	9·54	10·56	4·27	9·08	9·09	8·84	4·45	5·22	13·37	8·19	8·63
August . .	7·95		4·70	11·62	10·16	10·86	16·22	16·81	5·90	10·53	16·42	9·41	12·30	10·85	14·77	12·75	12·14
September .	7·82		6·60	12·39	4·23	5·24	7·70	15·60	3·64	7·90	5·15	11·55	4·80	6·67	7·41	7·12	7·51
October . .	6·84		9·73	9·36	5·66	10·15	7·57	10·47	5·92	7·36	7·43	9·40	4·15	10·43	6·93	7·67	7·51
November .	3·85		4·20	6·67	8·60	10·51	5·94	10·69	5·86	7·04	4·40	5·50	6·55	9·47	4·12	6·01	6·52
December .	5·89		5·40	3·70	7·60	5·20	2·95	6·84	9·92	5·94	4·59	5·55	9·00	8·74	9·03	7·38	6·66
	62·93	61·82	57·91	69·42	74·29	79·68	73·82	91·14	58·12	71·12	71·72	74·26	60·47	69·24	68·50	68·84	70·20

K

TEMPERATURE.

Temperature at the Botanic Gardens, St. Ann.

Thermometers.	Monthly Means.				Extreme.	
	Dry-bulb.		Maximum.	Minimum.	Maximum.	Minimum.
1880.	9.30 a.m.	3.30 p.m.	9.30 a.m.	9.30 a.m.	9.30 a.m.	9.30 a.m.
June	79·5	80·1	82·8	69·7	86·3	67·0
May	80·8	81·0	84·2	69·7	88·0	67·0
April	80·1	80·5	83·9	68·5	86·0	65·3
March	79·0	79·8	83·2	67·9	86·3	63·7
February	76·7	77·9	80·6	67·0	85·7	60·7
January	76·7	77·3	80·1	67·6	83·6	62·3
					86·0	65·2
1879.						
December	78·3	78·0	82·3	68·0	84·7	66·3
November	80·1	80·6	83·8	69·6	88·1	67·7
October	81·5	81·6	85·6	71·1	88·4	67·3
September	80·9	79·7	84·6	70·3	88·2	67·0
August	80·0	80·1	83·3	69·8	87·0	67·3
July	79·7	79·4	82·7	65·7	86·4	66·2
June	79·7	80·4	83·6	70·3	87·3	68·5
May	82·7	84·5	87·8	69·9	89·9	62·2
April	82·3	83·2	86·6	68·8	88·9	66·7
March	79·9	80·9	85·0	68·0	88·2	64·5
February	79·6	81·5	84·7	66·8	88·5	64·0
January	78·9	80·7	84·8	68·3	87·2	65·8
					87·7	66·1
Mean Maximum Average		...	...		88·1	
Mean Minimum Average		...	...			67·2
1878.						
December	80·5	82·0	85·4	69·8	87·4	65·3
November	81·7	81·8	85·9	70·2	88·0	67·6
October	83·0	81·5	87·7	71·4	89·9	68·0
September	82·2	82·8	87·3	71·4	91·3	68·7
August	80·7	80·1	84·4	70·8	87·0	69·0
July	80·3	81·4	84·4	71·2	88·3	68·2
June	82·0	81·9	85·0	71·1	88·5	68·7
May	83·3	83·9	87·2	72·2	91·9	67·7
April	85·2	86·5	90·5	73·0	95·5	64·6
March	84·6	85·6	90·3	68·4	93·8	64·6
February	82·3	83·9	88·4	67·5	90·7	64·7
January	80·7	82·1	85·5	67·3	88·0	60·1
					90·0	66·4

TEMPERATURE AT THE BOTANIC GARDENS, ST. ANN.—*continued*.

THERMOMETERS.	Monthly Means.				Extreme.	
	Dry-bulb.		Maximum.	Minimum.	Maximum.	Minimum.
1877.	9.30 a.m.	3.30 p.m.	9.30 a.m.	9.30 a.m.	9.30 a.m.	9.30 a.m.
December	81·1	80·7	84·9	70·2	87·6	67·6
November	82·5	81·7	86·7	71·1	88·8	68·9
October	83·0	82·0	87·0	71·3	89·9	69·4
September	83·0	82·7	87·6	71·5	90·1	67·0
August	83·3	82·6	86·7	70·8	88·9	67·4
July	82·5	81·7	85·7	71·1	88·7	69·1
June	81·8	81·7	86·3	71·7	90·7	67·5
May	84·7	84·2	88·6	71·8	92·0	68·3
April	83·0	83·0	87·6	70·0	90·4	66·7
March	81·7	81·4	86·5	68·0	90·7	61·0
February	81·1	82·6	86·3	65·3	89·0	60·3
January	79·6	80·0	85·0	66·6	86·9	61·1
					89·5	66·2
1876.						
December	80·3	80.9	85·7	67·8	87·3	64·9
November	83·1	83·0	86·8	72·3	89·1	69·8
October	81·2	82·2	85·9	71·6	88·4	67·0
September	80·6	81·9	85·6	72·7	88·9	71·0
August	79·9	81·0	84·7	71·5	88·0	69·9
July	80·5	81·5	84·8	72·0	87·2	70·5
June	79·7	81·2	84·3	72·5	89·6	69·5
May	80·7	83·5	85·6	72·1	89·0	69·5
April	80·6	83·0	85·6	70·2	89·0	67·9
March	78·5	80·9	83·7	70·1	87·0	66·3
February	78·1	80·6	83·1	68·3	86·2	63·7
January	78·9	80·3	83·3	71·0	85·3	69·3
					87·9	68·3
1875.						
December	78·4	80·8	84·2	70·0	86·3	67·6
November	79·7	81·3	85·2	70·8	88·0	68·3
October	79·5	81·4	85·4	71·4	88·4	69·7
September	80·0	81·6	85·8	71·7	89·1	69·3
August	80·7	82·4	86·3	72·0	88·5	69·9
July	79·9	81·5	84·8	71·9	88·9	69·4
June	80·6	83·1	85·9	71·7	88·3	69·3
May	80·0	83·0	86·0	70·9	88·4	68·0
April	80·7	82·9	85·4	69·1	88·7	65·0
March	78·3	80·6	83·7	68·4	86·3	64·9
February	78·2	80·1	82·7	67·0	84·8	61·7
January	77·6	79·6	82·8	68·7	85·9	65·2
					87·7	67·4

TEMPERATURE AT THE BOTANIC GARDENS, ST. ANN.—*continued.*

THERMOMETERS.	Monthly Means.				Extreme.	
	Dry-bulb.		Maximum.	Minimum.	Maximum.	Minimum.
1874.	9.30 a.m.	3.30 p.m.	9.30 a.m.	9.30 a.m.	9.30 a.m.	9.30 a.m.
December...	79·0	80·5	84·1	70·0	87·2	68·3
November...	80·0	81·7	85·4	71·2	88·4	68·3
October ...	81·0	82·2	86·2	72·5	89·3	69·3
September	80·5	81·0	85·8	72·5	88·3	70·5
August ...	80·1	81·6	85·2	72·2	88·3	70·2
July ...	80·5	80·9	84·5	72·0	88·3	70·0
June ...	80·1	81·1	84·5	71·8	88·3	68·3
May ...	81·0	83·5	86·1	71·3	89·0	68·3
April ...	79·4	80·9	84·1	70·4	87·1	67·4
March ...	78·9	81·1	84·1	70·0	86·3	65·9
February ...	78·3	80·9	84·0	69·6	86·4	65·9
January ...	78·1	80·4	83·7	...	86·3	65·9
					87·7	68·2
1873.						
December...	79·0	81·0	84·3	70·3	87·9	63·8
November...	80·0	81·8	85·5	71·3	88·4	68·0
October ...	80·8	82·9	85·9	72·3	89·9	70·2
September	81·5	82·9	86·7	72·5	89·4	70·1
August ...	81·3	82·6	86·0	72·1	89·0	70·1
July ...	81·0	83·0	86·2	72·3	89·4	70·3
June ...	81·3	83·1	86·6	72·3	89·4	69·9
May ...	83·3	85·7	89·2	71·6	91·2	67·4
April ...	80·2	83·2	86·6	69·3	89·9	65·3
March ...	78·3	80·9	83·7	68·2	87·3	62·5
February ...	76·9	79·8	83·0	67·3	86·2	64·3
January ...	77·0	80·6	83·1	68·7	87·2	64·6
					87·9	67·2
1872.						
December...	79·7	79·4	83·2	70·1	87·4	64·8
November...	79·6	81·0	84·3	74·9	87·7	67·4
October ...	81·5	84·1	87·3	72·9	90·1	69·8
September	81·4	83·4	87·5	73·3	90·0	71·2
August ...	80·1	81·2	85·3	72·3	88·7	69·0
July ...	80·5	82·7	86·0	72·2	88·8	68·8
June ...	79·8	81·8	84·2	72·4	88·1	69·3
May ...	82·4	83·7	86·8	71·8	91·6	69·7
April ...	80·2	83·3	86·2	69·9	88·7	65·2
March ...	79·6	82·8	85·5	69·3	87·9	67·2
February ...	79·0	82·6	85·1	69·1	88·9	64·5
January ...	77·2	80·5	83·6	69·1	85·9	65·0
					88·6	67·7

TEMPERATURE AT THE BOTANIC GARDENS, ST. ANN.—*continued.*

THERMOMETERS.	Monthly Means.				Extreme.	
	Dry-bulb.		Maximum.	Minimum.	Maximum.	Minimum.
	9.30 a.m.	3.30 p.m.	9.30 a.m.	9.30 a.m.	9.30 a.m.	9.30 a.m.
1871.						
December	78·4	80·4	83·7	70·3	86·2	67·3
November	79·9	81·5	85·4	71·2	88·7	67·7
October	81·7	83·2	86·2	73·5	89·3	69·8
September	80·7	81·7	85·6	72·6	89·0	69·8
August	80·7	81·7	86·1	73·5	89·0	70·9
July	79·7	81·2	84·6	72·1	88·2	70·2
June	80·9	82·5	85·7	73·2	89·5	70·7
May	82·1	84·6	87·6	71·3	90·1	69·3
April	80·4	83·4	86·2	70·1	89·6	67·0
March	78·6	81·6	84·6	69·7	88·3	63·1
February	77·2	80·4	83·1	69·5	85·9	65·5
January	78·6	80·1	83·1	70·9	85·5	68·5
					88·3	68·3
1870.						
December	77·8	80·1	83·5	70·5	86·6	66·2
November	80·6	81·9	85·8	71·7	88·7	70·2
October	81·2	81·9	86·0	72·6	91·0	70·0
September	82·9	82·3	83·7	71·1	88·7	67·8
August	80·3	81·1	84·3	73·0	90·6	70·0
July	79·8	81·3	83·5	72·4	86·4	70·2
June	79·1	80·3	83·3	72·4	86·2	69·3
May	80·7	82·7	85·0	72·8	87·5	70·2
April	79·9	82·5	84·9	69·8	87·1	65·7
March	78·4	80·0	82·6	70·1	85·6	67·5
February	78·0	79·8	83·2	70·1	86·7	66·9
January	77·2	79·3	81·9	70·5	83·9	64·2
					87·4	68·2
1869.						
December	78·6	80·5	82·9	71·7	86·1	68·6
November	80·0	81·5	84·0	73·0	87·2	70·2
October	80·9	82·4	84·8	73·9	87·5	68·3
September	81·1	81·8	84·9	73·8	87·9	70·3
August	80·5	81·6	84·1	73·6	87·3	71·5
July	80·8	82·4	84·7	73·9	87·4	71·8
June	81·7	82·6	85·6	74·8	89·2	72·0
May	83·4	86·7	88·7	74·2	90·8	68·6
April	82·1	86·1	88·0	72·6	90·1	68·0
March	79·2	81·7	83·8	70·3	85·6	67·6
February	79·3	82·0	84·1	69·4	87·2	65·4
January	78·5	81·0	83·3	70·1	85·8	66·5
	80·5	82·5	84·9	71·8	86·8	69·1

TEMPERATURE AT THE BOTANIC GARDENS, ST. ANN.—*continued.*

THERMOMETERS.	Monthly Means.				Extreme.	
	Dry-bulb.		Maximum.	Minimum.	Maximum.	Minimum.
	9.30 a.m.	3.30 p.m.	9.30 a.m.	9.30 a.m.	9.30 a.m.	9.30 a.m.
1868.						
December ...	79·0	81·6	84·2	71·1	85·9	67·1
November ...	81·4	82·2	84·9	73·3	86·7	70·6
October ...	80·9	82·6	85·2	73·7	89·8	71·1
September ...	81·3	82·5	85·3	74·7	87·1	70·3
August ...	80·8	82·4	84·7	73·6	86·9	70·8
July ...	79·9	80·8	83·3	76·3	85·9	70·6
June ...	80·4	81·5	84·2	73·8	87·3	69·0
May ...	80·4	82·8	84·8	72·3	86·5	69·6
April ...	80·2	82·9	84·8	70·7	87·1	67·8
March ...	78·9	81·0	83·1	71·1	85·5	67·0
February ...	77·4	80·1	81·6	69·0	85·0	64·4
January ...	78·2	80·2	81·8	71·1	85·3	67·8
	79·1	81·7	83·9	72·5	86·6	68·8
1867.						
December ...	79·5	81·3	83·1	71·7	84·8	69·2
November ...	80·6	82·8	84·7	74·6	86·2	68·9
October ...	80·6	82·2	84·4	73·3	85·7	70·2
September ...	81·2	81·9	84·3	74·3	86·4	71·8
August ...	80·3	85·3	83·8	73·2	86·3	71·0
July ...	80·5	81·3	83·8	75·9	85·7	71·2
June ...	80·6	82·9	84·9	73·9	87·2	71·0
May ...	82·5	84·6	86·5	74·2	89·7	71·5
April ...	80·3	83·4	84·8	71·7	87·8	69·3
March ...	78·2	81·3	82·6	70·8	85·9	67·8
February ...	77·8	79·3	81·5	71·5	84·3	68·4
January ...	77·7	80·3	82·1	70·0	84·1	66·3
	79·5	82·2	83·9	72·7	87·0	69·7
1866.						
December ...	79·2	80·0	82·1	72·9	83·9	68·3
November ...	80·2	81·2	83·4	72·7	85·6	68·9
October ...	80·1	82·0	83·9	74·2	86·1	70·0
September ...	81·4	82·6	84·6	75·1	86·7	68·3
August ...	79·9	81·5	83·4	73·5	86·4	71·6
July ...	80·3	81·6	83·6	73·2	85·7	70·8
June ...	80·4	82·1	84·0	74·0	86·7	71·8
May ...	81·6	83·9	85·8	73·5	89·0	68·7
April ...	80·5	82·2	83·8	72·6	86·2	69·1
March ...	78·6	80·1	81·7	71·2	84·5	65·0
February ...	76·9	78·9	80·4	71·0	82·8	67·5
January ...	77·8	79·7	81·2	70·8	83·3	67·1
	79·7	81·4	83·1	72·9	86·0	68·9

TEMPERATURE AT THE BOTANIC GARDENS, ST. ANN.—continued.

THERMOMETERS.	Monthly Means.				Extreme.	
	Dry-bulb.		Maximum.	Minimum.	Maximum.	Minimum.
	9.30 a.m.	3.30 p.m.	9.30 a.m.	9.30 a.m.	9.30 a.m.	9.30 a.m.
1865.						
December ...	78·8	80·3	82·0	71·5	84·4	66·3
November...	79·6	81·2	83·4	72·8	85·9	70·8
October ...	79·9	81·0	83·0	73·0	85·4	70·7
September	80·9	81·7	83·9	74·0	87·4	72·1
August ...	80·7	81·5	84·1	73·9	87·1	71·7
July ...	80·1	81·4	83·6	72·6	86·8	71·8
June ...	81·0	82·5	84·3	74·3	86·0	72·0
May ...	81·6	83·6	84·8	74·6	86·6	72·6
April ...	79·7	81·2	83·7	73·7	85·5	71·0
March ...	78·7	80·8	82·0	72·0	86·7	67·5
February ...	77·6	80·5	82·0	71·1	86·4	65·6
January ...	77·7	80·5	82·4	71·1	84·3	68·0
	79·7	81·3	83·2	72·9	86·1	70·0
1864.						
December ...	79·0	80·0	82·1	72·9	84·4	69·3
November...	80·6	81·7	83·8	73·4	86·3	71·0
October ...	81·3	82·9	84·7	73·7	87·3	68·0
September	81·5	81·7	84·7	74·8	86·4	71·4
August ...	79·6	80·5	82·7	73·5	85·5	71·3
July ...	79·4	80·7	83·1	73·5	85·9	71·0
June ...	79·9	81·7	83·6	74·4	86·0	71·0
May ...	81·8	84·4	86·0	74·2	89·0	70·3
April ...	80·3	83·7	85·1	71·6	88·0	68·7
March ...	78·0	81·6	82·7	68·8	86·2	67·1
February ...	75·8	79·4	80·3	69·5	82·5	66·8
January ...	76·1	79·5	80·1	70·6	82·2	68·0
	79·5	80·7	83·7	72·7	85·8	69·5
1863.						
December ...	77·1	79·4	80·7	71·7	83·9	69·0
November...	79·2	80·8	82·9	73·3	85·1	71·3
October ...	80·5	81·3	83·5	74·1	86·5	71·3
September	79·7	81·2	83·2	73·7	87·2	71·2
August ...	79·4	80·9	82·9	73·7	85·0	71·6
July ...	78·8	80·3	81·9	73·1	85·0	70·8
June ...	80·2	81·5	83·7	74·0	87·5	70·3
May ...	81·3	83·4	84·9	73·1	87·5	70·0
April ...	79·3	81·9	83·1	71·5	86·0	68·8
March ...	77·7	80·3	81·3	70·9	84·2	68·5
February ...	77·0	79·5	80·7	71·7	83·1	68·3
January ...	76·3	78·9	80·0	71·1	82·2	67·0
	78·8	80·8	80·7	72·6	85·2	69·8

TEMPERATURE AT THE BOTANIC GARDENS, ST. ANN.—*continued.*

THERMOMETERS.	MONTHLY MEANS.				EXTREME.	
	Dry-bulb.		Maximum.	Minimum.	Maximum.	Minimum.
1862.	9.30 a.m.	3.30 p.m.	9.30 a.m.	9.30 a.m.	9.30 a.m.	9.30 a.m.
December ...	78·0	80·2	81·9	72·3	83·4	67·0
November...	78·8	80·0	82·1	73·7	85·5	70·3
October ...	80·2	81·3	83·4	74·8	85·4	72·2
September	80·4	81·2	83·3	74·5	86·2	73·3
August ...	79·2	80·2	82·2	74·8	84·7	73·0
July ...	79·8	81·0	82·6	74·9	85·3	72·5
June ...	79·9	81·7	83·0	74·2	86·0	72·0
May ...	82·4	84·5	85·9	75·2	88·5	72·0
April ...	79·9	82·3	83·2	71·8	86·2	69·0
March ...	78·4	81·0	82·3	71·2	85·0	69·0
February ...	76·8	79·9	81·0	71·8	84·5	67·5
January ...	—	—	—	—	—	—
	79·4	82·1	82·8	73·6	85·5	70·7

CHAPTER V.

POPULATION—ETHNOGRAPHY—RELIGION—EDUCATION—CRIME.

THE history of the population of a country is at all times an interesting topic, but it becomes particularly so under certain circumstances. In this respect, a descriptive outline, or general view of the early settlement of Trinidad, and the gradual development of its population, is replete with interest, though, at the same time, involving a complicated problem which cannot be easily solved, from want of precise data and unprejudiced observation. I can, therefore, present only partial results; but such as they are, I hope they may prove useful and acceptable.

During the time of slavery, the records of births and deaths were kept with accuracy; but, immediately after emancipation, everything was neglected in this as in some other essentials. In the year 1847, however, an ordinance was passed for registering births and deaths, and a registrar-general appointed, as also local registrars. The provisions of the ordinance were made neither sufficiently comprehensive nor stringent, particularly as regards the registering of births; so that the ratio is not exactly what it appears to be in the yearly returns, the number of births particularly being in reality greater than that recorded. Neither is there any provision for distinguishing legitimate from illegitimate children—a classification most essential, in so far as it affords the means of testing the progress of a people in morals; for the proportionate number of marriages is, to a certain extent, one undoubted criterion of the morality of a population.

When first discovered by Columbus, Trinidad was apparently well populated, being then inhabited by various tribes of the Carib-Tamanaco family—Yaos, Salivas, Cumanagotos, Chaymas, Tamanacos, and others. These tribes did not receive from the invaders a much better usage than their unfortunate brethren of the other islands and the neighbouring continent. At a later period, however, their remnant groups were formed into several missions throughout the island—namely, at Tacarigua, Arouca, Caura, Cumana, Siparia, Montserrat, Savanna Grande, Arima, and Toco. But in Trinidad, as in other parts of the New World, the poor Indians have resisted the pressure of civilisation, and finally sunk under the ascendancy of a more intelligent race. In the year 1783, the indigenous population amounted to 2,032 souls, who, at the capitulation of the island, had declined, according to official returns, to 1,082 individuals. In the year 1830 there still existed 689 survivors of that race, the ratio of mortality being, among them, in the same year, 3·49, and that of births 3·75 per cent. At present there cannot be above fifty to one hundred Indians in the colony; so that the aborigines may be said to be almost extinct. The natural inquiry arises, what were the causes productive of this general decrease? Did they emigrate to the neighbouring continent, or did they die away in the island? It is highly probable that many did seek a refuge and a home in the virgin forests of Venezuela; but I also coincide in opinion with some judicious observers, who trace this extinction of our Indian population partly to the preference manifested by the Indian women towards the whites and the negroes, by whom they were kindly treated, whilst they were regarded by their husbands, of kindred race, more as slaves and beasts of burden than as equals or companions. As a consequence of those connections, there exists at present in the island a certain number of individuals of Indian descent, but of mixed blood.

I have already mentioned that it was only from the granting of the second cedula by the Spanish Government, in the year 1783, that Trinidad may date any ostensible settlement. Encouraged by the liberal offers made under that cedula, colonists began to throng from Grenada, St. Vincent, and the French islands, succeeded by a few refugees from San Domingo, with some *émigrés* from France, and even from Canada. Their example was followed by many respectable coloured families from the above-mentioned islands, who gladly availed themselves of the protection afforded, and the opportunity offered of bettering their condition, by becoming landowners in Trinidad; and as late as the year 1829, if my information is correct, there were scarcely more than six or eight white proprietors in Naparima, whilst nearly two-thirds of. Port-of-Spain belonged to the coloured class.

A few thousand Africans only had been directly introduced by slavers, the great majority of the labouring class having either accompanied their masters, or been clandestinely introduced by them, from the neighbouring islands. About 4,000 Africans, liberated from slavers, had been added to that class since emancipation; 24,280 Asiatics, East Indian Coolies and Chinese, formed part, in 1871, of our permanent population. The total population may be estimated at present at 154,000 souls.

The population of Trinidad, therefore, consists of a motley aggregation of Africans, Asiatics, Europeans, and a few individuals of American blood, together with their mixed descendants. By Africans, I mean not only those born in Africa, and introduced here as slaves or indentured labourers, together with the emigrants from the sister islands and the United States, but also those born in the island of African parents, and usually called Creole Negroes. The European section is formed of British (particularly Scotch), of French, Spaniards, a few Germans, and some Portuguese from Madeira, with the respective descendants of those various people. The Asiatics consist of Hindoos and Chinese, introduced partly at the public expense, as agricultural labourers, for the cultivation of staples, and especially of the sugar cane.

Heterogeneous as this population is, and has always been, the greatest harmony long prevailed among the different sections of which it was composed—a result which should be attributed to the liberal policy of the local government, and which, if it did not originate at the Colonial Office, was certainly sanctioned there. Equal protection was afforded to all, and all were content to live under what they considered to be really and truly a paternal rule. No distinction was drawn between those who were of foreign origin and those of British birth or descent; and I daresay no essential difference of feeling prevailed.

But there always had existed in the colony a party desirous to upset this state of things, and to establish a purely British —*i. e.*, Protestant—ascendancy. They were, for many years, too much in a minority to cause any uneasiness.

A variety of circumstances, however, at length combined to

strengthen that party, which was led by men who knew how to turn every event to the best advantage. General embarrassment, if not utter ruin, had resulted from the emancipation of the slaves; and the Creole proprietors found themselves either deprived of their estates, or suffered nominally to retain them as the mortgagees of capitalists in Great Britain, who, with scarcely an exception, were Protestants. In either case, the prestige and influence of the class were utterly lost.

The first overt act of those who longed for a change was the introduction, under the government of Sir Henry McLeod, of Ordinance No. 6, 1844, known as the "Ecclesiastical Ordinance." By this ordinance, the laws, ordinances, and canons ecclesiastical of England were declared to be in force in the colony; and the Church of England became the Established Church of Trinidad, in defiance of the long-established custom which tacitly admitted the Roman Catholic Church as the Church of the island, it being that of the immense majority. Trinidad was then placed under the spiritual charge of the Bishop of Barbadoes.

In 1855, Sir Charles Elliott, the then Governor of the colony, went a step further, and did not hesitate to show unmistakable signs of active hostility towards the Catholics, nearly all of whom were of foreign descent.

He was succeeded by Governor Keate, who held on the same course; and their narrow and most injudicious policy produced much social as well as political disunion.

Fortunately for Trinidad, that policy, which had been partially modified by the late Lord Canterbury, was completely reversed by Sir Arthur Gordon, his successor, and the feeling of antagonism which it had created almost immediately disappeared.

But I regret to be obliged to remark that there appears to be a tendency in certain quarters to revive, in its most mischievous form, the policy inaugurated under Sir Henry McLeod, and which we hoped had been crushed by Sir Arthur Gordon.

That such should be the case is deeply to be regretted. In a colony like Trinidad diversity of races will probably continue to exist for many years—a contingency which some may deplore, but which should not disturb their equanimity. In fact, it would be a most suicidal policy on the part of the Government to allow, much less to encourage, any one class of colonist to arrogate to itself a superiority over the rest. Mere difference of origin, or religion, or of social habits, should not be permitted to raise barriers between different sections of the community; still less should they form an excuse for hedging in a few as a superior caste.

No matter whence their ancestors came (and many of them can point to most respectable connections in the Old World), the descendants of the first settlers in Trinidad cannot forget that their fathers were the pioneers of civilisation in the island; that the dense wild forest was first cleared by their energy and perseverance; and that there was a time when they had their full share of influence in the affairs of the colony. They form, even now, the great majority of the resident proprietary body, and as such have every claim to be treated with consideration, instead of being looked down upon by those who, at least, are but transient residents.

It is not, perhaps, unnatural that those who consider themselves as the English *par excellence* should deem ascendancy and the largest share of the loaves and fishes their birthright; but it does not by any means follow that they are right in their pretensions. They should do well to remember what has occurred in other dependencies of Great Britain which once owed allegiance to other flags.

Whenever an attempt has been made to establish a spurious aristocracy of nationality, the result has invariably been disunion, jealousy, and disappointment. But should they rest content with the traditions of our own colony, they may find that even in their own days such attempt, though successful for a time, was eventually defeated, although carried on by men superior to them in position, in talent, and, above all, in personal influence. Let us toil together in peace, and side by side; it will be for the advantage of all.

The entire population of the island, according to the census taken on the first of April, 1881, was estimated at 153,128 souls, of which 83,716 were males and 69,412 females. It was classed as follows: Under ten years, 32,724; from ten to twenty, 27,717; twenty to forty, 59,994; forty to sixty, 25,673; sixty to upwards, 5,577; not described, 1,443.

In 1871 the population amounted to 109,638, of which

60,405 were males and 49,233 females: 1861, 84,438—males 46,074, females 38,364.

The national distribution was as below:—

	1881	1871
Natives of Trinidad	82,553	56,692
,, Africa	3,035	4,250
,, Asia	37,280	24,280
,, British Colonies	24,047 }	
,, Venezuela	2,277 } 30,259	
,, Other parts	2,873 }	
,, United Kingdom	1,06 }	

If we add to Asiatics the children born in the colony of Indian parents, and who are classed as natives, we shall have a grand total of 50,000 in this class.

The increase of Asiatics may be calculated, in round numbers, at 13,000; that of emigrants from other parts, especially the British Colonies, is about 10,240.

The few aborigines yet remaining in the colony are leading an isolated life in the forests, depending for their subsistence upon hunting and fishing—in short, retaining their ancestral habits. A few families of Indian descent are still, however, to be met with in different parts of the island, all speaking the Spanish language, and having preserved Spanish habits—fond of smoking, dancing, and all kinds of amusements, but, above all, of the *dolce far niente*. They are, generally, owners of *conucos*, that is to say, of a few acres of land, which they cultivate in provisions and coffee, but particularly in cacao.

Newly imported Africans are, generally speaking, industrious and laborious, but avaricious, passionate, prejudiced, suspicious, many of them still adhering to heathenish practices. The *Yarribas* or *Yarrabas* deserve a particular notice. They are a fine race, tall and well proportioned; some of them with fine features, intelligent, reflective, and can appreciate the benefits of civilisation and Christianity. They are laborious, usually working for day-wages on estates, but preferring job-work. The women are mostly occupied in petty trade and huckstering; some also in the culture of ground provisions: their houses are comfortable, and kept in perfect order within. In character they are generally honest, and in disposition proud, and even haughty; so that the cases are rare where a *Yarraba* is brought before the magistrate for theft, breach of contract, or other misdemeanour. They are besides guided, in a marked degree, by the sense of association; and the principle of combination for the common weal has been fully sustained wherever they have settled in any numbers; in fact, the whole *Yarraba* family in the colony may be said to form a sort of social league for mutual support and protection.

The emancipated class and their descendants bear the distinctive characteristics of the three European nations with which they were more intimately connected; and these characteristics are, to a certain extent, borne out by the external appearance and deportment of the three specimens: the French negro resembling in these respects a French European; the Spanish, a Spaniard; and the English negro, an Englishman. There are, however, some general traits which may be taken as an index to the distinctive peculiarities in the character of the emancipated class.

For too many years the recollections of slavery seemed to have acted on their faculties as an incubus, and for many years they remained, in general, averse to predial occupations, and to the hired labour of the cane fields especially. Lately, however, there has been an improvement in this respect: they no more nourish a sort of repugnance to all kinds of agricultural pursuits, giving preference and precedence to any petty trade and pedling occupation or handicraft. This improvement I mainly attribute to the example set by labourers from the sister colonies, who come here every year to assist in taking up the crop; also by the class of small proprietors, who cultivate their own grounds and can show their profits. They begin to understand that agricultural occupations are not degrading whilst they can be made profitable.

Excessively fond of display and of appearing to the best advantage in dress, they mistake vanity for that rational pride which ought to govern human actions. Singularly improvident, they do not seem to think for a moment of the necessity of economy, in order to meet and alleviate cases of sickness, accidents, or other contingencies of the future. They are indolent, and great amateurs of amusements; pleasure is apparently their main affair, for which they will neglect more serious occupations; and yet it cannot be said that the negro is lazy, as he can and does work hard at times. He is generally of gay disposition, but highly sensitive, and will raise quarrels for a trifle, especially if incited by friends. He is capable of gratitude and self-devotion; capable also, when required, of generous efforts. Being robust and abstemious, he can endure privations and climatic exposure, I will not say with fortitude, but with an apathy that is almost inconceivable. I could say, with some reason, in the year 1856, that few individuals among the emancipated had sensibly progressed; but I can now record that a marked change has been worked since, and if the lowest among them may be said to be still grossly ignorant in respect of their social and religious duties, even of their own true interest, I gladly recognise that for the last twenty years the emancipated, as a class, have progressed most satisfactorily. Though inconstant and inconsistent, the African is, nevertheless, susceptible of improvement to an extent which, perhaps, has not been fairly tested. He is, I consider, a being of pre-eminently religious feelings; though defective in the powers of reflection, he is possessed of a quick intelligence.

The descendants of the emancipated, and young men of colour in general, manifest a strong desire to gain public estimation, and look anxiously to social advancement. They are ambitious of success, and have proved that they can attain it. Not a few occupy respectable positions in the public service. They are particularly anxious to become enlisted in the liberal professions; and the white Creoles should look to them as not unworthy antagonists in the field of competition.

Immigrant Asiatics at present form the great body of our available agricultural population, and are almost the sole resident labourers on sugar and cacao estates.

The Chinese are few in number—about 500. Of them, as far as observation goes, it may be said that they are stubborn, and prone to suicide; but they are highly intelligent and discerning, steady labourers, and well versed in the tillage of the soil; in fact, they may be considered as the best gardeners in the colony. They are those who supply our markets with vegetables.

The Hindoos, such as I have been able to observe them in the colony, are a mild and timid race, obsequious, wanting in firmness and perseverance, more prudent and wily than energetic and straightforward. They are intelligent, rather industrious and saving; more manageable and steady, they are not so robust as the Africans. They have no dislike to agriculture. A distinctive trait in the character of the Coolie is insincerity; one cannot depend upon what he says. The private life of those who have not yet been influenced by civilisation is, generally, depraved and disgusting. It is highly encouraging, however, to find that not a few among those who have settled in the island have adopted a better mode of living; the change is especially remarkable among the women. In fact, the contrast between the *new* and the *old* Coolies is very striking in many respects. They are much attached to their cattle, especially the cows, and from them mainly the public get their supply of milk. A Coolie will never sell any of his cattle to the butcher for slaughter.

The Hindoos of the Mahometan faith have been found, on the whole, more intelligent, active, and industrious and orderly than those of the Gentoo and other castes of India. Many among them can read and write. These Asiatics still adhere to their own peculiar creeds and habits; they even continue, with rare exceptions, to wear their country costume, and but few have become converts to Christianity, or have persevered in the new faith. Sometimes they ask to be baptized, with a view to secure some worldly advantages, and persevere in their old practices. This may be attributed partly to the unfortunate arrangement which insures their return to India after a term of ten years' residence in the colony. They are thus naturally led to retain most of those habits which they expect to resume in full force on revisiting their native land. The Coolies seem disinclined to send their children to the public schools, except they are established purposely for them.

Notwithstanding the surrounding influences of civilisation, the belief in sorcery is generally and strongly entertained among the more ignorant classes of the population, either Asiatics or Africans. This is a fact which is deplorable indeed, but which I should not let pass unnoticed. Obeahism, or witchcraft, is still practised by many unprincipled individuals of both sexes who know that they will acquire influence and derive undu advantage by inspiring the poor, the ignorant, and the credulous with a dread of their practices, however disgusting or foolish. Sir Emerson Tennent had the opportunity of observing, in Ceylon, the same practices; and I believe that I cannot do better, with reference to this painful subject, than to quote what he relates in his book on that island:—"The professors of sorcery," he remarks, "turn the practice of witchcraft and

L

charms to lucrative account, pandering to the worst passions of degraded humanity, by the secret exercise of pretended arts and the performance of revolting ceremonies.

"In December, 1848, the police vidahn of Vannerpoone, in the suburbs of Jaffna, came to the magistrate in much mental agitation and distress, to complain that the remains of his son, a boy of about eight years of age, which had been buried the day before, had been disinterred during the night, and that the head had been severed from the body, to be used for the purposes of witchcraft. Suspicion fell on a native doctor of the village, who was extensively consulted as an adept in the occult sciences; but no evidence could be produced sufficient to connect him with the transaction.

"The vidahn stated to the magistrate that a general belief existed among the Tamils in the fatal effects of a ceremony performed with the skull of a child, with the design of producing the death of an individual against whom the incantation was directed.

"In this instance a watch was kept upon the proceedings of the suspected doctor, and it was ascertained that he and his family were engaged in the most infamous practices. His sons were his assistants in operations similar to that which has been described, and in the preparation of philters to facilitate seductions, and medicines for procuring abortion. . . . . The skulls of infants were applied, as occasion required, for the composition of love potions and the performance of incantations.

"In the course of the following month, a second complaint against the same individual was brought before the magistrate of Jaffna, to the effect that, on a stated morning, he had murdered an infant, in order to possess himself of his head, and that at the moment of bringing the charge a second child was detained in his dwelling, and destined for a similar fate. . . . . Unfortunately the criminal was permitted to escape. His papers were seized by a magistrate, among which was a volume of recipes for compounding nefarious preparations and poisons; and along with these a manuscript book containing the necessary diagrams and forms of invocations to 'Siva the Destroyer;' for every imaginable purpose: 'to seduce the affections of a female,' to effect a separation between a husband and wife, to procure abortion, to possess with a devil, to afflict with sickness, and innumerable directions for procuring the death of an enemy. In this remarkable treatise on domestic medicine there was not one single recipe for the cure of disease amongst the numerous formulas for its infliction; not one instruction for effecting a harmless or benevolent purpose, amidst diagrams and directions for gratifying the depraved passions, and encouraging the fiendish designs of the author's dupes."

To seduce the affections of a female, to effect a separation between a husband and wife, to possess with a devil, to afflict with sickness, to procure the ruin or the death of an enemy—such are the objects of Obeahism in Trinidad, as they are of sorcery in Ceylon. The practices are not so vile and monstrous here as in Ceylon; but they may be said to be highly foolish and absurd. There are, unfortunately, many who actually believe in the efficacy of the incantations performed. Such efficacy, as we must suppose, results from natural, but most nefarious, practices. Poison—in most instances vegetable—is administered to the party whom they wish to get rid of. The health is destroyed, and death may ensue. If the object is the ruin of an enemy, poison is given to his fowls, to his cow, or donkey. Of cours? the poor man becomes nervous and discouraged at his loss, and abandons his holding, or sells it at a loss. It is only natural that practices of Obeah should inspire the most ignorant people with dread; and such dread will always act as an obstacle to discovering and bringing to punishment the impostors. And yet, though thus dreaded, they are held in contempt, and shunned by the people generally. Some pretend to cure diseases; they invariably declare that such diseases are produced by wicked practices, and, of course, can be cured only by the administration of medicines aided by incantations; and such incantations are accordingly performed, with the accompaniment of cabalistic words and signs. The medicines are prepared beforehand, and administered in secret—sometimes in a dark room—when the poor deluded victim will be made to cast up centipedes, scorpions, spiders, pins, &c., to the great amazement of those present, and the entire satisfaction of the poor dupe. Some of those quack doctors and Obeah practisers have a wide reputation, and practise extensively; they are generally negroes from Africa.

The least that I can say of such people is this: they are impostors of the worst kind, having mainly one object in view—obtaining money under false pretences. Some even will not recoil from administering poisons to satisfy their hatred, or with the view of proving their power. I contend that, in general, the magistracy makes too light of Obeahism.

The Europeans and their descendants do not offer any peculiar traits beyond those which prevail among the nations of their respective ancestries. In the mass, however, Creoles may be characterised as improvident, fickle, and by no means exempt from the censure I have attached to the emancipated class—that of disliking agriculture, and other occupations which require exertion and steadiness of purpose.

It is impossible correctly to trace the progress of population in Trinidad, from the capitulation to the present day; and I have no documents wherefrom to ascertain even the increase of that population by natural causes. Captain Mallet's official return states the population to have been in 1797, 17,718; viz., 2,151 whites, 4,476 free coloured, 10,009 slaves, and 1,082 Indians. Previous to the cedula of 1783, it was 2,763: whites, 126; free people of colour, 295; slaves, 310; Indians, 2,032. In 1790 it had increased to a total of 10,422. I find in Alcedo's dictionary that, in the year 1805, it amounted to 25,245 souls, divided as follows: whites, 2,261; people of colour, 3,275; slaves, 19,709. It appears also that in the year 1825 it had increased to 43,262 inhabitants.

The census of 1851, although incorrect in several minor respects, may be regarded, however, as containing a fair return of the population of the island, which then amounted to 69,600 souls. Ratio of births, 3·50 per cent., or one birth for every 2,850 inhabitants. Population, according to census of 1861, 84,438; 1871, 109,638; 1881, 153,128.

The following Tables show the number of births in the island for two periods, from 1848 to 1853, and from 1870 to 1879, for each quarter in every year, and the ratio of males to females.

TABLE OF BIRTHS, 1848—1853.

Years.	MALES Registered Quarter ending				Quarterly Totals.	FEMALES Registered Quarter ending				Quarterly Totals.	Yearly Totals.
	Mar.	June	Sept.	Dec.		Mar.	June	Sept.	Dec.		
1848	148	256	280	274	958	124	256	277	273	930	1,888
1849	266	289	294	304	1,153	279	253	309	307	1,148	2,301
1850	245	315	315	270	1,145	305	271	270	236	1,082	2,227
1851	308	310	301	308	1,227	294	309	341	270	1,214	2,441
1852	292	290	316	303	1,201	260	256	312	306	1,134	2,335
1853	309	289	312	304	1,214	268	314	353	278	1,213	2,427
1854	—	—	—	—	—	—	—	—	—	—	2,828
Grand Totals	1,568	1,749	1,818	1,763	6,898	1,530	1,659	1,862	1,670	6,721	16,447

TABLE OF BIRTHS, 1870—1879.

Years.	MALES Registered in the Quarter ending the last day of					FEMALES Registered in the Quarter ending the last day of					MALES AND FEMALES Registered in the Quarter ending the last day of				
	March.	June.	Sept.	Dec.	Total.	March.	June.	Sept.	Dec.	Total.	March.	June.	Sept.	Dec.	Total.
1870	377	374	460	496	1,707	407	380	385	525	1,697	784	754	845	1,021	3,404
1871	571	467	445	503	1,986	510	444	385	517	1,856	1,081	911	830	1,020	3,842
1872	483	539	462	467	1,951	429	551	494	466	1,939	912	1,090	956	932	3,890
1873	568	582	526	596	2,272	516	538	525	526	2,105	1,084	1,120	1,051	1,122	4,377
1874	577	557	522	559	2,215	517	535	450	519	2,021	1,094	1,092	972	1,078	4,236
1875	528	524	502	525	2,079	492	481	450	494	1,917	1,020	1,005	952	1,019	3,996
1876	598	581	508	584	2,271	618	590	517	610	2,335	1,216	1,171	1,025	1,194	4,666
1877	581	603	537	608	2,329	570	556	516	625	2,267	1,151	1,159	1,053	1,233	4,596
1878	549	590	546	588	2,273	566	544	537	541	2,188	1,115	1,134	1,083	1,129	4,461
1879	657	541	612	702	2,512	557	566	597	680	2,400	1,214	1,107	1,209	1,382	4,912
Totals	5,489	5,358	5,120	5,628	21,595	5,182	5,185	4,856	5,502	20,725	10,671	10,543	10,036	11,130	42,380

By adding the totals of these two periods we have, for sixteen years, 55,239 births. By referring to the above tables, we find that out of a grand total of 55,239 births, there are 26,993 males and 27,446 females; so that the males are to the females as 100·68. Hufeland pretends that the ratio of the sexes for the whole world is as 21 males to 20 females, or as 105 and 100. The result in Trinidad is somewhat contrary to what has been observed elsewhere; the number of males being always greater than that of females.

By reference to the above tables we have the number of births per quarter, and therefore can ascertain the months wherein a larger average of births takes place.

Thus we have 13,769 for the first quarter ending 31st March; 14,223 for the second quarter; 13,706 for the third quarter; and 14,563 for the fourth quarter.

The months showing a majority of births are therefore October, November, and December; July, August, and September.

MARRIAGES.

Table showing the number of marriages throughout the first period:—

1848.	1849.	1850.	1851.	1852.	1853.	1854.
364	324	358	391	382	329	1,625

Table showing the number of marriages during the second period:—

1870.	1871.	1872.	1873.	1874.	1875.	1876.	1877.	1878.	1879.	1880.	1881.
369	416	477	453	391	449	437	465	436	585	632	559

Average for the twelve years, 472. The average of six years for the first period was 360. I have not included in my calculation the year 1854, which exhibits 1,625 marriages, a very startling result if it could not be easily accounted for. But in this memorably calamitous year (1854), cholera raged in the colony for about four months, and not only were several persons married *in articulo mortis*, but the terror created by hourly impending danger of almost sudden death induced many who were living in concubinage to submit to the holy rite; hence the disproportionate number of marriages in that year. The population being 109,638 in 1871, and the number of marriages

416, we have one marriage per 263 inhabitants. In England the ratio is 1 per 134. The number of marriages being 632 the year preceding the census, we have 3·96 per 1,000.

Mortality.—This is a subject of the greatest importance, and for the analyses of which we fortunately possess correct and precise data.

TABLE SHOWING THE NUMBER OF DEATHS QUARTERLY, FOR BOTH SEXES, OVER A PERIOD OF SIX YEARS.

Years.	MALES Registered Quarter ending				Quarterly Totals.	FEMALES Registered Quarter ending				Quarterly Totals.	Yearly Totals.
	Mar.	June	Sept.	Dec.		Mar.	June	Sept.	Dec.		
1848	275	324	314	303	1,216	159	214	264	206	843	2,059
1849	327	303	340	271	1,241	221	189	233	191	834	2,075
1850	322	328	375	321	1,346	263	236	307	208	1,014	2,360
1851	285	397	414	308	1,404	245	321	405	204	1,175	2,579
1852	269	379	358	263	1,269	193	224	263	214	894	2,162
1853	322	382	573	381	1,598	229	244	337	264	1,074	2,672
Grand Totals.	1,800	2,113	2,374	1,847	8,074	1,310	1,428	1,809	1,287	5,834	13,907

Table showing number of deaths for ten years (1870 to 1879):

1870.	1871.	1872.	1873.	1874.	1875.	1876.	1877.	1878.	1879.
3,085	3,370	6,366	3,311	3,449	3,745	3,972	3,792	3,964	3,738

Adding the totals of the two periods (sixteen years), we have 52,700 deaths, or a yearly average of 3,293·75; 2,318 in the first period, and 3,879 in the second period. If we take the mortality in 1871 (the year of the census), we have one death in 30·73 inhabitants, or again 30·73 per 1,000. If I omit the mortality of the year 1872, during which a most severe epidemic of small-pox prevailed, we have for the nine years an average of 3,615 deaths. If we take the mortality in 1880 (the year preceding the census), we have the proportion of 2·55 per cent. Dr. Gavin, in his "Report on the Sanitary Measures necessary to be taken in the Colony of Trinidad," June, 1852, states that the mortality among children under five and ten years is the true cause of the excessive mortality of Port-of-Spain, it being one in every 17·10. "However, when further inquiries are made," says the learned inspector, "it is found that the mortality in Port-of-

Spain among adults is not very dissimilar to the mortality of London."

If we take the mortality of 1871 (the year of the census), we have rural districts' population, 81,067, Port-of-Spain and San Fernando, 28,566, or 2,491 for the rural districts and 868 for the two towns.

As regards the influence of months on the general mortality, we have the following results: First quarter, 10,147; second quarter, 8,304; third quarter, 10,143; fourth quarter, 9,578; so that the months of the first quarter, or January, February, and March, present a greater mortality; the lesser mortality would be in April, May, and June.

With regard to sexes, the number of deaths in the ten years is: Males, 22,447; females, 16,345; yearly average, 2,244·70, and 1,634·50.

The following Table will show the influence of age on the mortality:

PORT-OF-SPAIN AND SAN FERNANDO.

Periods.	Under 10 years.	10 to 20.	20 to 30.	30 to 40.	40 to 50.	Above 50.	Yearly Totals.
1848	270	69	152	133	152	204	980
1849	224	89	168	137	118	128	864
1850	286	91	138	110	104	125	854
1851	506	64	116	122	97	142	1,047
1852	234	62	126	126	91	166	805
Grand Totals	1,520	375	700	628	562	765	4,550

Out of a grand total of 4,541 deaths, 1,520 took place under ten years, which gives the ratio of 33·47 per cent., or one-third; from ten to twenty, 366 or 8·05; from twenty to thirty, 700, or 15·41, nearly double; between thirty and forty, 625, or 13·38. The greatest mortality is under ten years; then, successively, between twenty and thirty, thirty and forty; least between ten and twenty. These results coincide pretty exactly with those obtained in Europe, Cuba, New York, and Baltimore. Here, as in those places, the period between twenty and thirty is that of the passions and adventurous life.

The following Table, drawn up by the Registrar-General,

shows the rate of mortality from birth to the age of ten years:

Periods.	Under One Month.	1 to 3.	3 to 6.	6 to 12.	1 to 5 Years.	5 to 10.	Yearly Totals.
1848	58	8	19	25	72	18	200
1849	37	11	19	27	107	33	234
1850	52	13	30	38	118	35	286
1851	45	20	30	51	294	65	505
1852	61	10	18	38	99	25	251
Totals of Ages	253	62	116	179	690	176	1,476

Thus, of the grand total of 1,476 deaths, 610 took place under twelve months, which gives the rate of one death per 2·42—that is to say, that of 242 deaths which took place from birth to ten years, 100 occurred between the ages of one and twelve months. The rate is very moderate between one and three, and also between three and six months, but very great between one and five years, this being not only the period of weaning, but also that wherein children are subject to the many diseases incident to infancy and early youth.

When seeking to establish a comparison between the number of births and deaths, we come to the following results:—

Births (10 years) 42,220
Deaths   „   38,792

Difference 3,428

The difference, 3,428, is in favour of births—that is to say, that within ten years the population has increased from natural causes by nearly 343 every year. It may be remarked, that in the year 1872 the mortality was double that of the other years; in that year, 1872, the colony suffered severely from an epidemic of small-pox.

I wish now particularly to call attention to a few conclusions which naturally flow from the above statistical facts.

The number of females being in the whole island 69,413, and that of males 83,716, it is evident that, *cæteris paribus*, the ratio of births must be smaller in Trinidad than in other countries where the sexes are equal, or nearly so. In the year 1881, the population was distributed as follows in the counties:—St. George, 43,559 males, 38,156 females; Victoria, 22,446 males, 16,887 females; Caroni, 13,946 males, 9,533 females.

A rather interesting fact is the great overplus of females residing in town as compared with the number of males. The towns of Port-of-Spain and San Fernando exhibit the following figures:—Males, 18,443; females, 19,750; rural districts— males, 65,273; females, 49,662; the proportion being 106 females to 100 males in the towns, and 100 males to 76·08 females in the rural districts. For the year 1851, the proportion was, in towns, 100 females to about 74 males; and in the rural districts, 100 males to about 75 females. This disproportion between males and females I consider to be very deplorable, both in a moral and social point of view.

The gathering of females in towns may be explained by the following considerations:—Females are customarily more employed as household servants than males, as they are satisfied with lesser wages, and indoor occupations being more in accordance with the habits of their sex, they not only prefer that service, but are more at home, as it were, in the performance of its duties. There is, in addition to these, a very large proportion of washerwomen, seamstresses, hucksters, cigar makers, and petty traffickers, who more than compensate for the number of tailors, shoemakers, and other artisans of the male sex. On the other hand, it cannot be denied that many of the female sex resort to towns for the purpose of either private or public prostitution.

The larger number of males in the rural districts evidently results from the disproportion of sexes among the imported immigrants.

I beg to be allowed to borrow from the Reports of the late Protector of Immigrants, Dr. Mitchell, some very interesting facts in connection with the mortality of our Indian labourers:— In 1872, the mortality was 302 on a total of 7,949 under original contract, or 3·8 per cent. Total average death-rate on contract servants of all classes, 380 on 11,017·02, or 3·2 per cent. Death-rate on children, 1·9—on boys, 2·2; on girls, 1·6.

1872–1873: Death-rate, 3·17. Children, 2·05: boys, 2·3; girls, 1·8; percentage of five years for both sexes, 1·04. It would seem that, in the Ward of Tacarigua (a healthy district), the comparative mortality among Coolies and Creoles would be 10 adult Creoles to 3 adult Coolies; 9 Creole children to 1 Coolie child; 8·33 Creole infants to 1 Coolie infant.

1873–1874: Mean death-rate :—Adults, 3·7; children, 2·1. The total mortality of the 22,000 Indians resident on estates may be calculated at 2 per cent. 1878–1879: 163 deaths on 8,384 contract servants, or 1·34 per cent of the adults. On 52 estates out of 105, the death-rate was only 0·5 per cent.

If we take the quinquennial period terminating on 30th September, 1879, we have the following results :—

Year.	Immigrants.	Deaths.	Percentage.
1875	10,155	296	2·90
1876	9,422	289	3·06
1877	9,020	270	2·99
1878	8,515	201	2·36
1879	8,384	163	1·94
Mean rate for the five years			2·65
Average of eight years			2·72

I unhesitatingly endorse the remark of Dr. Gavin, that the mortality (5·58 per cent.) among children under five and ten years is the true cause of the excessive mortality of Port-of-Spain; but the remark is evidently not applicable to Indian children, the mortality among them being only 1·94 per cent.

Let me observe, in explanation, that the Coolies located on estates receive regular medical attendance, and the required medicines and food when sick. Young children are placed under the care of some nurse when their mothers are at work; they are allowed to suck as long as they please. Their usual food is cow's milk and rice—not highly nutritious, perhaps, but well adapted to delicate digestive organs. Their parents at all times take good care of them.

On the other hand, the Creoles, in general, have only precarious medical attendance, because of their own unwillingness to remunerate a regular practitioner; in lieu of this, they prefer the assistance of a class of impostors, both male and female, who unite the practice of Obeahism and quackery, exact little from their patients, but are commonly satisfied with the amount and mode of remuneration tendered for the nostrums they administer and the incantations they perform. When sick, very many of the labouring class are, solely through previous improvidence, in need of almost everything. The children, generally speaking, receive only coarse food, and are much neglected in every other respect.

RELIGION.—Although Christianity is the professed religion of the people, yet immigration has been instrumental in introducing Mahometans, Gentoos, and other heathen sects. In this respect the religious community may be divided as follows :—

CENSUS, 1871.

Heathen Gentoos and others...	27,000
Christians	80,300

There were in the colony at the time of the last census, 1881, 37,280 Coolies and Chinese. I do not believe that, out of these, more than 3,000 had become Christians, leaving as heathens 34,280.

The census of 1861 had given the following numbers:— Christians, 65,053; Mahometans and heathens, 4,547.

Catholicism may be said to be the religion of the majority of the people, since Trinidad having been settled by Spaniards and French, they brought up their slaves in the religion which they themselves professed.

Episcopalians and Dissenters came in after the capitulation of the island; but it is since emancipation that their number has increased, by the influx of immigrants from the other colonies, as well as from North America, Great Britain, and Madeira—the immigrants from the latter country being, in fact, refugees, in consequence of a change of religion.

For some years the Church of England enjoyed all the privileges of an Established Church; it was, however, disestablished in the year 1868, and the various Christian communities existing in the island placed on the same footing. The Anglican and the Catholic clergy had always been paid a stipend from the Treasury. In the year 1869 the sum thus paid was consolidated into an Ecclesiastical Fund, from which are now paid the Anglican and Catholic clergy, also the Wesleyan ministers, according to the numbers of their congregation. The Presbyterians and Baptists declined the aid offered.

The Episcopalian establishment consists, locally, of a bishop, an archdeacon, four rectors, and three island curates; one assistant curate.

The Roman Catholic establishment consists of one archbishop, a coadjutor bishop, a vicar-general, twenty-one curés or parish priests, and seven assistant curés.

Some of these parishes are extensive; and yet, in many cases, so difficult is the communication between their different parts, that it is a matter of impossibility for the most zealous and robust clergyman fully to attend to the multifarious duties of his charge. As a consequence, not only is religious instruction almost utterly, because unavoidably, neglected, but it may be said that too many in those districts live and die like heathens.

EDUCATION.—During the period of slavery, a few private teachers of the lowest standard, in point of qualification, were employed in instructing the children of the free classes. After the passing of the Act of Emancipation in the year 1834, schools were established in several districts with the aid of funds bequeathed by Lady Mico for educational purposes; but they were soon afterwards broken up. Other schools were then projected in connection with the Anglican and Roman Catholic churches, and under the auspices of the local government; but the system of tuition not being based upon any comprehensive or systematic plan, and being conducted, with few exceptions, by incompetent persons, proved very inefficient. The adoption of a general and liberal system of primary instruction had become necessary after emancipation, not only to eradicate the ignorance so deeply rooted in the soil of slavery, but also to impart a knowledge of the English language to a population of foreign origin. This Lord Harris perceived at once, and in the year 1851 the following resolutions were, on his proposition, adopted in a committee of the Board of Council for the establishment of schools throughout the island.

First. A Board of Education to be formed, consisting of the Governor, with such members of the legislative council of government and other persons, being laymen, as may be appointed, from time to time, by the Governor.

Second. An inspector of schools to be appointed, with a salary.

Third. A training school, with a master and mistress, to be established for the educational training of teachers; the expense of maintaining such school, with suitable accommodation for the teachers, to be defrayed from the public funds of the colony.

Fourth. Public schools to be established at once in each ward of the colony, and at such places most suitable for the convenience of the population.

Fifth. The training and primary schools to be under the control of the Board of Education, and subject to the supervision of the inspector.

Sixth. The expenses of erecting and maintaining the schoolhouses, with suitable accommodation for teachers, and the salaries, to be defrayed from the funds of the wards.

Seventh. No person to be appointed master or mistress unless such person has produced a certificate of good character to the satisfaction of the Board of Education, and until such person has undergone an examination by the Board, and has received a certificate of efficiency.

Eighth. At the primary schools instruction to be provided for day scholars, and for evening and adult classes.

Ninth. Admission to the primary schools to be gratuitous.

Eleventh. Instruction to be given at the training and primary schools to be secular, and without direct religious or doctrinal teaching.

These resolutions formed the basis of the system proposed by his Excellency Lord Harris. This system was strongly objected to, on account of the resolution which made the instruction purely secular; and experience has proved, I apprehend, that it was neither intrinsically the best, nor the most suitable to the requirements of the population.

Two training or normal schools were established, one for males and another for females, and to each was attached a model school.

In the year 1863 Mr. Keate, the then Governor of the colony, established the Queen's Collegiate School, for secondary education, on the plan of the Queen's Colleges in Ireland.

Sir Arthur Gordon, finding that the system of primary education established by Lord Harris in 1851 had only partially effected the object for which it was designed, proposed for the adoption of the Legislative Council certain important modifications.

Schools established by private persons became entitled to receive aid from the Government, on compliance with the following conditions :—

First. That the property and control of the schools is vested in a local manager, or managers, having the power (A) to appoint the teacher, provided he or she be one duly certificated by the Board of Eduction ; (C) to make use of the schoolhouse for any lawful purpose, before and after school hours; (D) to grant holidays and vacations, provided the school be kept open not less than 200 days annually.

Third. That the teacher of the school is one duly licensed by the Board of Education.

Fourth. That the school is open to all children, without distinction of religion or race.

Fifth. That no child receives any religious instruction objected to by the parent or guardian of such child ; or is present whilst such instruction is given.

Sixth. That free access is given, under regulations approved by the Board of Education, to all ministers of religion who may desire to afford religious instruction to children of their own persuasion being pupils in such schools.

Seventh. That the school is, at all times, open to inspection.

Tenth. That the rules and books of secular education are subject to the approval of the Board of Education.

Eleventh. That the aid to which such schools are to be entitled shall consist of :—

1st. Provision for the remuneration of teachers, by (a) a fixed salary dependent upon the possession of a first, second, or third class certificate, obtainable by examination; (b) a capitation grant, paid proportionately to the educational results certified annually by the inspector of schools; (c) a capitation grant paid proportionately to the attendance of pupils, certified quarterly by the local manager or managers.

2nd. Grants in aid of the erection of buildings and supply of necessaries proportionate to the amount obtained from private sources.

7th. That reformatory and industrial schools for criminal and vagrant children be established at the cost of the colony.

Though more in accordance with the general feelings of the population, this modified system cannot be said to have answered the expectations of the introducer.

Further and more important modifications were, therefore, introduced in our system of primary education by our last Governor, Sir Henry Irving. He caused an ordinance to be passed in 1875, by which schools of primary education became entitled to receive aid from the public funds of the colony on the following conditions :—

First. That provision, to the satisfaction of the Board of Education, be made for the control and management of the schools by a local manager or managers.

Second. That the school be open at all times to inspection or examination by the inspector of schools, or by any officer appointed by Government for the purpose.

Third. That the average daily attendance at the school, computed on a period of a year, be not less than twenty-five.

Subject to the provisions of the ordinance, the aid to which any school becomes entitled consists of a certain annual capitation grant, according to the results of an annual examination of the school in secular instruction by an inspector of schools, such annual capitation grant being at the rate of :—

(1) One pound sterling for each pupil passed in the First and Second Standards.

(2) Twenty-five shillings for each pupil passed in the Third and Fourth Standards.

(3) Thirty shillings for each pupil passed in the Fifth and Sixth Standards.

Governor Irving's system of primary education is, in my opinion, an improvement upon the systems of Lord Harris and Sir Arthur Gordon, inasmuch as it does not interfere with the religious feelings of the people, and gives facilities for the establishment of purely denominational schools; and tends to create a wholesome spirit of emulation among the different religious communities existing in the island. Anybody may, on complying with the provisions of the ordinance, establish a school, and become entitled to receive aid from the funds of the colony. Under this new system the number of schools has increased, as also the attendance of children.

Sir Arthur Gordon had not rested satisfied with the changes which he had introduced into the system of primary education established by Lord Harris; and in 1870 he had an ordinance passed changing the name of the "Queen's Collegiate School" to that of the "Royal College of Trinidad." The college was placed under the management of a council; and it was made lawful for the college council to declare any school of secondary education to be a school in connection with the Royal College, on compliance with the provisions of the ordinance. And the pupils of every affiliated school became students of the Royal College, it being made optional for them to be relieved from the obligation of attending the classes of instruction, provided they can show to the satisfaction of the committee that they receive sufficient instruction in classics, mathematics, natural science, and modern languages, in the school which the student is attending.

Any school in connection with the Royal College becomes entitled, from year to year, to aid from the funds of the colony, to consist of: (1) A fixed salary to the principal, or head, of the school; (2) Of a capitation grant for each student over nine years who has received from the principal of the Royal College a certificate of having given, during the preceding twelve months, a fixed number of attendances; (3) Of a capitation grant on the results of an annual examination, at the college, of the pupils of the affiliated schools. Four exhibitions are granted to the students of the Royal College who pass with honours the Cambridge local examinations.

Free admissions are annually granted to six pupils of the primary schools receiving Government aid who pass the best competitive examination, provided such pupils are at the time of such examination under fourteen years of age.

As may be seen from the above sketch, our system of education, both primary and secondary, rests on a sound foundation, and may be said to be very liberal.

The number of schools in operation at the end of 1880 was as follows:—

Secondary Education	3
Normal with Model Schools	2
Primary Education, Government Schools	52
„ „ Assisted Schools	39
	96

Total number of children on the rolls :—

Secondary—Royal College	80	
„ College of Imm. Conception	142	
„ Convent Girls	110	
		332
Primary—Model and Normal Schools	408	
District or Government Schools, including the San Fernando School	3,964	
Assisted Schools	3,807	
Estates Schools (mainly Coolies)	590	
Orphan Asylums	119	

Males, 4,906; Females, 4,001 = 8,907.

The report of the inspector of schools for 1878–79 affords the following information :—

Years.	No. of Schools.	No. of Pupils.	Average Attendance.
1868	35	2,836	1,333
1877	72	5,801	3,695
1879 (6 months)	88	6,290	4,228

Net expenditure by Government in 1878 :—

Government Schools	£6,913
San Fernando Schools	221
Assisted Schools	769
Royal College	2,160
Affiliated Schools	1,000
Education Department	1,035
Examinations, &c.	208
	£12,306

Taking the population at the end of 1880 at 145,000, we have 4·48 pupils per 1,000 inhabitants.

ASSISTED SCHOOLS.

Expenditure	£2,961
Income	2,689
Contributed by the Managers	272

There are, in addition to the above public establishments, several private institutions, in which is afforded education superior to that which is imparted at the public schools. They may be said to be schools where infants of the better classes are trained for a higher course of instruction.

I should be allowed to say a few words respecting the Seminary of Saint Joseph, known here as the "Convent." It was established here in the year 1836, for the education of young ladies, by the Congregation of Saint Joseph de Cluny, a religious sisterhood originating in France not many years ago, for the special purpose of diffusing instruction throughout the colonies. The Seminary of Saint Joseph has a complete appointment of nuns for the different branches in the education of youth. The English and French languages are taught therein, together with sacred and profane history, geography, and arithmetic. Needle and fancy work also form an essential part of the training. Music and drawing constitute separate branches, as accomplishments. The pupils are boarded, or received as day scholars. The boarded pupils are divided into two classes: those who are found in all necessaries by the establishment, and those who are dieted by their parents. The average charges for the former may be estimated at 200 dols., and for the latter at 120 dols., a year. Day scholars pay from three to four dollars per month.

The Seminary of Saint Joseph may be regarded as a blessing to the colony, and certainly is an institution unique in the British West Indies. Unaided as it is, it supplies gratuitous education—consisting of reading, writing, Scripture history, the four rules of arithmetic, needlework, and the Church catechism—to more than 300 poor girls yearly. The Saint Joseph nuns, at present, keep six girls' assisted schools.

Connected with the subject of education, I should mention here the "Public Library," formed in the year 1851. It is supported by the Colonial Government and private subscriptions. The terms are moderate, the subscription being only £1 sterling per annum.

The library is under the control of a Committee of Management, chosen by the Governor and the subscribers, in the proportion of one member to every £50 of contribution. The stock of books consists of 10,500 volumes, English and French. There are besides a few Spanish works, also maps, periodicals, and reviews. In the year 1856, the stock of books consisted of 2,887 volumes; increase in twenty-three years, 7,613.

The library is open from seven to ten in the morning, and from eleven to six o'clock in the evening. The regulations may be considered as very liberal.

Of the "press" I have very little to say. There are at present published in the colony, besides "The Royal Gazette," five weekly papers: "The Port-of-Spain Gazette," "The San Fernando Gazette," "The New Era," "The Palladium," and "The Fair Play"; bi-weekly paper, "The Chronicle." "The San-Fernando Gazette" is issued in that town; the others in Port-of-Spain. The Trinidad "Official and Commercial Register and Almanac," which is published yearly, is a very useful and creditable compilation.

CRIME.—This is a subject the examination of which is of great importance, and particularly so in an island wherein is congregated such an admixture of so many different races, and in which there exists such a diversity of religious creeds. But this examination is, at the same time, replete with difficulty, inasmuch as comprehensive details are wanting in order to a thorough investigation of the subject. Such as I have been able to obtain, however, will lead to some interesting conclusions.

The following is a return of persons committed to the Royal Gaol of Port-of-Spain, from the 1st of January, 1872, to the 31st December, 1878, with particulars of sexes, country, and religion :—

Years.	Males.	Females.	Total.
1872	1,923	208	2,131
1873	2,239	265	2,504
1874	—	—	2,092
1875	—	—	2,764
1876	2,061	396	2,457
1877	2,072	435	2,507
1878	2,483	460	2,943
Grand Total			17,398

In this grand total are not comprised adjourned cases, debtors, &c. Annual average number, 2,424.

If we take the total of the five years, 1873, 1874, 1875, 1876, and 1877, we have, after deducting as above, adjourned cases and debts, 12,950 persons committed, and these may be classed as follows :—

	1873.	1874.	1875.	1876.	1877.
Felons	128	159	120	123	135
Misdemeanants	2,002	2,933	2,644	2,334	2,372

With respect to felony and misdemeanour, we find, during the whole period, 42 commitments for murder and manslaughter, viz., 3 in 1873, 9 in 1875, 5 in 1876, 8 in 1877, and so many as 17 in 1874; 5 commitments for arson; 10 for burglary; 111 for cutting and wounding; 251 for receiving stolen property; and for obtaining money under false pretences, 66. Of lighter offences we have: Assaults and battery, 1,117; drunk and disorderly, 726; fighting, 1,039; larceny, 2,136; violent and obscene language, 483; riotous and disorderly conduct, 598.

Murder and manslaughter are generally the results of revenge. The cases are very rare where a man is murdered with the view of appropriating money. Wife murder is a crime very common among the Coolies; any wife forsaking her husband may be said to do so at the risk of her life. The crime of arson is of very frequent occurrence: megass houses, in which the cane refuse or megass is stored as fuel, are generally selected as being the more easily fired. It is with the greatest difficulty that the perpetrators can be discovered or apprehended. There were, in the period recorded, an annual average of 22 cases of cutting and wounding, and how many more were and are never brought before the magistrate? For the negro very much resembles the schoolboy, who prefers silently to suffer rather than call for the interference of the master. The weapon most commonly used in such cases is the cutlass—an agricultural tool which the peasant generally carries about with him, and, in case of any quarrel, is too often turned into a deadly weapon. The negro is irritable and obstinate, and whenever his passions have been roused by contention or stubborn opposition, he becomes unmanageable, and strikes his opponent with whatever weapon he can grasp. We have also 1,117 cases of assault and battery; 1,039 cases of fighting, or an average of 431 cases a year. We record 2,136 cases of larceny; 251 for receiving stolen goods, and 66 cases for obtaining money under false pretences; altogether 2,453 cases, or a yearly average of 490, showing to what an extent the practice of stealing is carried. But in how many cases is information not lodged on the offended party recovering the stolen goods? or how many more are disposed of by the injured party's summary procedure of inflicting corporal punishment on the thief? "Taking is not stealing," is a common saying among all classes of servants; that is to say, carrying off that which may be left within reach, is not larceny in the opinion of those people.

There appear on the list 752 cases of drunkenness, and 598 of riotous and disorderly conduct, or a yearly average of 275. Obscene and violent language, 483 cases. The individuals committed for riotous and disorderly conduct are generally members of those societies which are a regular pest. If we deduct from the number of offences committed by Asiatics those which may be regarded as breaches of the immigration regulations, we shall then have about 3,300 cases of ordinary offences.

The interval between the present year and the year 1871, when the census of the colony was taken, is too great to allow me to establish by comparison the proportionate number of offenders belonging to each country which sends us emigrants. I, nevertheless, can say this, and I say it with regret, Trinidad occupies a very unenviable position as compared with the year

1851. Number of natives then, 40,584; average annual number of offences, 156: for the five years I have recorded it is 625. Surely the native population has not increased fourfold: it has not even doubled.

If we take the religion of the offenders as a starting point for comparison, we arrive at the following results:—

Non-Christians ...		6,693
Christians—		
Anglicans	3,565	
Roman Catholics	3,829	
Other Christian Communities	94	
		7,488

I wish to call special attention to the following facts, viz., the large increase of female and of juvenile offenders. The years 1850, 1851, 1852, 1853, 1854, had given an average of 104 female offenders; the five years 1872, 1873, 1876, 1877, 1878 give an average of 353, more than treble that of the first period. Again, the number of female offenders, which in 1873 was only 208, had swelled up to 460 in 1878.

The number of juvenile offenders, which in 1873 was 51, had increased to 84 in 1877. This is, indeed, a sad progression.

I cannot do better than quote here some passages of the reports of the Inspector of Prisons for 1874 and 1877; and I do so the more readily as I entirely concur in whatever he says on this subject and on prison discipline generally.

"The question of female crime," he remarks, "is a very serious one; and when it is considered that by far the greater number of our female prisoners are committed for riotous behaviour, obscene language, drunkenness, and other offences of that type, I cannot but think that it would be worth while to consider whether women of this class should not be treated somewhat in the same way as juvenile offenders, and sent to a penitentiary for a term of years, instead of being allowed to spend their lives in alternative short spells of liberty and imprisonment.

"These short periods are, in reality, nothing more than intervals of rest, during which the female convicts gather health and strength at the public expense, and come out with renewed energies to recommence the same round of vice and debauchery. It is painful to be obliged to make such an assertion; but I am bound to state that each succeeding year shows a rapid spread of prostitution, and no one can pass through the streets of our towns without having ample evidence of the utter degradation of our lower class females."

With reference to juvenile offenders the inspector remarks: " I regret to have to report a very large increase under this head, there having been sixty-two boys and twenty-two girls committed in 1877, as against thirty-five boys and eleven girls in 1876.

" I had entertained sanguine hopes that the commencement of this year would have seen the opening of the much-needed reformatory and industrial schools; but I regret that objections raised by one or two individuals against the proposed site have caused the whole question to be indefinitely postponed.

" In the meantime the evil is increasing and developing, and before long we shall reap the bitter fruits of this procrastination.

" A very large proportion of our criminals here are not of what, in England, is called the criminal class. I do not mean to assert that there is no such class here; unfortunately, one of the results of our increasing civilisation and prosperity is, that such a class is rapidly increasing; but we even yet have neither a distinctly criminal class any more than a thieves' quarter.

" There is no shame here attached to the fact of having been an inmate of a criminal prison; and so long as this will be the case, it is vain to hope that the gaol will have much reformatory effect.

" The labourer in these colonies, whether African, Creole, or Asiatic, works as little and sleeps or idles as much as he can, and his ordinary food consists of plantains, corn-meal, salt fish, and rice, washed down with rum when he can get it.

" He lives on, or near, an estate, in a hut, and neither his employer nor any one else cares much if he lives or dies, unless, indeed, he be an indentured immigrant.

" If such a man commits a crime, and is sent to gaol for twelve months, can it be contended that, physically, he is worse off than when working on the estate?

"In the gaol he is well lodged and fed at the public expense, with food identical with that which he consumes when at liberty, and clothed (also at the public expense) in a way which, to a labourer in the old country, would be a mark of disgrace, but which to him conveys no such feeling. He has medical attendance when ill, and what to the Creole and Asiatic is an immense enjoyment, he can sleep from 6 p.m. to 5 a.m. next morning.

"The labour to which he is put is not more severe than that to which he has been accustomed on the estate or roads of the island, and certainly can in no case be considered penal, or even in the light of a punishment. What, then, does such a prisoner suffer by imprisonment?" Let me add that you can hear that class of people declare that they are quite content to be sent to gaol, as they are better off there than they can be when at liberty.

The inspector again remarks that "imprisonment in the gaol, when accompanied by hard labour, is not looked upon as a disgrace; and a convict who comes out of prison after one or two years of penal servitude, resumes his place in society with no more difficulty than if he had been absent for the same period in a neighbouring colony."

The remark is unfortunately but too well justified by facts. "Of course," adds the inspector, "in such a state of things there is one advantage—the facility which a discharged prisoner has here of obtaining work on his release. Whereas, in the old countries, the reverse has been one of the greatest difficulties with which those anxious for the future well-being of the man have had to contend; but this advantage, great though it be, cannot compensate for the fact that no sense of moral degradation attaches here to the prison dress, or even to the fact of having been an inmate of the gaol."

Generally, when such prisoners as are members of the societies or bands alluded to are discharged from the gaol, they are met at the gate by friends, male and female, and received with demonstrations of joy, but with not the faintest exhibition of shame; and they are accompanied home with triumph. When taken to gaol, they had been escorted by a retinue of followers. For the last two years, however, they have been conveyed to the prison in a closed van. Yet it is really painful to hear them—the female prisoners especially—singing at the top of their voices, as if in defiance of the law and of all decency. It cannot be surprising that the conduct, in prison, of creatures so callous to any feeling of shame is extremely bad, and that "a fearful amount of depravity is practised between them when in an unwatched association." Are they not, in the majority of cases, members of *bands* notoriously formed for immoral purposes, and there practically taught to scorn all that society respects and appreciates, and to indulge in unbridled licentiousness?

Of course, I cannot pretend, in a book like this, to suggest any definite remedy; but I may be pardoned for quoting from the report of the inspector the words of Sir Joshua Jebb:— "The deterring elements of punishment are hard labour, hard fare, and a hard bed; and, for the lowest class of prisoners, these elements should be applied, as far as they can consistently, with a view to deter men from crime." Let hard labour, therefore, be enforced.

I shall again say, in the words of the inspector: "As for females undergoing short sentences, nothing but severe punishment will have the slightest effect upon them.

"The present hard labour (?), which consists of sewing and washing, can have no terrors for women who have utterly lost all sense of shame, and who glory in their degradation. . . . . I certainly recommend complete separation, by night and by day, work in association, but perfect silence."

The first step, however, to be adopted, and the most important, is to have a separate prison for females; and we may reasonably expect that, when the new lunatic asylum has been built, and the lunatics transferred there, the present buildings will be adapted to the reception of our female criminals.

As to the juvenile offenders, there are but poor chances of obtaining their reformation, unless industrial schools are founded for their reception. In the year 1876 an ordinance was passed for the establishment and regulation of industrial schools. Such schools may be established either by Government or by private individuals. As this is a question in which I took some interest, and had opportunities to talk over the matter with Governors Sir James Longden and Sir Henry Irving, I trust that I shall be excused. for saying a few words on the subject.

Governor Irving was fully alive to the great difficulties that must attend the creation and management of a Government reformatory school. In his opinion, the only chance of success lay in the foundation by religious communities of such reformatories.

He, therefore, felt some anxiety in having two such schools

simultaneously established by the Protestant and the Catholic communities. By the ordinance of 1876, it had been made lawful for the Governor to order payment to the managers of the schools of a capitation fee, not exceeding £10, for each child sent thereto. It was also agreed that funds would be advanced by the Government in aid of the establishment of the schools, such advance to be reimbursed within a fixed period.

The Catholics succeeded in obtaining the co-operation of a religious body, had found a suitable site, and were prepared to begin at once; but the Anglican bishop and clergy having declared that they were not ready yet to start their school, the whole affair was dropped—but not for ever, as I sincerely hope and desire.

Offences, as it appears, are not so common in those counties where the number of small proprietors is larger; and this is easily accounted for. The social condition of individuals must have its influence, and that a powerful one, on the perpetration of crime, particularly of offences against property. It is, hence, undeniable that the small cottager who can live independently by cultivating his own land is less exposed to the commission of crime than the day labourers, who live in a crowded state on a sugar estate, and are wholly dependent upon money wages, paid weekly or fortnightly, for their subsistence. It may be objected that the estate labourer is, in more than one respect, more comfortable, generally speaking, than the cottager; his lodging is free, and he neither pays taxes nor is burdened with house repairs; whereas, on the other hand, the cottager, though conscious that the pressure of these very burdens should urge him to increased exertion, does not seek to realise his independence by cultivating his land to the degree he might and ought.

Evidently, however, this cannot invalidate the principle I have laid down; and I have no doubt that, were it practicable to induce the labourers located on estates to cultivate their own small patches of garden-land, the number of offences would greatly decrease in the rural districts.

I cannot conclude this chapter without giving again expression to a regret that there is not, in connection with the Royal Gaol, a house of correction for young offenders, or, what would be better still, a *penitentiary farm*, where they would receive primary instruction, religious education, and industrial training;

also a reformatory for female criminals. I must, however, in justice, say that the gaol of Port-of-Spain is conducted on excellent principles.

The majority of the male prisoners are employed on public works, to the great benefit of the country and of their own health, as shown by the low rate of mortality of prisoners. The expenditure of the gaols (salaries included) for 1877 amounted to the sum of £8,340; valuation of labour performed, £5,731. The expenditure in 1876 was £7,920; value of labour, £5,788. Expenditure for 1878, £8,947; labour, £5,953.

The following Table, showing the proportion and the particulars of the principal offences for which prisoners were committed during the five years already mentioned, will prove interesting to the reader:—

Offences.	1873.	1874.	1875.	1876.	1877.
Arson	1	2	3	—	5
Assault and Battery	158	207	267	220	265
Burglary and Breaking into Houses	12	9	7	10	5
Cutting and Wounding	28	12	30	15	26
Drunkenness	102	155	159	156	189
Resisting and Assaulting Police	52	66	25	48	35
Murder and Manslaughter	3	18	10	5	8
Riotous and Disorderly Conduct	3	2	1	1	2
Exposure and Indecent Behaviour	44	67	33	32	54
Larceny	343	436	440	440	477
Embezzlement	2	5	7	10	5
Obtaining Money under False Pretences	17	12	13	16	10
Fighting	141	207	200	166	215
Vagrancy	37	108	75	69	41

CHAPTER VI.

GENERAL ADMINISTRATION—GOVERNMENT—CIVIL, JUDICIARY, ECCLESIASTICAL, AND FINANCIAL DEPARTMENTS.

UNDER the Spanish dominion, Trinidad was a dependency of the "Capitania-General de Caracas," and was administered by a Governor, assisted by the "illustrious cabildo"—a kind of municipal corporation, vested with extensive powers, and enjoying great privileges.

This corporation was a self-elected body, exercising jurisdiction partly general, partly municipal and judiciary. It consisted of the Governor, as president, and twelve members—two of whom were elected "alcaldes" of the first and second election, or "alcaldes" in ordinary. It was lawful for the cabildo to levy duties and impose taxes, but their municipal jurisdiction did not extend beyond the limits of Port-of-Spain. The town had been divided into four "barrios" or wards, and an "alcalde de barrio" was appointed to each by the cabildo. Their functions were similar to those of the commandant, which I will define hereafter. The "alcaldes" in ordinary had special charge of the streets and markets. The alcaldes in ordinary exercised their judicial powers in criminal as well as in civil matters, assisted by a Spanish lawyer, acting as assessor or adviser; and for nearly eight years—from 1808 to 1814—they held both the civil and criminal sessions. No case, however, involving forfeiture of life was ever decided by these judges after the island became a British possession.

Don Jose Maria de Chacon—the last Governor under the Spanish rule—had divided the island into numerous small districts called "quarters;" to each was appointed "a commandante" as chief and sole magistrate; for he was, at the same time, police magistrate, justice of the peace, and administrator of his district, charged with the return of population and property, and the collection of taxes. They held petty sessions, and had the power of fining and condemning to prison; they acted also as coroners. All judicial summonses and citations were sent from the supreme courts in Port-of-Spain to these officers, whose certificate was a sufficient proof of service. These important functionaries were allowed an "alguazil," or constable, as an executive officer, who was paid a small salary, raised by an alguazil-tax levied on every estate. The commandant was always one of the most respectable inhabitants of the quarter, and his office purely honorary.

Colonel Picton, on taking charge of the island after its capitulation, made no alteration in that administrative arrangement, but chose, in addition, from amongst the most influential inhabitants, "assessors," who formed a "council of advice," which may be regarded as the origin and foundation of the "Council of Government" which succeeded, and was afterwards changed into the present "Legislative Council."

The powers and duties of the "illustrious cabildo" and "commandants of quarters" were gradually modified, until they became extinct in the years 1840 and 1849, by the adoption of the ordinance constituting the "Town Council of Port-of-Spain," and of the territorial or wardens' ordinance.

The "Court of Alcaldes in Ordinary" was abolished in the year 1823, and the judicial jurisdiction of the cabildo became extinct. In the year 1840 an ordinance was passed for "regulating the powers and constitution, and settling the mode of election of the members of the corporate body called the 'Illustrious Cabildo' of the town of Port-of-Spain, and changing the name thereof to that of the Town Council of Port-of-Spain." The qualifications for electors were, residence in or within three miles of Port-of-Spain, and the payment of an annual house-rent to the amount of ninety-six dollars; in addition to which, councillors were to be worth £500 free of all debts. The council was thus rendered elective; but the Governor still retained the presidency over, and an absolute veto on, the proceedings of the town council. In the year 1852, a petition was addressed by the town councillors to the Governor in council, praying for a new constitution based on the same principles as those embodied in the Municipal Act of England. The prayer was granted, and the name of the "Town Council" changed into that of the

"Borough Council of Port-of-Spain." The franchise, at present, is, for electors, the occupancy of a house within the borough, rated to the house-tax at an annual rental of not less than twenty pounds sterling; for councillors and auditors, to be on the burgess list, and to be possessed, as absolute owners or tenants for life, of some household or other estate or freehold of real property assessed to the house-tax at an annual value of no less than £50, or at a rental of no less than £75 per annum. The council is presided over by a mayor. It appears, from this statement, that the town of Port-of-Spain has been in the enjoyment of municipal institutions since before the conquest of the island by the British forces. Similar privileges were granted to San Fernando in the year 1840. The qualifications for burgesses are the same as in Port-of-Spain; for councillors and auditors they are £30 and £40, instead of £50 and £75.

When protectors of slaves were appointed, a part of the powers of the commandants was transferred to those officers; in the year 1834 the stipendiary magistrate superseded them in their judiciary functions; the appointment of commissioners of roads, in 1846, contracted their jurisdiction within still narrower limits; and, finally, the "quarters" having been consolidated into wards, in the year 1849, the functions of the commandants ceased entirely; and, let it be remarked, without the slightest compliment on, or remuneration for, their services, although several of them had performed their gratuitous, onerous, and multifarious duties for upwards of twenty years, and had expended much of their private funds in the service of the colony.

At present the government is somewhat differently constituted from what it was under our first Governors; and the changes introduced are chiefly due to Sir Henry MacLeod, and to his successor, the Right Honourable Lord Harris.

Trinidad is a "crown colony," under the control of the Colonial Office, the government of which is administered, locally, through a resident Governor, assisted by an island executive, and a legislative council. On several previous occasions attempts had been made to obtain a representative form of government; and, for the last time, in the year 1853, but without success; they were opposed both here and at the Colonial Office.

Executive Council.—It consists of the Colonial Secretary, the

Attorney-General, and the Commander of the Forces, under the presidency of the Governor. It is a mere consultative body, which the Governor calls together on important occasions, in order to have their opinion, which he may follow or not, as he pleases.

Legislative Council.—This council consists of the Governor, as president, and fourteen members, of whom six are "official" and eight "non-official." The official members are the Colonial Secretary, the Chief Judge, the Attorney-General, the Solicitor-General, the Receiver-General, and the Protector of Immigrants. The non-official members must be British-born usbjects; they are nominees of the Crown, and chosen from among the most respectable inhabitants of the colony.

The position of the chief judge, as a member of the legislative council, is a rather delicate one, since he may be called upon to give at the board his opinion on matters which will have afterwards to be decided on the bench.

The legislative council discusses and adopts such ordinances and measures as are introduced or proposed by the Governor, or any member of the council. To become law, all measures passed by the council must receive Her Majesty's sanction. Ordinances which have been neither disapproved, nor formally approved within two years of their having been passed, become void and null. Generally, whenever any member proposes a legislative measure, he must himself prepare it in a legal shape—an objectionable course, in my opinion, because it is almost impossible that, under such circumstances, errors should not creep in and render the law defective. It may also happen that such a measure, though passed in council, is not transmitted home for confirmation, and thus becomes null after two years. This was the case with the ordinance establishing vestries for the Roman Catholic churches in this island. And yet it was seriously stated that it was the fault of the Roman Catholics, since they ought to have asked for its transmission home, and for its confirmation.

The legislative council discusses also and votes the estimates for each following year. The items may be ranged under two heads, viz., the fixed and the unfixed establishments. The estimates, as regards the fixed establishment, are laid before the board as a mere matter of form, and are not submitted for discussion. Members, however, may propose alterations in the shape of resolutions, which are transmitted to the Colonial Office for consideration. The unfixed establishment is regulated every year. All motions for money must come through the Governor. There are regular meetings of the board on the first day of each month, or on the day following, should the first be a Sunday, and at any other time the Governor may think proper to call the members specially together; and the board is to sit from day to day until the standing business is disposed of; the president and eight members to form a quorum. In the absence of his Excellency, the senior member presides. The sittings are public, and the proceedings reported in the newspapers of the colony.

It is before this board, then presided over by the chief judge, or, in his absence, by the senior member of the council, that each new Governor takes the oath previous to entering into office.

The Governor is vested with extensive powers; and, as he has the uncontrolled appointment of all officers who are not on the fixed establishment, he can suspend and dismiss them without referring to the Colonial Office. All others he can suspend from office—even the members of council—until her Majesty's pleasure is made known. He may require the attendance at the council-board of all the members, and exact that of the official section. The chief judge being by position the only independent member of this section, the Governor may be said to have the command of the votes of the officials; and he can, with a little stratagem and his own casting vote, form a majority on any important question he wishes to carry or oppose. He has also the control of the public funds; and the receiver-general, it seems, is justified in paying out any sum of money on the Governor's warrant. By royal instructions he is not authorised —except in urgent cases—to order the payment of any sum of money above £200, without special authority from the secretary of state, and previous sanction by the board. He can also veto any measure passed by the legislative council.

GENERAL ADMINISTRATION.—This may be considered under five different heads: Administrative. civil, judicial, ecclesiastical, and financial.

Administrative Section.—As I have already stated, Lord Harris introduced in the year 1849 a new territorial division of the island, which was accordingly partitioned into two grand sections, the northern and the southern, each being sub-divided into four counties, each county into two districts, and each district into wards, according to their population.

The common boundary of the two grand divisions is formed by a line running from Point Manzanilla westward, and following the course of the River Lebranche; then along the summits of the Middle Range to Mount Tamana; thence, west-south-west to Montserrat; and from that point due west to the Gulf of Paria, south of Point Savanetta.

The four counties in the northern section are St. George and Caroni, St. David and St. Andrew.

The four counties in the southern section are Victoria and St. Patrick, Mayaro and Nariva.

There exist at present forty-one wards, viz., twenty-six in the northern, and fifteen in the southern section. The county of St. George comprises the larger number of wards, viz., eighteen; Caroni, five; St. David and St. Andrew, two each; Victoria and St. Patrick, six each; Nariva and Mayaro, one each.

Before leaving the colony, Lord Harris had admitted, in a review of the various acts of his administration, that the wardens' ordinance had, on the whole, worked satisfactorily, but that it required amendments—such amendments as experience had suggested. What amendments his Excellency would have introduced it is difficult to say. Changes, however, have been made, first by Sir Charles Elliott, and later by Governor Sir Henry Irving, radically altering the scheme of Lord Harris.

In 1854 Sir Charles Elliott had an ordinance passed " making certain amendments and alterations in the wardens' ordinance, and making it lawful for the Governor to form such and so many wards as he shall see fit into ward unions, and to appoint one warden for the several wards comprised in each union."

The Governor accordingly ordered the distribution of the several wards of the colony into the following unions, viz. :—

Diego Martin Union, comprising the wards of Chayuarasmos, Chacachacare, Carenage, Diego Martin, Mucurapo, and Morraval.

Saint Ann Union, comprising the wards of Saint Ann, Laventille, Cemaronero, Aricagua, and Santa Cruz.

Tacarigua Union, comprising the wards of Saint Joseph, Maracas, Tacarigua, Caura, and Lower Caroni.

Arima Union, comprising the wards of Arima, Upper Caroni, Guanape, Turrure, and Manzanilla.

Mayaro Union, consisting of the two wards of Mayaro and Nariva.

Toco Union, formed of the wards of Toco and Blanchisseuse.

Couva Union, comprising the wards of Chaguanas, Carapichaima, Couva, Savonetta, and Point-à-Pierres.

North Naparima Union, extending over the wards of Naparima, Savanna Grande (northern and southern).

South Naparima Union, comprising the South Naparima eastern and South Naparima western wards, also the ward of Oropuche.

Cedros Union, including the wards of La Brea, Guapo, Irois, Cedros, and Erin.

In the year 1878 an ordinance was introduced by Sir Henry Irving "for further amending the law with regard to wardens." The ordinance makes it lawful for the Governor to form so many unions as he thinks fit into provinces, and to appoint a commissioner for each province; the commissioners having, each in his province, all the powers and authorities granted by the previous ordinances to wardens; he can also appoint assistant wardens.

The different ward unions of the colony have accordingly been formed into two provinces, the Northen and Southern, corresponding to the northern and southern divisions of Lord Harris, and two commissioners appointed, with a salary of £800, and £100 for travelling expenses. Salary of the assistant wardens, £250 to £350, and £50 allowances.

The Governor made another and more important change. The assessment of five shillings an acre on cultivated, and three pence an acre on uncultivated land, has been converted into a uniform tax of one shilling an acre, whether cultivated or uncultivated. Houses of which the annual value does not exceed £5 are rated at four shillings; and houses of which the annual value exceeds £5 are rated at £7 10s. for every £00. Barracks occupied by immigrants or other labourers are assessed at the rate of four shillings for each separate apartment.

Previous to the passing of the ordinance of 1879, the monies belonging to the wards were paid over to the Colonial Treasury, and carried by the treasurer to the credit of each ward. At present, all monies collected by the wardens are merged into the general funds of the colony, and the ward's expenses defrayed from those funds. They are, however, charged separately for constables, paupers, medicines, and other sundries, to the amount of about £5,220, as appears by the estimates for 1880. The principal sources of revenue are: Land tax, £14,500; house tax, £10,230; spirit and wine licences, £8,860. Total local revenues, £35,000.

The duties of the wardens have also been contracted into narrower limits. On this subject Sir Henry Irving remarks, in his message of 22nd January, 1878: "In 1854 it was found necessary to employ salaried officers as wardens . . . a salaried warden being appointed to each union. A radical change was thus introduced into the scheme of Lord Harris; but no corresponding adequate change made in its administration. With the exception of their being paid instead of unpaid, the position and the duties of the wardens remained unchanged. They were still regarded as local officers. . . . The appointments were left to be filled up locally by gentlemen who were left without guidance or control by superior authority, to perform, in respect of large populous districts, the multifarious duties which, under the original scheme, were to be performed on a comparatively trifling scale and within a limited area. . . . The interior administration of the country became dependent on the ability of fourteen gentlemen to discharge successfully the whole range of executive duties—from supervising excise, for example, to civil engineering. It is not surprising that a system, dependent for its success on impossible conditions, should have proved a comparative failure." The duties of the wardens are now limited to those which properly attach to a revenue officer, their duties of road officers having been transferred to the public works department.

The Governor, in his message of 3rd November, 1879, commented thus on the changes which he had effected: "The system of assessment has acted as a discouragement to cultivation. It has been a fruitful source of error, inequality, evasion, and fraud. By the conversion of the assessment into a uniform acreage rate, a system of taxation will be substituted which will encourage the acquisition of land and stimulate its cultivation, which will minimise error and inequality, and render evasion and fraud impossible. This reform of system would, however, be incomplete were it not to be accompanied by a change also in the method heretofore in force for the recovery of taxes on real property. That method has hitherto been regulated by the warden's ordinances of 1852 and 1854, which provide that, where default is made in payment of the ward rates, the warden shall proceed against the defaulter by distress; and in case of there being no sufficient levy to meet the distress, shall return the warrant to the secretary of the intendant, by whom, after advertisement, the property is sold at auction. Practically, no attempts have been made to levy under these warrants of distress; or if made, have been evaded by the ratepayer by the temporary concealment of his property. The issue of the warrant, and the return to it of no sufficient levy, have become to be regarded as mere matter of form; and the collection of so much of the rates as are not voluntarily paid to the wardens has been left to the secretary of the intendant, to be recovered by him under the pressure of an immediate and peremptory sale. By the great bulk of the ratepayers this system has been understood, and has by many of them been taken advantage of to postpone payment of their rates till the last moment; but in individual cases it has resulted in gross illegality and wrong, and its general effect has been to depreciate the security of real property. It is not surprising that a mode of procedure, which was based on trickery and evasion on the part of the smaller ratepayers, and on the acquiescence on the part of the wardens in a sort of chartered perjury on the part of their bailiffs, should have yielded its fruit in malpractices, which have culminated finally in frauds such as those which have recently been brought before the Supreme Criminal Court of the colony. By the public land charges' ordinance recently passed, the root of these abominations will be cut away. The wardens will be compelled to collect their revenues, instead of handing this over to be effected by a Government auctioneer of real property."

I unreservedly concur in the above remarks and criticisms. In my review of the Territorial Ordinance (first edition of this work, 1858), I had expressed similar views, and suggested changes which I am glad to see have been introduced since. I only find excessive the percentage exacted in cases of non-payment of the ward rates.

The towns of Port-of-Spain and San Fernando are administered by elected councillors. At the end of 1878 their financial affairs stood as follow :—

PORT-OF-SPAIN.

Expenditure.	Dollars.	Receipts.	Dollars.
Street Scavenging	11,131	House Tax	29,559
Repairs	9,627	Markets	13,107
Charity—Asylum	7,905	Real Property	4,603
Lighting and Watering	1,275	Licences	3,729
Markets	2,368	Improvement (Town)	7,206
Gutters (Town)	9,583	Miscellaneous	1,759
Cemetery	2,272	Balance from previous Year	16,950
Salaries	5,228		
Purchase of Property	4,816		
Miscellaneous	4,352		
	58,557		76,913

SAN FERNANDO.

Expenditure.	Dollars.	Receipts.	Dollars.
Streets	5,384	House Rate	10,877
Tramroad	1,134	Licences	1,772
Charities	1,289	Markets	1,310
Horses and Carts	1,594	Wharf Dues	5,604
Markets	506	Tramroad	888
Cemetery	665	Cemetery Building Lots	1,031
Salaries	1,898	Miscellaneous	1,640
Schools	1,226		
Tramroad Wharf Water Dues	2,724		
Miscellaneous	2,056		
	18,476		23,122

At the end of 1878 the borough of San Fernando had become largely indebted to the Colonial Government in respect of debentures issued for the construction of a branch tramroad to Cipero, which they were even unable to maintain in proper repair. An amicable arrangement was entered into by which the Government took over the tramroad, assuming at the same time the liabilities incurred by the borough on that account; so that at present the borough has no interest in the tramroad, and part of the wharf dues is retained in reduction of the debt—a very fair arrangement, as I believe.

CIVIL ESTABLISHMENTS. — His Excellency the Governor, £5,000; private secretary, £300 : total £5,300.

Colonial Secretary, £1,000; provisional and personal, £200; chief clerk and clerk of council, £600; second clerk, £300; third clerk, £200; fourth clerk, £140; two messengers, £220; allowances, £65; contingencies, viz., postage and telegrams, £150 : total, £2,875.

RECEIVER-GENERAL.—Receiver-General, £800 ; provisional, £175: total, £975. Chief clerk and accountant, £360; second clerk and cashier, £340; three clerks, £530; two messengers, £110; allowance to cashier, £40; excise officer, £229 19s. 2d.; lockers, £140 ; San Fernando sub-receiver, £450 ; clerk, £200. Excise: locker and extra clerk, £220 ; allowance to cashier £10; supervisors, £100; contingencies, labour at bonding warehouses, £142 10s.: total, £3,847 9s. 2d.

IMMIGRATION.—Protector of immigrants, including travelling expenses and personal, £1,000 ; inspector, £500; sub-inspector and assistant inspector, £400 ; five clerks, £1,060; interpreters, £385; messenger, £40; travelling allowances to inspector and sub-inspector, £250 : total, £3,637.

AUDITOR-GENERAL.—For many years the Colonial Secretary had also the title of Auditor of Public Accounts. Some years ago, however, an audit office was organised, and the staff now consists of an Auditor-General, with a salary of £700 ; chief clerk, £450 ; clerks, £1,450; messengers, £70 : total, £2,670.

REGISTRAR-GENERAL.—This office was established by Ordinance 12, 1847. The Registrar-General is mainly registrar of deeds. A fee of ten shillings to twenty shillings is exacted for the registration of deeds, and from twenty shillings to two shillings for that of wills, probate, and letters of administration; also a fee of one shilling for office copies of any deed, will, or other document; from twenty shillings to five shillings for certificates, and one shilling for examining any deed, will, or other document. There is also a registrar of births, deaths, and marriages for the towns of Port-of-Spain and San Fernando, and for each ward respectively ; these are paid from the funds of the two boroughs and the wards—a sum of one shilling for each registry of birth and death. In case such registration has not been made in due time, the party in default pays a fine not exceeding £5. Registrar-General, £500 ; chief clerk, £300 ; clerk, £50; pay of copying clerks, local newspapers, £115 : total, £965.

PUBLIC WORKS AND SURVEY.—An office of public works had been established in the year 1845. Previous to its formation, the Surveyor-General had the superintendence of all the public works. The engineer officer of the garrison, however, was occasionally employed ; and he was particularly so engaged in superintending the construction of the Government and Court houses. It became necessary, on the introduction of railways in the island, to re-model the department. On the resignation of the late superintendent, in 1875, the entire staff of the establishment consisted of a superintendent, an assistant superintendent, a draughtsman, and a clerk—a staff quite insufficient and inadequate to the work. The title of superintendent was changed to that of Director of Public Works, and the department now comprises the following branches : Railways, public works, including buildings and ordinary roads; surveys. The staff of the department consists of the following officers and subordinate employes : Director of Public Works, £1,200 ; assistant director, £800 ; first assistant engineer, £500 ; second assistant (temporary), £500; accountant, £250 ; clerk to director, £200; financial assistant, extra assistant engineer, draughtsman, storekeeper, &c., twelve employes altogether, £2,802 10s. These appointments are provisional— four road officers, £700 ; messenger, £37. Allowances : Director of Public Works, £200 ; assistant engineers, £500 ; road officers, £200 ; paymaster, San Fernando, £70. Total, £7,959.

SURVEY DEPARTMENT.—Engineer in charge of surveys, £500; two assistants, £900; draughtsman, £120; allowance, £400 : total, £1,920.

Superintendent of transport train, £350; steam tug, £375; dredger and five barges, £570 ; water-works and sewerage, £573 10s.; saw-mill, £302; keeper of buildings, £100: total, £2,270 10s.

Total Public Works, £12,129.

CUSTOMS. — Port-of-Spain : Collector, £700 ; chief clerk, £450 ; three other clerks, £480. Landing waiters, lockers, and tide surveyors: principal, £300 ; other waiters, two surveyors, &c, £2,090 ; boatmen and porters, £559 ; allowance to cashier, £25 : total £4,606. San Fernando: Landing waiter, £170 : total, San Fernando, £170. Contingencies, viz. : Repairs of boats, boatmen's clothing, &c., £180. Total Customs, £4,956.

POST-OFFICES.—It was under the government of Lord Harris' that a regular postal communication was established between the different parts of the island. The mails are made up for certain districts every day except Sundays and public holidays; for others, two or three times a week, and only once a week for the remotest parts. The General Post-Office in Port-of-Spain is open from 7 A.M. to 4 P.M., and 7 to 8 A.M. on Sundays and public holidays. Our present postmaster has had pillar-boxes put up in different parts of the town; they are cleared daily at 6 A.M., 10 A.M., and 3 P.M., except on Sundays. All letters must be posted with stamps. There is but one district—the chief town—where letters are delivered by letter carriers; in the other districts the parties must send for them to the different post-offices. Trinidad is comprised within the general postal union.

Postmaster-General, £600; postmaster, San Fernando, £270; chief clerk, £250; second clerk, £150; two additional clerks, sorters, letter carriers, &c., £835; contingencies, viz., extra labour, lighting, &c., £175; district postmasters, £415; clerk, San Fernando, £100; total, £2,795. Harbour-master of the island, £500; assistant, £250; harbour, San Fernando, £100; signalmen, £320; allowances, £70; contingencies, viz., buoys, lighthouse, &c., £575; steam launch, £332: total, £2,147.

Crown Lands Department.—Both under the Spanish and British Government, the Governor of the island acted as intendant of crown lands.

Under the Spanish rule, there existed the Court of Intendant, consisting of the Governor as Intendant, his assessor—a lawyer, and a secretary, or escribano. The court sat in two capacities—as guardian and judge of crown lands; and in all matters relative to land sales, quit-rents, the Queen's revenue, &c. All petitions for lands, all claims, &c., were sent and submitted to the assessor by the escribano. He examined into the matters referred to him, heard the parties, and issued his orders; he, however, occasionally consulted with the Governor previous to issuing final orders. All such orders were transmitted by the escribano to the parties concerned. There existed also the office of "Surveyor-General and Commissary of Population." All Government surveys were made by the Surveyor-General, or by his orders.

The whole system was remodelled some years ago; there is no such thing now as a Court of Intendant; and the office of Surveyor-General, such as it existed, has been done away with.

The Governor, however, is still intendant of crown lands; but a new department has been formed, consisting of a sub-intendant, a secretary, and clerks. Rules have been adopted for the survey and sale of crown lands. The following are the most important:—

No person can survey, or begin to survey, any crown lands without being directed by the Governor to do so.

No block is to be measured out unless it bounds on lands already estimated.

All measurements are to be made in chains and links, with what is known as the Gunter's chain of 66 feet, or 100 links in length, a standard of which is fixed at the Government House.

Proper boundary marks—such as stones, pieces of iron, or other lasting objects, with broken bottles buried underfoot—are to be placed at the corners of every block.

The surveyors must give the petitioners due notice of the date of survey, and that their presence will be required at it.

Parties wishing to become purchasers of crown lands will apply to the commissioner of the province, at his office, where the necessary forms of petition can be supplied and filled up, the petitioner giving the boundaries and his address.

Petitions for less than ten acres are not received, except under special circumstances.

Each petition must be accompanied by a deposit of the upset price of the land prayed for, together with the fees payable for its survey and grant.

Every petition shall be reported on by the warden, or assistant warden, of the ward in which the land is situated; and the commissioner shall certify his approval or disapproval of the petition.

If disapproved, he will submit the same to the intendant for his instructions, stating his reasons for disapproval.

If approved, the petition is transmitted to the Surveyor-General.

It will be the duty of the Surveyor-General to cause the boundaries given in the petition to be certified, referring the petition back to the commissioner should material alterations be found necessary.

The petition must be submitted to the intendant for approval.

If disallowed by the intendant, it will be returned to the commissioner, who will prepare a referred warrant for the deposit money.

If approved by the intendant, an order for survey is issued.

Sales of crown lands are held at the office of the sub-intendant, at Port-of-Spain, on the first Tuesday of every month, or at such times as his Excellency the Governor may direct.

The sub-intendant shall, at least twenty-one days before any sale of crown lands, publicly advertise and post up in his office a list of the lands to be offered for sale on each day, and shall also notify the applicants.

All crown lands petitioned for, where the petition has been approved, the survey duly executed, and due notice of sale given, are offered at such sale for public competition, and disposed of to the highest bidder for cash. When the highest bidder for any land fails to pay the amount of his bid immediately after the sale, the next higher bidder, on paying the amount of his bid, becomes the purchaser. The upset price for ordinary crown lands is £1 per acre. The Governor may fix the upset price of any specially-designated crown lands at any higher rate than £1 per acre, and for any swamp lands at a rate not less than 10s. per acre. Village lots are sold under separate and special regulations.

When land applied for by one person is purchased by another, the whole of the money deposited by the original applicant is returned to him.

Sub-intendant and commissioner of Northern Province, £800; secretary to intendant, £500; four clerks, £960; porter and messenger, £75; allowance to sub-intendant for travelling expenses, £200; total, £2,235.

WARDENS AND SUPERVISORS.—Northern Province: four wardens, £3,050; three assistant wardens, £900. Southern Province: Commissioner and warden of Naparima, £800; three assistant wardens, £950; clerk to commissioner, £180; travelling allowance, £100; to assistant wardens, £150: total, £6,130.

COLONIAL STOREKEEPER. — Storekeeper, £450; clerk and porter, &c., £65: total, £515.

BOTANIC GARDEN. — This garden was laid out under Sir Ralph Woodford, at the Governor's residence, St. Ann, mainly with the object of encouraging the propagation of spice-trees. Well selected as forming part of the Governor's ground, and for its proximity to Port-of-Spain, this spot is in other respects ill-adapted to its destination, the soil being poor and barren and the supply of water scanty.

Flowers and ornamental shrubs are extensively cultivated; and lately, I am glad to say, the cultivation and amelioration of fruit-trees by selection and grafting has been successfully attempted. Nurseries have been established of coffee and lime plants, also of several varieties of sugar-cane; the latter, however, with only partial success, on account of the poverty of the soil. I must, in fairness, acknowledge that our present botanist, Mr. Prestoe, has turned to the best account the scanty resources thus afforded. I am under the impression that by damming one or two small gullies in the grounds, a sufficient supply of water could be obtained for gardening and other agricultural purposes.

Botanist, £300; clerk and two gardeners, £455: total £755. Examiner of animals, £450.

PRINTING.—Printer, £400; foreman, £200; compositors, binders, £505; other employes, £772; binding, repairs, &c., £200: total, £2,077.

JUDICIAL DEPARTMENT.—I have already stated that the "illustrious cabildo," or, more properly speaking, the "alcades in ordinary," were vested with judiciary powers, which they exercised with the assistance of a lawyer, and within very narrow limits, since the majority of cases were decided by arbitration, each party choosing a friend as arbitrator; in case these did not come to an agreement, they chose an umpire, who sided with either one or the other.

Immediately after the capture of the island, Mr. J. Nihell, a resident, was appointed Chief Justice, deciding all cases *according to his conscience*. In 1800, Governor Picton established the "Court of Consulado;" in 1807, Governor Hislop abolished this court and re-appointed Mr. J. Nihell chief judge. In 1808, however, the Colonial Office sent out Judge Smith to Trinidad, with authority over all the tribunals of the island; he was also empowered to *hear appeals from his own decisions*.

In the year 1814, John Bigge, Esq., Barrister-at-Law, arrived in Trinidad as Chief Justice in both civil and criminal matters, and associated to himself in criminal matters Dr. Ramon Garcia, the assessor to their honours the alcades. Appeals were allowed from his decisions to the Governor, as judge of the Court of

Appeals. The alcades in ordinary, however, continued to entertain actions in civil matters until the year 1828, when the "Court of Alcades in Ordinary" was abolished by an Order in Council of September, 1822.

By this and another order of the same date beneficial alterations were made in the judicial administration of the colony. The powers united in the decision of civil and criminal cases were separated; "Courts of Criminal Trials" and "First Instance of Civil Jurisdiction" were established, and a judge of "Criminal Enquiry" appointed. A "Court of Appeal," both in criminal and civil matters, was organised, with the Governor as judge, assisted by an assessor, who acted also as assistant to the chief judge in the "Court of Criminal Trial" and that of "First Instance of Civil Jurisdiction."

Judge Bigge was succeeded in the year 1820 by Ashton Warner, Esq., of the Middle Temple; he died in September, 1830, much esteemed and universally regretted, both as a judge and gentleman. His successor (in 1832) was his Honour George George Scotland, of the Middle Temple, a talented barrister, who retired from the colony in the year 1849 on a pension, leaving as his successor George William Knox, barrister, a native of the island, a scholar, and a highly-respected judge. Our present Chief Justice is Sir Joseph Needham; there are besides the Chief Justice two puisne judges—their Honours Horace Fitzgerald and Henry Court.

The English practice and the English laws were gradually introduced into the colony. In the year 1844 the criminal law of England and trial by jury were adopted; trial by jury in civil cases was adopted in 1848.

The Judicature Act was introduced, with some modifications, in the year 1879. Our present judicial establishment now consists of the Supreme Court, which is a court of record; it has the same jurisdiction within the colony as the High Court of Justice has in England, except in admiralty and divorce and matrimonial causes.

The Supreme Court.—Jurisdiction in all cases of lunacy and bankruptcy; it has an appellate jurisdiction, both in civil and criminal cases, from the decision of a single judge, whether sitting in court or in chambers; also from the decisions of stipendiary or other justices of the peace where the penalties imposed by such stipendiary justices amount to or exceed £5; or where imprisonment, even for a week, is imposed.

This court is presided over by the Chief Justice of the colony, assisted by the two puisne judges.

The "Supreme Court" has a primary jurisdiction in all cases where the subject matter does not exceed £200, or in actions for the recovery of the possession of lands where the annual rent or value does not exceed the sum of £20.

This court is held every fortnight in Port-of-Spain, and once a month in the town of San Fernando. It is presided over by one of the judges, and is governed by the same rules, with some slight modifications, as the "Supreme Court."

The "Supreme Court" sits five times a year for the disposal of criminal matters and gaol delivery, and every fortnight for the disposal of cases not triable by jury.

Jurors are empanelled to try all criminal and civil cases pending before the "Supreme Court." In the summary jurisdiction of this court any judge has the power to order a jury of five to be empanelled in any case pending before such court.

The "Supreme Court" has power to sit at any time except during the long vacation, which commences on the 26th of June, and ends on the 3rd of October in each year.

Appeals to Her Majesty in her Privy Council lie in all cases in the "Supreme Court" where the claim exceeds £500 sterling.

Court of Vice-Admiralty.—This court is presided over by the Chief Justice of the colony, and derives its jurisdiction and powers under the 2nd William IV., entitled "An Act to regulate the practice and fees in the Vice-Admiralty Courts abroad, and to obviate doubts as to their jurisdiction."

Petty Civil Court.—This is a court having a summary jurisdiction in all pleas of personal actions, both in the town of Port-of-Spain and the rural districts, where the debt or damage claimed does not exceed £10 sterling. This court has no jurisdiction in ejectment, or where the title to land arises, or as to the validity of any devise, bequest, or limitation under any will, or in cases of trover, or in any action of tort. In the town of Port-of-Spain it is presided over by a commissioner, and in the town of San Fernando and the rural districts by the stipendiary justices of San Fernando and such rural districts. No appeal lies from the decisions of the Petty Civil Court of Port-of-Spain, or of the stipendiary justices in their respective districts; but by a recent ordinance in Judicature Act of 1879, the Supreme Court has power, on the motion of the Attorney-General, to order all proceedings from inferior courts to be sent up to it, there to be reviewed.

Rural Districts Courts.—There are in the island seven of these courts, presided over by stipendiary justices, who reside in their respective districts.

Every stipendiary justice has jurisdiction over the whole island.

The Rural Districts Courts have a summary jurisdiction in all cases of a criminal or quasi-criminal nature, where the offence committed is not of an indictable nature. When the offence committed is of an indictable nature, the stipendiary justices take preliminary depositions, and forward the same to the Attorney-General, who determines whether the party charged should be indicted or not.

The power of imprisonment by a stipendiary justice is limited to six months, with or without hard labour.

A court of similar jurisdiction to those of rural districts sits daily in Port-of-Spain. It is presided over by the stipendiary justice of the western district of the county of St. George and the town of Port-of-Spain.

The important duties of coroner are performed by the stipendiary justices. The verdict of the jury must be unanimous, or the jurors are confined for several hours, until they concur in a final agreement, or are dismissed on some good ground.

As there are many foreigners in the island—Spaniards, French, Portuguese, Hindoos, Chinese—there are interpreters attached to the different courts.

Executions take place within the precincts of the Royal Gaol, in the presence of all the prisoners assembled, and a certain number of the public admitted for the purpose.

Chief Justice, £1,800; first puisne judge and commissioner of Petty Civil Court, Port-of-Spain, £1,200; second puisne judge, £1,000; clerk to the judges, £200; messengers, porter, £145; allowance and contingencies, £130 : total, £4,475.

Registrar of the Courts.—Registrar, £600; four clerks, £455: total, £1,055.

Attorney-General.—Attorney-General, £1,000; clerical assistance, £300 : total, £1,300.

Solicitor-General.—Solicitor-General, £200.

Crown Solicitor.—Crown solicitor, £300.

Marshal.—In lieu of fees in criminal processes, £200.

Petty Civil Court.—Judge of Petty Civil Court, first puisne judge; clerical assistance, £330.

Complaint Court, San Fernando.—Clerk, £50; registrar in bankruptcy (provisional) £300.

MAGISTRACY.—Stipendiary justice of the western district, county of St. George, and magistrate of Port-of-Spain, £700; eastern district, £600. Stipendiary justice, San Fernando, £600; county of Caroni, £600; Savannah Grande, Oropuche, &c., £600; Cedros, £500; two other magistrates, £600. Total magistracy, £4,200.

Clerks of the Peace, £2,325; bailiffs, £1,457; interpreters, £480; pound keep and office keeper of courts, £138 10s.; travelling allowance to magistrates, £477 : total, £4,877 10s. Grand total of judicial establishment, £16,105 10s.

EDUCATION.—For many years, and until the changes introduced by Sir Henry Irving, the Government contributions towards education were confined to the salaries of the inspectors of schools, of the superintendent, and the teacher of the boys' and girls' model schools, and the secretary of the Board of Education—altogether a sum of £1,150. The primary schools were maintained out of local funds. At present, the expenses of public education, either secondary or primary, are altogether or partly defrayed from the general funds of the colony. I need not point out the many advantages of this system.

Secondary Education.—Royal College : Principal, £700; house-rent, £100; masters, £1,350; professor of chemistry and Government analyst, £500; principal, affiliated school, £500; porter, £90; contingencies, viz., prizes, books, stationery, repairs, &c., £300 : total, £3,340.

Primary Education.—Superintendent of boys' model school, £300; of girls' model school, £250; district masters, £2,755; inspector of schools, £500; travelling expenses, £200 : total, £4,005. Expenses exclusive of establishments, £10,900. Total primary education, £14,905.

MEDICAL DEPARTMENT.—This may be said to be a newly-constituted department, organised with the object of affording medical assistance to the poor in the rural districts, and securing effective attendance to the indentured immigrants. It consists of a surgeon-general and twenty-four Government medical officers. The medical staff of the Colonial Hospital consists of a resident-surgeon and three assistant-surgeons. To the San Fernando Hospital there is only one resident-surgeon attached; there should be at least one assistant. There is also to each hospital a consulting surgeon.

I must say that, to my view, the present arrangement is open to serious objections. In general, the house-surgeon and his assistants are young men, some fresh from the medical schools, more or less ignorant of the diseases of the country, and quite inexperienced in their treatment. They may be clever and willing, and good operators; but they have not yet acquired that experience which is gained only by several years' practice. In my opinion there should be appointed to each hospital a visiting-surgeon and a visiting-physician, who have been some years in the island, and who would have the greatest share of responsibility, and a sufficient number of resident surgeons and physicians, who would act under the control and direction of the visiting practitioners. All young men coming to the colony should, before obtaining employment under the Government, pass through the colonial hospitals. Many appointments are only temporary, and the district medical officers may be removed at will. My objection to this is, that the medical officer cannot take an interest in the district to which he is temporarily appointed, nor has he the opportunity of becoming acquainted with the people he is called to serve. As a rule, all appointments should be made permanent, unless the occupant asks for a change in case of any vacancy.

The district medical officers are expected to attend at certain places, on regular days and hours, to prescribe for persons applying for medical advice—a very humane provision.

Paupers producing a certificate of pauperism from the warden or assistant-warden of the district are prescribed for gratuitously, and the medicines ordered furnished free of charge.

Applicants producing a certificate of poverty, signed by a burgess or a respectable ratepayer, are prescribed for on prepayment of a shilling; and the medicine ordered can be procured at certain appointed shops at a reduced rate.

Persons applying for advice without certificate are regarded as private patients.

In the case of paupers and others unable to pay, the medical officer will visit on the order in writing of the warden, and will be entitled to payment from the ward funds of a single fee of 4s. per visit, with 1s. mileage allowance.

He is responsible for attending, whether prepaid or not, in any case of extreme urgency, or on the summons of any warden, magistrate, or police officer.

Similar provisions have been made for the boroughs of Port-of-Spain and San Fernando. Let me observe that the certificate from the warden is not always easily obtainable, as he may reside several miles from the patient's residence; and many find it too inconvenient or too tiresome to walk several miles to obtain the necessary document. Thus the good intentions of the Government may be defeated. The only remedy that I can discover is the following:—Let a list of all the paupers in each ward be prepared, and left at the different places appointed for giving advice; the list should be revised every year. There cannot be much difficulty in doing this. I would also suggest the formation of categories, in which to include all those who might be considered as poor—for instance, of people residing on estates, or day labourers, assistant masons and carpenters, &c.

Surgeon-General, £1,000; twenty-three medical officers, £300 each: £6,900; three supernumeraries, £900. Resident-surgeon, Colonial Hospital, £200; senior assistant, £50. Resident-surgeon, San Fernando Hospital, £200. Medical officer of shipping, &c., £150. Medical officer, lunatic asylum and gaol, £200. Medical officer, leper asylum, £150. Consulting surgeon, San Fernando Hospital, £100. Surgeon to Chaguanas depôt, £50. Total, £1,100. For several medical officers for residence and houses, £1,925. Personal allowance to seven medical officers, as compensation, £950. Total, £12,175.

HOSPITALS.—Colonial Hospital: dispenser, £200; assistant, £100; clerk, £200; assistant, £50; stewards and issuer, £195; matron, £150; superintendent of nurses, £248 15s.; sixteen nurses, £680 10s. 11d.; six supernumerary, £195; other inferior employes, £742: total, £2,761.

o

San Fernando Hospital.—Dispenser, £150; clerk, £50; steward and issuer, £105; head nurse and matron, £115; nurses, £312 10s.; two supernumerary, £70; wardsmen, &c., £255; St. Joseph Infirmary, £80 : total, £1,107 10s.

Leper Asylum.—Resident superintendent, £200; dispenser, £75; five nurses, £150; wardsmen, cook, baker, laundress, &c., £262 10s.: total, £687. The Leper Asylum is placed under the care of Dominican nurses.

Lunatic Asylum.—Head attendant, £175; assistant, £52 10s.; teacher and clerk, £200; dispenser and steward, £62 10s.; six male attendants, £286; four probationary, £150; three female attendants, £142 10s.; two probationary, £75; cook, laundress, &c., £297 10s.: total, £1,402 10s.

House of Refuge.—The House of Refuge was established purposely for the reception of paupers and infirm persons in the rural districts, the Borough Council of Port-of-Spain having their own asylum for the poor of the town.

PUBLIC HEALTH DEPARTMENT. — Port-of-Spain : Sanitary inspector, £250; four assistants, £345; two district medical officers, £100; San Fernando sanitary inspector, £100; assistant, £75; district medical officer, £50 : total, £920.

Surgeon-General.—Chief clerk, £220 ; other clerks and employes, £400 : total, £620.

POLICE AND GAOLS.—The general police force consists at present of an inspector commandant, two inspectors, two sergeant-majors, superintendent staff clerk, superintendent sergeant, instructors, &c.; twenty-five sergeants, twenty-five corporals, twenty-five lance corporals, two hundred and fifty constables, captain volunteer fire brigade, and eight firemen. There is, besides the police force, a certain number of rural constables.

Inspector commandant, £700; inspector northern division, £370; inspector southern division, £450; superintendent staff clerk, £200; sergeant-major northern division, £200; sergeant-major southern division, £140; sergeant-inspector, £140; two sergeant-superintendents, quarter-master, and armourer, £610; twenty-five corporals, £2,062; twenty-five sergeants, £2,737; twenty-five lance-corporals, £1,487; two hundred and fifty constables, £14,250; captain volunteer fire brigade, £200; eight firemen, £456; female teacher, £20; allowances, house-rent for inspectors, &c., £558; clerical assistance, £30 : total police force, £24,630.

ROYAL GAOL.—The Royal Gaol is not on the separate system. Separation by night is carried out as far as the cell accommodation permits. By day all male prisoners work in association; the females are, in great measure, separated from each other. All prisoners in association by day are under the constant supervision of warders. There are in the Royal Gaol 126 separate cells: wards and cells in association, 37. At the Royal Gaol religious service is performed every Sunday, and religious instruction given on one evening in each week by the chaplains. A schoolmaster attends four evenings a week to give instruction to male prisoners who are sentenced to twelve months and upwards; also to juveniles.

Besides the Royal Gaol there are two convict depôts, where male prisoners, under hard labour, are sent; one at Chaguanas at the entrance of an extensive forest. Separate cells at the depôt, 126.

The prisoners are there employed in carrying railway sleepers, hauling logs, cutting wood, cutting traces through the forest, and cultivating provisions. Carrera's Island is a small calcareous islet at the entrance of the Bay of Chaguaramas, where prisoners are employed in quarrying stones and breaking road metal. Separate cells, 56.

All the Royal Gaol male prisoners are utilised in quarrying stones and breaking road metal at the Government quarries, keeping the grounds of Government institutions in order, working at trades within the prison walls; female prisoners in needlework, washing clothes, and breaking stones.

Inspector of prisons, £100; superintendents, £400; clerk and teacher, £50; overseer, £170 : £720; eighteen warders, £1,220; hospital attendant, matron, messenger, £320 : total Royal Gaol, £2,260. Chaguanas convict depôt : superintendent, £300; ten warders, watchmen, £740 : total, £1,040. Carrera's Island : Five warders, £370; allowances, inspector of prisons, and keeper of gaol for travelling expenses, £100; warders for quarters, £400 : total, gaol and depôts, £4,170.

RAILWAYS.—This section belongs to the Public Works Department. So far back as the time of Lord Harris, a company had been formed in England with the object of constructing, in

Trinidad, a regular network of railways, under the condition that the colony would grant the company, on each side of the line, where traversing crown property, a certain extent of land proportionate to the extent of miles constructed; also that the colony should guarantee to the shareholders a minimum interest of six per cent. This was found to be a much too onerous condition, and the scheme, besides, was deemed much too comprehensive. The matter dropped in consequence.

At a later period, another company suggested the adoption of a more restricted scheme, but under conditions pretty similar to those which had been formerly rejected. The offer was declined.

Sir Arthur Gordon, whilst administering the Government, had recognised the great difficulty of constructing roads and maintaining them in good condition, on account of the nature of our soil and the difficulty of procuring good road materials, and come to the conclusion that, after all, railways might prove cheap means of communication. He had not time, however, to initiate the measure, but when in London mooted the question.

His successor, Sir James Longden, had the good fortune of beginning the work—viz., the construction, eastward, of the line to Arima, a distance of sixteen miles; but it devolved on Sir Henry Irving to complete this our first railway. It succeeded beyond all expectations; and it was decided almost immediately to extend the line from St. Joseph southward to Couva, and later on to San Fernando, a distance of about twenty-five miles, thus connecting the southern and northern divisions of the island and its two principal towns.

Passenger fares.—First class, eight cents a mile; second class, four cents a mile; third class, two cents a mile; children under twelve years, half-price; goods, according to classes, from half a cent to two cents per 100 lbs., or portion of 100 lbs., per mile. Sugar, molasses, cocoa, rum, and coffee, are carried under special arrangements.

General superintendent, £300; clerk to superintendent, £250; messenger, £37 10s. : £587 10s.; lithographic press printer, &c., £256.

Traffic Department.—Traffic manager, £450; assistant, £250; clerks, collector, head guards, under guards, police, gatekeepers, signalman, porters, £2,257 : total, £3,017.

Stations.—San Juan, collector, porter, £108; St. Joseph,

£226 8s. 4d.; Tunapuna, £185 18s.; Tacarigua, £107 16s.; Arouca, £183 16s.; D'Abadie, £88; Arima, £256 16s.; Caroni, £98; Couupia, £88; Chaguanas, £286 8s. 4d.; Carapichaima, £126; Couva, £456 0s. 4d.: total, £3,052.

Locomotive Department.—Locomotive superintendent, £450; drivers, firemen, cleaners, shedmen; clerk, storekeeper, coalmen, watermen, turner, fitter, blacksmith, £4,070 5s.: total, £4,521 5s.

Carriage and Waggon Department.—Cleaners and greasers, £382 12s.

Engineering and Maintenance Department.—Engineer, £250; two foremen, eight gaugers, thirty-two platelayers, weeders, £3,035 : total railway, £14,259.

ECCLESIASTICAL.—Grant to Church of England, £3,770; to Roman Catholic Church, £6,500; to Wesleyan body, £500: total, £10,770. This grant will be ultimately reduced to £10,435.

Expenditure, exclusive of establishments.—Administration of justice: Expenses of Solicitor-General, advocates, witnesses, medical practitioners giving evidence in criminal cases, &c., £3,000.

Registration fees to registrars, £320.

Education.—Normal schools; districts and assisted schools, result fees, exhibitions, &c., £10,900.

Police.—Clothing, horses, and mules, £3,720; lighting police barracks and station, travelling allowance, stores, necessaries, &c., £2,375.

Gaols.—Royal Gaol: Food, clothing, &c., for about 350 prisoners, £3,325. Chaguanas and Carrera depôts: Food, clothing, &c., for 180 prisoners, £1,710. Total police and gaols, £11,130.

Hospitals.—Provisions, stimulants, medicines, clothing, &c., £21,400; vaccination, £600. Grand total, £22,000.

Convict Depôt, Chaguanas.—Railway and tram-roads charges, &c., £677 10s.; Carrera, £72 10s. Total depôt, £750.

Rents.—Police stations, district schools, bonding warehouses, Port-of-Spain and San Fernando post-offices, £2,891 5s.

Contract Gulf steamer, £3,000; transport of public officers and special services, £200; local mails, £650: total, £3,650.

Postage.—Share of postage payable to Imperial Government, £1,200; commission on sale of stamps, £200 : total, £1,400.

Immigration. — Cost of introducing 2,400 immigrants, £24,000; surgeon fees, £2,800; return ship, £5,500; district medical officers, £4,800; collecting 2,400 immigrants, £9,600; salary and travelling expenses of agents in India, £2,000; captains' and officers' gratuities, orphan homes, hospital and house of refuge, medical inspectors, expenses at depôt, pay of cooks, &c., grant of £5 instead of return passage, £1,000. Total of immigration, £55,091.

Miscellaneous services.—Allowance for maintenance of Government House and grounds, furniture, grant to library, &c., £2,221.

Interest on Savings Bank deposits, £1,100.

Drawbacks and refund of duties, £3,500.

Interest on debentures, £855; redemption of debentures, £5,150: total, £6,005.

Railway Working Expenses.—Arima, Couva, £11,000; interest and sinking fund, £15,000.

Telegraph.—Subsidy to West Indies and Panama Telegraph Company, £2,500; local telegraph, £300: total, £2,800.

Stationery, £2,300.

Botanic Garden.—Maintenance of garden and plantations, £1,350.

Census expenses, £1,000.

Roads and bridges, £34,000; road extension and improvement, £14,000; works and buildings, £13,300; miscellaneous, £3,700. Grand total, £55,000.

WARD UNIONS. — Arima, £486 6s. 8d.; Chaguanas, £292 14s. 2d.; Couva, £322 1s. 8d.; Diego Martin, £328 16s.; Mayaro, £206 5s.; Montserrat, £180 16s.; St. Ann, £583 6s. 8d.; Tacarigua, £719 11s. 8d.; Toco, £179 3s. 4d.; Naparima, £989 11s. 8d.; Cedros, £328 2s. 6d. Total Wards, £4,616 15s.

The following Table exhibits the Receipts and Expenditure of the colony for a series of years, and at different periods:—

Year.	Revenue.	Expenditure.
1850	£88,084	£77,362
1860	184,861	187,220
1870	233,585	241,148
1871	264,352	234,170
1872	281,570	285,384
1873	296,060	326,282
1874	376,320	365,760
1875	341,619	352,488
1876	316,070	311,508
1877	310,338	318,586
1878	346,997	343,400
1879	419,885	375,986
1880	430,583	443,824
1881	419,999	414,598

If we take the three periods, 1850, 1860, 1870, we have—Revenue, £506,530; expenditure, £505,730—nearly equal. The nine years, from 1871 to 1880 exclusive, give the following results:—Revenue, £2,888,836; expenditure, £2,820,650; leaving a balance of £68,186 in favour of revenue.

The colony has contracted a heavy debt for the construction of railways—say £400,000—viz.: £150,000, 1874, at 5 per cent., for the construction of the railway from Port-of-Spain to Arima; £100,000, in 1878, at 5 per cent., for extending the railway to Couva; a further sum, in 1880, of £150,000, at 4 per cent., for further extension to San Fernando. Amount repaid on the loan of 1874, £5,840. Total debt now due for railways, £392,380. To this debt should be added the following sums, for which the colony is responsible, viz.: £12,800, residue of a sum of £86,510, borrowed at 6 per cent., 1856-65, for the formation of tram-roads; £1,600, also residue of a sum of £7,000 taken at 6 per cent., in 1860-61, for the repair of roads in South Naparima; £7,500, balance due on £15,000, borrowed for the construction of a tram-road at San Fernando. Total amount due, or guaranteed by the colony, £414,280. This debt is repayable as follows:—

Loan of 1874, by half-yearly appropriation out of the general revenue equal to 3 per cent. on the total nominal value of all debentures previously issued.

Loan of 1878, by half-yearly appropriations out of general revenue for payment of interest, and one-half per cent. on total nominal value of all debentures issued on account of their redemption.

Loan of 1880. Half-yearly appropriations out of general revenue for payment of interest, and one-half per cent. on total nominal value of all debentures issued on account of the redemption.

Loan of 1856-65. Yearly payments by estates deriving benefit from the undertakings, to meet interest and redemption.

Loan of 1860-61. Yearly payments by the estates in the locality.

Loan of 1864-65. Annual payments by the Borough Council for interest, and £600 for redemption. The balance of the loan (£7,600) has been taken over by the Government, together with the tram-road, in the expectation of being reimbursed from the profits of the undertakings.

The capital account of the two railways (about forty-two miles) may be said to stand at £392,300. Working expenses estimated at £11,000; interest and sinking-fund, £15,000: total, £26,000—a sum which it is reasonable to expect the receipts will amply repay. They were, in 1878, £22,036; in 1879, £25,085. Working expenses, in 1878, £12,421; in 1879, £13,925, leaving a net revenue of £9,614 for the former year, and of £11,089 for the latter. The receipts for the last ten months of the present year (1880) are highly encouraging. Total debt of the colony on 31st December, 1882, £591,760. Railways: debt, £585,360.

By published returns of available assets and immediate liabilities of the Colonial Government, on the 31st December, 1879, the financial position of the colony appears to stand as follows:—

	£	s.	d.
Cash in hands of Custodes on Deposit Accounts	55,000	0	0
,, ,, Receiver-General	2,890	4	10
,, ,, Sub-Receiver	1,380	3	4
,, ,, Crown Agents	10,170	2	0
Investment in Port-of-Spain Improvement Debentures	4,500	0	0
Advances to Sundry Pensions	30	0	0
,, on Account of Couva Railway	3,000	0	0
,, ,, Guaracara Tram-road	8,034	3	11
,, ,, San Fernando Tram-road	248	11	4
,, ,, the Arima, Couva, and San Fernando Railway	57,925	15	3
Due by Couva Extension Railway for Sleepers and Transfer Entries	4,000	0	0
By Borough Council of Port-of-Spain for Hospital dues	1,875	0	0
Borough Council for Education and Metal from Gaol	1,676	13	2
Sundry Persons for Hospital Dues and Establishments	2,847	15	4
Arrears of Water Rates	998	6	7
Police Superannuation Fund	312	10	0
	£154,887	5	9

LIABILITIES.

	£	s.	d.
Deposits	69,225	12	5
Due to Borough Council of Port-of-Spain for Coffins, Rent, &c.	958	4	7
Balance on Immigration Account	2,799	10	4
	£72,981	7	2
Balance in favour of the Colony	£81,905	18	7

This is, undoubtedly, a very satisfactory financial condition, especially when it is considered with reference to the general progress of the colony. The amount of specie in circulation in the colony is taken in the Blue Book of 1879 at £50,000—evidently mere guess than from any accurate information. The amount of paper currency was estimated in previous years at £50,000, which is probably very much below the mark. If under this head be included promissory notes discounted by the bank, the amount may be roughly estimated at between £300,000 and £400,000 sterling.

The accounts are kept by the merchants and the bank in dollars and cents; by the public departments in sterling.

The only silver coin in circulation is the English coin. Besides the English gold coin, United States and Spanish gold are received in payments by merchants at their value. The par of exchange, however, has been fixed by Order in Council at $480 per £100. Gold coins: sovereigns, $4·80; half-ditto, $2·40; United States eagle ($10), £2 1s.; half-eagle ($5), £1 0s. 6d. Silver coins: half-crown, 60 cents; florin, 48 cents; shilling, 24 cents; dollar, 4s. 2d.

Sterling money was rendered the standard coin in the year 1845, previously to which period the Spanish or Mexican medium had prevailed. This consisted of the dollar and its subdivisions. There was also for several years in circulation a colonial coin— viz., the quarter dollar and its subdivisions, the smaller of which was equal to six cents and a half. The gold coin long continued to be purely Spanish or Hispano-American—viz., the doubloon, or $16 piece, the 8, the 4, and 2 dollar pieces.

BANKING.—The Colonial Bank is the only establishment of the kind transacting business here, and, as I believe, a very profitable business. The exchange varies from 470 to 480 dollars, allowance being made for time and amount; deposits taken at three per cent.; money discounted at eight per cent. Rate of interest, 8 and 10 per cent. on good security; small sums, however, are often borrowed, on note, at 15, 20, and even 30 and 40 per cent.

MEANS OF COMMUNICATION—Roads and Bridges.—It cannot be expected that a country but recently settled—only a bit along the sea-shore under cultivation—should possess a superiority of internal communication; and this is precisely the case with regard to Trinidad. Moreover, materials for making roads and keeping them in repair are not only scarce, but the metal being in general limestone, is not very durable, and is procurable only from a few localities. The very nature of the soil itself—it being, in many places, clay or clay-loam—is, when coupled with our heavy rains, a very great obstacle to the formation of good roads.

During the prevalence of slavery, the *commandants* had the charge of making, repairing, and keeping in repair the roads; the construction of bridges was out of the question. The free inhabitants of each *quarter* were compelled by law to keep the roads, in their respective districts, in good order, and for that purpose a certain amount of days' labour was exacted, according to their amount of property; the *commandant* made an estimate of the number of days necessary for the repairs, and summoned each proprietor to furnish his quota, the roads being partitioned among the different individuals, and, as a rule, the portion nearest to each individual's estate allotted to him as his share; the work was afterwards inspected, and if not properly executed, was required to be perfected.

Immediately after emancipation, it became necessary to change that system, and no less than *four* ordinances were enacted between the months of October, 1839, and March, 1844. In the year 1846, however, an ordinance was passed providing for the making and repairing, and keeping in repair, the roads, bridges, and fences in the island of Trinidad. This ordinance was made very comprehensive, and fully entered into the details of the subject. The colony was divided into twenty-nine road districts, and commissioners were appointed who had the management and care of the roads in their respective districts, with authority to regulate the roads already laid out; to alter or even discontinue those they might regard as useless; to ascertain and define others. A portion of the roads was allotted to each commissioner, and funds assigned.

Bridges were to be kept in repair by joint contributions from adjoining districts. Although very comprehensive, this ordinance never worked well; nevertheless, it was changed only and consequent on the new territorial division in the year 1849.

The new enactment divided the roads of the colony into royal and ward roads. The roads termed royal were five in number. They were placed under the superintendence of surveyors and inspectors appointed by the Governor, while the wardens of the several wards were charged with the superintendence and keeping in repair of all other public thoroughfares not being royal roads. The expenses of the ward roads were defrayed from the ward funds, and those of the royal roads partly from the ward funds and partly from the general revenue.

This ordinance was partly repealed by the Act of 1854; at present all the roads of the colony are placed under the management of the Public Works Department, and the expenses defrayed from the public funds.

The frequent alterations of our roads' ordinances, the apparent uncertainty which so long governed this most important branch of the public service, must be a subject of surprise, and nevertheless are easily accounted for, when matters are duly considered. Laws may appear unexceptionable on paper, but their execution may be so full of difficulties as to render them null and nugatory. It would seem, on reading our road ordinances, that provision is made for everything, except what is most essential—viz., persons qualified to determine, direct, and superintend the making and repairing of the roads. The wardens had each in his district the charge of the roads and bridges; and yet many before their appointment had been merchants, clerks, or planters at the best; in fact, anything but fit agents for this special duty. I must acknowledge, however, that it was a prevailing opinion in the colony that any individual might be turned into a good road officer—a great mistake, as I think. The making and repairing of roads, especially the construction of bridges, should be entrusted to persons having special knowledge.

The Public Works Department has lately been remodelled, and a staff of competent engineers appointed; yet I apprehend that the department has not been properly organised in all its details, a great deal being still left to untaught subaltern officers. We should not lose sight of this; a small portion of our roads only is as yet macadamised or even properly drained; not a few are mere bridle paths, and bridges generally are very primitive structures. It will require time and money before our highways are put in proper order. As I conceive matters, an engineer should be appointed to each province, and take charge of the roads of his province, especially of the main roads. The local Road Boards should have the superintendence of the local or ward roads, under the control and guidance of the engineer of the province, it being their interest to have them in good condition. They might be of invaluable service.

CHAPTER VII.

PRODUCTIVE INDUSTRY—AGRICULTURE—EXPORTABLE ARTICLES: SUGAR, CACAO, COFFEE, ETC.—ALIMENTARY ARTICLES: LIVE-STOCK, VEGETABLES, PLANTAIN, MAIZE, RICE, MANIOC, YAMS, ETC.—FRUITS—COMMERCE.

THIS subject, from its importance, will be noted as fully as possible under the two following heads—1st, Agriculture ; 2nd, Commerce.

AGRICULTURE.—Trinidad is an exclusively agricultural country, and such it must continue to be for an unlimited period, inasmuch as its prosperity entirely depends on the cultivation of the soil and the exportation of colonial produce.

Agriculture, therefore, is of vital importance to the island, and ought to be encouraged, and even aided at any expense. This has already been done within certain limits. The immigration ordinance and the exemption from duty of machinery and implements of husbandry are measures calculated to benefit the agricultural interest. To these I may add the trespass ordinance, and the clause of the law which makes the stealing of sugarcanes or provisions an offence punishable by a heavy fine or imprisonment.

The sugar interest being, by far, the most important, is entitled to, and ought to receive, the largest share of protection ; not, however, to the extent and the form it was once granted, when all other cultures were made subordinate to that sole branch.

The territorial ordinance was passed avowedly with the object of penning up the labouring class on the existing plantations. But instead of locating on, or returning to, sugar and cacao estates, the emancipated bondsmen gave themselves up to petty traffic, and devoted their children likewise to mechanical trades ; or, again, took illegal possession of the public lands. The towns and villages became crowded with a swarm of idlers and swindlers; and avenues to honest industry were obstructed by those who, abandoning field occupations, originated a ruinous competition in the various crafts to which they resorted. Hence arose at the same time a scarcity of labour, not only in carrying on the cultivation of our staples, but even the production of alimentary articles.

Setting aside the discouragement created by the heavy charges which, for so many years, weighed upon landed property, there was, as there is still, a dislike among all classes to agricultural pursuits. On the part of the emancipated, this was too natural to be blamed, however much to be regretted. In their estimation, slavery had stamped field labour with infamy, so much so that servile in-door occupations were deemed more *respectable* than any field work. On the other hand, agricultural pursuits are disliked by the educated, both on account of the precarious nature of the crops, and the difficulty of procuring continuous labour; also, because such pursuits require unremitting attention and application. In fact, I really know of no occupation more laborious than that of an overseer during the crop season.

The tiller of the soil is, however, more independent, and his occupation less precarious, than that of a clerk, or even of a mechanic, carpenter, mason, or any other; these latter are entirely dependent on chance openings in their respective callings, whereas the former is always certain of obtaining employment and remuneration proportionate to his exertions.

"O fortunatos nimium sua si bona nôrint!"

These are causes which have hitherto acted, and still continue to act, in fomenting a prejudice against *the sole branch* of industry which we can follow here, and which may be regarded as the only foundation of our prosperity. For commerce itself entirely depends on agriculture; and the consumption of imported articles of manufacture is in direct ratio with the prosperous or adverse condition of the agriculturists.

I must acknowledge, however, that things, as they existed in 1856, have been modified, and important changes introduced, first by Sir Arthur Gordon, and more recently by Sir Henry Irving. Governor Gordon opened the crown lands to competition, and, as a parallel measure, issued stringent measures against squatters or illegal occupiers of crown lands. At present, land may be purchased at a comparatively low price, say £1 an acre, exclusive of expenses for survey and registration. By an ordinance introduced by Sir Henry Irving in 1879, the tax has been rendered uniform on all lands, whether cultivated or uncultivated, and at present no houses or buildings are exempted from taxation. An impetus has thus been given to the cultivation of the soil, and industrious habits fostered.

Agriculture, nevertheless, may be said to be very backward. Not only are agricultural operations difficult in lands newly cleared, and full of stumps and roots, but the classes connected with agriculture are not, generally, guided by any method, and the most primitive routine is the sole guide of the great majority of husbandmen. The emancipated negro and the Indian immigrant may be said to be ignorant, as they were always employed as mere mechanical agents, and had, besides, no interest to become skilful. The great majority of the planters themselves may be said to be unskilled. During the time of slavery, there was no necessity for the display of agricultural skill; and since emancipation they have been so incessantly engaged in struggling for their daily bread, as to have had but little time to devote to its acquisition, either in theory or as a practical study.

What I have stated concerning agriculture is, *a fortiori*, applicable to manufacture. Improvements in the manufacture of sugar required expensive and complicated machinery; means and skill to work the same; and, consequently, a large outlay of capital, which the sugar planters had not, and could not procure under difficult circumstances.

On the other hand, the cacao planter could scarcely eke out a livelihood, even with the utmost exertions; he dared not improve his article, since he might not have found, on the spot, purchasers ready to pay a higher price for a more costly article; nor would he run the risk of shipping any quantity on advance of money, lest he should, at a future reckoning, be liable to a reimbursement.

However, for some years past, great attention has been given to the preparation of cacao, and little remains to be achieved under this head. Except, perhaps, the *conuqueros*, or small cottagers, cacao growers devote great care to the curing of the seeds; sweating or fermenting rooms are built, in which they are almost hermetically heaped and allowed to undergo a thorough process of fermentation; proper houses are erected for the reception and drying of the article on its being removed from the sweating room. As a consequence, Trinidad cacao is well received on the markets of Europe and the United States. It is generally shipped by the proprietors to agents in Europe, the inferior article only being sold in the colony.

Besides the two species or varieties—the *Cacao Criollo* and the *Forastero*—there are not a few other sub-varieties exhibiting distinct qualities, and, in my opinion, selection should be attended to in the formation of any new plantation.

For many years drainage had been completely disregarded; lately, however, it has been found not only useful, but absolutely necessary in certain localities; and, where resorted to, the results have been most remarkable.

At one time, and that of not a far back date, the cacao plantations were negligently weeded with the cutlass twice a year, mainly to facilitate the gathering of the crop. They were not methodically pruned, nor cleared of parasites, mosses, and lichens. I have often thought that the horse-hoe might be employed in the cacao walks with advantage. Generally speaking, the weeds to be found on cacao plantations are soft and not very deep-rooted, whilst the mould being deep, there would be very little obstruction to the working of that instrument. The work done by the horse-hoe would certainly be better and cheaper also, I believe, than that performed with the cutlass; for, with the latter, the grass and weeds are only cut at from one to two inches above the ground, the surface not being even scratched; whereas, with the former, there would be a thorough deep weeding. But the horse-hoe could not be used in old-established cacao estates, where the roots of the " Bois Immortel " and those of the cacao trees themselves form an inextricable network of impediment to a surface action. Such practice should be resorted to primarily in young plantations, and then might be continued as they advanced in growth; this I throw out as a suggestion to any enterprising cacao planters. The common hand-hoe, however, ought to be used *immediately around* each plant. This is, also, as far as I know, the practice on the Spanish main, where the cultivation of the cacao plant is better understood than in any other country. A friend of mine tried the fork in his cacao plantation, and with very beneficial results, as he informed me.

Sugar is found in many plants; but it is mainly manufactured from the sugar-cane and beet-root. The sugar industry has, of late years, made rapid and signal progress; the beet-root has, by careful cultivation, and scientific appliances to the manufacture of sugar, become the source from which is obtained nearly one-half of the whole quantity of sugar produced in our days, so much so that the chances are that we will succumb in the competition, unless we pay greater attention to the culture of the cane and the manufacture of sugar. Our sugar industry, I grieve to say, is going to ruin on account of the imperfect methods followed. The time has arrived which imperatively calls for a change of system.

The science of husbandry is no longer that confused congeries of incoherent precepts, which for so long a period formed its fundamental structure. Taught by chemistry and meteorological observations, it has, by degrees, assumed among the other sciences the high position to which it is eminently entitled. But the precepts of that science vary in their application with the climate, the soil, and the different properties of the plants themselves; so that methods of culture, though based on uniform principles, are but the digested result of a series of individual observations, made under the same climate and in various localities, not only respecting tillage, manuring, planting, drainage, &c., but also regarding the economical management of properties. Hence the great utility of agricultural societies, of agronomic stations, or at least of occasional agricultural meetings, at which any member possessing aught of interest to communicate might contribute his quota of information to the general stock. I am sorry to say, however, that the proceedings of our planters are generally governed by egotistical individualism. Instead of widening the circle of his observations, each individual seems satisfied with contracting it within the bounds of the estate which he manages. Further still, not a few conceal from their nearer neighbours their success as well as their failures; for they are under the impression that their knowledge is more enlarged, their experience more sound, and their system superior; some even refrain from friendly intercourse, lest they should be taken by surprise, and thereby disclose some important secret, of which each conceives himself the sole possessor. But let those who imagine they have little or nothing to learn from others, or believe themselves in possession of secrets, be at once undeceived, for this is the sure symptom of an ignorance blind to its own errors and defects, or of a vanity which dreads being eclipsed by contact with a superior intelligence. It is an undoubted fact that the most skilful and best-informed *can*, and *do* at times, derive profit from the experience of others, even of the most ignorant. For, in agriculture, the field of observation is unlimited, and what had escaped the attention of the most superior mind, may have been remarked by one vastly inferior in intellect; or that which was but superficially observed by one individual, may have been deeply examined by another.

I readily acknowledge that the cultivation of the sugar-cane has made some progress; that inquiries have been instituted; but a great deal more remains undone. We should follow the example set us by the beet growers. Selection is now considered as a necessary ingredient in the successful cultivation of plants.

There are, as I think, several species, and many more than twenty varieties, of cane, each having its peculiarities—some growing better in poor soils, and resisting better the effects of droughts; others thriving in stiff lands: some richer in sugar; others containing a larger proportion of foreign matter; and yet I am not aware that any series of experiments have been instituted with the object of obtaining reliable data on the subject.

The Tahitee cane is universally held as the best for all purposes, so much so that by many inquiries are considered as futile; but comparative experiments would either corroborate the general opinion, or might show that, under peculiar circumstances, some other variety should obtain preference, and the matter would then be finally settled. It has been ascertained that the cane not only grows better and more vigorous in soils rich in lime salts, but yields a juice which is more easily manipulated. The composition of the sugar-cane is pretty well known at present, and that composition is far from being uniform; in this respect, the variety cultivated has its influence; the component parts of the juice vary not only in the different varieties, but in the same variety, according to circumstances. Our knowledge of the general composition of the cane should teach us the manure most suitable to its perfect growth.

P

On every estate, therefore, there should be kept a book showing the composition of the different cane-fields—such knowledge being, in my opinion, the only rational means of determining the best manure applicable to each field.

I would urge, in order to obtain the best results, the necessity of co-ordinately performing agricultural operations. It is very generally assumed that it suffices, for securing success, to perfect one of those important operations which modern agricultural science counsels, the others being neglected. This is a great mistake. Those various operations—viz., drainage, manuring, the pulverisation of the soil by the means of implements, &c.—however important they are, may signally fail if performed singly; or, at least, they will not produce permanent and complete results. For instance, we do not derive from drainage all the benefits we should expect if the ground has not been preliminarily well prepared. Hence the great utility of modifying the physical properties of the soil by the means of correctives, and the addition of proper manures; by deep ploughing, disintegration of the subsoil, and by irrigation. Equally so with the uses of the plough; performed singly, and without the aid of correctives, manures, &c., ploughing ultimately impoverishes the land. On the other hand, manuring has not its full effect if other circumstances do not favour vegetation; in fact, manures may then turn waste agents.

It is, therefore, most important that all agricultural meliorations should be performed concurrently and in unison.

But it is only by adopting the system of intensive culture that we can expect to carry out the above suggestions. On the other hand, the adoption of the *intensive* system pre-supposes the disjunction of agriculture and manufacture. In fact, they are two distinct branches; and it is not entirely due to the agriculturist that the beet-root has been able successfully to compete with the sugar-cane; a great deal of that success is attributable to the assistance of chemistry and chemists, which taught the beet growers the most scientific and most profitable method of working. We know how to obtain the best sugar. Improvements, however, should begin in the field, and planters should look to one ton and a half, and even two tons, per acre, as an average.

ALIMENTARY ARTICLES.—Cerealia.—Indian corn or maize

(*Zea mais*). Inferior to wheat only, in point of nutritive qualities, the Indian corn is one of the most nourishing grains, and superior to rice, rye, barley, or potatoes : the proportion of starch is 67·55 per cent.; of gluten and other azotised substances, 12·50; of fatty matter, 8·80; whereas that of bran is only 5·90. —(Payen). It has been ascertained that individuals subsisting on this grain are, in general, stronger and more robust than those using either rice, barley, or potatoes. Indian corn is also a very wholesome aliment, and forms the principal article of food of nearly one half of the southern population of Europe, of a very large proportion of that of Asia and Africa, of nearly the whole population of South America, and of a great part of North America. Maize grows well in Trinidad, and thrives remarkably in good soils: the average yield per acre is from twelve to fifteen barrels in ears; its price varies from 80 cents to 2 dollars per barrel, and the cost of raising the crop per acre from the seed is about 8 dollars—under our present imperfect system of culture. Corn is raised either in high or low lands; when in the former, it is planted at the commencement of the wet season, and in the latter part of May; in low lands, in January or February—so that two crops may be commanded every year. It is planted in holes of slight depth, being made with the point of a cutlass or a sharp-pointed stake, at a distance of four feet apart, from three to five grains being cast into each hole. When at about three weeks' growth, it is well hoed, and weeded once more when two months old : it comes to maturity within four or four and a half months. During the wet season the plant is bent, so that the ripe ear hangs downwards, and thus the infiltration of rain-water within the husk is obviated. The maize of Trinidad is different from that cultivated in the United States and Europe; it grows here from eight to ten feet high; the grain is smaller, less flat, and of a deep yellow hue. As an article of food, it is preferred both by man and animals, the latter seeming to fatten much more solidly and readily on it. With all these advantages, maize is but sparingly cultivated, mostly on account of the difficulty of protecting the grain against the ravages of the cereal beetle, that spoils it in a very short time.

True, no method has yet been adopted for its preservation. Both the grain and meal are imported annually from the United States of America and Venezuela. Corn-meal is imported to the amount of 8,988 bushels, value £5,906 sterling. The price of United States corn varies from 1 dollar 80 cents to 3 dollars per bag of two bushels, and that of meal from 4 dollars to 6 dollars per barrel.

In the present position of the colony, and with a very scanty agricultural population, it cannot be expected that corn should be cultivated for exportation; but it certainly might and ought to be produced in a sufficient quantity for home consumption.

Rice (*Oryza sativa*).—This grain grows very well in Trinidad, and yields from six to seven barrels per acre. The culture of rice, as conducted here, does not require any great amount of labour or care; whereas, the land should be well and thoroughly prepared before the seed is committed to the soil. Rice is either sown or planted: planting is a more tedious but much more profitable operation. It should be planted at intervals of eight inches, from three to five grains being put in each hole. Transplanting is unknown. Rice is sown or planted at the beginning of the wet season, and may grow without the aid of artificial irrigation. It is cultivated either in high or low grounds; in the latter it grows more vigorous, and is very prolific. There are two distinct varieties of rice cultivated here. The one (*nelou kar*, Ind.) is of a reddish colour, and small in size; it seems to be hardier than the other sort, but is not so prolific, and grows in the worst soil, provided the latter has been thoroughly burned. The other species (*nelou samba*) is more vigorous, but requires a better soil, and thrives in low lands, where it shoots up, at times, to the height of from five to six feet; its grain is as large and white as that of the Carolinas.

Rice comes to maturity within three months and a half; heavy showers prostrate it to the ground, and, in that state, if not cut within a few days, it germinates.

The inhabitants cultivate this grain generally for their own use; they reap and preserve it in the straw till required for use, and then bruise it in a wooden mortar to separate the grains from the husk—a very tedious, imperfect, and consequently, a very expensive process.

The proportion of starch in prepared rice is 89·15 per cent.; of gluten and other nitrogenous substances, 7·05; of fatty matter, 0·80; bran, only 1·10—(Payen)—and yet it forms the basis of the alimentary diet of the eastern populations. We import annually 15,899,319 lbs. of rice, value £132,543; duty paid in 1879, £17,224. The importation from the East Indies has greatly increased with the immigration of labourers from that country; the quantity imported in 1879 was 14,762,749 lbs. Rice might be produced here in sufficient quantity for the island consumption, without any danger to the public health; and large tracts of land, which now lie comparatively waste, either from their infertility or from the difficulty and consequent expense of draining the soil, might be thus rendered highly productive.

We cannot, however, hope for such a desirable consummation unless some person undertakes the cultivation of rice on a certain scale; or, again, several persons might join in the undertaking, and import at the same time the necessary machines for the thrashing and cleaning of the grain. A gentleman recently imported one such machine, in the hope that he might obtain from Coolies a sufficient quantity of rice in husk to make a fair experiment, either by buying from them, or by inducing them to send their rice to be cleaned. I am under an impression that he has not yet had the opportunity of making a trial. I wish him God speed.

Guinea Corn (*Andropogon sorghum* and *Andropogon saccharatus*).—Two species are cultivated here to a very slight extent, and that not as an aliment, but rather as fodder; they are very prolific, and might be raised as a supply of grain for poultry. Indian corn, however, will always be preferred.

Musaceæ.—Plantain (*Musa paradisiaca*).—Like all cultivated plants, the plantain has many varieties: there exist, however, three distinct species. The *Horn* plantain (*Musa paradisiaca*)— from the resemblance the fruit bears to the horn of a young bull; the *French* and the *Dominica* plantain (*Musa regia*); Bananas (*Musa sapientum*). The *Horn* plantain is more extensively cultivated than the other species, being hardier and not requiring frequent replanting; but though the fruit is much larger, whence it also obtains the *sobriquet* of Horse plantain, its bunch is not so well supplied, having ordinarily but twenty-five, and often fewer, plantains or fingers to the bunch; as an edible, it is also much coarser than the other species. *French* or *Maid* plantain: the body of this plant is of a dark violet colour, as also the nerves of the leaves; the fruit is smaller than that of the former, but the bunch is supplied with a much greater number of plantain-fingers, averaging about sixty and eighty, but sometimes from one hundred to one hundred and thirty. This species is regarded as more delicate than the others, particularly when ripe. *Dominica* plantain: this is a variety of the latter; though the body is exactly like that of the *Horn* plantain, the bunch, however, resembles that of the *French;* but the fruit is somewhat shorter and plumper. The plantain is extensively used in Trinidad, and on the neighbouring continent: it is a cheap, wholesome, and nutritious diet, and perhaps the most productive of all alimentary plants—in fact, field labourers contend that it is better suited to the support of their strength, in manual labour, than bread—at any rate, it forms the *staff of life* to the generality of Creoles. Its nutritive value has not yet been ascertained, but Boussingault considers it superior to that of potatoes; it is also superior, in general opinion, to that of cassava and rice: it may rank as a farinaceous aliment, containing albumen and gum. The plantain is used either in the ripe or green state: in the former it is eaten either as a fruit, or prepared in various ways with sugar and spices, as confectionery. When green, it is either roasted, dressed with meat, or simply boiled, and afterwards crushed in a mortar, so as to form a thick paste, which is used instead of bread. Plantain may be regarded as the most productive of all alimentary plants; the yielding per acre is, according to Humboldt, 155,000 pounds; and 125,000 pounds, according to Boussingault. The plantain requires a good deep soil and a sheltered position, being easily prostrated by strong winds. It is propagated by sprouts (improperly called *slips*) which are planted at ten feet apart. From five to seven of these young shoots or suckers spring out of and around the parent stem. The fruit, or rather the bunch of fruits, makes its appearance between eight, nine, and twelve months. The young shoots then give their fruit in succession, for two, three, or even many years, according to the climate, fertility of the soil, and the care bestowed on them. A plantain *walk* requires only occasional weeding and pruning. We import from Venezuela about 7,000,000 plantains annually—value, 53,000 dollars.

Bread-fruit (*Artocarpus incisa*).—*Artocarpaceæ*.—The breadfruit, so invaluable to the inhabitants of the Polynesian Islands, is perhaps too much neglected in the western archipelago; for although little nourishing, it is a wholesome aliment. A few trees only are met with in the island, and yet it would form an invaluable resource for the poor; or, at least, it might serve to feed or fatten swine. The bread-fruit tree thrives in good or even poor soils, and requires very little or no attention. It is very prolific—each tree bearing, every season, from seventy-five to one hundred and sixty pods, and each pod affording sufficient for a meal for two persons. They sell at about two cents each. It is propagated by cuttings from the roots; the root is severed from the tree, and raised from under the ground; after about three weeks, buds begin to appear on the part thus raised; it is then taken up and separately planted. Incredible as it may appear, the poorer classes profess a great contempt for this article of food : it is only good, they say, for pigs ; and cooks in respectable houses object to buying bread-fruits at the markets ; it is a vulgar vegetable.

Tubercles (*Dioscoreaceæ*).—Yam (*Dioscorea*).—This is the most important of colonial tubercles. It is farinaceous and wholesome, containing, according to Payen, twenty-seven per cent. of nitrogenous principles. It may be used as a substitute for bread, either boiled or pounded after boiling, or dressed with meat: another advantage is that it keeps for several months, provided it be laid up in some dry place. There are two species of Yams—*Dioscorea Triphylla*, and *Sativa*, the hard and the soft leaved. Amongst the former, the *Portuguese* and *Guinea* Yams are the best varieties, and most farinaceous. The Guinea Yam gives the best and quickest return, but it germinates early in March. The Portuguese sort comes in later and preserves better, but does not give so good a return. Both varieties also resist the attacks of the parasol-ants much better than any other kinds.

The different varieties of *water* yams, or the soft-leaved species, are more prolific but not so delicate : they come in later, and keep until the middle or end of July. With proper care and attention yams grow well in any land, but they thrive best in good soils, particularly in loam and on hills. The soil must be well prepared for the reception of plants; generally, large holes or trenches from eighteen to twenty-four inches deep and two feet in diameter are dug, and filled with decaying vegetable matter, or *trash*, then covered with earth and the plant placed below in the hole, or trench. Some people are content with raising mounds about two feet high, in which they lay the plants; they are commonly set at four feet apart with a prop stuck in the central interval of every four plants, to serve as a support to the vine. Yams are generally laid in when *they ask to be planted*, to use a local expression—that is, when they send forth shoots, which they infallibly do, however dry may be the place where they have been kept. The tubercles may be dug up in December, or after nine months; they weigh from twelve to twenty-five pounds; and an acre of land, well prepared and properly attended to, may yield from 7,000 to 9,000 pounds. The outlay may be calculated at from sixty to seventy dollars per acre. Yams commonly sell at three dollars per 100 pounds.

Cush-cush (*Dioscorea alata*).—The cush-cush is very different from the yam, and is perhaps the most delicate of all known tubercles; but, with the drawback of not keeping beyond a few days, it cannot be expected that it will ever be cultivated to any great extent. The tubercles weigh from two to four pounds, and a single plant may give from forty to sixty pounds. The cush-cush requires a good light soil, and the same care as the yam; it grows from tubercles which must be planted immediately after being dug. The crop is from February to May.

Euphorbiaceæ.—Manioc or Cassava root (*Jatropha manihot*). —This is divided into *bitter* and *sweet* cassava; the latter of which is an edible root, very farinaceous, and may be used either boiled or roasted. The *bitter* cassava is poisonous, and must undergo certain processes before it can serve for food; there are three varieties of the bitter kind. From the roots are prepared flat cakes called cassava bread, and also a coarse meal known as *farine*, or manioc meal; both of these are extensively used as a substitute for bread, especially the farine, which keeps a long time when properly stored. From the same part of the plant is also prepared a fine starch, which is in great request among washerwomen.

To be made into these various preparations the roots are first scraped clean, then washed, and grated; after this, the pulp is pressed so as to extract nearly all the juice it may contain. When the pulp is to be made into cakes, it is laid on an iron plate over a fire, and baked to the required point; when to be converted into meal, it is placed in a sort of large pan, or on a similar plate with a low rim, and stirred backwards and forwards, as well to favour the regular diffusion of heat throughout the mass, as to prevent its burning or uniting in lumps. The juice is allowed to subside for two or three days, and then drawn off, when a fine starch is found deposited in the vessel. From this juice is also prepared a pungent sweetish sauce called *cassaripe*, which is much esteemed by the natives, and also highly relished by Europeans. The *bitter* cassava is highly poisonous, and no culinary process will deprive the pulp of its deleterious properties, unless the juice be previously expressed. All kinds of animals as well as man are poisoned by eating the roots, but particularly by drinking the juice of the bitter cassava. Agoutis, however, lapas, and even pigs, may and do feed on the roots fresh in the soil, and when covered with earth, without apparent injury. Pigeons have been seen to drop dead, without even tasting it, from merely perching on the margin of the vessel containing the juice. The active principle, or poisonous agent of the *bitter* cassava is hydrocyanic acid, which is distinctly perceptible from its strong smell. The best counterpoison, perhaps, is salt water. *Sweet* cassava comes to maturity within six or nine months, *bitter* cassava within ten or fourteen months; the latter may also be allowed to stand over for two years and above, when planted in a well-drained soil. The cassava may be grown in soils of moderate fertility; it however thrives best in clay loam, and an exposed situation, as on the slope of hills. It is propagated by cuttings, which must be planted in the driest season—in March, for instance. The soil having been well prepared, holes are dug about six inches deep, and the cuttings thrust in. The yield in good soil is from fifteen to twenty barrels an acre. Cassava does not keep more than two or three days, and must be manufactured into cakes and meal as soon as possible. A large quantity of the starch is imported from the Main, particularly from Maturin.

Convolvulaceæ.—Sweet potato (*Batatas edulis, Ipomea batatas*).—This is a very delicate and wholesome tubercle, which is very extensively cultivated in some of the old islands; but in Trinidad it is raised on a very small scale, although it thrives well in the light loams of the colony. Barbadoes, St. Kitts, Grenada, and St. Vincent have the privilege of supplying the market of Trinidad with yams and sweet potatoes to the amount of nearly £1,200 sterling yearly.

Araceæ—Tanias (*Caladium esculentum* and *Colocasia antiquorum*).—Several species of *caladium* are cultivated in Trinidad; some of them, as the *plantain tania* (so called from its size and form), grow very large, and are an excellent food. The tania may be ranked amongst farinaceous substances, and is very wholesome: the part used is the rhizoma, or underground stem, which is generally boiled.

Vegetables.—Most of the vegetables of temperate climates may be grown in Trinidad, from December to May or June; but during the rainy months they suffer from excessive humidity, and are liable to rot; native vegetables, on the contrary, thrive well during the wet season. Good carrots and turnips are grown, as also excellent cabbages, though small. Three different beans, being species of *Phaseolus*, are cultivated here—the French, the red or dwarf, and the black bean; the latter is very prolific, but on account of the dark colour of the husk, is commonly prepared as French beans, or as salad; it is particularly abundant during the wet season. Together with these may be classed several species of peas (*Dolichos*)—of which three different kinds are much used; they are known by the French under the respective names of *pois-souche* or the *stump* pea, the black-eyed, and *pois chiches*, all of which, with the pigeon or angola pea (*Cytisus cajanus*), are commonly sold in our markets. It is to be regretted that more attention is not paid to the cultivation of the latter pea.

The Cajan is a shrub which may be planted on the borders of cane-fields, or of any other cultivation, so as to have the benefit of the tillage necessary for the growth of more important plants. It is a very good vegetable when dressed soon after being gathered. The pigeon pea is also excellent for restoring the fertility of fallow lands.

The Ochro (*Hibiscus esculentus*) is abundant; tomatoes (*Solanum lycopersicum*) and melongens (*Solanum melongena*) are plentiful, and require but little attention. Pumpkins and squashes (*Cucurbita maxima* and *melopepo*), as also the christophine or chouchow (*Sechium edule*) require no other trouble than that of planting. Jerusalem artichokes (*Helianthus tuberosus*), cucumbers (*Cucumis vulgaris*), and radishes (*Raphanus sativa*) are likewise brought to market, together with the following culinary herbs :—Lettuce, parsley, thyme, and water-cresses ; onions and shallots (*Allium ascalonicum*), spinach (*Spinacia oleracea*), goment (*Solanum morella*), and the foliage of tanias.

We import annually a large quantity of vegetables, either as preserves or fresh. Preserves are imported mainly from France. The total quantity imported may be estimated at £31,975 sterling —from France, £3,374 ; Portugal (potatoes and onions), £3,711 ; United States (potatoes, cabbages, beet-root, &c.), £8,183 ; British West Indies (yams, sweet potatoes), £5,304 ; Venezuela (plantains, peas), £7,217.

Animal Food.—The animal food of the population consists of salt provisions and fresh meat, including game of all kinds.

Salt Provisions.—We import from the British Colonies of North America and the United States, besides cod or salt fish (local term), mackerel, herrings, and salmon, to the amount of about one million two hundred thousand pounds—value £60,713, of which £40,623 is imported from British North America. Salt fish may be said to be the staple of the animal diet of the population ; the richest as well as the poorest inhabitant of Trinidad must have his salt fish at breakfast, and many use it at dinner also. So constant and extensive is its use in the rural districts, that it has long borne the flattering designation of "Planter's Ham."

Salt beef, pork, and hams are imported from the British Isles and the United States ; corned fish, salted hog, and *tasajo* or jerked beef, from Venezuela. We import of meats (salted and dried), 8,085,036 lbs.—value £45,353. We get our supplies of butter from France and the United States mainly (483,781 lbs. and 98,600 lbs.) ; total quantity imported, 619,949 lbs.—value, £25,170 ; total quantity of lard imported, 610,686 lbs., of which 540,432 lbs. are from the United States—value, £10,163. Olive oil, 34,668 bottles—value, £11,256, of which quantity France sends us 31,690 bottles.

Live Stock and Fresh Meat.—Except poultry, the island rears almost no animal food—nearly every ox slaughtered in the colony being imported from Venezuela. The beef is not of the best quality, as the animals, on arrival, are generally wild and lean ; it sells at from 20 to 24 cents per pound. About 4,305 oxen are imported annually, of which 3,652 come from Venezuela—value,

£55,302. To these should be added 14,466 heads of other animals (pigs, sheep, and calves)—value, £12,616. The cattle, however, from the mainland, may be considered as an exchange for goods, most of them being imported as remittances. Veal is very scarce, and sells at 20 cents per pound. Goats and swine are imported chiefly from Margarita and the province of Maturin; they sell at 20 cents; sheep from the United States, Cariacou (one of the Grenadines), and some of the old islands; mutton may be said to be scarce and of average quality, except American mutton; it sells at 30 cents, and even 35 cents. Except in a few privileged localities, such as Icacos, Mayaro, and the Cocal, sheep do not thrive in Trinidad. Swine succeed very well, indeed, and can be easily fattened; but people seem to find the rearing too troublesome.

Poultry.—Although poultry is bred abundantly, particularly on cacao, coffee, and provision estates, yet a large quantity is imported from Margarita, and even from Grenada. Chickens are subject to *yaws* (local term), and a very severe catarrh, or *chack*, both of which destroy a great number at certain seasons; it is almost impossible to preserve young turkeys from the attacks of the former distemper. Ducks are much less liable to disease, but the breed is confined mainly to the musk species (*Anas moschata*), though a few of the European species are here and there to be met with. The opossum, the tiger-cat, and a large species of falcon or hawk are great enemies to grown fowls, and a large lizard, the *mato* (local), to young ones; alligators, also, sometimes make havoc among ducks. However, except turkeys, the island produces poultry in nearly sufficient quantity for its own consumption.

Pigeons are scarce, and are seldom sold in the markets. The price for a pair is 50 cents; for a fowl, from 50 to 70; for a capon, from 80 cents to 1 dollar; ducks (a pair), 1 dollar to 1 dollar 50 cents; turkeys (a pair), from 2 dollars 50 cents to 3 dollars 50 cents; the latter are mostly from the Main, and are sold on board of the launches from 1 dollar 60 cents to 2 dollars; Guinea birds, from 1 dollar 50 cents to 2 dollars per pair.

Fish.—The market is tolerably well supplied with the following, viz., snappers, king-fish, groupers, mullets, baracoutas, and lébranches. A species of carangue, known here by the name of anchovy, is very abundant from the end of June to the middle of July. During the dry weather, the cascaradura (a pond fish) is also sold in the markets; it is much esteemed by the natives.

There is, in addition to the above, a good supply of turtle, principally from the Main; morocoys, or land tortoises, are also sold during Lent, and at other seasons.

Crustacea and *Mollusca*.—The following are in great and general use:—Sea and land crabs, cray-fish, shrimps, lobsters, *palourdes*, or mussels, cockles, and *chipchips*; oysters, although good and plentiful, are seldom offered for sale in the market.

Milk is not so plentiful as it ought to be; but it may be had, of good quality, for ten cents a quart bottle.

Fruits.—In Trinidad are found all those fruits which are the produce of tropical climates:—Bananas (*Musa sapientum*), five or six varieties; mangoes (*Mangifera indica*), in abundance; for the last few years grafted trees have been introduced from Martinique and Cayenne—viz., Reine Amelia, Mangue Divine, sans parielle, Mangue d'or, and Julie (the best of all); also from India, the Gordon, the Peter, and the Bombay; excellent oranges (*Citrus aurantium*), five or six varieties; Malacca apples (*Eugenia*); pine apples (*Ananassa sativa*); mammee apples (*Mammea Americana*); four or five varieties of sapodillas (*Achras sapodilla*); Chili and Governor's plums (*Spondias* and *Flacourtia*); granadillas and water-lemons (*Passiflora Alata, P. laurifolia*); sugar apple, soursops, custard apples (*Anona squamosa, A. muricata, A. reticulata*); three varieties of caimit (*Chrysophyllum Caimito*); musk melons and water-melons (*Cucumis melo, Cucurbita citrullus*), the former scarce, the latter abundant; pomegranates (*Punica granatum*); papaws (*Carica Papaya*); cashews (*Anacardium occidentale*); Pommecythere (local), or cytherine apple (*Spondias cytherea*); and several other sorts of tropical fruits.

Avogado Pear (*Persea gratissima*).—The *avogado* or *aguacate* pear—the latter being preferable as the original Carib designation—is extensively used; hardly, however, as a fruit, but rather as a sort of *vegetable marrow*, which term has not inaptly been applied to it. From it may also be extracted an oily substance, which might be brought to serve for various purposes. The flesh of the aguacate pear, when ripe, is remarkably soft, and forms an excellent salad. The process of boiling, however, seems to develop in it a bitter principle, which renders the oil prepared by ebullition unfit for culinary purposes. It is presumable, however, that this oil, when cold drawn, might be used at table as a condiment. Such of it as has been obtained is limpid, of a greenish colour, and has answered very well for burning in lamps. The pulp contains from fifteen to sixteen per cent. of oil; but only eleven per cent. has yet been extracted. Although the aguacate tree thrives best in good land, yet it grows in almost any soil; it requires very little care, and yields well. It begins to bear at between five and six years, and continues in full bearing for about twenty or thirty years. The fruit weighs from one pound to a pound and a half. I have seen some weighing as much as three pounds two ounces.

Grapes and European figs are very scantily cultivated; probably on account of the parasol-ants, which are particularly fond of the vine, and of an insect which attacks the fig-tree. Limes and lemons (*Citrus vulgaris, Citrus limonum*) are very common; the balata fruit (*Mimusops globosa*) is also sold in town and country.

EXPORTABLE ARTICLES.—The principal and almost sole articles of export are sugar, molasses, and rum; cacao, coffee, and coco-nut oil. The cotton, hides, &c., exported from Trinidad, come from the neighbouring cantons of Guiria and Maturin, though some of the former is cultivated in the island.

Sugar is, by far, the most important article of exportation; it is, in general, of inferior quality. For the last six or eight years the vacuum pan has been adopted on several estates; on Sevilla and Frederick estates, belonging to Messrs. Gr. Turnbull & Co., on Waterloo, the property of Mr. J. Cumming; and a usine has been established on the Saint Madeleine estate by the Colonial Company, capable of manufacturing 5,000 tons of white crystallised sugar. It is calculated that this year (1881) they will manufacture from 9,000 to 10,000 tons. A good deal of the sugar thus manufactured is consumed in the island. The total quantity of sugar exported in the year 1879 was equal to 66,818 tons. Trinidad has a large extent of good sugar land; there are now 52,163 acres under cultivation. Average yield per acre, 2,600 lbs.; maximum, 5,000 lbs.

In good soil canes ratoon—*i.e.*, are reproduced from the original stools without replanting—for seven or eight years; in superior virgin land, newly cleared, for fifteen years and upwards.

Canes are cut at a growth of between twelve and fifteen months. The crop commences as soon as the weather permits—say, in the beginning of January, and continues till June, when the rainy season sets in. Advantage is also taken of good weather towards the end of the year—in the fall, as it is called—viz., in October and November.

A system of culture had obtained in Trinidad during the time of slavery, the apparent advantages of which are, in my opinion, more than counterbalanced by its disadvantages; it is known as the *stand-over* system. Canes, though ripe, are allowed to stand over for the next crop, at which time they are from twenty to twenty-two months old. This system was mainly followed in the Naparimas, and it is only there that some of its advantages become apparent; the yield per acre is undoubtedly better, but the canes have been left growing for, at least, eighteen or twenty months, instead of being cut at twelve and fifteen months; and a larger acreage should be kept under cultivation. The system shows its advantages only where the soil is clayed, as in the Naparimas, for instance; but canes do not *stand over* in light soils, even of the best quality; they dry up or decay before they can be cut, as has been experienced in Tacarigua, St. Joseph, and Chaguanas.

It is only lately that the plough has passed into general use; for many years only a few planters would employ it; even now some object to its adoption. The pretext for retaining the hoe was the nature of the soil, in some districts it being clayey and the ground undulating, also the damage caused by the heavy showers which prevail during the planting season, by which the loosened soil is washed down the slopes. The steam plough has been introduced, and is worked with marked advantage in flat districts. Another useful instrument is the fork; it is especially employed in turning up clods in the cane pieces, where other implements could not be worked without injuring the growing crop; also in burrying the cane tracts. The horse-hoe and cultivator are used for weeding the young plants. So far, much progress may be said to have been achieved during the last fifteen or twenty years.

There are two planting seasons—from May to the end of July; the practice should be followed only on those estates where soil is gravel or sandy, as by February the plants are strong enough to resist the droughts of March, April, and May; but, on the other hand, they are not fit for cutting in the following year. The best planting season is from October to January. During the dry months planting may be experimented in the low damp localities.

I have said that Trinidad sugar is of inferior quality; and yet, unless we improve that quality, we cannot expect to obtain remunerative prices. The adoption of improved apparatuses and methods is, by far, the safest plan. But improved apparatuses are costly, and a series of unfavourable years and unremunerative prices have had the effect of impoverishing the planters, who, however willing they may be to introduce improvements, find it impossible to do so; nor can they expect, under the circumstance, assistance from capitalists. They should not despair, however, and relinquish all hope. Let them try the possible. In Barbadoes, and Porto Rico, in Brazil, they do manufacture, with a common set of coppers, moscovado, which sells readily and with profit. What can prevent us doing the same? I see no reason why, with care and attention, we should not obtain similar results.

If we could obtain from the cane a juice composed solely of water and sugar, how easily could we, with the aid of heat, eliminate the former to obtain the latter! Unfortunately, cane juice is not so simple in its composition, as it contains, in a greater or less proportion, all the matters which its organs require for their development and healthy growth—those which its apparatuses needed for the normal performance of their functions; those generated during the process of vegetation. Not only these substances may vary with the different varieties of the plant, with cane grown in different soils and under different atmospheric influences, but they may also vary in the same cane, as is easily ascertained by analysis. The unripe part of a cane—the top, for instance, differs in many respects from the lower or ripe part; it contains those bodies which are found in young or unripe canes. And one may form an idea of that different composition by referring to the analysis made by Payen:—

Ripe cane—water, 71·04; sugar, 18·00; alluminous and other azotised substances, 0·55; salts, 0·28; other matters, 0·37.

Unripe cane—water, 79·70; sugar, 9·06, or 50 per cent. less; azotised substances, 1·17, or more than 50 per cent.; salts, 1·95;

other matter, 1·09. Thus not only the unripe cane, say the top, contains 50 per cent. less sugar, but the proportion of foreign and fermentable matters is much larger. The unripe portions of the cane yield only a poor juice, and difficult to operate upon, and give sugar of inferior quality. Again, in canes which have suffered injury, there are found anormal matters more or less injurious. The cane juice is a liquor easily affected by external influences, and quickly undergoes chemical changes, especially under the action of heat. Planters, therefore, should be extremely careful to avoid anything which may bring such changes; they should, without hesitation, cast out all injured canes and unripe portions of healthy ones ; as little trash as possible should be allowed to pass through the mill. The greatest cleanliness should be enforced in every department of manufacture—from grinding to potting; all utensils used in the manufacture should be washed several times in the day ; also the gutters and coppers well, so as to prevent fermentation and the formation of acids and inverted sugar. It will be objected that such minute precautions will entail trouble and expense. Undoubtedly; but the question is, whether a better article and more remunerative prices would not be obtained. Of this, again, I have no doubt.

There are but few water-mills in the island; no wind-mills ; steam-engines are preferred, some turning twelve to eighteen hogsheads a day, the majority from six to ten. The sugar is put up in hogsheads, tierces, and barrels.

The quantity of molasses shipped in 1879 amounted to 1,777,540 gallons, of which 727,418 gallons were shipped to the United Kingdom ; 548,465 to British North America; 314,506 to the United States ; and 116,100 to the French West Indies.

The Trinidad rum has been much improved lately, owing to the introduction of the most approved stills. The quantity exported in 1879 was 73,892 gallons, which, however, might be much increased.

Cacao * (*Theobroma cacao*) is the article which ranks next in importance to sugar. Quantity exported in 1879, 11,614,170 lbs., of which 7,646,878 lbs. went to the United Kingdom ; 3,283,460 lbs. to France, and 660,690 lbs. to the United States.

From its first settlement, Trinidad exported cacao ; and that

* "Cacao, not Cocoa," as remarked by Professor Lindley, "ought to be the name for the *Theobroma*."

cacao soon gained a reputation on account of its delicious aroma. According to Gumilla, it was superior to that of Caracas and other places, so much so, that the crops were bought and paid for beforehand. In the year 1727, however, a terrible epidemic spread in the cacao plantations. The trees were apparently healthy and vigorous; the flowering abundant, giving fruits; but none of them came to maturity, as the young pods dried up before full growth. Cacao being the only article of export, the commerce of the colony was crippled at once, complete and irretrievable ruin soon following. The ruined and starving colonists were compelled to seek refuge on the neighbouring continent, taking with them their slaves, plate, and jewellery; the population was reduced, exclusive of the Indians, to the scanty number of 162 adults; the public revenue fell to the derisory sum of 231 francs. Thirty years later, some Aragonese Capuchin fathers were successful in their attempt to revive the culture of the cacao in the island. They imported from the continent a new species, the *Cacao forastero*, which, though giving a produce of inferior quality, was, nevertheless, promptly propagated as being hardier; that is the cacao at present cultivated in the island.

Here, as in Venezuela, growers admit two distinct species or varieties; they are the Creole cacao (*Cacao criollo*), and the foreign cacao (*Cacao forastero*). Whether distinct species or mere varieties, they have distinct characteristics. The former produces the best specimens, and is extensively cultivated in the province of Caracas. It is somewhat more delicate than the Forastero, requires the best soil, and does not bear so abundantly. It is otherwise pretty healthy and fruitful; the pod is in shape roundish, the shell thinner, the beans plumper and larger, from twenty-five to thirty in number in each pod; the mucilaginous covering of the seeds less abundant, so much so, that two days sweating will suffice to deprive it of such, whilst two days, or two days and a half exposure to the sun will dry the beans; kernels of a cinnamon tint, light.

Cacao Forastero.—The tree is hardier, more robust, and yields more abundantly; the pod is elongated, the beans smaller and flattened, of a darker colour inside, exhibiting a somewhat astringent taste, whilst that of the Criollo is soft.

There evidently exist several species of Theobromas. Martius, in his monography, mentions the following: The *Guayaneuse* (Aublet), the *Bicolor* (Bompland), the *Ovalifalium* (De Cand.)— this Theobroma, according to some, is the celebrated Soconusco— *Th. speciosum* (Wildenow), *Th. sylvestre, Th. microcarpum, Th. glaucum,* and *Th. cacao* (Linnæus). This latter, according to most botanists, supplies the cacao exported to the European and American markets. It should be considered as the parent stock of the numerous varieties now cultivated, all of which are the products of hybridism.

As remarked by Mr. Prestoe: "Under the proceeds of cultivation, no matter how rude, for a very long period, the different species having been brought together, an interminable intermarriage has been set up, and of course sustained to the present day, in which we have varieties, not one of which is so constant, that one can take the seed and be perfectly certain that the progeny will be like the parent." This is the popular impression, and growers of cacao will tell you that it matters not much whether you select for propagation an apparently fine variety, as the progeny is not invariably like the parent. Yet I think it a sound practice to look for those varieties which are deemed the best. I may mention, in connection with this subject, that a friend reported to me that he once planted some seeds of the beautiful *Sangre Toro;* out of many plants, one gave yellow pods, these being, however, in every other respect, shape, seeds, &c., similar to the parent fruit. I may as well remark here that the red cacao often turns yellow.

"There are," adds our botanist, "various names uttered in reference to various kinds of cacao; but I do not find, even with persons who seem to be able to understand that there are different varieties of cacao, that the few names made use of are uniformly applied; but with the majority of growers, there are neither different varieties nor names to distinguish such, beyond, perhaps, ' red cacao' and 'yellow cacao.' As to cacao criollo, it is either one of the twenty-two varieties known to me."

Of those many varieties he has eliminated a few, the most prominent characteristics of which he briefly notes as follows :—

1st. (*Forastero*). Pods, ten ribbed or ten grooved, restricted at base; colour, generally red; beans oblong in the long section and round in short section.

2nd. (*Colorado*). Pods, five ribbed or grooved, more or less ovate and cordate; colour, red; beans, as foregoing, but somewhat irregular and elliptical in cross section.

3rd. (*Cayenne*). Very long and pointed pods; very rugose; ten grooved; beans, roundish; pods' tissue ligneous.

4th. (*Verdecico, or smooth pale green*). Pods, five grooved, thick pod substance; colour, glaucous unripe: yellow ripe; beans, small rounded.

5th. (*Reticulate, or Yellow Criollo*). Pods, obovate, five grooved, reticulated; beans, angular, flattish; colour, pale green : yellow, ripe.

6th. (*Calabacillo*). Pods, rounded, five grooved, shell ligneous; beans, very angular and flat; yellow when ripe.

In the race No. 1 is included the beautiful bright red cacao, I take to be true Cundinamarca variety. Touched with No. 2, it has a shorter pod with a fine bean. It is this variety which gives the high characters to San Antonio; touched with No. 5, it gives the feature in the Torrecilla cacao.

No. 2 includes the big fleshy podded "Sangre Toro" (Bull Blood).

I may well remark that Calabacillo is discarded by all careful planters. *Verdecico* I hold as identic with *Truxillano*; this latter is cultivated in preference along the Gulf, more particularly at Yrapa and Yaguaraparro; also *Cundiamor*. It would appear that the five-grooved pods are more common in the best races, a character easily recognisable.

The quantity of land under cultivation for the cacao is about 22,000 acres; in 1856 it was only 7,000 acres. Cacao thrives in rich deep light soil, such as valleys and the banks of rivers. Heat and also shade are necessary for its healthy growth. The mean yearly temperature should be 27·50 centig., and trees must be planted at intervals in the cacao walks, to afford protection against the sun and strong breezes. Again, cacao plantations prosper mainly in virgin lands, and should not be made to succeed any other cultivation, if possible.

After the land has been cleared, it is picketted off at a distance of twelve or fifteen feet; the beans are then planted by the pickets at twelve inches apart, and covered with plantain or balisier leaves, which are removed so soon as the seed has germinated. If the two plants succeed, one is removed altogether, or for supplying a failure elsewhere—this being done at a growth of between twelve and eighteen months. The planting season is in July; the seeds should be taken fresh from a ripe pod. A nursery is, at the same time, formed for the future supply of those plants which may have not succeeded.

Previous to the laying-out of a cacao walk, plantain shoots are set throughout, for the benefit of their shade to the young plants; a crop of maize is also raised, which, with the plantains, assists in defraying the expenses of the first two or three years. Some growers plant the slips of manioc round the young plants; they afford shade for a year or eighteen months, when the roots are manufactured into cassada cakes, or meal. Slips, or better, seedlings of *bois mortel* are also planted for the protection of the more mature plants in future years. There are two species of bois mortel, or *Madre de Cacao:* the anauco (*Erythrina velutina*) and the bucare (*Erythrina umbrosa*). The Erythrina umbrosa is harder and has a denser foliage than the E. velutina, but the latter is preferred. However, the Umbrosa is preferable wherever the soil is not of the best quality. The cacao tree grows from twenty to thirty feet high; it begins to bear a few straggling fruits between three and four years, is in full bearing at twelve, and continues to give good returns for a duration of thirty years, after which period it declines. The cacao plant is very delicate, and has, besides, many enemies. The north wind, as also the irregular showers that may fall during the dry season, are injurious to the tree itself, but chiefly to the blossoms and young fruits, which they blight. The healthy growth of the young plants may be arrested by the parasol-ants devouring the tender leaves, or the deer nipping the terminal bud, and even twisting the young tree. It has also an enemy in an insect of the genus *Prionites*, which lays its eggs on the inner bark, where the larva feeds, destroying the *cambium*. A species of woodpecker (*Dendrocolaptes*), as well as squirrels and surmulots, destroy a large number of pods annually in search of insects, or to feed either upon the sweet acidulated pulp which covers the beans, or upon the beans themselves. The cacao tree is also very liable to become covered with parasites, mosses, and lichens.

The average yield per acre throughout the island is 600 lbs., or about 2 lbs. per tree, the *maximum* being as much as 1,080 lbs. per acre, or little more than 3 lbs. per tree. There may be said that there are two regular crops or *pickings* in the year, viz., the June and the December crops, extending over two months; there are, however, partial pickings in the intervals. The pods come to maturity within three months and a half, rain hastening ripening. They are detached from the tree with a knife or with a blade of peculiar form, attached to the end of a long pole, so as to reach the highest branches. They are afterwards gathered into heaps, and each pod is opened with a strong knife or short cutlass. The beans are then taken out, put into baskets, and carried to the curing-house, there to be cured and dried. Different methods may be adopted for curing and drying cacao for the market. According to one method, the beans are immediately spread out in large flat boxes or *trays*, or on an earthen floor, left exposed to the action of the sun, put under shelter for the night, to be spread out again the next day; this is repeated till they are sufficiently dried to be packed into bags.

The cacao thus prepared is of a red colour, flinty, heavy, and bitter; in fact, the worst sample from which to prepare chocolate, but by far the best to bear adulteration, by admixture with amylaceous substances.

The beans (when recently taken from the pods) are covered with a sort of sweetish acidulated pulp, which it is necessary to destroy; this is done by submitting them to fermentation; in fact, no cacao can be pronounced a good marketable article which has not undergone the process of fermentation or *sweating*. With this object in view, the seeds are gathered in heaps, and covered with plantains or balisier leaves, or blankets, and left in that condition for four, five, six, or even seven or eight days, according as the prevailing weather is dry or not. When they have gone through a thorough process of sweating, they are spread for a few hours, put in heaps again, and allowed a few hours' more fermentation, say eighteen hours. They are then spread on a drying earthen floor, and left exposed to the sun for a shorter or longer period. This is the plan preferred on the Main, and it is undoubtedly the best when there is fair weather and no danger of rain; but in no place, as I believe, is cacao buried as a preparative for drying. When dried in trays or on a plank floor, the beans are sometimes sprinkled with finely-pulverised earth, when still damp from the sweating heaps. The plan adopted in Trinidad is the following:—One or more curing-houses are erected, according to the extent of the estate. A curing-house consists of a floor, generally twenty-five or thirty feet long, by fifteen or twenty feet wide, elevated three or twelve feet from the ground; two running roofs of thirty or thirty-five feet long are made to run in opposite directions on rafters supported on pillars or wood posts. Under the floor, or by the side of the curing-house, is a sweating-room, more or less spacious; it is so made as to close hermetically, with a lattice bottom through which the juice or acidulated liquor from the fermenting mass is allowed to run off and escape outside. When the cacao has fermented a sufficient time, it is taken from the sweating-room and spread on the floor; the roofing is then run off, to allow the direct action of the sun; it is put in heaps at night, and spread again next morning, and so on for three, four, or five days or more, till the beans are sufficiently dried; they are then put in bags and sent to the town.

Cacao has been analysed by several well-known chemists, and we may say that it contains, as essential components, 1st, a fatty substance—cacao fat—ranging from 36 to 46 per cent.; fecula, from 6 to 14 per cent.; nitrogenous compounds, about 12 per cent.; *Theobromine*, 1 to 2 per cent. *Theobromine* is an alkaloid characteristic of cacao; as *Cafeine* and *Theine* are characteristic of coffee and tea, and yet very similar in their properties.

"When we see," says Payen, "that the cacao bean, in its composition, presents more nitrogenous matter than wheat; about twenty times as much of fatty substance, a notable proportion of fecula, and a pleasant aroma which stimulates appetite, we are inclined to admit that such substance must be eminently nourishing. Experience has proved that it is really so. In fact, cacao, intimately mixed with equal quantity or two-thirds of sugar, to form the well-known beverage, chocolate, is a substantial aliment under all circumstances, and capable of supporting human strength during travelling."

Trinidad cacao now sells from 70 to 90 shillings, the best marks as high as 110 shillings per cwt. During the revolutionary war of the Spanish colonies, the best Trinidad cacao sold for 28 dollars a *fanega* of 110 lbs., and continued to sell at a high price —from fourteen to sixteen dollars—for several years. The price began then to decline till, in 1827, it fell as low as three dollars, planters not taking the trouble of gathering their crops, the expenses of attendance thereon being greater than the price offered. This falling off in the price of Trinidad cacao may be attributed to various causes, general or local. The European and British markets especially became glutted with importations from Brazil and Guayaquil; Spain, then at peace with her old colonies, began to import cacao from Venezuela and Nueva Grenada, so that the article became a mere drug, except the best Caracas cacao. Unscrupulous speculators in the island also resorted to most nefarious practices to defraud purchasers, not only by the admixture of damaged and inferior with good cacao, but by the addition of weighty substances; remunerative prices being paid by them for the heaviest sort, the production of a bad article was thereby encouraged, the Trinidad cacao gradually lost its reputation, and the producers were ruined.

Encouraged by the example of the late Mr. Charles Maingot, the generality of planters have tried their best to improve the quality of the article. Undoubtedly that quality has been and may be still further improved by proper care and attention being paid both to selection and the process of curing the seeds. But, with all possible improvements, it seems a mistaken idea to expect that, under present circumstances, "Trinidad might supply cacao equal to anything produced in the best markets of the Magdalena, Soconusco, and of other places on the Spanish Main," as assumed by Dr. Lindley in his lecture "On Substances used as Food, illustrated by the Great Exhibition." "Cocoa, or cacao, as we should call it," says the learned professor, "is an article of very large consumption. Enormous quantities of it are now used in the navy, and every one knows how much it is employed daily in private life. It is, moreover, the basis of chocolate; but we have evidence that we never get good cacao in this country. The consequence is, that all the best chocolate is made in Spain, in France, and in countries where the fine description of cocoa goes. We get a cocoa which is unripe, flinty, and bitter, having undergone changes that cause it to bear a very low price in the market." This may have been true at the time Professor Lindley delivered his lecture; and let me add that this "unripe, flinty, and bitter cocoa" was the one prepared for the British market. The English consumer did not know then the difference between good and bad cacao : not the case now, however.

Undoubtedly Dr. Lindley is fully aware that if proper attention to culture and preparation can improve the quality of cacao, there exist also local conditions—that is to say, " the temperature, the soil, the exposure, and other circumstances "—which have their share in modifying the quality. There are, moreover, several varieties of the Theobroma, and the plain fact is that, although Trinidad cacao may be classed next to that of Caracas, it cannot bear comparison with cacao from Orituco, Guigue, Cupira, &c., in the province of Caracas, or from Pedraza, in the province of Varinas, and Rio Chico, in the province of Maracaybo, much less with that of Soconusco, which, during the Spanish dominion, was exclusively reserved for the use of the royal family.

Coffee (*Coffea Arabica*).—As Trinidad has never exported much coffee, that which is grown in the island has not yet acquired any repute. Nevertheless, very good coffee might be produced here, and in abundance; the coffee plant thrives on our hills, at Saint Ann, Diego Martin, Laventille, and along the southern coast, at Erin, and Moruga. If the culture of coffee ever extend in Trinidad, the valleys of Caura and the heights of Arima, Guanape, Aripo, and Oropuche will afford a magnificent field for its cultivation. The coffee, like the cacao tree, requires shade and protection, and the bois mortel or the pois-doux (*Inga*) is planted along with the seedlings, as also plantain shoots. The quantity of coffee exported in 1879 was not more than 14,605 lbs., and the quantity imported equal to 178,163 lbs., of which 146,243 lbs. were from Venezuela. Trinidad, therefore, would not produce enough coffee for its own consumption. Few of us, I expect, were prepared for this conclusion. The price varies from fifteen to twenty cents a pound. The cultivation of coffee may be carried on without much outlay, but a large number of hands becomes necessary in crop time for the gathering in of the berries, as they come to maturity all together and germinate very quickly when they are left on the ground. Women and children may be employed in picking and 'gathering the crops. The berries are made to pass through the coffee-mill to separate the seeds from the soft outer husk; they are afterwards washed and dried, and made again to go through the mill to be winnowed from the inner husk or parchment, before being packed for exportation. These are operations too numerous and troublesome to leave any fair hope for the extension of coffee cultivation in Trinidad—at least, with its present scanty agricultural population. The Asiatic islands and Brazil will, therefore, probably long enjoy the privilege they have gained of supplying the markets of the world with coffee. We should aspire to this at least, to producing sufficient for our own consumption.

The coffee plant is subject to diseases which, in certain localities, have proved most destructive. The fine coffee groves of Martinique, Guadeloupe, and other West India islands were thus completely destroyed; and occasional attempts to revive coffee cultivation have failed. At present the fine coffee plantations of Ceylon suffer extensively from the leaf disease.

For the last few years there has been a disposition to cultivate coffee in the colony, a few persons trying the experiment on a rather large scale with varieties supplied from the Botanic Gardens mostly. Those varieties are the following, as characterised by Mr. Prestoe :—

Liberian (*Coffea Liberica*).—"This extraordinary coffee has become generally known to colonists from the accounts given of it in the newspapers; the large size of the beans, and the high price realised for this coffee, having first attracted the attention of persons desirous of promoting coffee cultivation in the British tropical colonies.

"It is indigenous to the West Coast of Africa, about Sierra Leone and Liberia, where it appears to be almost the only kind cultivated, and with much success, in hot and moist lowlands, or hills of no great altitude. . . . This kind of coffee may be regarded as a perfectly safe and most valuable introduction to this island.

"The soil in which the plants in the Botanic Gardens have thriven, is the ordinary red gravelly loam or clay-like deposit found associated with quartz and schists throughout the northern parts of the island.

"A glance at the Liberian coffee plant impresses one with the great difference in the character of the plant and that of the common or creole coffee, and suggests a method of culture somewhat different. . . . With a size and general robustness of habit at least three times that of the ordinary coffee, it assumes the character of a small tree much more distinctly than any other of the better known varieties. Its first branches and leaves are few and gross, becoming smaller and more numerous and dense with age. These peculiarities indicate that a system of rather wide planting must be resorted to, and such treatment in pruning as will induce a lateral development, viz., topping the leaders permanently at seven feet, and the leading branches first at three feet from the stem, and subsequently at one and two feet at subsequent toppings, when the growth does not promise to be sufficiently dense." Mr. Prestoe recommends planting at a distance of sixteen feet, and interlocating the common creole coffee; these intermediate to be removed at a later period, when the ground will have become completely covered.

"The narrow-leaved, from the Java Botanic Gardens, probably quite as new to western cultivation as the Liberian.

"A species eminently adapted for cultivation in poor, rocky, or gravelly soils. Resist droughts that would prove fatal to the ordinary creole coffee; remarkably prolific, the size of beans only second to that of the Liberian.

"The foliage is remarkable from being spare and drooping, the leaf being much longer, but only one quarter the width of an ordinary creole coffee leaf, and of very leathery texture. It is adapted for resisting the attacks of fungoid and insect blight to which the moka and common coffees seem becoming more and more liable.

"*Soufrière Coffee.*"—This coffee has been so named from the district in which it was found growing in Dominica. "My attention," says Mr. Prestoe, "was attracted from a distance to trees of this kind in the Soufrière hills by their uniform fruitfulness and health, whilst being surrounded by trees of creole and moka coffee, all more or less affected with blight, and impoverished by drought and barren soil. On examining the trees, I found they were quite distinct from any other variety I had yet seen, in the general sturdiness of habit, distinctly pendulous branch, deep green of the foliage, and the leathery texture of leaf. Moreover, the trees were evidently proof against insect attacks. The size of the bean of this variety is unusually large, nearly equalling that of the narrow-leaved coffee.

"This variety is eminently adapted for cultivation on steep and barren hillsides, where it will develop much more quickly and thrive when the creole coffee would fail.

"Moka—varieties, *Major* and *Minor*. The variety distinguished as Minor is inferior in robustness of habit and size of beans. The rate of growth of the former (Major) is much faster, and it is also more prolific."

Mr. Prestoe adds : " It does not appear to be generally known that the moka coffee is rendered more prolific by scorching sun-heat up to a point of making the trees lose their leaves to some extent, and thus it is that in the East the operation of gathering is often effected by drawing the branches through the hand—not picking the berries off the branches. Moka coffee-trees in this island are often seen in the leafless condition alluded to laden with fruit."

There is no doubt that high-price coffee can be produced in Trinidad, all along the northern range, also at Erin and Moruga, where the plant thrives and fruits to perfection. For some years, in the beginning of the age, beautiful coffee plantations flourished on the Laventille hills, but the insalubrity of the locality caused their abandonment. The different degrees of excellence in quality depend mainly on variety. It is important, however, to take into consideration the conditions of soil and altitude.

I should recommend the cultivation of the *Liberian* variety in our lowlands, of the *Java narrow leaved*, the *Soufrière* and the major moka varieties on our hills, as they seem to be less liable to disease, hardier, and more prolific.

Cotton (*Gossypium herbaceum*).—Cotton was once extensively cultivated in Trinidad—viz., at Mayaro, Chacachacareo, and Guayaguayare; and a few individuals made their fortunes by its growth and exportation. This cultivation, however, was afterwards abandoned for the more lucrative production of sugar. Whatever cotton is now exported from the colony is the product of Venezuela. The soil and climate of Trinidad, though rather damp, seem to be well adapted to the growth of cotton of the best quality; but the scarcity of manual labour and competition with countries better situated in that respect, will, for a long time, if not for ever, prevent the restoration of that cultivation here.

Coco-nuts (*Cocos nucifera*).—The coco-palm thrives remarkably in Trinidad, and is cultivated to advantage in several districts, either for sale in the nut, or for the manufacture of oil. In a green state, the nut affords a pleasant cooling beverage, and is sold at the rate of five cents for three nuts; and at the rate of one dollar per hundred in the dry state. The price of the oil ranges between $1 to $1 50 c. per gallon. The quantity of oil manufactured in the island had greatly diminished lately, in consequence of large importations from the United Kingdom; but the price being unremunerative, the importation has decreased, or even ceased, to a great extent, and there is now a tendency to a rise in the price.

The coco-palm grows best along the sea-shore, in the blown sand, especially where it is mixed with vegetable *debris;* salt and a saline atmosphere are necessary for its healthy growth and full development. The cultivation of the coco-palm has been in progress lately, and new walks have been formed at Irois and Guapo, at Oropuche and elsewhere. The whole of the eastern coast, Guayaguayare and Jicacos are lined with groves of coco-palms. The plantation now existing between the mouths of the Lebranche and the Ortoire, known as the *cocal,* was primarily formed accidentally by nuts being washed on shore from the wreck of some vessel. The finest specimens, however, are to be found along the Mayaro beach, some of the trees being seen to flower at the early age of three years, which is very unusual indeed, this palm beginning to bear fruit generally at five or six years. The period of full bearing is at eight years and upwards, when it brings forth a bunch of flowers every month, each bunch having nine nuts on an average, some as many as twenty. Every tree is calculated to yield at least one dollar net every year from the sale of the nuts. Coco-palms are planted at twenty-four feet apart, and require very little or no care, except when they are quite young. When arrived at maturity a *cocal,* or coco-nut grove, forms an excellent pasture-ground for sheep, cattle, or other grazing animals; poultry, pigs, &c., also fatten very readily on the coco-nut meal after the oil has been expressed. The almond, or pulp, contains, according to Brande, 25 per cent. of oil, and the shell 26 per cent. of the pulp. It is calculated here that thirty-three nuts give one gallon of oil. The plan generally adopted here is the following:—Any person undertaking to manufacture oil, gives a gallon for sixty nuts.

The cultivation of the coco-palm evidently suits our people, as it requires little labour and attention. There are many varieties of the coco-palm, some giving rather small nuts, others very large ones; some more robust, others more delicate. The larger nuts are naturally preferred by the buyer, and sell more readily. I would advise those who wish to engage in the cultivation of the coco-palm to select the best varieties, and avoid the indiscriminate planting of indifferent kinds. We may estimate at 250,000 the number of trees existing in the island; in 1881 we exported 4,227,276 nuts, worth £13,278.

There exist in Pulo Pinang, Ceylon, and other places in the East, fine coco-palm plantations, or, as they are termed here, coco-walks. These are formed, according to S. Itier, in the following manner: the nuts required for plants are selected from healthy full-grown trees; they are laid in the ground in a shaded place, and barely covered with fine earth: as soon as the leaves become pinnated and the roots begin to appear out of the husk, they are removed and planted at intervals of from 33 to 40 feet. The young trees are manured with stale fish, guano, or compost containing a certain proportion of salt. On the coast of Coromandel, they place a handful of salt in each hole. In the best localities, the coco-tree begins to bear at between six and seven years' growth; and it is calculated that each tree yields annually eighty nuts, which generally sell at the rate of 1 dol. 50 c. per hundred on an average: 5,000 trees would therefore give 400,000 nuts, yielding about 13,700 gallons of oil, or at the rate of one gallon for thirty nuts, each tree yielding three gallons. The price being 42 cents per gallon, each tree would then give a gross revenue of 1 dollar 26 c., or a net return of 84 cents per annum, allowing 33 per cent. for expenses. The chief enemy of the coco-tree is a species of *coleoptera*, which fixes its abode at the base of the leaves, and, by degrees, penetrates into the central bud and the very heart of the palm. If not promptly removed, the tree soon withers and dies. So destructive were the ravages of this insect at Singapore, that the inhabitants were thereby compelled to abandon the cultivation of the coco-palm. It is destroyed either by using an iron rod, hooked at the extremity, and by which the hole bored by the insect is thoroughly probed, or by pouring a strong solution of salt into the tuft of leaves.

Tobacco (*Nicotiana tabacum*).—Trinidad tobacco, from the district of Siparia, was judged at the Exhibition as inferior only to the Havanna, and yet its cultivation is limited to a few acres of land, and the quantity thus raised is consumed on the spot where it is grown, whilst a sufficiency might be easily raised for the entire island consumption. The annual quantity of tobacco imported is 318,300 pounds, equal to £10,000 sterling. The tobacco-plant requires a light, dry, and rich soil; it is sown in September, and the young plants transplanted when about six or seven weeks old: they are generally planted two by four feet apart. When five feet high, the upper bud is cut off, as also the young shoots which spring from the axilla of the leaves: from seventeen to twenty of the latter are preserved, and, as they gradually arrive at maturity, are picked off, successively, to undergo the process of curing. This process, although most essential to the good quality of the article, is very carelessly performed here. The soil and climate of Venezuela being very similar to that of Trinidad, it will not be amiss to furnish such information on the culture of this plant there, as may prove acceptable to tobacco growers in this island. The seeds are sown in very rich and deep soil, and after forty or fifty days the plants are taken up and transplanted at about two feet apart, and in rows of nearly four feet interval; from ten to fifteen leaves only are left on each plant, in order to obtain tobacco of a superior quality. When a space of dark blue shows itself near the pedicle, the leaves are sufficiently mature to be plucked, and are carried under sheds, where they are spread out in layers, on hurdles ready for the purpose. The tobacco now becomes yellow, and quite soft; the stems of the leaves are then removed, the leaves themselves twisted together, and put up in bundles of seventy-five or one hundred pounds. These bundles are next placed on a larger heap, made of damaged tobacco leaves, and the stems stripped off; the whole heap is then covered over and allowed to ferment for forty-eight hours, the leaves being sprinkled with water, should the tobacco become too dry. After the *twists* have undergone sufficient fermentation, they are unfolded, and the leaves hung up under the shed, in order to promote the evaporation of any superfluous humidity. If the tobacco is found to possess the requisite qualities, it is then made into *manojos*, or small packages of five pounds each. In case the fermentation has not been sufficient, it is caused to undergo a second process of the kind. Although proper attention to the cultivation and curing of tobacco greatly improves its value, yet it is incontrovertible that climate exercises the main influence as regards the quality of the article, which is particularly good in those localities where the temperature is not beneath 75°. In Venezuela, they calculate that eight plants yield two pounds. It is to be regretted that sufficient attention has not yet been directed to the cultivation of tobacco in Trinidad, and particularly in Siparia, where the soil seems to be admirably adapted to its growth.

Indigo (*Indigofera tinctoria J. anil*).—No indigo is at present manufactured in the island, although that plant grows wild almost everywhere along the road-sides, and might, therefore, be cultivated with success; in all probability, however, years will elapse ere the production of indigo is attempted in Trinidad; it is, therefore, unnecessary to offer any remarks on that branch of agricultural economy.

Arrowroot (*Maranta arundinacea*) and touloman, or tulema, *Canna coccinea*, or, according to Dr. Lindley, *Canna achiras*.—From the roots, or *rhizomas*, of these two plants is extracted a large quantity of nutritious starch, extensively used as food for young children, and particularly for convalescents and persons of irritable stomachs. Arrowroot and tulema are, in medical opinion generally, preferable to sago and tapioca, and may be used in the preparation of blanc-mange and other dishes. Arrowroot is a much smaller plant than the tulema, and thrives only in very good moist soil; it is generally planted two feet apart, and each plant or stool must be carefully moulded in order to a good return. The tulema, on the contrary, grows almost in any soil, provided it is properly planted and due attention paid to its cultivation. The plants are laid in rows, and at three feet distance. The flowers of the tulema are of a brilliant crimson, those of the arrowroot, white. This plant is usually called "tous les mois;" but this is a misappellation, and *touloman*—the carib term for the "balisier"—is its true name. At whatever time touloman and arrowroot are planted, they yield their starch only in the dry season. The planting season is generally in May: one acre gives from 2,500 to 3,600 pounds. Touloman gives no trouble in its culture; but the parasol-ants are very partial to it.

Castor-oil seed (*Ricinus communis*).—In the climate and soil of Trinidad the castor-oil plant grows to the height of twelve and twenty feet. There are two varieties, the *red* and the *white*, distinguishable not only by the colour of the plant and its pedicles, which is violet in the one and whitish green in the other, but by several other characteristics. The red castor-oil plant is more vigorous, its seeds larger, and of a darker hue: the seeds of the white, though smaller, are in general more plump, and also contain, as is asserted, more oil. The castor-oil plant is not cultivated here with a view to commerce, but many poor people have two or three trees near their houses from which to prepare their own oil. In this preparation they follow the old system:—The seeds are grilled, then crushed and formed into a paste, which is afterwards boiled in water; this mixture is allowed to cool, the oil skimmed off, and again boiled. Oil obtained by this process is of a dark colour, has a strong scent and taste, and, as a purgative, is somewhat irritating. The best plan, certainly, is to crush the seeds and express the oil from the paste by means of a screw-press; but an improvement on the former plan, although not rendering it equal to the latter, would be to crush the seeds without grilling, and then boil the paste, as already mentioned. The seeds of the castor-oil plant might be exported to England with advantage, for it is very prolific, requires but little or no attention, and the gathering of the seed is a most simple task.

Carapa oil, yielded by *Carapa Guianensis*, and *C. Touloucouna*. —The carapas are lofty forest and timber trees, bearing pods as large as a husked coco-nut, and containing from twelve to fourteen seeds of the size of the walnut. The seeds are gathered in June and July, boiled for about six hours, then laid in heaps for eight or ten days, during which time they undergo a sort of fermentation; they are then broken, and the pulp they contain carefully taken out and kneaded into lumps of thick paste, each about fifteen pounds. This paste is laid on boards slightly incurvated and inclined, and placed in a sheltered place, when the oil oozes through the mass, and runs into a vessel placed for its reception. The paste is carefully remoulded every morning and evening, so as to favour the disengagement of the oil. After twelve days, boiling water is poured on the mass, and a fresh quantity of oil of inferior quality is thereby obtained. One

R

barrel of seeds gives about twelve bottles, or about 264 ounces of oil. Carapa oil is thick, excessively bitter, and keeps a long time. It is especially used in destroying insects, and particularly *tics*, which are at times very troublesome to animals, hundreds of them sticking to the hides of mules and oxen in the pastures on estates. This oil is also applied by friction, as a remedy in rheumatism. It has been remarked, as a singular effect, that whenever animals that have been rubbed with carapa oil are exposed to rain, the rubbed part becomes swollen. The agouti and lapa are very fond of the carapa seeds.

Sesame (*Sesamum orientale*).—Although sesame, or *Gigeree* as it is called by creoles, is cultivated here only by a few Africans for its oily seeds, yet it is well known that large quantities of it are imported into France—particularly from Egypt and the East. The sesame oil is sweet, pleasant, and keeps a long time; it will even bear comparison with the best olive oil, and as a substitute for the latter may be used for culinary purposes; in fact, Thunberg says that in Japan it replaces butter and lard. The people here use it in preparing their food: they first heat, then bruise it, and in that state mix it with their food. Sesame grows in almost any soil; it is planted in the beginning of the wet season, and comes to maturity within four months or four months and a half; for its reception the land must be well prepared and thoroughly cleared of weeds. As the fruits or capsules ripen gradually, and grow along the upper part of the stem, the latter is cut as soon as the lower capsules are ripe; otherwise these split when dry, and the seeds are then lost. When reaped they are tied in bundles, so as to keep the capsules together and prevent their splitting; they are then stored up in some cool place. The seeds are very small and flat, and are separated by merely beating or rubbing the bundles with the hand. It is stated that sesame contains as much as 50 per cent. of oil; and there is no doubt it might be cultivated here to advantage—if not for exportation, at least for culinary purposes.

Spices—nutmegs (*Myristica moschata*).—The nutmeg may be said to be perfectly acclimatised in the colony, and it yields nuts as good and fine as any which can be imported from the Asiatic Islands; it has not yet, however, been cultivated with a view to commerce. The nutmeg tree requires a good moist soil and plenty of shade; it grows particularly well under protection of the saman-tree. At St. Ann's government-gardens it yields about 15 pounds per tree. Nutmegs sell here at 60 to 80 cents (2s. 6d. to 2s. 10d.) per pound.

Cloves (*Caryophyllus aromaticus*).—The clove has also been naturalised, and thrives well; it requires a good, but rather dry soil, and, contrary to the nutmeg, is injured by too much shade; it is very scantily cultivated.

Cinnamon (*Cinnamomum zeylanicum* and *C. cassia*).—The latter species, or variety, is cultivated here by several persons, but a few only prepare cinnamon from it. There are to be found at St. Ann's a few plants of the *Cinnamomum zeylanicum*; they look very healthy, although planted in rather poor soil, and yield excellent cinnamon.

Pimento (*Eugenia pimenta*).—Though not indigenous to the island, the pimento thrives admirably; there are two distinct species or varieties here. Pimento is largely exported from Jamaica, and such might be the case with Trinidad also; yet it is only cultivated for its leaves or berries, which are used in culinary or confectionery preparations.

Black pepper (*Piper nigrum*) thrives very well indeed, but is cultivated by a few individuals only, and more as an object of curiosity than utility.

Cayenne pepper (*Capsicum annuum*).—All sorts of capsicums, and the *bird-pepper* (*Capsicum baccatum*) especially, are so common here, that the people take no care in preparing them for preservation as a condiment.

Vanilla (*Vanilla planifolia*).—The vanilla grows wild in our forests, but it is not the best kind. There are, it seems, two distinct species distinguishable, not only by the size of the fruit, but also by its fragrance; the larger species is more fragrant, and also more common. The vanilla grows on those trees which do not shed their bark, generally creeping along the trunk in a straight line, the extremity and divisions hanging downwards. Rats, oppossums, and squirrels are very fond of the vanilla, and it is difficult to save it from their attacks, as they eat it as soon as it arrives at maturity. The vanilla might be cultivated here to advantage, although it eventually causes the death of those trees to which it adheres.

Ginger (*Zingiber officinarum*), Turmeric (*Curcuma longa*),

Guinea pepper (*Amomum granum Paradisi*).—These plants are only cultivated for domestic purposes, not for exportation; but they succeed very well. To the above catalogue of useful plants might be added as great a number; such as the musk ochro (*Hibiscus abelmoschus*), which grows wild here, and the seeds of which are extensively used for perfuming in France, under the name of "Ambrette;" the senna plant (*Cassia obovata*), which is cultivated by the inhabitants of Mayaro, Erin, and some other places, for their own use; the noyau (*Prunus*), the seeds and leaves of which might replace, for distillation, the cherry laurel. Many others might be given, but their enumeration would swell this sketch to too large a volume.

The following dye-woods may, however, be mentioned, viz., log-wood (*Hæmatoxylon campechianum*); this is not indigenous to the island, but grows very well in dry spots. Arnotto (*Bixa orellana*); the arnotto is indigenous, and thrives best in good soils and cool localities; it is very prolific, but is used here only as a condiment. Fustic (*Broussonetia tinctoria*) is indigenous, and thrives best in good soils and hilly districts; it is used here in wheelwork, especially for naves.

COMMERCE.—The commercial movement consists mainly, if not entirely, of imports and exports. In the year 1713, the whole trade of the island was carried in a vessel of 150 tons, a little cacao and indigo being bartered for some coarse cloth and other necessaries. In 1797, fourteen years after the granting of the second cedula by Charles III., the colony exported 7,800 hogsheads of sugar (1,000 lbs. to 1,200 lbs. each); 330,000 lbs. of coffee, 96,000 lbs. of cacao, and 224,000 lbs. of cotton—the produce of 159 sugar plantations, 130 coffee, six cacao, and 103 cotton farms. In 1802, the number of sugar plantations had increased to 192, producing 15,461 hogsheads; quantity of coffee exported, 358,000 lbs; of cotton, 263,000 lbs.; of cacao, 97,000 lbs.; tonnage, 15,000. In 1809, the exports had increased to 18,235 hogsheads of sugar; 460 gallons of rum, and 100,000 gallons of molasses: quantity of coffee, 500,000 lbs.; of cacao, 358,000 lbs.; of cotton, 800,000 lbs. 1819.—Exports: 30,205,724 lbs. of sugar; 534,626 gallons of rum; 545,400 gallons of molasses; 1,205,445 lbs. of cacao; 258,220 lbs. of coffee, and 131,990 lbs. of cotton. 1829—59,089,421 lbs. of sugar, 400,321 gallons of rum; 1,362,605 gallons of molasses, 2,206,467 lbs. of cacao; 226,123 lbs. of coffee; 25,203 lbs. of cotton. Increase: sugar, molasses, and cacao. Decrease: rum, coffee, and cotton. Quantity exported of the latter article, 25,203 lbs., instead of 800,009 lbs. in 1809. From 1839, the quantity of sugar was reckoned in hogsheads instead of pounds, and molasses and rum in puncheons instead of gallons:—

Years.	Sugar.	Molasses.	Rum.	Cacao.
	hhds.	punchs.	punchs.	lbs.
1839	21,422	18,051	112	2,914,068
1849	30,579	13,151	718	4,378,186
1850	26,075	9,884	273	3,816,728
1851	30,407	10,792	528	5,008,920
1852	35,220	12,077	817	4,216,851
1853	33,835	13,306	216	3,757,352
1854	37,746	11,748	267	5,427,354
1855	31,548	6,316	3,733	4,842,075
1860	34,284	6,541	1,353	3,733,521
	lbs.	galls.	galls.	
1865	62,718,710	1,000,633	85,583	6,760,287
1870	91,732,830	1,459,247	6,219	7,176,588
1871	120,046,000	2,159,205	36,341	6,422,038
1872	103,092,200	1,716,930	20,806	6,985,904
1873	133,489,078	1,621,998	16,644	7,482,091
1874	99,739,550	1,697,131	39,761	9,396,531
1875	129,801,172	2,423,049	52,162	6,272,540
1876	114,921,284	2,004,508	13,400	9,477,123
1877	102,713,036	1,464,472	1,775	9,726,742
1878	116,587,351	2,184,918	7,264	9,911,365
1879	149,674,017	1,777,540	73,892	11,641,170

The hogshead may be taken as weighing 1,800 lbs. net; the puncheon of molasses as containing 110 gallons, and the puncheon of rum as containing 100 gallons. In 1839, the year immediately following emancipation, the quantity of sugar was only 21,422 hogsheads, or about 38,559,000 lbs; in 1829, ten years previously, it was 50,089,221 lbs. It seems that the proportion of molasses ought to correspond to the quantity of sugar. Such, however, is not the case, as may be ascertained by reference to the above table, the quantity drained from the muscovado varying each year, being larger or lesser, according to the condition of the canes.

Table showing the value of exports and imports for a period of fifteen years:—

Years.	Imports.	Exports.
	£	£
1850	476,000	319,394
1860	829,304	714,603
1867	859,389	1,086,901
1868	987,796	1,116,198
1869	920,607	1,118,695
1870	1,042,678	1,227,574
1871	1,213,024	1,492,811
1872	1,233,771	1,439,904
1873	1,324,432	1,733,615
1874	1,342,992	1,412,260
1875	1,507,794	1,625,082
1876	1,666,268	1,636,618
1877	1,708,457	2,093,650
1878	1,901,401	1,839,067
1879	2,223,952	2,264,744
	19,237,865	21,121,116
Balance in favour of Exports, £1,883,251.		

Thus within ten years the imports and exports have doubled—imports 2·40, exports 2·02.

Our exports consist mainly of sugar, molasses, rum, and cacao, as they represent a gross amount of £1,304,824, the other articles representing the comparatively low figure of £142,887, in which are included £23,560, value of 25,938 tons of asphaltum, and £25,191, value of 5,039,070 coco-nuts, and 4,880 lbs. of coco-nut fibre.

Table showing imports, exports, and re-exports:—

Years.	Countries.	Imports.	Exports.	Re-exports.
		£	£	£
1875	United Kingdom	531,612	1,220,446	
,,	British East Indies	91,133	nil	
,,	France	85,738	63,946	
,,	United States...	278,209	107,926	
,,	Venezuela	311,887	129,992	
,,	Other Countries	209,215	102,774	505,455
	RECAPITULATION.			
,,	United Kingdom	531,612	—	
,,	British Colonies	251,923	—	
,,	Foreign Countries	724,259	—	

COMMERCE. 263

IMPORTS, EXPORTS, AND RE-EXPORTS—*continued*.

Years.	Countries.	Imports.	Exports.	Re-exports.
		£	£	£
1876	United Kingdom	571,720	1,248,367	
,,	British East Indies	83,942	741	
,,	France	97,720	88,674	
,,	United States	301,783	86,881	
,,	Venezuela	374,573	122,479	561,289
	RECAPITULATION.			
,,	United Kingdom	571,720	—	
,,	British Colonies	251,023	—	
,,	Foreign Countries	843,525	—	
1877	United Kingdom	492,769	1,416,592	
,,	British East Indies	77,644	1,100	
,,	France	88,853	117,027	
,,	United States	360,350	196,441	
,,	Venezuela	405,750	252,690	
,,	All other Countries	282,981	—	741,929
	RECAPITULATION.			
,,	United Kingdom	492,769	—	
,,	British Colonies	289,927	—	
,,	Foreign Countries	925,761	—	
1878	United Kingdom	643,543	1,246,567	
,,	British East Indies	116,038	1,672	
,,	France	70,679	105,865	
,,	United States	341,560	168,804	
,,	Venezuela	449,000	—	
,,	All other Countries	603,182	—	156,812
	RECAPITULATION.			
,,	United Kingdom	643,543	—	
,,	British Colonies	201,808	—	
,,	Foreign Countries	1,378,601	—	
1879	United Kingdom	773,849	1,180,944	
,,	British East Indies	129,609	nil	
,,	British North America	80,213	23,487	225
,,	France	155,483	126,602	155,907
,,	United States	367,774	79,291	24,258
,,	Venezuela	525,508	4,178	331,149
,,	All other Countries	891,516	—	391,424
	RECAPITULATION.			£902,963
,,	United Kingdom	773,849	—	
,,	British Colonies	331,367	—	
,,	Foreign Countries	1,118,736	—	

EXPORTS OF CACAO.

Years.	United Kingdom.	France.	United States.	N. American Colonies.	Other Parts.
	lbs.	lbs.	lbs.	lbs.	lbs.
1875	3,746,353	1,585,977	670,783	160	—
1876	6,043,518	707,767	128,560	—	4,320
1877	5,516,205	3,387,747	690,147	—	18,919
1878	7,283,510	1,073,981	831,670	1,950	4,863
1879	7,646,878	3,283,460	660,669	16,694	10,423

Total quantity of exports, and value in pounds sterling—1875, 6,003,278 lbs., value £159,602; 1876, 6,884,165 lbs., value £259,480; 1877, 9,613,018 lbs., value £281,252; 1878, 9,195,974 lbs., value £336,074; 1879, 11,618,124 lbs., value £490,490.

The following Table of imports for the year 1879 shows the nature and quantities of the articles imported, also the countries whence imported:—

1879.—ARTICLES IMPORTED.

Bread Flour, 93,357 brls.; Rice, 15,899,319 lbs....	£254,773
Live Stock, 21,366 heads	118,616
Fish (dried and pickled)	60,713
Meats (salted and dried) 3,085,036 lbs.	45,353
Vegetable Products	31,975
Olive Oil, 34,668 gals.; Butter, Lard, Cheese, 1,416,147 lbs.	54,300
Malt, 79,518 gals., 97,054 quarts	43,350
Wines, 267,647 gals.	45,751
Spirits, 78,913 gals.	30,474
Sugar (refined) 673,599 lbs....	11,226
Timber (shooks, shingles, staves, &c.)	22,550
Lumber	78,675
Cottons, Linens, Silks	261,543
Hardware, Machinery	99,580
Bricks and Tiles, 2,087,519 (no Lime)	10,846
Tobacco (manufactured and unmanufactured), 363,117 lbs.	19,696
	£1,189,421

In this Table I have included only the principal articles of import, leaving aside the least important. Value of alimentary articles imported, £574,300; of building materials, £89,500.

I am indebted to the kindness of Mr. Norman, the harbour-master, for the following return of articles imported from Venezuela during the year 1880 :—

Horses	105
Mules	48
Assos	705
Oxen	3,618
Sheep	63
Goats	829
Pigs	1,826
Turkeys	826
Plantains	7,172,160
Coco-nuts	587,000
Cacao	5,870 bags
Corn	685 barrels
Tobacco	6,265 bales
Starch	20,714 packages
Coffee	2,351 bags
Hides	2,558
Tannias	2,629 barrels
Stuffed Birds' Skins	24 packages
Hummocks	50 ,,

The cacao imported is for exportation, especially to France; the hides and coco-nuts are likewise re-exported. Our Venezuelan trade is chiefly with Bolivar and Barancas, or Puerto Jablas on the Orinoco; with Guiria and Maturin within the gulf, and the Island of Margarita. This trade might be greatly augmented by the adoption of a more liberal tariff and a less selfish policy on the part of the Venezuelan Government.

By seeking to establish a comparison between imports and exports from and to different countries, we are led to the following conclusions :—

UNITED KINGDOM—AVERAGE OF FIVE YEARS.
Imports ... ... £602,698 | Exports £1,262,583
Difference—Favour Exports ... £659,885.

BRITISH COLONIES.
Imports ... £277,209 | Exports £129

UNITED STATES.
Imports .. ... £349,923 | Exports £127,876
Difference—Favour Exports ... £222,047.

FRANCE.
Imports ... ... £99,696 | Exports £114,423
Difference—Favour Exports ... £14,729.

VENEZUELA.
Imports ... ... £413,343 | Exports (three years) £168,353
Difference—Favour of Exports (approximately) £132,755.

Thus the only countries to which we sent more than we received are the United Kingdom and France. As to our other commercial connections, taken collectively, the foregoing comparison shows that we really disburse in their favour, and that in hard cash, a yearly average (more or less) of £630,000. Our trade with the United Kingdom would certainly seem to be the most advantageous, since the colony apparently receives, as annual remittances, the sum of £659,885. But this advantage is only apparent, as proved by a close examination ; for the greater part of that sum remains in Great Britain, either as an income to absentee proprietors, or in payment of the interest and capital money advanced. A return of the total value, in pounds sterling, of the imports and exports of the colony of Trinidad in the year 1880, has just been published, which I beg partly to transfer to these pages.

Countries.	Total Import therefrom.	Produce and Manufacture of the Colony.	British, Foreign, and other Colonial Produce and Manufactures	Total Export.
	£	£	£	£
Total United Kingdom ...	830,799	944,760	219,030	1,163,791
British East Indies ...	112,525	—	9	9
British North America ...	80,358	47,126	93	47,219
British West Indies ...	72,286	3,191	19,419	22,610
All other British Colonies	20,643	3,194	4,587	7,781
Total British Colonies ...	285,814	53,512	24,108	77,621
France	176,135	86,793	223,945	310,738
Germany	20,175	9,932	13,028	22,960
Spain, including Colonies	18,614	341	971	1,312
Portugal, including Colonies	2,497	6,661	—	6,661
U. S. America ...	408,145	223,649	38,267	261,917
Danish West Indies ..	718	1,399	—	1,399
French West Indies ...	56,298	8,988	7,815	16,803
Spanish West Indies ...	11,836	—	31	31
South America	3,445	2,338	20	2,358
Venezuela	568,099	1,906	317,754	319,660
Total Foreign Countries ...	1,266,019	342,265	601,833	944,099
Grand Total	2,382,632	1,340,538	844,973	2,185,512

I have left aside some figures which cause the grand total copied from the return not to agree exactly with the total put down by me, the difference between the two not being over £10,000.

Balance in favour of imports, £197,120; a result less favourable, in my opinion, than that of the preceding years.

This return shows correctly, I believe, the value of re-exports, amounting to the large sum of £844,973. The export of produce and manufactures of the colony is shown in the following Table :—

EXPORTS.

Produce of the Cane (Sugar, Molasses, Rum)	£905,448
Cacao	321,906
Coco-nuts and Coco-fibre	14,231
Asphaltum	25,314
Total	£1,266,899

SHIPPING—1879.

	British.	Foreign.	Total.
Tons—Entered	276,174	128,663	404,837
,, Cleared	272,877	130,349	403,226

The following Table of comparative imports and exports may prove interesting :—

1879.	Trinidad.	Barbadoes.	British Guayana	Jamaica.
Imports ...	2,223,271	1,023,397	2,065,045	1,347,342
Exports ...	2,264,744	1,259,158	2,715,535	1,357,671

Population of Trinidad in 1881, 153,128. Estimated population at the end of 1880, of Barbadoes, 180,000; of Guayana, 248,110; of Jamaica, 560,000.

Proportion of imports and exports to each inhabitant :—

	Trinidad.	Barbadoes.	British Guayana	Jamaica.
Imports ...	14·10	5·69	8·32	2·49
Exports ...	14·78	6·99	10·94	2·51

Average ratio (per inhabitant) of imports—Trinidad, £14 1s.; Barbadoes, £5 10s.; British Guiana, £8 7s.; Jamaica, £2 10s. Exports—Trinidad, £14 15s.; Barbadoes, £7; British Guiana,

£10 10s.; Jamaica, £2 10s. Thus, taking into account the number of inhabitants, we import nearly three times as much as Barbadoes, nearly double the quantity imported by British Guiana, and six times as much as Jamaica; we export exactly twice as much as Barbadoes; twenty per cent. more than British Guiana; and six times more than Jamaica.

This shows the importance of Trinidad in a commercial point of view. In fact, its proximity to Venezuela will ever make it one of the most valuable possessions of the British empire in these seas.

Note.—Justified by etymological and botanical analogy, encouraged also by Dr. Lindley's example, I have, throughout, made use of the word cacao instead of cocoa, to designate the Theobroma cacao; and of the term coco instead of cocoa-nut, to distinguish the cocos—the botanical name of the coco-nut palm. Moreover, it is impossible that the application of the same term to two plants so widely different in all respects as the cacao-tree and cocos-palm should not create confusion in the mind.

CHAPTER VIII.

TOPOGRAPHY—NORTHERN DIVISION: COUNTIES OF ST. GEORGE, ST. DAVID, ST. ANDREW, AND CARONI.

1. County of St. George.—This county is bounded on the east by the rivers Aripo and Madamas, and a line connecting the same across the mountains; south, by Aripo and Caroni, and by the Gulf of Paria, from the mouth of the Caroni down to the Dragon's Mouths; and north by the sea, from the river Madamas to the *Boca Grande*. It is divided into eighteen wards.

Port-of-Spain, the chief town of Trinidad, is situated in this county, just at the angle formed by the junction of the north-west prolongation of the island with its main land, and about two miles northward of the mouth of the Caroni river, at the corner of a small semi-circular plain encircled by two spurs running from the northern range towards the sea. It is from two to two and a-half miles wide and nearly four miles in length, along the sea-shore, towards which it declines in a gradual slope of about fifty feet per mile. The St. Ann and Marava valleys open on this plain.

The town is well laid out, its streets running due E. and W. and due N. and S., thus intersecting at right angles. They are thirty to thirty-five feet wide, with paved gutters at the sides, the centre being macadamised and gravelled.

There are in Port-of-Spain but few places of general resort. Brunswick Square, between Abercrombie and Frederick Streets, is a pleasant promenade, surrounded by an iron railing and planted with large trees, such as poui, roble, angelim, and other densely foliaged trees or shrubs. It has nine entrances, with corresponding alleys. There is in the centre of the square a fountain with a bronze group, the gift of the late Mr. Gregor Turnbull.

The promenade between King Street and Marine Square

is a fine walk, also planted with rows of large trees. It is about a hundred feet wide, and extends from the Saint Vincent or Queen's Wharf to the Dry river, eastward of the Catholic cathedral, running parallel to the sea. A square has been lately formed at its eastern extremity, with the statue of Christopher Columbus in the centre, placed on a high pedestal in an ornamental fountain. The statue is the gift of Mr. Hippolyte Borde, a native of the island. The promenade is divided nearly in the middle by an open plot, which is used as a cart-stand. There is in the centre a fountain, ornamented with a diminutive group—a child holding a swan by the neck. From the cart-stand the Almond Walk—an alley planted with almond trees (*Terminalia catalpa*)—leads to the South Quay and the old jetty, or King's Wharf, whilst Frederick Street runs up in an opposite direction to the Circular Road, a distance of more than a mile in a straight line. To the eastward of the town, between George and Nelson Streets, is the market-place, which was, for a long time, appropriated to the sale of vegetables, but has been since formed into an open square. At the north end of the town, an open space—Belliard's Orchard—has likewise been laid out as a square.

To the north of Port-of-Spain, and forming part of the town, is a fine extent of level pasture or meadow land, called the Queen's Park, well fenced in with hard wood posts and iron bars; it is used as a grazing ground, for milch cows particularly; though other animals are admitted at a monthly fee. It forms one of the finest race-courses in the West Indies; the great defect is the want of a sufficient number of trees for shelter to the animals pastured there.

Between the Queen's Park and the town there are two other plots of land enclosed by iron railings and separated by the avenue leading to the Circular Road; the one bordering on the St. Ann's Road is designated as the Small Savanna; on the other is constructed the Prince's Building, an unsightly structure, which is used by the pupils of the Royal College.

Westward of Brunswick Square, between St. Vincent and Abercrombie Streets, stand the Government and Court-houses—two massive edifices on the same line and set due north and south. In point of architecture and solidity, they are far from being creditable to the architect, and can never, by any contrivance, be made an ornament to the town. The bonding warehouse on the south quay is a low building, but shows a very good appearance. A custom-house has been lately erected on the south quay. The buildings connected with the railway cover a large space between the Dry river and the prolongation of the Almond Walk. The gaol, at the north end of the town, between Clarence and Kent Streets, is a massive, ugly construction, well adapted, however, for its object. The market-house, between George and Charlotte or St. Ann's Streets, is a good-looking building, consisting of a stone pavilion, a large central and two smaller lateral sheds, imported from Great Britain.

The finest erections, however, in Port-of-Spain, are the Roman Catholic cathedral, Trinity Church, the police barrack, and the colonial hospital. The police barrack is situated in St. Vincent Street, south of the Court-house; it is a lofty substantial structure, with arched openings, a tower and clock, railed in on two sides. Attached to the building are the police-court and the dwelling of the inspector commandant; it abuts upon streets on three sides. The colonial hospital, constructed by Mr. Samuel, a native of the island, is perhaps the finest structure in Port-of-Spain. It stands in a large open ground eastward of the St. Ann's Road; the grounds in front are well kept, and the building shows a fine façade. It is a two-storied house, neat and substantial; but its internal distribution might have been made more suitable to its destination. It is now found to be too small for the number of patients who apply for admittance. Two additional wings, or separate buildings, might be constructed to accommodate a double number of patients.

The Catholic cathedral stands at the eastern end of the Marine Square promenade, at one of the angles of the town, and is, consequently, very inconveniently situated; but it is a large, substantially-built temple, in the form of a cross, with a nave and two aisles; also two small towers in front. The wood materials are of the best country timber—cedar, balata, purple-heart, &c. Trinity Church is a very neat edifice, built of stone and the hard wood of the country, with a fine square tower on the north, surmounted by a spire with a gilt cross; it has no aisles. It is situated south of Brunswick Square, in a spacious yard inclosed within a handsome iron railing, and having a broad pavement of slab stone, leading from the great western entrance to the street. In addition to these two cathedrals, I may mention the following chapels or places of worship :—The Parochial Chapel of the Rosary ; the Chapel of the Sacred Heart, not yet completed; the Church of St. Patrick, New Town; the Chapels of St. Joseph and the Immaculate Conception—all Roman Catholic; All Saints' Chapel of Ease (Church of England); the Wesleyan, the Baptist, and Portuguese Chapels; and the Scotch or Presbyterian Kirk.

The quays of Port-of-Spain are good, solid constructions, being built of heavy blocks of stone strongly united by clamps. There are two jetties : one on iron pillars, projecting into the sea to a distance of 600 feet; it is 30 feet wide. The other is not more than 150 feet, and is used mostly as a landing place for boats.

With three or four exceptions, all the houses in Port-of-Spain are one or two stories high. In the lower or commercial part of the town they are pretty regularly and closely built; they are more scattered in the upper part, many houses having large lots attached, which are planted with trees and flowers. These dwellings being generally low and almost hidden amidst the foliage, the town assumes a peculiar and, in some parts, a rather rural aspect. The view of Port-of-Spain from the harbour is not imposing, as the ground on which it stands is, on an average, not more than 30 or 40 feet above the level of the sea. Vessels anchor from half a mile to one mile and a half and even two miles from the shore; goods are landed in *flats*, and so smooth is the water that all kinds of lumber are made into rafts and towed to the wharves.

To the west of the town, between the St. James's Road and the sea, is the public cemetery, divided into two sections—the Catholic and Protestant. This cemetery is the property of the corporation, and placed under its exclusive control.

Port-of-Spain is built on a light soil, which permits a quick and easy filtration of the surface water to the sea, whenever it has not been carried off by the surface drains. The lower or southern part of the town consists of land which has been *made* or claimed from the sea within the last forty years. Grumblers did not fail, at the time, to sneer at the folly and extravagance of the Government, though the work was avowedly commenced with the object of filling up and doing away with a long swampy belt, which extended from the tolls-gate to the Almond Walk, a distance of nearly half a mile, and which was a permanent source of insalubrity; and had not the work been completed, it is difficult to say where and how we could have established the railway terminus in Port-of-Spain.

The town is effectually protected to the eastward against the effluvia of the great Caroni swamp by the hills forming the eastern spur. Bordering on these hills is the Dry river—a deep ravine almost always dry, except during some heavy showers in the rainy season. The Ariapita or St. Ann's river had primitively its course through the town, about where Brunswick Square and Trinity Church now stand. In the year 1787 it was diverted to its present bed by order of Governor Chacon, with a view to improve the town. It may be said, however, that the object he had in view was not attained, since the Dry river may, in our days, be regarded as an almost irremediable source of noxious effluvia; it is a receptacle for filth. Nevertheless, Port-of-Spain and its harbour may be considered as healthy. Seven bridges establish a communication across the Dry river with the neighbouring districts.

The town of Port-of-Spain was divided, in the year 1853, into five wards, each electing three councillors to form, together with two auditors for the whole, the council of the borough of Port-of-Spain. Every male person of full age, occupying a house rated to the house-tax at a rental of not less than £20 sterling within the borough is a qualified elector; and every elector paying a house-rent of £75, or being possessed of an annual fixed revenue—household or landed—of £50 sterling, is eligible to the office of councillor. The revenue of the town consists of the house-tax, market dues, revenues from real property, and licences; total, in 1880-81, 74,427 dollars. The annual expenditure is for salaries of officers, streets, charities, hospital dues, lighting the town, &c.; total, 74,271 dollars. The councillors elect the mayor every year, on the 3rd of November.

Port-of-Spain is supplied with water from the St. Ann's and Maraval rivers. Three reservoirs have been constructed in the

s

latter valley at about three miles from town, and a main pipe of 12 inches bore, reduced to 10 inches, brings the water to the lowest end of the town and the wharves. It is then distributed through every street by sub-main and branch pipes, varying from six to two inches in diameter; hydrants are also disposed at every 500 feet, more or less, for protection against fire. There are 276 such hydrants, and they can be made to throw water over the highest houses. The local supply is calculated at 2,500,000 imperial gallons per day, or 77 gallons per individual, the population being 31,858 inhabitants. There are, at present, 3,802 service pipes, supplying about 3,700 houses. The length of line from the reservoirs to the town is three miles; general fall, 122 feet. A dam and a reservoir have also been built at the entrance of the Fonds Amandes glen, with the object of procuring for the town a further supply of water from the St. Ann's valley. The pipe is eight inches in diameter, reduced to six, and supplies water to several private residences in the ward, to three public fountains, to two tanks in the Government pastures, to the Governor's residence, to the lunatic asylum, and to several houses along the Circular Road. The main pipes from the two reservoirs are made to communicate by a connecting pipe through the small savanna. General supply from St. Ann's about 300,000 gallons.

The colonial hospital, a wash-house with 137 troughs, and two large public bath-houses are supplied with water from the water-works. When constructed, they were intended to afford a continuous supply to the inhabitants; large baths were erected in several private lots, also jets d'eau; from these causes, and mainly from the carelessness of the people, the waste is very great indeed, and the more to be regretted, as, in case of fire, the water may fail—not an improbable occurrence, as already proved.

Port-of-Spain became the capital of the island in the year 1783; to that time San Jose de Oruña was the seat of the Government. In 1757, Governor Don Jose de la Moneda, finding it impossible to procure a house in San Jose, removed to Port-of-Spain, which, from that date, virtually became the chief town; it was in 1783, however, that Governor Chacon proclaimed it the capital of the island. On the 24th of March, 1808, under the government of Sir Thomas Hislop, it was almost entirely destroyed by fire. The loss was estimated at £500,000 sterling. The town was rebuilt on a better plan, and much improved by Sir Ralph Woodford, who made regulations to prevent wooden constructions; which were unfortunately overlooked by his successors. Population of the town according to census of 1881, 31,858 : males, 15,324; females, 16,534.

To the north of the Queen's Park, and bordering on the Circular Road, stands the Governor's residence, or St. Ann's House. It is built of the limestone of the island properly dressed, with a square tower above the grand staircase. The house may be said to be distributed into two distinct sets of apartments : one for public receptions on the lower storey, consisting of a large hall, followed by a splendid dancing-room, and a fine cool dining-room facing the last; a billiard and several sleeping rooms; galleries on the east and south. The upper storey is occupied by the Governor's private apartments. The pleasure-grounds are well laid out; forming part of these grounds are the Botanic Gardens, where are cultivated some rare and useful plants, such as several varieties of coffee, the cinnamon, nutmeg, clove, vanilla, specimens of the sugar-cane, &c., &c.

Ward of St. Ann.—This ward is comparatively well populated, and possesses several neat country houses. It is inhabited by many small proprietors, who cultivate ground provisions and vegetables; fruit-trees are plentiful; a few acres planted in coffee and cacao. The soil is generally good, but nearly the whole ward is mountainous or hilly, the highest summit being 2,140 feet. Good timber was, for a number of years, cut in the mountainous part, viz., poui, cyp, cedar. The ward of St. Ann is formed of three small glens, each having its stream. Roads, practicable partly for carts and partly suited only to horse or mule passage, lead to the head of the glens.

Some forty years ago, the river St. Ann had, even during the dry season, a sufficiency of water for washing purposes. The river is now, and has been for some years past, dried up, in consequence of the destruction of timber on the ridges. I had suggested to Governor Sir Arthur Gordon the feasibility of making, with the proprietors on the heights of St. Ann, an exchange of their lands against double the quantity of crown land in any district they might prefer. Under proper regulations and strict surveillance, these lands would soon become sufficiently wooded so as to afford an increased supply—an object the more desirable, as the St. Ann's water does not appear to possess the incrusting properties of the Maraval water. Of course it is difficult to say whether the offer would have been accepted; I nevertheless regret that it was never made. Successive and superlaying reservoirs might be formed in the glens, even at Cascade, with the object of collecting water for the supply of the town. St. Ann's is a Roman Catholic parish —population, 1881, 872; 1871, 808.

Westward of Port-of-Spain is the ward of Mucurapo—flat, with a light soil of average quality. There is at present only one sugar estate in this ward, viz., Woodbrook estate. The St. Clair estate has been lately bought by the Government, with the object of parcelling it into building lots, and preventing its occupation by the coolies and the poorer classes. This ward is traversed by the western Royal Road and the Maraval river. On the right bank of the Mucurapo, or Maraval river, between the Royal Road and the entrance of the Maraval valley, are the St. James's Barracks, about two miles from Port-of-Spain. These fine barracks stand on a flat, permeable ground, with underground sewerage to the bed of the river, just opposite the opening of the Maraval valley, and are, consequently, exposed to the direct action of the northerly wind, which, as is well known, is dangerous. To this injudicious position is mainly attributable the much-talked-of unhealthiness of these barracks. The selection, I must say, was an unfortunate one, both in site and proximity to the town. Let me recall here the opinion of Captain Tulloch:—"The mortality (in Trinidad) is under the average of the whole command (Barbadoes), being only about 60 per 1,000, or 1 per 16·66." Population, 1881, 2,789.

Westward of Mucurapo is the ward of Cocorite—mainly hilly, and soil generally bad; a few acres planted in provisions and guinea-grass. A large conical-shaped hill (1,830 feet), called Fort George Mountain, seems to tower over the whole ward; on a summit somewhat lower (1,120 feet) is the fort of the same name, as also the signal-post, which corresponds with a similar post (740 feet) on the north side of Diego Martin, and, by notice from the latter, signals the arrival of vessels long before they enter the gulf. At the base of Fort

George is the hamlet of Cocorite, which occupies a small portion of this plain towards the sea-side, and is traversed by the Royal Road. At the back of the village, some extensive buildings, formerly occupied by the Ordnance department, are now used as a leper asylum. The number of inmates at present in the asylum is 133. A female quarter, quite distinct and completely separated from the male quarters, has been built lately. The establishment is altogether under the management of European Dominican nuns, and admirably conducted; the poor patients are tended and nursed by the good nuns with maternal solicitude. Both Mucurapo and Cocorite are subject to intermittent fever. The village is flanked on the west by an extensive swamp; it is, however, to a certain extent, protected from malarial effluvia by a spur of the Fort George Mountain.

Northward of Mucurapo and Cocorite are the two wards of Maraval and Diego Martin, and westward of Diego Martin, Carenage and Chaguaramas. The three wards of Maraval, Diego Martin and Carenage have the same general aspect, being formed respectively of the three valleys of the same name, with their intervening hills; they are therefore partly flat and partly hilly—highest peak 1,830 feet. The soil is light in the valleys, loamy on the hills, and, in general, fertile; the soil of the valley of Maraval, however, is not so good as that of Diego Martin and Carenage. Sandstone, slate, and limestone are met with in the ridges, which also grow valuable timber—such as poui, cip, cedar, &c. There is, in the Maraval ward, one small sugar estate, and one in Diego Martin. Diego Martin was one of the first districts of the colony in which the cane was cultivated. Coffee, cacao, and provisions are grown in the hilly parts of the three wards. A good ward-road branches off from the Circular Road, and leads up the valley to the Moka estate. There the ridge, separating Maraval from Santa Cruz, becomes rather lower at the place called *La Silla*, or the Saddle. At this point the road crosses over to Santa Cruz. The dam and the reservoir forming part of the Port-of-Spain water-works are built near the road on the right bank of the river, about two miles and a half from the town. Another road follows up the ridge between Maraval and Diego Martin to the north coast, near Sant d'Eau, sending a branch to Diego Martin; these are mere bridle-paths.

The ward-road of Diego Martin is a good carriage-road. At the extremity of the valley a signal-post has been established, which corresponds with that of Fort George. Since emancipation, a free village has been formed in the ward of Diego Martin, and a school established in 1853.

The ward of Carenage extends to the sea on the south. Besides the small river of Cuesa, which traverses the valley from one end to the other, another mountain torrent descends the hills, not far from the mouth of the Diego Martin. There are coco-palm plantations along the beach, and a village has been formed in the neighbourhood of the Catholic church, which is a neat stone building, and on which the inhabitants of that impoverished district have spent *in labour* above 3,000 dollars.

Our enterprising townsman, Mr. William Tucker, has purchased the whole valley of Cuesa, where once flourished four sugar estates, and has commenced there the formation of an extensive cacao estate, the belt along the bay being planted in coco-nut palms. On the north coast, and corresponding to the valley, is the bay of Maqueripe, where has been landed the telegraphic cable connecting Trinidad with the other Antilles and North America.

The port of Carenage belongs to this ward. Population, 1881, 1,329.

The district is unhealthy, as also the ward of Chaguaramas. This latter consists of the extremity of the north-western peninsula, together with the islands of Monos and Gasparillo, and a few other diminutive islets. It is entirely hilly, scantily inhabited, and more scantily cultivated. Chaguaramas is, as already stated, a fine land-locked port with bold water. A stream of pure, never-failing water runs down the hill into the bay. This latter is separated from Carenage by a limestone promontory, connected with the mainland by a mere neck, 2,000 feet wide, through which a canal has been cut for small boats.

The islet of Gasparillo, or Gaspar Grande, is well known, on account of its extensive caves, which are haunted by vampires and countless bats. The islet is of limestone formation, and the soil good; but vegetation suffers part of the year from scarcity of water. Carrera's Island, lying at the entrance of the bay of Chaguaramas, has been turned into a convicts' depôt, the prisoners being employed in quarrying and breaking stones. Monos belongs to the borough of Port-of-Spain, as also Huevos and Pato. Monos has several wells of wholesome water; it is a place of resort for sea-bathing. The population consists chiefly of fishermen. Nothing can be cultivated there except during the wet season, and even then it is with the greatest difficulty that one can grow provisions, on account of the ravages of the parasol-ants or *Bachacos*.

The ward of Chacachacareo consists of the islands of Pato and Huevos—uninhabited—and Chacachacareo. The latter island may be said to be formed of two smaller islets or ridges, converging towards the north till they meet, being there connected by a neck of land a few yards in breadth, and a few feet above the level of the sea—a fine little cove, with deep water, being formed between the two ridges. Chacachacareo is well populated, fertile, and once produced fine cotton; it is now cultivated in vegetables and fruits, and is noted for its fine sugar-apples and melons. Guinea-grass grows in luxuriance, and is used by the residents for thatching their cottages. Alum has been found both there and at Huevos. On the south side of Chacachacareo is a large pond of salt-water, which might be advantageously made to yield a home supply of salt. A small Catholic chapel had been erected by the inhabitants in a commanding position, and a few houses scattered around form a kind of hamlet. There was also at Chacachacareo a whaling establishment. There were, not many years ago, four such establishments on the *Bocas* islands. The species of whale caught in the Gulf is a balaenoptera (razor-back). Whales arrive in December, but they are then so wild that they cannot be easily approached : the whaling season was from February to May, at which time the balaenoptera leave these shores for other climates. In taking the whale, peculiar boats only are used, so that the whalers do not venture beyond the placid waters of the Gulf. The method followed here is the same as that pursued on the ocean; but, no large vessels being engaged in the pursuit, when the animal has been killed it is towed to the establishment by the boats : this is a very tedious mode of procedure, and should the wind and tide be against the boatmen, it often occupies twenty-four hours. The animal is brought as near the shore as possible, the blubber cut into long slices and carried to the boilers; even this, however, is not accomplished without much trouble. Very often immense troops of sharks attack the carcase of the whale, and devour part of it before it can be removed to the establishment; but they particularly swarm around when the operation of slicing is commenced, from 1,500 to 3,000 sharks sometimes collecting in an incredibly short time, so that some of the men are then employed in killing them with harpoons and hatchets. Great waste often takes place from imperfect resources; one-fourth of the available parts of the animal being sometimes left on the spot. The number of whales caught annually was from twenty-five to thirty; quantity of oil, about 20,000 gallons. Sometimes whales come in accompanied by their young, and as the female is very fond of its offspring, the whaler aims at wounding the calf with the least possible injury. The mother, in this case, never abandons her young, but continues swimming round, so as to be easily approached and harpooned.

Huevos is uninhabited, on account of the immense number of rats which have made it their abode. On the north side of the islet is a cave, the resort of guacharos.

At Monos, Huevos, and Chacachacareo grows the lignum vitæ (*Guayacum officinale*), and, what is locally called here country bark (*Portlandia hexandra*), an emeto-cathartic, used in the cure of fevers. These islets, as well as Pato, are noted for their centipedes, some of them being from eight to ten inches long.

Proceeding eastward from Port-of-Spain are the following wards:—Laventille; this is immediately contiguous to the town, partly hilly, partly swampy, sloping down towards the Eastern Royal Road and the Caroni river. Soil, generally good; a few cacao and coffee plantations, with provision-grounds and an abundance of fruit trees. The hills are of limestone, which protrudes in several parts, of a bluish colour, with veins of pure carbonate. From these hills are quarried stones for building purposes, and for macadamising the streets of the town and the roads adjoining; excellent lime is also manufactured from the same. Fine gypsum may be procured at the foot of the hills. Several fresh-water springs are found in this ward. Laventille has gained the well-merited reputation of being one of the most unhealthy districts of Trinidad, which it owes to its proximity to an extensive mangrove swamp; the most elevated part of it, however, is less unhealthy. No whites can live there; the coloured people suffer much, and Africans and Chinese are the only people who enjoy comparatively good health. It is assumed that a white man who sleeps *one* night on the Laventille heights must necessarily get fever. If correctly informed, a certain number of white families from Dominica and St. Lucia were induced by Sir Ralph Woodford to settle on the Laventille hills and establish coffee estates. In less than eight years they were mowed down by fever, and coffee cultivation was abandoned. Population, 1881, 4,472; in 1871, 1,775.

Next to Laventille comes the ward of Cimaronero, very much resembling the former in general position and unhealthiness; however, it is not placed so much within the reach of the malaria, and its soil, near the Aricagua river, is of a better quality.

The ward of Aricagua, which follows, is partly hilly, partly flat, and very much resembling the preceding one. The Aricagua river has its outlet into the Caroni. On the right bank of the Caroni, and extending into the Cimaronero ward, is a natural savanna, called Bordonal; it is under water for a certain part of the year. The small village of San Juan stands on a high ground, northward of the Royal Road, about 200 yards from the river Aricagua, and is traversed by a ward-road conducting into the valley of Santa Cruz. It is a miserable-looking village, with a stone-built Catholic church, and a curé attached. Besides San Juan, there are two small hamlets along the Royal Road, opposite to the Aranguez and Le Vivier estates; an Anglican chapel has lately been built at the latter, and a curate appointed.

The ward of St. Joseph, which comprises the small town of St. Joseph, with a population of eight hundred and eighty-eight inhabitants, together with the quarter of the same name, comes next; it is partly hilly and partly flat; soil very much resembling that of Aricagua, and very fertile along the banks of the St. Joseph river. On the flanks of the hills are several natural savannas, looking at a distance like prairies, and which can be seen from the harbour of Port-of-Spain. Large blocks of milky quartz are scattered all over these savannas, which stretch, at intervals, along the ridges to the river Arima. The small town of St. Joseph was founded towards the year 1577, and was for a long time the chief town of Trinidad. It stands on a narrow eminence at the entrance of the Maraccas valley, has some few neat and comfortable houses, and is mainly inhabited by Spanish families, descendants of the former possessors of the island. Two streets, pretty steep, lead from the Royal Road into the interior of the town. At the north end of St. Joseph's were once barracks, in which was generally stationed a company of white troops; in 1838, however, they were occupied by a corps of blacks, recently formed of Africans liberated from slavers. On the night of the 17th of June, 1838, these savages revolted, fired on their officers, and part of them succeeded in making their way eastward, in march, as they fancied, to their native country. They were met at Arima by an armed militia force, and several were killed; in fact, this attempt at rebellion ended in the death of forty of those deluded men, of whom three prisoners underwent military execution.

In 1595, Sir Walter Raleigh having entered the Gulf of Paria, sent some of his boats up the river Caroni, from which he passed into the St. Joseph tributary, and, having landed his men near the town, captured and burnt it. St. Joseph is a Catholic parish, with a neat stone-built church, from the tower of which one has the command of a most extensive view. The Maraccas ward-road joins the town near the barracks.

The hilly parts of the above wards are inhabited by small proprietors, the majority of them being emancipated labourers; they cultivate provisions, some coffee and cacao, and generally work out on hire. The plains are cultivated in canes; and in Laventille is found one sugar estate; in Cimaronero two estates; two in Aricagua, on one of which is a water-mill; six in St. Joseph. A quarry of excellent building-stone has been lately discovered in the ward of Aricagua, and supplies macadam for the adjoining portion of the Royal Road; very pure gypsum may also be obtained from the hills near St. Joseph, and a snow-white clay, at the foot of the high ground on which the town is built. This latter is used for whitewashing.

Northward of the above wards are the following:—Santa Cruz, Maraccas, and Las Cuevas—the latter stretching along the sea-shore, and bounded on the south by Santa Cruz and Maraccas. They bear the greatest resemblance to each other in every respect, and are for the most part hilly—Maraccas and Las Cuevas especially. The soil is in general of the best quality—light and sandy in the valleys, and a clayey loam resting on schists and limestone on the hills; these are generally steep, and the valleys rather damp and warm. The valley of Santa Cruz—in all respects the richest, and also the largest, in Trinidad—is entirely cultivated in cacao, and contains some of the finest cacao estates to be found in the island. They were once exclusively owned by the Spaniards—the first settlers and proprietors of the island—but the greater number have changed hands within the last twenty years. Coffee and provisions are cultivated on the hills. The valley of Santa Cruz branches off into several smaller glens, each being irrigated by its respective stream, which carries off its water to the Aricagua river. The road to Santa Cruz once traversed the village of San Juan. Its direction has been altered, and it now runs up along the right side of the stream to the head of the valley. A branch road establishes a communication over the *saddle* with Maraval, while another section crosses the mountains at the end of the Gasparillo glen to Maraccas bay, in the ward of Las Cuevas; it is but a mere path through the high woods. Population, 1881, 2,191; 1871, 2,252.

The valley of Maraccas extends northward of the town of St. Joseph, from which it is separated by an elevation of the land; it is much more contracted than Santa Cruz, and the surrounding ridges are higher, particularly at its extremity. Cacao, coffee, and provisions are the only cultivations. The vale of Acono is a dependency, or branch, of the Maraccas valley.

Las Cuevas is still more hilly than Maraccas, and does not contain above 800 acres of flat land: these form the two estates of Maraccas and Las Cuevas, situated respectively on the bays of the same name, and separated by a steep ridge. These two estates are cacao plantations, drained by the two streams of Maraccas and *Quebrada de Hierro,* or the iron ravine. Produce from Las Cuevas is conveyed to town in small sloops; that from Maraccas bay is carried through to Santa Cruz on mule-back, and from thence carted to town.

The highest mountain of the colony is situated between Las Cuevas and the extremity of Maraccas valley; it is called Las Cuevas, or *el Tocuche,* and is 3,100 feet high. At the bottom of Maraccas valley is a waterfall, from a height of about 340 feet, and remarkable for the nearly perpendicular cliff of the mountain from which it descends; this may be regarded as the source of the St. Joseph river. About one mile and a half from the cascade, on the right bank of the river, almost within its bed, and at the foot of a high hill, is the mineral spring of Maraccas; it contains a small proportion of sulphuretted hydrogen gas, epsom salts, &c. These mineral waters have not yet been tested to an extent sufficient to warrant a decision on their medicinal properties; but they have been used in a few cases of nervous debility, and have proved efficacious; this spring, therefore, will be found of great advantage to invalids. It is in that part of the mountains, stretching between Santa Cruz and Maraccas bay, that Galena was found, as pretended, by Mr. Darmany. Very valuable timber abounds in these wards.

Tacarigua, to the eastward of St. Joseph, is, in general, more level than the latter ward, a small section only to the north being hilly; the plain slopes very gradually towards the Caroni. The banks of this river are somewhat higher than the adjacent plain, which, being in some parts of a retentive nature, is not easily drained. The soil of the ward is, in general, light—too much so in a few spots.

Tacarigua, strictly so called, is more fertile than Arouca. It is here proper to remark that the quality of the land gradually improves from Port-of-Spain to St. Joseph; but from St. Joseph, eastward, it becomes gradually poorer, until we reach the table-land between Aripo and Cuare. Eastward of Cuare, it again improves, until meeting the fertile districts of Oropouche and Manzanilla. The hilly parts of Tacarigua, and also portions of the plain, are cultivated in provisions, the rest in canes, there being eleven sugar estates in this ward. The river Tacarigua traverses this ward, flowing from the valley of Caura. On the left bank of the river, and immeditely southward of the Royal Road, is the parish church of St. Mary, not far from which is the country seat of the late Mr. Burnley. Between St. Joseph and the Tacarigua river, houses scattered on each side of the road form a rude village. Another village, on a more regular plan, is situated opposite the Orange Grove and Dinsley estates, on lands of the Paradise estate. Two miles further eastward is the village of Arauca, with a Catholic church and a Presbyterian chapel.

Next to Tacarigua are Arima and Guanape, very much resembling each other in point of soil and general features. Of these wards, a small part only is hilly, the greater portion being flat; the soil is in general very poor, except on the hills and along the rivers—such as those of Arima and Guanape—where there is a belt of alluvium, very rich and well adapted to the cultivation of the cacao. The soil of the plain consists, in most parts, of a coarse, yellow clay, very retentive, and consequently cold; cortaderas, melastomaceæ, and timites grow in abundance, as also fine poui and balata timber. Between the Guanape and Aripo, the soil is of the worst description; wild pine-apples, cortaderas, and timites are particularly abundant—some of the *timitales*, or timite-groves, resembling marshes. A small section of Guanape is covered over with silicious pebbles and a meagre vegetation. Arima and Guanape are almost exclusively cultivated in cacao; they also produce some coffee; but the growth of provisions is much neglected, though maize, plantains, yams, manioc, &c., grow to perfection in the best tracts. There is also a great abundance of good timber, such as carapa, yoke, olivier, and tapana, besides poui and balata, already mentioned. These two wards are sparingly cultivated, and the population scanty, on account of their bad soil. Guanape, Arima, and Tacarigua form, perhaps, the most healthy districts of Trinidad, and newly-arrived Europeans are not therein subject to the usual country fevers, unless imprudent or addicted to intemperance. Several natural savannas are found in the ward of Arima — viz., Piarco, Piarquito, Arima, and O'Mara; they produce but a coarse grass, upon which animals do not thrive. The village of Arima, situated at the foot of the northern range, on the right bank of the river Arima, and at the head of an extensive plain, sixteen miles from Port-of-Spain, is well laid out; its streets are wide, and intersect each other at right angles, with a large square in the centre of the village. It has its police-station; and at the eastern side of the square stands the Catholic church, built of mason work.

The village of Arima was for a long time an Indian mission. Soon after the settlement of the island by the conquerors, the Indians, with the consent of the Government, had been drawn together by the Capuchin monks, mainly with the object of bringing them under the civilising influence of Christianity, also of protecting them against the exactions of the colonists. Four such missions were formed at Tacarigua, Caura, Arouca, and Arima; but as the establishment of *ingenios*, or sugar estates, was carried eastward, the Indians located at the above places were removed to Arima, where one thousand quarrees of land had been reserved on the right side of the river as their full and inalienable property. The present village of Arima owes its origin to the mission. This was settled and governed on the same plan as all such establishments in the Spanish colonies. These Indians had their own municipal government, the first and second Alcades being chosen from among themselves, but under the control of the missionary priest. At the conquest of the island, and subsequent to the death of the *padre*, or missionary priest, a *corregidor* was appointed, as also a *protector*, to whom the Indians would appeal against any arbitrary act of the *corregidor*. All able-bodied Indians were obliged to work two days in the week, for the support of the aggregate members of the community, who, in general, were employed in keeping the village clean and cultivating the land in common, the proceeds being distributed to each house or family equally; each head of a family had, besides, his own allotment, or *conuco*, which he cultivated for his own private benefit and advantage. They were not, strictly speaking, subject to taxation, but were bound to assist in performing any public work within the limits of the mission, when ordered by the corregidor; they had also to accompany him whenever required, on wages. The Indians were considered in the light of minors, and could not sell or otherwise dispose of their property, which, however, descended to their natural heirs: a very wise provision indeed, since the moment they became emancipated, they sold what property they had for a mere trifle. Once every year they elected, with the sanction of the corregidor, a king and queen to preside over their festivities, and to act as their principals on solemn occasions. In 1834, when a stipendiary magistrate was appointed, the Indians were brought under the common law, and the corregidorship was abolished. In 1840, after the passing of the territorial ordinance, the lots in the village were put up for sale at an upset price—a measure the legality of which is highly questionable, as far as the Indians were concerned, since the lands and lots in the mission had been granted to them as compensation for property of which they had been deprived. The Indians of Arima called themselves *Califournans;* some twenty-five years ago a few of them were still alive. I knew then the one which could be called the patriarch (about one hundred years old), and his wife; they were good specimens of the race, or tribe. The old man was short and square-built, with high cheek-bones, good eyes, and straight, white hair. His wife bore a similar appearance, and was borne down by the weight of years. Pascual was always gay, and apparently satisfied with his lot; he was fond of spirits, and became drunk whenever an opportunity was afforded. He was otherwise most honest and peaceable. The old man had sold his *conuco*, and depended upon the *padre*, or parish priest, for his maintenance. Two schools—one for boys and another for girls—were once maintained for Indian children, but the attendance was always very scanty.

The village of Arima was formerly, and remained for a long time, celebrated for its festival of Santa Rosa, the patron saint of the mission. On that day the Indians elected their king and queen—in general, a young man and young girl—and all appeared in their best apparel and most gaudy ornaments. The interior of the church was hung with the produce of their industry—bunches of plantains, cassava cakes, and the fruits of the season; game of various descriptions, coincos, lapas, parrots, &c., and draperied with the graceful leaves of the palm-tree. After mass they performed ceremonial dances in the church, and then proceeded to the *Casa real*, or royal house, to pay their compliments to the corregidor, who gave the signal for dancing and various sports—among others that of archery—in which the men exercised themselves until a prize was adjudged to the best marksman. People from all parts of the country would resort to Arima for the purpose of witnessing the festivities, which were invariably attended by the Governor and staff. Sir Ralph Woodford, in particular, always took the greatest interest in the mission, and every year would distribute prizes to the children of both sexes who deserved them by their good behaviour, and their improvement at school. Santa Rosa's day was really a gay anniversary, at which the poor Indians, the simple children of yore, were, for the time, the principal actors, and during which they forgot both the loss of their heritage and their own individual serfdom.

The 30th of August is a holiday still, but bears quite a different character. People still crowd to the village from different parts of the island, but there are no more Indians, neither are their oblations to be seen adorning the church; their sports and their dances have passed away with the actors therein, and, in their stead, quadrilles, waltzes, races, and blind-hookey are the present amusements of the village.

Arima is sixteen miles distant from Port-of-Spain. Since the year 1879 it has become the terminus of a railway from that town; three passenger trains each day; transit, one hour. Arima will ultimately become an important centre of population and commerce. Produce from the adjoining mountains will find its way to Arima, to be transported afterwards to town. All the cacao from Cumuto, Tumpuna, Cunape, and even Oropuche must be carted there, until, at least, the projected tramway along the left bank of the Caroni is fairly established, when the inhabitants of those localities will find it more advantageous to use the tramway. Population of the ward in 1871, 3,295; houses, 1,883. Population in 1881, 4,687.

Northward of Tacarigua, Arima and Guanape, are the wards of Caura and Blanchisseuse. They are hilly, but the soil is, in general, very fertile—particularly that of the valley of Caura. This valley, which is watered and drained by the river Tacarigua, is considered as the most picturesque spot in the whole island— in fact, it is described by visitors as a perfect *paradise*. It is cultivated in cacao, coffee, and provisions; the inhabitants are mostly of Spanish descent, and the Spanish language is universally spoken. Blanchisseuse stretches along the sea, and is entirely hilly. The ward-road of Caura has been lately extended to that ward, but it is barely more than a bridle-path. Blanchisseuse communicates with Port-of-Spain by sea, or by Santa Cruz, through Las Cuevas and Maraccas; a bridle-path across the mountains connects it with Arima. When this path has been converted into a regular road, Blanchisseuse will send its produce to Arima.

It may be seen from the above description that the county of St. George is, for the most part, hilly; the soil excellent in some parts, and altogether barren in others. Cacao is the chief produce, and is cultivated in the valleys and the river-hollows; the roads are generally good. Population in 1871, 39,659; in 1881, 80,761; increase, 41,102.

2. County of St. David.—Only two wards have been formed in

this county, one in the north and the other in the southern division; the district itself is but imperfectly known, as the greater part of it is still covered with high virgin forests. It is in general hilly, and the high-lands would appear to be very fertile, whilst the level are of the worst description; but a tract of undulating land, near the river Oropuche, is of the best quality. The ward of Toco, in the northern division, extends along the sea-shore; this ward is entirely hilly and uneven, some of the hills being 500, 850, and 1,230 feet high, the depressions between being well sheltered and cool. This ward is particularly well adapted to the cultivation of cacao, coffee, and provisions. The cultivation of coco-nuts should be tried along the shore, and on those localities most exposed to the sea-breeze. The soil near Rio Grande and along Tumpire is of the best quality. There was formerly at Toco bay a sugar estate, which was abandoned soon after emancipation. The want of proper harbours and the difficulties of communication with the bay and Port-of-Spain will be felt for a long time as a serious obstacle to the progress of this ward, which otherwise would soon rise in importance as a cacao and provision-growing district. Great progress, however, has been made within the last few years, and the crops are larger than they were. Governor Gordon, always alive to the best interests of the colony, had encouraged steam communication around the island. I must say, however, that he failed in his endeavour to benefit this remote district. The inhabitants would not improve the opportunity afforded under very frivolous pretexts. They would not make any previous arrangements, but would complain that the steamer would not wait for their convenience. I think that they are sensible of their mistake, and would now prove wiser and more discreet. Means of communication, however, should be improved by the formation of good roads in the district, one especially from Rio Grande to Sans Souci, and another one to the bay of Cumana. A contract for steam communication between Port-of-Spain and the eastern coast has been advertised, touching at Toco, Manzanilla, Mayaro, &c. I hope that the contract will be taken up by some enterprising person, and I have no doubt that it will prove remunerative. I would suggest the necessity of touching at Cumana, Balandra Bay, or Salibia. There exists at present a land communication between Toco and Port-of-Spain along the sea-shore, and across Tumpire, Matura, and Oropuche;

T

but it is a mere track, and scarcely fit for mule traverse. The ward of Toco abounds in excellent timber, and cedar-boards are a regular trade commodity. Population, 1881, Toco and Blanchisseuse, 2,025; 1871, 1,278.

The ward of Turure, in the southern district of this county, is partly hilly, partly level; the settlements of Cuare, Turure, and La Ceyba, with a few plantations along the banks of the Matura and Oropuche were for many years the only inhabited parts of this ward, its central part, traversed by the eastern road, being highly infertile. Lately, however, many acres have been bought from the Government along the road towards Sangre Chiquito and Morne Calabash; also on the banks of Sangre Grande, Cunape, and Upper Cumuto. The soil along Cunape and Upper Cumuto may be pronounced of the best quality, and cacao cultivation is fast gaining ground in those localities, almost to the foot of Tamana. This district may before long become one of importance. I have said that the central part of Turure is highly infertile; nothing, in fact, can be worse than the tract lying between Aripo and La Ceyba.

The settlements of Cuare, Turure, and La Ceyba were formed, in the year 1816, of disbanded soldiers from the 1st West India Regiment. These settlements or villages ranged along the banks of the rivers bearing their respective names; and the soldiers were located thereon with a grant of sixteen acres of land to each man. They were placed, to a certain extent, under the supervision of their sergeants, who were allowed a larger and more commodious house, on condition of admitting travellers to a temporary lodging when requested so to do. Sergeant Brooks had, for many years, the privilege of entertaining travellers to *Bande de l'Est.* Some of the locations also bordered on the road, with the object, it seems, to keep that road in good repair; also to place labour within the reach of neighbouring proprietors. The experiment proved a complete failure, the *King's men*, as they called themselves, being too proud to work as day-labourers. In the year 1849, after the passing of the territorial ordinance, the lands of these and other settlers were surveyed, and fifteen acres granted free to each settler or his descendants; but the lands of Cuare, La Ceyba, and Turure being of the very worst description, the occupants gradually gave up their grants for better land elsewhere.

Cacao, a little coffee, and provisions, are the only productions. The cacao plantations are on the banks of the rivers Oropuche and Matura, and have lately been extended to Cumuto and Cunape. Produce is brought to Arima on mules. The Oropuche is a fine stream, receiving, on the right, Cuare, with its effluents Turure, La Ceyba and Guayco, Cunape, Sangre Grande, and Sangre Chiquito; on the left, Melao and Rio Grande. It is not, however, accessible to crafts, in consequence of the bar at its mouth and the heavy surf along the Matura shore. This river is also noted for the large number of *Huillias*, or water boas, which find shelter there. Population, 1881, 956; 1871, 599.

The county of St. David, as may be inferred from the above sketch, is thinly populated and scantily cultivated. The hills and undulating parts of this county are fertile, but the plain is desperately barren, consisting of a variable mixture of clay and sand, and stratified detritus containing an excess of quartz. One single ward-road, or rather trace, branching off the eastern road between Valencia and Aripo, connects Matura and Oropuche with Arima; from the village of Matura it follows an easterly direction to the bay of Salibia, and thence, across the hills, leads to Toco. Population of the county, by last census, 2,025; in 1871, 1,877.

3. County of St. Andrew.—Only one ward has been formed out of this county, viz., that of Manzanilla, including Morne Calabash. These were once settlements like those of Cuare, Turure, and La Ceyba, formed of disbanded black soldiers, on the same plan and with the same views; they were brought under the common law in the year 1849, fifteen acres being granted to each settler or his descendants. For many years, the settlers of St. Andrew had as their superintendent a medical man. They were on half-pay, and every month a drogher was despatched from Port-of-Spain with provisions for the settlement, and, in return, took the produce to town, the owners of the articles travelling generally by land.

The ward of Manzanilla, and the county of St. Andrew in general, are fertile; in fact, Manzanilla and Morne Calabash may be classed among the best districts of Trinidad. " Plant a stampee "—the smallest silver coin—" and a doubloon will grow," was a common saying of the inhabitants, whereby to express their opinion of the fertility of the soil. And really the whole tract bordering on the sea, and from about six to eight miles inland, including the Lebranche hills, is of the best description. The surface is undulating, and the district lavishly produces those natural indexes of fertility—carats, cedars, wild fig-trees, balisiers, &c. This section of the island would now be densely populated were it not for the great difficulty of conveying the produce to market, since, except the small harbour under Point Manzanilla, there is no shipping-place along the whole line of coast. At one time it was in contemplation to cut a canal of communication between the rivers Oropuche and Caroni; the survey was actually made, in 1804, by Colonel Rutherford. The projected canal was made to start from the junction of the Sangre Chiquito with the Oropuche, and reach the mouth of the Cumuto; then following the left bank of the Caroni to its junction with the Arouca. Such canal would have afforded the advantage of draining the country which it traversed; but I doubt very much whether, during the dry season, it would have had sufficient water to be of any utility in the way of transport. A tram-road would be by far the most advantageous medium of connecting the counties of St. Andrew and St. David with the Gulf of Paria. Population, 1881, 570; in 1871, 350.

All that has been said of Manzanilla is pretty applicable to the greatest part of the county in general. The part contiguous to St. George and Caroni is generally poor; but from the river Cunape eastward, the quality of the soil improves from a deep clay to a black loam, near Morne Calabash, where, as already stated, it becomes of a very superior, and even of first-rate quality. The land in the whole county is undulating, or generally hilly. It is traversed by the high road leading from the capital to the eastern coast; at Morne Calabash it branches off in two directions—to Manzanilla on the north-east, and to the beach on the east, thus establishing a communication along the sea-shore with Mayaro.

It is in this ward, at Pointe Noire, that the coal formation of the island was first traced by Messrs. Wall and Sawkins. There are, as it appears, three series of beds exhibited in the cliffs, commencing one and a quarter mile south of the mouth of the river Oropuche, and proceeding to the south, and separated by spaces of low and swampy land. It has been ascertained that this coal formation extends to the Gulf of Paria, constituting what Messrs. Wall and Sawkins term the Caroni or carbonaceous series.

4. County of Caroni.—This county has been divided into seven wards: Upper and Lower Caroni, Chaguanas, Carapichaima, Savanetta, Couva, and the ward of Montserrat. Upper Caroni possesses a great variety of soils, from the worst to the best; the level section is, at times, a poor sandy soil, sometimes argillaceous; the *vegas*, or river hollows, and the undulating land towards the east and the south are excellent. Maize and cacao are almost the sole cultivations; plantains also thrive in the vegas, but are not extensively grown. The parts under culture are along the banks of the rivers, such as the Tumpuna and Caroni, or in their immediate vicinity. The produce was taken down the river to town, or brought to Arima on mules. For many years all the properties in this ward were owned by the mixed descendants of Indians and Spaniards, many being emigrants from Venezuela; and little or none but the Spanish language was spoken throughout this district. Of late years many have changed hands, and become the property of usurers. The parasol-ants, or *Bachacos*, are there a regular pest. This ward abounds in good timber, and there are groves of cedars towards the upper course of the Tumpuna. Cacao yields more abundantly in this ward than, perhaps, in any other part of the island. I know an instance of 1,000 trees, about 18 years old, yielding 32 fanagas, or 3,500 lbs., whilst the average returns, in other parts, for the same number of trees, is about 1,500 lbs. only. Maize is cultivated during the dry season.

Three roads connect this ward with the Royal Road: one from the junction of the Guanape and Aripo, which reaches Royal Road just at the south-eastern boundary of the Arima village— this is the Cocorite Road; another runs a little westward of Tumpuna, meets the Arima railway station, and crosses the O'Mara savanna—it is known by the name of O'Mara Road; the third leads from the mouth of the Maujico to d'Abadie's village, and by another branch through the Piarquito savanna to the village of Arouca. For years the Caroni river was the real highway to Port-of-Spain. It is in this ward that the Guanape and Aripo join to form the Caroni; half a mile lower down it receives the Tumpuna. The banks of the Caroni are high and steep; its course extremely winding. After its junction with Tumpuna, the depth of water varies from one to three feet down to the point reached by the tidal flow, and from four to twelve feet below that point to its outlet. The shallow mud bar at its mouth can be crossed only at high tide. The mean time descending in a corial from Tumpuna to the sea is eight hours; but going up, or against the current, is very tedious, as the canoe is pushed up by the means of a long pole.

During the wet season, after any heavy showers, the Caroni and its effluents overflow their banks, inundating the country around for many hours, and leaving, on retiring, a fertilising deposit. Between the left bank of the Caroni and the undulating ground to the eastward, there is a hollow, which serves as a recipient for the surplus water of the Caroni and surface water of the surrounding country. This is the Guaymare, which runs parallel to the river in the direction of the Grand Savanna. When the water of the Guaymare and Conupia—a stream which runs from the Montserrat hills—meet together, they cover for several miles the flat lands adjoining the Caroni savanna, and have more than once already put to a severe test the solidity of the railway between the Caroni and Conupia stations. Population in 1881, 1,326; in 1871, 668.

The Chaguanas and Lower Caroni wards may be said to be entirely level, a great part of their extent being occupied by what is called the Grand Savanna, and an extensive mangrove swamp, which forms, as it were, the Delta of the Caroni. The eastern part of the Lower Caroni ward is under cultivation, cacao and sugar being the staple productions. The estates generally are situated on or near the banks of the Caroni. The soil is partly light and partly clayey, and the district rather damp. Presently nearly the whole produce will be conveyed to town by railway. There are, in Chaguanas, on both sides of the river Capparo, a fine cacao estate and several sugar plantations.

A convict depôt has been formed in this ward for some years past, at the entrance of the extensive forest extending to the Montserrat hills. The prisoners are employed in cutting wood, hauling timber, and conveying logs to the railway station. A tramway, about six miles long, from the depôt to the sea, has been established, and is maintained partly by the Government and partly by the planters, for the transport of timber, supplies to the estates, and produce. Chaguanas owes its prosperity—nay, its very existence as an agricultural district—to this tramway. Cartage by the road during the wet season was simply impossible. There is a station at Chaguanas, seventeen miles from town.

From the south-eastern boundary of Port-of-Spain to the ward of Chaguanas included, for about eleven miles along the sea-shore, and from three to five miles in depth, extends an immense mangrove swamp, and further inland the Grand Savanna. This latter covers an area of several miles, say 20,000 acres. It is more or less completely submerged during the rainy season, and to such an extent at times as to preclude communication across. Some portions are boggy, so that a sort of undulating movement is communicated to the entire surface by a person walking or even treading on the treacherous crust. The savanna may be said to commence a few hundred yards from the river Caroni.

About two miles south of the river is a large pond of fresh water, called the *Bejucal*; this pond swarmed with fish, and immense quantities of *Cascarduras* (Callichthys) were taken in it annually. The quantity has lately greatly diminished, the coolies damming out or even poisoning the streams for the purpose of securing even the smallest fry. The manner adopted for fishing in the Bejucal was as follows: The fisherman made a sort of raft of rushes, and then anchored out in the deep water, throwing his cast-net, which he generally withdrew fully laden with fish. It is from the Bejucal that Dr. Court procured the two specimens of the *Pipa frog*, which can be seen at the council-room. Westward of the Bejucal is the *Cascarduras hole*, in the centre of a bog.

The savanna extends westward to the river Chaguanas, or *Madame Espagnole*. Westward of the savanna, and along the sea-board, is that extensive mangrove swamp, already mentioned, dotted over with ponds of salt or brackish water—some of them pretty large—and cut up by a network of canals. Cipriani's canal was opened by the proprietor of the Felicité estate to carry his produce to the Chaguanas river for shipment to town.

The Caroni, or Grand Savanna, was for many years regarded as a public pasture-ground, to which cattle were sent from various estates for the advantage of grazing out of crop. It may be said that at present it is not used for the purpose, and the Government is now prepared to parcel it out and sell the land to public competition. Every year in March (or sooner or later, according to the dryness of the season) fire is set to the rank grass, which burns readily. The fire sometimes keeps alive for weeks, the dark, dense smoke spreading and hanging at the horizon like an immense cloud.

It has been observed, as the beneficial result of this yearly burning, that the quality of the grass improves, and the shade-trees grow more thickly. When the colony was first settled, the Grand Savanna was renowned for the immense quantity of aquatic game and parrots which thronged there, and which were eagerly hunted for sport or profit by the inhabitants.

Some of the white settlers and French emigrés made a living from their chase. Ducks, teals, herons, flamingos (*Red Ibis*), &c. then swarmed in the ponds; the mangroves and guava trees were literally covered with ramiers and parrots. The quantity, however, has diminished in an incredible degree, particularly since the firing of the long grass, which afforded shelter to the feathered and other game. From the mangroves along the Caroni, Port-of-Spain gets a good supply of fuel. Lower Caroni and Chaguanas: population in 1881, 7,118; in 1871, 4,046.

Wards of Carapichaima, Couva, and Savanetta.—Next to Chaguanas lies the ward of Carapichaima, and in succession, southward, Couva and Savanetta; these wards are bounded on the north by Chaguanas, on the south by Pointe-à-Pierre, on the east by the ward of Montserrat and undefined crown lands, on the west by the Gulf. These wards very much resemble each other in point of soil and general disposition, and may be said to form a perfect level, except towards the interior. The soil is not of the best description, being generally sandy, except on the banks of the rivers, where it is pretty rich alluvial; also near the sea-shore. The soil of Couva is considered, on the whole, as being of a better quality; also the lower part of Savanetta. Carapichaima is the worst, being a poor stratified detritus.

These wards, being flat, may be considered as damp, at least during part of the year; they are partly still in high woods or brush woods. The water is very shallow along the whole length of coast, and mangrove swamps occur at frequent intervals; as a necessary consequence, malarial fevers are rather prevalent.

During the last few years cane cultivation has been increased in these wards, and much improved. Steam-ploughs have been used apparently with signal advantage, inasmuch as the average yield per acre has been increased, and the cost of cultivation diminished. But the soil, as a rule, is sadly deficient in lime salts.

The first vacuum pan and turbines ever worked in Trinidad were put up on the Brechin Castle estate (Savanetta), and with good results to the proprietor, I assume, since he has been induced to repeat the experiment on the bank of the Caroni. These two factories, as compared with our ordinary establishments, are undoubtedly great improvements; not such, however, as I would like to see permanently adopted.

Mr. J. Cumming has erected on the Waterloo estate, in Carapichaima, an improved manufactory, capable of turning out more than 5,000 tons of white crystallised sugar.

Indeed, this is a progress which we should hail with deep satisfaction. Carapichaima, Couva, and Savanetta: population, 1881, 11,305; 1871, 7,477.

Ward of Montserrat.—This is a newly-constituted ward, the limits of which are not yet well defined, at least on the north and east. As the formation of this ward is intimately connected with the suppression of squatting in the island, I beg to enter into some details on the subject.

Not many years ago, the district or quarter of Montserrat was mostly, if not entirely, occupied by individuals of Spanish descent—*peones* of the best class—who had been allured thereto by the fertility of the soil, and the facility of getting land. Not ten could show any title to the land they occupied. They were therefore squatters, but squatters of the good sort, who aimed at becoming proprietors and permanent settlers. They cultivated provisions, cacao, and coffee. This class, numbering at least four hundred, comprised, besides the Spanish peones already mentioned, a few descendants of persons who were free before emancipation—amongst them some tradesmen, especially carpenters.

When they became aware of the determination of the Government to check squatting, they sent to the acting Governor, Mr. Rushworth, a memorial, in which they represented their case fairly enough, alleging that they had had the undisturbed enjoyment for many years of their holdings, acquired in some instances by inheritance or by purchase from former occupiers, pleading long occupation and the payment of ward rates for a number of years, as some justification for their belief that they were in legal possession. While declaring their inability to pay the whole amount of the value of the lands occupied by them, they expressed their readiness to pay for the same by annual instalments, to extend over a period of four years, under such restrictions as might be imposed upon them.

After some hesitation, the following arrangements were made :—In justice to the *bond fide* occupiers, the holdings were not put up for competition. To those who preferred to pay by four equal instalments, the land was sold at £2 per acre; those who were prepared to pay cash, or within the year, were allowed to purchase at the rate of £1 an acre.

Such among the squatters as had cacao plantations were entirely dependent for the necessary supplies for the support of themselves and families on merchants in the town, who made advances against the coming crop. This incident greatly aided in settling the question. Those merchants and others who had advanced money, finding that the Government was prepared to make arrangements with the squatters, readily advanced the purchase-money, in order to secure their debt and prevent the holdings passing into other hands.

Many actually occupied a larger extent of land than they had declared; so that the Government judged it necessary to have nearly all the lots' re-surveyed. The whole affair was conducted with prudence, firmness, and forbearance; and great indulgence shown throughout to the squatters, especially to those who had families, and evinced their readiness to comply with the law. In less than five years, the whole district was formed into a prosperous ward. Only two persons, having declined to comply with the orders of the Government, were ejected from their holdings.

The success which accompanied the measures enforced at

Montserrat made it an easy task to deal with squatting in other parts, as proved by subsequent proceedings against that class of offenders.

However, to carry out those measures, the Governor required the co-operation of active, intelligent officers; and such officers, I dare say, he found out in Mr. Robert Mitchell (afterwards immigration agent in Calcutta for many years), and in his successor, Mr. St. Luce d'Abadie. They were appointed to act as wardens and commissioners of crown lands in the district. Both these gentlemen had the advantage of understanding and speaking, besides the English idiom, the French and Spanish languages. In addition, Mr. d'Abadie had surveyed most of the lots in Montserrat, and thus was well acquainted with the district; and to the squatters he was not altogether unknown. The matter was thus settled, not only to the satisfaction of the Government, but also to the ultimate advantage of the settlers themselves: their titles to their holdings were legalised, roads were made where none existed previously, and new and extensive sales of crown land continued to be effected. Seven coolie settlements have been formed in the district, comprising nearly 3,000 acres. The number of grants made in 1879 amounted to 63, and the number of acres granted to 1,090. Population in 1871, 3,388; in 1881, 7,354—more than double; number of Indians, 1,738.

The Aragonese Franciscan fathers had selected Montserrat as a proper site for the establishment of an Indian mission. The village of San Jose was accordingly laid out, near the river Mayo, where the present village of Mayo now stands. This mission was broken up about the year 1824, when the Indians dispersed in the neighbouring districts.

The evils arising from the illegal and indiscriminate occupancy of public land are self-evident, especially with a population as that of this colony. Of those evils, the loss of crown property revenue is the least; while lawless habits, and the tendency to deviate from the paths of civilisation, are the greatest. By many the suppression of squatting was regarded as almost impossible; but it always was my opinion that this could be easily effected. Under a system of *Laissez faire* and *Laissez aller*, many violate the law who submit when it is firmly and considerately enforced, as proved by the Montserrat experience, where the Government had to deal with not a few, but with more than four hundred, squatters.

The land in Montserrat may be said to be of the best quality. It belongs to the Tamana series, the limestone producing a reddish brown to a dark brown loam, and the calcareous sands affording a loose, generally blackish, soil. It is particularly well adapted to the cultivation of cacao and coffee; provisions of all kinds thrive well, especially tanias.

The wards of Carapichaima, Couva, Savanetta, and Montserrat still abound in good timber—balata, poui, copaiba, carapa, cedar. They are drained by the following water-courses: the Arena and Couva, which latter separates the ward of Couva from Savanetta. It is the largest river of the whole district, and has for its principal tributary the Savanetta brook: they flow from the adjoining hills.

On the southern sloping of the Montserrat hills there is a spot of highly sandy and sterile land, designated as the "white land," on account of the colour of the soil. Here has been discovered a bed of beautiful glance pitch, which might be worked to advantage when the means of communication are improved and the facilities of transport increased.

Several villages have sprung up in the above wards since emancipation—among which, Camden and California villages. The Royal Road from Port-of-Spain to San Fernando traverses these wards, running parallel to, and about one mile and a half from, the sea-shore. From this main road branch off several ward-roads, viz., those of Upper Couva and Montserrat. The railway from St. Joseph to San Fernando runs nearly parallel to the Royal Road; there are four stations, viz., at Carapichaima, Camden village, California village, and Claxton bay.

The county of Caroni is generally level, and even flat. The quality of the soil is very varied, being, in general, a light sandy loam, resting on a substratum of clay; as a whole, it is not considered as very rich, except towards the interior, where the land is undulating. The vegas, or river hollows, are also of excellent quality. Cane, cacao, and provisions are pretty generally cultivated. There are, perhaps, more Spanish families of mixed blood in this county than in any other. Population, according to the last census, 25,777; population in 1871, 14,911.

CHAPTER IX.

TOPOGRAPHY—SOUTHERN DIVISION: COUNTIES OF VICTORIA, ST. PATRICK, MAYARO, AND NARIVA.

THE southern division comprises four counties, viz., Victoria, St. Patrick, Mayaro, and Nariva.

1. County of Victoria.—Bounded on the N. by the county of Caroni; on the S. by a line running E.N.E. from Siparia, and intersecting the Guataro or Ortoire at about 10° 13′; on the E. by a line drawn from the latter point to Mount Tamana; and on the W. by the sea and part of the south-western side of the lagoon of Oropuche. This county is naturally divided into four sections: the section of Pointe-à-Pierre, N. of the Guaracara; that of N. Naparima, N. of the river Cipero; that of S. Naparima, S. of the same river; and the district of Savanna Grande, to the eastward of the Naparimas.

The section of Point-à-Pierre is bounded on the N. by the ward of Savanetta; on the S. by the river Guaracara; on the W. by the Gulf; and on the E. by Montserrat. This district is level or gently undulating on the S.W., and hilly on the N.N.E., towards the Montserrat hills. The soil is generally gravelly, or a light loam, with the exception of some veins which are clay, and not very productive; the soil in this ward is derived from the older Parian, which nowhere presents very encouraging evidence of fertility. However, its quality improves, and it is very productive along the banks of the Guaracara. The principal productions are sugar and ground provisions. Population, 1881, 4,393; in 1871, 2,756.

The river Guaracara rises, as previously stated, in the Montserrat hills, between two spurs, one of which terminates at Pointe-à-Pierre on the N., and the other at the Naparima hill on the S.; it is a tidal stream, with a bar at its mouth, and yet navigable a short distance for flats and boats.

On the Plaisance estate and in its vicinity are to be found the thermal and chalybeate springs I have already mentioned. After Port-of-Spain had been almost entirely destroyed by fire, in the year 1808, it was in contemplation to erect a new capital at Pointe-à-Pierre, on the La Carriere estate, both on account of the depth of water and the direct line of its position, S. and N. with the *Bocas* or Dragon's Mouths. If this district and the adjoining country ever become thoroughly settled, a town built in that locality would possess advantages, of which San Fernando must for ever be deprived, viz., a good port, excellent building materials, and the proximity of good water.

The railway to San Fernando is carried through the ward of Pointe-à-Pierre, at a short distance from the sea. Would it not be possible, and even advantageous, to have a landing-place at Bon Accord or La Carriere? and would the building of a quay and jetty there be in any way injurious to the interests of San Fernando? I do not believe that it would, if liberal arrangements were made for the transport by rail of goods from and to the landing-place. The merchants might have offices on the spot, and continue to carry on business at San Fernando. Captains of vessels, I presume, would prefer to land at Pointe-à-Pierre instead of San Fernando. The sea-wall once built, the gravelly soil could be easily made to fall in, to form the platform. Produce from the southern part of Montserrat, even from Savanna Grande, the Guaracara valley, also from part of Savanetta and Naparima, would find their way to this port, where vessels, on account of the depth of water, would have every facility for loading and unloading, the flats being able to approach the wharf at all times.

North Naparima.—This section is bounded on the N. by the Guaracara; on the S. by the South Naparima eastern road; on the W. by the Gulf; and on the E. by Savanna Grande. It comprises the only ward of N. Naparima. This ward presents everywhere an undulating surface, and is traversed, from the Naparima hill to Savanna Grande, in a N.E. direction, by a ridge which declines towards the Cipero on the S., and towards the Guaracara on the N.; it is easy, therefore, to trace the connection of the Naparima hill with the central range. The soil of this district is, in general, clayey, of a good quality, and of a blackish colour towards the Cipero; towards the Guaracara, it is of a reddish appearance and retentive, not so productive as the marl soil of S. Naparima and Savanna Grande. In some spots, the soil seems to be superposed by layers, and after heavy showers or continued rain, it is not rare to see patches of the upper layer, from two to three feet in thickness, and several yards in extent, slide down the flanks of the undulations with the canes they support. These are the land-slips so detrimental to roads and cultivations. The Guaracara river and several ravines drain the northern division of this section, and the Cipero the southern portion. Very little or no cacao is cultivated in this district, and but few ground provisions raised; it may be said that cane only is cultivated.

The Naparima mountain or hill is nearly insulated, sloping down towards the E.N.E., and, though only 600 feet high, remarkably conspicuous. It is entirely formed, according to all probabilities, of silicate of alumina, covered with a fine vegetable mould. At its foot stands San Fernando, the chief town of the southern division of the island. It is partly built in a sort of small recess, formed by two spurs stretching from the hill towards the sea, and partly round the basis of the hill. Houses, generally poor and miserable, are scattered over this site of the town, except, however, along the principal street, which leads from the wharf to the foot of the hill; it has a rather winding direction. To the southward is a high ground, upon which stand the Roman Catholic church, the hospital, the town-hall, and the court-house. An alley planted with trees forms a promenade; the promenade was projected by Lord Harris, and bears his name. This part is the most pleasant section of the town, as it commands an extensive view of the harbour and adjacent country. A pier of 300 feet, built of hard-wood, with a flooring of carapa and cedar planks, had been erected by a private company, for the convenience of passengers by the steamer; it has become public property, the Government having paid money compensation to the said company. Though the soil is of a retentive nature, San Fernando is, nevertheless, easily drained, on account of the peculiar disposition of the ground; the ravines which traverse the town may, by proper precautions and gradual improvements, be made useful sewers; whereas if due attention be not paid to their banking and cleansing, they must be to San Fernando what the Dry river is to Port-of-Spain—an intolerable nuisance.

The soil in the town and at the base of the hill is strongly impregnated with bitumen, which oozes out in several places, and forms between St. James and San Fernando streets a small pool; the bituminous nature of the substratum prevents the sinking of wells, since the water becomes so strongly impregnated with bitumen as to be unfit for use. Lately wells have been sunk at the base of the hill, and an adit carried some distance, with the object of procuring water for the use of the inhabitants; thirty-seven public fountains or dippers have been established, at which the people can get water. The supply is intermittent : main pipe, six inches; thirty-four hydrants; fourteen stop-cocks. The total quantity thus supplied may be calculated at 18,000 gallons per day. The wells are made to communicate; the water is pumped up by machinery and sent to a reservoir, from which it is conducted to the fountains. When pumped up from the wells, this water has a marked smell and a faint taste of bitumen, which, however, disappears when it has been kept for some time in the reservoir. The water flowing from the adit has a similar taste and smell, and that of sulphur besides, which is found deposited in a very thin layer. The water has been analysed, and found to contain a large proportion of bitumen, also of sulphur, it being thereby rendered more or less unfit for drinking and domestic purposes. It should be forbidden, by all means, to denude the hill and establish cultivation on its flanks. This is a subject fully worth the attention of the Borough Council.

This question of supplying San Fernando with water is one of great importance, also beset with difficulties, and which is not solved yet. For it is evident that the present supply is not only inadequate, but is of very bad quality—in fact, unfit for ordinary domestic purposes. But wherefrom to get the required supply? From Montserrat? The distance (twelve miles), and serious difficulties to be surmounted, and the consequent large outlay, without a corresponding return, are, in my opinion, an insuperable obstacle. From Pointe-à-Pierre? It would then become necessary to construct collecting reservoirs, and to make use of machines for forcing the water up to the town.

But there are at several places round the San Fernando hill wells with springs, and gullies which might be dammed and turned into reservoirs. " It has been supposed," says Mr. Wall, "that a reservoir might be formed by embanking the open extremity of the Coulée ravine, and thus collecting a considerable amount of spring and surface water. The feasibility of this plan is an engineering question; but it may be remarked that the porous nature of the subjacent gravel would render careful, perhaps expensive, cementing necessary to prevent leakage." I am far from pretending any engineering knowledge, but I have always been under the impression that the gullies around the San Fernando hill might be embanked, and thus made into reservoirs. I deeply regret that the experiment has not been made at the Coulée ravine : had it been successful, how easy to supply San Fernando with water! Some of the gullies opening at the base of the hill might be embanked in succession, and the springs and wells there existing properly controlled, so as to give a sufficient supply of wholesome water, and, as I imagine, at a reasonable cost. It is objected that the porous nature of the gravel would render the undertaking nugatory; but careful cementing would act as a remedy. I am very much mistaken if they will not be compelled ultimately to adopt the plan here suggested.

A tramway having been established between the Mission or Princestown and the Cipero landing-place, the Borough Council of San Fernando thought it a profitable undertaking to connect the tramway with the wharf, through the town. Unfortunately, the work was conducted by incompetent persons, and turned out an unpaying concern. The deep trench they were obliged to cut through the borough has, ever since, been a source of anxiety respecting the safety of adjoining buildings, and will, in the future, I fear, give occasion to repeated expenses, unless measures are adopted to prevent the impending evils. The Government has been induced to take over the San Fernando tramway, in the expectation of being able to work it to advantage in connection with the railway, which has just been opened to the public. The terminus is on the wharf.

San Fernando is about thirty-two miles south of Port-of-Spain ; a daily communication, excepting Sunday, exists between both towns by means of a small steamer ; the passage is three hours; the cabin fare one dollar; steerage passengers pay fifty cents. The sea is very shallow off the town, as also along the neighbouring coast, except at Pointe-à-Pierre, and vessels are compelled to anchor at two or two and a half miles from the shore. San Fernando was founded as early as the commencement of 1786, but has obtained only lately the municipal privileges of a council and mayor. Population in 1881, 6,335 : males, 3,119 ; females, 3,216, of which 873 are Indians. Population in 1871, 5,006. There are two suburbs attached to the borough : the *Café*, on the North Naparima road, and *Bushy Park*, on the South Naparima road.

From San Fernando three main roads lead respectively northward to Pointe-à-Pierre, southward to Mosquito Creek and Oropuche, and eastward to Savanna Grande or Princestown. From these main roads branch off several ward-roads, leading to the east and south-east, and affording means of communication between the estates and the different landing-places ; also two main bridle-paths to Mayaro on the east, and Moruga on the south. The South Naparima eastern ward marks the limit between the districts of North and South Naparima. Population in 1881, 4,824 ; in 1871, 3,305.

South Naparima.—This section is divided into two wards, viz., South Naparima eastern and South Naparima western wards. It is bounded on the N. by the district of North Naparima ; on the S. by the Oropuche lagoon ; on the E. by Savanna Grande ; on the W. by the Gulf. It is gently undulating, and the whole of it may be said to be under cane cultivation. If not the largest, at least the best, sugar estates of the colony are to be found in this district. Maize, rice, and edible roots, such as tanias, yams, and sweet cassada, thrive remarkably well, but are very scantily cultivated.

The soil in this district may be classed under three heads— black, or *figuier* soil ; dark brown, or *zapatero ;* and white, or marly. The black soil is called *figuier* on account of the large number of the *figuiers*, or wild fig-trees which grow therein ; and the dark brown, *zapatero*, because the *zapatero* tree is there found in great abundance. The *figuier* soil is of the very best description, and of lasting fertility ; it extends, in the form of a zone or belt, from the sea-board and the lagoon, along the river Cipero, to Savanna Grande, and in a nearly due east direction, to the mouth of the Guataro or Ortoire. It varies in breadth from four to five miles. Not only do the canes *ratoon* in this soil for many years, but it does not seem to be favourable to the growth of rank weeds; from three to four annual weedings only are required to keep the cane-fields clean and in good condition. The canes generally do not grow to a very large size; but from twenty to thirty shoots from the same stool; and the richness of the juice varies from sixteen to twenty-two per cent. of sugar. The *zapatero* soil, though good, is not of the same extreme fertility. The white soil forms, in a manner, the substratum of the whole district; it is a magnesian marl. Wherever it predominates, the canes are liable to wither from drought during the dry season, but they grow and thrive during the rainy weather. The principal defect of this soil seems to result from its colour, which acts in checking the free absorption of heat, while its power of reflection acts injuriously on the foliage of the cane. Stable manure is the best corrective of this defect. That the magnesian marl forms the substratum of a large tract becomes evident wherever the superstratum has been removed by one cause or another. Patches of this substance are met with both on the brown and black soil.

The river Cipero, which may be taken as the natural boundary between North and South Naparima, is a small brook, muddy and dried up during part of the year; it is formed by the accumulation of waters that collect in the depressions of the undulating land on both sides; its bed is deep and the bottom muddy. It is a tidal stream and, at high water, becomes navigable for canoes and flats for about a mile from its entrance. It has its outlet a little southward of San Fernando. The *embarcadere*, or shipping-place, is at the extreme end of the navigable part, with storehouses for receiving the sugars from many estates in the interior, ready for shipment. There are, besides this, two other shipping-places which can also be approached at high tide, viz., Aly's Creek on the Bel-air estate, at the mouth of a small ravine; and Mosquito Creek, at the northern entrance of the Oropuche *lagoon*. This lagoon—known also by the name of the Great Lagoon—may be considered, as I have already stated, as the main draining reservoir of the western division of the southern basin. Many small streams bring down, from the adjoining districts, the tribute of their water to the lagoon; part of this flows from the hills in the vicinity of Savanna Grande, and part from the district of Siparia and the southern range. The lagoon is about twelve miles in length, from east to west, and from a half to three and even four miles in breadth. Its ground surface swells up at intervals into mounds, which form so many islets with which the lagoon is studded. They are covered with a rich vegetation. The largest among them are cultivated in provisions. They are separated by natural channels and a labyrinth of ponds covered with rushes, reeds, and other aquatic plants : four or five larger canals meander amidst this intrication of islets, and ponds, serving as outlets to the water which accumulates in the lagoon. Near the sea-shore, and even in the interior, mangroves grow in great abundance. During the dry season, that portion of the lagoon lying to the eastward remains dry. The land adjoining the lagoon, and such parts of it as remain uncovered at low tide, are of the same black colour as the *figuier* soil of South Naparima. It is, therefore, probable that, in the course of years, and by the slow but regular process of natural agencies, fresh alluvia will be gradually added to those already deposited, and new land be formed, whilst the waters will collect into some main channel, and form a river, it may be, of considerable size.

At present two principal outlets carry off the waters of the lagoon to the sea, viz., Mosquito creek or Blazini's river, on the Naparima side, and Godineau's river on the Oropuche side—by far the most important of the two. M. Godineau was a French colonist who had formed a settlement at Oropuche, immediately adjoining the lagoon. He first opened a canal, by which to transport his canes to the mill in punts, and afterwards cut through a small neck of land, which acted as an embankment, in order to procure a water communication with the sea, and a freer discharge of the waters of the lagoon. The enterprising Frenchman was unfortunately ruined in an undertaking too arduous for his resources, but which, under favourable auspices, might have terminated successfully, and which would, undoubtedly, have proved of incalculable benefit to the adjoining districts, not only as conducive to their salubrity, but in regard to facility of transport and other advantages. Such as it is, however, the Godineau is a pretty large stream, and the principal outlet of the lagoon.

The area of the Oropuche lagoon or swamp may be estimated at fourteen square miles.

In the year 1852, a corduroy road was laid out across the

lagoon, closely parallel with the sea-shore. It is two miles long, and cost the sum of £1,855 sterling. Two bridges have been thrown over the Blazini and Godineau rivers, the latter a fine iron structure; also many culverts along the line. This corduroy road is a necessary connecting link between the Naparimas, Oropuche, La Brea, and Cedros, and yet it is not sufficiently wide; and, as an embankment, is not very solidly laid.

The lagoon is frequented at certain seasons by large numbers of water-game—white and gray herons, crimson spatulas, red ibis, teals, ducks, water-fowls, &c. The mangrove ramiers and flocks of parrots resort to the islets and the mangroves as their places of rest; and at such times the chattering of the latter is really deafening. The lagoon is also inhabited by alligators; mangrove dogs are not uncommon. Large oysters are found in some of the channels, sticking to the roots of the mangrove trees.

The Oropuche lagoon is an inexhaustible source of malaria, which spreads over the neighbouring districts and renders them very unhealthy, especially that part of the ward of Oropuche which stretches along the coast. Intermittent and remittent fevers are endemic in those localities. Population of the two wards of S. Naparima, 1881, 10,057; in 1871, 8,787.

Savanna Grande.—To the east of the wards of North and South Naparima is the district of Savanna Grande, divided into two wards. It is bounded on the W. by the Naparimas, and on all other sides by Crown lands. The ground in this district is highly undulating, rising into hillocks near the Mission. The Mission and the settlements around extend over the table land which stretches to the S.E., and, after skirting the head of the lagoon, join the southern range, so as to form, in a manner, a dividing ridge between the Ortoire and the Oropuche lagoon. This section is, in general, fertile, and tracts of it may bear comparison with the best soils of Naparima—in fact, the zone of the *figuier* soil may be traced to some of the sugar estates of this district, which are considered as equal to any in the colony. In several places are found beds of marl, containing hard nodules, with infusoria and bivalve shells. In the eastern ward are the mud volcanoes, or salses, which I have already mentioned. Sugar and provisions are the principal, not to say the sole, products.

There are in this district, besides the Mission—now Princestown, with a population of 3,991—two settlements, formed about the year 1817 by the location of some hundred American black and coloured people, captured during the last war, and brought to Trinidad by Admiral Sir A. J. Cochrane. A few acres of land were allotted to each individual, in fee, on paying a quit-rent. In the year 1848, these allotments were re-surveyed, and each settler was granted six acres of land, in full property, subject to the ward rates. These settlements, I must confess, have not answered the object for which they were intended; and to these American settlers may be addressed the same reproach which I have attached to the disbanded soldiers located at Manzanilla and Turure. They cultivate some provisions, it is true, and occasionally employ themselves as jobbers on estates, mainly as axe-men, cane-cutters, and trenchers; but their principal occupation is the chase, their hunting ground extending from Tamana to Moruga, and from the Mission to Mayaro. They generally belong to the Baptist persuasion.

Savanna Grande communicates with San Fernando by means of a main road which follows the winding of the ridge extending from the Naparima mountain to the Mission. It is seven miles long, without a bridge; and this same ridge continues to run nearly due east for ten miles further, without a gap or ravine. A track, or bridle-path, through the virgin forest leads southward to Moruga; and another one eastward to Mayaro.

Population of the two wards, 1881, 11,765; 1871, 8,974.

The county of Victoria, though second in population to that of St. George, may be regarded as the most important, in an agricultural point of view. Its surface is uniformly undulating, gradually rising from the sea-shore southward of San Fernando, and from the lagoon, in an .E.N.E. direction, for about sixteen miles, with a few hillocks here and there above the general level of the country. Every ridge sends its streamlet down hills to the right and left, and small brooks or ravines collect the diminutive tributaries from every depression. On the N., the watercourses bend towards the valley of the Guaracara; on the S.S.E. towards the lagoon, and contribute to the formation of the Cipero in the centre. Those parts which are not under cultivation abound in cedars, robles, savanettas, &c., and the carat palm, for thatching. There is also a great abundance of cabbage palms; many are preserved in the cane-fields, sending forth their column-like stems, surmounted by a crest or crown of undulating foliage.

With fortunately but few exceptions, the soil is excellent throughout the whole extent of the county, and is well suited to the growth of almost every product—provisions, cacao, and sugar; but it seems particularly well adapted to the production of the latter article. If it ever be the good fortune of Trinidad to extend its cane cultivation, new sugar estates will decidedly be established in the county of Victoria. The only drawbacks against this district are the difficulty of establishing good roads, and of keeping them in proper repair. The roads now existing are pretty good; but for many years it was nearly impossible, during the rainy season, to cart one single *barrel* of flour to any distance; even an empty cart could not, in the wet weather, force its way through the deep and adhesive mud of most of the roads; and it often became necessary to pack the flour in small parcels of forty or fifty pounds, each parcel being then carried by a labourer to the estate. It was not unusual to see carts left lying, or rather sticking, in the mire on the high road, from the sheer impossibility of taking them back to the estate. This soil, which becomes so soft and adhesive when saturated with water, is of brick-like consistency when exposed for some weeks to the action of the sun and the wind, and, by the gradual process of evaporation, breaks into deep fissures in all directions, and becomes dangerous to man and beast. In consequence of this property in the soil of the Naparimas and Savanna Grande, there is no good pasturage in these districts; and, in former times, the loss of animals was very great—nearly 20 per cent. per annum. It has, however, materially decreased since the planters have adopted the plan of hand-feeding their stock in stables during part of the day.

Nearly the whole tract westward of Savanna Grande is under cultivation. From some of the elevated spots, the aspect of the country is enchanting. All around cane-fields are seen waving under the gentle influence of the breeze, surmounted by their beautiful panicles of flowers, and concealing the saccharine treasures which the industry of man will soon make available for freighting the vessels awaiting in the placid gulf their annual cargo of sweets. Lo! on whatever side the observer turns, the black, curly smoke escaping from the lofty chimneys, and carried away by the evening breeze, is an indication that the manufacture of sugar is going on throughout the whole district; and whithersoever he bends his steps, the wholesome balsamic odour of new-made sugar is wafted in a tide of perfume towards the spectator.

In the year 1876 a usine was established on the Sainte Madeleine estate, capable of manufacturing 5,000 tons of white and crystallised sugar—a beautiful establishment, formed under somewhat difficult circumstances, but which is, nevertheless, prosperous.

Since emancipation, several villages have sprung up in this district, viz., Victoria village, on the Cipero river, and on the South Naparima eastern road; Bamboo, or Canaan, at the head of Ally's creek, and on South Naparima main road; Bourg Mulatresse, or Rambert, on the South Naparima central road; the village of St. Joseph, on the Pointe-à-Pierre's road; those of Sainte Madeleine and St. John, in North Naparima, and of Monkey Town in Savanna Grande.

Population of the county in 1881, 36,474 : males, 20,391; females, 16,983. Indians and children, 18,351.

2. County of St. Patrick.—Bounded on the N. by Victoria county and the Gulf; S. by the sea; E. by a line running from the Ortoire, down and along the river Moruga, to the sea; W. by the Gulf. This county has been divided into six wards, viz., Oropuche, La Brea and Guapo, Irois, Cedros, Erin, and Moruga.

The ward of Oropuche, which comprises the quarter of Oropuche and the Mission of Siparia, is bounded on the N. by the Gulf and the lagoon; on the S. by crown lands; on the E. by the lagoon and crown lands; on the W. by La Brea, from which it is separated by the Roussillac.

The surface of this ward is highly undulating, rapidly elevating towards the east. In no part of the colony, perhaps, is the quality of the land more variable; veins of the *figuier* soil or Naparima marl are met with in tracts of a coarse clay, or of a poor sandy soil. It is, on the whole, more retentive than that of Naparima and Savanna Grande. Towards Siparia, it is a light sandy soil of average quality, being well adapted to the growth of cacao, coffee, plantains, and all sort of ground provisions; as also of tobacco, which, when properly prepared, is of excellent quality. The tract of land between Oropuche and Siparia is very much broken up by ravines, which have their courses through thick *Timitales*. The principal productions are, in Oropuche, sugar and provisions; lately, they have commenced planting coco-nuts; in Siparia, a little cacao, coffee, tobacco, and provisions. The cane cultivation extends along the sea-shore, from Godineau to the Aripero river, and not further than two miles inland. Besides the Godineau river, the ward of Oropuche is drained by the Aripero, or silver stream, and the Roussillac, which receives the waters of a considerable hollow or depression, known as the Roussillac swamp, between Oropuche and La Brea. The Aripero is a tidal stream, and admits of the entrance of flats to unload estates' supplies and take off produce. Between the mouths of the Godineau and Aripero rivers lies a shallow bank, formed by the washings of the lagoon and surrounding district. At the fall of the spring tide, this bank extends upwards of a mile out to sea, impeding the approach of the smallest boat. The Rio Perro and the Negro discharge their waters into the lagoon, as also the San Francisco, which may be regarded as the outlet of the Bertrand lagoon. Just at the foot of the Siparia table-land, there is a small streamlet called *lavapies*. They all flow from S.S.E.

The quarter of Oropuche is very unhealthy, not only on account of its proximity to the lagoon, but also in consequence of the prevalence of mangrove swamps all along the line of coast.

The village of St. Mary stands on a small natural savanna, between the Bellevue and the Otaheite estates, about a mile from the Godineau river, and a mile and a-half from the sea. It is well laid out, but the constructions are miserable; the ground upon which it stands is rather sandy. Besides this village, there are a few isolated settlements, viz., at Freeman's Bay, the public landing place; the Yarraba village, the Krooman village, the Avoca, and the Fyzabad—the latter a Coolie settlement. In all these nooks and corners are herded together bands of immigrants imported into the colony, particularly Congoes and Kroomen. In fact, the population of Trinidad may be characterised as a heterogeneous collection of inhabitants of different countries—Congoes, Yarrabas, and Kroomen from Africa; Coolies and

Chinese from Asia; Americans from the United States; Spaniards from Venezuela; emigrants from the British and French colonies, with a limited number of natives of Trinidad. Not many years ago, the population of Oropuche was a pretty fair representation of the worst class of squatters. Scattered far and wide, throughout the vast extent of the district, removed from the influence of civilising institutions, and left to the unfettered indulgence of a half savage life, moral depravity and ignorance of all social responsibility formed their chief characteristics. Bound together by the ties of nationality, or tribeship, they generally banded in distinct settlements, where nought was to be found beyond the primary elements of social aggregation. Many were squatters, regarding with suspicion and as intruders those who entered their settlements. On more than one occasion they behaved riotously, and even tried to resist the agents of the Government. Things, however, are now very much altered; the population of Oropuche has become more steady and more industrious. The proportion of Asiatics has very much increased—from 348 in 1871 to 560 in 1881.

The Mission of Siparia is situated on a table-land, about seven miles and a half eastward of St. Mary's village, with a descending slope of about 200 feet on all sides. The village is 235 feet above the level of the sea. The Mission of Siparia had been established about the year 1758 by the Aragonese Capuchin fathers, under the name or vocable of "La Divina Pastora." The capabilities of the soil, the abundant natural resources of the locality, the beauty of the scenery, had attracted the attention of Sir Ralph Woodford, who attempted the re-organisation of the Mission by locating therein royalist emigrants from the Spanish colonies of South America. After the war of independence, its population received new accessions, and finally rose to nearly 500 souls. They had then a resident *padre* or priest, a corregidor, and a schoolmaster. The present condition of the Mission is far from affording the same pleasant aspect, its population being reduced, cultivation neglected, houses in a dilapidated state; no school, no resident priest: Siparia is now completely neglected. The retired position of Siparia and bad roads are the great obstacles to the progress of this district. Lately, however, the road to Oropuche has been improved; but it may be said to be still a mere bridle-path. Siparia, from its elevation and inland position, is cool and very healthy. Population of Oropuche and Siparia in 1881, 4,393; 1871, 1,646.

The ward of La Brea, which comprises the quarters of La Brea and Guapo, is bounded on the N. by the Gulf; on the S. by crown lands; on the E. by the ward of Oropuche; on the W. by Irois. The surface of this ward bears some resemblance to that of Oropuche—undulating towards the coast, and swelling into elevations towards the interior, where it meets Morne l'Enfer, 327 feet high. From Pointe La Brea eastward, the ground rises into a sort of dividing ridge, expanding towards Siparia on the E., and towards Guapo on the W. The waters thus separated contribute to form, on the N.N.E., the Roussillac and Silver Stream, and on the W.S.W. the Vessini or Bravo river, and the Guapo. In the vicinity of and skirting the Roussillac exists an extensive marshy plain, or hollow, which, in the wet season, becomes flooded to the depth of nearly four feet. The whole line of coast, extending between the mouth of the Roussillac and Pointe d'Or, is thickly studded with mangroves. The soil is not of very good quality, being an admixture of reddish retentive clay, or unproductive sand, with asphaltum, very poor in organic matter, and therefore easily exhausted. It improves towards the interior; but even there the abundance of *limites* shows that it is still rather infertile. La Brea is distinguished for its fine and delicious pine apples. Guapo very much resembles La Brea; the soil, however, may be rated as of better quality, particularly on the slopes towards the rivers. Besides the Vessini, or Bravo, and Guapo rivers, there are two or three smaller brooks. Once flourishing districts, La Brea and Guapo began to decline shortly after emancipation, and may be considered now as almost abandoned. In 1840, there were in the district of La Brea seven sugar estates and eleven in Guapo, all under the management of their resident proprietors; now only provisions are cultivated, and even these on a very reduced scale. Lately, however, abandoned tracts have been purchased, with the object of forming coco-nut plantations. The inhabitants of the ward are generally poor, but moral and peaceable. The population of La Brea and Guapo, which amounted to 439 inhabitants in 1871, is now 621, with only two Indians.

The quarter of La Brea, which owes its name to the large

quantity of asphaltum, or pitch—*brea*, in Spanish; *brai*, in French—which is found everywhere in this district, and forms the Pitch lake, is, on this account, one of the most interesting districts of the island. Every stranger who can spend a few days in Trinidad will do well to pay a short visit to this great natural curiosity of the country. A steamer which plies between Port-of-Spain and Cedros, stopping at San Fernando, touches three times a week at La Brea, viz., every Monday, Thursday, and Saturday, on its way to Cedros, so that there is sufficient time to visit the lake during the interval of its return. The early morning, however, is the best time for visiting the lake, as the heat on its surface becomes almost insufferable after nine o'clock. The best plan, perhaps, would be to sleep at San Fernando, and start early next morning for La Brea in a boat. This might be attempted on one of the three days that the steamer goes to Cedros, so as to catch it on its return.

The lake and its scenery have already been described by so many persons, that it would be a work of supererogation to enter into many details here. I shall, therefore, limit myself to offering only a few remarks. The Pitch lake, or great asphaltum deposit of Trinidad, is situated at Pointe La Brea, at about one mile from the sea, and at an elevation of 138 feet; it covers an area of about 100 acres. The road to the lake is the ward-road of the quarter.

The appearance of the lake is that of a dull, still, dark waste —*atra regna*. It is irregularly circular, and its surface perceptibly convex, being more elevated in the centre, and thence insensibly declining on all sides. In the centre also the asphaltum is quite soft, in fact, semi-fluid; but it becomes more and more hardened as it approaches the circumference. Excepting the soft central parts, the surface is intersected in all directions by numerous fissures or chasms, varying in breadth from two to twelve feet, and from a foot to five feet in depth. The sides of these fissures are slanting downwards, thus forming inverted angles; these crevices are at all times filled with rain water. The insulated spaces between the chasms exhibit a slight curvature, of which the apex occupies the centre. Here and there, where the asphaltum is mixed with earthy matters, grow lichens and mosses, with a few coarse grasses (*graminea* and *cyperaceæ*), whilst stunted jicacos, some annonaceæ, etc., and caratas form clusters, either completely or partially surrounded by water.

The centre of the lake—the pitch-pot, or cauldron, as it is called—is at all times so soft, that any person remaining on it would run the risk of sinking, more or less, in the thick substance. There a slow but constant bubbling and puffing is perceptible, accompanied by the emissions of gaseous substances, and the throwing up of a yellowish mud, quite cold and of an acrid saltness. Over the entire extent, the degree of hardness varies with the intensity of the solar rays, at early morn the whole surface, excepting at the centre, is hard; whilst, at midday, it becomes so much softened that it retains the stamp of the lightest impress.

Whenever any quantity of bitumen has been dug and taken up from the lake, the excavation soon fills up, and a perfect level is restored within a short time. The deeper the digging, the quicker the restoration. In the centre trees or branches are sometimes seen emerging to the surface, to be submerged soon afterwards. Casks placed near the spot to receive bitumen have also disappeared.

It is evident, from the above observations, that the operation going on in the Pitch lake may be ascribed to a revolving motion, a sort of *ebullition* which continually presses up the asphaltum from the centre to the surface. There is no difficulty in admitting this process, as the mass thus thrown up is semifluid, owing to an admixture of an oily substance. It has been noted that the surface of the lake is divided into a number of small bituminous areas, each owing its existence, undoubtedly, to a centre of emission from which the asphaltum has been pressed up. On reaching the surface, it spreads slowly; the oily substance gradually evaporates on exposure to the direct action of the sun, the outer portion becomes harder and less fluent than the inner, which continues to ascend—to "roll under," as expressed by Mr. Manross—thus giving to the sides of the chasms their curved forms. Messrs. Wall and Sawkins, however, do not admit that explanation; but they suggest that " when two adjacent masses come in contact, and are not sufficiently plastic to unite or join together, they leave a division, which originates the depression in question."

The Pitch lake is not the only spot where bitumen exists in

Trinidad. I may mention asphaltic deposits as existing at Montserrat, on the southern side of the hills, at Naparima, Oropuche, especially on the Aripero estate and Pointe d'Or: it abounds everywhere in the wards of La Brea and Guapo, where springs of semi-liquid asphaltum or petroleum occur in the high woods. We meet with bitumen at Quemada, Moruga, Guayaguayare, where the tourist will do well to pay a visit to *Lagon Bouff*. There are also at times regular eruptions of liquid bitumen in the Gulf, opposite Guapo, at Guayaguayare, and even in the bay of Mayaro, on the eastern coast. The places where it issues are indicated by the oily part floating on the surface of the water, and a very strong odour of asphaltum. After such eruptions, lumps or cakes of this substance are washed on to the beach. It is highly probable that bitumen is disseminated in seams or veins throughout the whole southern division of the island.

Now, what is the origin of the asphaltic deposits at Trinidad? The same as that of coal and peat. It has been remarked that, where exist lignite and brown coal, there the sources of asphalte are more abundant. Such is the case in Trinidad. Vegetable *débris* are the only substances containing carbon and hydrogen in sufficient quantity to form asphalte; and this formation takes place by a process of conversion. "The first department of the process," say Messrs. Wall and Sawkins, "consists in the formation of a black oily substance, and has been termed asphaltic oil. . . The residue, after the separation of this material, consists of the ordinary asphalte, usually containing the oils in sufficient quantity to render it highly plastic. The purer varieties—such as approach, or are identical with, asphaltum glance—have been observed in isolated masses. In this case no displacement from the original position has ensued, and consequently the material is free from earthy impurities."

Three principal varieties of asphaltum are found here—asphaltum glance, the purest of all, hard and brittle; ordinary asphaltum, by far the most common; and asphaltic oil or petroleum. This is not so common as the ordinary asphaltum; it generally rises to the surface through cones having orifices in the centre.

The Pitch lake, however, ought not to be regarded solely as a curiosity; it may turn out a permanent source of profit to the island. Numerous attempts have been made to utilise our asphalte locally, but without any marked success. For one reason or another, it has not succeeded as a suitable material for pavement or for flooring. Until further researches are made, I deprecate its use for such purposes. The fact is that it contracts or shrinks, and after a time the layer becomes uneven, or even breaks when exposed to the rays of the sun. It has given some satisfaction, however, when used together with megass as a fuel. Oils of different consistency, and for various adaptations, can be extracted from our asphaltum, especially for lubricating purposes. Asphaltum glance is a more valuable material; mixed with turpentine oil, it gives a fine black varnish. Asphaltum is exported either as a raw material or as épuré.

Quantity exported in 1879:—

Raw	17,416 tons
Epuré	6,144 ,,
	23,560 tons

of which 4,396 raw and 3,021 épuré went to the United Kingdom, 9,565 raw to the United States, and 2,626 épuré to Germany. Value in sterling £25,938.

Ward of Irois.—This ward bears, in point of soil and general aspect, the closest resemblance to that of La Brea; it is highly undulating, particularly towards the interior. The soil is deep, but generally poor, being sandy, and in some places of a reddish colour, deficient in organic matters. Nearly the whole of this ward is crown property, and scanty crops of ground provisions only are cultivated by a few scattered settlers; it nevertheless once could boast of its sugar plantations, among which *La Paix* was the largest and most productive. An extensive forest of mora trees lines the course of the river Irois, and probably spreads out in the interior to a great distance; there are besides a few locust, carapa, guatecare, and olivier trees. This forest of moras had attracted the attention of Sir Ralph Woodford; it was, however, eventually lost sight of, and it may be said, in some measure, to have been discovered anew by Mr. Purdie, Government botanist. Governor Elliott decided at once on taking advantage of this natural wood-yard, and turning the mora and other timbers to useful purposes. A penal depôt was formed on the right bank of the river, on an elevation at a few yards' distance from the sea. The labour exacted from the convicts was the felling and preparing the timber for water transport to the capital. The mora is a social plant, and grows in great numbers on the same spot; whilst the young plants are as thickly set under the grown-up trees as in a well-supplied nursery. The trees were felled and cut into logs, the larger sized being squared on the spot; they were then formed into rafts and towed to Port-of-Spain, a distance of forty miles. It was contemplated to erect a saw-mill at the depôt, but the plan was left unexecuted.

This ward is watered by several small streams, among them the Capdeville, which is the largest, the Irois and Cimetierre, all having their rise in the high lands of the interior, and pursuing a northerly course. The steamer from Port-of-Spain, on its way to Cedros, lands and takes passengers at Capdeville. A road to Erin, called Chatham Road, has also its terminus at Capdeville. That road is an important one, as it establishes a communication between the ward of Erin and the Gulf, and must greatly facilitate intercourse between these two points. Population of La Brea, Guapa, and Irois, 1881, 621; 1871, 439.

Ward of Cedros.—This ward is bounded on the N., S., and W. by the sea, on the E. by the ward of Irois, and may be said to occupy the whole of the south-western peninsula of the island. It comprises the three quarters of Cedros to the north, Quemada to the south, and Icacos to the west. In general features and disposition this ward is nearly similar to the preceding, except in possessing the advantage of greater fertility. The ground is chiefly waving, and the surface rather broken, particularly towards Point Cedros and the east; but it becomes more even as the quarter of Icacos is approached; the latter is a dead level. The soil is everywhere deep but light. Quemada is, however, very fertile, its soil, though light, being at certain spots somewhat similar to the black soil of Naparima. L'Envieuse, Beaulieu and Columbia estates in Quemada, and Loch Maben in Cedros, are equal to any in the colony. The soil of Icacos is a light sandy loam, containing a very large admixture of organic matters. It is very fertile, but vegetation suffers to a great extent whenever any drought is prevailing. However, all sorts of ground provisions thrive admirably. The coco-palm grows beautifully and yields large crops; for the last few years many acres have been brought under cultivation, and the number of trees may be calculated at some fifty thousand. The whole of Icacos might also form an excellent sheep-run, or can be converted into a *hato*, or stock farm, though still continued as a coco-walk. The breeding of swine would, I imagine, be very profitable. Icacos is obliquely traversed from E.S.E. to W.N.W. by several lagoons, which would supply water for the animals at graze; these lagoons might also be partially drained, and turned into meadow lands; one of them—the largest—opens into the sea to the leeward of Los Gallos, and is known by the name of the Los Gallos lagoon; the others discharge their superfluous waters in the Bay of Quemada. A natural savanna stretches between two of these lagoons.

On the l'Envieuse estate there is a pitch or petroleum cone; and I have observed in the pasture several blocks of sandstone protruding in several places. On the Columbia estate are to be seen the mud volcanoes or salses which I have already mentioned. They are on an elevated spot, in all probability raised gradually by the agency of the self-same volcanoes. The area is limited, and within it, here and there, small conical mounds are formed, from the centre of which oozes or bubbles forth a greyish mud; it is quite salt, and spreads around in a thin layer, which is traversed in all directions by irregular cracks. It is said that there are, at certain periods, regular eruptions of this mud; but I could not see any symptoms of this; the ground bordering the base of the mounds can be trodden with perfect safety.

The ward of Cedros is nearly all private property; the cane, coco-nut trees, and provisions are the only cultivations. There is no river in this ward; but fresh water can be easily procured by the sinking of wells, even to the high-water mark. Besides the lagoons at Icacos, several others of diminutive dimensions are met with at different places, some of which might be drained, and the salubrity of the district thereby improved. I should mention the shallow marsh to the eastward of Saint Mary estate. The sea is shallow all along the coast, except round Point Icacos, where the water is sufficiently bold to afford anchorage to large vessels within hail of the shore. This, however, does by no means render it a safe harbourage, owing to the existence of very strong currents. A heavy surf breaks along, from Point

Icacos to Point Cedros, during the prevalence of the northerly winds, rendering landing rather difficult, and menacing, at any moment, the drifting of the craft. Point Icacos had been denominated by Columbus *Punta Arenal* (Sandy Point). It was at this point that the admiral lost an anchor; that anchor was found, some years ago, buried in the sand on Constance estate, and exhibited at the last Paris Exhibition.

There is at Cedros but one village between the Perseverance and Loch Maben estates, though a few scattered houses at Granville, and on the lands of Saint Mary estate, are honoured—I must say most undeservedly—with the name of villages.

A steam communication exists between Cedros and Port-of-Spain, the steamer leaving town every Monday, Thursday, and Saturday, at seven o'clock in the morning, touching, on its way, at Couva, Naparima, La Brea, and Irois, and arriving at Cedros about two p.m.; it then leaves at three for Port-of-Spain, where it arrives at about seven in the evening. There is also a land communication, partly along the beach and partly through the forest, over some of the points which project into the sea; this road is a mere bridle-path, and the traveller must always time his journey with the ebb of the tide, unless he should prefer being exposed to be drenched by the waves at the flow, or even prevented altogether from proceeding. Population in 1881, 3,420; in 1871, 3,802.

Wards of Erin and Moruga.—These two wards extend along the sea-shore, Erin being bounded on the W. by Cedros; on the E. by Moruga; on the N. by Guapo and Irois. Moruga, on the W. by Erin; on the E. by Guayaguayare; on the N. by undefined crown lands; and both wards on the S. by the sea. The surface of these two wards is very uneven, particularly towards the interior. The soil is, generally, light, too much so to be considered as of average fertility, except where interstratified shales and calcareous sandstone occur; such tracts are very fertile, though liable to suffer from any prolonged drought. Only a narrow belt, along the sea, is under cultivation. Erin was once pretty extensively cultivated—sugar, cacao, coffee, and provisions being the staple production; the Erin coffee is still regarded as equal to any grown in the colony. Some of the estates have been abandoned, owing mainly to a want of easy communication with the town; the comparative unhealthiness of the district is also a serious drawback. Dwelling-houses should be built more in the interior. At present cacao and provisions may be said to be the only articles cultivated; lately they have commenced planting coco-nuts, which thrive admirably. Moruga is still more scantily inhabited, and produces only a little cacao and provisions.

Colonel Hamilton once attempted, under the Government of Sir Ralph Woodford, the establishment of a *hato*, or stock-farm, principally for the breeding of horned cattle and horses, in the natural savanna of Erin; the farm did not succeed, if public rumour is to be believed, owing to the ravages among the animals of bats (vampires) and ticks; it is, however, very probable that the whole concern was ill managed. Seams of lignite exist along the south coast, from Cedros to Guayaguayare, the extent of which has never been ascertained. Near Moruga, it occurs in layers; the beds at Erin contain the carbonaceous matter diffused throughout their whole extent.

Produce is brought to town by droghers or *pirogues*, after rounding Point Icacos—a tedious, expensive voyage. A path through the Virgin Forest leads from Moruga to the Mission of Savanna Grande, or Princestown. The telegraphic wire, connecting Trinidad with Demerara, is laid along this track. I have already mentioned Chatham Road; it is highly desirable that it should be, as soon as possible, transformed into a good cart road. I have no doubt that, when this road is completed, and the contemplated steam communication round the island is established, many applications will be made for crown land in this district.

The above two wards abound in excellent timber, particularly fustic and cedar. They are drained by several small streams, and, among others, the Erin, La Ceiba, Siparia, Luna, and Moruga; the latter, a tidal stream. They have all a southerly course. Population in 1881, 1,573; 1871, 396.

The county of Saint Patrick consists partly of waving and partly of hilly lands, being traversed from E. to W. by the southern range. The greatest part of it is crown property. Except at Oropuche and Cedros, the population has rather decreased than increased. As regards the soil, it may be divided into two zones: from La Brea to Cedros it is generally light, poor in organic matter, as shown by the extensive *timitales*, or timite groves, abounding at Guapo and Irois; from Point Luna, its eastern boundary, to Quemada, along the sea, it is either a light or clayey loam, generally fertile. This is evidenced by an abundance of a species of palm (*Attalea speciosa*), its presence being a sign of a rich, light soil; and by the successful cultivation of cacao, and the natural growth of carats and cedars. This county, notwithstanding its relative disadvantages, is highly interesting, as being the grand receptacle of our bitumen deposits and lignite formation.

The great obstacle to the development of this county is the want of facilities for land communication. It is only quite lately that the Government has undertaken the formation of cart roads between Oropuche and La Brea and at Cedros. A few villages have arisen in the county of St. Patrick, viz., at Oropuche, Guapo, and Cedros; the Missions of Siparia and Erin have a nominal existence. Siparia, however, may be said to be a resort for pilgrims. Population of the county in 1881, 7,209: males 4,350, females 2,859; increase on last census, 2,635.

3. County of Mayaro.—Bounded on the N. by the river Ortoire; on the S. and E. by the sea; and on the W. by the counties of Victoria and St. Patrick. It comprises two wards—that of Moruga, which I have already described, and that of Mayaro, which comprises the quarters of Mayaro and Guayaguayare, extending along the eastern and southern coasts from Point Mayaro to Point Casa Cruz. Only a part of the county—a long, narrow belt—is cultivated, and it is very thinly inhabited. Mayaro preserves a level all along the sea-shore from Point Mayaro to Lagon-doux, but runs into waving land in the interior. The level tract along the beach is a light sandy loam, of excellent quality, compounded largely of organic matter, with a goodly proportion of comminuted marine shells; the undulating tract is a brown clayey loam, resembling the Naparima Zapatero soil. The sugar-cane, rice, plantains, and roots succeed admirably, and yield abundant returns; sweet potatoes also and yams are of particularly fine growth and of excellent quality. The coco-palm thrives better along the Mayaro beach than anywhere else, perhaps, in the island. Cotton was once extensively cultivated, but the high price of sugar, coupled with the depredations of caterpillars and locusts, induced the proprietors to abandon its

cultivation for that of the cane. Six sugar estates were then settled in the quarter. Immediately after emancipation, however, a large number of the emancipated labourers abandoned the cane-fields for other pursuits, the planters being thereby compelled to make the most urgent sacrifices to procure immigrants. But the difficulties of communication with Port-of-Spain, and the high freight paid for the carriage of produce thither, as well as for articles of food therefrom, influenced, or rather necessitated, the labourers to retire from the quarter; in fact, they were sometimes left without salt provisions, or even flour, for weeks. The remoteness of Mayaro from a proper market, therefore, was the chief cause of its utter ruin, all the sugar estates having in succession gone out of cultivation. The plantation of coco-palms, however, has extended, and is still extending, to the advantage of the proprietors and the prosperity of the ward. The quarter of Guayaguayare has progressed in the same ratio, and the number of coco-nut trees may be estimated at 60,000.

During the time of slavery, cotton only and provisions were cultivated at Guayaguayare. The soil is of excellent quality, being a light loam; and it may be said that no part of the island has been found better adapted to the growth of corn, plantains, and other articles of food, than this quarter. Guayaguayare, moreover, is well watered, an advantage of which Mayaro, Nariva, and Manzanilla are deprived. When Guayaguayare becomes a productive district, there will be no difficulty in taking whatever it produces to Port-of-Spain by droghers; for the anchorage under the lee side of Point Galeota is safe enough. It is much to be regretted that the name of Point Galeota has been substituted for that of Point Galera, as denominated by Columbus when he discovered the island, as this change may induce people to believe that Columbus first sighted the N.E. point of Trinidad, whilst it was the S.E. point. It cannot be easily explained how this change of designation was accomplished. I fear, however, that there is no remedy, since in all the maps of Trinidad the N.E. cape is marked Galera, and the S.E. cape Galeota.

I have already mentioned the two rivers which discharge their waters into the bay of Guayaguayare, viz., Lizard and. Pilot rivers; they are tidal creeks, with mangroves at their outlets. A few diminutive brooks course through the undulating ground of Mayaro, and, owing to their being regularly dyked by the sand thrown up by the surf, expand at their mouth into small lagoons; of these only one is worth notice—the Lagondoux.

I must now say a few words of the Guataro or Ortoire. My information is drawn partly from Captain Columbine's survey, and partly from reliable private sources. The Ortoire has its mouth to the northward of Point Radiz, after rounding which point it runs for some miles in the rear of Mayaro, and thence takes a W.N.W. direction. Its lower course winds in the most eccentric manner, particularly towards its mouth, where the country is very flat. Its banks are low, and the bed muddy; but the former rise proportionately with the elevation of the adjacent lands. The Ortoire is navigable for large canoes for eighteen miles. Captain Columbine surveyed it for twelve miles upwards, and, at that distance, found it thirty feet wide and eighteen deep. It does not seem that the Ortoire receives any considerable affluent from the south; the great body of its water descends from the central range, between Tamana and Montserrat; its tributaries in that direction being Pure (not Poole) or Upper Ortoire, Guarapiche, Guanapure, Anapa, and Caranache.

Moras grow abundantly in the low lands along the Ortoire; in the best tracts, cedars and robles. Should this part of the island ever become settled, a village might be formed at the head of the river navigation, and a tram-road laid down from that point to La Brea, or rather to Pointe-à-Pierres. Or, again, produce might be carried down to the landing-place at Mayaro, since a distance of only 1,270 yards across the Mayaro estate separates the river Ortoire from the beach; a tram-road should then be laid down as a connecting-link between the river and the sea, thereby avoiding the difficulties, not to say the impossibility, of entering the Ortoire, and the dangers of a navigation to the northward of Point Radiz.

Except a narrow belt along the shore, the entire county of Mayaro is crown property; its surface, to all appearances, is uneven, rising into hillocks towards the S. and S.E; it is said to be rugged, and everywhere cut up by deep ravines, especially to the rearward of the Mayaro ward and the three sisters.

The two counties of St. Patrick and Mayaro belong to the

Newer Parian group, as termed by Messrs. Wall and Sawkins; and to the Moruga or Arenaceous series. "From the S. coast to the valley of the Ortoire," say these gentlemen, "and even further N., an extensive series of strata, usually of a loose sandy nature, are observed. These are well exposed in cliffs all along the southern shore. Thick strata of massive sand, generally loose and pulverulent, are the most prevalent beds; and, indeed, sand may be said to be in great excess.

"Shales are numerous, but clays are of rarer occurrence.

"Calcareous sandstone is extensively diffused in beds, not exceeding six to eight feet thick, and often only a few inches. There is, at the sources of the Moruga river, an isolated tract of the Naparima marl."

The geological formation of the southern range is evidently different from that of the northern and middle range. Shales, sandstone, and calcareous sandstone are the materials of which the southern range is formed. The nucleus of Point Mayaro seems to be of sandstone, with an admixture of limestone; and the entire promontory represents a rather peculiar disposition, being an insulated headland, bounded on the N. and W. by the river Ortoire; whilst the ground is so low southward that it cannot be more than thirty or forty feet above the level of the bay or river. Point Mayaro is very rugged, being rent in all directions by ravines, though the soil is a loam of excellent quality. Its connection with the ridge followed by Mr. d'Abadie, when cutting the Mayaro track, can be easily traced. The disposition of Point Galeota is very similar to that of Point Mayaro, and its geological formation probably identical. It is in the quarter of Guayaguayare, longitude of Casa Cruz, N. of the three sisters, that the pitch deposits and salses called "Lagon Bouff" and "Terre Bouillante" are to be found. The three sisters are the three summits of the mountains sighted from the *Pinta*.

The surface of the Moruga series occupies more than one-fourth of the total area of the colony; and "it is essential," say Messrs. Wall and Sawkins, " to arrive at some understanding as to what productions would be best suited for it. After full consideration, it seems that many, if not all, the natural conditions requisite for the growth of *cotton* are present. The surface is dry, the soil light and sandy, and the district not characterised by an excess of moisture. This production of the tropics and sub-tropical regions is more in demand than any other at the present time, and the consumption is likely to continue equal to the supply. Should the time arrive when this staple can possibly be raised to advantage in this colony, experiments in the district would be advisable, as affording the best chances of success.

"Tobacco has succeeded in Siparia, the quality produced there being regarded as superior.

"There is abundance of analogous soil, and this article might doubtless be advantageously cultivated on a more extended scale.

"If the uneven country, and that adjacent to the coast, should be devoted to the above staples, the interior districts might be found adapted for cacao; and the level and richer valley of the Ortoire even for sugar, as the extent to which that fine river is navigable would afford the means of readily transporting the produce raised along its course. The districts adjacent to the Ortoire seemed amongst the finest in the island, and it was a matter of regret that time did not permit their more complete exploration."

Population of the county, 2,006 : males 1,075, females 931 ; increase on 1871, 1,669.

4. County of Nariva.—Bounded on the N. by the county of St. Andrew, on the S. by that of Mayaro, E. by the sea, and W. by the county of Victoria. Although one of the most extensive, this county is the least populated, and consequently the least cultivated of all the island divisions. The only inhabited part is the *Cocal* or coco-walk, a very narrow belt along the sea, planted in coco-nut palms, and which constitutes the ward of Nariva. The whole, or nearly the whole, of this county is crown property, except the Cocal, which belongs to the Borough Council of Port-of-Spain, and nothing is cultivated in the county but coco-palms and some provisions.

This coco-palm plantation, extending from the mouth of the Lébranche to that of the Ortoire, was, as it appears, accidentally formed years ago. Among the many traditional accounts of that event, the following bears a very plausible aspect; it is to the effect that a schooner, laden with coco-nuts, was wrecked on the coast, and the nuts washed ashore by the surf. The locality being favourable, they sprouted, grew up, and spontaneously propagated to a large extent. Whatever its origin, the Cocal consists of about 60,000 coco-nut trees, more or less, some of them very old, others quite young, and a great many in full bearing.

A manufactory has been erected about midway between the rivers Lébranche and Mitan, so that the carriage of nuts across the Mitan, from near the Ortoire, to the establishment, is a tedious affair. It is worked by a steam-engine of six-horse power. The kernel extracted from the shell is bruised by means of grooved rollers, then reduced to a pulp by a mill-stone; the pulp is next placed in double-bottomed pans, heated by steam, which process has for result the evaporation of a certain proportion of water, and the coagulation of the albuminous ingredients of the pulp. The mass is then submitted to the action of an hydraulic press, and the oil allowed to run off; it is finally drawn off into casks, carted to the landing-place at the mouth of the Lébranche, and put on board of vessels anchored under lee of Point Manzanilla, for transport to Port-of-Spain.

The sea has a tendency to encroach upon the land at the Cocal, while the Mitan is gradually eroding southward to a considerable extent; the destruction of a good number of coco-trees is the result of this process. The plantation, however, may not only be preserved in its natural area, but it might be extended by steady planting, when two establishments might be maintained—one as at present existing, and the other between the Mitan and the Ortoire. The Cocal is leased for a term of years, at the annual rate of 2,000 dols.

The county of Nariva may be said to consist altogether of virgin land; it is partly level and swampy, partly undulating and hilly towards the central range. Both the level and hilly tracts are very imperfectly known. I may say, however, that this county is most varied in its geological formation. E. of Tamana, S. of Lébranche, and in the ward of Manzanilla, we meet with tracts of the Tamana calcareous soil; a long belt of the Naparima marl, extending from the Guarapiche to a few miles from the beach; a tract of stiff ferruginous clays, lying between Tamana and Manzanilla, and between the Upper Ortoire and the swamp, affording soils of a more or less red colour, not very productive; a tract of low land of good quality along the left bank of the Ortoire; and the swamp, which might be made productive by drainage—not an easy task, I admit. This swamp may be estimated at 34,560 acres.

Several streams originating in the central range have their course towards the swamp; the principal of these, pretty large, bears the name of Nariva.

The swampy part of Nariva presents, from the sea, a striking appearance, it being a perfect level from the beach to the foot of the Lébranche ridge; and, though covered with a luxuriant vegetation, it looks like a still waste, with the mountain-cabbage towering above the tall grasses and the copse-woods around; close to the beach, mangroves and balatas grow in clusters. The vapours which rise early in the morning, forming long hovering streaks of wreathy mist, indicate the *locale* of the swamps which intersect these lowlands in all directions, whilst in the background, the Lébranche hills seem to emerge abruptly from the plain. In front, the Nariva or Mitan stretches along the beach, immediately beyond the Cocal, for several miles. It is a fine deep sheet of dark water, expanding near its mouth into a sort of basin. The Nariva, as I have already stated, takes a northerly course until it meets the southern spur of the valley of Lébranche, when it turns nearly abruptly southward; it is formed by the accumulation of the waters which descend the Lébranche group, from Morne Calabash to Tamana. They collect first in swamps and canals communicating with each other, ultimately to unite in one stream. There is, besides the Nariva, the *Jean Paul*, or *Doubloon* river; it owes its existence and names to the following circumstance: Mr. Carter, the lessee of the Cocal, finding that, during the rainy season, the quantity of water received by the Nariva was disproportionately large, came to the determination of opening a new channel for the surplus waters, and made an arrangement with a man of the name of *Jean Paul* to cut a canal through the sandy beach, for which he paid him a doubloon; hence the names of *Jean Paul* and *Doubloon* given to that canal, which may be said to form, at present, a second mouth to the Nariva.

In the year 1849, Messrs. M. Sorzano, surveyor-general, and L. d'Abadie, also a land-surveyor, received instructions from Lord Harris to cut a track from Tamana to the Cocal. They began their survey on the 15th of April, and reached the beach on the 2nd of May. This track is a straight line, its direction being E. ¼ S., and its entire length fourteen miles. For nearly four miles from Tamana, the country is undulating, the superstratum resting on limestone. The lower portion is seven miles in length, and varies alternately from gently waving to flat; the last three miles present a marshy plain. In this section, mangroves were observed first, then, in succession, a dry savanna, a tract of very rich land, of about one mile and a half in breadth, covered with carats and wild plum-trees; next, an extensive savanna, with clusters of the moriche-palm; several mangrove swamps, separated by dry savannas and belts of dry land; a fine dry savanna, swamps, and mangroves; again, a small savanna; and finally, cabbage-trees and balatas bordering on the Cocal. The track opened on the beach about midway between the Nariva and the Ortoire.

All the water-courses met with during the survey, had a northerly or north-easterly direction. Four of them only bear names, viz., the Cunape, about one mile and three-quarters, and the Canqué, five miles from Tamana; the Carapa, one mile and a quarter, westward of the first savanna, and the Caratal immediately after the same. About six miles from the starting-point, Messrs. Sorzano and d'Abadie met with a low wet tract; and, soon after, with an impassable swamp, which compelled them to alter their line by nearly a mile to the southward. These gentlemen observed, on their route, several cacao-trees: were they accidentally planted, or are they the natural growth of the country? They fell in also with brush-wood, and a few lime-trees; such being evidence that, during slavery, the *maroons* or fugitive slaves resorted to that spot, as to a fastness.

In the following year, Mr. d'Abadie received further instructions to find a more direct road to the eastern coast, from Savanna Grande to the Cocal, or to Mayaro. He started from Monkey Town on the 19th of March, 1850, but completed his survey only the following year, when he reached the Cocal one mile northward of the mouth of the Ortoire—the whole length of the track being twenty-six miles. He followed, as far as possible, the direction of ridges, in order to avoid the low swampy grounds. For seventeen miles all the water-courses had their flow southward towards the Ortoire. The principal were the following: Guanapure, three miles from the starting-point; this river ought to be regarded as the true origin of the

Ortoire—not only because it is the first important stream which occurs on the track, but its position corresponds better to the range of that river as marked down on Mallet's map than to that of his Moura. Next to the Guanapure, and within a range of three miles, came in succession the following watercourses: Pure, the Poui, the Guarapiche, and the Guanapure—the Carib name Guarapiche induces me to admit the existence of bitumen in the neighbourhood. The Guanapure corresponds pretty well, in position, to the Moura of Mallet. Two and a half miles from the Guanapure flows the Caranache; about three miles from the Caranache, the Anapo; one mile and a half further eastward, the Agua-Clara; and, for about three miles, a series of smaller ravines or rivulets. Except the Guanapure, which has a gravelly bed, all these streams are muddy. For about six miles, a number of small brooks have their course to the northward, and a few to the southward, the road there following the dividing range. Among the former are the Guatecaro, about five miles, and the Cascaradura, about one mile and a half from the shore.

Mr. d'Abadie having received new orders to connect the Tamana with the Mayaro track, left the latter about eighteen miles from Monkey Town, and, after a run of little more than four miles in a northerly direction, met the former between the two first savannas, at that tract of rich land already mentioned. He encountered several water-courses, having an easterly direction, a swamp, and a tract of land partly level and partly waving, with a forest of moras; the ground bordering on the savanna was, in general, soft, and intersected with swamps. At a later period Mr. d'Abadie opened another track, about four miles from the beach, connecting the Mayaro path directly with the ward of Mayaro.

I have entered into these details, in order to indicate the real disposition of that extensive tract of low country stretching seaward of the Cocal, between the Lébranche and the Ortoire, and I have come to the following conclusions: From Tamana, a ridge extends in a south-easterly direction towards Point Radix, dividing the basin of the Ortoire from that of the Nariva; there exists no water communication between the two rivers—a fact which had already been ascertained by Captain Columbine and by Mr. J. Carter. The natural slope of the country is evidently from the S.S.W. to the N.N.E., as proved by the fact that all the water-courses—and mainly the Carapa and the Caratal—have their course in the latter direction, and that the swamps predominate towards the north, and the dry land towards the south. Moreover, Mr. Carter had already discovered that the upper stream of the Nariva tended northwards, and then, by an abrupt bend, inclined towards the south. The numerous lagoons which exist throughout the whole extent of that low tract evidently owe their origin to the accumulation of waters flowing partly from the Lébranche, and partly from the Tamana ridge.

Report fixes the soil of Nariva as generally good—and even, in some parts, of the best quality. The district also abounds in excellent timber. The cultivation of the coco-palm might be extended over all those localities which are within tidal influence; and the natural savannas might be turned to excellent account in rearing and feeding horned and other stock; also, with the refuse from the mills, swine might be fed in great numbers. Mr. Carter has tried the experiment, and succeeded sufficiently well to prove that, with good management, the rearing of animals might here become very profitable.

Population of the county, 1881, 274: males 156, females 118; decrease as compared with 1871, 18.

CHAPTER X.

PROSPECTS OF TRINIDAD—SUGGESTIONS.

To judge fairly of the prospects of Trinidad, we should take into account its geographical position and its many natural resources; we should not forget that it has already passed through periods of prosperity and great depression. Not later than the year 1848, Lord Harris wrote as follows to Earl Grey:—

"It is sad and painful to behold men expecting ruin quickly to overcome them; it is, perhaps, sadder and more painful to see them struggling and toiling against adversity, but with their energies dulled and their arms palsied from their knowledge that their labours must be unremunerative, and that failure can be the sole result; it is most distressing to witness this, and, at the same time, to be aware that much of the misery from which they are suffering, and which awaits them, is of a nature which they are unable to avert by any acts of their own.

"It is pitiable to witness a fine colony daily deteriorating—a land enjoying every blessing under heaven—suffering from a shock from which it does not rally. Did I not see a prospect—I think a better one than in any of the West Indies—of getting this colony through the present crisis, I should not venture to propose that advances should be made; but, looking at the fertility of the soil, and the almost certainty of favourable seasons, I believe that, with assistance, there can be little doubt of its ultimate success."

Not through advances, but with the assistance afforded by the Indian immigration, the colony was enabled to get over the crisis, and to attain a certain amount of prosperity; and yet its position, in consequence of the depreciation of its staple produce, may be said to be precarious. Trinidad, nevertheless, possesses many natural resources: what they are I have already stated; it only remains for me to add a few remarks.

The island of Trinidad may be considered as consisting of two great valleys, formed by three mountain ranges of various elevation. The middle and southern ranges are accessible on all sides, and might be passed over at many points by carriage roads. The northern range is accessible only on the south or land side, there being but a few landing-places on the sea-coast. The two valleys might be easily run through from E. to W. by tram-roads or railways, which would afford every facility for internal communication and for the transport of goods to our great sea-port, the Gulf of Paria.

On the hills, coffee, cacao, cotton, and spices might be cultivated with advantage, as exportable articles; plantains, corn, ground provisions, and the more delicate vegetables, for home consumption. The hills are generally healthy and cool, and might be settled and cultivated by a white population, and others, with a small capital. The plain might be reserved for the cultivation of the cane mainly; the cultivation of cacao and tobacco should be carried on in the *vegas* or hollows of river valleys, the low swamps and less fertile tracts might be planted or sown in rice. In the case of some other cultures being introduced, as indigo, sesame, the castor-oil plant, these could be tried in inferior lands.

Tramways might be laid down between the Oropuche river and Port-of-Spain in the northern basin; and between the Ortoire and La Brea, or Naparima, in the southern basin. Those are the local or intrinsic capabilities of Trinidad, but are not its sole advantages. Its geographical position, adjacent to the continent and the republic of Venezuela, almost at the mouth of the Orinoco, renders it, in a commercial and political point of view, as important as Cuba. Wherefore, though the fate of Trinidad be intimately connected with that of the other British colonies, yet her prospects may be greatly affected by extraneous influences; for they, in a great measure, depend upon the fate of the neighbouring republic of Venezuela. If ever Venezuela becomes tranquil and prosperous, Trinidad will share in that prosperity; for the magnificent Gulf of Paria is a vast harbour common to both: in fact, it is or can easily be rendered the great seaport of the rich and extensive basin of the Orinoco, as may be ascertained by glancing at the map of Venezuela.

The Andes form, southward of Popayan, and about the second

degree of north latitude, a trifurcation known by the name of the *Cordilleras of Nueva Granada*. The easternmost chain is the *Cordillera* of Venezuela, which traverses that republic from S.S.W. to E.N.E., from Almaguer to cape Peña, or even Point Galera, the north-eastern point of Trinidad. It runs, at first N.N.E. from San Miguel de Mocoa to Valencia; Pamplona, Merida, Truxillo, Barquisimeto, and even Valencia being left on the northern or sea-coast side, and San Juan de los Remedios, Casanare, with Varinas on the southern or Orinoco side of the chain. From Valencia, the *Cordillera* runs due east, and so close to the Caribbean sea that its very base is washed by the surf—Maracaybo, Puerto Cabello, Caracas, Barcelona, and Cumana being thereby separated by rugged mountains and high table lands from the basin of the Orinoco.

That immense basin extends from the Andes, eastward, to the mountains of Parima and the Atlantic; and southward, from the same *Cordillera* to the Rio Negro. Besides a number of less important streams, it is drained by the following large navigable rivers, viz.,—the Guarico, the Portuguesa, the Apure, Arouca, the Meta, the Vichada, and the Guaviare, all coming down from the Cordilleras; and by the Ventuari, the Caura, and the Caroni, which have their sources in the Parima system of mountains; all are tributaries of the mighty river.

This short description shows that the *Cordillera* of Venezuela has been thrown up by nature, as an unsurmountable barrier to commercial communication between the basin of the Orinoco and the Caribbean sea, so that either Angostura or Port-of-Spain must become the great emporium of Venezuela, and the Orinoco or the Gulf of Paria the outlet of the interior basin.

Angostura—now Bolivar—is a fine river-port with deep water, but about 300 miles from the Atlantic; the temperature there is oppressive, though the climate cannot be said to be unhealthy. The navigation against the stream is, however, very tedious, principally during the overflow of the river, viz., from April to October, when the currents are very strong; whilst the marsh effluvia, all along its banks, are very deleterious, particularly during the low-water season. There are, at the mouth of the river, low islands and sand-banks or shoals, which also render the navigation intricate and even dangerous; so much so, that large vessels would not find it safe to venture, without skilful pilots, through its many channels. To remove or even permanently to remedy those obstacles cannot be regarded as an easy undertaking. On the other hand, the Gulf of Paria is not only one of the safest harbours known, but is fully capable of sheltering the united fleets of the world; hurricanes are unknown here, and ground swells are felt but very seldom, and that, within a line drawn from the first Boca to Point la Brea; in fact, the navigation of the Gulf is, at all times, safe and easy; whilst dangers, if there be any, attending the passage of the smaller Bocas, or entrance mouths, can easily be avoided by passing through the largest, or Grand Boca.

The Gulf is considered healthy, and even the yellow fever, in its occasional and rare visitations, has made but a few victims among the shipping. There is a never-failing and plentiful supply of excellent spring and river water in the island, and fresh meat can be procured from the provinces of Guiana and Barcelona; dry docks might also be constructed at the Gasparil Islet, and warehouses erected there for ship stores.

The Gulf communicates with the Orinoco by means of the Caños, or channels, of Pedernales, Manamo, and Macareo. Small crafts bound to Trinidad from Bolivar pass generally through Caño Pedernales; the steamers, at present, take in preference Caño Macareo. These, or at least one of these natural channels might be rendered navigable for large steamers and other vessels, which would carry the produce of the immense and fertile basin into the Gulf, for the lading of vessels awaiting their cargo; or they might be tugged to Barrancas. The attention of his Excellency Lord Harris had been attracted to the subject, as proved by the following extract: "I have already, on several occasions, pointed out to your lordship the very great benefits which would accrue to this island if a more liberal policy could be adopted respecting the trade with other countries, more especially with France and Spain; a still greater one would be gained if the neighbouring republic of Venezuela could be induced to modify its Customs' duties.

"Should the steam communication between Port-of-Spain and Maturin—which I have shown every inclination to support—be established, it would prove very beneficial; but I am more anxious to see a similar one, only on a larger scale, set on foot between this and the City of Bolivar. There are many reasons for hoping that Port-of-Spain may eventually become the receptacle of the trade of that vast tract of country from which the Orinoco draws its waters. A steamer passing by the Caño Macareo could reach Bolivar in seventy hours and return in fifty, whereas merchant vessels take from five to twenty days to ascend to that place from the chief mouth of the river. An American company has already entered into contract with the Venezuelan Government to navigate the Orinoco, from Bolivar upwards, for a distance of 700 miles by steamer. It only requires, therefore, to connect Trinidad and Bolivar by similar means—only I hope by an English company—and the interior of the western part of that vast continent would be opened to enterprise, and an invaluable impulse given to the commerce of this island." (Lord Harris to Earl Grey, 21st February, 1848.) That connection has been established for the last eight or ten years, two trips monthly to and from Bolivar corresponding with the arrival of the English mail. Great, therefore, not to say unlimited, are the advantages enjoyed by Trinidad. How long will they remain only partially developed, God only knows! for numerous are the obstacles to be overcome. We have to deal with jealous neighbours, more or less prejudiced against foreigners, with a Government blind to its best interests; and yet, "under the fostering care of Great Britain (if she will foster it), this colony may become, not only prosperous, but may prove of vast importance in assisting to civilise the fine and extensive continent in its vicinity." (Lord Harris to Earl Grey.) It is, therefore, our duty to prepare ourselves for any favourable contingency which may arise, by adopting such measures as may improve our condition, and render this island a desirable home for all who may choose to bring hither their capital and industry.

Trinidad is a newly-settled country, with a scanty population, and imperfect means of communication; it is, therefore, most important that we should establish good roads where required. Without such, entire districts must remain altogether undeveloped or stationary. The perfection of means of communication does not, however, depend on the proper construction of roads, but also on the facility of procuring fit materials for their repair and maintenance. In our best agricultural districts, the ground is far from affording facilities for the formation and preservation of public ways, it being generally clayey and deficient in suitable material for road-making. On that plea, some persons are of opinion that it would be better to lay tramways rather than construct new roads and have them properly macadamised at an enormous cost. They contend that such tramroads would ultimately prove cheaper, inasmuch as they might be made to yield revenue, instead of being, as at present, a permanent cause of expenditure. That might be so, but the first outlay will always act as a serious obstacle to their establishment.

The staff of road engineers now in the colony is, I think, equal to all requirements. Far from me the pretention of suggesting what duties should be imposed upon them, or how they ought to proceed; but this I do not hesitate to say, too much of latitude is left to the inferior officers, and the principals are not seen on the highways as often as they should. The island has been formed into two principal divisions for administrative purposes— the northern and the southern. An engineer should be appointed to each division, and made responsible to the Director of Public Works, as head of the department. He should regularly visit and inspect the roads in his division, prepare estimates for their repair and the construction of bridges. He would determine whether any new roads were required, trace them, and superintend their formation. No bridge should be built in his division, except under his personal superintendence; he should regularly send reports, showing the conditions of the roads within his district, with such suggestions as he would consider useful. A code of rules and instructions should be prepared for the management of the public ways, which all inferior officers should be compelled to obey.

We have no fair chance of progressing unless we establish roads throughout the country; but we particularly need population, and to us immigration has become a matter of vital importance. The introduction of immigrants, immediately after emancipation, saved the colony from immediate ruin; and we must look up to immigration, and the introduction of field-labourers, if we are determined not to retrograde. But as the people so introduced gradually retire from field labour, either by leaving the island to return home, or by adopting other occupations, or by becoming land-owners, we must make provision for a continuous influx of immigrants, lest the cultivation of our staple articles should become restricted, or should even cease altogether.

This question of immigration is of such paramount importance, that I will be pardoned, I hope, for taking a short retrospective review of its history in Trinidad. Immediately after emancipation, so pressing had become the demand for agricultural labourers, in consequence of our scanty population and the preposterously high wages demanded for field labour—so palpable, so imminent had become the danger of ruin—that it was at once and almost instinctively resolved to call in immigrants by every mode of inducement. Labourers from the neighbouring colonies, attracted hither by the prospect of higher wages, began to immigrate to the island at their own cost. It was soon discovered that a regular current of immigration would set in if sufficient encouragement were afforded. The planters at once manifested their readiness to advance the passage-money, provided the immigrants would engage their services as a compensation.

On the other hand, a bounty was offered to those captains of small trading vessels who would introduce them, on condition they would use their influence to secure the services of the immigrants to the party paying the bounty. Several planters, themselves owners of vessels, despatched them to Grenada, St. Christopher, or Nevis, to bring over labourers for the crop season, and on many occasions undertook to send them back to their native island after their term of service. Moreover, money was invariably advanced to the immigrants, on the pretext that they required articles of food or clothing. But as there was no legal provision specifying the conditions of contract, or binding the immigrants and employer to their observance, many of the immigrants actually left, or were enticed to leave, the estates to which they were attached, the planters who had paid for their passage and made advances thus losing a part, or even the whole, of the money advanced. The planters had thus amply proved their readiness and determination to help themselves; but so defective was the system adopted, that they were compelled to desist. The Legislative Council was, under the circumstance, induced to make the introduction of labourers a public enterprise; and a "regular trade in immigrants" was established between Trinidad and the neighbouring islands, but especially with Grenada, Nevis, Montserrat, and St. Christopher. The captains who introduced them being entitled to a bounty, managed to bring over as many as possible; and, in order to keep up the trade, they would take back the very same people for whom they had received a premium on some former voyage, in order to have the opportunity of re-introducing them a second, or even a third and fourth time, thus converting the same individuals into an *ad libitum* bounty. This discreditable practice was carried on until, being discovered, the bounty system was discontinued. Thus ended the ill-contrived and injudiciously-managed intercolonial immigration.

The demand for labour, however, was still pressing. Immigrants came from Havre, Madeira, and the United States. Those from France were engaged either as house-servants or field-labourers. The former, after their term of service had expired, preferred a livelihood as shopkeepers, carters, or petty traffickers; only a very few succeeded. The latter were carried off by fever. The immigrants from the States did not succeed any better, inasmuch as being generally carpenters, bricklayers, &c., they had to compete with the same class of tradesmen, already too numerous in the colony. Immigrants from Madeira were more successful. The two sources, however, from which we have received the largest accession of labourers are Africa and Hindostan.

The Home Government having decided that the Africans liberated from the captured slavers would be sent to the West India colonies, Trinidad received a good share. A few hundred voluntary immigrants also came from the Kroo coast. It soon, however, became evident that we could not depend for any length of time on a supply of labourers from this source; and it was decided to follow the example of Mauritius, and to introduce Coolies from Hindostan. Accordingly the *Fatel Rosack* left Calcutta with a first cargo of Coolies, and anchored in the harbour on the 30th May, 1845. The pressure must have been great indeed to compel the colonists to seek labour from the far East; and such a determination certainly argues much in favour of their energy. Other vessels followed in regular succession; and in May, 1848, 5,162 immigrants from India had been landed in the island. The two or three first draughts answered the expectations which had been formed; but the others did not.

They had not been judiciously selected. Their introduction was a mere experiment, and as such surrounded with many difficulties. Again, the Coolies were perfect strangers in the island, and the relations in which they were placed with regard to the emancipated blacks quite novel. But no class of labourers has given more satisfaction than those subsequently introduced under a well-regulated system of immigration. The manner of dealing with that class of immigrants is now regulated by law, and in several respects very different from what it was at the commencement; added to which, their own countrypeople are here to advise, and to initiate them in the customs and occupations of the inhabitants; in fact, they are much less hampered in their habits and their own peculiar ideas. They, in consequence, work more successfully, because they fully understand their duties and their rights. When the Coolies were first introduced, it was found advisable to appoint a special magistrate for their protection. Major Fagan, who was acquainted with the language and customs of the people of India, was selected for the post. When the major arrived in Trinidad only a few inoperative regulations existed concerning immigrants of all classes; and it was consequent to that want of proper regulations that so much suffering was undergone by " those unfortunate people, in the shape of disease, starvation, and ultimate death," as expressed by Mr. Montgomery Martin; but not because, as stated by him, "the treatment of immigrants generally, and especially of the East Indian Coolies, had been most discreditable." This will become apparent on perusal of Lord Harris's despatches.

The Africans liberated from slavers had been appointed to the planters under certain conditions, viz., that they should work for a stated number of hours every day, on being provided with lodging, food, clothing, and medical attendance. They, however, did not consider themselves as party to the contract— the obligations of which they did not understand—and determinedly refused to work, and absconded into the woods, prowling about in the neighbourhood of plantations, on which they ventured, at night, for plunder. Others attempted to retrace their steps to their country, as they imagined, by travelling eastward. Not only did they avoid inhabited localities, but when they did encounter any of the inhabitants, being ignorant of the language spoken in the island, they could neither understand them nor make themselves understood. The Coolies, who had been landed in the interval, soon availed themselves of the bad example set to them, and of the laxity of the law. The contracts made were broken, first by the indentured labourer, and most willingly afterwards by their employers, who could in no wise consider themselves bound when the immigrant had freed himself from all obligations. Lord Harris having fully treated this subject in his correspondence with Lord Grey, I prefer giving his opinions in his own words to offering mine on the matter :—

"My desire has been impartially to study the interest of both parties, at the same time never to lose sight of the fact that the Coolies were placed here under peculiar circumstances, as utter strangers in a foreign land, and therefore requiring the zealous and increasing care of Government; that they are also far from being the best class of the Indian labouring population, are naturally dissolute and depraved in their habits if left to themselves, and much inclined to fall into habits of drinking and of wandering idly about the country, and therefore require the close supervision of Government, in order to correct, if possible—but, at all events, to prevent—any evident cases of vagabondage and licentiousness." (Lord Harris to Mr. Gladstone, July, 1846.)

"After having given my best consideration to the subject, it appears to me that, in the first place, the immigrants must pass through an initiatory process; they are not, neither Africans nor Coolies, fit to be placed in a position which the labourers of civilised countries may at once occupy. They must be treated like children—and wayward ones, too—the former, from the utterly savage state in which they arrive; the latter, from their habits and religion." (Lord Harris to Earl Grey, 1848.)

Lord Harris, therefore, had, with the aid of Major Fagan, the Coolie magistrate, prepared a code of regulations, which was published in 1846. A great outcry was raised here and in Great Britain against these regulations, some of which, on the assumption of his lordship himself, were "stringent." These regulations were disallowed by the Secretary of State for the Colonies, Lord Grey, not only because, in his lordship's opinion, "they had no legal validity," but also on the strong and not very judicious representations of the Anti-Slavery Society, so that the system of *laissez aller* was once more preferred to a more restrictive, but surely—as proved by the result—a more beneficial and more humane policy. However, certain heads were at the same time sent out by Lord Grey, which were digested into an ordinance for the encouragement of immigration, and made law in 1847.

With reference to the withdrawal of the regulations prepared by Major Fagan, Lord Harris observes : " Your lordship will remember that the withdrawal of some rules which I had established respecting the management of the Coolies was required by despatch dated 16th September, 1846, and they were accordingly cancelled on the 17th October following.

" Doubtless there were numerous faults in these rules. From the circumstance of the case, they had been drawn up at a very short notice; but all will allow, who had the opportunity of judging, that, during their operation, the Coolies were well clothed, healthy, generally contented, and improving daily in habits of industry.

" On the withdrawal of those rules, they returned to the habits which are natural to them : they left the estates, and were to be seen wandering about in the country in bands, and by the time that the immigration ordinance came into force, but few were remaining on the properties on which they had been generally located."

As to the ordinance of 1847, Lord Harris states :—" I cannot say that the ordinance No. 9 of 1847, for the encouragement of immigration, has succeeded to my satisfaction. The cause of its failure I attribute partly to the very depressed circumstances of the planters at the time of its being brought into force, and the general conviction that the Coolies would not remain on the estates, consequently inducing a small demand for the Coolies, and partly to its want of adaptation to the localities, and the population with which it was intended to deal.

" Many of the Coolies left the estates within a week of entering into contract, but no pains were taken to give the Government any information of it. Want of means was one cause why contracts were not generally entered into by the planters.

" But there was also a general feeling that the provisions of the ordinance were not sufficiently stringent to warrant their advancing the sum required. That such has turned out to be the case there can be no doubt. I shall proceed to explain why it appears to me that it was likely to happen.

"On entering into contract, the Coolies were liable, on breaking their engagements, to certain penalties. In order to enforce these it was necessary, first, that the delinquents should be caught, and then brought before a justice of the peace. Now, the great difficulty is, in this country, to get such penalties at all to bear upon the delinquents.

"The result has been that I know only of one instance in which the proprietor has attempted to recover the Coolies.

"The consequence of their readoption of their wandering habits has been most distressing. I was induced, from numbers being found destitute, sick, and starving in the roads, to establish two hospitals for their reception." (Lord Harris, February, 1848.)

In these words and observations of Lord Harris, we have the proof that it was not the fault of the planters if the first attempts at establishing and regulating a fair system of assisted immigration remained ineffectual. In this opinion Earl Grey seems to have concurred, for he says in his despatches to the Governor of Trinidad:—

"It is possible, indeed, that the code of Coolie regulations proposed by you might have been more successful than ordinance No. 9 of 1847; and the primary objections that I took to it, namely, that it had no legal validity, might have been obviated by the enactment of an ordinance. Such rules could not be enforced without a violation of the principles on which free labour is ordinarily regulated, nor without running the risk of great abuses. It is possible that the abuses would have occurred but seldom, and that they would have been a far less evil than the vice and suffering on the part of the Coolies, to which their unrestrained condition has given birth; but we have to bear in mind the sentiments to which the exposure of even one gross example of abuse might give occasion here, and the obstruction to all immigration, which might be the consequence, not only in Trinidad, but throughout the sugar colonies; and I doubt not that your lordship will perceive the serious difficulties under which we labour in the treatment of immigrants belonging to savage or half-civilised races, whose unfitness for unrestrained liberty is not generally understood or acknowledged in this country." (Earl Grey to Lord Harris, 15th April, 1848.)

Earl Grey writes again:—"It is exceedingly painful to me to learn that the immigration ordinance, though seconded by your lordship's zealous efforts, and by the order for the prevention of vagrancy, passed by her Majesty in council on the 7th of September, 1838, and the proclamation for the prevention of squatting, issued by you on 22nd June, 1847, has been ineffectual, and has not succeeded in preventing the Coolies from falling into fatal and dissolute ways of life; so that great numbers of them have ended by dying in the public hospitals, and not a few by the waysides and in the woods." (Earl Grey to Lord Harris, 15th April, 1848.)

The Secretary of State had laid down the principle that it should be sought "to place the immigrants in a situation in which they might be acted upon by the same motives by which men are compelled to labour in industrious countries." In answer, Lord Harris offers the following very judicious remarks:—

"I have great doubts whether the Coolie and African are morally or mentally capable of being acted upon by the same motives in this island, on their first arrival, as labourers are in more civilised countries. . . . .

"The only independence which they would desire is idleness, according to their different tastes in the enjoyment of it; and then the higher motives which actuate the European labourer (and we must remember the vast difference there is even in Europe with respect to the industry of various races), which are above and beyond circumstances, irrespective of mere self-interest, which he has received as his patrimony from previous generations, and which, I believe, even in this age, are still to be found prevailing amongst them—viz., that to be industrious is a duty and a virtue; that to be independent in circumstances, whatever his station, raises a man in the moral scale amongst his race; and that his ability to perform his duties as a citizen, and, we may add, as a Christian, is increased by it. These, and such motives as these, are unknown to the fatalist worshippers of Mahomet and Brahma, and to the savages who go by the names of Liberated Africans."

The immigration ordinance of 1849 has been since amended on several occasions, and, though still amendable in some minor points, may be said to afford full protection and to give satisfaction to the immigrants. I dare say that under the operation of the present ordinance the immigrants are "healthy, well clothed, and contented, and improving in habits of industry."

The Coolie on his arrival is to undergo the ordeal of acclimatisation. Those who are weak, or belong to the inferior castes, may suffer from the change; but those who are of good constitution, and disposed to toil, soon become inured, and work readily. Anemia and ulcers are their prevalent ailments; and these complaints are generally the result of improper food and filthy habits, seldom of protracted fevers. The mortality of Coolie children is less than of Creoles. Few Coolies have adopted the costume or mode of living of the country. They are, however, generally clean, and their dresses made of good materials—very different, in this respect, from their newly-arrived countrymen. How different, again, the low obsequiousness of the recently-landed Hindoo from the manly deportment of his compatriot after a few years' residence in the colony! Those who are ragged and filthy may be pronounced at once to be worthless fellows. That they are not overworked is proved by the fact that many re-engage for one year's further industrial residence on receiving a bounty of ten dollars; that they are contented is proved by their disposition to remain in the colony after they have completed their term of industrial residence. Many are shop-keepers, and a still larger number are licensed to sell spirits and other drinks. Others go about in the rural districts buying fruits and provisions, which they afterwards retail in towns and villages. Not a few have become landowners by purchase or by grants from the crown. Let me reiterate, therefore, that Coolie immigration, properly conducted, may yet aid in saving such of the West India colonies as have fertile lands; nay, may be the foundation, in this Archipelago, of industrious, peaceful, and happy communities.

We had also received, some time in the year 1853, a few hundred Chinese; but unfortunately they were the refuse of seaports, were unaccompanied by interpreters, and were in consequence exposed to many hardships, from their inability to understand or make themselves understood by their employers. Hence, incapable of making known any objections they would think reasonable, or any wish they might form, or of asking redress for any real or imaginary wrong they might have suffered, they on many occasions—and doubtless through ignorance—resisted the just claims of their employers. Some of the indolent among them would simulate illness in order to escape the necessity of labour, and yet would exact or expect the full allowance of food to which they were entitled in health. If I may judge of the Chinese from the few hundreds introduced here, I must say that they are proud, stubborn, and deceitful, bearing rebuke with impatience, and prone to revenge and suicide; they are also much addicted to stealing. On the other hand, when so disposed they worked hard, steadily, and well; in fact, they understand the tillage of the soil better than any other class of labourers we ever had; and they avail themselves of the smallest spot allowed them on estates to cultivate provisions. They are highly praised by some of the planters as even the best class of labourers, and are easily acclimatised. But it cannot be denied that the first importation of the Chinese did not, at the outset at least, succeed well, not being, I think, carefully selected; and we had, during the first months of their introduction, a repetition of the same difficulties which attended the initiation of the first imported Coolies.

I am aware that paid immigration is denounced by some persons as an artificial system, which, as such, should be discontinued. Undoubtedly paid immigration is an artificial means of supplying labour where population is scarce, but recourse has always been had to that system with a view to developing the resources of a new country. It has its drawbacks, but it has also its advantages, in which the immigrant shares as well as his employer. The great drawback is the temporary alienation by the immigrant of a portion of his freedom, inasmuch as he is bound to reside on some estate, and to do a certain amount of work, for which, however, he receives fair wages. On the other hand, his employer is bound to supply him with proper lodgings, and to take care of him and his children, both in sickness and health. After a term of industrial residence, he recovers his full freedom, and can adopt such course as he may consider more profitable and congenial to his taste. He has a right to a return passage home, but here in Trinidad can commute his return passage for £5 in money and five acres of land. Not a few make money during their indenture; and as long as the immigrant remains in the colony, he enjoys all the privileges of a British subject, and is, at all times, fully protected by the law. Of course under that system immigrants can be brought only from over-populated countries, such as India and China; the people are there more or less exposed to periodical famine and its consequent evils—starvation and epidemic diseases.

Intending immigrants from India to these colonies, as a rule, are sunk in the deepest misery, with not the slightest chance of bettering their condition. Again, the immigrant is transferred from a land where heathenism and despotism have full sway to a land of Christianity and civilisation—not a small advantage, at least in the eyes of reflecting men. Can it be said that such immigration would act as a drain on the country from which it flows? It should be rather considered in the light of a relief. For instance, what can be to India, teeming with millions of inhabitants, the abstraction, let us say, of 20,000 souls every year? Again, let it not be forgotten that paid immigration has been set on foot, and is continued to the present day, mainly with the object of averting complete ruin. "There can be no doubt," said Lord Harris, "that the prosperity, nay, the existence, of these colonies, depends on a cheap and steady supply of labour; the favourable solution of free against slave labour must depend on it; every means ought to be tried, more especially on the part of the mother country, to obtain it on as cheap terms as possible." There is this fact—the only sugar colonies of Great Britain that are still extant, as such, are Barbadoes, Mauritius, Demerara, and Trinidad—Barbadoes, on account of its large native labouring population; Mauritius, Demerara, and Trinidad, thanks to Indian immigration.

To keep up the production of our staple articles, to increase them, we must keep up a regular influx of labourers; we should even increase their number. If, therefore, the British Government considers it worth while to retain its colonies in this part of the world, as useful dependencies, it should not hesitate to foster immigration to these islands.

The Coolies are, I have said, entitled to a free return passage after ten years' residence in the colony, an arrangement which fully proves the interest the Indian Government takes in their subjects; but an arrangement much to be regretted, inasmuch as we are pledged to send back to their country the very people for the introduction of whom such heavy sacrifices have been made, and whose labour we urgently require. This is an evil to which we must submit.

The only reasonable pledge the colony should be expected to take is this: whenever a sufficient number of immigrants are found willing and ready to return home, to procure for them a vessel and a passage on the same terms as those on which they were introduced. We have tried to remedy this evil to a certain extent, by granting to the immigrants, instead of a free return passage, £5 in cash and five acres of land. Many have already availed themselves of the offer, and have thus become permanent settlers. At first they were granted 10 acres of land, worth £10, considered as equivalent to the passage-money. As a rule, a locality is selected, surveyed in lots of five acres, and a settlement is thus formed of Indian immigrants only; and an Indian name is given to the settlement. Thus we have the Calcutta, the Madras, the Barrackpoor, and the Fyzabad settlements. The immigrants are thus encouraged to form small communities, speaking the same language, and having the same habits and ways. Of course such arrangements must be received with favour by the Coolies; but this system is not without its inconveniences—the Coolies being more or less excluded from intimate intercourse with the Creoles will be more apt to retain their ways and superstitions, and less inclined to initiate themselves into our habits and civilisation.

I must add that, as a class, the Coolies have not proved very intelligent tillers of the soil. Generally they are satisfied with cultivating provisions—corn, rice, and tanias being the favourite articles. Corn and rice are exhaustive plants, and whenever they have been cultivated on the same spot for successive years, the land becomes impoverished, and remains unprofitable for some time; it must then be allowed to remain fallow for several years. The Coolie generally prefers to sell off, instead of waiting, with the object of buying new land somewhere else; or betakes himself to other pursuits. Of course our schools are open to Coolie children; but very few only attend, either because they reluctantly mix with the Creole children, or because their parents do not seem to appreciate the advantages of primary instruction. An American Missionary Society has, nevertheless, established on estates, and on several Coolie blocks, special schools for their instruction; these schools are better attended. I will here remark that the Hindoos seem to be highly indifferent in matters of religion, and, from sheer habit probably, steadily adhere to their pagan tenets and practices. Only an imperceptible minority have become converts, and I say with regret that little reliance can be placed on these converts.

For too many years the illegal occupation of crown lands, or squatting, had been regarded as an evil which was incurable. It may be considered now, I hope, as effectually suppressed by the enforcement of the wise measures adopted by Governor Gordon; and there is no fear of its recurrence, if the Government only manifests common vigilance. The opening of the crown lands at an upset price of £1 per acre, in paying the survey fees and grant, was, in my opinion, one of those wise measures. But no method seems to have guided the surveying and laying out of lots. Petitions were sent for the grant of lands in any part of the colony, and were received favourably. The form of the lots was not regulated, so that in certain districts, where good land was to be looked for, along the rivers, a string of lots (if I may use the expression) were surveyed and granted of every shape. It is inutile to point to the great inconveniences of such a practice; they are obvious even to the least observant. I would therefore, presume to suggest a more comprehensive, and, to my view, a more perfect plan. The island has been divided into eight counties, and each county is divisible into wards. The wards as at present formed are, some, very small—too small in fact—such as Mucurapo, Cocorite, and Cimaronero; others are left undefined, such as, for instance, the wards of Turure and Montserrat. What I propose is this, to have some of the counties—say Caroni, for instance, Victoria, St. George, and St. Andrew—at once surveyed and laid out into wards; and only part of St. Patrick, of Mayaro and St. David, all along the sea-side, for example. The wards should be of four or six miles square, or less, according to the extent and peculiar configuration of the country. The bounds of the different wards should be marked at the corners, and at every mile with worked stones or small iron pillars. Each ward should be laid out in sections of a square mile, containing 640 acres; and these, when required, into quarters, half-quarters, and even smaller divisions, to suit purchasers. As far as feasible, all lines should be run North and

South, and East and West, and should commence or start from the sea-side; all divisions to be rectangular.

I cannot see any serious objections to the plan I here suggest; even that of expense, I must say, does not strike me as insurmountable. In fact, I consider that the Government is bound to lay out and fix the limits of new wards, as the sale of crown lands progresses. Outline maps of the county might be prepared; there cannot be any difficulty in this. Now, on these maps the wards might be provisionally marked out. Wards and sections once laid out, subsequent surveys will become much easier; also the sub-divisions of the sections and the disposal of the crown lands. The sub-intendant or commissioners and principal surveyor will be able, on looking to the county maps, to know exactly the position of the land petitioned for. As an essay, the plan which I suggest might be experimented in the counties of Caroni and St. George, where large tracts have already been granted. As a matter of detail, I would propose that the wards be named after the rivers running through, or the mountains standing within, their limits.

The question naturally suggests itself whether it would not be wise and prudent to reserve, in certain wards, a few sections which afterwards might be bought entire to form sugar estates or central usines.

I grant that prospects, in this peculiar branch of agriculture, are not very encouraging; and yet who can positively say that the cultivation of the sugar-cane will be ultimately abandoned and cease altogether in these parts?

There are certain measures, the adoption of which I consider not only as beneficial but as absolutely essential, either as preventive enactments, or with a view to the correction of certain existing evils; amongst others, a stringent vagrant act and provisions for its enforcement. The order in council of September, 1838, may be said to be a dead letter: it should be revived and rigidly enforced.

In civilized societies all men are bound to contribute their quota to the necessities of the state, in order to enable the Government to afford that protection which civil and social institutions demand; the man of capital, his resources; the man of art, his skill; the owner of the soil, his produce; the tiller of the ground, his labour. In addition, all are bound so to employ their faculties and exert their energies, that they do neither become a helpless charge on the State, a burden to their fellow citizens, indolently and criminally live at the expense of the commonwealth. The man who possesses not an income, an independent freehold or a rent-roll, must labour, in accordance with his ordinary vocation. The artisan must work, the tiller of the soil must toil : if he works not, if he toils not, want and distress must inevitably be his companions. Food he must have : true, he may obtain it on credit, but with a detriment to the community by non-payments : if not attainable in this wise, he must steal.

To what cause, principally, is to be ascribed the neglect of, and even aversion to, the growth of provisions? To the system of plunder which is carried on in the rural districts. And by whom? By the *far niente* class of vagrants. In a country like ours, with an heterogeneous population and scattered cultivation, agricultural interests can be protected only by stringent laws.

Corn and plantain are carried off ere ripe; yams, potatoes and other edible roots are artfully dug out during the night, fowls are picked up with audacity. As a consequence the cultivation of provisions is neglected, as also the rearing of fowls. The stealing of cacao has lately become a most common offence. The marauder stealthily comes during the night with his bag, approaches the pile of fruits which has been made the day previous in the cacao walk, breaks the pods, and carries off his booty, which consists of the fresh beans, which, however, are marketable only after they have been cured and dried : this the depredator has seldom the opportunity to do, as he would run the risk of being detected. It is therefore admissible that he secures beforehand the connivance of some compeer who receives this cacao, and cures it for the market. He is, as a rule, a shopkeeper in the vicinity. Both have their profit in the transaction. All this is well known, but the difficulty is to trace the felony. I may as well mention that, in one of the cacao districts of the East, the cacao growers suffered this year from repeated depredations: fresh as well as cured cacao was audaciously stolen, either from the field or the curing houses. On enquiring, the people remained convinced that this was done by a band of marauders, who took their spoil to a man who himself is owner of a small cacao plantation: his average crop

x

is about 50 bags, and yet he ships nearly 100, some of which may have been purchased, the balance being stolen goods: but how to obtain a conviction, when you are asked, for instance, to identify the article as yours? As easy to identify cacao beans as to identify grains of corn or oats.

It is clear that, under such circumstances, some stringent and comprehensive measure ought to be adopted, and rigidly enforced, and some scheme devised for the more easy discovery of the offenders. The cacao planters are unanimous in recommending the adoption of the following plan as a remedy: all cacao dealers, especially the shopkeepers in the country and villages, should be bound to keep books in which they would enter the name of the vendor, the date of the purchase, the condition of the article when received, whether cured or uncured; the name, or designation of the property. This would afford the means, in case of need, to trace the origin of all cacao in stores. The matter is, at least worth the consideration of the legislature; agriculture is the mainstay, the foundation of our social fabric, and therefore calls for the fostering care and protection of the State. Mechanics' institutions are supported by the public for the instruction and improvement of artisans: apprenticeship laws are enforced for securing competent masons, carpenters, shoemakers, and other tradesmen: and why, in a country strictly agricultural, should not public establishments be formed with a view to teaching the elements of agricultural science, together with the art of husbandry? The tillage of the soil is generally regarded as the province of the ignorant. This is a prejudice, and one which must have an injurious reaction on the success of agricultural pursuits. To be well conducted, no operation, perhaps, requires more practical knowledge or greater proficiency, to be improved. This prejudice probably owes its origin to the following circumstance: the growth of plants is the result of the combined actions of natural agents and not of any mechanical appliances. If the intervention of man had not for effect to favour the action of those agents, then the ignorant, matter-of-fact ploughman would evidently be as good a husbandman as the well-informed and skilful agronomist, and of all occupations agriculture would be the simplest and easiest. But this is not the case : for agriculture consists in combining a series of operations, so as to obtain from a given quantity of land the largest possible return at the lowest possible cost. I would call planting the mere procedure of replacing by useful vegetables the natural growth of wild plants, the word planter expressing, in the case, pretty exactly the state of agriculture in these colonies. The sugar planter commonly possesses a certain amount of information : the provision grower is, in the majority of cases, an ignorant labourer; he cuts down the high wood or copse at a certain period, cleans the land by burning, and then plants the seed of his corn in holes made with the point of his cutlass or lays his manioc cuttings or plantain shoots in openings made by one or more strokes of the hoe. The provision ground is weeded once or twice, and in time, under God's providence, the crop arrives at maturity; if a good crop be obtained, he is considered skilful, if not, the fault is that of the weather or the land. And yet it is well known that an acre of indifferent land, properly and carefully cultivated will yield as much as 15,000 lbs. of yams, whilst the same extent of good soil slovenly planted and ill-managed, will yield perhaps but one-half of that quantity. Of this, however, the great majority of cultivators are not convinced, because, in their opinion, Nature is the sole agent of production ; and unless they have tangible proofs that care, skill and industry can effectually aid and second Nature in her operations, they will never give to the cultivation of their properties that attention and perseverance which are the instruments of success. Now, in case his land has been under cultivation for years, and has become exhausted, the provision grower gets but a miserable return : but he knows of only one method for restoring to his fields some of its former fertility, and even this for a short period only—to leave it fallow. Did he possess experience and theoretical knowledge, he could obtain from his land, by proper management, all sorts and successions of crops in greater or less abundance.

In agriculture, as in commerce, skill and industry are capital vested at a high rate of interest; but in agriculture as in commerce, none become skilful except by proper training. In both teaching is necessary ; and in both the result of teaching is too apparent to be denied. Exhausted land, judiciously treated, may give as good—nay, better—returns and larger profits than virgin soil thriftlessly laboured; whilst under injudicious management the richest soil may soon become impoverished. Any measure, therefore, that would tend to afford practical experience and theoretical knowledge must be beneficial. This object, in my opinion, will be obtained mostly, if not wholly, by the establishment of model farms or estates, whereon cultivation, not only of the staples, but of all the alimentary articles, would be conducted according to the most approved methods. It is more than probable that many who now hesitate to devote time and attention to the culture of provisions, or who consider such occupation as unremunerative, and therefore not worth the attempt, would gladly resort to the same if it were satisfactorily proved by authentic data that the raising of provisions is as profitable—perhaps more so—on a proportionately smaller scale than the cultivation of the grand staples. Any risks, at least, would be greatly lessened. I have no doubt that all the branches of our agricultural industry would benefit by the establishment of model farms.

We might, besides establishing model farms, found here at once an *Agronomic Station*. Such stations exist in Germany, in France, and elsewhere in Europe; they were founded mainly for the benefit of the best growers, who, in a great part owe to them their success and the supremacy they have obtained in the markets of the world. Our agronomic station ought to be connected with the Botanic Gardens, and should be organised on a plan somewhat different from the one adopted in Europe. It should be established for the advantage of the whole colony. Cane, cacao, coffee and spices should be experimentally cultivated; also rice, tobacco, and sesamum. We can fortunately dispose of part of the St. Clair estate, recently bought by the Government; the portion on the north, along the river Maraval, might be set apart, and turned into an experimental farm. It would be within proximity of the town; and the prisoners, especially the juvenile offenders, might be employed for all cultural purposes. The cultivation of the best varieties of the sugarcane might be experimented there with different manures, after the soil had been carefully analysed. When ripe, the canes should be analysed, with a view to ascertaining the proportion of sugar, albuminous matter and salts in reference to the manure supplied. The best varieties of cacao and coffee should also be cultivated, and different manures tested. A fair trial should be given to the cultivation of tobacco and rice. We import annually 462,000 lbs. of tobacco, worth £12,600 sterling; and 15,900,000 lbs. of rice, worth £132,550 sterling. Nobody has yet made a decisive attempt at the growth of these two articles— no doubt because the attention of the people has not been directed to them; nor are there sufficient data by which their efforts can be guided.

I will only remark that Creole rice, as an article of food, is preferred—except, however, by the Coolies, who give precedence to their own grain. If the quality depend upon the variety cultivated, how easily can seeds be imported from India; if from the method followed in its preparation, how easily again can we adopt the method. The cultivation of tobacco has not yet been made an object of speculation, simply because, as I fear, its preparation or curing requires a certain degree of practical knowledge in which we are wanting. We should encourage, as they have done in Jamaica, the importation of skilful labourers in that branch, by assisting the immigration here of some hands from Cuba. The agronomic station should be placed under the direction of the Government botanist, assisted by the professor of chemistry.

To the agricultural establishment of Hoffwil, formed and conducted for a number of years by that distinguished philanthropist, the late Mr. De Fellenberg, Switzerland owes its progress in the art of husbandry. To the model farms of Roville and Grignon, France is greatly indebted for the advance she has lately made, and the position she now occupies as an agricultural country. I have known young gentlemen of rank, fortune and education, spending months at Roville, under the tuition of Mr. Mathieu de Dombasle, in order to acquire sound information on agricultural chemistry, and a practical knowledge of farming operations, which they afterwards successfully applied in the conduct of their own properties. Our model estates might be based on a plan submitted by me to His Excellency Lord Harris, in the year 1849, and the details of which are exposed in the Appendix.

The tillage of the soil ought to receive the larger share of encouragement. To this subject I cannot too often return; for, excepting the cultivation of the sugar-cane, all other growths are neglected. And yet upon the success of agricultural pursuits depends the prosperity of all classes—not of the hired labourer only, but of the artisan, of professional men, and of the mercantile body. Their profits must be in proportion with those of the cultivators of the soil. Encouragements given to the growths of provisions and minor staples would tend to retain in the colony a large amount of specie. Under present circumstances we must encourage the production of articles other than sugar, inasmuch as, if we direct all our energy to the production of one, or even two, articles, and they should become valueless, the whole community must participate in the ruin of the planters.

I may add besides, in the words of Lord Harris, that "Inattention to raising provisions is an evil of serious import, operating unfavourably against reduced cost of production, by rendering the labourers totally dependent upon high money-wages to pay for imported articles of consumption." Again, the provision grower, the small proprietor, must of necessity become a fixture in the island, there accumulating his savings and concentrating his affections. Such a class will consist of those already possessed of a small capital, those who emigrate to the island at their own expense, and, finally, of imported immigrants, who may have made money by persevering industry, or obtain grants in lieu of return passage.

The geographical position of Trinidad and its natural resources are, as I have elsewhere observed, surpassed only by those of Cuba. Trinidad is a new country, laid open to successful enterprise. Squatting has been rooted out of the land. Crown land is offered for sale at a reasonable price, even in small parcels; our means of communication are being steadily and energetically developed; paid immigration is encouraged, and the colony is open to voluntary immigrants; education, both primary and secondary, is placed within reach of the people; we have perfect freedom of religion. Let us now have agricultural reformatories and model farms; let us have a *modicum* of representative government, at least in matters of taxation, and we may then look with some confidence to the future.

CHAPTER XI.

NATURAL HISTORY—ZOOLOGY—BOTANY.

MAMMALIA.

TRINIDAD fully realises what has been said of tropical regions in general; organic life is there at its *summum*, and some specimen of existence is everywhere to be found. Not only is the surface of the ground covered with some plant or other—here shrubs, there gigantic trees; here grasses, there lianes—but in every pool, in the running stream, some alga is to be picked: the trunks and branches of trees not only support lichens and mosses, but also bromelias, epidendrons, ferns, and caladiums. Under the bark of living and decaying trees, in the calices of flowers, on the stems and leaves, are to be observed hosts of insects; they are met with again at the surface of the soil, and on turning up the vegetable *débris* which contribute to form its rich superstratum of mould, hundreds of the Entomological tribes are discovered. In the copses and the recesses of forests, quadrupeds—above in the dense foliage, birds—representatives of nearly all the genera of their classes, are to be found: reptiles are to be seen coiled up, or motionless on the watch, or stealthily gliding away. Not only do our rivers, lagoons, ponds, and pools swarm with fish, alligators, snakes, batrachians, and even chelonians, but they also afford a receptacle for myriads of the larvæ of mosquitoes and libellulæ, as well as of other insects and tadpoles. In the atmosphere, and buzzing around, are heard coleoptera, hemiptera, hymenoptera, and diptera, whilst beautiful lepidoptera are everywhere in quest of flowers wherein to plunge their long spring-like suckers, and arachnidans in constant ambush within their subtle webworks.

Evidently it would require many years of the lives of several individuals to give an accurate and complete description of the numerous and various creations which thus animate our island; nor can I have the presumption or pretension to offer within the following narrow compass, other than an imperfect summary of our Fauna and Flora. I only wish to show how rich is this small spot in objects of Natural History, and how much allied, in this respect, to the neighbouring continent.

VERTEBRATA.

CLASS I.

Within the limits of Trinidad are to be found the following mammifers, or MAMMALIA:—

ORDER II.—QUADRUMANA.

Howling-monkey,
  Singe-rouge *Mycetes*. 1 species.
              Mycetes Barbatus.
Sapajou or Grey-
  monkey, Singe-
  blanc . . . . *Cebus*. 1 species.

ORDER III.—CARNARIA.

Bats . . *Cheiroptera*. 4 genera.
        Molossi
        Noctilions.
            Noctilio leporinus.
        Phyllostoma.
        Mormops.
Carnivora *Plantigrada*.
Racoon, or
  Mangrove-
  dog . . . *Procyon*.
          Procyon cancrivorus.
Glutton . . *Gulo*.
Gato-Melao,
  or Taïra . *Mustela Barbara*.
Chien-bois, or
  wood dog . *Viverra vittata*. (?)
      Digitigrada.
Otter, or
  Loutre . *Lutra*.
          Lutra insularis.
Cat . . . *Felis*.
Tiger-cat, or
  Chat-tigre. *Felis Pardalis*.

ORDER IV.—MARSUPIALIA.

Opossums or
  Manicous . *Didelphys*. 3 species.
        Didelphys Opossum.
          „   *Cayopollin*.

ORDER V.—RODENTIA.

Squirrel . *Sciurus*. 1 species.
Rat . . . *Mus*.
      Echymys. 2 species.
        Echymys chrysuros.
          „ *rufus*. (?)
Rats, properly
  so-called . *Mus*. Several species.
Porcupine . *Synetheres*.
Porcupine, or
  Coendou. *Synetheres prehensiles*.
Agouti . . *Chloromys*.
      Chloromys Acuti.
Lape, or lapa *Coelogenys*.
      Cavia Paca.

ORDER VI.—EDENTATA.

Armadillo or
  Tatou . *Dasypus*.
Cachicame . *Cachicamus novem-
       cinctus*.
      „ *septemcinctus*.
Ant-eater . *Myrmecophaga*.
Great Ant-
  eater, or
  Sloth . . *Myrmecophaga tri-
       dactyla*.
Small Ant-
  eater, or
  Sloth . .   „ *didactyla*.

ORDER VII.—PACHYDERMATA.
Cuenco, or
  Pecari . *Dicotyles*.
Collared Cu-
  enco . . *Dicotyles Torquatus*.
Red Cuenco   „   *Labiatus*.
ORDER VIII.—RUMINANTIA.
Deer or Biche *Cervus*.
        Cervus simplicicornis,
        or *Guazoupita*.

ORDER IX.—CETACEA.
HERBIVORA.
Manati, or La-
  mantin . . *Trichecus Manatus*.

CARNIVORA.
        Balænoptera.
Whale, or
Balcine. *Balæna Boops*.

These are the mammifers which are known to exist in Trinidad. Of several of them there are varieties: for instance, two agoutis, distinguishable by their colour, one being much darker than the other, and perhaps smaller in size; two lapas, likewise differing in colour, one being fawn, and the other brown coloured; the former also with whitish feet, and of a larger size. There are, again, two varieties or even species of the guazoupita, one larger, of a darker colour, with antlers covered with a soft skin, and having habits somewhat dissimilar from those of the more common kind; it is apparently more solitary, and when chased by dogs, starts off at once in a straightforward direction: albinos are not rare among the guazoupitas.

The habits, aliments, and resorts of these mammifers are varied. The opossum, agouti, and deer seem to prefer the neighbourhood of plantations, where they find an abundance of food—viz., the opossum, fruits and fowls; the agouti, fruits and roots; and the deer, maize, peas, manioc, &c. In the same localities squirrels, lapas, and tatous are met with; the squirrel chiefly infesting cacao plantations, in which it sometimes commits great ravages. The pecari is always found in the high forests, where it feeds upon roots, fruits, and leaves, and even upon snakes and reptiles. The tiger-cat, taīra, great and small ant-eaters, and the tatou, also haunt the high woods—the latter preferring, generally, low and soft ground, where it can grub in search of worms, which form its principal food. The racoon does not venture out of the mangrove swamps, where it finds an inexhaustible supply of crabs. The otter is found in ravines, where it can easily seize the fish upon which it preys. Both the howling and weeping monkeys shun the presence of man; the latter may be said to abound principally in the south-eastern part of the island, whilst the former is often heard in Cimaronero, and the northern mountains at Carenage and Diego-Martin. The echymys is met in the vicinity of cacao plantations and provision grounds. The whale frequents the Gulf from January to May, and, as far as I am aware, the manati has been seen only in the Guataro, which it ascends for a certain distance in search of food.

The agouti, pecari, racoon, and monkeys, are accustomed to seek their sustenance during the day, and particularly in the morning and towards evening. The deer, lapa, cachicame, tiger-cat, and great ant-eater, roam about during the night, leaving their recesses or the woods about one or two hours after sunset. Similarly timed is the opossum, and particularly on fine moonlights, which afford the best opportunities for taking them, as several may be surprised on some fruit-tree, and their retreat being cut off they are easily shot. From six in the evening, to eight and ten at night, are also very favourable hours for *watching* the deer in their feeding grounds.

Nearly all these animals produce but one at a birth—viz., monkeys, the deer, lapa, and pecari: the agouti in general brings forth two; the cachicame, from four to five; and the opossum, from five to seven. The monkeys and opossum carry their offspring about; and should the mother be killed, the young continue to cling to the parent corpse, and are thus easily captured. Like other ruminantia, the deer conceals its fawn in some thicket, but runs to its succour when called upon by its distressed bleating; and though ordinarily proverbial for timidity, it has been known, in some cases, to give battle to the aggressor. It is particularly attached to its male offspring.

The agouti and lapa are easily tamed; they, however, always retain something of their natural wild dispositions, particularly the latter, which remains concealed in some corner of the house during the day, and only ventures out after sunset; they are never very pleasant guests, as they gnaw everything which comes within their reach, such as furniture, wainscoting, &c. The deer, pecari, and mangrove dog, particularly the two latter, are easily domesticated, and become as tractable as dogs. Although perfectly docile, however, and even much attached to its master and the household, the pecari rushes fiercely on strangers, and is, in fact, an admirable watch. The racoon becomes so familiar as to be troublesome from its caresses. The deer is likewise an annoying favourite, as, besides destroying garden-plants, it nibbles books, cloth, &c. I know an instance of a female deer, which grew so tame, that it was allowed to roam at large about the neighbouring plantations, and became large with young; it was unfortunately shot one night, and, being dangerously wounded, ran to its mistress as for aid and protection; but it died a few days after, bitterly regretted by the young lady, who had taken great pains in rearing it. The squirrel can be easily tamed also, but it will carry off anything it can lay hold of to some hiding-place, and on one occasion the first part of the "Gazza ladra" was realised in a respectable house in the colony. A servant had been severely reprimanded on account of some missing plate, and even her reputation for honesty called in question; the articles were, however, found a few months after, in some holes, where a squirrel had concealed them.

The deer, agouti, pecari, lapa, and cachicame, the two latter particularly, are very fine game. The flesh of the deer is rather dry, except, however, when the animal is young and fat, particularly the doe. The agouti may be said to be flavourless, and never fat. The pecari, when young and fat, is an excellent dish, as is also the cachicame: the manati is excellent eating, either salted or fresh.

As it is difficult to preserve meat for any length of time in our climate, those who make hunting an occupation adopt the following plan. The bones of the animal are disjointed, the flesh deeply incised, and sprinkled with salt; the flesh is next laid on a *boucan*—a sort of stage made of green sticks, resting on four posts about three feet above the ground; a slow fire is then kindled beneath, and the carcase thoroughly smoked; the flesh thus prepared is dry, tough, and unsavoury; though that of the lapa and cuenco are, in this state, sold at high rates. The taste is not very unlike that of hung beef.

Tatous and lapas are taken in traps, the latter more frequently, as they generally follow the same beaten track to get at their food. This track once discovered, a falling trap, composed of heavy logs, is carefully disposed along the passage, and rarely fails to crush or retain the animal. Another very dangerous method is the following: a gun is *set*—as it is said—by being fixed on a couple of rests, and a twine attached to the trigger, also connected with a bait at the muzzle, commonly an ear of maize; when the lapa, or any other animal, attempts to gnaw or disengage the corn, it necessarily pulls the trigger, and generally receives the contents in the head. Not a year passes during which some person is not dangerously wounded, and sometimes killed, from the setting of such unlawful snares. The most common method, however, is the chase, in which the best dogs for tatous and lapas are the pointer, the terrier, and our common breed, some of which are capital hunters, especially those crossed with the *Guarauno* races. I have no doubt, however, that the basset would prove superior. Whenever the lapa has a long run to its retreat, or, more generally to the river, whither it invariably resorts for safety, it may be caught by fleet dogs; otherwise it is killed in its own fastness, which is commonly a hollow tree, or a cave in the midst of a labyrinth of roots, or under the bank of some stream—the two latter with several outlets. The tatou is always killed in its burrow, and it is necessary to dig or smoke it out when there is too great a difficulty in reaching it. The agouti is either shot, when pursued by dogs, or on the watch; sometimes also in its retreat—almost invariably the hollows of the decayed interior of some fallen timber, or beneath the roots of trees.

The chase of the pecari resembles, on a small scale, that of the wild boar in Europe. When in numbers, the pecaris not only show fight to the dogs, but sometimes give them chase, should the latter be few and of small size; several of these animals may be shot, when met in a *band*; but they are generally killed with the spear or cutlass when at bay, seldom with the fowling-piece. The most pleasant sport, however, is deer-hunting, for which the best dogs are unquestionably hounds. The deer behaves, when chased, exactly like the roebuck: after an hour or more of chase, it returns, by a circuit, to the very spot whence it was started, and then makes a dart in a straight line. If within the proximity of a river, it crosses the stream several times; or, if shallow, walks down the bed, probably with a view, by checking the scent, to set the hounds at fault, or to divert the pursuer from the track; if on the sea-board, it generally seeks refuge in the water, and sometimes swims out for more than a mile; it is nevertheless easily caught, if a canoe be at hand, as in that element it is slow in its movements; or it may be turned, and again compelled to seek the land. The deer is also very commonly shot on the watch, particularly during the full moon; and this method is preferred by the peons, as they find the chase of this animal very trying to their dogs. The manati is, in a like manner, shot whilst at graze: but if only wounded, it rushes to the water, and thus escapes; it is sometimes watched at the mouth of the Guataro and speared with the harpoon.

BIRDS.

AN ESSAY ON THE ORNITHOLOGY OF TRINIDAD,

By Antoine Leotaud, M.D.P.

THE study of the birds of Trinidad is far from being devoid of interest. The number of genera to be found in the island is sufficiently large to render the correct determination of species a service to ornithological science. Respecting nearly 300 species which have fallen under my observation, there are errors to correct, and facts to record, such as to constitute these researches a matter of no idle curiosity.

We lie so contiguous to the southern continent, that our ornithology must necessarily differ from that of the other West India islands. This is a point of geographical distribution which has its importance, both as regards the science in general, and in questions of pure locality. So luxuriant and varied is our vegetation, so extensive our forests, so numerous our insects, and the disposition of the country is itself so far from being uniform, that the vastness of our ornithological treasures cannot form a matter of surprise; and should I but enumerate the species, that alone would be to register facts which, at a remote period, may acquire an immense local interest. Our vegetation will change, our soil become impoverished, our forests will diminish in extent, as they yield to the axe; our marshes will disappear, and our insects cease to swarm in such numbers as at present, and, as a consequence, the ornithology of the island will then present in its aspect a change which is even already perceptible.

But this is a range which I am far from proposing to bring within the limits I have prescribed to myself. I must, therefore, confine my remarks to a few general considerations and some restricted details.

Taking Cuvier as a guide, the following are the genera and sub-genera I have observed here:—

Raptorial or birds of prey.
- Diurnal.
  - Noble.
    - FALCONIDÆ.
      - Falcons (properly so-called). Two species. *Falco Bidentatus.*
      - Goshawk-Eagle (*Morphnus*). One species. *Spizaetos Ornatus.*
      - Cymindis . . . . Two species.
      - Goshawks (*Astur*) . . . . Five species. *Astur Plumbea. Falco Melanops.*
      - Kite (*Milvus*) . . . . . One species. *Falco Furcatus.* (a)
  - Ignoble.
    - VULTURIDÆ . . . . . Three species. *Vultur Papa.* (b) *Vultur Urubu.* (c) *Vultur Catus.*
- Nocturnal.
  - STRIGIDÆ: Owls (*Strix*) . One species. (d)
  - Sparrow-owls (*Scops*) . . Three species. *Strix Nudipes.* (e)

Passeres. Dentirostres.
- SHRIKES (*Lanius*)
  - Shrike (properly so-called) . . . Many species. *Thamnophilus Major. Thamnophilus Doliatus.* (f)
  - Becarde (*Psaris*) . . . . One species. *Lanius Cajanus.*
- FLY-CTCHERS (*Muscicapa*).
  - Tyrants (*Tyrannus*) . . . . . Several species. *Lanius Pitanga.* (g) *Tyrannus Ferox.* (h) *Tyrannus Solitarius.* (i) *Tyrannus Savanna.* (j)
  - Fly-catchers (*Muscicapa*). . . . Several species. *Muscicapa Ruticilla.* (k)
  - Platyrhyncos . . . . One species. *Platyrhyncus Cancromus.*
  - Muscicapida . . . . Several species.
  - Tersine (*Tersina*) . . . . . . One species. *Tersina Cœrulea.* (l)

(a) Excepting a kite and a sparrow-hawk, known here respectively as the scissors-tail and the Gri-gri, all our falcons bear the name of Gavilans, viz., the speckled, the white, the black Gavilan, &c.
(b) The King of the Corbeaux.
(c) Common Corbeaux; one with a red head is called the Governor of the Corbeaux.
(d) Cent-coups de couteau.
(e) A large owl inhabiting churches and other large solitary buildings.
(f) Wood-Pintade, or Carate-bird.
(g) Qu'est-ce-qui-dit.
(h) Pipiri.
(i) Id.
(j) Longue-queue, or long-tail.
(k) Officer.   (l) Cutinga.

		Procnias	One species.
			Ampelis Carunculata. (a)
		Averano (*Casmarhynchos*). . .	One species.
			Ampelis Variegata. (b)
		TANAGERS (*Tanagra*).	
		Tanagers euphonious.	
			Tanagra Violacea. (c)
		Tanagers (properly so-called).	
			Tanagra Mexicana. (d)
		Cardinal Tanagers.	
			Tanagra Gyrola. (e)
	Dentirostres.	Rhamphoceline Tanagers . . .	Many species.
			Tanagra Nigerrima. (f)
			Tanagra Rubra. (g)
			Tanagra Episcopus. (h)
			Tanagra Jacapa. (i)
		BLACKBIRDS or **MERLES** (*Turdus*).	
		Blackbirds (properly)	Four species.
			Turdus Flavipes. (j)
		Ant-catchers (*Myothera*) . . .	Two species.
		WARBLERS.	
Passeres.		Fauvettes (*Curruca*)	Several species.
			Sylvia Æ-tiva. (k)
			Sylvia Torquata. (l)
		Wrens (*Troglodytes*)	Two species.
			Troglodytes Eudon. (m)
			Troglodytes Rutilus. (n)
		Titlarks (*Anthus*)	One species.
		Manakins (*Pipra*)	Two species.
			Pipra Gutturalis. (o)
			Pipra Erythrocephala. (p)
		Swallows and Martins (*Hirundo*)	Several species.
	Fissirostres.	Goat-suckers (*Caprimulgus*) . .	Four species.
			Caprimulgus Caripensis. (q)
		Grosbeaks (*Coccothraustes*) . .	Several species.
			Coccothraustes Rufiventris. (r)
			Loxia Minuta. (r)
			Loxia Jacarini. (s)

(a) Capucin.
(b) Campanero.
(c) Louis-d'or.
(d) Diable-enrhumé.
(e) Vert-vert tête cacao, or brown-headed.
(f) Père-noir, or black father.
(g) Cardinal.
(h) Oiseau bleu, or blue bird.
(i) Bec-d'argent, or silver-bill.
(j) Black thrush; the other species being also known by the name of thrush
(k) Canary, or serin.
(l) Mountain sucrier.
(m) Rossignol, or nightingale.
(n) Bush nightingale.
(o) Casse-noisette.
(p) Manakin-à-tête-jaune, or yellow-headed.
(q) Guacharro, or diablotin
(r) Cicis.   (s) Sauteur, or jumper.

TRINIDAD.

Passeres.
- Conirostres.
  - Bullfinch (*Pyrrhula*) .... One species.
  - Cassicans (*Cassicus*) ..... Three species.
    - *Cassicus Cristatus*. (a)
    - *Cassicus Icteronotus*. (b)
    - *Cassicus Ater*. (c)
  - Carouges (*Icterus*) ..... Three species.
    - *Oriolus Xanthornus*. (d)
    - *Oriolus Icterocephalus*. (e)
  - Starling (*Sturnus*) ..... One species.
    - *Oriolus Ruber*.
  - Nuthatches (*Sitta*) ..... One species.
    - *Neops Ruficauda*.
  - Anabates .... Several species.
  - Sinallaxis .... One species.
    - *Sinallaxis Ruficapilla*.
- Tenuirostres.
  - Picucule (*Dondrocolaptes*) .. Four species. (f)
  - Creepers (*Certhia*) ..... Several species (remarkable for their brilliant colours).
    - *Certhia Cyanea*. (g)
    - *Certhia Cœrulea*. (h)
    - *Certhia Atricapilla*. (i)
  - COLIBRIS and HUMMING-BIRDS   Eighteen species (some of them with the most dazzling plumage).
  - Colibris (*Trochilus*).
  - Humming-birds (*Orthorhynchus*).
    - *Trochilus Superciliosus*. (j)
    - *Trochilus Pectoralis*. (k)
    - *Trochilus Viridis*. (l)
    - *Trochilus Hirsutus* (m)
    - *Trochilus Mango*. (n)
    - *Trochilus Leucogaster*.
    - *Trochilus Ornatus*. (o)
    - *Trochilus Mellivorus*. (p)
    - *Trochilus Longirostris*. (q)
    - *Trochilus Moschitus*. (r)
    - *Trochilus Bicolor*. (s)
    - *Trochilus Amethystinus*. (t)

(a) Merle-à-queue-jaune, or yellow-tailed corn-bird.
(b) Merle moqueur, or mocking merle.
(c) Merle cavalier, or black corn-bird.
(d) Cassique.
(e) Merle-à-tête-jaune, or yellow-headed merle.
(f) Mangeur de cacao, or cacao-eater.
(g) Grimpereau pieds-rose, or pink-footed grimpereau.
(h) Vert-de-gris.
(i) Vert-vert-à-tête-noire, or black-headed vert-vert.
(j) Supercilious humming-bird, or brin-blanc.
(k) Hausse-colvert, or green humming-bird.
(l) Vert-pré.
(m) Colibri balisiers, or hirsute humming-bird.
(n) Plastron, or mango.
(o) Huppe-col, or tufted-necked.
(p) Jacobine.
(q) Carmine.
(r) Rubis-topaze, or ruby-crested.
(s) Sapphire-emerald.   (t) Amethystine.

ORNITHOLOGY. 369

<table>
<tr><td rowspan="11">Passeres.
Syndactyles.</td><td>Mot-Mot (Prionites) . . . . .</td><td>One species.
Prionites Brasiliensis. (a)</td></tr>
<tr><td>King-Fishers (Alcedo) . . . .</td><td>Two species.
Alcedo Alcyon.
Alcedo Americana.</td></tr>
<tr><td>Jacamars (Galbula) . . . . .</td><td>One species.
Galbula Paradisea. (b)</td></tr>
<tr><td>Wood-Peckers (Picus) . . . .</td><td>Five species.</td></tr>
<tr><td>Cuckoos (Cuculus) . . . . .</td><td>Four species.
Cuculus Cayanensis. (c)
Cuculus Cayanus. (d)
Cuculus Naevius. (e)</td></tr>
<tr><td>Couroucoui (Trogon) . . . .</td><td>Three species.
Trogon Viridis. (f)
Trogon Collaris. (g)</td></tr>
<tr><td>Anis (Crotophaga) . . . . .</td><td>Two species.
Crotophaga Major.
Crotophaga Ani. (h)</td></tr>
<tr><td>Toucan (Ramphastus) . . . .</td><td>One species.</td></tr>
<tr><td>Maccaws (Aras) . . . . . .</td><td>Two species. (i)</td></tr>
<tr><td>Parrots (Psittacus) . . . . .</td><td>Two species.</td></tr>
<tr><td>Paroquets (Cornurus) . . . .</td><td>Two species. (j)</td></tr>
</table>

<table>
<tr><td rowspan="3">Gallinaceans.</td><td>Yacou (Penelope) . . . . . .</td><td>One species.
Penelope Pipile. (k)</td></tr>
<tr><td>Tinamoo (Tinamus) . . . . .</td><td>One species. (l)</td></tr>
<tr><td>Pigeons (Columba) . . . . .</td><td>Ten species.
Columba Speciosa. (m)
Columba Cinerea. (n)</td></tr>
</table>

Grallatoriæ.
<table>
<tr><td rowspan="2">Pressirostres.</td><td>Plovers (Charadrius) . . . .</td><td>Two species.
Charadrius Pluvialis (o)
Charadrius Hiaticula. (p)</td></tr>
<tr><td>Savacoo (Cancroma) . . . .</td><td>One species.
Cancroma Cochlearia. (q)</td></tr>
</table>

<table>
<tr><td>Cultrirostres.</td><td>Courlan (Ardea) . . . . . .</td><td>One species.
Ardea Scolopacea. (r)</td></tr>
</table>

(a) Voutou.
(b) Jacamar.
(c) Petit coucou manioc, or small manioc cuckoo.
(d) Grand coucou manioc.
(e) Trinité, from its note.
(f) Couroucou ventre-jaune, or yellow-bellied cuckoo.
(g) Couroucou ventre-rose, or pink-bellied cuckoo.
(h) Merle corbeau, or tick-bird.
(i) Blue maccaw and red maccaw.
(j) Blue-headed paroquet and perruche-aux-sept-couleurs, or the seven-coloured paroquet.
(k) Pajui, sometimes called the *wild turkey.*
(l) Quail.
(m) Ramier ginga, or speckled ramier.
(n) Ortolan bleu. Our pigeons are divided here into ramiers (2 spec.); doves, or wood-pigeons (5 spec.); and ortolans, or ground-doves (3 spec.).
(o) Golden plover.   (p) Ring plover.   (q) Boat-bill.   (r) Croja.

Y

		Herons (*Ardea*)	Nine species. *Ardea Major.* (a) *Ardea Egretta.* (b) *Ardea Garzetta.* (c) *Ardea Leucogaster* (d) *Ardea Tigrina.* *Ardea Lineata.* (e) *Ardea Nycticorax.* *Ardea Sexcetacea* (f) *Ardea Agami.* (g)
Grallatoriæ.	Cultrirostres.	Wood-Pelican (*Tantalus*) . . .	One species. *Tantalus Loculator.* (h)
		Spoonbill (*Platalea*)	One species. *Platalea Ajaja.* (i)
	Longirostres.	Ibis (*Ibis*)	One species. *Scolopax Rubra.* (j)
		Curlews (*Numenius*) . . .	Two species. *Scolopax Armata.* (k) *Scolopax Phæcopus.* (l)
		Snipe (*Scolopax*)	One species. *Scolopax Gallinago* (m)
		Godwit (*Limosa*)	One species.
		Sandpipers (*Calidris*)	Five species.
		Sanderling (*Arenaria*)	One species. *Charadrius Calidris.*
		Turnstones	Two species. *Tringa Interpres.* (n)
		Chevaliers (*Totanus*) . . .	Six species. *Totanus semi-palmatus.* (o)
		Grallus	One species. *Hemantopus Charadrius.*
Palmipedes.	Macrodactyles.	Jacana (*Jacana*)	One species. *Parra Jacana.* (p)
		Kamichi (*Palamedea*)	One species.
		Rails (*Rallus*)	Eight species. *Rallus Longirostris.* (q) *Rallus Stolidus.* (r)
	Divers.	Water-hens (*Fulica*)	Two species. *Gallinula Chloropus.* (s) *Porphyrio Tavoua.* (s)
		Grebe (*Podiceps*)	One species. *Podiceps Carolinensis.*

(a) Aileronne. (b) Garce. (c) Tufted egret. (d) Blue egret.
(e) Crabier de montagne, or mountain crab-eater.
(f) Crescent crab-eater.
(g) Agami.
(h) Soldat, or soldier.
(i) Roseate spatula.
(j) Flamant, or flamingo.
(k) Crooked-bill.
(l) Bécard.
(m) This snipe is identical with that of Europe.
(n) Sea plover.
(o) Aile-blanche, or white-wing.
(p) Surgeon.
(q) Poule-de-bois, or wood-hen.
(r) Several species, called here poules savanne, or savannah hens.
(s) Seal water-hens.

Palmipedæ	Totipalmatæ / Longipennes	Coot (*Podoa*)	One species.
		Sea-swallows (*Sterna*)	Three species.
		Scissor-bill (*Rhynchops*) . . .	One species. *Rhynchops Nigra*. (a)
		Pelicans (*Pelecanus*)	One species.
		Cormorant (*Halieus*)	One species. *Halieus Carbo*.
		Man-of-war-bird (*Tachypetes*) .	One species. *Pelecanus Aquilus*.
		Booby (*Sula*)	One species. *Pelecanus Sula*.
		Darter (*Plotus*)	One species. *Plotus Anhinga*.
	Lamellirostres	Ducks (*Anas*)	Ten species. *Anas Clypeata*. (b) *Anas Americana* (c) *Anas Marila*. (d) *Anas Dominica*. (e) *Anas Moschata*. (f) *Anas Autumnalis*. (g) *Anas Viduata* (h) *Anas Discors*. (i)

(a) Bec-en-ciseaux, or scissors-bill.
(b) Shoveller, the same as in Europe.
(c) Jensen.
(d) Millouin.
(e) Vingeon.
(f) Musk-duck, but commonly and erroneously termed Muscovy-duck.
(g) White-winged ouikiki, or vicissi.
(h) Ouikiki bouriqui.
(i) Crescent-teal.

In glancing over this catalogue, it will be observed that the raptorial order is largely represented, in proportion to the extent of the island; for, not only is the number of species not inconsiderable, but one of them, the *Spizaetus Ornatus*, is of a pretty large size: the fact of their number is undoubtedly a consequence of the facility afforded these birds in the procuring of food. They prey upon the smaller species which abound in the island, and feed upon their young or their eggs. Bats, which are far from being scarce, supply food to one of our falcons, and a few species feed upon reptiles and our largest insects: the black-backed goshawk is constantly on the watch, along the sea-shore and the banks of rivers, ready to seize upon the fish which form its main aliment.

The insectivorous tribes, however, are the true representatives of our ornithology, as regards number. There are so many species which feed upon insects and their larvæ, that it may be asked, with much reason, what would become of our vegetation, of ourselves, should these insect-destroyers disappear? Everywhere may be perceived one or other of these insectivora in pursuit or seizure of its prey, either on the wing, or on the trunks of trees; in the coverts of thickets, or in the calices of flowers. Whenever called to witness one of the frequent migrations from one point to another so often practised by ants, not only can the *Dendrocolaptes* be seen following the moving trail, and preying on the eggs and the ants themselves, but even the *Tanagra Nigerrima* abandons his usual fruits for this more tempting delicacy. Our frugivorous and baccivorous genera are also pretty numerous, and most of them are so fond of insect food, that they unite, as occasion offers, with the insectivorous tribes.

Marsh birds (*Grallatoriæ*) are remarkable, not only for their number, but also for their large size; the kamichi is the size of a turkey; the heron (*Ardea Americana*) stands more than four feet when erect; the great egret (*Ardea major*) is as tall, and the tantal, of the same height, is larger in body.

As to the granivora, the number of species is scarce; and it cannot be otherwise, when the nature of our vegetation is taken into consideration.

We have eighteen species of humming-birds; and this large variety of these charming creatures which draw from the calices of flowers the honey-dew which affords their sustenance, proves that the country is not altogether destitute of flowers. They also share in the prey of the insectivora, and whilst sucking their nectareous aliment, they swallow together with it the small insects that have been entangled in the viscous liquor which, by agglutinating their wings, has rendered their escape impossible. It is scarcely probable that these insects are found accidentally in the digestive tube of humming-birds, as those have thought who would have their sole food to consist of the juice of flowers: on the contrary, they would appear to constitute the essential part of their alimentary diet. On opening the crop of a humming-bird, one is struck with the large quantity of small flies which it contains; they are met with also, and in as great a number, in the stomach of the nestlings that are wholly fed by the parent bird. Besides, are there really in the juice of flowers all the organic and inorganic elements which are indispensable in restoring the losses of organism? Doubtless the insects must contain those elements as a supply for the bird. The juice of flowers would then be a purely respiratory aliment; and there is no ground for wonder at the large consumption of this aliment by the humming-bird; for it spends in some measure the greatest portion of its existence in the open atmosphere. Almost ever on the wing, and moving with that quick motion which renders it almost invisible, it repairs from flower to flower; and whilst apparently most stationary during the suction of its food, the motion is in reality the most excessively rapid. Such short incessant strokes of the wing on the air must necessarily cause a more rapid circulation of the blood, a more active respiration, and, as a consequence, must require a larger amount of materials suited to combustion.

It has been pretended that these birds hover about spiders' webs with a view to despoil them of the insects entangled therein. I have often witnessed humming-birds thus manœuvring, but never observed them seizing insects; they were only purloining a few threads wherewith to aid in the weaving of their nests.

On reflecting on the circumstances which thus regulate the alimentation of our birds, we are led to a first inference, viz., that this colony being still new, and subject therefore to the changes which time may produce, our ornithology will hereafter lose its present characteristics. Not only will the number of species diminish in proportion to the reduction of alimentary resources, but new species will perhaps be naturalised, as new cultures are introduced. A species of grosbeak seems already to have become one of our guests, since the cultivation of rice has been introduced.

A second consequence, arising from the preceding, is that many genera cannot of necessity observe any permanency as regards their *habitat*. Frugivorous and baccivorous are met with wherever fruits and berries may answer their requirements. Hence, one of the means employed by the sportsman for procuring certain species: knowing that, at such periods, and at such spots, certain trees will attract certain species, he resorts thither for the purpose of shooting them; of these trees are the *Gommier*, the haunt of ramiers, and the *Pois-doux* (*Inga*), of paroquets, &c.

The insectivorous tribes are likewise largely distributed; but as fruits and certain berries are rarely found but in the neighbourhood of inhabited places; as insects seem even to swarm in greater abundance in the skirtings of wood-lands, never will the chirpings and twitterings which announce the coming dawn be heard amidst the density of the forests. At all times there reigns in those solitudes a stillness which one would be far from expecting.

There is more, however, to be considered in this flitting life, on the one hand, and in this attachment to cultivations on the other, than the mere support of existence. Certain species, though frugivorous or baccivorous, are not met with except in very remote and wooded localities; they never approach our abodes. If some species seem to shun the solitude of the woodlands, and do not dread the neighbourhood of man, it is quite the reverse with others, though belonging to the same genus. The *Diable enrhumé* (*Tanagra Mexicana*), the *brown-headed Vert-Vert* (*Tanagra gyrola*) are met in the fruit and berry trees which grow near our clearings; whilst another tanager (*Arrivant*) flies to conceal its beautiful plumage in the depths of forests. One of our blackbirds enlivens our copses, whilst another (*Turdus flavipes*) seems to avoid our abodes.

The *Troglodytes eudon* is so much attached to the society of man, that it never deserts him, and it is even under his roof that it establishes its nest. Never does its note salute the ear of the wanderer in the forest. More than once, after a long jaunt, and thinking myself still near the starting point, I have been quite surprised at finding myself approaching the end of my journey—the song of a wren being a sure sign I was in the proximity of some inhabited place. And yet the other species is met with everywhere.

Certain flowers which are eagerly sought by some species of humming-birds are far from being scarce in those localities which suit their growth: and yet it is well known that, in order to procure these humming-birds, the naturalist must seek them in other and well-determined spots.

The black-headed *Urubu* is found in all parts, whilst the red-headed species is never seen in towns, but is met with only at a distance in the country. The former may be said to be mainly urban, and the latter rustic; still, their habits are the same; and if I can depend on information which has been furnished me, there are parts of the neighbouring continent, in the towns of which none but the red-headed urubu is to be seen. The former swarm in Port-of-Spain, and, from the tops of houses, they are constantly on the watch for the smallest prey which may fall in the streets; but never is there seen among them a red-headed urubu. Whenever, in the country, some dead animal attracts the vultures, both species assemble in a band, and seem to act on good terms.

The *habitat* of birds, therefore, is not determined by the alimentary substances which suit them : there are other secondary but indispensable conditions which escape observation.

Nidification.

The study of the constructive instinct in birds would undoubtedly afford much gratification to any one who might devote attention to the subject; but nothing is more difficult than an investigation of that which refers to this part of Ornithology. The luxuriance of our vegetation is such that, wherever forest-trees have yielded to brushwood and its accompanying variety of plants, the foliage forms a dense screen, impervious to the sight, and concealing within its recesses every possible object; in fact, it is by mere chance that even a close scrutiny can discover the fabrics which so many species repair thither to construct, and dispose with such artistic skill and care. Even when they are built on large trees, the foliage invariably shrouds them from the eye. There are, however, a few species, such as the *carouge* and the *cassique*, which seem to avoid those retreats, and, in preference, append their nests to the extremity of branches, and in the full glitter of the sunbeams. Many pairs of the above congregate at the season of laying, and make choice of the same tree. They give to their nests the shape of an elongated pear, or rather of a long pouch, the smaller end hanging from the branch by means of a few threads from the tissue of the nest itself. The entrance is lateral, and a little beneath the point of attachment; the whole being light and graceful, and recalling to the mind that admirable instinct of the feathered tribe, which we cannot but admire in such constructions. Nothing, however, equals the effect which the assemblage of those pendent nests produces, forming, as they do, to the tree another sort of covering, which is as agreeably striking as the foliage itself.

As to the humming-birds' nests, they are perfect miniatures; the frame-work is of dry grass-blades, bound together by spiders' threads; there is but little variation in their configuration—the minuteness of the fabric and the perfection of the workmanship alone calling for deserved admiration.

There is a bird—the *Sinallaxis ruficapilla*, only four inches long, that constructs a nest which, if differently shaped, might accommodate a lodger of twenty times its size. It is difficult to conceive how so small a creature can carry the twigs which serve in the construction, they being several lines in diameter; and what is still more striking, these twigs hold together by mere interweaving; no bond unites them, and yet they are twisted into a shape which reminds one of a gourd—there being left a lateral and upper opening, which is another marvel in this astonishing construction. The sinallaxis begins by the framework, and the framework alone constitutes the whole nest. What an amount of instinct must the bird develop in order to attain its object, particularly in laying down and fitting together the first pieces of its edifice!

Many nests, instead of being laid on the bifurcation of branches, are hung in a manner as light and as frail as the sword of Damocles. Undoubtedly this is a precaution taken with a view to protect the young against snakes, in the same manner as the nests buried in bushes and the dense foliage of trees escape the eye of the birds of prey. I do not, however, understand how birds can protect their nestlings against ants; for so large is the number of these insects in our climes, that it would seem as if everything must become their prey.

MIGRATION.

All our birds do not make a permanent stay in the island; and, as regards certain species, there are two very distinct annual migrations. When the wet season has fairly commenced, the following alight on our shores: sandpipers, knots, plovers, &c.; they are emigrants from South America. These birds swarm in the extensive *llanos*, or plains, which skirt the Orinoco; as soon as these become inundated, their inhabitants are compelled to depart elsewhere in search of food. Several species of ducks follow the example of those Grallatoriæ. After the rainy season is over, all return to the continent, save a few individuals which continue to frequent our marshes.

In November, other species appear. These are principally ducks, viz., the poachard, shoveller, jansen, &c., that seek a shelter against the cold of North America.

There are other species whose migrations cannot be accounted for in the same satisfactory manner. In July, the *Tyrannus savanna* arrives here from Venezuela, in immense flocks, and leaves us in October. These birds feed on insects only, and surely such a prey cannot be wanting on the continent. Similar is the case of the speckled ramier, which comes in and returns at the same periods; and yet the berries on which it feeds must also be abundant on the mainland.

GAME.

As an article of food, our birds exhibit one main characteristic —they are utterly deficient in *flavour*. The ramier, dove, quail, and parrot, which are occasionally served on our tables, do not in any way recall to one's mind the flavour of the partridge; and the amateur must forget that ordinary stimulant of appetite, in order to relish that *something* which makes a young parrot a delicious dish. The speckled ramier is much prized, and with good reason; and the ortolan is also very acceptable to the epicure : as far as these are concerned, however, we yield the palm to Europe, to claim it, notwithstanding, for our ducks. The individuals which come from South America particularly leave nothing more exquisite to be desired; those which migrate from North America are not all so excellent; such as they are, nevertheless, they are far superior to those of the old continent.

Among the smaller species, several have been remarked by connoisseurs : the *Tyrannus savanna* is a ball of fat, and a *brochette* of these small birds yields, in no one particular, to the *becafico* of Europe. Some of our merles, when feeding upon aromatic berries, possess a *goût* which is not inferior to the flavour in which they are deficient.

I ought not to pass unnoticed the guacharo (*Caprimulgus caripensis*). The young ones, which are literally a mass of fat, are highly praised and relished by amateurs. I have on several occasions partaken of them, but must candidly confess that, in consequence of a certain cockroachy flavour, which is the reverse of tempting, I have, for a long time, discarded that dish.

There is, however, in this island a bird which verifies the proverb, "All is good that is rare"—this is the yacou, or pajui. With all the good qualities of the pheasant, it possesses besides the advantage of being far more juicy; and any one who has once been treated to this truly *récherché* gallinacean, only regrets that it is not more plentiful. Thus, some species cause us to be unmindful of that in which they are all deficient, viz., *flavour*. Whatever be their defects, however, the main deficiency is that they are not prepared by some *Vatel;* for, when in Europe they praise the snipe, they really mean that they have good cooks.

NOTE AND SONG.

It is well known that song is the heritage of the birds of the north; whilst under our brazen sky, the beauty and richness of plumage replace the melodious notes of the nightingale. True, the ear is not greeted by notes warbled in simple trills, or in full-toned cadences: but the eye cannot be satiated with admiring those colours, the variety of which can alone vie with their vividness. The form itself seems to have been sacrificed, and Nature's efforts concentrated in painting the plumage of our birds with the prism's hues. None of them possess the slimness of the wagtail, the fairiness of the titmouse, or the grace of the fauvette; there is no charm in their movement, none in their flight: and nothing in them recalls to the mind the skylark hovering on high above its nest. Every gift has been lavished on their gorgeous attire, the brilliant plumes of which often add somewhat more of distinctiveness to our birds. The tufted humming-bird, besides the tuft, wears on each side of the head slender feathers, maculated at their extremity with spangles of the brightest emerald. The heron-agami can, at pleasure, erect its long neck so as to display those fine, long, and narrow blue feathers which, in their crescent-like layers, present an admirable *ensemble*. Even when we direct our attention to the birds inhabiting Asia, Africa, or Australia, and which unite singularity to their richness of plumage, we find that ours have something markedly distinctive, whenever a comparison is instituted between them and birds of metallic hue. Everywhere else there is some really metallic reflection of the plumage, whilst here there is nothing more dazzling than our ruby-crested humming-bird. On the one hand the metal, on the other the gem, reflects the light.

Let us acknowledge, nevertheless, that this luxuriousness does not speak to the imagination, does not reach the heart, does not move it. Our admiration is kept alive, but we yet commune with this world, which it is so sweet to forget in the forest recess whilst the ear imbibes the plaintive notes of the nightingale!

Our forests are not, however, altogether silent, nor our copses either. Often in the depth of our woods our attention is awakened by sounds which remind us of those of a bell. Hark! those two or three notes, loudly and several times repeated, are those of the averano, calling forth its mate from the summit of some tree towering to the clouds. The metallic tone, and the fulness of the bird's call, produce a complete illusion; it resembles the toll of a far-ringing bell; wherefore, the Spaniards have given it the name of *campanero*, or bell-ringer. It perches chiefly on trees which clothe the mountain sides, and the sounds of its voice, re-echoed by the adjoining mountains, so intermingle, that it becomes difficult to find out precisely the spot occupied by the bird itself. This, though a purely physical effect, the vulgar assign to the instinct of the averano, which thus modifies its note in order the better to conceal its retreat.

Here, as elsewhere, our doves pour forth their tender moan, thus rendering still more melancholy the stillness of our woods: one of them particularly, the partridge, imparts to its cooing the impress of sadness; it resembles the complaint of suffering humanity, so complete is the illusion.

The early morn is welcomed by the qu'est-ce-qui-dit (*Tyrannus pitanga*), whose song, or rather cry, though containing nothing of melody, yet rings in sounds of pleasantness around our dwellings. The cry is clear, and is answered by the voices of several others of these birds, which are the better heard, as they perch at the extremity of some branch. Sometimes the united notes become a regular uproar, though far from being unpleasant. We hear, without attending to them, the twittering of other smaller birds that also welcome the dawning light. But our attention is still attracted by the gay tumult of the qu'est-ce-qui-dit: there is a cheerfulness in their cry, and man is never more disposed to be cheerful than in the morning.

In the woods, curiosity alone will impel one to ascertain the cause of a singular noise, which can be ascribed to a bird only on sight; it is made by the *casse-noisette*, or nut-cracker (*Pipra gutturalis*). These small manikins, crowded on a shrub, are continually on leap from the branches to the ground, and from the ground to the branches. During these short passages of a few feet they emit the noise, which is a short and sharp rolling produced with the aid of their bills. So great an uproar on the part of such small birds is not easily understood, and less so their end in producing it; for the ordinary note or call uttered by them under all other circumstances has in it nothing particular. At those periods, when joy alone seems to move them, they remove from the ground everything which lies on it, so as to make a perfect clearance of a small spot, which is always circular. This is again an enigma; and yet this manœuvre they will continue for hours entire.

There is a bird, the song of which announces man's dwelling, viz., the *Troglodytes eudon*, which is a wren, but is called here *rossignol*. Though no rival of the European night songster, yet it is the only one among our birds that may induce one to think there must be a charm in listening to a bird pouring forth the harmony of its notes. However, it is respected much less for its melody than for its habits, which attach it to our dwellings: a sort of veneration is even felt for the little creature, which is shown by its very popular name, for it is called " Oiseau du Bon-Dieu," or God's bird. Several nocturnal birds of prey disturb the stillness of night by their shrieks, and in those shrieks there is here, as everywhere else, something so dismally lugubrious, as to cause the unfortunate to shudder in his hut; for, to him they are ominous of death. But it is rather curious that a diurnal bird, the trinité (*Cuculus naevius*), sometimes makes its cry to be heard during the night : whilst its companions of the day are in deep repose, it wakes on the branch, and each hour gives forth its notes, which night renders querulous, but which in turn make night more mournful still.

Some other particulars may be remarked in the call of our birds; but as a characteristic of this point of Ornithology, they may be said to whistle rather than sing, whilst some of them produce with their bill singular noises. Thus our cassique, by rapidly moving its bill along the quills of its wing-feathers, produces a noise which must strike any one who hears it for the first time; this it repeats frequently. Whenever perched on a branch, it indulges in a chattering which imitates, even to deception, the mewing of a cat, the light laughter of children, the cackling of hens, the whistling of man, &c. It is a treat, surrounded by a few of these birds, to listen to the different modulations into which they are capable of inflecting their voice.

REPTILES.

THE four grand divisions of reptiles have their representatives in the island, viz., the chelonia, the sauria, the ophidia, and the batrachians. Of these a few are to be met with in the other West India Islands, whilst many are common to Trinidad and the neighbouring continent, but none seem to be peculiar to this island alone.

CATALOGUE OF REPTILES.

By Dr. J. Court.

ORDER I.—CHELONIA.

FAMILY I.
Land Tortoises—
  Testudo. 2 species.
    Testudo Tabulata. (a)
    „ *Carbonaria.* (a)

FAMILY II.
Fresh-water Tortoises—
  Emys. 2 species. (b)

FAMILY III.
Sea Tortoises—
  Chelonia. 3 species.
    Testudo Mydas. (c)
    Testudo Marina. (d)
    Testudo Imbricata. (e)

ORDER II.—SAURIA.

FAMILY I.
Crocodilians—
  Alligator. 1 species.
    Alligator Sclerops. (f)

FAMILY II.
Lacertidæ—
  Geckos. 2 species.
    Platydactylus Thecconyx. (g)
    Hemidactylus Mabuia. (h)
  Iguanidæ. 4 species.
    Polychrus Marmoratus. (i)
    Anolius Alligator. (j)

(a) The land tortoises are known here by the name of morocoy, and (b) fresh-water tortoises by that of galapa.
  (c) Common turtle.   (d) Caouane.   (e) Caret, or tortoise.
  (f) Alligator, or babiche.
  (g) Plantain Mabuia, or mabouia des bananiers.
  (h) Wall Mabuia, or mabouia des murailles.
  (i) (j) Generally considered here as chameleons.

FAMILY II.—*continued.*
  Iguana Tuberculata.
    (a)
  Hypsibatus Agamoides. (b)
  Salvator. 1 species.
    Salvator Merianæ. (c)
  Ameiva. 2 species.
    Ameiva Vulgaris. (d)
    Ameiva Major. (d)
  Chalcides. 2 species.
  Amphisbœna Fuliginosa. (e)
  Amphisbœna Alba. (e)
  Scincoideæ. 1 species.
    Eumeces Spixii. (f)

ORDER III.—BATRACHIANS.
  Raniforms. 1 species.
    Pseudis Merianæ. (g)
  Hylæforms. Several species.
    Hyla Viridis. (h)
  Bufoniforms. Several species.
    Bufo Strumosus. (i)

ORDER III.—*continued.*
  Pipæforms. 1 species.
    Pipa Americana. (j)

ORDER IV.—OPHIDIA.
Non-venomous. Several species.
  Tortrix. 1 species.
    Tortrix Scytale. (k)
  Boa. 2 species.
    Boa Constrictor. (l)
    Boa Murina. (m)
  Coluber. Several species.
    Coluber Variabilis.(n)
  Dendrophis. 2 species.
    Dendrophis Liocercus. (o)
    Dendrophis Aurata. (p)
Venomous. Several species.
  Elaps. 1 species.
    Elaps Corallinus. (q)
  Trigonocephalus. 1 species.
    Trigonocephalus Jararaca. (r)
  Crotalus. 1 species.
    Crotalus Mutus.

(a) Common guana, or lésard.
(b) A lizard, remarkable for an inflated head and spinous or pencilled-like groups on the vicinity of the ear.
(c) Mato, or mate.   (d) Ground anolis, or lizards.
(e) Double-headed serpent, or serpent-à-deux-têtes.
(f) A pretty sleek little lizard, to be seen on trees, of a brown colour on the back, and greenish below; also with blackish points scattered along the back, and a brown band on each side, imperfectly terminated.
(g) Frog-fish, paradoxal-frog.
(h) A beautiful frog of rather large size, green above, and a light pink beneath.
(i) Our common crapaud.
(j) A large ugly frog, caught in the Bejucal.
(k) Rouleau.
(l) Macajuel.
(m) Huillia.
(n) Clibo, or cribo noir.
(o) Ash-coloured horse-whip, or rigoise-argentée.
(p) Green horse-whip, or rigoise-verte.
(q) Coral-snake, or serpent-corail.
(r) Cascabel.

The reptiles mentioned in the above catalogue are not met with in all parts of the country indifferently. A few seem to prefer the vicinity of man's habitation—such as the ameivas, geckos, lizards; the clibo, toads, and some tree-frogs; also the mato or safeguard, and smaller lizards. Others, as the land and fluviatile tortoises, are encountered in the high woods; and some are almost universal, of which are the frogs, alligators, iguanas, boas, crotals, and other serpents, provided, however, the locality suits them. The alligator, for instance, shows a preference wherever there are pools of stagnant or dormant waters; they are, nevertheless, particularly numerous at Mayaro, and in the county of Caroni. The iguana generally delights in the vicinity of the sea-shore, and sandy spots, where it can deposit its eggs in safety; and large numbers of them are met with on the Bocas islets, and at the mouths of rivers, particularly along the eastern coasts. The boa constrictor, or macajuel, seems to prefer low damp places, and the boa-murina, or huillia, never strays far from the river or pond which it has selected as its abode. They are specially plentiful in the Oropuche river, and its affluents, viz., the Cunapo, Sangre-grande, and Sangre-chiquito; nor are they scarce at Cedros. The mute crotal, or mapepire, shows a· predilection for high grounds, whilst the cascabel, or trigonocephalus, is commonly met with in damp, low lands. The only specimen of pipa which I have seen came from the Caroni Savannah, and that of the paradoxal-frog from Cedros.

The sea-tortoises, or turtles, deserve no peculiar notice. The morocoy and galapa live on soft plants, fruits, and insects; the morocoy seems to be particularly partial to the wild plum, which it swallows entire; during the ripening season, several of them may be met with under one tree. Being very slow in their movements, the morocoy and galapa are easily caught; if near a pond or river, however, the galapa at once dives and escapes under water. Dogs often detect the morocoy by barking at it; also when coupling they emit a peculiar grunt, which likewise serves to discover them. I may here mention a few particulars regarding the capture of turtle. They are caught either in nets, or on the beach when crawling ashore to deposit their eggs. For this purpose they come forth at night, and are watched by the catchers. As soon as a turtle is aware of any danger it immediately takes to the sea. The safest plan in that case is to gain the seaward of the animal, and seize it by the fore-flaps; it then continues to urge against the catcher, and is, with its own aid, easily turned up. If approached and held by the side, it makes a powerful resistance, and in the struggle throws up a cloud of fine sand, which, almost blinding its antagonist, causes him to lose his hold. A very ingenious contrivance is sometimes adopted to bring a turtle of the largest size from a distance. One of the fore-flaps is secured to the carapace, or shell, with a line, and the animal placed in the sea, the bound flipper shoreward, so that it is thus easily led along the beach to any distance. The turtle may also be harpooned whilst rising to, or lying on, the surface, and sometimes it may even be taken asleep in that position.

The common iguana, but particularly the mato, are not to be rejected from the table. Iguanas are either shot on trees, or caught when laying; their fore and hind feet are then tied behind, so that they cannot move; they can live many days without food. Matos are hunted down with dogs, and taken either in holes, or in some hollow tree, wherein they seek a temporary refuge; the best mode, however, is shooting them; they are then watched about mid-day in some copse or bushy spot, whither hens are accustomed to lead their broods, or, during the dry season, along the dried beds of ravines, where they lurk for fish. The iguana lives on insects, eggs—those of the tortoise principally—young birds, and the tender buds of plants; the mato is exclusively carnivorous, and fish, young birds, mice, insects, eggs, and even small snakes become its prey; it generally lays in the nests of termites. Both these saurians are excellent divers, and can remain for a long time under water.

Some of our serpents attain very large dimensions. The boa-constrictor may reach the length of twenty-two feet, and will swallow agoutis, lapas, and young deer; a huillia killed in the river Cunapo measured seventeen feet eleven inches; it, however, attains to twenty and even twenty-four feet. The clibo, or cribo, reaches from ten to twelve feet; and a mute crotal, or mapepire, killed at Couva, and now in the possession of Dr. Court, measures eleven feet. These are the largest species.

It is well known that snakes live upon such animals as they are enabled to seize; this prey—generally taken by surprise—consists of small quadrupeds, birds, and even other reptiles. Rats and opossums are the great treat of the macajuel; and as many as seven of the latter were once found in the stomach of a boa-constrictor. The huillia preys on even larger game—such as the lapa, young deer, &c. A gentleman being once engaged in the chase, near the river Oropuche, a young deer was started, and its distressed bleating soon proved it was caught. On approaching to the river, whence the cries arose, he saw the animal struggling in the water, and at first was unable to account for its movements; but, on a nearer view, he ascertained that it was held in the folds of a young huillia; both animals were killed, and the serpent was found to measure only seven feet and a few inches.

The rigoise, or horse-whip snake, is generally met in thick copses or under brush, and may be seen gliding along the tops of the crowded and interlaced plants. The cascabel is found in low, damp localities, and along river borders, where it selects its abode among the clumps of bamboos. The mapepire shows a preference for high grounds, and is very common in Mayaro, as also between Caroni and Tamana, near the river Tumpuna. It is often found together with the lapa in the same hole; and, in certain localities, hunters are obliged to act with great caution, in order to protect their dogs or themselves from its poison fangs. There is, I believe, no authentic record of a lapa having ever been found killed in its recess by a mapepire.

These serpents, as well as the coral snake, are highly venomous; in fact, the mapepire is quite as formidable as the rattlesnake. The description given of the habits and exterior appearances of the *Crotalus mutus*, by Schlegel, and of the *Lachesis mutus*, by Dumeril, accurately corresponds to our mapepire; and the *Trigonocephalus jararaca*, and the *Bothrops jararaca*, by the same authors, to our cascabel. Dr. Court possesses three specimens of the *Trigonocephalus lanceolatus*, or the Martinico's fer-de-lance, and of the Trinidad cascabel and mapepire, respectively—in which the characteristic differences of these three serpents are very well delineated. The scales of the mapepire are oval, and carinated as those of the others, but they are not so flat, and there is besides on each a prominence, giving it the appearance of a pine-apple eye; hence its local name of "Mapepire Ananas;" head triangular and thick. The head of the fer-de-lance, or lance-headed trigonocephalus, is more elongated; and that of the cascabel more so, particularly the muzzle. The mapepire may almost be said to be torpid, or at least so sluggish and indolent as to require provocation before it acts on the offensive; but once roused, it is very fierce, and will spring on, or

z

even pursue, its enemy. This serpent generally warns by a peculiar rattling sound, caused by the rapid movements of its tail—probably against the dry leaves, as it has no articulated rattle, like that of the *Crotalus horridus*, but only a white horny spur, and may be considered as establishing a link between the trigonocephalus and the crotalus. The mapepire is much more dreaded than the cascabel. Though very sluggish, this latter serpent shows occasionally much determination, and after inflicting a first wound, it sometimes immediately recoils for another attack. The ground-colour of the cascabel is brown, with deep transversal stripes; the belly has a tesselated appearance, black squares symmetrically alternating with others of a lighter colour.

I may repeat here, what Prince de Neuwied says of the coral snake—that it can be taken and handled without any danger, children very often playing with this viper, encircling it round the neck. I have myself, more than once, carried about corals, not suspecting they were venomous. The apparent innocuity of the coral arises from the peculiar conformation of its head and mouth; the head is of the same growth with the body, and not separated by a distinct neck; nor can it, on account of its anatomical organisation, open its jaws sufficiently to seize and bite any bulky body. It is nevertheless highly poisonous. The clibo and rigoise are very common; of the former, there are three species or varieties—the black or speckled, the yellow-bellied, and the yellow-tailed; the first is of a glossy lead colour, and the under parts of a light yellow, with dark stripes; the second, of a deep lead colour above, and a fine yellow beneath; the body of the third is also of a lead colour, and the belly, together with the tail, of an orange tinge; they generally attain the same dimensions, though the last may be found of a somewhat larger size.

The rigoise, or whip-snake, would appear to pertain to the tribe of poisonous serpents, but its bite would not be deadly; it is called *rigoise* or *horse-whip*, not only on account of its long slender form, but also from the current belief among the negroes that it uses its tail as an instrument for flogging its antagonist.

Besides the above-mentioned, and well-known serpents, there are several others which we have not been able to classify, from the many difficulties which attend the study—among others, the mangrove-cascabel, or *dormilon;* it bears the greatest resemblance to the true cascabel, but, on all accounts, is not poisonous; it is very common all along the lower Caroni, and may often be seen sluggishly extended on some branch that stretches over the river. A small serpent, from twelve to sixteen inches in length, is met with occasionally in courtyards, and among rubbish, also in pasture-grounds; it is called the ground-snake, and is probably a cœcilia; another smaller one, provided with a sting at the end of the tail, may possibly be the *Stenostoma albifrons* of Dumeril. The *Cuaïma* is reported as being a deadly viper; I have never seen it, and only mention it on hearsay.

Besides the toad here mentioned, there are several other species, differing not only in size, but in general configuration. Of real frogs I know but one, the paradoxal or fish-frog, so remarkable for the large size of the tadpole, which is several inches long, and has some resemblance to the cascaradura; its body—which is smooth and not scaly—exhibiting oblique bands exactly like those of that fish. It still retains the tail some time after the four limbs have grown, which gives it the grotesque appearance of a fish provided with a toad's feet; hence the erroneous impression among the vulgar, that the cascaradura is ultimately metamorphosed into a toad. There exist in the colony many tree-frogs, or hylæ-forms; besides the one already mentioned, I know a very small one, of a brown colour above and grey beneath; another, of nearly the same colour, but much larger, and found in cacao plantations, generally sticking on the under surface of some leaf (*Hyla xerophylla?*); a third, of a milky colour (*Hyla lactea?*).

The pipa is a large batrachian, very remarkable on account of its singular form, but more, and chiefly so, from its mode of generation. The female carries on its back the eggs or semina which the male has placed there; a sort of inflammation is the consequence of such application, and each egg becomes as imprisoned in a cell, which gradually increases in size, so as to accommodate the growth of the semen. When hatched, the young escape from the cells, the back of the mother remaining for some time as if honey-combed.

A pretty little lizard, about four inches long, which we have not been able to determine, is very common in town, along fence-walls, in the crevices of which it dwells. It is easily distinguishable by its large lustrous eyes, and a bright white streak extending from the point of the muzzle to the extremity of the tail; also by the lighter colour of the neck and head, as compared with the body.

I have also seen a curious little animal resembling an amphisbæna, but having four limbs; it is probably a ceps.

FISHES.

THE great class of fishes supplies many individuals remarkable for their varied forms, their beautiful colours, their habitat, and the benefits which are derived from them as articles of food. I found it impossible to make a detailed list of all the species which inhabit our seas, streams, and ponds; the following catalogue, however, compiled by my friend Dr. Leotaud, exhibits nearly all the genera which may be said to belong to the island :—

ORDER I.—ACANTHOPTERYGIANS.

FAMILY I.
Percoides—
    Centropomus. 1 species.
    Centropomus Undecimalis. (a)
    Mesoprion. 2 species. (b)
    Rypticus. 1 species.
    Anthias Saponarius. (c)
    Priacanthus. 1 species.
    Polynemus. 1 species. (d)
    Sphyræna. 2 species.
    Sphyræna Barracuda. (e)
    Upeneus.

FAMILY II.
Mailed Cheeks—
    Prionotus. 1 species.
    Dactylopterus. 1 species. (f)

FAMILY II.—*continued.*
    Scorpæna. 1 species. (g)

FAMILY III.
Scienoïdes—
    Otolithus. 1 species. (h)
    Eques. 1 species. (i)
    Haemulon. Several species. (j)

FAMILY IV.
Sparoïdes—
    Pagrus. Several species. (k)

FAMILY V.
Menides—
    Gerres. 1 species. (l)

FAMILY VI.
Squammipennes—
    Chætodon. 2 species.
    Ephippus. 1 species. (m)

(a) Pike, or brochet.
(b) Gruper, or vieille.
(c) Soapwort, or savonette.
(d) Paradise-fish.
(e) Barracuta, or bécune.
(f) Flying-fish.   (g) Vingt-quatre-heures.
(h) Salmon, or saumon.   (i) Sea-horse.
(j) Red-mouth or gueule-rouge.   (k) Pagres.
(l) Fresh-water pike, or brochet.   (m) Horseman.

FAMILY VI.—continued.
   Holacanthus. 1 species.
   Psettus. 1 species.

FAMILY VII.
Scomberoides—
   Auxis. 2 species. (a)
   Cybium. Several species.
   Xiphias. 1 species.
     Xiphias Gladius. (b)
   Istiophorus. 1 species (c)
   Elacate. 1 species. (d)
   Trichiurus. 1 species. (e)
   Temnodon. 1 species.
   Chilodipterus Heptacanthus.
   Caranx. 5 species.
     Scomber Carangus. (f)
   Vomer. 1 species. (g)
   Zeus. 2 species. (g)

FAMILY IX.
Theutyes—
   Acanthurus, 1 species. (h)

FAMILY XI.
Mugiloides—
   Mugil. 3 species. (i)
   Atherina. 1 species.

FAMILY XII.
Gobioides—
   Clinus. 1 species. (j)
   Opisthognatus.

FAMILY XII.—continued.
   Gobius.
   Gobioides. 1 species.

FAMILY XIII.
Pediculated Pectorals—
   Antennarius.
   Malthacus.
   Batrachus. (k)

FAMILY XIV.
Labroides—
   Labrus. 1 species. (l)
   Lachnolaimus. 1 species. (m)
   Scarus. 1 species. (n)

FAMILY XV.
Flute-mouth—
   Fistularia. 1 species. (o)

ORDER II.—MALACOPTERYGIANS.

FAMILY I.
Cyprinoides—
   Anableps. 1 species.
     Cobitis Anableps. (p)
   Pœcilia. 2 species. (q)

FAMILY II.
Esoces—
   Belone. 1 species. (r)
   Hemiramphus. 1 species. (s)

FAMILY III.
Siluroides—
   Mystus. 2 species. (t

(a) King-fish, or tassard, and Spanish mackerel, or carite.
(b) Espadon, or saw-fish.
(c) Maman-balaou.
(d) Cod-fish, or morue.
(e) A fish found in ponds and ravines, resembling the lamprey; hence its name of cutlass-fish, or coutelas.
(f) Carangues: the common carangue (*Scomber Carangus*), is the largest and most abundant: the carangue grasse is not so large, but more delicate, as are also the two others; a fifth species is our anchovy, or anchois.
(g) Dories, or lunes.
(h) Surgeon.
(i) Lebranche, large and common mullet.
(j) Gruper, very large, found in rocky places.
(k) Crapaud, or toad-fish. The three genera of this family are known by the name of anglers.
(l) Lippe.
(m) Captain.
(n) Parrot, or paroquet.
(o) Trumpet-fish, or poisson-trompette.
(p) Large-eyed fish, or gros-yeux.
(q) A small fish found in rivulets, and even in wells, in Port-of-Spain.
(r) Gar-fish.   (s) Balaou.
(t) The common cat-fish, or machoiran, and the barbe, an inhabitant of our rivers.

FAMILY III.—*continued.*
   Callichthys. 2 species. (a)
   Hypostomus. 1 species. (b)

FAMILY IV.
Salmonides—
   Hydrocyon. 2 species. (c)
   Saurus. 1 species.

FAMILY V.
Clupeæ—
   Clupea. 1 species. (d)
   Odontognathus. 1 species.
   Engraulis. Several species. (e)
   Butyrinus. 1 species.
     Butyrinus Banana. (f)
   Erythrinus. 2 species. (g)

FAMILY VI.
Sub-brachians—
   Flat fishes.

FAMILY VI.—*continued.*
   Solea. 1 species. (h)
   Echeneis. 1 species. (i)

ORDER III.—APODAL-MALACOPTERYGIANS.
Anguilliforms—
   Murœna. 1 species. (j)
   Symbranchus. 1 species. (k)

ORDER IV.—LOPHOBRANCHII.
   Syngnathus. 1 species.
   Hippocampus. 1 species. (l)

ORDER V.—PLECTOGNATHI.
FAMILY I.
Gymnodontes—
   Diodon. 1 species. (m)
   Tetrodon. Several species. (n)

FAMILY II.
Sclerodermes—
   Balistes. 1 species.
   Ostracion. 1 species.

(a) Cascaradura, and a small fish found in clear streams.
(b) Anne-Marie.
(c) Fresh-water sardines.
(d) Cailleu-tassart.
(e) Anchovies.
(f) Banana, or banane.
(g) Guabine and yarrao, two fresh-water fishes; the former very common in ponds, ravines, and rivers; the latter found only in clear rivulets.
(h) Sole.
(i) Pilot-fish.
(j) Conger-eel, or congre.
(k) Dog-headed eel, or anguille-tête-chien, abundant in ponds and ravines.
(l) Hippocamp.
(m) Mailed-fish, or poisson-armé.   (n) Chouf-chouf, poisonous.

There are, besides the above-mentioned genera, several others which have not yet been ascertained; they must, however, be few. I will say nothing of the varied forms of our fishes, because it would be but to mutilate what has been written in professional works on the subject. Their habitat, utility, and the noxious properties of a few, are nevertheless matters of interest, and which require some elucidation.

As to habitat, I will separate the fresh-water from the salt-water fishes. The former are few in number; they are the pike (*Gerres*), the cutlass (*Trichiurus*), pœcilia, barbe (*Mystus*), cascaraduras (*Callichthys*), Anne-Marie (*Hypostomus*), sardines (*Hydrocyon*), guabine and yarrao (*Erythrinus*), dog-headed eel

(*Synbranchus*). Besides the above, there are the common eel (*Anguilla*) and the *Coscorob*, very common in ponds and rivers, the cats (*Callichthys ?*). I have also been told that a *trout* is not scarce in our mountain streams ; this fact I have not been able to ascertain.

Except the pœcilias and cats, together with a very small callichthys, all our fresh-water fishes are used as food. The river pike attains about eight inches, is met with in clear limpid water, and is generally caught with the hook. The cutlass fish—about twelve inches in length—inhabits muddy ravines, and is caught in nets, or, during the dry seasons, in isolated pools formed by the partial drying up of ravines ; it is indifferent eating. The barbe is generally taken in nets, but also with the hook—it is a good fish ; also the Anne-Marie, about eight inches long, and scaly, very common in clear streams. The sardines are of small size, resembling the European sardine in form, but more compressed ; the smaller sized is so familiar, as sometimes to attack the legs of persons standing in the water, or bathing ; they are found in the clear and shallow streams of our valleys, and are generally caught by means of cast-nets ; for which purpose a handful of manioc-meal is thrown into the water, and the sardines rush in shoals to the bait. The guabine is the largest of our fresh-water fishes, measuring from twelve to twenty inches in length ; it is very voracious, and bites severely. As already stated, the guabine is found in rivers and deep ponds, particularly in the Bejucal, and other ponds in the neighbourhood of Caroni, and the Cocal. It seems that the spawning season is about the month of July ; they then creep into all the small rills of water which have a communication with the ravines and rivers, and are easily caught. They nibble at the hook, or are caught in *fish-pots ;* the latter are long, conical net or basket works, made of roseau or bamboo, which are let down into the centre of the current of some stream, a regular dam being otherwise formed across, by which the fish are forced, in their passage down the stream, into the only opening afforded by the entrance of the pot ; and having once entered, egress is impossible. The yarrao resembles the guabine in form, but is smaller in size. The dog-headed eel is caught in nets, in which it entangles itself in pursuit of other fish ; for the guabine is, perhaps, the only adversary it does not overcome ; it attains from three to four feet. The bait placed in the nets is generally the manioc root; several intoxicating plants are also used to poison fish in pools and ponds. But, of all our fresh-water fish, the cascaradura is, by far, the most noted. Its length is from six to ten inches; the body nearly prismatic, and covered with very hard horny scales—whence its name. The flesh is of an orange colour, and very delicate; it ought not to be confounded with the cat-fish, which resembles it very much, but the flesh of which is white and unsavoury. The cascaraduras are found in immense numbers in nearly all our large ponds, but particularly those in the Caroni savannah, and the marshy parts of Nariva, where even a small ravine bears the name of Cascaradura.

Our salt-water fishes are far more numerous, and of much greater importance, on account of their paramount utility as articles of food; there are also among them several which are naturally, or may accidentally become, poisonous. Some of them are caught in the open sea, others near the shore, and at the mouths of rivers or creeks, and a few in rocky localities. The king-fish and Spanish mackerel are taken with tan-lines, either in the Gulf, or outside, along the north coast; they are caught chiefly during boisterous weather. The anchovy (*Caranx*) is caught in the harbour; it is of the size of a sardine; an immense quantity is taken every year during the month of July; but they are migratory, and disappear in about three weeks. The pike (*Centropomus*), salmon (*Otolythus*), and codfish (*Elacates*) are also taken in the open sea. The lebranche, mullets; the balaou, gar-fish, crapaud, and rays are caught near the shore—the former at the mouths of rivers and estuaries or small creeks, which they ascend with the flow, and generally retire from with the ebb; drag-nets are then laid at the entrance, and the lebranche easily caught; the mullets are taken with the cast-net. The balaou and gar-fish are commonly caught at night by torch-light, or with the seine; carangues also, sometimes in enormous quantities, with the same; they are easily announced by their gambols at the surface of the water, and not unfrequently quite close in shore, so as to be then easily surrounded and dragged to land. It is not, perhaps, amiss to mention here a case, wherein about 3,000 carangues were thus made prisoners and secured in a net: about 500 were sent to the markets the first day, and from 300 to 400 each subsequent day. One of our grupers (*Mesoprion*) haunts, in preference, the mouth of our larger rivers—the Caroni, the Guataro, &c.; it comes to a very large size, weighing above four hundred pounds; another species (*Clinus*)—the largest of all—is fond of rocky places, where it hides in some hole; the third species (*Mesoprion*) is also found in such localities. The crapaud (*Batrachus*)—a very ugly-looking fish, particularly about the head, whence its name—is found imbedded in the mud-flats, or under large stones, where it is taken at low water. The red-mouths or crocros (*Haemulon*) are caught in weirs all along the coast; the snappers are hooked from the sandy banks about the bocas, as also the sardes—all excellent fish. The barracuta (*Sphyraena*) and conger-eel (*Muraena*) generally choose some haunt in the middle of rocky points, and there watch for their prey. The barracuta, when grown to a large size, is nearly as ferocious and voracious as the shark itself; it attains to seven or eight feet in length, and is abundant all along our shores. There is, on the eastern coast, a rocky point called "Barracuta Point," or "Pointe Becunes," on account of the large number of sphyraenas which are there found; they are reported to be more voracious than in any other place, and it is said there are but poor chances for any one falling overboard in that locality; he is soon devoured by these shark-like fishes. The dorie or lune, the parrot, and paradise fishes, together with a few others, are caught only by chance. The gros-yeux (*Cobitis anableps*) is a small fish, about eight inches; they may be seen leaping in shoals above the surface of the water, in the shallows quite close to the shore, with quick successive jerks; they are then easily shot, and picked up when dead. The rays are plentiful, but seldom offered for sale; poor people, and the Coolies especially, feed upon the young sharks. Besides the fishes above enumerated, there are three or four others of undetermined genera, viz., the *Paoua*, rather common, but not generally eaten—except by the poorer classes; the *Aileronde*, met with at Mayaro chiefly; it is about the size of a sole, but resembling the dorie in flesh, and is, perhaps, our most delicate fish; the *Zapatero* is also of good quality; the *Grande-écaille* is common but neglected. Another large fish—weighing upwards of 100 lbs. when of full size—is common in estuaries, on the northern and eastern coasts; it is called by the Spanish peons *Bagre-sapo*, or *toad-pagre*, and is excellent eating.

Some of our fishes deserve peculiar notice on account of their poisonous nature, or from their sometimes dangerous and even fatal encounter with man; I have already mentioned the barracuta; the sharks are too well known to deserve any lengthened notice. The fishes of the above description to be met in the Gulf, and on the coast, are the common shark (*Carcharias*), the pantoufflier (*Zygaena*), and the rays. The number of sharks in the Gulf is surprising, particularly during the whaling season; and they, at times, occasion great loss to the fishers, as many as several hundreds being said to prey on a dead whale, so that people are specially employed in killing them; this is done with a hatchet, or a sort of sharp spade, by which means the spine is divided at one single blow; large numbers are thus despatched. The armed, or sting-ray, is often the cause of serious accidents. The barracuta and a small fish called *coulirou* are occasionally poisonous; but the only evil effects brought on are vomiting and purging, accompanied with urticaria, and which easily yield to proper treatment. The scorpaena, or "Vingt-quatre-heures," is also considered a dangerous fish, and is much dreaded on account of the accidents it causes. Dr. Leotaud was twice wounded by the scorpaena, and thus describes the symptoms he felt: "on the first occasion, when wounded in the toe, the pain was at first very severe locally, but soon retired to seize on the ankle-joint, then the knee, the hip, and the shoulder, in succession—the pain gradually dislodging from the parts primarily affected. From the shoulder, it extended to the corresponding side of the chest, at which period the respiration became laboured, the pulmonary functions apparently ceased, and I fainted. A fever followed that lasted twelve hours, after which health was restored by the entire cessation of the pain, which disappeared in like manner as on its access, though following an inverse course." On the next occasion, the scorpaena being of a very small size, the symptoms were similar in kind, but much less in intensity.

The accidents brought on by the tetraodon, or "Choufchouf," are of a different nature; the flesh itself is poisonous, as proved by the following facts: a large tetraodon having been boiled, in order to get the skeleton, the flesh was thrown away in the courtyard, and two cats, as many ducks and pigs, on accidentally eating of the same, died from its effects. Again, sometime in the year 1854, two young children died, within a few hours, after having partaken of the liver of a tetraodon. It is rather remarkable that the voracious corbeau, as if warned by instinct of its poisonous nature, will not touch that fish.

The gar-fish, or orphie, though neither voracious nor poisonous, may be accidentally the cause of very serious sufferings. When disturbed, the orphies dart out of the water with great force, and should their course happen to be across or in the direction of a canoe, may come into contact with one of the persons therein. The snout of this fish, being long and serrated, pierces deeply into the part they hit; it then generally breaks, a bony fragment remaining in the flesh, or even in the plank of the boat: several accidents of this kind have been known, and in such cases it became necessary to make a deep incision, in order to extract the fragment broken in the flesh.

Short and concise as is the above sketch, I yet hope that but few genera have been omitted of the great and remarkable class of vertebrated animals. It is true that but few species have been determined, an act of prudence, on account of the great difficulty in procuring objects of comparison, and of distinguishing the sexes and ages, among birds. How many errors have arisen from the latter cause! for, sometimes the female is more different from the male, and the young from the parent bird of the same species, than is genus from genus. From the above, also, the naturalist may form a pretty good opinion of our zoological riches, whilst some of the details into which I have entered may prove entertaining to the general reader.

One remark more; many of our animals (whether quadrupeds, birds, reptiles, or fishes) have no local English designations, and all the names are either Spanish or French, some Indian; so that I have been induced to use such terms as I know to prevail, either in the above languages, or in the English.

BOTANY.

OUTLINE OF THE FLORA OF TRINIDAD.
By Herman Crüger.

TRINIDAD exhibits—if not on a grand scale, at least within striking and well defined limits—the distinctive characteristics of an intertropical American country. The variety of its soil and formations, the abundant supply of water with which it is blessed, give to the vegetable covering of this island the glowing colours, the richness and grandeur of forms which astonish and charm the admirer and lover of Nature, and invite the thoughtful and scientific mind to study and meditation. No wonder that the grateful Indian called this spot a paradise, swinging away his eventless life in the *chinchorro*, whilst below and around the teeming soil spontaneously afforded him not only the necessaries, but even the luxuries, of life.

> "Mollia securæ peragebant otia gentes;
> Ipsa quoque immunis, rastroque intacta, nec ullis
> Saucia vomeribus, per se dabat omnia, tellus."
>
> Ovid i. 12.

"The character of a population depends greatly, though not solely, on the aspect of the vegetable world of a country," says Von Humboldt, in his "Views of Nature." Were I possessed of the pen or pencil of a Humboldt, I would essay to place in their mutual relation the luxuriance and grandeur of our forest-woods, with the careless though amiable character of the Trinidadian; but this is hardly within the scope of these pages. I may here, however, as well enregister my conviction that Trinidad—like other fertile tropical countries—will, from its own boundless luxuriance, never nourish a very industrious population.

The general character of our flora approaches that of Guiana; partaking, however, more or less, of that of the West India islands in general, as will appear hereafter. The botanical traveller will therefore find the works of Aublet as useful and necessary to him in his researches as those of Swartz, Bonpland, and Kunth. This is, however, not to be understood in the sense that we have absolutely the same *species* of plants that grow in and characterise Guiana and the Antilles, for I have found this to be true in respect of *genera* only; but as genera, in most cases, exhibit the same vegetative characteristics in all, or most of their species, this is quite sufficient to demonstrate and explain the similarity of general aspect between our island, its continental neighbour, and the sister-islands.

With regard to species, I must say that of them I have not been able to determine a great number, and have, therefore, limited myself to giving in the annexed catalogue the names of genera only. Species can only be determined with absolute accuracy in large cities, where collections of plants, and libraries of reference, can supply all comparative information. I could give only approximate determinations, which would prove of no real use ; I have, therefore, preferred giving none.

The lists of species which I have seen of other islands, such as Barbadoes and St. Thomas, fully corroborate the truth of what I assert; for they are replete with errors of all sorts, merely because the writers thought it incumbent on them to particularise the species.

Forest-growths take the most predominant place in our vegetation; and that which at once strikes the European on reaching our shores is the multiplied variety of forms and foliage they present. A large number of families contribute their quota to these formations; among which may be mentioned Palms and Lauraceæ, Rubiaceæ and Apocynaceæ, Verbenaceæ and Cordiaceæ, Myrsinaceæ and Sapotaceæ; as also Ebenaceæ, Myristicaceæ and Anonaceæ, Capparidaceæ, Malvaceæ, and Sterculiaceæ; with Tiliaceæ, Ternströmiaceæ and Clusiaceæ, Meliaceæ and Cedrelaceæ, Malpighiaceæ and Sapindaceæ, Euphorbiaceæ and Burseraceæ, Simarubaceæ and Diosmeæ, Melastomaceæ and Myrtaceæ, Chrysobalanaceæ, and, lastly, perhaps the richest family, Leguminosæ, or Fabaceæ, including Swartzieæ, and Mimoseæ. A glance at this list of families shows at once the difference which exists between these forests and those of higher latitudes, where, not only a few families, but also a few species, form the whole woodland vegetation. Nor ought it to be believed that only a paucity of the above families is met with in each forest, for the aggregate is almost everywhere of the same variety, whilst the species, and genera, perhaps, are different. In plains, with a fertile soil, for instance, certain forms predominate, without altogether excluding others; and the like arrangement occurs in other localities. A rich soil is generally indicated by the cabbage-palm (*Areca oleracea*), and the carat (*Copernicia*); whereas, the timit (*Manicaria*) grows in light sandy soils, generally in company of a variety of trees of the myrtle tribe. In general, palms are indicative of the quality of the soil, and of the respective productions which can be raised on a given spot.

The northern chain of mountains, covered nearly everywhere with dense forests, is intersected at various angles by numbers of valleys presenting the most lovely character. Generally each valley is watered by a silvery stream, tumbling here and there over rocks and natural dams, ministering in a continuous rain to the strange-looking river-canes, dumb-canes, and balisiers, that voluptuously bend their heads to the drizzly shower which plays incessantly on their glistening leaves, off which the globules roll in a thousand pearls, as from the glossy plumage of the stately swan. Amid such Dryad-haunts as these, well might the poet realise the myth of the bathing nymph, and gloating Pan behind some broad-leafed fern concealed, with all the emotions of the Satyr-God!

One of these falls deserves particular notice—the Cascade of Maraccas—in the valley of that name. The high-road leads up the valley a few miles, over hills, and along the windings of the river, exhibiting the varying scenery of our mountain district in the fairest style. There, on the river side, you may admire gigantic pepper trees, or the silvery leaves of the *Calathea*, the lofty bamboo, inclosing, perhaps, as in a leafy frame, a group of girls bathing beneath its many-stemmed shade, or the fragrant *Pothos*, the curious *Cyclanthes*, or frowning nettles, some of the latter from ten to twelve feet high. But how describe the numberless treasures which everywhere strike the eye of the wandering naturalist? Here, on the steep hill-side, the hut of the *Conuquero* emerges from a few fruit trees, such as the orange, lime, mangoe, and avocado; and, if he be a Spaniard, you may perceive him sitting on a bench before his door, near a rose or other flower-tree, meditating on better, bygone times, or saddened by the untimely death of a favourite game-cock.

To reach the *Chorro*, or cascade, you strike to the right into a "path" that brings you first to a cacao plantation, through a few rice or maize fields, and then you enter the shade of the virgin forest. Thousands of interesting objects now attract your attention: here, the wonderful *Norantia*, or the resplendent *Calycophyllum*, a *Tabernæmontana*, or a *Faramea*, filling the air afar off with a fragrance of their blossoms; there, a graceful *Heliconia* winking at you from out some dark ravine. At the margin of the latter let us take our seat, and, after having had a draught of the crystal element, I will tell you, during our rest, the names of the fairy forms that surround us; whilst a host of crickets and lizards chirp and whistle under concealment of the decaying leaves, making holyday the whole year round. That shrubbery above is composed of a species of *Bœhmeria*, or *Ardisia*, and that scarlet flower belongs to our native *Aphelandra*. In the rear, there are one or two *Philodendrons*—disagreeable guests; for their smell is bad enough, and they blister when imprudently touched. There also you may see a tree-fern, though a small one. Nearer to us, and low down, below our feet, that rich panicle of flowers belongs to a *Begonia;* and here, also, is an assemblage of ferns of the genera *Asplenium, Hymenophyllum* and *Trichomanes,* as well as of *Hepaticœ* and mosses. But, what are those yellow and purple flowers hanging above our heads?— They are *Bignonias* and *Mucunas*—creepers straying from afar, and having selected this spot, where they may, under the influence of the sun's beams, propagate their race. Those chain-like, fantastic, strange-looking lianes, resembling a family of boas, are *Bauhinias;* and beyond, through the opening, you see in the abandoned ground of some squatter's garden the trumpet-tree (*Cecropia*), and the groo-groo, the characteristic plants of the *rastrajo*.

Now, let us proceed on our walk; we are near the cascade:— Here it is opposite you, a grand spectacle, indeed! From a perpendicular wall of solid rock, of more than thirty-three feet, down rushes a stream of water splitting in the air and producing a constant shower, which renders this lovely spot singularly and deliciously cool. Nearly the whole extent of this natural wall is covered with plants, among which you can easily discern numbers of ferns and mosses, two species of *Pitcairnia*, with beautiful red flowers, some aroids, various nettles, and, here and there, a *Begonia*. How different such a spot would look in cold Europe! Below, in the midst of a never-failing drizzle, grow luxuriant ardisias, aroids, ferns, costus, heliconias, centropogons, hydrocotyles, cyperoids, and grasses of various genera—tradescantias and commelynas, billbergias, and, occasionally, a few small rubiaceæ and melastomaceæ.

From near this spot we may start to ascend the Tocuche, our highest mountain—it is about 3,100 feet. There I shall be afforded another opportunity of pointing out some natural beauties. Through dense forests—composed of some of our choicest timbers, such as the locust, poui, and cedar, with here and there a wild plum tree or a sterculia, and in which the under-wood is made up of melastomaceæ (*Clidemia* and *Miconia*), rubiaceæ, peppers, grasses, and cyperaceæ—you reach, about 1,500 feet higher up, a region where the aspect of the woods begins to change. Winds must blow here with great violence, at times, since the ground is strewed with small branches; humidity also is greater, as indicated by the number of mosses and ferns that clothe the trunks of the trees. Here is a kind of bamboo (*Chusquea*), a climbing plant which is not to be met with in the lower parts, and also very rarely on other mountains. The growth and size of the trees decrease as we gradually ascend higher and higher until we reach the summit, where they become stunted and scarce, being replaced by a small palm (*Geonoma*). Here occurs a new and interesting vegetation, which exhibits some of the characters of the mountain districts of South America, as described by Humboldt and others; here, also, we meet with one or two tree-ferns of a goodly size, a *Thibaudia*, and the beautiful *Utricularia montana*, growing on trees like other parasites. Nearly all the stems are covered with jungermannias and mosses, ferns and small orchids; some spots are covered, exclusive of all other plants, with another bambusaceous grass, viz., the *Platonia elata*.

As has already been remarked, the woods of the plains do not differ very materially from those of the lower mountains. There are only two species of our forest trees that are gregarious in growth, and that may be termed *social*—the *Mora*, which covers extensive tracts of land in different parts of the island; and the mangrove (*Rhizophora*), which grows in the saline swamps that border the sea; the rhizophora is, however, generally accompanied by the other species of mangrove, viz., the *Avicennia* and the *Conocarpus*. The conocarpus appears to be a salt-plant, for I also found it near the mud-volcanoes, together with a few other shrubs, and amarantaceous plants which thrive near the sea-shore.

Next to our forests, our so-called "natural savannahs" deserve notice. Four different classes may be distinguished, all more or less denuded of trees and shrubs. The first class is the periodically inundated savannahs of the coast, immediately in the rear of the mangrove forests of Caroni and Chaguanas. Coarse grasses and cyperoids, together with a slight sprinkling of convolvuli, hibisci, sesbaniæ, echites, and a few others, characterise these tracts; as they stretch towards the interior and the high woods, these plants become mixed up with grasses of a finer kind —an *Ambrosia, Malachra, Mimosa,* &c. Next to the above comes the savannah on the eastern side of the island, at a rather considerable distance from the sea. Here again the principal growth is of grasses and cyperoids, but of a different kind, though those of the former are not altogether excluded; but the finer sorts are more prevalent here, and the whole district bears a different appearance, particularly as this savannah is enlivened by the mauritia palm. There exists, in its vicinity, an extensive swamp covered with many trees, among which I have remarked the *Virola* in great numbers, together with the *Moronobea* of Aublet. Here also is to be found a splendid *Crinum,* from eight to ten feet high when in bloom, the umbel of flowers measuring more than a foot in diameter.

The savannah of Aripo differs from the above-mentioned; it is, in the interior, subject to periodical but partial inundations, and covered with grasses and herbs altogether different, and, to the naturalist, of a much higher interest than the former specimens. The soil is a kind of sand covered with vegetable *detritus*. It is impossible to describe the feelings of the botanist when arriving at a field like this, so much unlike anything he has ever before seen. Here are full-blowing large orchids, with red, white, and yellow flowers; and, among the grasses, smaller ones of great variety and as great scientific interest; melastomaceous plants of various genera (*Arthrostemma* and *Osbeckia*)—utricularias, droseras, rare and various grasses, and cyperoids of small sizes and fine kinds, with a species of *Cassytha;* in the water, *Ceratophyllum* and bog-mosses. Such a variety of forms and colours is nowhere else to be seen, or met with, in the island. This scenery is enlivened by groves of moriche and cabbage palms, growing here and there in great luxuriance in the more inundated spots.

The transition from this kind of savannah to the dry savannahs of the plain, or plateau, is exemplified in those known by the name of O'Mara and Piarco. They do not exhibit that variety of plants which adorn those already mentioned, but they still retain the same striking features, and the soil is undoubtedly of

A A

the same composition. The grasses are higher and coarser, and the savannahs themselves interspersed with two small trees—the *Chaparro* (*Curatella*) and a *Bunchosia;* here and there also a shrub of *Miconia*, or *Vismia*, with byttnerias, ruellias, and osbeckias. In the water-courses are to be found two plants, viz., an *Eriocaulon* and *Tonina*, which are perhaps to be found also at Aripo, together with the following: *Xyris, Mayaca, Hydrolea*, and, bordering on the high wood, *Rapatea*.

Somewhat resembling the above, but more destitute of similar shrubs, are the savannahs of Icacos, and those of Savanetta and Couva. The driest, however, as also the least interesting of our "natural savannahs," is that situated near Arima. It is overgrown with chaparros, under whose scanty shade grow coarse scrophularaceæ, principally *Beyrichia*, with a smaller quota of grasses and cyperoids; and, in moist spots, an abundance of *Heliconia psittacorum*.

I would not, without much hesitation, class the savannahs on the mountains—from St. Joseph to Arima—among *natural* savannahs. They may possibly owe their origin to the destruction of forests by fire, in parts where the layer of soil was too thin to nourish a fresh generation of trees. They offer little interest to the botanist, and yet their exploration is rather difficult, the high rank grass they produce—*Pennisetum, Setaria, Andropogon*, &c.—being mixed up with cutting sclerias and others. However, whenever these savannahs have been cleared by burning, a more interesting vegetation succeeds; and I have found there, among other plants, several orchids, *Buchnera*, &c.

After thus endeavouring to present a picture of our forests and savannahs, as far as their botanical character is concerned, I will now proceed to give an account of the rivers and swamps.

Rivers with a rapid stream are of little interest to the botanist, and we have already noticed what plants are met with on their banks, when speaking of ravines and waterfalls. As to plants vegetating altogether in water, there are hardly any beyond a few algæ adhering to the roots of trees: those of a larger size would be carried away by freshets during the wet season. But those watercourses which are rather mere estuaries, since their waters become salt during the dry season, deserve peculiar notice.

As soon as the wet season sets in, they are seen covered with a thick carpeting of nymphæas, utricularias, pontederias, and azollas. This vegetation is nearly identical with that of our swamps or lagoons, for instance, those of Erin and Quemada; they exhibit, however, a few other plants which are not found at the above place, viz., *Salvinia*, *Limnobium*, *Ceratophyllum*, besides *Lemna* and *Pistia*. The half-salt or brackish swamps nourish principally large rushes, typhas, banisterias, and *Echites biflora*, *Acrostichum aureum*, and, nearer to the sea, *Crenea* and *Antherylium*. In small water-pools or rivulets, in the plains of the interior districts, may be found *Ammania* and *Jussieua*, *Spilanthes*, several species of *Nerpestes*, *Mayaca*, and *Conobea*.

On sandy beaches, we observe, before all, the beautiful *Ipomea Pes Capræ* and another species with white flowers, a *Pancratium* and a *Remirea*; also several grasses of the following genera:— *Paspalum*, *Cenchrus*, *Stenotaphrum*, Cyperoids, and others. Further inward we meet with a dense shrubbery of *Chrysobalanus*, *Conocarpus*, *Paritium*, and *Bactris*; and beyond these, we may, perhaps, observe fields of *Gynerium saccharoides*, or the white roseau.

The vegetation of the pitch-lake has its peculiarities, although no particular species grows there within my knowledge. In the middle of this curious spot there is, of course, no vegetation whatever, since the pitch is there in a state of ebullition; farther off this centre, and in the water of the many crevices which intersect the lake in every direction, the first traces of vegetation become perceivable—such as a few confervæ and a *Chara*; at a still greater circumference, the pitch, having been long exposed to the agencies of sun and rain, has become disintegrated, and in this kind of soil are found a few lichens, mosses, grasses, and cyperoids. In other places, where this layer is looser and thicker, we find the following:—a *Clusia*, *Chrysobalanus icacos*, *Anona palustris*, *Xyris*, bromeliaceæ, and ferns. The lake itself is bounded on one side by a kind of savannah—the sterility of this spot being marked by an undue proportion of sclerias, ferns, and melastomaceæ (*Osbeckia* and *Spennera*), together with bromelias dotting everywhere the rank grasses.

The islets of the Bocas are overgrown with plants which are, as it were, peculiar to them, and on that account they deserve a distinct notice. These islets are, for the most part, drier than the mainland of Trinidad, which circumstance is, undoubtedly, the great modifying cause inducing a botanical resemblance between the former and the Windward Islands; whereas the flora of Guiana preponderates on the mainland. Any person landing on one of these islets must be struck at once with the difference: large bromelias, cactuses, and agaves everywhere shoot up, with their characteristic features; and the thickets of brushwood are composed of helicteres, crotons, capparis, and mimosas, under whose shade thrives a luxuriant vegetation of evolvulus, ruellias, various commelynaceæ, amarantaceæ and compositæ, with only a very few grasses. One ridge is wholly occupied by the beautiful *Coutarea speciosa*, one of the bark-trees of the West Indies.

The primæval forests of these small islands were probably destroyed at an early period, so that we cannot now affirm what they then were; but we must conjecture they were different from those of the mainland. The few plants which are now standing are of trifling interest to the botanist: besides, they do not display that marvellous vigour exhibited by the general vegetation of Trinidad. Almost constantly buffeted by strong blighting winds, they exhibit a ruffled appearance, just as the man, harrowed by habitual passions, bears a peculiar cast of features. These trees belong to the genera bursera, gomphia, sabinea, bombax, and others.

Having thus, and as far as my abilities would allow, sketched the general features of our vegetable world in its natural state, I must now offer a few remarks on the appearance it takes under the fostering care of man, and the modifying influence of cultivation. The plants which are grown, directly or indirectly, for the purpose of ministering to the sustenance and convenience of man, have been fully noticed in the work to which the present paper forms an appendix: they are therefore not to be considered here. But a few plants formerly introduced into Trinidad have been since allowed to degenerate into a wild state; of these I shall first speak. I must premise, however, that my data are not sufficiently authentic, and, of course, this part of my sketch, at least in a few instances, admits of doubts.

The first family which claims our attention is that of grasses —either as having produced a few troublesome intruders, or as having supplied useful individuals. The Guinea-grass (*Panicum jumentorum*), though not, I believe, indigenous to Trinidad, is now found wild in some localities. A panicum grows at the Bocas islands, *called* Guinea-grass; it is very nearly allied to the former, but I am dubious as to their complete identity. Next to this comes the Para-grass, also a panicum, introduced here at some trouble, and which soon became an intolerable nuisance. I must also mention the Bahama-grass (*Cynodon Linearis*); this, however, was not perhaps intentionally introduced or propagated in the island. The same observation applies to the coco-nut tree.

A few amarantaceæ—for instance, *Amaranthus spinosus*—were probably of foreign extraction, and accidentally imported. *Sesamum orientale* grows wild here and there, but only in single specimens.

Among crassulaceæ, the *Bryophyllum calycinum* deserves to be mentioned.

A few cucurbitaceæ were also brought in, no doubt, originally, as an article of sustenance; but from their immense spread they may now be considered almost as indifferent weeds; such are the common pumpkin and the mexicain (*Momordica balsamina*).

Several species of opuntias and cereus are to be found everywhere; these certainly are not indigenous.

Two species of clerodendron are regular pests all round Port-of-Spain.

If, now, we turn to those plants which grow wild, although not indigenous, being of fortuitous introduction, our knowledge becomes more restricted still.

An European poa grows wild in the streets and courtyards of Port-of-Spain, and I am inclined to believe that scourge of the gardener and planter—the nut-grass (*Cyperus hydra*)—to be a foreigner.

A number of so called cosmopolitan plants—such as the *Emilia sonchifolia*, *Eclipta erecta*, *Erigeron canadense*, *Datura stramonium*—are, in all probability, accidentally imported species.

Another class of plants calls for a few remarks in this place —I mean those which follow or accompany man on his path of settlement and in his cultivations, which cover the walls of neglected or abandoned dwellings, and are, for the most part, sure symptoms of his former residence in their localities. They are hardly to be met with anywhere else; so much so, that we can judge with certainty, by the mere presence of certain plants, that a plantation must have existed in such or such a place; in fact, that we are in a RASTRAJO. Now where, I would ask, were the germs of these plants previous to the eradication or decay of the original vegetation?

The streets of Port-of-Spain are overgrown by a number of plants of the genera cynodon, eleusine, cyperus, alternanthera, and euphorbia; these appear to become the more vigorous the more they are trodden upon. Others could not resist or survive this treatment, and, therefore, retire into vacant courtyards and abandoned lots—as, for instance, the peperomia, several urticas, and amaranthi, the *Elephanthopus spicatus, Eclipta erecta, Parthenium hysterophorus, Synedrella nodiflora*, a *Hedyotis, Leonurus Sibiricus*, solanum, datura, and physalis, *Scoparia dulcis, Capraria biflora*, a portulacca, a sida, and others less common. On crumbling roofs and dilapidated mason-work we may remark a barbula, *Gymnogramma calomelanos, Dactyloctenium Ægyptiacum, Poa ciliaris, Tradescantia discolor*, urtica, and parietaria, *Boerhavia paniculata* (Rich.), eupatorium, and sonchus, borreria, and verbena, &c. Two vines, a cissus and the *Luffa operculata*, cover nearly every old wall.

On road-sides, we meet with certain of the same plants we have just now enumerated, mixed up with a variety of species belonging to different families. Where the road traverses cultivated land, the following genera prevail:—Setaria, cenchrus, sporobolus, chloris, saccharum, andropogon, cyperus, and fuirena; in moist situations, spermacoce and barreria, spigelia, asclepias, schultesia, and sabiea, hyptis and salvia, rivinia, sida, urena, euphorbia, and croton, osbeckia, crotalaria, æschynomene, and hedysarum: these grow in company with shrubs of the genera hamelia, randia, rauwolfia, and lantana; also with lianes and vines, such as convolvulaceæ, bignoniaceæ, echites, stigmophyllum, paullinia, and leguminoseæ. A somewhat different assemblage prevails where the path lies through a forest: there we find ferns of the genera adiantum, lindsæa, trichomanes, lycopodium, and selaginella; xiphidium, piper, böhmeria, various rubiaceæ, acanthaceæ, and bignoniaceæ; petiveria, triumfetta, melastomaceæ, and others.

The sides of ditches are, generally, clothed with the following :—Bartramia, jungermanniaceæ, hemionitis, asplenium and acnemia, lycopodium and selaginella; various grasses and cyperoids; dorstenia, leria, cephaelis, hedysarum, and mimosa.

Cultivated grounds have also their peculiar inhabitants. Polypodium, aspidium, lindsæa and adiantum, large setarias, commelynaceæ, pupalia, centropogon, hedysarum and aroideæ delight in cacao plantations; paspalum and panicum, cyperus and mariscus, conyza and ageratum, eryngium, indigofera, hedysarum and desmodium, herpestes and drymaria, and, but too frequently, the alectra, or cane-killer, in sugar plantations: the alectra, however, is not limited to cane-fields. In provision grounds and recently burnt land, the following genera occur :—Poa, panicum, cyperus, erigeron, porophyllum, emilia, spilanthus, neurolæna, erechtites, solanum, mitreola, priva, oxalis, wedelia, cenchrus, *Scoparia dulcis, Eryngium fœtidum,* microtea, and croton.

In abandoned lands will grow, at first, the foregoing weeds, and soon after, the following shrubs :—Lantana, varronia, psidium, ochroma, cecropia, and abroma, and, among palms, the groo-groo, *acrocomia,* and astrocaryum.

The vegetation of our pasture-lands is composed, in addition to grasses and cyperoids, of hypoxis, cipura, araceæ, elephanthopus, spermacoce, spigelia, echites, *Asclepias curassavica,* marsypianthes, solanum, achetaria, sauvagesia, osbeckia, hedysarum, and mimosa.

It now remains for me to enter upon the enumeration of all the genera I have had an opportunity of observing in the island — a list that will interest the general reader much less than the scientific man, or the student seeking information. Before, however, commencing this task, I will give a general sketch of what Humboldt calls " Forms of Vegetation," and how far each of these is represented in Trinidad.

PÁLMS.—These are largely represented here, and among them we have the small geonoma, from three to four feet in height, as well as the stately *Oreodoxa,* or *Areca oleracea,* with its lofty crest towering above our forest giants, and the climbing desmoncus winding upwards and downwards among its neighbours, sometimes to an enormous length. The pinnated-leaved genera outnumber, by far, those with fan-shaped leaves, of which there are only three species, to my knowledge. Our palms are seen to the best advantage in the savannahs at Aripo and the Cocal, where they form groups at shorter or longer intervals.

BANANAS.—This form embraces the plantain and banana, or Indian fig, as well as the balisiers, the ginger and arrow-root plants. We have a rich supply of these, and no doubt, in conjunction with the palms, they impart to our landscape some of its choicest features. Every person of taste must have been struck with the exquisite beauty of some of our glens and river hollows, in the composition of whose scenery the balisiers contribute an important item.

MALVACEÆ.—Humboldt finds the type of this form in those gigantic trees known here under the common name of silk-cottons. The latter we have in the island, as also a few others, viz., the wild chestnut (*Carolinea*) and the cork-wood (*Ochroma*). The first of these trees, the bombax, presents this striking peculiarity, that, besides its enormous proportions, it affords a hospitable home to a multitude of parasites from numerous families—such as ferns, wild pines, orchids, and cacti, besides a host of mosses and liverworts.

MIMOSÆ.—The elegance of this form, both as regards branches and foliage, cannot fail to attract the attention of an observer. Of these, the tamarind tree is the most common example, but certainly not the most beautiful. This is to be found in the ingas and the genera deriving from them.

HEATHS.—We have nothing like this form.

CACTUS.—Excepting on the Bocas islands, these have but few representatives here, on account of the great fertility of the soil and the abundant atmospheric moisture.

ORCHIDS.—It is well known that we possess many individuals of this strange family, though they are becoming more rare in the vicinity of cultivations—at least their finer kinds. But in the forests they occur at every step, displaying their graceful forms and gorgeous hues.

CASUARINAS.—There are a few of these—cultivated.

PINES.—We have no pines, except a few cultivated specimens, stunted and miserable-looking, as if longing for " sweet home." There is a ridiculous exhibition of them in front of Trinity church, Port-of-Spain.

POTHOS AND AROIDS.—We are very rich in this form, there being all imaginable varieties of them. From the numerous species of anthurium, growing like parasites on trees, various species of caladium and others; from the widely known and useful mamure (*Carludovica*), which furnishes the settlers with natural twine and rope, down to the dumb-cane (*Dieffenbachia*) and smaller aroids growing on river-sides, together with the curious cyclanthus—all are equally interesting and attractive. Tanias and seguines belong to this form. An interesting plant of this class is the *Montrichardia*, the largest of all, covering our half-salt, brackish swamps for miles: its seeds supply a sort of chestnut, which certainly no one would have expected.

LIANES.—We have already had occasion to observe how rich our forests are in this form—the truly distinctive feature of the tropical woods. A great number of families supply examples—the most prominent being bignonias, malpighiaceæ, bauhinias, and dilleniaceæ: they assume all possible forms, sometimes being twisted together like ropes, or flattened like tapes; sometimes they creep up the highest trees, thence to hang down in elegant festoons, or coil around the stems, like giant serpents, attempting to stifle their supporters. A few run along the ground, their hooks and thorns catching or tearing the incautious hunter, who, in return, has honoured them with the appellation of *Boyaux-Diable* (devil's-guts) and *Crocs-chien* (dog's-teeth). Others hang a few feet only from the ground, in readiness to cut and tear the clothes of the treader of their mazes. A great many, on the other hand, supply, in case of need, as I have more than once experienced during my rambles in our forests, an abundance of fresh water of a deliciously cool and refreshing quality. A large proportion of our lianes bear the finest flowers; I need only mention the bignonias, dolichos, norantea, the passion-flowers, and the securidaca.

ALOES.—There is but one plant here as a representative of this form—the agave—which grows principally at the Bocas islands, in great numbers and with much vigour.

GRASSES—mainly arborescent.—Although the bamboo, which chiefly represents this form in our island, is a foreigner, yet it has spread all over the colony to such an extent that it becomes, in many places, an indispensable adjunct to our island landscape. We possess, however, an indigenous bamboo, which may be seen at Caroni, Chaguanas, and Couva, and also the elegant chusquea, which we have noticed on the *Tocuche*.

FERNS.—We have a few tree-ferns, as I have already mentioned; but as they grow on the top of our highest *mornes*, they are not easily reached. Notwithstanding, the form of ferns has here a large number of representatives, and in many localities they add no inconsiderable charm to the refreshing scenery of our valleys and ravines.

LILIES.—Although we have a number of very elegant pancratiums, crinums, and amaryllides, yet a South American island is not exactly the spot in which a botanist would seek or expect a rich assemblage of these plants. The only part where the importance of this form is exhibited to any advantage is the swamp near the savannah at the Cocal.

WILLOWS.—Not represented here.

MYRTLES.—In dry and somewhat sterile spots, we generally meet with a peculiar vegetation, characterised by not very large trees, with slender branches, small leaves of a dark shining green, and a roughness of the stem, owing to the shedding of their bark. These are myrtles. But the myrtle form does not possess here that importance it assumes in higher latitudes, and in New Holland.

MELASTOMAS.—If we are rather poor in myrtles, this deficiency is compensated by the melastomaceæ, a form not very remote from the preceding. The plants belonging to it are, generally, shrubs or small trees, with dark green leaves, distinguishable by very prominent longitudinal ribs. The flowers commonly form large rich clusters, and are frequently very fragrant. They are closely allied to the next class.

LAURELS.—This closes the list of forms as enumerated by Von Humboldt. He adds to this form that tribe of plants to which belong the mammee and the *Matapalo* of our forests—distinguishable by a very fine foliage and large flowers, generally fragrant. We are, therefore, induced to aggregate to them the moronobea—one of the finest ornaments of our woods—the different species of clusia, also the rose-apple tree, though an exotic.

There is one form of trees which Von Humboldt has omitted, and which cannot fail to attract the notice of the least attentive, as very peculiar and highly characteristic. I would call it the Papaw form.

PAPAYAS.—A naked trunk, or branches, crowned by a cluster

of large leaves with long stalks, will characterise this form. Besides the type-form—the papaw—we must notice the trumpet-tree (*Cecropia peltata*) and a species of panax, common in cultivated grounds.

I have now nearly arrived at the conclusion of my task, since it remains for me but to give a list of all the genera I have, up to the present time, had opportunities of observing. However long and learned this list may appear to the general reader, yet its perusal will afford but little satisfaction to the scientific man. It is therefore natural that, for the information of the latter, I should prefix this bare classification by a few words of explanation. Though I have been engaged now more than fourteen years in researches connected with the vegetable world of Trinidad, I have rather given preference to the study of morphology, anatomy, and physiology, contributing the results of my investigations therein, from time to time, to the scientific papers of Germany. To the lower families of plants, in particular, I have not been able to devote that time and attention they deserve; and, as a consequence, it will appear that they have been neglected. I have also already explained the reason for my having refrained from determining the numerous species of plants which compose the flora of Trinidad.

A CATALOGUE OF THE DIFFERENT FAMILIES AND GENERA OF PLANTS EXISTING IN TRINIDAD, AS HAVING PASSED UNDER MY OWN OBSERVATION.

Algæ—
  Oscillaria.
  Zygnema.
  Conferva.
  Vanchoria.
  Ulva.
  Sphærococcus.
  Zonaria.
Characeæ—
  Chara . . . . . . Ag.
Lichens—
  Cænogonium.
  Parmelia.
Fungi—
  Uredo . . . . . . Pers.
  Torula . . . . . . Pers.

Fungi (continued)—
  Phragmidium . . . Link.
  Didymosporium . . Nees.
  Coryneum . . . . Fries.
  Tubercularia . . . . Tode.
  Psilonia . . . . . Fries.
  Fusisporium . . . . id.
  Bacridium . . . . Kunz.
  Oidium . . . . . Link.
  Sporotrichum . . . id.
  Botrytis . . . . . Mich.
  Aspergillus . . . . id.
  Eurotium . . . . . Link.
  Pilobolus . . . . . Tode.
  Isaria . . . . . . Pers.
  Erysibe . . . . . Rcb.

Fungi (continued)—
Stemonitis	Gled.
Physarum	Pers.
Geaster	Mich.
Nidularia	Fries.
Clathrus	Mich.
Phallus	id.
Hysterium	Fries.
Sphæria	Hall.
Hypoxilon	Bull.
Tremella	Dill.
Peziza	id.
Helvella	L.
Hydnum	L.
Polyporus	Fries.
Agaricus (a)	L.

Hepaticæ—
Riccia	Mich.
Anthocera	Mich.
Marchantia	March.
Jungermannia	Dill.

Musci—
Sphagnum	Dill.
Fissidens	Hedw.
Bryum	Dill.
Bartramia	Hedw.
Calymperes	Sw.
Syrrhopodon	Schu.
Barbula	Hedw.
Macromitrium	Br.
Dicranum	Hedw.
Hypopterygium	Brid.
Miuadelphus	C. Mül.
Neckera	Hedw.
Polytrichum	P. Bea.
Hookeria	Sw.
Hypnum	Dill.

Filices—
Gleichenia	Smith.
Mertensia	Willd.
Cyathea	Presl.
Cnemidaria	Presl.
Alsophila	Br.
Lastrea	Pres.
Oleanara (b)	Cavan.
Nephrolepis	Schott.
Polystichum	id.
Aspidium	id.
Blechnum	L.
Asplenium	L.
Diplazium	Sw.
Davallia	Smith.

Filices (continued)—
Lindsæa	Dryan.
Dicksonia	Pr.
Lomaria	Willd.
Pteris	L.
Allosorus	Bernh.
Adiantum (c)	L.
Cheilanthes	Sw.
Vittaria	Smith.
Polypodium	L.
Marginaria	Bory.
Campyloneurum	Pr.
Pleopeltis	Hum.
Phymatodes	Pr.
Monogramma	Sch.
Hemionitis	L.
Pleurogramma	Bl.
Grammitis	Sw.
Meniscium	Schreb.
Gymnogramma	Desi.
Polybotria	Hum.
Olfersia	Raddi.
Acrostichum	L.
Parkeria	Hook.
Hymenophyllum	Sw.
Trichomanes	L.
Aneimia	Sw.
Schizæa	Sw.
Lygodium	Sw.
Ophioglossum	L.

Hydropterides—
Azolla	Lam.
Salvinia	Mich.

Lycopodiaceæ—
Lycopodium	L.
Selaginella	Pal.

Balanophoraceæ—
Helosis	Rich.

Graminaceæ—
Leersia	Sol.
Oryza	L.
Pharus	P. Br.
Zea (d)	L.
Coix (e)	L.
Paspalum (f)	L.
Olyra	L.
Eriochloa	Kunth.
Panicum (g)	L.
Stenotaphrum	Trin.
Oplismenus	Pal.
Pennisetum	Rich.
Cenchrus	L.

(a) Our edible mushroom.
(b) Hart's-tongue.
(c) Maiden-hair.
(d) Maize.
(e) Job's tears.
(f) Lancet-grass.
(g) Guinea-grass.

Graminaceæ (continued)—
Sporobolus . . . . R. B.
Gynerium (a) . . . H.B.K.
Cynodon (b) . . . . Rich.
Dactyloctenium . . . Willd.
Chloris . . . . . Sw.
Leptochloa . . . . Pal.
Eleusine (c) . . . . Gaert.
Poa . . . . L.
Orthoclada . . . . Pal.
Streptogyna . . . . id.
Chusquea (d) . . . Kunth.
Nastus (e) . . . . Jus.
Tripsacum . . . . L.
Eriochrysis . . . . Pal.
Saccharum (f) . . . L.
Anthistiria . . . . L.
Andropogon (g) . . . L.
Ischæmum . . . . L.
Cyperaceæ—
Scleria (h) . . . . Berg.
Rhynchospora . . . Vahl.
Dichromena . . . . Rich.
Remirea . . . . . Aubl.
Diplasia . . . . . Rich.
Fuirena . . . . . Rottb.
Fimbristylis . . . . Vahl.
Isolepis . . . . . R.B.
Cyperus (i) . . . . L.
Eriocaulonaceæ—
Eriocaulon . . . . Gron.
Tonina . . . . . . Aubl.
Xyridaceæ—
Xyris . . . . . . L.
Mayaca . . . . . Aubl.
Commelynaceæ—
Commelyna (j) . . . Dill.
Aneilema . . . . . R. B.
Callisia . . . . . Löeffl.
Tradescantia . . . . L.
Dichorisandra . . . Mich.
Juncaceæ—
Rapatea . . . . . Aubl.
Pontederiaceæ—
Pontederia . . . . L.
Smilaceæ—
Smilax (k) . . . . Tourn.
Dioscoreaceæ—
Rajania . . . . . L.
Dioscorea (l) . . . Plum.

Hydrocharidaceæ—
Limnobium . . . . Rich.
Burmanniaceæ—
Dictyostega . . . . Miers.
Iridaceæ—
Cipura . . . . . . Aubl.
Hæmodoraceæ—
Xyphidium . . . .
Hypoxidaceæ—
Hypoxis . . . . . L.
Amaryllidaceæ—
Amaryllis (m) . . . L.
Crinum . . . . . L.
Pancratium . . . . L.
Alstrœmeria . . . . L.
Agave (n) . . . . . L.
Bromeliaceæ—
Ananassa (o) . . . . Lindl.
Bromelia (p) . . . . L.
Bilbergia (q) . . . . Thun.
Pitcairnia (q) . . . Herit.
Tillandsia (q) . . . L.
Gusmannia . . . R. & P.
Orchidaceæ—
Pleurothallis . . . . R. B.
Specklinia . . . . Lindl.
Lepanthes . . . . Sw.
Stelis . . . . . . id.
Liparis . . . . . . Rich.
Bolbophyllum . . . Tho.
Polystachya . . . . Hook.
Epidendrum . . . . L.
Isochilus . . . . . R. B.
Cattleya . . . . . Lindl.
Nanodes . . . . . id.
Trizeuxis . . . . . id.
Ornithocephalus . . . Hook.
Maxillaria . . . . R. & P.
Bifrenaria . . . . Lindl.
Catasetum . . . . Rich.
Stanhopea . . . . Hook.
Gongora . . . . . R. & P.
Coryanthes (r) . . . Hook.
Peristera . . . . . id.
Cymbidium . . . . Sw.
Cyrtopodium . . . R. B.
Cyrtoptera . . . . Lindl.
Notylia . . . . . id.
Ionopsis . . . . . H.B.K.
Rodriguezia . . . R. & P.

(a) White roseau.
(b) Bahama-grass.
(c) Pied-poule.
(d) Vine bamboo.
(e) Common bamboo.
(f) Sugar-cane.
(g) Lemon-grass.
(h) Sword-grass.
(i) Nut-grass.
(j) Herbe-grasse.
(k) Sarsaparilla.
(l) Yam.
(m) Lily.
(n) Langue-bœuf.
(o) Pine-apple.
(p) Caratas.
(q) Wild pine-apple.
(r) Macaque.

Orchidaceæ (continued)—
Burlingtonia . . .	Lindl.
Macrodenia . . .	R. B.
Cryptarrhena . . .	id.
Oncidium (a) . . .	Sw.
Fernandezia . . .	R. & P.
Dichæa	Lindl.
Brassia	R. B.
Angræcum . . .	Thou.
Habenaria . . .	Willd.
Spiranthes . . .	Rich.
Pelexia	Poit.
Prescottia	Lindl.
Cleistes	Rich.
Epistephium . . .	H.B.K.
Vanilla	Sw.
Schomburgkia . .	Lindl.
Batemania	id.
Paphinia	id.

Zingiberaceæ—
Alpinia (b) . . .	L.
Costus (c)	L.

Cannaceæ—
Thalia	L.
Maranta (d) . . .	Plum.
Calathea (e) . . .	Meyer.
Canna (f)	L.

Musaceæ—
Heliconia (g) . . .	L.

Naiadaceæ—
Zostera	L.

Lemnaceæ—
Lemna	L.

Araceæ—
Pistia	L.
Caladium (h) . . .	Vent.
Philodendron (i) . .	Schott.
Dieffenbachia (j) . .	id.
Monstera (k) . . .	Adans.
Montrichardia . . .	Crüger.
Massowia	Koch.
Anthurium	Schott.

Typhaceæ—
Typha	Tourn.

Pandanaceæ—
Carludovica (l) . . .	R. & P.
Cyclanthus	Poit.

Palmaceæ—
Oreodoxa (m) . . .	Willd.
Mauritia (n)	L. son.
Geonoma	Willd.
Manicaria (o) . . .	Gaert.
Copernicia (p) . . .	Mart.
Thrinax	L. son.
Desmoncus (q) . . .	Mart.
Bactris (r)	Jacq.
Guilielma (s)	Mart.
Acrocomia (t) . . .	id.
Astrocaryum	Meyer.
Elaïs	Jacq.
Cocos (u)	L.

Taxaceæ—
Podocarpus	Herit.

Piperaceæ—
Piper (v)	L.
Peperomia (w) . . .	R. & P.
Ottonia (x)	Spreu.

Ceratophyllaceæ—
Ceratophyllum . . .	L.

Ulmaceæ—
Celtis	Tourn.

Moraceæ—
Morus (y)	id.
Ficus (z)	id.
Dorstenia (aa) . . .	Plum.

Artocarpaceæ—
Brosimum (bb) . . .	Sw.
Cecropia (cc)	L.
Coussapoa	Aubl.
Trophis	P. Br.

Urticaceæ—
Urtica (dd)	Tourn.
Boehmeria	Jacq.
Parietaria	Tourn.

Lacistemaceæ—
Lacistema	Sw.

Amarantaceæ—
Iresine	Willd.

(a) Butterfly and flies.	(k) Ceriman.	(u) Coco-palm.
(b) Mardi-gras.	(l) Mamure.	(v) Black pepper.
(c) Canne-de-rivière.	(m) Mountain cabbage.	(w) Herbe-couresse.
(d) Arrow-root.	(n) Moriche.	(x) Potomo.
(e) Aruma.	(o) Timit.	(y) Fustic.
(f) Tuluma.	(p) Carat.	(z) Wild fig-tree.
(g) Balisier.	(q) Groo-groo.	(aa) Contra-yerva.
(h) Tanias.	(r) Black roseau.	(bb) Moussara.
(i) Seguine.	(s) Pirijao.	(cc) Trumpet-tree.
(j) Seguine-diable.	(t) Groo-groo.	(dd) Nettle.

Amarantaceæ (continued)—
Alternanthera (a) . . Forsk.
Gomphrena . . . . L.
Pupalia . . . . . Mart.
Amaranthus (b) . . L.
Chamissoa. . . . . H.B.K.
Polygonaceæ—
Polygonum . . . . L.
Coccoloba (c) . . . Jacq.
Nyctaginaceæ—
Boerhaavia . . . . L.
Pisonia . . . . . Plum.
Monimiaceæ—
Siparouna. . . . . Aubl.
Tetratome . . . . Pöpp.
Lauraceæ—
Aiovea. . . . . . Aubl.
Ocotea. . . . . . id.
Cassytha . . . . . L.
Hernandiaceæ—
Hernandia (d)
Proteaceæ—
Rhopala (e) . . . Aubl.
Aristolochiaceæ—
Aristolochia (f) . . Tourn.
Plantaginaceæ—
Plantago (g) . . . . L.
Plumbaginaceæ—
Plumbago . . . . . Tourn.
Compositæ—
Odontoloma . . . . H.B.K.
Sparganophorus . . Vent.
Vernonia . . . . . Schre.
Elephanthopus . . . L.
Rolandra . . . . . Rottb.
Liabum . . . . . Adans.
Pectis . . . . . . L.
Isocarpha. . . . . R. B.
Ageratum . . . . . L.
Hebeclinium . . . . de C.
Eupatorium (h) . . . Tourn.
Mikania (i) . . . . Willd.
Erigeron . . . . . de C.
Conyza . . . . . Less.
Baccharis . . . . . L.
Pluchea (j) . . . . Cass.
Eclipta. . . . . . L.
Clibadium (k) . . . L.

Compositæ (continued)—
Ambrosia (l) . . . . Tourn.
Parthenium . . . . L.
Wedelia . . . . . Jacq.
Melanthera . . . . Rohr.
Wulffia . . . . . Neck.
Gymnopsis . . . . de C.
Leighia . . . . . Cass.
Bidens . . . . . . L.
Cosmos . . . . . Cai.
Verbesina . . . . Less.
Spilanthes . . . . Jacq.
Syncdrella . . . . Gaert.
Porophyllum . . . Vail.
Calea . . . . . . R. B.
Neurolæna (m) . . . id.
Erechtites . . . . Raffin.
Emilia. . . . . . Cass.
Leria . . . . . . de C.
Sonchus . . . . . L.
Lobeliaceæ—
Lobelia . . . . . L.
Laurentia. . . . . Neck.
Centropogon . . . . Presl.
Pongatieæ—
Pongatium . . . . Jus.
Rubiaceæ—
Borreria (n) . . . . Meyer.
Spermacoce . . . . L.
Diodia . . . . . . L.
Cephaelis . . . . . Sw.
Palicourea . . . . Aubl.
Psychotria . . . . L.
Coffea (o) . . . . . L.
Faramea . . . . . Rich.
Chiococca (p) . . . P. B.
Lygodisodea . . . . R. & P.
Nonatelia . . . . . Aubl.
Sabicea . . . . . id.
Hamelia . . . . . Jacq.
Isertia . . . . . . Schreb.
Gonzalea . . . . . Pers.
Hedyotis . . . . . Lam.
Sipanea . . . . . Aubl.
Calycophyllum . . . de C.
Manettia . . . . . Mutis.
Hillia . . . . . . Jacq.
Coutarea (q) . . . . Aubl.

(a) Herbe-à-vache.
(b) Spinach.
(c) Sea-side grape.
(d) Mirobolant.
(e) Aguatapana.
(f) Snake-root.
(g) Plantain.
(h) Herbe-à-pino.
(i) Guaco.
(j) Guérit-tout.
(k) Barbasco.
(l) Altamisa.
(m) Herbe-à-pique.
(n) Macornette.
(o) Coffee.
(p) Petit branda.
(q) Bocas bark.

TRINIDAD.

Rubiaceæ (continued)—
Nauclea . . . . . L.
Bertiera . . . . . Aubl.
Randia . . . . . Houst.
Genipa . . . . . . Bl.
Amaioua . . . . . Aubl.
Oleaceæ—
Linociera . . . . . Sw.
Loganiaceæ—
Strychnos . . . . . L.
Apocynaceæ—
Allamanda . . . . L.
Vallesia . . . . . R. & P.
Thevetia . . . . . L.
Rauwolfia . . . . . Plum.
Tabernæmontana . . L.
Echites . . . . . P. B.
Dipladenia . . . . Al.
Asclepiadaceæ—
Metastelma . . . . R. B.
Sarcostemma . . . id.
Philibertia . . . . H.B.K.
Asclepias . . . . . L.
Gonolobus . . . . Rich.
Marsdenia . . . . R. B.
Gentianaceæ—
Voyria . . . . . . Aubl.
Schultesia . . . . . Mart.
Lisianthus . . . . P. B.
Coutoubea . . . . Aubl.
Slevogtia . . . . . Rich.
Mitreola . . . . . L.
Spigeliaceæ—
Spigelia (a) . . . . L.
Labiateæ—
Ocimum (b) . . . . L.
Marsypianthes . . . Mart.
Hyptis (c) . . . . Jacq.
Salvia . . . . . . L.
Leonurus . . . . . L.
Leonotis . . . . . Pers.
Verbenaceæ—
Lippia . . . . . . L.
Verbena (d) . . . . L.
Priva . . . . . . Adan.
Lantana (e) . . . . L.
Tamonia . . . . . Aubl.
Hosta . . . . . . Jacq.
Vitex (f) . . . . . L.
Citharexylon . . . L.
Duranta . . . . . L.

Verbenaceæ (continued)—
Petræa . . . . . . Houst.
Amasonia . . . . . L.
Ægiphila . . . . . Jacq.
Myoporaceæ—
Avicennia (g) . . . L.
Bontia . . . . . . Plum.
Cordiaceæ—
Cordia (h) . . . . R. B.
Ehretiaceæ—
Ehretia . . . . . L.
Beurreria . . . . . Jacq.
Tournefortia . . . . R. B.
Heliotropium . . . L.
Convolvulaceæ—
Evolvulus . . . . . L.
Convolvulus . . . . L.
Calonyction . . . . Chois.
Quamoclit . . . . Tourn.
Batatas (i) . . . . Chois.
Pharbitis . . . . . Chois.
Hydroleaceæ—
Hydrolea
Wigandia
Solanaceæ—
Nicotiana . . . . . L.
Solandra . . . . . Sw.
Physalis . . . . . L.
Solanum . . . . . L.
Cestrum . . . . . L.
Scrophulariaceæ—
Browallia . . . . . L.
Brunfelsia . . . . Plum.
Capraria (j) . . . . L.
Herpestes . . . . . Gaert.
Achetaria . . . . . Cham.
Buchnera . . . . . L.
Scoparia (k) . . . . L.
Alectra (l) . . . . Thunb.
Acanthaceæ—
Thunbergia . . . . L.
Hygrophila . . . . R. B.
Ruellia . . . . . . L.
Aphelandra . . . . R. B.
Eranthemum . . . id.
Blechum . . . . . P. B.
Dicliptera . . . . Jus.
Trichanthera . . . Kunth
Bignoniaceæ—
Tecoma (m) . . . . Jus.
Spathodea (n) . . . Pal.

(a) Brinvilliers.
(b) Petit baume.
(c) Frombasin.
(d) Verveine.
(e) Cariaquite.
(f) Fiddle-wood, or bois-lézard.
(g) Mangrove.
(h) Cyp.
(i) Sweet potato.
(j) Thé-pays.
(k) Sweet broom.
(l) Cane-killer.
(m) Poui.
(n) Cable-vine

GENERA OF PLANTS.

Bignoniaceæ (continued)—
  Bignonia (a) . . . . Jus.
Gesneriaceæ—
  Columnea . . . . . Plum.
  Besleria . . . . . Plum.
  Drymonia . . . . . Mart.
  Gesnera . . . . . id.
  Gloxinia . . . . . Herit.
  Rytidophyllum . . . Mart.
  Couradia . . . . . id.
Crescentiaceæ—
  Crescentia (b) . . . L.
Utriculariæ—
  Utricularia . . . . L.
Myrsinaceæ—
  Myrsine . . . . . L.
  Ardisia . . . . . Sw.
  Jacquinia . . . . . L.
Sapotaceæ—
  Chrysophyllum (c) . . L.
  Sabatia . . . . . Sw.
  Achras (d) . . . . P. B.
  Lucuma . . . . . Jus.
Ebenaceæ—
  Diospyros . . . . . L.
Ericaceæ—
  Clethra . . . . . L.
  Thibaudia . . . . . Par.
Umbelliferæ—
  Hydrocotyle . . . . Tourn.
  Spanantho . . . . Jacq.
  Eryngium . . . . . Tourn.
Araliaceæ—
  Panax . . . . . . L.
Ampelidaceæ—
  Cissus . . . . . . L.
Loranthaceæ—
  Viscum . . . . . L.
  Loranthus . . . . L.
Menispermaceæ—
  Cissampelos (e) . . . L.
Myristicaceæ—
  Myristica (f) . . . . L.
Anonaceæ—
  Uvaria (g) . . . . . L.
  Anona (h) . . . . L.
Dilleniaceæ—
  Curatella (i) . . . . L.

Dilleniaceæ (continued)—
  Doliocarpus . . . . Rol.
  Tetracera . . . . . L.
Ranunculaceæ—
  Clematis . . . . . L.
Papaveraceæ—
  Argemone . . . . Tourn.
Cruciferæ—
  Nasturtium (j) . . . R. B.
  Lepidium . . . . . id.
  Sinapis . . . . . . Tourn.
Capparidaceæ—
  Cleome . . . . . de C.
  Capparis . . . . . L.
  Cratæva (k) . . . . L.
  Hermupoa . . . . Löeffl.
Nymphæaceæ—
  Nymphæa (l) . . . . Neck.
Droseraceæ—
  Drosera . . . . . L.
Violaceæ—
  Alsodeia . . . . . Thou.
Sauvagesiaceæ—
  Sauvagesia . . . . L.
Turneraceæ—
  Turnera . . . . . Plum.
Samydaceæ—
  Samyda . . . . . L.
  Casearia . . . . . Jacq.
Bixaceæ—
  Bixa (m) . . . . . L.
  Flacourtia (n) . . . Comm.
Passifloraceæ—
  Ryania . . . . . . Vahl.
  Passiflora (o) . . . Jus.
Papayaceæ—
  Carica (p) . . . . . L.
Cucurbitaceæ—
  Feuillea (q) . . . . L.
  Melothria . . . . . L.
  Anguria . . . . . L.
  Bryonia (r) . . . . L.
  Luffa (s) . . . . . Tourn.
  Momordica (t) . . . L.
Begoniaceæ—
  Begonia (u) . . . . L.
Cactaceæ—
  Cerus . . . . . . Hau.

(a) Cable-vine.
(b) Calabash.
(c) Cainito.
(d) Sapodilla and Balata.
(e) Pareira-brava.
(f) White cedar.
(g) Fruta de Burro.

(h) Sour-sop.
(i) Chaparrio.
(j) Water-cress.
(k) Toco.
(l) Water-lily.
(m) Arnotto.
(n) Governor-plum.

(o) Granadilla.
(p) Papaw.
(q) Secua.
(r) Bryony.
(s) Torchon.
(t) Mexicain.
(u) Wood-sorrel.

418   TRINIDAD.

Cactaceæ (continued)—
 Rhipsalis . . . . . Gaert.
 Opuntia (a) . . . . Tourn.
 Pereskia (b) . . . . Plum.
 Phyllocactus . . . . Link.
Portulaceæ—
 Sesuvium . . . . . L.
 Cypselea . . . . . Turp.
 Portulaca (c) . . . Tourn.
 Talinum . . . . . Adans.
Caryophyllaceæ—
 Drymaria . . . . . Willd.
Phytolaccaceæ—
 Petiveria . . . . . Plum.
 Rivina , ... L.
 Microtea . . . . . Sw..
 Phytolacca . . . . Tourn.
Malvaceæ—
 Urena . . . . . . L.
 Pavonia . . . . . Cav.
 Hibiscus (d) . . . . L.
 Paritium . . . . . A. Jus.
 Thespesia . . . . . Corr.
 Sida (e) . . . . . Kunth.
 Malachra (f) . . . . L.
Sterculiaceæ—
 Pachira . . . . . Aubl.
 Bombax (g) . . . . L.
 Ochroma (h) . . . . Sw.
 Helicteres . . . . L.
 Sterculia (i) . . . . L.
Byttneriaceæ—
 Byttneria . . . . . Löeffl.
 Guazuma (j) . . . . Plum.
 Waltheria . . . . . L.
 Melochia . . . . . L.
Tiliaceæ—
 Sloanea . . . . . L.
 Apeiba . . . . . . Aubl.
 Triumfetta . . . . Plum.
 Muntingia . . . . L.
Ternstroemiaceæ—
 Marila . . . . . . Sw.
 Quuna . . . . . . Aubl
Clusiaceæ—
 Clusia (k) . . . . . L.
 Calophyllum (l) . . . L.

Clusiaceæ (continued)—
 Moronobea (m) . . . Aubl.
Marcgraviaceæ—
 Norantea (n) . . . . Aubl.
 Marcgravia . . . . Plum.
Hypericaceæ—
 Vismia (o) . . . . Vell.
Meliaceæ—
 Trichilia . . . . . L.
 Guarea . . . . . . L.
 Carapa (p) . . . . Aubl.
Cedrelaceæ—
 Cedrela (q) . . . . L.
Malpighiaceæ—
 Hiræa . . . . . . Jacq.
 Triopteris . . . . . L.
 Tetrapteris . . . . Car.
 Banisteria . . . . L.
 Stigmaphyllon . . . A. J.
 Bunchosia . . . . Rich.
Erythroxylaceæ—
 Erythroxylum . . . L.
Sapindaceæ—
 Cardiospermum . . . L.
 Seriana . . . . . Plum.
 Paullinia . . . . . L.
 Sapindus (r) . . . . L.
 Melicocca (s) . . . . L.
 Dodonæa . . . . . L.
Polygalaceæ—
 Polygala . . . . . L.
 Catacoma . . . . . Bent.
 Securidaca (t) . . . L.
Hippocrateaceæ—
 Hippocratea (u) . . . L.
 Tontelea . . . . . Aubl.
Rhamnaceæ—
 Gouania . . . . . Jacq.
Chailletiaceæ—
 Chailletia . . . . . de C.
Euphorbiaceæ—
 Pedilanthus . . . . Neck.
 Euphorbia (v) . . . L.
 Dalechampia . . . . Plum.
 Hura (w) . . . . . L.
 Hippomane (x) . . . L.
 Microstachis . . . . A. Jus.

(a) Prickly-pear.
(b) Gooseberry.
(c) Purslane.
(d) Ochro.
(e) Broom-plant.
(f) Mallow.
(g) Ceyba.
(h) Cork-wood.
(i) Mahaut.
(j) Elm.
(k) Matapalo.
(l) Galba.
(m) Mountain-mangrove.
(n) Prince of Wales' feather.
(o) Bois-sang.
(p) Carapa, or crapaud.
(q) Cedar.
(r) Savonette.
(s) Quenepe.
(t) Liane-paques.
(u) Sto. Domingo-nut.
(v) Euphorbs.
(w) Sand-box.
(x) Manchineel.

Euphorbiaceæ (continued)—
  Tragia . . . . . . Plum.
  Acalypha . . . . . L.
  Omphalea. . . . . L.
  Mabea . . . . . . Aubl.
  Jatropha (a) . . . . Kunth.
  Curcas (b) . . . . . Adans.
  Croton . . . . . . L.
  Phyllanthus . . . . Sw.
  Stillingia . . . . . Gard.
Anarcadiaceæ—
  Anarcadium (c) . . . Rottb.
Spondiaceæ—
  Spondias (d) . . . . L.
Burseraceæ—
  Icica . . . . . . Aubl.
  Bursera . . . . . Jacq.
Connaraceæ—
  Connarus . . . . . L.
  Omphalobium . . . Gaert.
Ochnaceæ—
  Gomphia . . . . . Schreb.
Simaroubaceæ—
  Quassia (e) . . . . de C.
Rutaceæ—
  Esenbeckia (f) . . . Kunth.
Oxalidaceæ—
  Oxalis . . . . . . L.
Combretaceæ—
  Bucida (g) . . . . L.
  Terminalia (h) . . . L.
  Conocarpus (i) . . . Gaert.
  Poivrea . . . . . Comm.
  Combretum . . . . Löeffl.
  Cacoucia . . . . . Aubl.
Rhizophoraceæ—
  Rhizophora (j) . . . Lam.
Legnotideæ—
  Cassipourea . . . . Aubl.
Onagraceæ—
  Jussieua . . . . . L.
Lythraceæ—
  Ammannia . . . . Houst.
  Crenca . . . . . . Aubl.
  Antherylium . . . Rohr.
Melastomaceæ—
  Spennera . . . . . Mart.
  Heteronoma . . . . id.
  Chaetogastra . . . de C.

Melastomaceæ (continued)—
  Arthrostemma . . . Par.
  Osbeckia . . . . . L.
  Pterolepis . . . . de C.
  Clidemia . . . . . Don.
  Tchudya . . . . . de C.
  Ossaca . . . . . . id.
  Sagræa . . . . . id.
  Conostegia . . . . Don.
  Diplochiton . . . . de C.
  Pogonorhynchus . . Cr.
  Henriettea . . . . de C.
  Loreya . . . . . . id.
  Tetrazygia . . . . Rich.
  Miconia . . . . . R. & P.
  Glossocentrum . . . Cr.
  Cremanium . . . . Don.
  Chaenopleura . . . Rich.
Myrtaceæ—
  Psidium (k) . . . . L.
  Myrtus (l) . . . . Tourn.
  Myrcia . . . . . de C.
  Marlierea . . . . . St. Hil.
Lecythidaceæ—
  Lecythis (m) . . . . Löeffl.
  Couroupita (n) . . . Aubl.
Drupaceæ—
  Prunus (o) . . . . L.
Chrysobalanaceæ—
  Chrysobalanus (p) . . L.
  Hirtella . . . . . L.
  Parinarium . . . . Jus.
Papilionaceæ—
  Crotalaria . . . . L.
  Psoralea . . . . . L.
  Indigofera (q) . . . L.
  Tephrosia . . . . . Pers.
  Sabinea . . . . . de C.
  Sesbania . . . . . Pers.
  Æschinomene . . . L.
  Desmodium . . . . de C.
  Rhadinocarpus . . . Vog.
  Clitoria . . . . . L.
  Neurocarpum . . . Desv.
  Centrosema . . . . de C.
  Galactia . . . . . P. B.
  Canavalia . . . . . de C.
  Mucuna (r) . . . . Adans.
  Erythrina (s) . . . L.

(a) Manioc.
(b) Medicinier.
(c) Cashew.
(d) Wild-plum, or monbin.
(e) Bitter ash.
(f) Gasparil.
(g) Olivier.
(h) Almond-tree.
(i) Black mangrove.
(j) Red mangrove.
(k) Guava.
(l) Pimento, or bois d'Inde.
(m) Guatecare.
(n) Bomb-tree.
(o) Noyau.
(p) Icacos.
(q) Indigo.
(r) Cowhage.
(s) Bois-immortel.

Papilionaceæ (continued)—
  Phaseolus (a) . . . . L.
  Dolichos (b) . . . . L.
  Eriosema . . . . . de C.
  Rhynchosia . . . . id.
  Abrus (c) . . . . . L.
  Amerimnum . . . . P. B.
  Drepanocarpus . . . Mey.
  Machærium (d) . . . Pers.
  Andira (e) . . . . Lam.
  Mora (f) . . . . . Bent.
  Cæsalpinia . . . . Plum.
  Parkinsonia . . . . id.
  Cassia (g) . . . . . L.
  Hymenæa (h) . . . L.
  Caulotretus (i) . . . Rich.

Papilionaceæ (continued)—
  Bauhinia (j) . . . Plum.
  Macrolobium . . . Schr.
  Copaifera (k) . . . . L.
  Brownea (l) . . . . Jacq.
  Swartzia . . . . . Willd.
  Pentaclethra . . . . Bent.
  Entada . . . . . L.
  Desmanthus . . . . Bent.
  Mimosa (m) . . . . L.
  Acacia (n) . . . . Willd.
  Calliandra . . . . Bent.
  Inga (o) . . . . . P. B.
  Pithecolobium . . . Mart.
  Enterolobium . . . id.

(a) Beans.
(b) Stump-pea.
(c) Liquorice.
(d) Roble (?).
(e) Angelim.
(f) Mora.
(g) Stinking-weed, and others.
(h) Locust.
(i) Tasajo-liane.
(j) Pata-de-vaca.
(k) Balsam-capivi.
(l) Palo-rosa.
(m) Sensitive-plant.
(n) Acacia.
(o) Pois-doux.

CHAPTER XII.

HISTORICAL OUTLINE.

I HAVE been urged by some friends to render this new edition more complete by adding an historical sketch of Trinidad. I must confess that I would never have attempted the task had I been left altogether dependent on my own resources; but I fortunately found in the "History of Trinidad," by E. L. Joseph, and specially in Mr. G. Borde's "Histoire de la Trinidad," the information and assistance which otherwise I would never have been able to procure. Mr. Borde was even good enough to place at my disposal the MS. of the second volume of his history. To Mr. Fraser, also, I am indebted for information respecting the government of the Commissioners and Sir Thomas Hislop. However, I am alone responsible for what is reported from the time of Sir Henry Macleod to the present day. This sketch I publish for what it is worth; a mere record of the more interesting events connected with the annals of the colony.

As already stated, Trinidad was discovered on the 31st of July, 1492, by the great navigator, Christopher Columbus. "About mid-day," says Washington Irving, "a mariner at the mast-head beheld the summits of three mountains arising above the horizon. As the ships drew nearer, it was seen that these three mountains were united at the base.

"Columbus had determined to give the first land he should behold the name of the Trinity. The appearance of these three mountains, united into one, struck him as a singular coincidence, and, with a solemn feeling of devotion, he gave the island the name of 'La Trinidad,' which it bears at the present day." These mountains, rising at the back of Punta Tablas, are known as the "Three Sisters." The south-eastern point was next sighted, and received the name of "Point Galera," instead of "Point Galeota," by which it is now known.

Columbus immediately sailed westward along the southern coast, looking for a safe roadstead and water. He anchored in a small bay, probably that of Moruga, where he took a supply of water. The next day he again dropped anchor, most likely in the bay of Erin. On landing he saw on the sandy beach human footsteps, and picked up some fishing implements.

Here and there were thatched huts and patches of cultivated grounds. It was during his navigation along the coast that Columbus discovered, towards the south, a low land, which he designated by the name of "Isla Santa." This Isla Santa was nothing else but part of the Delta of the Orinoco, or of the continent of South America; and from that day we should date the discovery of the Continent, not by Amerigo Vespucci, but by Columbus. The next day he was off Point Jicacos, or "Punta Arenal," as he termed it, forming with a line of rocks a narrow pass, near which he anchored his vessels. To the principal of these rocks he gave the name of "El Gallo," and to the pass itself that of "Boca de la Sierpe," or the serpent's mouth. Whilst at anchor his caravel was approached by a large canoe with some twenty-five islanders; they, however, stood at a distance, and soon paddled off to the shore.

During the night of the 2nd of August he had the opportunity of witnessing the phenomenon of a ground swell; his vessels were lifted up by the surge, whilst one of the caravels lost its anchor. Some time in the year 1877 an anchor was found imbedded in the sand at Constance Estate, Point Jicacos, and deemed to be the anchor lost by Columbus. Mr. Fr. Agostini, the owner of La Constance Estate, had the same sent to the Paris Universal Exhibition of 1878.

Columbus on leaving his anchorage at "Punta Arenal," entered the Gulf of Paria, and, on finding its water nearly fresh at places, came to the conclusion that some large rivers must discharge their contents into it, and gave the Gulf the name of "Mar Dulce"—the fresh sea. After some days' sailing in the Gulf, Columbus debouched into the Atlantic, through the Grand Boca.

The island, of which the name was "Caïri," as reported by Sir Walter Raleigh, or "Yere"—the land of humming-birds—according to Joseph, was, as it appears, well settled and pretty densely inhabited by Caribs, who were subdivided into smaller tribes; viz., the Nepoios, Yaios, Carinapagotos, and Cumanagotos; also by Aruacas, Chaymas, Tamanacos, Chaguanas, Salivas, and Quaquas. As it appears, these people were formed into two confederacies, or leagues, with two chiefs, Buchumar and Maruane. These aborigines were well made and brave.

The island was visited in succession by several adventurers. In 1499 by Ojeda, in partnership with Amerigo Vespucci and Juan de la Cosa; a little later by Pedro Alonso Niño; in December, same year, by Vicente Yanez Pinzon, both companions of Columbus in former voyages; and in 1500 by Diego de Lope. It appears also that Christobal Guerra, the companion of Niño, sailed in 1501 for the Gulf of Paria. In 1502, Alonzo de Ojeda made a second voyage to Trinidad. Pearls seem to have been the principal, if not the sole, article of trade.

To the year 1510 no attempt had yet been made to conquer or civilise the island. In that year, however, the Provincial of the Dominicans sent two of his religious to Trinidad, with the object of converting its inhabitants to Christianity. They were at first successful, as the Indians manifested a willingness to become Christians and be baptized. A Spanish vessel having anchored in the Gulf meanwhile, the Indians, instead of keeping aloof as they were wont to do, received the new comers with great demonstrations of friendship, as compatriots of the reverend fathers. They were easily induced to come on board to bargain; but when a sufficient number had been thus enticed, the captain weighed anchor, and sailed with the poor deluded creatures. The natives, being convinced that the monks had connived at the treacherous act, would have massacred them on the spot but for their promise that they would obtain the release of the prisoners. They were allowed a few months of respite; but the release of the prisoners having been refused at Santo Domingo, the poor monks were made to atone for the crime of the kidnappers. Subsequently unscrupulous adventurers did not hesitate to resort to the nefarious practices of their predecessors; and the poor natives of Trinidad were either carried off and sold into slavery, or killed by thousands whilst defending their independence.

Some thirty years had elapsed since the discovery of Trinidad, and no attempt had yet been made to settle it permanently. The time, however, was near at hand when, from its geographical position, it began to attract attention. The Royal Treasurer at Porto Rico, Don Antonio Sedeño, asked for, and obtained, a licence to conquer the island; and, in the year 1528, the king, by letters patent, appointed him Governor and Captain-General of Trinidad. Sedeño then returned to Porto Rico to make his preparations; and in the beginning of the year 1530 he left that island with two vessels and seventy men. He was, on his landing on the southern coast—at Erin, it is supposed—cordially received by the natives and one of their caciques, or chiefs, called Chacomar.

His first act was the construction of a fortified building. He treated the natives conciliatorily, and paid generously for whatever assistance they gave him. But both provisions and money became scarce; and Sedeño, being unable to pay for food, did not scruple to plunder the provision grounds of the natives. The exasperated Indians resisted, and came to the determination of driving the invaders away by all means. Fighting began in earnest, and the Spaniards were reduced to the last extremities. Sedeño in this stress sought and obtained advice from his friend Chacomar; and, by following his directions, was, for some short time, relieved from starvation and left undisturbed. Fighting, however, was soon resumed, and the fortified barracks furiously assailed; but the assailants were repulsed with great slaughter. The position had become most critical, and it was agreed that Sedeño should go to Porto Rico for provisions and fresh reinforcements, and that his companions should temporarily retire to the neighbouring continent, where they expected to be left unmolested. In order, however, to be prepared for all eventualities, they erected a fortified enclosure, where they collected whatever provisions they could procure. This enclosure, or fort, was built near Caño Perderuales. He appointed as his lieutenant and commander of the fort one Juan Gonzales, and sailed for Porto Rico. Soon after his departure, the Spaniards were attacked by the Indians, and reduced to the last straits. They were timely relieved by Geronimo de Ortal, a rival of Sedeño, who induced them to break faith to their Governor, with the exception of Gonzales and a few others. Sedeño, who had returned from Porto Rico, retook possession of the fort by misleading its commandant, Captain Agustin Delgado, whom he took as his associate; he then sailed for Trinidad, after appointing Bartolomeo Gonzales commandant of the fort. It was not long before he was compelled to return to the continent to retake possession of the fortified house on the coast of Paria, which had been delivered up to one Alonzo de Herrera, by Gonzales. Herrera and Gonzales were made prisoners and taken over to Trinidad, and Delgado appointed commander. Sedeño had constant quarrels, now with Herrera, then with the Royal Audiencia of Santo Domingo. He was of violent temper and rather unscrupulous. His own men revolted against him and made him prisoner, but, dissensions having occurred among them, he was soon relieved. Finding himself in a precarious position, he decided on again returning to Porto Rico, leaving Agustin Delgado as his lieutenant in the island. During his absence, Diego de Ortal landed in Trinidad, and was joined by Delgado; they then both left the island for the continent.

Sedeño, finding it difficult to enrol people for the conquest of Trinidad, began to give countenance to the reports respecting the marvellous riches of the neighbouring continent, and thus succeeded in enlisting 140 men and procuring fifty horses, which troop he directed to the main where he had been authorised to establish his head-quarters. There he attempted to dissuade his men from going in search of the promised treasures, and to induce them to complete the conquest of Trinidad, but in vain. He was compelled to follow them, but was soon after poisoned by a slave woman, and died in 1540. Thus ended the first Spaniard who had attempted the conquest of Trinidad, and who may be said to have been its first Governor.

From the death of Sedeño to the year 1570, say during a period of thirty years, the Gulf of Paria was visited only by slave dealers, who had but one object in view—Indian slave trading.

About this year, 1570, a creole of Santo Domingo, Juan Ponce, made application to the Spanish Government, and obtained letters patent permitting the conquest, and granting to him the government of Trinidad. Being bent on success, Ponce took with him some monks and a few emigrants, and arrived safely in Trinidad some time at the end of 1571. The natives showed resistance, and had, as effective auxiliaries, mosquitoes and other vermin, which played mischief with the intruders; they died by scores, a small number only having succeeded in leaving the island. As to Don Juan Ponce, it is not known what became of him. He probably succumbed to the cachexy which had decimated his people.

In 1576 two missionaries, members of the Society of Jesus, came to Trinidad, and settled at Puerto de los Hispanioles (Port-of-Spain), where they began to preach the Gospel to the Indians; but they soon abandoned the task, and retired to the continent.

It is a well-known fact that the great object of those who flocked to the New World was to enrich themselves by the discovery of precious stones and precious metals. About this time the Dorado was the great attraction. It was supposed to lie in Guiana, and many already had been the efforts directed towards the discovery of that inexhaustibly rich country, according to the rumours propagated by the Indians and one Juan Martinez, otherwise Juan Martin de Albujar.

The province of Guiana formed part, as it seems, of the Government, or Capitania-General, of New Grenada, of which Gonzalo Ximenes de Quesada was Captain-General. He had as companion one Antonio de Berrio y Oruña, an enterprising and upright man of great energy. Don Antonio de Berrio, having married Quesada's niece, was left by him sole heir of his large fortune, on condition that he would prosecute the conquest of the Dorado. He, therefore, set on his undertaking in earnest, and came down the Meta and the Orinoco, losing on his way down the rivers a large number of men and beasts. There he heard more of the Dorado. Being, however, unable to commence the conquest of that fairy land, he came to Trinidad, there to make his preparations. It was about the year 1584. De Berrio, after firmly establishing himself in Trinidad, went to Margarita and Cumana in search of reinforcements; he then returned to the island, and succeeded in subjugating the natives, and establishing a regular form of government. He then decided on building a town, some six miles to the eastward of Puerto de los Hispanioles, and gave it the name of "San Jose de Oruña," which was for several years the capital of the island. The site was well chosen on an eminence, with the river Saint Joseph running by, to the Caroni, which it joined about two miles southward. He also built another town on the right bank of the Orinoco at the spot known as "San Tome de Guiana," or "Vieja Guiana."

Spain pretended to be the sole power which had a right to

the lawful possession of the New World; and it may be said that she was mistress of the continent from Mexico down to Chili. The other nations being jealous of her dominion and covetous of her great riches, privateers—French, English, and Dutch—were suffered to organise a regular warfare against her commerce; and whenever Spain was at war with any foreign country, they joined in attacking her merchant navy at sea and her dependencies on land.

More intimately connected with the history of Trinidad, at this period, are the two expeditions of Sir Walter Raleigh in search of the Dorado. It was in the year 1594 that he preluded his expedition by sending Captain Widdhon to Trinidad, with the object of getting information respecting the Dorado. It seems that, whilst anchored off Port-of-Spain, a party of English ventured out in the neighbourhood, but were never seen again. The probability is that they were killed by the Spaniards, or at their instigation.

On the 22nd of March, 1595, Sir Walter Raleigh arrived at Trinidad, and anchored in the Gulf. He was well received by the Spaniards, which did not deter him from entering into relation with the Indians, from whom he received full information respecting the small number of men in the island, the town of San Jose, where de Berrio was then staying, and directions for reaching the capital. De Berrio, who had reason to suspect the intentions of the English, had sent messages to the Governors of Margarita and Cumana asking for assistance. On the other hand, Sir Walter Raleigh, who had found ready concurrence among the caciques, or chiefs of the Indians, decided on attacking de Berrio and his town. As related by him, "taking a time of much advantage, he set upon the Corps de Garde, Port-of-Spain, in the evening, and having put the soldiers to the sword, he sent Captain Culfield onward with sixty men, and soon followed with forty more, to the attack of San Jose de Oruña. The city was taken at daybreak, and set on fire at the request of the Indians. Don Antonio de Berrio fought bravely at the head of his men, but was made prisoner." Sir Walter then returned to Puerto de los Hispanioles, bringing with him de Berrio and one of his lieutenants as prisoners.

Raleigh then set off on his expedition to the Dorado, taking de Berrio with him; the Governor was, however, released when

Sir Walter left the island to return to Europe. Having decided to remain at San Tome, de Berrio left one of his lieutenants in command of the island. The latter, with the aid of the few soldiers who had escaped and other inhabitants, began rebuilding San Jose. De Berrio meanwhile was making preparations for the discovery and conquest of the Dorado; but he met with only disastrous results, and died at San Tome in 1597, disappointed.

"This Berrio," says Walter Raleigh, "is a gentleman well descended, and has long served the Spanish King in Milan, Naples, the Low Countries, and elsewhere, very valiant and liberal, and a gentleman of great assuredness, and of a great heart."

He was succeeded by his son, Don Fernando. Don Fernando, having been deprived of his command, was superseded by Don Sancho Alquiza, who acted as Governor to the year 1615. However, Don Fernando succeeded in obtaining his restoration to power; but, as a successor had been meanwhile appointed to Don Alquiza—viz., Don Diego Palomeque de Acuña—it was agreed that the latter should retain the government of Trinidad and Guiana for two years—from 1616 to 1619. Don Diego Palomeque had instructions to protect Guiana against the premeditated invasion of Sir Walter Raleigh. Lieutenant Ramo took command of the island

At the end of the year 1617, Sir Walter Raleigh came to anchor under El Gallo, and from there sent boats to attack San Tome. The town was taken by storm after a stern resistance, and the brave Acuña was killed.

After the capture of Santo Tome, the English began to search for supposed hidden treasures; but they were incessantly harassed by the few surviving Spaniards and the Indians. They then decided on ascending the Orinoco and its affluents, in the hope of finding provisions and discovering gold; none could be found, and, after a few weeks, they returned to San Tome, where they were again attacked by the Spaniards and Indians. Sir Lawrence Keymis, seeing no prospect of succeeding, rowed down the river and arrived at Trinidad. He was scornfully received by Sir Walter, and committed suicide.

This was the last attempt to conquer Guiana and occupy the Dorado. For many years this region of Dorado was regarded as a myth; but it has proved, in our days, to be a reality. The province of Guiana seems to be very rich in the precious metal. Gold has been found in many places; the Callao mine is reported as very rich; quite lately nuggets have been found at a place called La Pastora.

Don Diego Palomeque being dead, de Berrio resumed his government in 1618 and died in 1622, after a somewhat quiet government.

What was the condition of Trinidad at the death of Don Fernando? The native population had been thinned by war, starvation, and kidnapping, and the European population was still very small. There was not any regular trade between the island and foreigners. San Jose, the capital, had about six hundred inhabitants.

It was about this time that the various European nations, jealous of the power acquired in America by Spain, and annoyed at their systematic exclusion, began to show opposition and try their strength in the Antilles. French, English and Dutch adventurers, secretly encouraged and supported by their respective governments, contrived to occupy the smaller islands, and to form regular associations under the name of Buccaneers and Filibusters. These combined to make depredations on the Spaniards, both on land and at sea. In 1640 the Dutch attacked Trinidad, and captured the town of San Jose. The inhabitants had abandoned the place, and the enemy was disappointed at finding no booty. On descending the river Caroni they were met by the Spaniards and Indians, who inflicted on them heavy losses, compelling them to retire to Essequibo unsuccessful. In 1672 the British attacked the island, under the leadership of Sir Tobias Bridges from Barbados. He had landed his troops on the eastern coast, but suffered heavily in his attempt to reach St. Joseph, through the thick forest which covered the whole island. In 1677 Trinidad was once more invaded by the French, under the command of the Marquis de Maintenon, who had orders to attack the Spaniards and their colonies. De Maintenon ransacked the colony and carried away the spoils. The progress of the island was thus arrested, and great misery prevailed.

Trinidad was then a dependency of the government of Nueva Andalusia, and was governed by delegates from Cumana. The following gentlemen, according to Salcedo, acted as Governors during the period extending from 1640 to 1687 : Martin de Mendoza y la Hoz ; Juan de Urpin ; Christobal de Vera ; Pedro de Brizuela ; Pedro de Padilla ; Juan de Viedena ; Jose de Aspe y Zuñiga ; Francisco Ventura y Rada ; Juan Bautista de Valdez ; Juan Bravo de Acuña ; Diego Ximenes de Aldama ; Francisco de Rivera y Galindo ; and Juan de Padillā y Guardiala.

It was about this time (1687) that one Rodriguez Leite, conceived the idea of bringing the Indians to civilisation, not by compulsion, but by persuasion. He, therefore, prepared a plan of evangelical missions, and addressed a memorial to the Bishop of Porto Rico, which was, by him, forwarded to the Court of Spain with pressing recommendations. Accordingly a Royal Cedula was issued in 1687, prescribing the formation of villages or missions of convert Indians, who were declared exempt from all taxation for a period of twenty years. They could no more be compelled to work on private properties. These missions were established by the Aragonese Capuchin Fathers. It was also about this time that a Governor was appointed for Trinidad, Don Antonio de Leos y Echales, the colony still remaining a dependency of Cumana. To him we may trace a regular civil organisation. Before his appointment the Spanish colonists took unauthorised possession of the public lands, whether they worked them or not.

Five missions, or villages, were established by the Capuchin Fathers ; viz., that of Purissima Conception, where San Fernando is now built ; that of Annunciacion of Savanna Grande, now the village of Savanna Grande or Princestown ; that of San Jose, in Montserrat, near the Mayo river, at a spot where there still exist a few vestiges of the old village ; that of Santa Anna de la Savanetta, on Rivulet Estate ; and that of San Francisco de Arenales, somewhere near Tumpuna. The Indians of this village, having heard that the Governor was coming on a visit of inspection, took fright and traitorously murdered the missionaries, after which they laid in ambush for the Governor and his suite, whom they also massacred. However, they paid dearly for their treachery, as they were chased like wild beasts, and killed almost to the last man.

In the year 1690 the French attacked Trinidad, under the conduct of Levassor de la Touche. The leader was severely wounded at the attack of San Jose de Oruña, but was allowed to retire unmolested.

The colony at last began to enjoy some peace, and agriculture to receive some share of attention. The principal article cultivated was cacao, which was proclaimed by Gumilla as superior, for its fine aroma, to the cacao of Caracas and other places. It was so much praised that the crops were bought beforehand. The Governors, at this period, were Felipe de Antieda, Christobal de Guzman, Pedro de Yarza, Martin Perez de Anda y Salazar. Don Felipe de Artieda it was who, at the urgent request of the colonists, obtained such changes in the organisation of the missions as permitted the employment of the Indians as labourers on private properties. The Reverend Fathers strenuously opposed the change, but a Royal Cedula, dated 15th August, 1703, changed the then existing missions into doctrinal missions, with a civil chief appointed by the Governor, under the title of corregidor, or magistrate. Three doctrinal missions were then established; viz., that of Tacarigua, among the Tacariguas tribe; that of Cuara or Caura, at the entrance of the valley of the same name; and that of Arauca or Arouca, on the territory of the Aruacas Indians.

The prosperity of the colony had now reached its culminating point, cacao selling at a very high price. But in the year 1727, according to Gumilla, not a disease of the trees exactly, but a blight attacking the pods under certain atmospherical influences, destroyed the crops. The trees were apparently healthy, got flowers and young fruits, but none came to maturity. Cacao cultivation being the only resource of the island, complete, irretrievable ruin followed. The starving people abandoned the colony, and the population, exclusive of the Indians, had been reduced, in the year 1733, to the scanty number of 162 adults; of these twenty-eight only were white. The colonists had sought refuge on the neighbouring continent, taking with them their slaves, plate, and jewellery. The public revenue fell to the derisory sum of 231 dols. Rank vegetation overran the cultivated fields and covered the dwellings.

The Governor, Don Aredondo, had retired from the government in 1730, and delivered it up to Don Bartolomeo de Adunate y Rada, who died three years later. Under his administration, Trinidad had sunk in the deepest misery.

Gumilla mentions that about the year 1732 the soil sank at Point la Brea, and gave origin to the lake; but it is well known that asphaltum existed there before the occurrence.

After the death of Don Bartolomeo, the colony was administered by the two alcades, Jose Orbay and Pedro Ximenes. It was about this time that the Capitania-General of Caracas was established, of which Trinidad became a dependency.

The colony, however, was slowly recovering from its depressed condition, and the census of 1733 had given, exclusive of the Indians, 2,000 inhabitants, of whom 500 were whites, and about 1,500 blacks and mestizos, slaves and free people. The revenue had risen to 1,200 dols.

In October, 1735, Don Esteban Simon de Liñan y Vera took from the alcades, Orbay and Ximenes, the government of the island. Twelve years after the cacao blight, in 1739, a terrible epidemic of small-pox ravaged the colony. The Governor left for Cumana, without notification to the Cabildo, but had appointed Major Espinosa to act during his absence. The Cabildo, considering his appointment illegal, would not recognise his authority. The major called out the militia; the Cabildo interfered, and the militia sided with the popular authorities. The two alcades, Orbay and Ximenes, then took in hand the administration of the colony. On his return to Trinidad, Don Esteban met with strong opposition on the part of the people: virulent accusations were brought against him; matters waxed worse and worse; the Governor was arrested, sent to Port-of-Spain, and put in irons. The Cabildo, which, meanwhile, had remained inactive, issued a decree, declaring Don Liñan fallen from his position of Governor and an usurper, proving by this and other harsh measures its connivance with the mob. Meantime Major Espinosa had gone to Cumana to report the events. The Governor of Cumana was ordered to proceed to Trinidad, and to release the prisoner. Don Feliz Espinosa landed at Port-of-Spain at the head of a strong body of troops, and released the Governor. The latter, however, broken down by his long captivity and cruel sufferings, was unable to resume his functions. The two alcades, M. Lozado and Soto, were sent to prison and put in irons, whilst their accomplices were sentenced to ten years' banishment. The goods of the two alcades were confiscated, and the proceeds applied to defraying the expenses of the suits instituted and the expedition.

Captain Feliz Espinosa administered the colony as Acting Governor for a period of six months, when Juan José de Salcedo was appointed Governor. He also had to quarrel with the Cabildo, but, in order to have peace, let things alone. The inhabitants who had been banished were allowed to return. The Governor having been laid prostrate by an attack of apoplexy, the alcades came forward, claiming the administration of the colony. Don Juan de Salcedo was succeeded by Captain Francisco Nanclares. He also, as his predecessors, had to suffer from the interference of the Cabildo in the administration of the public affairs of the colony. Governor Nanclares had for his successor Colonel Don Pedro de la Moneda (1757). Unable to find a suitable house in San José de Oruña, de la Moneda retired to Port-of-Spain, which thereby became the chief town, the illustrious Cabildo being left in peaceful occupation of San José.

It was about this time that an attempt was successfully made to re-introduce the cacao plant. A new species, the *Cacao forastero*, which being hardier, though not yielding the same fine quality, succeeded beyond expectation. It is this cacao which is still cultivated in our days. It was also about this time that the Aragonese Capuchin Fathers formed new missions, by congregating together the native Indians; viz., at Arima, Toco, Siparia, and, on the eastern coast, at Matura, Cumana and Salibia.

The Cabildo, nothing daunted, persevered in showing seditious dispositions; a conspiracy was even planned against the Governor; but being discovered in time, miscarried, on which occasion the Governor addressed to the Cabildo a most severe and cutting rebuke. Colonel de la Moneda governed wisely, and was promoted to the government of Popayan.

Captain Don Jacinto San Juan was appointed his successor, and fixed his residence in Port-of-Spain. It appears that against this Governor also the Cabildo conspired; and he had to resign in the hands of Don Antonio Gil, about the year 1762. A conspiracy was weaved against this new Governor also, at San Tome de Guiana, but failed. The Governor having left for Margarita, appointed Don Juan de Bruno to act in his place. Don

Juan was relieved from his functions, in 1766, by Captain Don Jose de Flores. He also, during the whole time he was Governor, had to resist the pretensions of the Cabildo, apparently intent to throw difficulties in the way rather than assist in conducting the affairs of the colony. Thoroughly disgusted with the people, Governor Flores asked repeatedly to be relieved from his office; but it was only in 1773 that Don Juan Valdez y Varza assumed the government of the island. He was energetic, and succeeded in defeating the ill dispositions of the Cabildo.

It may be said that, during a period of fifty years, and from the failure of the cacao crop, the colony had dragged on a miserable existence, and suffered from the persisting antagonism of the Cabildo, which evidently could not have been actuated by a sense of patriotic opposition, but by vanity and interested motives.

Thus had Trinidad been gradually reduced to the state of marasmus, from which it could not be expected to recover except by an infusion of healthy blood. The population was scanty, amounting to about 1,000 souls, exclusive of the Indians. Immigration, therefore, seemed to be the only remedy. But where to seek immigrants, and by what allurements induce them to come and settle in the colony?

In November, 1765, Charles III., the successor of Ferdinand VI., had issued a decree allowing commercial intercourse between the islands of Cuba, Santo Domingo, Porto Rico, Margarita, and Trinidad. The trade of these colonies, hitherto restricted to Cadiz and Sevilla, and to the importation of national manufactures, was permitted with all the principal ports of the mother country and the Balearic and Canary islands, without any distinction of products, except wines and other spirituous liquors. It abolished all vexatious restrictions on navigation, imposing a duty of three per cent. and seven per cent. respectively, on all national and foreign articles, either as exports from or imports to the Spanish ports.

Several of the French colonies—viz., Tobago, Grenada, St. Vincent, and Dominica—had been ceded to England by the Treaty of Paris in 1763. National prejudices, stronger then than at present, had inspired harsh measures, and made the domination of the conquerors felt to the utmost. The conquered communities became downcast and sulky. Several of those islands—

Grenada in particular—had suffered from the ravages of a most destructive ant (the Parasol ant?), and discouragement everywhere prevailed.

There lived then in Grenada a colonist of good birth, married to an English lady, one Philip Rose Roume de Saint Laurent. On hearing favourable reports of Trinidad, Saint Laurent decided on trying his fortune in that island. Before doing this, however, he thought it prudent to visit the island, and have an interview with the Governor. Saint Laurent might have led a quiet and honoured life in his native land; but his noble heart had bled at the sight of his countrymen's sufferings, and he came to the determination of attempting something for their relief.

Roume de Saint Laurent landed in Trinidad May, 1777, and began at once the visit of the island. He was highly pleased with all that he saw—with the fertility of the soil and the many natural advantages it possessed. He, therefore, entered into relations with Governor Falquez, and endeavoured to persuade him that, however encouraging the cedula of Charles III., it could not have for its effects to induce foreigners to migrate in any numbers. He then insisted on the prospects of a large immigration from the French islands, if sufficient inducements were proffered; otherwise they would emigrate to the United States. Falquez listened to him with interest, and advised him to address a memorial embodying his views to the Court of Madrid. Before leaving the island, and as a token of his earnestness, Saint Laurent bought some land in the valley of Diego-Martin.

On his return to Grenada he depicted Trinidad as a most desirable country, and urged his countrymen to cast their lot in that colony. Luckily the memoir of Saint Laurent has been preserved, and may be read in Mr. Borde's "Histoire de la Trinidad." Governor Falquez died in Port-of-Spain about this time, July, 1797.

Roume de Saint Laurent had submitted his memoir to Falquez before forwarding the same to the Court of Spain; the Governor had approved and endorsed it. Lieutenant-Colonel Don Martin de Salaverria was then sent to Trinidad from Caracas, with instructions to adopt such measures as could advance agriculture, increase the population, and develop commerce.

The Court of Spain had not yet come to any decision respecting Saint Laurent's scheme; they, nevertheless, had appointed two Governors, a civil administrator, and a commander of the troops, viz., Don Rafael Delgado and Colonel Salaverria. Don Rafael advised Saint Laurent to go to Caracas and try to secure the good-will and concurrence of the intendant of that town. But Saint Laurent preferred, as a preliminary measure, to pay a cursory visit to the smaller Antilles, with the view to inducing immigration to Trinidad. He took with him for distribution French and English copies of the cedula granted by the king. On returning from this voyage he started for Caracas, with the object of submitting his plan to the intendant, Don Jose de Sabalos, and obtaining his acquiescence in the same. Don Sabalos approved the plan, and promised his support at the Court of Madrid. Saint Laurent, in order to avoid further delays, decided to go to Spain. Passing through Paris, he saw there Count d'Aranda, who approved his decision, and urged him to continue his voyage. Saint Laurent's plan was approved, and the Cedula of Colonisation was issued shortly after. Pending the arrival of Captain Don Jose Maria Chacon, appointed Captain-General, Don Juan Franciso Machado acted as Governor, with instructions to carry into effect the plan of colonisation adopted by the Government, the cedula promulgating the same having been signed in November, 1781.

As we may trace the colonisation of Trinidad to this cedula of 1783, the reader will, no doubt, be glad to know its principal clauses. This document consisted of twenty-eight articles, some of which are unimportant as referring to general matters. The first article enacts that all new colonists must be Catholics. Article 2 requires the new comers to take the oath of allegiance to the King of Spain, and to observe the laws of the Indies, the king then granting them, gratis and in perpetuity, the lands they may have a claim to. Article 3 determines the quantity of land to which every new comer will be entitled, viz., each white person of either sex to four fanegar and twenty-sevenths (thirty-two acres); half that quantity for every slave he may introduce, the grants being prepared in such manner that all grantees may have land of bad, indifferent, and good quality; these grants to be registered in a book of population, showing the individuality and name of each colonist, the date of his admission, the number of persons composing his family, his quality, and lineage; and authentic copies of all such grants shall be delivered to them, which shall serve as titles of property. Article 4 enacts that every free negro and persons of colour shall be entitled to one-half of the quantity granted to white people. Article 5 stipulates that, after five years' residence, the new colonists shall become naturalised Spanish subjects, they and their children, and that they shall be eligible for public employment. Article 6 stipulates that no capitation or personal tax shall be enacted from the new colonists; they shall only pay a yearly tax of one dollar. By Article 7 the new colonists are authorised to retire from the island, on forfeiting their grants and paying ten per cent. on all that they may have accumulated. Article 8 relates to such as may die in the island; their heirs may inherit, provided they are Roman Catholics, and agree to reside in the colony; if the heirs do not choose to reside, they pay 15 per cent. Articles 9 and 10 grant power of bequeathing, and permission to leave the colony, under certain restrictions. Article 11 exempts the colonists from tithes for a space of ten years. Article 12 also exempts the people from all duties on articles sold. Article 13 obliges the new settlers to be armed, though not obliged to join the militia, except in urgent cases. Articles 14, 15, 16, 17, 18, 19, and 20 regulate commercial intercourse with the French islands.

It was also under that cedula that a code was issued for the good government of the slaves, a code as liberal as any previously published anywhere else.

Article 21 orders that, from the province of Caracas, animals —viz., horned cattle, horses, and mules—shall be sent to the island, to be sold there at first cost. Articles 22 and 23 regulate commercial transactions in certain cases, and the admission, free of duty, of agricultural implements. Article 24 is relative to the admission of priests speaking foreign languages. By Articles 26, 28, the colonists are permitted to lay before the king regulations for the government of their slaves; also to send memorials to Madrid, through the Governor, praying for the redress of any grievances.

Spain, being not in a position to colonise Trinidad with her own people, did wisely in attempting its colonisation with the concourse of foreigners.

Two months after the date of the cedula, the government of the colony was assumed *ad interim* by Captain Barruto.

In September, 1780, Don Jose Maria Chacon, captain of the navy, arrived in Trinidad, with the title of Governor and Captain-General. Governor Chacon was the man to carry into execution the plan suggested by Roume de Saint Laurent. He was well informed, clever, and prudent—a perfect gentleman, who could speak French and English fluently enough. He at once caused copies of the Cedula of Colonisation to be circulated in the French and English colonies. Soon immigrants from St. Vincent, Martinique, Guadaloupe, Dominica, and Grenada—but from the latter island especially—began to flock to Trinidad in search of a home, and with the object of bettering their condition.

Governor Chacon, being anxious to execute the conditions of the cedula, gave to the immigrants a ready and warm reception, treated them with consideration, and thus succeeded in securing the confidence of the new settlers. But he met, as natural, with opposition on the part of the Spanish colonists. They had taken possession of, and divided among themselves, large tracts of the best land of the island. They, of course, showed a determination to retain possession of entire districts, which, however, had never been surveyed or granted, and were not under cultivation. When it was attempted to grant lands to the new comers, claims were proffered and suits instituted. The Governor had to proclaim, in July, 1785, a law regulating their position, and protecting the public demesne. It was ill received by the Spaniards, and created dissensions between the two classes of colonists. Governor Chacon, nevertheless, persevered; and so successful was this immigration, that, from 1784 to 1789, the population of Trinidad had increased from 1,000 to 10,422. This immigration consisted not only of white families, with their slaves, but of most respectable black and coloured people.

Governor Chacon extended to all equal protection; and the provisions of the cedula were enforced, it may be said, without fear or favour. Nor did he lose sight of the aborigines, but managed to group them under *corregidors*, or magistrates, and, with that object in view, formed the existing missions into two villages, viz., Arima—consisting of the missions of Tacarigua, Arouca, Caura, and Arima; and of Savana Grande—comprising Montserrat, Savanetta, and Naparima. He also brought together the black Caribs of St. Vincent, who had emigrated to the island, at Salibia, on the eastern coast.

It was Governor Chacon who diverted the course of the Ariapita river (to-day, St. Ann) from its former bed to the foot of the Laventille Hills, where it bears the name of Dry river. This was done at the cost of 3,600 dollars, of which the Governor generously contributed 1,000 dollars. This took place in 1787.

The greatest accord prevailed; and the new colonists, among whom were men of talent, and most honourable, grateful for the benefits conferred, gave their ready support to the Governor. Many were appointed *commandantes*. It was Mr. de Laforest who prepared the slave code, and who suggested the building of a wharf. Mr. de Deshayes had proposed to bring to town the St. Ann's water.

Governor Chacon had to organise the whole administration of the colony, and, aided by the concourse of the immigrants, succeeded beyond expectation. Several royal decrees were issued, diminishing the duties on goods, and extending the privileges which had been granted for only a short time.

As a consequence of the French Revolution war had been proclaimed, and the archipelago had become the theatre of bloody warfare, viz., at Martinique, Guadaloupe, St. Lucia, St. Vincent, and Grenada.

Governor Chacon, naturally enough, began to feel anxious about the safety of the colony entrusted to his care; he particularly distrusted some French refugees nourishing republican predilections, and was in perpetual fear of some disturbance.

A British expedition had left England and sailed for Barbadoes, with the object of attacking the French colonies; St. Vincent, St. Lucia, Grenada, and Martinique had been compelled to submit. But Victor Hughes, delegate of the Convention and Governor of Guadaloupe, had resisted the attack of the English, and organised a fleet of privateers, who attacked the enemy's merchant vessels wherever opportunity offered. Hardly pressed by the British navy, some of them had taken refuge in the Gulf. Captain Vaughan, of the *Alarm*, and Captain Skinner, of the *Zebra*, received orders to chase them. Some of their vessels were destroyed by the *Zebra*, but the crews escaped and retired to Port-of-Spain, where, soon after, they had a row with some men of the *Alarm*, on which occasion Captain Vaughan landed with a party of armed marines—thus committing a breach of the neutrality of Trinidad. In October, 1796, war was declared between Spain and England. In January of the same year a Spanish squadron, consisting of four ships and a frigate, with about 800 men, had entered the Gulf, under the command of Don Ruiz de Apodaca, a chance being thus given to Chacon of defending the island.

On the other hand, the British fleet, having left Martinique with orders to take possession of Trinidad, entered the Bocas on the 16th of February, 1797. It consisted of eight men-of-war, two frigates, and eight sloops, besides two transports, carrying 900 guns and 6,700 men.

It must be acknowledged that Governor Chacon had made no defensive preparations, but no defence was possible. This he and Apodaca clearly saw. They therefore agreed to offer no resistance, and to put the vessels on fire to prevent their falling into the hands of the enemy. Chacon surrendered without firing a gun. A capitulation was signed, and the island delivered up to General Abercrombie and Admiral Harvey. Thus ended the dominion of Spain over Trinidad. Chacon and Apodaca were tried by court-martial and condemned, the former for not having defended the colony as he ought to have done, and the latter for having prematurely burnt his ships. Trinidad was finally ceded to England by the Treaty of Amiens in 1802.

At the time of the capture of Trinidad by the British, colonisation had made fair progress under the conditions of the cedula of 1785. The population, which in 1773 was only 1,000 inhabitants, exclusive of the Indians, had increased to 18,600 in 1797. The conqueror made no changes in the administrative organisation of the island; but, on the contrary, adopted the policy of the late Governor, and treated the colonists with due consideration. The colony continued to prosper under the new government. The colonists, particularly those of French descent, being energetic and industrious, had introduced various cultures, and when the island was transferred to Great Britain there existed a grand total of 468 estates, of which 159 were sugar estates, 130 coffee, 103 cotton, 70 tobacco, several indigo, 6 cacao plantations, besides a good many young cacao cultivations, representing a cultivated area of 37,960 acres.

Immediately after the surrender of the island, Sir Ralph

Abercrombie issued a proclamation assuring the inhabitants of the full and entire security of their persons and property as held under the articles of the capitulation, informing those who considered themselves as French citizens that means would be provided for their safe conveyance to some other colony; and calling upon all those who chose to remain in Trinidad to make oath of allegiance to his Britannic majesty.

All muskets and ammunition were called in, and ordered to be brought to the nearest fort and delivered to the commandant.

He also issued a commission to Mr. Nihell, an Irish gentleman, and owner of El Dorado estate, and who had held the office of alcade of the first election, or chief magistrate, appointing him magistrate, judge, and auditor in and over the whole island. Mr. Nihell's honesty and integrity were unquestionable, and his nomination was well received. Under the Spanish rule, the Governor was the chief magistrate, but he had a legal counsel who assisted him whenever he sat as judge.

About two months after the signing of the capitulation, General Abercrombie took his departure from the island, leaving as Governor and Commander-in-Chief his *aide-de-camp*, Colonel Thomas Picton, whom he vested with ample powers, and directed to execute the Spanish law as well as he could, and to do justice according to his conscience. He left with him about 1,000 men, of whom 500, mostly Germans, belonged to the Hompesh regiment. This number was, soon after, reduced to 520 by desertion and maladies. Of those only 260 were Germans, the rest having deserted.

Picton's task was a most difficult one. He had to deal, in a conquered country, with a motley aggregation of various nationalities, races, and languages. He knew that the Spanish Government were anxiously looking for an opportunity to resume the island. The Governor had, therefore, to display foresight and uncommon energy to protect the colony against hostile attacks, and keep internal peace. He saw at once that he ought to look for support to the old colonists, and he did not hesitate to seek advice from those best acquainted with the people. The population was composed mainly of immigrants who had suffered from the evils of war, and had sought refuge in Trinidad, with the object of bettering their condition. Such men must have looked with confidence to a soldier like Picton, who had proved, by words and deeds, his determination to crush disorder and uphold peace. They proved his firmest supporters. Having succeeded in obtaining the confidence of the most respectable inhabitants of the colony, he did not hesitate to venture in forming a militia, which proved very useful in enforcing order in the rural districts, whilst it permitted the disposal of the troops for more important duties.

On the 29th of June, 1801, General Picton was appointed by the home Government "Civil and Military Governor" of Trinidad. He was at the same time notified that the Courts of Judicature which existed before the capitulation should be continued in the exercise of all the judicial powers belonging to them in criminal and civil cases, and that he was vested with all such judicial powers as belonged to his predecessors, and should exercise them in like manner as they were exercised previous to the surrender of the island.

The Governor called a meeting of the principal inhabitants, communicated the royal will, and then appointed a council of advice, consisting of five members, comprising a Spaniard, a Frenchman, and three Englishmen.

On the proclamation of the Treaty of Amiens, which finally ceded Trinidad to Great Britain, a number of Scotch and British adventurers actually poured into Trinidad from the neighbouring colonies, especially those which had been temporarily occupied by the British forces—men of doubtful character, who, however, considered themselves entitled to all sorts of consideration, as British-born subjects. They formed, as they thought, the English party. They at once declared themselves opponents of Picton, who, on the other hand, found staunch supporters in the old colonists, who had given unmistakable proof of their loyalty. The Governor was not the man to be cowed by such opposition, and he deprived two of their leaders of their commission in the Trinidad militia. They tried by all means to detract the government of Sir Thomas Picton and to injure his character, and it must be conceded that their efforts were not unsuccessful. Colonel Fullarton found in them ready auxiliaries in his war against Picton.

Mr. Pitt having been compelled to resign, Lord Sidmouth became Premier. It was then decided, by way of experiment, I suppose, to place the government of Trinidad in commission; an

HISTORICAL SKETCH. 443

unwarrantable experiment, as proved by the results. Three commissioners were named, Colonel Fullarton, Governor Picton, and Commodore Samuel Hood. Why was Fullarton, a man in every respect inferior to Picton, appointed first commissioner? This is a mystery. The government of the colony was transferred to the commission in January, 1803, the first commissioner having arrived at that time. General Picton had governed the colony for a period of nearly six years, from April, 1797, to January, 1803, under trying and most difficult circumstances. The condition of the colony, when it was placed under commission, may be fairly judged by the following figures :—

POPULATION, 1797.

	Men.	Women.	Boys.	Girls.	Total.
Whites	929	590	301	266	2,086
Free coloured	1,196	1,624	895	751	4,466
Indians	305	401	190	186	1,082
Slaves	4,164	3,505	1,232	1,108	10,009
	6,594	6,120	2,618	2,311	17,643

POPULATION, 1803.

Whites.
English	663	
Spanish	505	2,261
French	1,093	

Free coloured.
English	599	
Spanish	1,751	5,275
French	2,925	

Indians	1,054	21,618 ... Total 29,154
Slaves	20,564	

PRODUCE, 1796.   Hhds.
159 Sugar estates   7,800
130 Coffee   „   130,000
 60 Cacao   „   96,000
103 Cotton   „   224,000

From the pamphlet, "Political Account of the Island of Trinidad," I take the following figures :—

1799—Sugar   ... ... lbs. 9,895,634
      Rum   ... ... gals.   194,488
      Melases ... ...   „   142,637
      Cacao   ... ... lbs.   258,390
      Coffee   ... ...   „   335,913
      Cotton   ... ...   „   323,415
1800—Sugar   ... ...   „   9,895,534
      Rum   ... ... gals.   194,488
      Melases ... ...   „   128,507
      Cacao   ... ... lbs.   284,170
      Coffee   ... ...   „   469,614
      Cotton   ... ...   „   317,395

1801—Sugar	...	...	...	...	lbs.	15,461,912
Rum	...	...	...	...	gals.	343,113
Molasses	...	...	...	...	,,	173,369
Cacao	...	...	...	...	lbs.	324,720
Coffee	...	...	...	...	,,	328,664
Cotton	...	...	...	...	,,	262,997
1802—Sugar	...	...	...	...	,,	14,164,984
Rum	...	...	...	...	gals.	350,049
Molasses	...	...	...	...	,,	143,237
Cacao	...	...	...	...	lbs.	138,699
Coffee	...	...	...	...	,,	278,274
Cotton	...	...	...	...	,,	190,210

The colony had, therefore, made fair progress under the stern, but at the same time judicious, administration of Governor Picton. The existing roads had been improved, and new ones established. When the commission took charge of the government there was found in the public chest the very fair sum of 100,000 dols.

It would seem that Colonel Fullarton had left England with the mission, assumed or real, to find fault with the general administration of the Governor and to thwart his actions, for he had scarcely been in the island a few weeks than he began to censure the conduct of his brother commissioner, and to institute a sort of inquiry into his administration. He actually brought most serious charges against Picton; very soon all turned to confusion and bickering. Colonel Fullarton had clandestinely left the island, and Picton, unable to bear any longer the vexations to which he had been submitted, sent in his resignation in February. It was accepted, and in June he left the colony, highly regretted by those whom he had saved from anarchy. Before leaving Trinidad, he read to the council an address which contained a full *exposé* of what he had done, upon which a resolution was passed, expressing the regret of the council at the departure of the Governor, and their apprehensions with regard to the tranquillity and the safety of the colony. He was also presented with an address, signed by a large number of the most respectable inhabitants of the colony. Commodore Hood, who had seldom acted in his capacity of commissioner, had also left for active service; so Fullarton remained sole commissioner, virtually Governor-in-Chief.

The council having declined meeting him on his return to Trinidad, was dismissed, and a new one appointed. Fortunately, however, this distressing condition of affairs was not allowed to continue long. On the 20th of July Brigadier-General Hislop landed in Port-of-Spain, with the commission of Lieutenant-Governor.

When Colonel Fullarton arrived in Trinidad as first commissioner in January, 1803, the colony was just emerging, thanks to the prudent and energetic measures of its Governor, from a disturbed and very difficult situation. Instead of showing common discretion in his proceedings, he at once began to manifest his opposition to General Picton, criticising his general conduct, and bringing against him sweeping charges of the most serious character. The result was discord and mistrust; the good understanding so necessary between the different classes of colonists was disturbed, and the progress of the colony arrested. His departure was hailed as a relief. General Maitland, who had been appointed commander of the forces under the commission, also left the island, on which occasion he received an address from the Cabildo. In his reply we find the following words: " I will not throw away this opportunity of expressing, in union with you, that I greatly honour and esteem Brigadier-General Picton. In a period of public danger, when the colony was beset with traitors and shaken by the unruly behaviour of a disorderly soldiery, his undisturbed mind awed the factions, subdued the danger, and saved the colony."

General Hislop was a good soldier, but possessed little abilities as a civil governor, and may be said to have taken little interest in the administration of the affairs of the colony. Fortunately he had secured the services of an able, active secretary; but that secretary was not over-scrupulous, and the accusation of corruption brought against him, as it appears, was but too well founded. Sir Thomas Hislop, on taking the government of the island, re-appointed, with the consent of the home Government, the council which had been dismissed by Colonel Fullarton. On his arrival he found it necessary to stop the construction, at Point Gourde, of considerable fortifications, as wholly ineffective for the protection of the harbour; but at once proceeded to erect, at the Fort George mountain, strong military works. I should here mention that about the middle of 1805 the combined fleets of France and Spain had been despatched to the West Indies; Nelson at once followed in pursuit. Having received false information respecting the movements of the enemy, he came to seek them in Trinidad. On his vessels appearing off the north coast, alarm spread through the land, it being thought that they were the combined fleet. Martial law was at once proclaimed, and the militia called out. The town was declared untenable, and the inhabitants were invited to send any valuable property to the fort, and the merchants their books. The Governor marched up to the batteries with the regular troops, militia, and volunteers, leaving the town at the mercy of the supposed enemy. Nelson entered the Gulf and immediately retired. It was only then that the mistake was discovered, when the inhabitants and the military returned to Port-of-Spain.

Towards the end of this year, in December, a plot was discovered amongst the slaves in Diego-Martin, having for its object the massacre of the white men, and in which a great part of the negro population was implicated. It had originated, as it appears, with some French negroes from the old colonies. Four slaves were executed, and others severely punished by flogging and banishment.

It was under Governor Hislop that a first attempt was made to introduce into the island Asiatic immigrants.

Sometime in the year 1806 the ship *Fortitude* left Macao for Trinidad with 192 men and one single woman. She anchored in the harbour on the 12th of October, but the poor deluded Chinese would not stay, and, with the exception of twenty-three who remained in the colony, the rest re-embarked for China in the very same vessel which had brought them. These twenty-three individuals were located at Cocorite, a very unhealthy locality. They eventually turned gardeners, fishermen, or pork-butchers. Of course this first attempt at introducing immigrants from the East was a complete failure.

In 1807 the slave trade was abolished by Act of Parliament.

In 1809 an event occurred which sadly illustrated the state of legislation in Trinidad, and the wanton negligence of the Government in that very important matter. One Mr. Lebis, having flogged one of his slaves to death, was brought before the court. Judge Smith presided. The advocate of the defendant, Mr. George Knox, argued in his defence that Lebis could not be judged by the slave law of 1789, that law having never been confirmed by the Audiencia at Caracas; that he could not be judged by Picton's slave law, as that law had not received in time the royal sanction. Judge Smith was obliged to admit the validity of the argument, and Lebis was discharged. Of course laws had been framed: they actually existed; but having never been confirmed, they could not be enforced. The very appointment of Judge Smith was discussed, and the legality of his commission called into question. Beset with difficulties, he was almost constantly at war, now with the Governor, now with the Council or Cabildo. He left Trinidad worried, and was replaced by Judge Bigge. The colonists on that occasion became convinced that new legislation was required, and decided on petitioning Government for English laws. Subscription lists were circulated, and a committee appointed, consisting of the most respectable white inhabitants of the island. It was agreed to send to England Mr. G. Knox, barrister, as a delegate, to plead the cause of the colonists. But as it appears the coloured class was virtually excluded from participation in the advantages of the measure, they therefore met and prepared a counter petition, not because they wished to retain the Spanish laws, but because they were averse to special legislation. The ministers, who wished to keep Trinidad as an experimental colony, took advantage of this circumstance to refuse the prayer, under the plea that it was not the wish of the majority to have English laws.

The West India body in London was averse to granting English laws and a British constitution to Trinidad. They looked with some jealousy at the newly-conquered colony, with its foreign elements.

Mr. Marryat, however, presented in Parliament two motions, one for extending to the island English legislation, and one for granting a constitution. They were both lost on a division.

On the 24th of March, 1808, Port-of-Spain was almost completely destroyed by an accidental conflagration, as it appears. The buildings were of wood, and three-fourths of the town were burnt down; thousands were ruined, and hundreds turned to beggary. It must be acknowledged that faint efforts were made to arrest the conflagration, probably from the conviction that without water all efforts were unavailable. The loss was about £500,000. Assistance came from many quarters: Parliament voted £50,000; Governor Hislop gave £1,000; Picton generously contributed £4,000—a sum which the colonists had given him as a token of their appreciation of his services as Governor; the sum was declined. The neighbouring islands contributed largely. As a consequence of the calamitous occurrence, a law was passed forbidding the building of houses with inflammable materials.

General Hislop, as well as Governor Picton, had made it a duty to encourage insurrectional movements in the continental dependencies of Spain. In 1806, Miranda, encouraged by the British Government, attempted to revolutionise that part of the Spanish Main nearest to Trinidad. He had at his disposal several vessels and a troop of about 200 men; he was also joined by a considerable number of volunteers from Trinidad, and had also the assistance of Admiral Cochrane. Miranda, as is well known, failed in his attempt.

General Hislop, who had left on leave in January, 1810, returned in March, to leave finally in May. He had for successor Major-General W. Monro, who was sworn as Lieutenant-Governor in May.

General Monro, in his civil capacity and social dispositions, very much resembled his predecessor. He left almost entirely the cares and toils of government to his secretary and a Member of Council. This secretary was not better than the one at the service of Sir Thomas Hislop. He indulged in convivial parties with his friends, but would not trouble himself much about the administration of the colony entrusted to his care.

It was during his government, in the year 1811, that a royal order was issued to enforce the registration of the slaves. The measure was opposed by the planters, as fraught with most injurious results. It was, nevertheless, enforced.

The war waged by the colonists against Spain on the neighbouring continent was still raging, though with adverse vicissitudes. Trinidad was then—as it ever was, and still is—the asylum of the weaker party—not, perhaps, to its advantage, as proved by the rash measures adopted against the commerce of the island by the reigning president, Guzman Blanco (1883). England was at peace with Spain, and could not, without a breach of faith, encourage the insurgent colonists. However, Santiago Mariño, with several others, managed to prepare, in some valley of the north coast, an expedition, which landed on the opposite coast of the Gulf, and took possession of Guiria. These few men were the nucleus of a force of about 5,000 men, which joined Bolivar, and materially assisted the insurgents. On this occasion Governor Munro issued a proclamation, threatening to confiscate the property of any who would join in the enterprise.

The rebuilding of Port-of-Spain was, in the meantime, proceeding satisfactorily.

General Munro left in May, 1813, having thus governed the colony for two years.

He had for his successor a civilian, a man in every respect different from him—active, abstemious, and deeply interested in the government of the colony entrusted to his care. Sir James Ralph Woodford, Baronet, landed in Trinidad on the 14th June, 1813, and governed the island during fifteen years—from June, 1813, to April, 1828. He died at sea on the 16th of May, that year, during his return passage to England.

Sir Ralph was a perfect gentleman, having refined and aristocratic manners, which he knew how to value in others, and the example of which must have imparted to society that polish which for so many years distinguished Trinidad society. He was in his person graceful and dignified. No Governor was ever more amiable in domestic relations, and these kind dispositions he manifested towards the colonists, whatever their nationality or origin—a trait, let me say, characteristic of our best Governors, Sir Ralph Woodford, Lord Harris, and Sir Arthur Gordon. He always exacted to the utmost what he considered due to his position as Governor. Though fond of display on public occasions, Sir Ralph accepted, with perfect good grace, the scanty hospitality which at times was offered him in the country by poor planters. Sir Thomas Picton had, by his stern energy, preserved the colony to the British Crown. Sir Ralph Woodford, by his activity and high administrative qualities, improved it beyond expectation; always ready, indefatigable, constantly on the alert in the interest of the colony, he would inquire into all matters connected with the welfare of Trinidad. He was always prepared to listen to those whom he knew took an interest in the island. He had made it a rule occasionally to visit the different quarters into which the colony was divided, and to inquire into their wants, and the condition of the roads especially. Sir Ralph was a man of taste, and never considered it beneath his dignity to enter into details. He particularly took a pride in the rebuilding of Port-of-Spain and the embellishment of the city, which owes to him its present appearance; he would ride over the town to see with his own eyes before taking any decisive steps. He laid out Brunswick Square, and had Marine Square Promenade planted after the land had been recovered from the sea and made up; he saw the New Market House finished. He also directed the formation of the Botanic Gardens at Saint Ann, which he placed under the management of Mr. Lockhart.

In 1816 he laid the foundation-stone of the Catholic cathedral, and of Trinity Church, the Anglican cathedral. He had also laid, in 1815, the foundation-stone of the Church of San Jose de Oruña.

It was under the government of Sir Ralph Woodford, and at his request, that a Catholic bishop was appointed for Trinidad, which previously formed part of the diocese of Guiana, or Angostura. Doctor Buckley, Bishop of Gerren *in partibus infidelium*, arrived here in March, 1820, as Vicar-Apostolic for the British and Dutch West Indies; he lived on the most friendly terms with the Governor, and died, two months before his friend, in March, 1828, much regretted by persons of all denominations.

Dr. Coleridge, who had been appointed Bishop of Barbadoes and the Windward Islands, visited Trinidad in March, 1825, on a pastoral tour.

I should here mention that Sir Ralph Woodford always showed the greatest respect for the Catholic Church, of which, as Governor, he was patron; and consideration also for the Catholic inhabitants. Of course Sir Ralph was not without his faults: he was haughty, bore opposition with impatience, had of his magisterial powers an exaggerated idea, and at times administered arbitrarily; yet it cannot be said that he was tyrannical. He, I believe, never did aught but that which he thought to be for the good of the colony; in fact, during his long administration, Sir Ralph Woodford proved an efficient and good Governor. He has left his imprint on the colony, and may be proposed—in important matters at least—as a model administrator. To judge him fairly we should go back to the epoch in which he lived; he may not have been in advance of, but surely he was not behind, his time.

I have said that Trinidad always was a safe asylum for the refugees from the Spanish Main. I must acknowledge, however, that Sir Ralph Woodford on all occasions manifested his preference for the royalists, whom he treated with consideration; not so the republicans, whom he distrusted. But it was never proved that he treated them harshly, or refused them admittance into the island.

To the first Spanish settlers the Crown had made grants of land under certain conditions; but, as a rule, those grants were not regularly surveyed or registered, so that the occupants could not, in the greatest number of cases, exhibit their titles to such concessions. They, nevertheless, contended that they were lawful owners, and either refused to sell at all to the new comers, or demanded exorbitant prices. Governor Chacon, who was determined to carry into execution the provisions of the cedula, and to protect the new colonists, instituted a searching inquiry into the titles of the occupants, and then issued a proclamation calling upon them to prove the validity of their occupancy; failing which, they were to obtain new grants. Of course the proclamation was ill received, and the measure which it proposed to enforce regarded as highly arbitrary. This interference of Governor Chacon created discontent and rancour.

Sir Ralph Woodford, who, of course, could not be ignorant of the fact, did not hesitate—in an evil hour, no doubt—to revive the unpleasant question. He knew well that many of the colonists would not be able to produce indisputable titles; and he made up his mind to search for those titles, and to inquire into the grants made by the Crown of Spain—not only those made during and since the year 1783, but also before that epoch. The grantees were called to satisfy the Governor as to the legality of their occupancy; or, in case they could not do so, to take new grants on paying certain fees. This interference was viewed with jealousy, and strenuously opposed. More; the Governor aimed a blow at those who possessed lands by virtue of the cedula of 1783, but had neglected to register them in the *Libre Becerro*, as prescribed. The law required also that at least one-fifth of the lands granted should be under cultivation. Sir Ralph threatened to resume possession of the whole, or part of all such lands whenever this condition had not been fulfilled Again, quit-rent was exacted for all the grants; and other vexatious measures were adopted. Soon after, however, the quit-rent was remitted on all lands granted before the conquest.

The Governor had not it all his own way; pamphlets were written and petitions signed, supporting the rights of the landowners. These measures of Sir Ralph Woodford had their evil consequences. Discontent prevailed, and the titles of property being questioned, confidence was shaken, and the value of property lowered. This was an egregious error of Governor Woodford, and a political blunder, especially as the question might have been easily settled by simply causing the disputed grants to be re-surveyed and registered.

The whole matter was laid before Parliament, when Mr. Hume moved for the appointment of a Commission to report on the state of the island. Messrs. H. Maddock and Fortunatus Dwarris were appointed commissioners, and ordered to proceed to Trinidad to inquire into and report upon the state of the lands and the land question. Subsequently Mr. Jabez Henry was appointed chief commissioner, Mr. Maddock having been obliged to leave. The question was fully considered by the other commissioners, and finally settled to the entire satisfaction of the colonists, after twelve years of incessant litigation. We ought to suppose that Governor Woodford acted either at the instigation or with the tacit support of the Government.

On two different occasions, in 1819 and 1823, there were rumours of a rising amongst the negroes; fortunately matters were not as bad as first reported; the alarm soon subsided—only some wild talking among a few discontented slaves, but no actual plot.

In 1824 a law was passed for the protection of slaves; and in 1826 a royal proclamation was published removing certain vexatious regulations respecting the free blacks and people of colour.

In May, 1818, the town of San Fernando was destroyed by fire. Liberal sums were subscribed in aid of the sufferers.

In 1813 the minutes of the Cabildo were ordered to be kept in English; and in 1814 the English language was, for the first time, used in the law courts.

An Order in Council was also published in 1823, making changes in the tribunals of the island.

Sir Ralph Woodford was absent from the colony a short time in 1820, during which absence Lieutenant-Colonel Young acted as Lieutenant-Governor; again, in 1821–22, Colonel Young was Lieutenant-Governor. When he left, in 1828, on sick leave, Major Capadose was sworn in as Lieutenant-Governor, but acted only for a very short time, and was superseded by Sir Charles Smith, who, in turn, was supplanted by Colonel Farquharson.

The successor of Sir Ralph Woodford, Major-General Sir Lewis Grant, was a man of little energy, and never cared much for the colony. There is nothing interesting to record during his government. The constitution of the council was modified in 1831, and it was made to consist of six official and six unofficial members, all nominees of the Crown.

In 1832 several laws were enacted regulating the treatment of the slaves; organic changes were also introduced in the organisation of our courts of law, the Honorable George Scotland being then Chief-Justice. Governor Grant left the island in April, 1833; he had been twice in England on leave, and was replaced *ad interim* by Colonel Doherty and by Sir Charles Smith, who had been appointed, acting after the death of Sir Ralph Woodford.

Governor Grant was succeeded, in 1833, by Sir George Fitzgerald Hill, Baronet, colonel of the Londonderry Regiment of Militia. Like his predecessor, Sir George Hill governed peaceably, and never paid much attention to the exigencies of government; he evidently had a preference for the *laissez aller* system.

Two remarkable events, however, marked the period of his administration. On the 1st of August, 1834, the abolition of slavery and its transformation into apprenticeship were proclaimed. The ignorant negroes could not understand the subtle distinction between apprenticeship and slavery, nor the motives for establishing prædial and non-prædial apprenticeship; they could not understand why domestics, who worked under cover, and whose occupations were more comfortable, were apprenticed for only four years, whilst they, who worked outside, exposed to the inclemencies of the seasons, were condemned to two years more of apprenticeship. They, of course, manifested their discontent by refusing to work; a certain number repaired to the capital to ask for redress, and there behaved riotously. A few leaders were arrested, and punished by flogging. This act of severity had its salutary effect, and order was soon restored. The resistance of the apprentices was, as a rule, rather passive than otherwise.

The four years of non-prædial apprenticeship were drawing to a close; it was thought prudent and only fair to proclaim emancipation of all, prædial as well as non-prædial; and a resolution was passed by the Legislative Council granting complete freedom, as from the 1st August, 1838—a measure which had become unavoidable, and had the approbation of the planting body.

The other event to which I desire to refer is the mutiny, at St. Joseph, of the soldiers belonging to the 1st West India Regiment. They were newly-liberated Africans, who had been induced to enlist as soldiers, but who knew nothing of the obligations they had contracted. They revolted, because they considered they were not treated as free men. About 280 of them were barracked at St. Joseph : on the night of the 17th of June, 1837, they rose, and at once set fire to some huts which served for their use; they next attacked the officers' quarters, and fired at them—fortunately with no effect, as they knew not how to handle their muskets. A party of them left the town about seven o'clock, marching eastward, in the hope, as they thought, of reaching their country. They were met at Arima by the militia; some were killed, and the rest dispersed in the woods. That wild, unjustifiable mutiny, cost about thirty lives, including three chiefs, who were sentenced to death and executed.

In 1834 a number of emigrants from Fayal and Madeira were landed in Trinidad; that immigration was not followed up.

It was under the government of Sir George Hill that a few Mico schools were established in the island. They, however, were not carried on for any length of time.

Sir George Hill died in Trinidad in 1839, and the government of the colony was assumed by Sir Murray Macgregor, Governor-General of the Windward Islands, for only a short time, and till the appointment of Colonel Sir Henry McLeod.

Of the Governors who administered the colony since emancipation I shall say very little, especially as some of them are still living. I will only notice the most interesting events as they occurred to the present day, and any important measure adopted.

Sir Henry McLeod governed the colony from April, 1840, to April, 1846. He was active and prudent, and his management of the finances of the colony highly satisfactory. When he retired he left a replenished chest—a fortunate circumstance, since the colony had to pass, during the government of his successor, Lord Harris, through a most serious crisis. Sir Henry, a staunch Protestant, was the first Governor, since the capitulation, who declined the title of Patron of the Catholic Church, and scrupled to perform the duties that title imposed; and yet, as Governor, he was simply discharging a perfunctory obligation.

The Bishop courteously acquiesced in the scrupulosity of the Governor, but had not on this occasion the full approval of the Catholics.

This act of Sir Henry McLeod was as a preliminary step to a more serious move.

Religious equality virtually existed in the colony. The Ecclesiastical Ordinance of 1844 should be regarded as an infringement of that equality.

It was proclaimed in February of the following year, and purported to be "for the better regulation of the duties of the united Church of England and Ireland in the colony, and for insuring the more effectual performance of the same." The island was divided into parishes, and rectories were constituted. To this there could not be any objection; but the amount of the different salaries was fixed by law. Salaries were also voted for clerks and sextons; glebe lands were attached to each rectory. The rectory house of Trinity Church was to be kept in repair at the public expense. It was further declared that "on the passing of the Ordinance all laws, ordinances, and canons ecclesiastical, which were then used and enforced in England, should be accepted, esteemed, and taken to be in full force and virtue within the island." This was establishing the supremacy of the Church of England in Trinidad. This Ordinance was strongly opposed by the Catholics, though they were well aware of the existence of the letters patent granted by her Majesty on the 21st day of August, 1843. The Ecclesiastical Ordinance created jealousy and an uneasy feeling in the colony, and had for its effect the perpetuation of existing differences. It remained in force till the year 1870.

Sir Henry McLeod had for his successor Lord Harris. He administered the colony from April, 1846, to March, 1854, a most critical period in the history of Trinidad. I do not hesitate to say it was fortunate that Lord Harris was called to govern during that critical time. The high position he held, as a peer of the realm, afforded him opportunities, which a man in a less exalted position could not have, of serving the interests of the colony. Lord Harris, in his despatches to Lord Grey, appears as an independent character and an unprejudiced man, always ready to plead the cause of the much-abused colonists; he resolutely and candidly exposed the difficulties resulting, not only from the depressed condition of the market and the poverty of the people, but mainly from the wandering dispositions of the emancipated class.

Lord Harris clearly perceived the dangers of the situation, but knew where to look for a remedy; that remedy he found in Asiatic immigration, which to all unprejudiced minds appeared as the only means of relieving the colony. He unhesitatingly set to work, and did not rest satisfied till, by dint of perseverance, he succeeded in removing all objections, and in conciliating the Colonial Office to our system of immigration. The first essays were not very encouraging, not through his fault surely, since he perseveringly insisted on the necessity of a serious control and the adoption of stringent regulations. "My desire," said Lord Harris, "has been impartially to study the interests of both parties, at the same time never to lose sight of the fact that the Coolies are placed here under peculiar circumstances, as utter strangers in a foreign land, and therefore requiring the zealous and increasing care of the Government; that they are also far from being the best class of the Indian labouring population; are naturally dissolute and depraved in their habits if left to themselves, and much inclined to fall into habits of drinking and of wandering idle about the country, and therefore require also the close supervision of Government." The Governor deserved to succeed, and he did succeed. I should not be just and fair if I did not recognise the effective assistance given to the Governor by Mr. Ch. Warner, the then Attorney-General; he may be said to have been the indefatigable, clever, and felicitous collaborator of Lord Harris in this question of immigration. To both the colony owes a debt of gratitude.

Lord Harris had undertaken the government of Trinidad eight years after emancipation had been proclaimed.

During those eight years things had been allowed to continue as before, and yet a new plan of administration had become necessary. The powers entrusted to the commandants had been much curtailed: the roads could be no more kept in repair by corvees.

Lord Harris had the island divided into two principal divisions, the northern and the southern; each division was subdivided into four counties, and each county into two districts and into wards; these wards were, in most cases, the old Spanish quarters. To each ward Lord Harris appointed a warden—a respectable inhabitant of the ward, as a rule; to each warden was attached a clerk paid from the funds of the ward. One of the objects of Lord Harris in establishing wards and appointing unpaid officers was to prepare the people for the exercise of municipal privileges.

It had become urgent, under the new *régime* of liberty, to provide local funds for local purposes—a land tax was established. It had also become necessary to provide for the maintenance of the public roads—road boards were formed. The warden, an unpaid officer, had unfortunately been entrusted with multifarious duties which he could not perform: he had to make yearly returns of produce grown or manufactured; to prevent squatting; to detain lumber, &c., suspected to be cut on crown lands; provide work for the poor; fix the rates; pay all moneys into the colonial treasury; he was road officer, payer, &c.—a great deal too much for a man who had to attend to his own private affairs.

This was a mistake of Lord Harris, which, later, led to many changes in the territorial administration of the colony, as organised by him.

Fully alive to the evils of squatting, or the illegal occupation of crown lands, the Governor attempted its suppression. An Order in Council dated October, 1838, gave power to the stipendiary magistrates for the removal of persons having taken, or who would take, possession of lands without probable claim. A proclamation had been issued in June, 1847, with the object of enforcing this Order in Council. Lord Harris determined to give all facilities for the removal of squatters; extended the summary jurisdiction conferred on the stipendiary magistrates to all justices of the peace; information, as regards public lands, was to be preferred by the Surveyor-General; in respect of private lands, by the owner; and in respect of abandoned lands, by any one. Where lands belonged to the Government, or were abandoned, possession was given to the warden or Surveyor-General; where land belonged to private persons, to the owner. It must be acknowledged that the object contemplated by the measure was not attained; probably because it was not properly enforced. Ten years later the well-directed efforts of Sir Arthur Gordon were crowned with signal success.

A most important measure introduced by Lord Harris was his system of primary education. I regret to be obliged to say that it was an altogether Godless system; ministers of religion were excluded from the school-room, so also all direct religious teaching. This measure of Lord Harris, when proposed, was disapproved by Catholics, and even by Protestants. It is still partly in force. I dare say that, in its results, it was not very encouraging. Certainly morality has not improved in the island; quite the reverse. The plan of Lord Harris was complete in its scope; for it contemplated the establishment of normal schools both for boys and girls, and of a school of secondary instruction, all on the same system. Of course Lord Harris meant well; but he allowed himself to be influenced by the then prevailing notion that Government owed to the subjects only secular instruction, at least in communities composed of various religious denominations. That in all such cases the State should be bound to give only secular instruction is safe enough, but that it should exclude religious teaching and the ministers of religion altogether from the school-room, is simply exorbitant. It was teaching the people that the State does not care about religion and the morals it teaches.

In the year 1851 an Ordinance was passed for supplying Port-of-Spain and vicinity with water, a benefaction which cannot be too highly appreciated. Previously the inhabitants of the town drew their supply of water from wells, the contents of which were, in most cases, contaminated by the percolation of privy stuff; or from tanks in which rain water was collected. Bathing was then a rare luxury. The rate payable was calculated according to the annual rental, an arrangement which was highly beneficial to the poorer classes; a house assessed at £100 sterling annually paying five times as much as a house rented at £20.

It was under the government of Lord Harris, in 1853, that an Ordinance was passed for the regulation of municipal corporations in the island. Port-of-Spain and San Fernando were constituted boroughs, under the title of Mayor and Burgesses of Port-of-Spain, and Mayor and Burgesses of San Fernando. Port-of-Spain was divided into five wards, each ward being represented by three councillors. Under the old constitution, the Governor was the president of the Town Council, but the meetings were presided over by a vice-president. The Governor signed the minutes, and had a right of *veto*. The exercise of that right of *veto* was, on more than one occasion, a cause of conflict between the Town Council and the Governor.

A much regrettable event occurred during the government of Lord Harris. A serious riot took place on the 1st of October, 1852; the military were called out, and had to make use of their arms; one person was killed, and several others were wounded. The immediate cause was the indiscriminate enforcement of certain regulations, which, however, were not applicable to debtors; they had been cancelled, but a public meeting had been called; the people became highly excited, and assembled riotously round the Government-house; there the conflict took place.

Lord Harris was unassuming, persevering, and straightforward. His charity was unbounded, and no poor were ever sent away unassisted; and more than one indigent respectable family received from him substantial pecuniary aid. The exports and imports of the colony had fallen off, and the revenue had decreased in proportion; the funds were hardly sufficient to pay the salaries of the public officers. The Governor had come to the determination of retrenching from those salaries, beginning with his own. The colony, however, was not brought to such an extremity.

During the whole time of his office, Lord Harris never left the island, thus devoting his whole time to the administration of the colony entrusted to his care. He is one of the few Governors of Trinidad who, on leaving, were accompanied by the regrets and good wishes of the colonists; even those who had disapproved some of his acts were afterwards compelled to recognise his sterling qualities.

Commodore Sir Charles Elliot succeeded to Lord Harris, and

governed the colony from March 1854, to October, 1856. In this year, 1856, he had an Ordinance passed "amending and consolidating the law with regard to the appointment of wardens and their powers and duties," and giving power to the Governor "to form such and so many wards as he should see fit into wards unions, and to appoint one warden for the several wards comprised in such unions." The wardens became salaried officers; and, remarkable enough, none of the thirty-two wardens who had served gratuitously under Lord Harris were appointed to the well-paid offices created by the Ordinance of 1856, though several, to my knowledge, would have gladly accepted the situation.

In August, 1854, cholera broke out in the island, and was most fatal. About that time the Court of Rome had sent, as legate to the West Indies, the Right Reverend Dr. Spaccapietra. Trinidad was one of the islands he had instruction to visit. Archbishop Smith had just died, and Bishop Spaccapietra was appointed archbishop in his stead. The good prelate soon won the sympathy and admiration of all by his unremitting exertions during the prevalence of the pestilence: energetic, indefatigable, he would respond, by night and by day, to the call even of the lowest; by the poorest class he was venerated as a father and a benefactor. But Dr. Spaccapietra was a foreigner, and Governor Elliot, no doubt incited by sectarian friends, would not recognise him as archbishop, and withdrew his salary. This was regarded by the Catholics as unjustifiable interference; public meetings were held all over the island; a committee was elected, called the Catholic Committee; petitions, most numerously signed, were addressed to the Secretary of State and her Majesty the Queen, claiming for the Catholics of Trinidad the rights guaranteed to them by the capitulation. In this they were supported by a party of Protestants. The Governor, nothing moved, persisted in his determination to annoy the Catholics. A committee had been appointed to collect funds for the relief of the orphans and widows of the Crimean war. All the ministers of religion, including the Baptist minister, were named members of the committee; but the Catholic archbishop was excluded, under the pretext that he was a foreigner and could not be recognised. This exclusion was, by the Catholics, considered as a gratuitous insult and a grievance; a petition was addressed to her Majesty, complaining of the indignity inflicted, and praying for redress. Soon after the reception of the petition, a despatch was sent to the Governor instructing him to recognise as head of the Roman Catholic Church in the colony any dignitary presenting credentials from the Court of Rome, and whom the Catholics would recognise as such. Thus ended—to the general satisfaction, I dare say—the unseemly and most unpleasant contention with Sir Charles Elliot. Archbishop Spaccapietra was recognised as head of the Roman Catholic Church in Trinidad, and the arrears of his salary were paid him; these he handed over to the Crimean fund. Sir Charles Elliot had governed the colony for a little more than two years.

On his retiring from the government of Trinidad, Robert William Keate, Esq., was appointed his successor. I regret to say that he allowed himself to be guided by coterie influences— a most dangerous mistake in a mixed community like this. Governors should always keep free from such influence, lest they should, by acting partially, create antagonism. The principal act of Mr. Keate was the establishment, in 1863, of the Queen's Collegiate School of Secondary Instruction, on the plan of the Queen's Colleges in Ireland. The Catholics were averse to the school, contending that they could not and would not avail themselves of the advantages it proffered, as it was a purely secular institution; that the school, though maintained at the public expense, would, in fact, be so maintained for only a portion of the population. They suggested that the Protestants and the Catholics should establish their own schools, which the Government would then assist. Their suggestions were disregarded, and no account taken of their complaints.

In August, 1863, an Ordinance was passed "for amending the law with regard to the solemnisation and registration of marriages." Such an Ordinance was needed to remedy abuses of a serious nature and rather demoralising. Some of the provisions of the Ordinance were such, however, as to cause uneasiness and anxiety in the minds of the Catholics, who otherwise approved the main object to be obtained. The Ordinance required that all buildings for the celebration of marriages should be registered; notice of every intended marriage was to be given to the district-registrar, who, twenty-one days after receiving such notice, would deliver a certificate, upon which the marriage ceremony could be performed by the minister, in the place named in the certificate. Marriages solemnised in any other place than the building specified in the certificate are declared null and void; ministers of religion unduly solemnising marriages are deemed guilty of felony, and made liable to imprisonment, with or without hard labour, for any period not exceeding three years. Marriages may be contracted before the district-registrar. Civil marriage was thus established; religious marriage in an unauthorised place decreed null and void at law; and the minister of religion unduly solemnising any marriage declared a felon. The Catholics strongly remonstrated against some of the clauses of the Ordinance, observing that they held marriage as a sacrament of the Church, and that the law, by some of its provisions, interfered with the free action of the clergy; that the delay of twenty-one days, and the obligation of solemnising marriages in registered places, hindered the administration of the sacred rite *in articulo mortis*, when such administration could not be delayed.

In the year 1865 an Ordinance was passed, altering in certain particulars the provisions of the Ordinance of 1863, and giving satisfaction to the Catholics, under certain conditions, with regard to the solemnisation of marriage *in articulo mortis*. Marriages contracted under these conditions were of no effect as marriages in law.

Governor Keate had made up his mind to establish underground sewerage in the town, which he had divided into districts for the purpose. The scheme was generally disapproved, on the plea of a scanty supply of water, insufficient declivity, and the careless habits of the people. Sewers were laid down in only one district.

Governor Keate was absent from the island from April, 1860, to May, 1861, during which time the Government was administered by Lieutenant-Governor James Walker.

The Honourable J. H. Thomas Manners Sutton succeeded Governor Keate. There is nothing worth chronicling during his government—which lasted from September, 1864, to March, 1866, about eighteen months—except the Ordinance already mentioned for amending the law of marriage.

Governor Manners Sutton had for his successor Sir Arthur Gordon. Previous to his arrival the colony had been administered—from April, 1866, to November, same year—by Edw.

Everard Rushworth, Esq. Governor Manners Sutton and Mr. Rushworth had their serious attention called to the question of squatting, a very important matter really.

The government of Sir Arthur Gordon may be said to have inaugurated a new era in the politics of Trinidad. It would seem that he had for mission to undo several things which had been done by some of his predecessors. He made important changes in the system of public education introduced by Lord Harris, the principal of which was the permission granted to impart religious teaching in the school-room. The Board of Education was remodelled, and an executive committee formed, consisting of the Governor and eight members, four of whom must be non-Catholics, and four Roman Catholics. Schools of primary education were divided into two classes—those established and maintained by the Government, and those established by local managers and receiving aid from the public funds of the colony. Ministers of religion, or persons appointed by them were permitted to give religious instruction in the Government schools. With the object of promoting secondary education, he established, in the place of the Queen's Collegiate School, a college, called the ROYAL COLLEGE OF TRINIDAD. The management of the college was vested in a council, styled the COLLEGE COUNCIL, with power, among other things, to declare any school of secondary education to be a school in connection with the Royal College, and entitled to aid from the public funds of the colony, such aid to consist of a fixed salary to the principal or head-master of the school—of capitation grants, under certain conditions, to the pupils. This was a liberal scheme, showing respect for the rights of the tax-payer and deference for the religious sentiments of the people, who had no more reason for refusing to participate in the advantages afforded by the Government.

In February, 1870, Governor McLeod's Ecclesiastical Ordinance was repealed, save a few sections, and religious equality re-established, all Christian denominations being called to share proportionately in the Ecclesiastical Fund.

Governor Gordon was particularly successful in his efforts to suppress squatting. He first declared an upset price of crown lands, viz., £1 per acre, and 10s. for lagoon lands. Next, squatters were not only allowed, but invited, to legalise their position by purchasing the lands they occupied. An Ordinance was passed in October, 1868, "for facilitating the plantation and settlement of crown lands," making it lawful for the Governor to constitute districts and appoint commissioners, such districts to be surveyed and settled under the direction of the commissioner. Persons desirous of petitioning for the ungranted lands they occupied were allowed six months for doing so from the appointment of the commissioner; those not petitioning remained liable to prosecution. The district of Montserrat was inhabited by a large number of squatters, mostly Spanish peons, anxious to retain their holdings. Mr. Robert Mitchell was appointed commissioner, and at once set to work visiting every corner of his district, and almost every squatter in it. Petitions soon poured in, and the district became settled in a very short time. Governor Gordon, by opening the crown lands for competition, and declaring an upset price for the same, cut short all pretexts for complaints, and, by forming districts and appointing commissioners, did, in my opinion, hit upon the best plan for checking squatting. The appointment of commissioners was especially a felicitous expedient.

Many amendments which successive experience had pointed out had been made to the first Immigration Ordinance; every Governor, in succession, had his share in improving the Act. Sir Arthur Gordon, however, may claim the honour of having consolidated in one Ordinance, June, 1870, the different Ordinances enacted up to that date. As consolidated by Governor Gordon, the Ordinance of June, 1870, is the law in force.

An important Act was enacted for rendering certain offences punishable on summary conviction.

An Ordinance was passed for enabling aliens to obtain the privileges of British-born subjects in the island—an Ordinance of some importance in a colony like Trinidad, which requires population and immigrants.

Governor Gordon established a house of refuge for the reception and relief of destitute persons residing in the rural districts. The destitute residing in Port-of-Spain were already provided for by the Municipality.

A most important measure had been introduced by Sir Arthur Gordon; this was the Ordinance "for the declaration of titles to land, and to facilitate its transfer." It was based on Mr. Torrens'

Act, in force in Australia. The execution of the provisions of the Ordinance was entrusted to the Registrar-General's department. Under the Act the Governor may appoint deputy registrars and examiners of titles, also lands titles commissioners. Land alienated in fee from the crown after the commencement of the Ordinance was subject to its provisions; but it remained optional to bring under the provisions of the Ordinance such lands as had been granted prior to the day it came into operation. It is indisputable that this Ordinance would have had for its effect to facilitate the transfer of land and to fix titles, and this would have been obtained at a very small cost to the landholders, and yet the Ordinance, though passed some twelve years ago, and declared as taking effect from the 1st of January, 1871, has never been put in force, nor has it been repealed, so far as I know. How are we to account for this oversight? It was insinuated that great difficulties would be encountered in enforcing its clauses in the case of lands granted before its passing; but such difficulties could not be anticipated as regards grants made after the 1st of January, 1871, and how many acres have been granted since that epoch? But had the law been put in force, the interests of the legal profession would have suffered, and naturally enough lawyers show themselves antagonistic to the measure. But as far as I can understand the economy of the Act, the public would have gained substantial advantage had it taken effect. Had not Sir Arthur Gordon left the colony almost immediately after the Ordinance had been passed, he certainly would have put it in force.

When Sir Arthur Gordon took the administration of the colony, Governmental influence was in the hands of a few personages having exclusive views. The reforms projected by the Governor were ill-received by the party, and they strove to obstruct his way; but Sir Arthur was not the man to desist from measures which he considered just and fair. Unable to tame his opponents into acquiescence, he did not hesitate to crush them.

I shall not presume to pass a judgment on the administration of Sir Arthur Gordon. If some of his reforms were hailed with undisguised satisfaction by the majority of the people, they were, on the other hand, censured and opposed by those who must grieve at the loss of their influence. This, however, I can say, since the adoption of those reforms, all unpleasant controversies and invidious recriminations on delicate subjects have apparently ceased.

Governor Gordon was absent from the colony from June to November, 1868; Cornelius H. Kortright, Esq., was administrator till the arrival, in 1870, of James Robert Longden, C.M.G., appointed Governor. Governor Longden was prudent and cautious. He laid the foundation-stone of Saint Ann House in July, 1873, and had the good fortune of sanctioning and fostering the construction of the first railway laid in the island, from Port-of-Spain to Arima. He left the colony before it was inaugurated.

He had an Ordinance passed to enable the West India and Panama Telegraph Company to land their cable and construct telegraphs in the island, thus connecting Trinidad with the other West India islands and with the United States and Europe. The first message was received here on 28th July, 1866.

In 1870 an Ordinance was passed, making it lawful for the Governor to appoint district medical officers. The medical officers have to visit all estates being worked by indentured immigrants, and all paupers in their district; they are also public vaccinators. Previous to the appointment of district medical officers, the medical attendants of estates were chosen by the proprietors. The object of the Ordinance was, evidently, to place under the control of the Government the medical service of all estates having indentured immigrants.

The Immigration Ordinance was amended, and a minimum salary of twenty-five cents fixed for day and night work in the field.

An Ordinance was passed for the establishment of reformatory schools, but nothing has been done yet.

Mr. W. H. Rennie, who acted as Administrator from July, 1872, to May, 1873, had the Income-tax Ordinance repealed.

In April, 1874, William Wellington Cairns, Esq., C.M.G., arrived in the island as Governor, but left almost immediately after, the Colonial Secretary, the Hon. J. Scott Bushe, being appointed Administrator.

Henry Turner Irving, Esq., C.M.G., was appointed Governor, and arrived in the colony on the 20th of November, 1874. Governor Irving was active, and finding that there was room for improvement in several branches of the public service, diligently set to work. The Department of Public Works evidently required remodelling. The old staff had become insufficient and inadequate to the requirements of the service; the establishment of railways, and the extension through newly-settled districts of roads, required a more numerous personnel. An Ordinance was therefore passed in June, 1875, for the appointment of a Director of Public Works, who should take the charge and management of all public works and public buildings, and the superintendence of all public roads, and perform such other duties as by any Ordinance might be imposed upon him. Authority was given to the Governor to appoint assistants, who would then exercise any of the duties imposed, or any of the powers exercisable by the Director of Public Works. The director was made a corporation sole, capable of suing and being sued.

The department has been unmercifully criticised. The criticism, however, did not bear on the creation of the department, but on the manner in which it was conducted. The works undertaken, including the formation of roads and the building of bridges, have not been, in many cases, satisfactorily completed. The amount expended has been beyond precedent. But, in the opinion of all sensible men, the director had too much to do, and of course could not exercise over his subordinates that control which alone can secure success and economy. The details of the service, especially with regard to roads, were never properly regulated. I believe that this important branch of the public service is open to great improvements. What those improvements should be, it is not for me to say in this short historical outline.

The most important measure introduced by Sir Henry Irving was Ordinance No. 15, of 1875, "to facilitate the establishment of schools of primary education." It was an improvement on the scheme of Sir Arthur Gordon. Schools of primary education established by private individuals, on being allowed by the Board of Education, became entitled to aid from the public funds of the colony on certain conditions, the aid consisting of an annual capitation grant. This called at once in existence a number of denominational schools. The measure was received with general satisfaction.

In May, 1873, an Ordinance was passed to amend the law with regard to immigrants; a mean death-rate was declared, calculated on the average death-rate of all indentured immigrants in the colony; in case of excessive death-rate on any plantation, no allotment of new immigrants; regulations were made respecting day and task work, and provisions introduced for offences of immigrants.

Another important measure was the Ordinance for the custody of lunatics. For many years only lunatics who had committed assaults or were dangerous were confined in the asylum. Under the new law all classes of lunatics became admissible.

In 1876 the law with regard to wardens was amended; again in 1878, power being given to the Governor to proclaim provinces; the colony was consequently divided into two provinces, the northern and the southern, and two commissioners appointed.

A volunteer force was also formed, subject, as far as possible, to the regulations for the voluntary force in England; the volunteers may be called on for military service in any emergency.

As an amendment to the Wardens' Ordinance, the rate leviable on lands was made an uniform tax, and buildings exempted under former Ordinances became rateable—a fair arrangement, which was well received by all landowners.

In 1879 an Ordinance was passed "for constituting one Supreme Court, and for other purposes relating to the better administration of justice"—an Ordinance imitated from the English law, and entitled "the Judicature Ordinance."

Governor Irving was absent from the colony once, from December, 1877, to February, 1878, when the colony was administered by the Hon. J. Scott Bushe, Colonial Secretary, and George William des Vœux, Esq., C.M.G. On his leaving finally in July, 1880, and pending the arrival of his successor, the colony was administered by Wm. A. G. Young, Esq., Lieutenant-Governor of British Guiana, from August, 1880, to November, same year.

The present Governor of Trinidad is Sir Sanford Freeling.

I will conclude this chapter with a few general remarks. Every Governor in succession had to revise, alter, and amend the Immigration Ordinance as first passed; this was natural enough, and is easily understood. The Ordinance was, at first, as an embryo measure, and has been gradually developed into a comprehensive mature scheme which, I believe, leaves little room for further improvement.

With regard to the management of the crown lands, great hesitation may be said to have prevailed since the abolition of the Court of Intendant. This court, as existing under the Spanish Government, was assisted by the Surveyor General or Commissary of Population, a well-organised department. It was finally done away with in 1868, and an Ordinance passed "for regulating the sale of crown lands." Regulations were made at different times, lastly by our present Governor, Sir Sanford Freeling; they are, in my opinion, well digested and comprehensive.

In all countries the construction and maintenance of public roads are subject to fixed rules. It was not so in Trinidad; for many years they were left in the hands of incompetent persons having no notions of civil engineering; road boards, either central or local, were established with certain powers, and soon after changed, because they were unsuccessful in their efforts to perform the work to the satisfaction of the tax-payers. The roads of the colony have been lately placed under the charge and superintendence of the Director of Public Works, and the direction of qualified officers. It is to be hoped that no more important changes will be required.

APPENDIX.

SUGGESTIONS

FOR

Organising a Central Agricultural Committee,

AND

ESTABLISHING MODEL FARMS IN THE ISLAND OF TRINIDAD.

To His Excellency the Right Honourable Lord Harris, Governor of Trinidad.

MY LORD,—Under the present depressed state of agricultural and other affairs in Trinidad, and at a time when entirely new principles seem to govern the policy of the British Government and the Colonial Office with regard to the colonies; when we are left, in total reliance on our own resources, to struggle with foreign slave-countries raising similar produce to our own—we must strain every nerve to continue the unequal contest and preserve to our children the landed property which is their sole inheritance.

We cannot depend upon a protection, which is most peremptorily refused to our demands; immigration and an adequate supply of human labour are precarious aids; the wisest step, therefore, as also the surest, is to avail ourselves of those means which are placed within our reach, namely—science and improved methods, both in cultivation and manufacture.

But, my lord, if individual information, and facts gathered by a few planters, may ultimately be of service to colonial agriculture, it is evident that facts carefully collected and collated by order of a competent body, systematically arranged by well-informed and practical men, so as to form a system of local husbandry based thereupon, and made public by means of the local press—must be of the greatest benefit to the landholders and the community at large.

In countries, such as England, where thousands of acres are the property of wealthy landlords, where scientific information is at ready command, private individuals may, either by their own exertions or by liberal encouragements, correct the theory or improve the practice of agriculture: and yet agricultural societies, even there, are of the greatest advantage.

But in countries, like France, where properties are subdivided into small allotments, and particularly in such colonies as the West Indies, where the proprietary body is either impoverished or actually bordering on ruin, individual exertions generally remain sterile, and voluntary societies are powerless to do good.

It has, therefore, been deemed necessary in France to form model farms, and to organise a "Central Board of Agriculture" under the control of the Government.

The West India islands, compared with France, are in a still worse position than the latter as compared with England; and model farms, with agricultural schools, supported by the Government, are the only channels through which to convey to the people theoretical as well as practical instruction, and the only means for eventually improving the art of husbandry in this archipelago.

Sincerely impressed with this conviction—myself a humble individual, but deeply interested in the prosperity of this fine colony—I presume to intrude on your lordship's valuable time by offering, for your perusal, the following ideas, or sketch of a model farm. Such an establishment, properly conducted, would, in my opinion, be of no less benefit to Trinidad than any past or present scheme for immigration.

At no other period, perhaps, will the Colonial Government have a better opportunity of purchasing, at a moderate rate, one of the numerous sugar-estates now abandoned, and investing the same as Colonial property. In case the Government could spare a sufficient sum of money, two model farms might be established —one in Victoria, and the other in St. George; say, in Naparima for the former, and Tacarigua, or St. Joseph, for the latter county.

The cultivation of the sugar-cane and the manufacture of sugar should be the chief object of those establishments; but the culture of cacao and the raising of ground-provisions should also be liberally encouraged; in fact, the farms would be expected to produce a full supply of vegetable food for the people thereon employed.

The farm should be placed under the management of a "director," a person conversant with the various sciences connected with agriculture; viz., with botany, chemistry, meteorology, and possessing a knowledge of soils, together with the principles of agricultural science; certain moral qualifications should also be exacted as a standard of character.

The whole administration and conduct of the farm should be placed entirely under his control and management.

It would be the duty of the "director" to keep correct books and accounts, referrible to the quarterly or monthly examination of a "Central Agricultural Committee," to be by them investigated and approved previous to payment.

The director to have a liberal salary—independent of which he should receive no allowance either for overseers, servants, or other dependents.

Whereas a model farm would be of very little avail to the community without a school being attached to it, from which, as a source, the youth of the colony might draw information, a building could be fitted up on the farm for the reception of nine or more scholars above the age of fourteen years; such scholars to be admitted on their producing a certificate of good character, and sufficient proficiency in reading, writing, and arithmetic.

The pupils to be governed by stringent regulations, and to be exclusively placed under the authority of the director.

The course of instruction to be both theoretical and practical.

Theoretical instruction to consist of lectures on the principles of botany, chemistry, meteorology, and agrology; also of explanations of the various implements and operations of husbandry. The lectures to be delivered once in the week, and to be public. The pupils to be furnished with elementary books on the various sciences; they might also be required to take notes of the lectures delivered.

The practical instruction to be conducted as follows:—

1st year.—The pupil to superintend everything connected with the live-stock and farming-implements. He should, under the control of the director, attend to the pasture, fences, stables, carts, ploughs, &c., and have under his authority the cartmen, crook-boys, &c. He should learn to break and train animals, to dress and bleed the same when sick, to drive a cart, conduct a plough, and to attain a ready skill, manual or directory, in the usage of other implements.

2nd year.—The pupil would superintend the field-work, the drainage and preparation of land, planting, weeding, cutting canes, and other operations—under the immediate control of one of the senior, or third year's pupils.

3rd year.—During the three months immediately following the end of the crop, say, during June, July, and August, the senior pupils will superintend the field-labours, together with the second year's pupils; they will then take under their charge all the preparations for the ensuing crop-season—such as the repairing and putting in order the mill and the boiling-house, preparing specifications for mason, cooper, and carpenter's work, including the necessary materials. During the crop it will be their duty to superintend the boiling-house, and to conduct all operations connected with the manufacture of sugar.

A public examination to take place at the end of the year, and a prize to be awarded to each class—unless, however, the pupils should not be found sufficiently improved.

Each pupil to pay a premium of 200 dollars for the first year, 100 dollars for the second, and to receive 100 dollars as overseer's salary for the third year. The money received to be placed to the account or credit of the farm. The pupils to be boarded at the expense of Government for the first two years, and by the farm during the third year—the latter as part of overseer's salary.

Although I attach great importance to chemical analyses, yet I am of opinion that superior and more economical results would be gained, without material difference to the colonists, by obtaining analyses of soils and plants from chemists in Europe, rather than by forming a laboratory and having a chemist attached to the establishment in the island.

"CENTRAL AGRICULTURAL COMMITTEE."—Events have fully

proved that voluntary societies do not and cannot beneficially operate, and the reasons are obvious. It then becomes the duty of the Government to take the matter into their own hands. A "Central Agricultural Board, or Committee," should be established by law, to consist of six or more members—the director or directors of the model farms, and the Government botanist, being *ex-officio* members; the others to be appointed by the Governor. All the members to be required punctually to attend the meetings of the "Committee," under a penalty of £1 for non-attendance unless good excuse is given: the botanist to act as secretary.

It would be the duty of the "Central Committee" to prepare a general plan for the management of the model farm; they should examine the books and accounts of the director, and approve the latter for payment, on being found correct. It would also be within the province of the "Central Committee" to collect facts connected with the agriculture of the colony; and, for that purpose, to prepare such local questions as may be deemed of importance, for circulation among the proprietors of estates and intelligent planters, in the different parts of the colony. A digest of interesting facts, observations, and contributions should be published, for general information, in a journal, to be entitled the "Trinidad Annual Register of Agriculture," the said journal to be aided and supported by the Government.

As the model farm ought to be made, as far as possible, a self-supporting establishment, all net revenues should be employed—first, to repay the purchase-money; and this being effected, the entire proceeds should thenceforth be kept as a reserve against contingencies, and for the general promotion of agricultural objects and interests.

Although the model farm and the "Central Committee" are here made to be mutually dependent, they may still exist separately and independently. I am, however, fully aware of the many difficulties which may attend the establishment of a model farm in Trinidad. Prejudice and routine will, under existing circumstances, raise their cry against such an institution; and but a few, it is to be feared, will be awakened to its advantages —I would say, to its blessings. On the other hand, the formation of a "Central Committee" rests entirely with the executive, and, if properly organised, would, I believe, work successfully.

Men are fond of distinction, and were the members of the "Central Committee" to derive some importance from the appointment, it is to be anticipated they would gladly devote time and attention to the object of the institution. I therefore suggest that the committee should be consulted on all matters connected with or affecting the agricultural interest of the colony, as is the case in France. That body would then be, not a mere sugar-planters' committee, but would include cacao and other planters. It would thus be enabled to turn its attention to the cultivation of ground-provisions, tobacco, and oleaginous plants, the growth of which could be encouraged by the sale of crown lands to such natives and immigrants as might be disposed to devote labour or capital to that species of culture.

The committee should be appointed, primarily, by the Governor —the vacancies to be afterwards filled from a list of candidates prepared by the committee, the qualifications for the distinction being of a peculiar description.

I beg, in continuation, to offer a few remarks on the model farms.

It is to be expected that any scheme for the formation of model farms in Trinidad will meet, if not with disparaging criticism, or even opposition, at least with perfect indifference. The capital to be invested in the purchase and improvement of the farm will be considered as so much cash abstracted from the public purse, to gratify a chimerical project. Partly to invalidate this objection, I consider that the formation of the "Central Committee" ought to precede the establishment of the farm. The control exercised by the former would be a sort of guarantee to the public of success in the latter.

We have already had superabundant proofs that it is difficult to rouse the planters even to a sense of their best interests. If, on the one hand, we find reasons for this in their ignorance of agricultural science and the art of husbandry, on the other, we may also trace this apathetic unconcern to the following cause :—

Perceiving, in the midst of their distress—brought on either by the present commercial crisis, or the glut of their staple, which has been thrown into, and still remains in the market—

that the British Government have abandoned their former policy with regard to slave produce, the colonists are induced to believe that the mother-country is determined to allow them to die a lingering death, rather than to afford them support by Protection. Strongly impressed with that conviction, they regard the new policy of the Government as the chief, nay, the sole cause of their present grievances, and they are still under the impression that no remedy will alleviate their distress, but the one coupled with measures of relief from the home Government. The consequence is, that very little has been attempted in the improvement of colonial agriculture; and whilst our eyes have been widely open to the dereliction of the mother-country, they have been closed, and are still blind, to our own faults and shortcomings.

I readily admit that the reproaches urged by her Majesty's ministers and our adversaries are, to a certain extent, justly grounded; but, however presumptuous I may appear in offering an opinion in a matter so grave, I dare contend that much credit is not due to our opponents at home for ascribing the sum total of our misfortunes to our ignorance, and our want of industry and energy. Wrong we *may* be in deducing our distresses from a single source; but still more faulty are those who trace the same to far less powerful causes; viz., lack of information and despondency—the latter of these being but a very natural consequence of our present position.

But, should it be for once admitted that ignorance and supineness are the real causes of our present miserable position, her Majesty's minister for the colonies could not offer any reasonable objection to the adoption of a plan, which, in all probability, would effectually and widely contribute as much to a diffusion of knowledge as to the general improvement of agriculture, and which must eventually advance the prosperity of the colony and the welfare of its inhabitants.

As to the probable success of the undertaking, I may refer to the beneficial results already secured by individual efforts, and from the encouragements so generously afforded by your Excellency. It is true that, on a candid examination of the *practical* advantages hitherto obtained, we are led to confess that little has, as yet, been realised; but, when we take into consideration that the stronghold of prejudice has been shaken, and that the minds of many have been opened to better doctrines, we have reason to rejoice at the result, and to hope for further improvement.

The formation of a school connected with the model farm is, in my opinion, the surest and speediest plan for sweeping away the accumulated rubbish of errors that has, for years, obstructed the path of progress, for creating a new era in our agricultural economy, and for facilitating the onward march of a steady reform.

In fact, there is no systematic or rational instruction or training, under our present routine, for those who look forward to agricultural pursuits. A youth is, for a few years, engaged as an overseer by a manager or proprietor, who takes but little or no trouble in schooling his subordinate, to whom, even otherwise, he could impart but very little information. If the youth be active, intelligent, and honest, he turns out to be a *tolerable* manager, after some three or four years of apprenticeship. But he, like his former master, must depend upon his ignorant boilerman for the quality of his sugar, and in the entire process of manufacture, since that branch of plantership—the most difficult and the most important—does not form a part of the practical instruction of the planter, but is entirely left to the blind routine of a man who knows nothing of the composition of the juice of the cane, or of the effects of those agents he daily employs to extract therefrom a saccharine compound. No wonder, then, if we send to the home market the filthy produce commonly called muscovado, with an immense percentage of uncrystallised sweets in the form of molasses. We have strong motives to complain of a scarcity of labour, but our opponents have also some reasons for asserting that we do not know how to make available the labour we already do, or can, command. So long as we hoped for Protection, such language might have been deemed treasonable to our own interests; but at the present crisis it is only true, and ought to have the influence of truth. Skill and science are, indeed, the grand *desiderata;* but, if science and practical instruction be not placed within the reach of the planters, they certainly cannot be expected to improve by mere desire or intuition.

This, however, is not all. If we bring ourselves to inquire and scrutinise, we may discover further difficulties arising either from absenteeism, or from that reluctance to agricultural pursuits which is characteristic of the emancipated population.

More than one-half of the sugar-estates of the colony has become the property of merchants at home—a natural consequence of the exorbitant rate of interest paid to those capitalists for loans of money, supplies, and other charges, a result, also, greatly encouraged and hastened by the extravagant tactics, and the *laissez aller* (almost allied to fatalism) of the planters. Those merchants who have by force become proprietors find themselves in nearly the same predicament as the former owners —a want of good managers, whilst attorneys unable efficiently to superintend or control the general management of their properties are active agents in their ruin. It is therefore to be anticipated that the absentee proprietors, labouring under the same disadvantages as the old proprietary body of the island, will be ultimately roused to a sense of their own interests, and adopt some better system for the management of their properties. The following would be, in my opinion, the best and most advantageous, both for that class of proprietors and for the general welfare :—The manager should become a participator in the net profits of the estate : but, as it would be but justice to insure him a regular maintenance, he should also receive a small fixed salary—say of 500 dollars—in addition to 10 per cent. of the net proceeds. Under this system, the manager would have the sole and entire superintendence of the property, except in such cases in which material changes should be required, such as alterations in the general disposition of the buildings, apparatuses, &c. He should be allowed to procure his supplies at the lowest rate, instead of drawing them from the attorney's store. The attorney would be furnished with the pay-lists and all other accounts; he would ship the produce and pay the necessary duties and expenses thereon; as also all amounts due by the manager in service of the property, after being furnished with authentic vouchers. The manager would prepare a detailed estimate of probable expenditure for the ensuing twelvemonths —from the 1st of July, each year. On the other hand, he should be entitled to demand and receive the exact accounts of the sales and proceeds of produce.

This plan is simple, just, and safe. The manager, placed in this position, will have the same interest in the estate as the proprietor himself. Some prospects will be thus afforded him of improving his condition by industry; he will be encouraged to settle himself comfortably in marriage, and may, eventually, become a proprietor in his own right; also, in case the absent proprietor should be desirous of parting with his estate, he could safely enter into an advantageous arrangement with his former manager.

Now it is evident that the absentee proprietor cannot adopt the proposed plan if the class of managers, generally, do not offer sufficient professional guarantees. The formation of an agricultural school, and certificates delivered by the "Central Committee," would afford such guarantees; and the adoption of the proposed plan would also be a powerful inducement to the youth of the colony to improve themselves in the science of agriculture and the art of husbandry.

The reluctance evinced by all classes to field occupations has its origin in a deep-rooted prejudice, the offspring of slavery. Rural occupations are generally deemed a loss of caste in plodding labourers, and are considered as the special province of the ignorant. The command of God is, "In the sweat of thy face shalt thou eat bread," but slavery had made the command of God a prescription of man; and the slave, obliged to toil for the benefit of his master, viewed the obligation of working as a curse, whilst the master regarded the occupations of a slave (except in an interested light) as unworthy of his attention. It is, to all, clear and evident that, whilst we are loudly demanding an increase of field-labour, there is a glut of tradesmen and petty shopkeepers in the island. An agricultural school would have the effect of ennobling rural pursuits, and of raising agricultural occupations in the estimation of the community. This is the reason that the strictest obligations should characterise the training and service of the pupils, as also a high salary be paid to the director of the farm—the former to insure the stability and promote the final objects of the establishment, the latter, to secure the services of a respectable and competent individual.

The pupils should be boarded by the director, on an adequate allowance being made for the necessary expenditure.

In conclusion, I suggest that the growth of fruit-trees, ground-provisions, and the more delicate vegetables—those of

Europe included—should be encouraged. In aid of this design better methods of culture could be easily and successfully substituted for the present routine, and superior agricultural implements be made to supersede the hoe and cutlass. Plantains, manioc, Indian corn—even tanias, yams, and potatoes, might be cultivated with the plough and the cultivator. Let the example be exhibited on the model farms, and many of the middle classes will be, at once, satisfied to cultivate their own lands, and thus secure an honourable subsistence to their families; whilst a cheap and abundant supply of wholesome provisions could be regularly furnished to our markets. The white man will, himself, prepare his field with the plough and harrow, and drive the cultivator through his plantain walks or young manioc rows; the coloured man, by improving his condition, will rise in the social scale, and those baneful prejudices—the greatest obstacle to the prosperity of this fine island—will then vanish like noxious exhalations before the rising sun.

I have the honour to be, my lord,
Your Excellency's most obedient humble servant,
L. A. A. DE VERTEUIL, M.D.P.

PORT-OF-SPAIN.

Such was the scheme I submitted for Lord Harris' consideration some time in the year 1850. My opinions have not since changed, and I am still strongly convinced that the establishment of a model farm, with a school of agriculture attached, would confer incalculable benefits on the community. Moreover, as juvenile depravity is on the increase, and the number of youthful criminals augmenting to an alarming extent, such an establishment might be rendered subservient as a penitentiary for that class of offenders, where they could receive primary instruction, religious teaching, and industrial training.

To the plan, in the abstract, no one, I believe, can offer any serious objection; by many, I know, its realisation will be deemed impossible: to the latter I answer—it has been realised elsewhere to the fullest extent, and with manifold advantages.

MINERAL COALS.

During their survey of Trinidad, Messrs. Wall and Sawkins discovered seams of coal, which they reported to be of very good quality. This fuel cannot fail to be a most valuable addition to the already numerous and valuable resources of the colony.

The coal has been found at *Pointe Noire*, between Manzanilla and the mouth of the river Oropuche. The coal district would extend, according to all appearances, from the eastern coast to the Gulf, across the counties of St. Andrew, Caroni, and part of St. George. Unfortunately it was surveyed on an extent of only nine miles.

At Pointe Noire the coal is quite near the surface, and consequently can be worked at little expense, and with prospects of immediate return.

From the work of Messrs. Wall and Sawkins I have the following information.

The geological conditions indicate that the fuels of the island are contained in strata of recent origin, the carbonaceous deposits of the eastern coast being probably middle Tertiary, whilst that of the southern coast may be of even later date. Preliminary experiments having established considerable diversity in the qualities of the coals, the leading varieties only were selected and subjected to as complete an examination as practicable. The results are summarised in the following paragraphs:—

The specific gravity of the whole of the local specimens is comprised within the usual limits—1·2 to 1·4.

Sulphur does not exist in excess in any of the island specimens; in some the amount is very trifling.

The colonial fuels are less perfectly mineralised than those of the English formation.

The whole of the specimens from Trinidad having been collected from the outcrops of the beds to which they belong are in a more or less deteriorated condition, on which account an improvement may be confidently anticipated in the following particulars: a decrease in the amount of ashes; a decrease in the water mechanically mixed; and an increase in the illuminating gas.

Should it be considered advisable to select some of these fuels for trial of their practical value on an extended scale, Nos. 18 and 13 from Pointe Noire seem best adapted for general purposes; but for steam navigation No. 2, from the same district, unites the valuable properties of superior density, only slight caking tendency, and holding together well under transit.

Specimens were sent to the Museum of Practical Geology for examination; and here is the verdict of Sir Roderick Murchison:—

"Having examined the *fossil remains* which are associated with the combustible, I may now inform you that they are of a very recent Tertiary age. Hence the combustible comes, geologically, within the class of lignites, which are of very inferior value to the coal of real Carboniferous age.

"At the same time it is right to state that some Tertiary lignites possess an amount of calorific value which, in tracts where the old coal does not exist, renders them of considerable importance. Thus nearly all the Austrian steamers in the Adriatic are worked by Tertiary coal, which in the relation of its calorific value to the old coal is about 60 to 100.

"No. 15 by distillation furnishes a considerable quantity of hydrocarbon, and No. 18 would probably be valuable for gas making; but a large quantity of material will be required to make satisfactory experiments in regard to their economic value.

"These results, favourable as they are, being obtained from surface specimens which have been deteriorated by weathering, do not convey a fair idea of the value of the fuel which may be obtained from subterranean workings.

"It remains, of course, to be ascertained in the island whether the beds of lignite can be easily worked by horizontal galleries; for if the fuel is attainable at a small cost, it may prove highly valuable to the colony.

(Signed) "RODERICK L. MURCHISON."

On a subsequent visit to the district adjacent to Pointe Noire, the surveyors managed to obtain about twelve and a half tons of coal. The whole of that quantity was conveyed by men to Manzanilla for embarkation to Port-of-Spain. A ton of the fuel was taken on board of H.M. steamer *Buzzard* for trial. In the following letter from the commander of the ship we have the results obtained :—

"H.M.S. *Buzzard*, at Barbados,
"January 6, 1859.

"I have the honour to inform you that the coals I took on board the *Buzzard* at Trinidad were fairly tried in one furnace on board this ship. The opinion of Mr. Gilham, the chief engineer, and my own also, is, they are far superior to what we expected.

"The small quantity that I had to burn had been so long exposed to the air, rain, and heat of climate, that they were very much deteriorated.

"The coals give a very bright flame, with great heat and little smoke, but burnt so fiercely that we expended at the rate of seventy-two tons per diem.

"I certainly am of opinion, and also Mr. Gilham, that if coals were dug deeper in the vein they would prove of great use to steamers with tubular boilers.

"I have the honour, etc.,
(Signed) "FRANCIS PEEL,
"Commander."

The same vessel having visited Trinidad a few weeks later, the residue of the coal was taken on board and tried in the Gulf. The particulars ascertained were that "whilst the steam was raised and retained at the requisite pressure with equal or greater facility than with the ordinary fuels used, the consumption was, however, much more rapid than in the case of the English, Scotch, or Welsh coals."

With such facts before me, I repeat what I have already stated, that it is a matter for regret that Messrs. Wall and Sawkins were not encouraged and assisted in completing their survey of the coal district. They might have come upon seams at such localities wherefrom the transport of the coals would have been easy and unexpensive. But when we look to the report of the surveyors, to the opinion of Sir Roderick Murchison, to the trial made on board the *Buzzard*, I believe I only express a reasonable opinion when I say that it is highly desirable that the local Government should put our mineral fuels to a fair test; and that, with such object in view, it should not shrink from expending a few thousand pounds in bringing our coals within reach of our planters, our railways, engines, or steam vessels. This could not be considered as a rash step, inasmuch as we have the opinion of Sir Roderick Murchison, that "some Tertiary lignites possess an amount of calorific value which, in tracts where the old coal does not exist, renders them of considerable importance," as exemplified on board the "Austrian steamers in the Adriatic, which are worked by Tertiary coal." It cannot be a rash step when we have the statement that the Pointe Noire coals were "far superior to what was expected;" that "they gave a very bright flame, with great heat and little smoke, and burnt fiercely;" that "the steam was raised and retained at the requisite pressure with equal or greater facility than with the ordinary fuels used," though "the consumption was much more rapid than in the case of the English, Scotch, or Welsh coals."

According to Sir Roderick Murchison, No. 18 would probably be valuable for gas making.

We have again the opinion of the surveyors, of Sir Roderick Murchison, and of Commander Peel, that the specimens, being more or less deteriorated by weathering, do not convey a fair idea of the value of the fuel which may be obtained from subterranean workings.

Of course let the Government obtain coals from such subterranean workings, and then, but only then, shall we be able to pronounce upon the importance and value of our coal formation.

www.ingramcontent.com/pod-product-compliance
Lightning Source LLC
Chambersburg PA
CBHW021416300426
44114CB00010B/515